The Drama Scholars' Index
To Plays and Filmscripts:

A Guide to Plays and Filmscripts in Selected Anthologies, Series and Periodicals

by

GORDON SAMPLES

The Scarecrow Press, Inc.
Metuchen, N.J.   1974

Library of Congress Cataloging in Publication Data

Samples, Gordon.
    The drama scholars' index to plays and filmscripts:
a guide to plays and filmscripts in selected anthologies, series, and peridodicals.

    1. Drama--Bibliography. I. Title.
Z5781.S17   016.80882   73-22165
ISBN 0-8108-0699-1

For My Sister

FRANCES

CONTENTS

INTRODUCTION

Another play index? the examiner may ask. The author's primary purpose in preparing The Drama Scholars' Index, an effort which has extended over the past twenty years, is suggested by the title itself. It has been designed to give the serious student of drama an advantage in finding plays and filmscripts, either out of the ordinary, or in out-of-the-ordinary versions, in their original languages, or in translations. Moreover, the user, whether a serious student of drama or not, will find those often much-needed critical essays, excerpts of reviews, and biographical information so typically included in the foreign theater periodicals but so typically excluded from our own.

No other drama index--indeed, probably no other index of any kind--includes such an aggregate of important foreign periodicals as L'Avant-Scène du Cinema, L'Avant-Scène du Théâtre, Cahiers du Cinema, Chinese Literature (Peking), Divaldo/Theatre (Prague), Italian Theatre Review, Plaisir de France, Supplement Theatral, Revista de Teatro (Rio de Janeiro), Theater der Zeit, and Theater Heute (Hannover). It also includes several important British and American periodicals not to be found in any other drama index, such as Cinema, Modern International Drama, Negro History Bulletin, Paris Review, Plays and Players, Review of English Literature, and Yale/Theatre. In order to be a selective index, yet comprehensive within that delimitation, and not just a supplement, it does include the significant, standard plays and filmscripts in their ordinary versions. In all cases, the selective indexing extends through 1972.

With respect to the collections indexed (books and series other than periodicals), The Drama Scholars' Index maintains the same kind of emphasis. The standard is there, but so is the unusual, and the coverage is balanced both historically and ethnically. It is intended to provide the drama student with a well-rounded picture through the ages. Unlike any other drama index, it has collections of the eighteenth and nineteenth centuries, including some unusual and rare items. It is unique also in its inclusion of a considerable number of collections of significant radio and television scripts. As with the periodicals indexed, there is a large proportion in foreign languages, making it possible to find a play both in its original language and in various translations. There is a good representation of traditional Asian plays, ancient Indian, modern Chinese and Japanese, ancient Roman and Greek, old and new short plays, early American, avant-garde in all languages, the new black playwrights, Soviet short plays, and recent Latin American, including those in Portuguese.

Finally, the emphases of The Drama Scholars' Index can be illustrated by a few examples of the kinds of items it will handle: the radio script of the famous Orson Welles' broadcast, "The Invasion from Mars"; all the dramatic works of Byron, Keats, and Shelley; the script reconstructed from Chaplin's silent film, "The Gold Rush"; the plays of Edward Albee in German, French, Italian, and English; the play "Xanthippe on Woman Suffrage"; a play version of Dostoevsky's The Idiot; "The Red Lantern" by the Peking Opera Troupe and "The Red Detachment of Women" by the Troupe and Chiang Ching, the wife of Mao Tse-tung; two recently published plays by Pablo Picasso; French filmscript versions of Poe's "The Gold Bug" and "The Pit and the Pendulum"; a new play about Goethe by Adolf Muschg, dealing with the political events of his life; four different scripts based on Stephen Vincent Benet's story "The Devil and Daniel Webster," including his own play, the radio script by Charles Jackson, the filmscript "All That Money Can Buy," and a new play "Scratch" by Archibald MacLeish; the libretto of the opera "Levins Mühle" by Udo Zimmerman; a new play by Peter Weiss, "Hölderlin," in the original language; and the scripts of the three related plays, Henry Fielding's "The Covent-Garden Tragedy," a burlesque of Ambrose Philips' famous pseudo-classical tragedy, and "The Distrest Mother," which was a free adaptation of Racine's "Andromaque."

More specifically, the way in which this index differs from other play indexes may be more clearly defined by a comparison of coverage. First of all, it is selective, with the object in mind to present a balanced collection. Ottemiller's Index to Plays in Collections begins indexing anthologies published in 1900; this index goes back to and includes anthologies published in 1700. By actual count, this index analyzes 121 anthologies that Ottemiller's index does not. Some of these are 35- to 45-volume sets; for example, Cumberland's British Theatre and Bell's British Theatre are two among many which were previously not indexed. Chinese, Japanese, and other Asian cultures are included in this index, but omitted from Ottemiller's index. This index includes some important experimental children's plays, selective one-act plays, radio, film and television scripts, adaptations in many languages of Shakespeare's plays, including plays about him as well as plays written in imitation of him, which Ottemiller's index does not do. Also, certain publishers' series of individually bound plays and filmscripts, not indexed elsewhere, are included in this index.

As to periodical coverage, this index includes plays and filmscripts from 39 periodical titles not covered by Keller's Index to Plays in Periodicals. Still further in difference, this index places emphasis on foreign language periodicals. For each play or filmscript the author of the original source and the film director is entered alphabetically in the index. Historical characters are also entered, making available plays and films about people either in an actual or fictional account. The main difference with respect to H. W. Wilson's Play Index is that that publication's coverage of plays, singles as well as collections, begins with those published in

viii

1949, and now lags about six years behind in supplements; also, it is not selective, and excludes plays in foreign languages.

The author wishes to express his appreciation to the following persons at San Diego State University: to Louis Kenney, Director of the Library, for his cooperation; to the Faculty Research Committee, for their assistance; to Thomas Gwinup, Research and Reference Department colleague, for his encouragement and editorial assistance; and to Lenora Thomason for her expert typing of a difficult manuscript.

Gordon Samples

San Diego State University
California
March 1973

NOTE TO THE USER

This bibliography is in one alphabetical arrangement
by author and title. Complete entry is given only
under the author's name. Titles, joint authors,
authors upon whose work the script is based, and
historical characters are all referred to the main
entry or author entry. Citations for anonymous works
are listed under title. Plays and films about historical characters are indicated by an asterisk at the
beginning of the title. Those scripts adapted from
another author's work are indicated by a double
asterisk.

If this be not a good play,
the Devil is in it.

--Thomas Dekker.

A BECKETT, Gilbert Abbott, 1811-1856
    Jack Brag
        (In Cumberland's British Theatre, Vol. 46, no. 4)
    Man-Fred: a Burlesque Ballet Opera (on Byron's work)
        (In Cumberland's British Theatre, Vol. 33, no. 5)
    The Man with the Carpet Bag
        (In Cumberland's British Theatre, Vol. 29, no. 9)
    The Mendicant
        (In Cumberland's British Theatre, Vol. 29, no. 1)
    The Roof Scrambler
        (In Cumberland's British Theatre, Vol. 42, no. 1)
    The Turned Head
        (In Cumberland's British Theatre, Vol. 44, no. 1)
A Bout de Souffle (see Godard, Jean-Luc)
A Nous la Liberté (see Clair, Rene)
A Valparaiso (see Ivens, Joris)
Abbie, the Bug Boy (see Conkle, Ellsworth Prouty)
ABBOTT, George, 1889-
    Broadway (see Dunning, Philip Hart)
    Damn Yankees, by George Abbott and Douglas Wallop, based on
        Mr. Wallop's novel, "The Year the Yankees Lost the Pennant."
        (In Theatre Arts, Vol. 40, Nov. 1956)
    Fiorello! (see Bock, Jerry)
    The Pajama Game (see Rosenberg, Jerold)
    Three Men on a Horse, by George Abbott and John Cecil Holm
        (In 20 Best Plays of the Modern American Theatre, Vol. 1)
Abe Lincoln in Illinois (see Sherwood, Robert Emmet)
ABECASSIS, Guy
    L'Homme de Rangoon
        (In Plaisir de France, supplement theatral, no. 343, May
        1967)
ABEL, Lionel
    Pretender
        (In Partisan Review, Vol. 26, Fall 1959)
ABELL, Kjeld, 1901-1961
    Days on a Cloud
        (In Genius of the Scandinavian Theater)
Abend di Anni Nouveau (see Lardner, Ring Wilmer)
ABERCROMBIE, Lascelles, 1881-1938
    The Deserter
        (In Theatre Arts, Vol. 6, 1922)
Abie's Irish Rose (see Nichols, Anne)
"Der Abiturmann" (see Leonhardt, Arne)

ABLEMAN, Paul
    Green Julia
        (In Evergreen Playscript Series, no. 2)
    Madly in Love
        (In Modern Short Comedies from Broadway & London)
Above Rubies (see Brighouse, Harold)
Abraham (see Hrotsvit, of Gandersheim)
Abraham and Isaac (Anon.)
        (In Genius of the Early English Theater)
Abraham Lincoln (see Drinkwater, John)
Abre a Janela e Deixa Entrar o Ar Puro e o Sol de Manha
        (see Bivar, Antonio)
Absalom (see Ahel, Lionel)
ABSE, Dannie
    House of Cowards
        (In Plays of the Year, Vol. 23, 1960-1961)
Absence of a Cello (see Wallach, Ira)
The Abstract Tragedy; a Comedy of Masks (see Olson, Elder)
The Abstract Wife (see Molinaro, Ursule)
L'Academia (Text in French and English) (see Fratti, Mario)
Accent on Youth (see Raphaelson, Samson)
Accident (see Pinter, Harold)
L'Accompagnateur (see Mithois, Marcel)
According to Law (see Houston, Noel)
L'Accusateur Public (see Hochwalder, Fritz)
ACHARD, Marcel, 1899-
    Rollo, adapted by Felicity Douglas
        (In Plays of the Year, Vol. 20, 1959)
    Turlututu
        (In Plaisir de France, supplement theatral, no. 297, July
        1963)
The Acharnians (see Aristophanes)
ACKLAND, Rodney, 1908-
    A Dead Secret
        (In Plays of the Year, Vol. 16, 1956/57)
    Strange Orchestra
        (In Famous Plays of Today, 1932-33)
The Acrobats (see Fleming, Berry)
Acrobats (see Horovitz, Israel)
Across the Border (see Clements, Colin Campbell)
Across the Jordan (see Culbertson, Ernest Howard)
Act Without Words I & II (see Beckett, Samuel)
Acte (see Durrell, Lawrence)
Action (see Patrick, Robert)
Actua Tilt (see Herman, Jean)
Adalen 31 (see Widerberg, Bo)
Adam und Eva (see Hacks, Peter)
ADAMOV, Arthur, 1908-
    As We Were
        (In Evergreen Review, Vol. 1, no. 4, 1957)
    The Big and the Little Maneuver
        (In Modern International Drama, Vol. 5, no. 1, Fall 1971)

En Fiacre
 (In Plaisir de France, supplement theatral, no. 299, Sept.
  1963)
The Invasion
 (In Modern International Drama, Vol. 2, no. 1, Sept. 1968)
ADAMS, Samuel Hopkins, 1871-1958
 **It Happened One Night (see Riskin, Robert)
Adam's Rib (see Gordon, Ruth)
The Adding Machine (see Rice, Elmer L.)
ADDISON, Joseph, 1672-1719
 Cato
  (In Cumberland's British Theatre, Vol. 2, no. 2)
  (In Bell's British Theatre, 1797, Vol. 3)
  (In The London Stage, Vol. 1)
 The Drummer; or, The Haunted House
  (In Bell's British Theatre, 1797, Vol. 22)
Adelgitha; or, The Fruits of a Single Error (see Lewis, Matthew
 Gregory)
Adieu Berthe! (see Murray, J.)
Adieu Philippine (see O'Glor, Michele)
ADLER, Jack
 The Bed
  (In First Stage, Vol. 2, Fall 1963)
ADLER, Richard, 1921-
 The Pajama Game (see Rosenberg, Jerold)
ADLER, Robert, 1919-
 Open Secret, by Robert Adler, George Bellak, and Louis N.
  Ridenour
  (In Best One-Act Plays of 1946/47, N.Y.)
The Admiral (see MacLeish, Archibald)
Adonai (see Luongo, Guiseppe)
The Adopted Child (see Birch, Samuel)
The Adored One (see Sellers, Irma Peixetto)
ADREIN, Philippe
 La Baye
  (In Plaisir de France, supplement theatral, no. 359, Sept.
   1968)
The Adventure of Five Hours (see Tuke, Sir Samuel)
Adventure Story (see Rattigan, Terence Mervyn)
Adventures in the Skin Trade (see Sinclair, Andrew)
Adventures of Marco Polo (see Sherwood, Robert Emmet)
AESCHYLUS, 525-456 B.C.
 Agamemnon
  (In Complete Greek Drama, Vol. 1)
  (In Tragedy: Texts and Commentary, 1969)
 Agamemnon 1-350, trans. by R. Fagles
  (In Arion, Vol. 5, Winter 1966)
 Agamemnon 503-680, trans. by R. Fagles
  (In Arion, Vol. 6, Summer 1967)
 **The Aulis Difficulty (see Baring, Maurice)
 The Choephori
  (In Complete Greek Drama, Vol. 1)

The Eumenides
(In Complete Greek Drama, Vol. 1)
The Oresteia; Agamemnon; The Choephoroe; The Eumenides
(In Masterworks of World Drama, Vol. 1)
The Persians
(In Complete Greek Drama, Vol. 1)
Prometheus Bound
(In Complete Greek Drama, Vol. 1)
Prometheus Bound, trans. by Edmund Blunden
(In Review of English Literature, Vol. 8, Jan. 1967)
Prometheus Bound, trans. by Edith Hamilton
(In Theatre Arts, Vol. 11, July 1927)
The Seven Against Thebes
(In Complete Greek Drama, Vol. 1)
The Suppliants
(In Complete Greek Drama, Vol. 1)
The Affair (see Millar, Ronald)
L'Affaire Manet (see Aurel, Jean)
The Affectionate Son (see Engel, Johann Jakob)
AFINOGENEV, Alexander Nikolaevich, 1904-1941
The Passer-By
(In Soviet One-Act Plays)
Afore Night Came (see Rudkin, David)
African Medea (see Magnuson, Jim)
The African Queen (see Agee, James)
After All (see Van Druten, John)
After Closing (see Marz, Roy)
After Euripides' "Electra" (see Baring, Maurice)
After the Fall (see Miller, Arthur)
After the Play (see Gogal, Nikalai)
After Twenty-Five Years (see Firkins, Oscar W.)
Afternoon Tea (see Gorgey, Gabor)
Against the Storm (see Michael, Sandra)
Agamemnon (see Aeschylus)
Agamemnon 1-350 (see Aeschylus, trans. by R. Fagles)
Agamemnon 503-680 (see Aeschylus, trans. by R. Fagles)
Agamemnon (see Seneca, Lucius Annaeus)
L'Age d'Or (see Buñuel, Luis)
AGEE, James, 1909-1955
The African Queen
(In Agee on Film, Vol. 2)
**All the Way Home (see Mosel, Tad)
The Blue Hotel
(In Agee on Film, Vol. 2)
The Bride Comes to Yellow Sky
(In Agee on Film, Vol. 2)
The Night of the Hunter
(In Agee on Film, Vol. 2)
Noa Noa
(In Agee on Film, Vol. 2)
(In Film: Book 1)
AGENOUX, Soren
A Christmas Carol; based on the book by Charles Dickens.

(In The Best of Off Off Broadway)
Agnes Bernauer (see Hebbel, Friedrich)
AGOSTON, Gerty, 1918-
     The Beast
          (In Best One-Act Plays of 1949/50, N. Y.)
     For Each Man Kills
          (In Best One-Act Plays of 1948/49, N. Y.)
     Three Persons
          (In Best One-Act Plays, 1950/51, N. Y.)
The Agreeable Surprise (see O'Keeffe, John)
AGUIRRE, Isidora, 1919-
     Express for Santiago
          (In Best Short Plays, 1959/60)
Ah, Wilderness! (see O'Neill, Eugene Gladstone)
Ahasverus (see Heijermans, Herman)
AHEL, Lionel
     Absalom
          (In Artist Theatre)
AHMAD, Dorothy
     Papa's Daughter
          (In TDR, The Drama Review, Vol. 12, Summer 1968)
AIDE, Hamilton
     Colour-Blind: A Comedy of Twenty Minutes
          (In Anglo Saxon Review, Vol. 5, June 1900)
AIKEN, George L., 1830-1876
     Uncle Tom's Cabin, based on the book by Harriet Beecher Stowe
          (In S. R. O., the Most Successful Plays...)
          (In Best Plays of the Early American Theatre, from the be-
          ginning to 1916)
Air Mail From Cyprus (see Hall, Willis)
Air Raid (see MacLeish, Archibald)
The Airborne (see Blitzstein, Marc)
Ajax (see Sophocles)
The Ajax Touch (see Aklom, Mikhail)
AKINS, Zoë, 1886-1958
     Portrait of Tiero
          (In Theatre Arts, Vol. 4, 1920)
AKLOM, Mikhail
     The Ajax Touch
          (In Best One-Act Plays of 1940, London)
     Flash-Back
          (In Best One-Act Plays of 1944/45, London)
     The Murder Scream, by Mikhail Aklom, adapted by Harold
       Brighouse
          (In Best One-Act Plays of 1935, London)
     Of Social Significance
          (In Best One-Act Plays of 1942/43, London)
Akogi, a Noh Play (see Zeami Motokiyo)
Aladdin; or, The Wonderful Lamp (Anon.)
          (In Cumberland's British Theatre, Vol. 38, no. 5)
L'Albatros (see Mocky, Jean-Pierre)
ALBEE, Edward, 1928-
     Alles Vorbei

(In Theater Heute, no. 2, Feb. 1972)
The American Dream
  (In Mademoiselle, Vol. 52, Nov. 1960)
Box
  (In Box and Quotations from Chairman Mao Tse-tung)
The Death of Bessie Smith
  (In Three Plays)
Delicate Balance (Text in French)
  (In L'Avant Scene du Theatre, no. 400, Apr. 1, 1968)
Kiste
  (In Theater Heute, Vol. 10, no. 3, Mar. 1969)
Quotations from Chairman Mao Tse-tung
  (In Box and Quotations from Chairman Mao Tse-tung)
The Sandbox
  (In Best Short Plays, 1959-60)
  (In Three Plays)
Tiny Alice
  (In Best American Plays, Sixth Series, 1963-67)
Werte des Vorsitzenden Mao Tse-Tung
  (In Theatre Heute, Vol. 10, no. 3, Mar. 1969)
Who's Afraid of Virginia Woolf?
  (In Best American Plays, Fifth Series, 1957-63)
Who's Afraid of Virginia Woolf? (Text in French)
  (In L'Avant Scene du Theatre, no. 339, Aug. 1965)
The Zoo Story
  (In Evergreen Review, Vol. 4, Mar./Apr. 1960)
  (In Famous American Plays of the 1950's)
  (In Three Plays)
Zoo Story (Text in French)
  (In L'Avant Scene du Theatre, no. 334, May 15, 1965)
  (In Plaisir de France, supplement theatral, no. 320, June
    1965)
Albert Gates (see Brighouse, Harold)
Albert's Bridge (see Stoppard, Tom)
ALBICOCCO, Jean-Gabriel, 1936-
  La Fille Aux Yeux d'Or, d'apres la nouvelle d'Honore de Balzac
    (In L'Avant-Scene du Cinema, no. 7, Sept. 17, 1961)
Albina, Countess Raimond (see Cowley, Mrs. Hannah Parkhouse)
An Albino Kind of Logic (see Zahn, Curtis)
The Albion Queen; or, The Death of Mary Queen of Scots (see
  Banks, John)
Albumazar (see Tomkis, Thomas)
L'Alcade de Zalamea (see Calderon de la Barca, Pedro)
The Alcaid; or, The Secrets of Office (see Kenney, James)
ALCORIZA, Luis
  L'Ange Exterminateur (see Buñuel, Luis)
ALCOTT, Louisa M., 1832-1888
  **Little Women, a Screenplay (see Mason, Sarah)
ALDIS, Mary
  Ten P.M.
    (In Drama, Vol. 11, Mar. 1921)
Ale Pacha; or, The Signet-Ring (see Payne, John Howard)

Aleichem, Sholom, pseud. (see Rabinowitz, Shalom)
ALENCAR, Jose de
   O Credito
     (In Revista de Teatro, no. 293)
   O Rio de Janeiro (Verso e Reverso)
     (In Revista de Teatro, no. 300)
ALENCAR PIMENTEL, Altimar de
   O Auto da Cobica
     (In Revista de Teatro, no. 370, July/August, 1970)
ALEXANDER, Hartley Burr, 1873-1939
   Kills-With-Her-Man
     (In Theatre Arts, Vol. 12, June 1928)
   The Singing Girl of Copan
     (In Theatre Arts, Vol. 17, Aug. 1933)
   Three Chinese Folk Dramas: "Princely Fortune"; "Meeting at
   the Well"; "Woman Song, " edited by Hartley Alexander and
   translated by Kwei Chen
     (In Theatre Arts, Vol. 14, Nov. 1930)
ALEXANDER, I. J.
   Enemy
     (In Theatre Arts, Vol. 28, Sept. 1944)
ALEXANDER, Ronald
   Time Out For Ginger
     (In Theatre Arts, Vol. 38, Feb. 1954)
Alexander III, known as, Alexander the Great, 356-323 B.C.
   *Adventure Story (see Rattigan, Terence Mervyn)
   *Alexander and Campaspe (see Lyly, John)
   *Alexander the Great (see Lee, Nathaniel)
   *The Death of Alexander (see Baring, Maurice)
   *The Rival Queens; or, The Death of Alexander the Great (see
   Lee, Nathaniel)
ALFIERI, Vittoro, 1749-1803
   Philip the Second, by Count Alfiere de Asti, trans. by Fanny
   Holcroft
     (In Theatrical Recorder, ed. by Thomas Holcroft, Vol. 1,
     no. 2, Jan. 1805)
Alfonso X, el Sabino, King of Castile and Leon, 1221-1284
   *Alfonso, King of Castile (see Lewis, Matthew G.)
Alfred the Great, King of England, 849-901
   *King Alfred and the Neat-Herd (see Baring, Maurice)
   *King Alfred the Cake Burner (see Sims, Alan)
ALFRED, William, 1922-
   Hogan's Goat
     (In Best American Plays, Sixth Series, 1963-67)
ALGER, Horatio, Jr.
   **Sink or Swim (see O'Malley, Neill)
Algiers (see Lawson, John Howard)
'Ali, Pasha of Jamina, 1711-1822
   *Ali Pasha; or, The Signet-Ring (see Payne, John Howard)
Ali the Cobbler (see Shepherd, Martin)
Alice dans les Jardins du Luxembourg (see Weingarten, Romain)

Alice's Restaurant   (see Herndon, Venable)
Alizon (see Vivran)
"All Aboard!" (see Bengal, Ben)
All at Coventry; or, Love and Laugh (see Moncrieff, William
   Thomas)
All Fools (see Chapman, George)
All for Love; or, The World Well Lost (see Dryden, John)
All in the Wrong (see Murphy, Arthur)
All Mistaken; or, The Mad Couple (see Howard, James)
All My Sons (see Miller, Arthur)
All on Her Own (see Rattigan, Terence)
All or None (see Giffords, Franklin Rent)
All Summer Long (see Anderson, Robert)
All That Fall (see Beckett, Samuel)
All That Money Can Buy (see Totherch, Can)
All the King's Men (see Rossen, Robert)
All the King's Men (see Warren, Robert Penn)
All the Way Home (see Mosel, Tad)
All Things Are Possible (see Rubinstein, Harold Frederick)
All-American Ape (see Kephart, William M.)
ALLEN, Woody, 1935-
   Death Knocks
      (In New Yorker, Vol. 44, Jul. 27, 1968)
   **Quoi de Neuf, Pussycat? ("What's New, Pussycat?") (see
      Donner, Clive)
Alles Vorbei (see Albee, Edward)
ALLINGHAM, John Till, fl. 1799-1810
   Fortune's Frolic
      (In Cumberland's British Theatre, Vol. 33, no. 8)
      (In The London Stage, Vol. 2)
   **Jack of All Trades (Anon.); adapted from "The Weathercock"
      by J. T. Allingham.
      (In 26 Short & Amusing Plays)
   The Weathercock
      (In Cumberland's British Theatre, Vol. 5, no. 4)
   The Widow; or, Who Wins ?
      (In Cumberland's British Theatre, Vol. 43, no. 7)
      (In Bread Loaf Book of Plays)
ALLIO, Rene, 1924-
   Les Camisards
      (In L'Avant-Scene du Cinema, no. 122, Feb. 1972)
Allison's House (see Glaspell, Susan)
Alma Mater (see Green, Paul)
An Almanac of Liberty (see Rose, Reginald)
ALMAR, George
   The Battle of Sedgemoor; or, The Days of Kirk and Monmouth
      (In Cumberland's British Theatre, Vol. .34, no. 1)
   The Bull-Fighter; or, The Bridal Ring
      (In Cumberland's British Theatre, Vol. 39, no. 8)
   The Cedar Chest; or, The Lord Mayor's Daughter; to which is
      added, The Silver Palace
      (In Cumberland's British Theatre, Vol. 33, no. 1)

The Charcoal Burner; or, The Dropping Well of Knaresborough
(In Cumberland's British Theatre, Vol. 45, no. 8)
The Earl of Poverty; or, The Old Wooden House of London
Wall
(In Cumberland's British Theatre, Vol. 33, no. 7)
The Good-Looking Fellow; or, The Roman Nose
(In Cumberland's British Theatre, Vol. 38, no. 4)
Pedlar's Acre; or, The Wife of Seven Husbands
(In Cumberland's British Theatre, Vol. 20, no. 7)
The Shadow! A Mother's Dream
(In Cumberland's British Theatre, Vol. 33, no. 6)
The Tower of Nesle; or, The Chamber of Death
(In Cumberland's British Theatre, Vol. 27, no. 7)
ALMA-TADEMA, Sir Lawrence, 1836-1912
The Merciful Soul, by Lawrence Alma Tadema
(In Anglo Saxon Review, Vol. 3, Dec. 1899)
ALMAZ, Michael
Every Number Wins
(In Best Short Plays, 1968)
ALMEIDA, Abilio Pereira de
...Em Moeda Corrente do Pais
(In Revista de Teatro, no. 324)
Moral em Concordata
(In Revista de Teatro, no. 296)
Rua Sao Luiz, 27-8o
(In Revista de Teatro, no. 306)
Almost Like Being (see Van Itallie, Jean-Claude)
Alphaville (see Godard, Jean-Lac)
Alphonso IV, King of Portugal, 1290-1357
*Queen After Death; How to Kill Women (see Montherlant,
Henry de)
Altitude (see Lawrence, David Herbert)
Altruism (see Ettlinger, Karl, Ritter von)
ALVARADO, Rafael
From 7:15 to 8:00, the Entrance is Through the Hoop
(In TDR/The Drama Review, Vol. 14, no. 2, Winter 1970)
Alvarez Quintero, Joaquin, 1873-1944 (see Alvarez Quintero,
Serafin)
ALVAREZ QUINTERO, Serafin, 1871-1938
A Sunny Morning, by Serafin Quintero and Joaquin Quintero
(In 30 Famous One-Act Plays)
(In 50 Contemporary One-Act Plays)
ALVARO, Corrado
The Long Night of Medea
(In Plays for a New Theater)
ALVES, Edward G.
Mulher Zero Quilometro
(In Revista de Teatro, no. 349)
Always With Love (see Harris, Tom)
AMADO, Joao Jorge
O Quati Papa-Ovo
(In Revista de Teatre, no. 379, Jan./Feb. 1971)
Amanha e' Dia de Pecar (see Wanderley, Jose)

Amanha Se Nao Chover (see Pongetti, Henrique)
L'Amante Anglaise (see Duras, Marguerite)
Les Amants (see Malle, Louis)
Les Amants Peurils (see Crommelynck, Fernand)
Amateurs and Actors (see Peake, Richard Brinsley)
The Ambitious Step-Mother (see Rowe, Nicholas)
AMBLER, Eric, 1909-
    Encore (see Clark, T. E. B.)
AMBROGI, Silvano, 1929-
    The Burosaurs; both French and English texts are included.
    (In Italian Theatre Review, Vol. 11, Oct. /Dec. 1962)
AMCOTT, Vincent
    Poisoned
    (In 26 Short & Amusing Plays, 1871)
Amadee; or, How to Get Rid of It (see Ionesco, Eugene)
Amelie ou le Temps d'Aimer (see Drach, Michel)
Amends for Ladies (see Field, Nathaniel)
American Atrocities in Vietnam (see Gottlieb, Saul)
The American Dream (see Albee, Edward)
American Hurrah (see Van Itallie, Jean-Claude)
An American Playground Sampler (see Estrin, Marc)
American Power (see Schevill, James Erwin)
AMES, G.
    Green Veil Passes
    (In Best One-Act Plays of 1944/45, London)
AMHERST, Jeffery Amherst, 1st Baron, 1717-1795
    Ireland--As It Was
    (In Lacy's Acting Plays, Vol. 81)
AMIDEI, Sergio
    Rome, Ville Ouverte (see Fellini, Federico)
Amor a Oito Maos (see Bloch, Pedro)
O Amor na Terra do Cangaco (see Menezes, Maria Wanderley)
Amor por Anexins (see Azevedo, Arthur)
The Amorous Goldfish (see Voysey, Michael)
L'Amour Existe (see Pialat, Maurice)
L'Amour Quelquefois (see Maupassant, Guy de)
Un Amour Qui ne Finit Pas (see Roussin, Andre)
Les Amours de Jacques le Fataliste (see Huster, Francis)
Les Amours d'une Blonde (see Forman, Milos)
Amphitryon (see Platus, Titus Maccius)
Amphitryon; or, The Two Sosias (see Dryden, John)
Amphitryon 1968 (see Diez, Bernard)
Amphitryon 38 (see Giraudoux, Jean)
Amyntas (see Tasso, Torquato)
An Anachronism at Chinon (see Pound, Ezra)
ANAGONOSTAKI, Loula
    The Town
    (In Chicago Review, Vol. 21, no. 2, Aug. 1969)
Anastasia (see Marcelle-Maurette)
Anatol; filmscript (see Graziani, Henri)
Anatol (see Schnitzler, Arthur)
Ancey, Georges, pseud. (see Curnieu, Georges de)

And Now--The Journey (see Carter, Conrad C.)
And Now There's Just the Three of Us (see Weller, Michael)
And the Boy Who Came to Leave (see Kalcheim, Lee H.)
And the Wind Blows (see Da Rocha Miranda, Edgard)
And They Told Us We Were Immortal (see Dragun, Osvaldo)
And Things That go Bump in the Night (see McNally, Terrence)
And We Own the Night (see Garrett, Jimmy)
ANDERSON, Lindsay, 1923-
    If, a filmscript by Lindsay Anderson and David Sherwin.
      (Classic Film Scripts Series)
    If.... de Lindsay Anderson et David Sherwin.
      (In L'Avant-Scene du Cinema, no. 119, Nov. 1971)
  **Secret People (see Dickinson, Thorold)
ANDERSON, Maxwell, 1888-1959
    Anne of the Thousand Days
      (In Theatre Arts, Vol. 33, May 1949)
      (In Best American Plays, Third Series)
    The Bad Seed, dramatized from William March's novel
      (In Theatre Arts, Vol. 39, Dec. 1955)
    Barefoot in Athens
      (In Theatre Arts, Vol. 36, Oct. 1952)
    Both Your Houses
      (In Pulitzer Prize Plays)
    Elizabeth the Queen
      (In Eleven Verse Plays)
    The Feast of Ortolans
      (In Best One-Act Plays of 1938, N.Y.)
      (In Eleven Verse Plays)
    Gods of the Lightning, by Maxwell Anderson and Harold Hicker-
    son (Sacco-Vanzetti case)
      (In 25 Best Plays of the Modern American Theatre, Early
      Series, 1916-1929)
    High Tor
      (In Eleven Verse Plays)
      (In Nine Modern American Plays)
      (In 20 Best Plays of the Modern Theatre, Vol. 1)
    Joan of Lorraine
      (In Theatre Arts, Vol. 32, Apr./May 1948)
    Key Largo
      (In Eleven Verse Plays)
    Letter to Jackie
      (In Best One-Act Plays of 1943, N.Y.)
    Lost in the Stars; dramatization of "Cry the Beloved Country"
    by Alan Paton
      (In Theatre Arts, Vol. 34, Dec. 1950)
    Mary of Scotland
      (In Eleven Verse Plays)
      (In Theatre Guild Anthology)
    The Masque of Kings
      (In Eleven Verse Plays)
    The Miracle of the Danube
      (In Best One-Act Plays of 1941, N.Y.)

(In Best Short Plays, 1956/57)
Night Over Taos
  (In Eleven Verse Plays)
Saturday's Children
  (In 25 Best Plays of the Modern American Theatre, Early
    Series, 1916-1929)
Second Overture
  (In Eleven Verse Plays)
Valley Forge
  (In Eleven Verse Plays)
**What Price Glory? (see Stallings, Lawrence)
The Wingless Victory
  (In Eleven Verse Plays)
Winterset
  (In 20 Best Plays of the Modern American Theatre, Vol. 1)
  (In Eleven Verse Plays)
ANDERSON, Robert Woodruff, 1917-
All Summer Long, adapted from the novel "A Wreath and a
  Curse" by Donald Wetzel.
  (In Theatre Arts, Vol. 39, Aug. 1955)
I Never Sang for my Father
  (In New American Library Screenplays)
The Shock of Recognition
  (In Modern Short Comedies from Broadway & London)
Silent Night, Lonely Night
  (In Best American Plays, Fifth Series, 1957-63)
  (In Theatre Arts, Vol. 45, Dec. 1961)
Tea and Sympathy
  (In Theatre Arts, Vol. 38, Sept. 1954)
  (In Best American Plays, Fourth Series)
You Know I Can't Hear You When the Water's Running: Four
  One-Act Plays
  (In Best American Plays, Sixth Series, 1963-67)
ANDERSON, Sherwood, 1876-1941
The Triumph of the Egg
  (In Best Short Plays, 1956/57)
The Andersonville Trial (see Levitt, Saul)
Andre (see Dunlap, William)
Andre Masson et les Quatre Elements (see Gremillon, Jean)
ANDRE, Michel
Virginie
  (In L'Avant Scene du Theatre, no. 144)
ANDREEV, Leonid Nikolaevich, 1871-1919
He Who Gets Slapped
  (In Theatre Guild Anthology)
Love of One's Neighbor
  (In 50 Contemporary One-Act Plays)
ANDREWS, Isobel
Goldfish
  (In Best One-Act Plays of 1948/49, London)
Andreyev, Leonid Nikolaevich (see Andreev, Leonid Nikolaevich)
Andrezejewski, Jerzy (see Wajda, Andrzej)

ANDRIEU DE LA VIGNE, 1450?-1515
    The Miracle of the Blind Man and the Cripple
        (In Representative Medieval and Tutor Plays)
        (In Masterworks of World Drama, Vol. 2)
Andromache (see Euripides)
Andromache (see Racine, Jean)
Andromana; or, The Merchant's Wife (Anon.)
        (In Dodsley's A Select Collection of Old English Plays, Vol.
        14)
Andromaque (see also the Distrest Mother; The Covent-Garden
    Tragedy)
Andromeda (see Simpson, Louis)
L'Ange Bleu (Der Blaue Engel) (see Von Sternberg, Joseph)
L'Ange Exterminateur (see Buñuel Luis)
An Angel Comes to Babylon (see Dürrenmatt, Friedrich)
Angel Street (see Hamilton, Patrick)
Anger (see Ionesco, Eugene)
ANGIER, Emile, 1820-1889
    Le Gendre de M. Porrier, by Emile Angier and Jules Sandeau
        (In Chief French Plays of the 19th Century)
Angot, Michele
    Amelie ou le Temps d'Aimer (see Drach, Michel)
The Animal Kingdom (see Barry, Philip)
Animal Magnetism (see Inchbald, Mrs. Elizabeth Simpson)
Anjinho Bossa Nova (see Silvino, Paulo)
Ann of Denmark, Queen of James I of England, 1574-1619
    *The Magnificent Entertainment given to King James (see Dek-
        ker, Thomas)
"Anna Christie" (see O'Neill, Eugene Gladstone)
Anna Kleiber (see Sastre, Alfonso)
Anne of Cleves, 3rd wife of Henry VIII, King of England, 1515-1557
    *Anne of Cleves (see Morris, Jean)
Anne of the Thousand Days (see Anderson, Maxwell)
The Anniversary (see MacIlwraith, Bill)
Anniversary Waltz (see Chodorov, Jerome)
The Annual Jumble Sale (see Darmady, J.)
The Annunciation (see Wakefield Mystery Cycle)
Anoli: The Blind (see Tomholt, Sydney)
Another Part of the Forest (see Hellman, Lillian)
Another Summer (see Snyder, William Hartwell, Jr.)
Another Way Out (see Langner, Lawrence)
ANOUILH, Jean, 1910-
    Antigone
        (In Makers of the Modern Theater, 1961)
        (In Five Plays, Vol. 1)
    Ardele
        (In Five Plays, Vol. 2)
    Augustus, by Jean Anouilh and Jean Aurenche. A trans. of
    "Humulus le Muet" by George Hauger.
        (In Best Short Plays, 1969)
    Becket; or, The Honor of God
        (In Introduction to Literature: Plays)

Catch as Catch Can
  (In Seven Plays, Vol. 3)
Cecile; or, The School for Fathers
  (In One Act)
  (In From the Modern Repertoire, Series Three)
  (In Seven Plays, Vol. 3)
Cher Antoine
  (In L'Avant Scene du Theatre, Sept. 1, 1970, no. 455)
Episode from an Author's Life
  (In Educational Theatre Journal, Vol. 16, Mar. 1964)
Episode in the Life of an Author
  (In Seven Plays, Vol. 3)
The Ermine
  (In Five Plays, Vol. 1)
Eurydice
  (In Five Plays, Vol. 1)
  (In Pieces Noires)
  (In The Modern Theatre, ed. by R. W. Corrigan)
The Fighting Cock
  (In Plays and Players, Vol. 13, July, 1966)
L'Hermine
  (In Pieces Noires)
The Lark
  (In Genius of the French Theater)
  (In Five Plays, Vol. 2 by Anouilh)
  (In Theatre Arts, Vol. 41, March 1957)
  (In 20 Best European Plays on the American Stage)
Madame de...
  (In Best Short Plays of the World Theatre, 1948-67)
Mademoiselle Colombe
  (In Five Plays, Vol. 2)
Medea
  (In Seven Plays, Vol. 3)
  (In The Modern Theatre, Vol. 5)
Ne Reveillez pas Madame!
  (In L'Avant-Scene du Theatre, no. 508, Dec. 15, 1972)
The Orchestra
  (In Seven Plays, Vol. 3)
  (In Best Short Plays of the World Theatre, 1958-1967)
Les Poissons Rouges
  (In L'Avant-Scene du Theatre, no. 478, Sept. 1971)
The Rehearsal
  (In Five Plays, Vol. 1)
Restless Heart
  (In Five Plays, Vol. 2)
Romeo and Jeannette
  (In Five Plays, Vol. 1)
La Sauvage
  (In Pieces Noires)
Thieves' Carnival
  (In Seven Plays, Vol. 3)
  (In The Modern Theatre, ed. by Eric Bentley, Vol. 3)
Time Remembered

(In Theatre Arts, Vol. 43, Feb. 1959)
(In Five Plays, Vol. 2)
Traveller Without Luggage
(In Seven Plays, Vol. 3)
Le Voyageur Sans Bagage
(In Pieces Noires)
Tu Etais Si Gentil Quand Tu Etais Petit!
(In L'Avant-Scene du Theatre, no. 499, July 15, 1972)
The Waltz of the Toreadors, trans. by Lucienne Hill
(In Theatre Arts, Vol. 41, Sept. 1957)
Ansky, S., pseud. (see Rappoport, Solomon)
Answers (see Topor, Tom)
Anthony, C. L., pseud. (see Smith, Dorothy Gladys)
Antigone (see Anouilh, Jean)
Antigone (see Cocteau, Jean)
Antigone (see Sophocles)
Antigone lo Cassio (see Gateschi, Rossana)
The Antiquary (see Marmion, Shakerley)
The Antiquary (see Scott, Sir Walter)
Antonio (see Zerboni, Roberto)
ANTONIONI, Michelangelo, 1912-
    L'Avventura
    (In Screenplays)
    (In L'Avventura)
    Le Desert Rouge (Il Deserto Rosso)
    (In L'Avant-Scene du Cinema, no. 49, 1965)
    L'Eclisse
    (In Screenplays of Michelangelo Antonioni)
    Il Grido
    (In Screenplays of Michelangelo Antonioni)
    La Notte
    (In Screenplays of Michelangelo Antonioni)
    Zabriskie Point
    (In Modern Film Scripts)
Any Other Business (see Ross, George)
Aoi no Uye (see Zenchiku Ujinobu)
The Apartment (see Wilder, Billy)
The Apes Shall Inherit the Earth (see Aspenström, Werner)
Apius and Virginia (Anon.)
    (In Old Plays, 1703-1764, Vol. 12)
Apollo (see Pixley, Frank)
The Apollo of Bellac (see Giraudoux, Jean)
Apolônio, o Astronauta (see De Almeida, Lyad)
The Apothecary (see Wells, Charles F.)
The Apple (see Gelber, Jack)
Apples (see Indick, Benjamin P.)
Apprehensions (see Oklam, Mikhail)
The Apprentices (see Terson, Peter)
Les Approches du Soir (see Suffran, Michel)
APSTEIN, Theodore Emanuel, 1903-
    Beams of Our House
    (In Best One-Act Plays, 1952/53, N.Y.)
    Before the Bullfight

(In Best One-Act Plays of 1947/48, N.Y.)
Fortuna Writes a Letter
(In Best Short Plays, 1956/57)
(In Best One-Act Plays of 1948/49, N.Y.)
Making the Bear
(In Best One-Act Plays of 1946/47, N.Y.)
Paradise Inn
(In Best One-Act Plays, 1951/52, N.Y.)
A Remittance from Spain
(In Best Short Plays, 1953/54)
Wetback Run
(In Best One-Act Plays, 1960/61, N.Y.)
Aquarelle (see Delouche, Dominique)
Arabella (see Strauss, Richard)
ARAUZ, Alvaro
Entre Medina et Olmedo
(In Plaisir de France, supplement theatral, no. 340, Feb.
1967)
Le Retour de Cid
(In Plaisir de France, supplement theatral, no. 316, Feb.
1965)
Arbeitgeber (see Kelling, Gerhard)
The Arbitration (see Menander)
The Arbitration (Epitrepontes) (see Menander)
L'Arbre (see Dutourd, Jean)
ARBUSOW, Alexej (Aleksej Arbuzov) 1908-
Märchen vom Alten Arbat
(In Theater der Zeit, no. 6, 1972)
Arbuthnot, John, 1667-1735
Three Hours After Marriage (see Gay, John)
ARBUZOR, Aleksir
The Promise
(In Plays and Players, Vol. 14, Mar. 1967)
ARCHARD, Paul
Les Miserables, adapted from the novel by Victor Hugo
(In L'Avant Scene du Theatre, no. 146)
ARCHER, Thomas, 1830-1893
An Eligible Situation
(In 26 Short & Amusing Plays, 1871)
ARCHER, William, 1856-1924
The Green Goddess
(In 16 Famous British Plays)
ARCHIBALD, William, 1919-
The Innocents; based on Henry James' "The Turn of the Screw."
(In Theatre Arts, Vol. 35, Jan. 1951)
Archie and Mehitabel (see Kleinsinger, George)
L'Architecte Maudit: Claude-Nicolas Ledoux (see Kast, Pierre)
L'Architecture et L'Empereur D'Assyrie (see Arrabal, Fernando)
Architruc (see Pinget, Robert)
Ardele (see Anouilh, Jean)
ARDEN, Jane
The Party
(In Plays of the Year, Vol. 18, 1958)

ARDEN, John, 1930-
  The Bagman; or, The Impromptu of Muswell Hill
    (In Scripts, Vol. 1, no. 8, June 1972)
  The Ballygombeen Bequest, by John Arden and Margaretta
  D'Arcy
    (In Scripts, Vol. 1, no. 9, Sept. 1972)
  The Happy Haven
    (In Evergreen Playscript Series)
  Ironhand, adapted from Goethe's "Goetz von Berlichingen"
    (In Evergreen Playscript Series)
  Left-Handed Liberty
    (In Evergreen Playscript Series)
  Live Like Pigs
    (In Evergreen Playscript Series)
  Serjeant Musgrave's Dance
    (In Evergreen Playscript Series)
    (In New British Drama)
  The True History of Squire Jonathan and His Unfortunate
  Treasure
    (In Plays and Players, Vol. 15, Aug. 1968)
  The Waters of Babylon
    (In Evergreen Playscript Series)
  The Workhouse Donkey
    (In Evergreen Playscript Series)
ARDREY, Robert, 1908-
  God and Texas
    (In Best One-Act Plays of 1943, N.Y.)
    (In Theatre Arts, Vol. 27, Aug. 1943)
Arena Conta Zumbi (see Guarnieri, Gianfrancesco)
ARENT, Arthur, 1904-
  Ethiopia
    (In Educational Theatre Journal, Vol. 20, Mar. 1968)
Aria da Capo (see Millay, Edna St. Vincent)
Ariadne (see Marcel, Gabriel)
Ariadne in Naxos (see Baring, Maurice)
ARIOSTO, Lodovico, 1474-1533
  Supposes: a comedie written in the Italian tongue by Ariosto,
  Englished by George Gascoyne
    (In Early Plays from the Italian)
ARISTOPHANES, c. 450-c. 385 B.C.
  The Acharnians
    (In Complete Greek Drama, Vol. 2)
  The Birds
    (In Complete Greek Drama, Vol. 2)
  The Clouds
    (In Complete Greek Drama, Vol. 2)
  Congresswoman, trans. by D. Parker
    (In Arion, Vol. 6, Spring 1967)
  The Ecclesiazusae
    (In Complete Greek Drama, Vol. 2)
  The Frogs
    (In Complete Greek Drama, Vol. 2)

The Knights
(In Complete Greek Drama, Vol. 2)
Lysistrata
(In Masterworks of World Drama, Vol. 1)
(In Complete Greek Drama, Vol. 2)
Peace
(In Complete Greek Drama, Vol. 2)
Peace: 289-955, translated by T. Reynolds
(In Arion, Vol. 6, Winter 1967)
Plutus
(In Complete Greek Drama, Vol. 2)
The Thesmophoriazusae
(In Complete Greek Drama, Vol. 2)
The Wasps
(In Complete Greek Drama, Vol. 2)
ARLETT, Vers Isabel, 1896-
The Tree
(In Best One-Act Plays of 1948/49, London)
ARMSTRONG, Anthony
Ten-Minute Alibi
(In Famous Plays of Today, 1933)
ARMSTRONG, Mrs. Louise (Van Voorhis), 1899-
Dolls, A Christmas Nonsense Play
(In Drama, Vol. 11, Nov. 1920)
The Old History Book
(In Drama, Vol. 12, Jan. 1922)
ARMSTRONG, Noel
Marthe
(In 50 More Contemporary One-Act Plays)
The Army and People are One Family (see Yung, Chun)
ARNAND, Georges
**Le Salaire de la Peur (see Clouzot, Henri-Georges)
Sweet Confessions
(In Evergreen Review, Vol. 1, no. 3, 1957)
ARNE, Thomas Augustine, 1710-1778
Artaxerxes
(In Cumberland's British Theatre, Vol. 14, no. 1)
ARNOLD, Paul
The Little Taylor
(In Tulane Drama Review, Vol. 5, Sept. 1960)
ARNOLD, Samuel James
Man and Wife
(In Old Plays, 1810)
AROUT, Gabriel
Beware of the Dog
(In Plays of the Year, Vol. 33, 1967)
Cet Animal Etrange, based on a story by Tchekhov
(In Plaisir de France, supplement theatral, no. 316, Feb.
1965)
Des Pommes pour Eve
(In Plaisir de France, supplement theatral, no. 373, Dec.
1969)

Laure et les Jacques
  (In Plaisir de France, supplement theatral, no. 307, May
  1964)
ARRABAL, Fernando, 1932-
  L'Architecte et L'Empereur D'Assyrie
  (In L'Avant Scene du Theatre, no. 443, Feb. 15, 1970)
  The Cages
  (In Drama & Theatre, Vol. 7, no. 3)
  The Groupuscle of My Heart
  (In TDR/Drama Review, Vol. 13, Summer 1969)
  Impossible Lover
  (In TDR/Drama Review, Vol. 13, Fall 1968)
  Picnic on the Battlefield
  (In Evergreen Review, Vol. 4, Nov./Dec. 1960)
  Solemn Communion: Panic Ceremony
  (In TDR/Drama Review, Vol. 13, Fall 1968)
  Strip-Tease of Jealousy
  (In TDR/Drama Review, Vol. 13, Fall 1968)
  Der Tausendjährige Krieg
  (In Theatre Heute, no. 8, Aug. 1972)
  Viva la Muerte
  (In L'Avant-Scene du Cinema, no. 116, July 1971)
ARRUFAT, A.
  Carnival Saturday
  (In Americas, Vol. 10, Oct. 1958)
Arsenic and Old Lace (see Kesselring, Joseph)
ARTAUD, Antonin, 1896-1948
  Les Cenci
  (In TDR/The Drama Review, Vol. 16, no. 2, June 1972)
  The Philosopher's Stone
  (In Tulane Drama Review, Vol. 9, Spring 1965)
  Spurt of Blood
  (In Evergreen Review, Vol. 7, Jan./Feb. 1963)
Artaxerxes (see Arne, Thomas Augustine)
Arthur, Timothy Shay, 1809-1885
  **Ten Nights in a Bar-Room (see Pratt, William W.)
ARTSYBASHEV, Mikhail Petrovich, 1878-1927
  War
  (In Drama, Vol. 21, Feb. 1921)
L'Arzigogolo (see Grazzini, Antonio Francesco, called Il Lasca)
As We Were (see Adamov, Arthur)
As You Desire Me (see Pirandello, Luigi)
Asaph (see Bates, William O.)
The Ascension (see York Tailors' Play)
ASCH, Shalom, 1880-1957
  Night, by Sholem Asch
  (In 50 Contemporary One-Act Plays)
ASHBERY, John
  The Heroes
  (In Artists Theatre)
Ashelbe, Detective, pseud. (see La Barthe, Henri)
Ashes and Diamonds (see Wajda, Andrzej)
Ashton, Ruth (see Beier, Carl)

ASHTON, Winifred, 1891?-1965
    A Bill of Divorcement
        (In Collected Plays of Clemence Dane, Vol. 1)
    Granite
        (In Collected Plays of Clemence Dane, Vol. 1)
    Scandal at Coventry
        (In Collected Plays of Clemence Dane, Vol. 1)
    Til Time Shall End
        (In Collected Plays of Clemence Dane, Vol. 1)
    Wild Decembers
        (In Collected Plays of Clemence Dane, Vol. 1)
O Asilado (see Figueiredo, Guilherme)
ASKE, Lake
    Non Nobis
        (In Best One-Act Plays of 1944/45, London)
Asmondee (see Mauriac, Francois)
ASPENSTRÖM, Werber
    The Apes Shall Inherit the Earth
        (In Tulane Drama Review, Vol. 6, Nov. 1961)
Assassin! (see Ball, David)
Assassins Associes (see Thomas, Robert)
The Assault upon Charles Sumner (see Hivnor, Robert)
Assemien Dehyle (see Dadie, Bernard)
Assis, Machado de (see Machado de Assis, Joaquin Maria)
The Astonished Heart (see Coward, Noel Pierce)
ASTRUC, Alexandre, 1923-
    Evariste Galois
        (In L'Avant-Scene du Cinema, no. 82, June 1968)
    Les Mauvaises Rencontres, by Alexandre Astruc et Roland
    Laudenbach
        (In Cahiers du Cinema, Vol. 9, no. 52, Nov. 1955)
    Le Puits et le Pendule, d'apres la nouvelle d'Edgar Poe
        (In L'Avant-Scene du Cinema, no. 64, 1966)
    Le Rideau Cramoisi, d'apres "La Premiere Diabolique" de
    Barbey D'Aurevilly
        (In L'Avant-Scene du Cinema, no. 38, 1964)
    Un Vie
        (In Cahiers du Cinema, Vol. 14, no. 90, Dec. 1958)
At the Chasm (see Frida, Emil Bohslav)
At the Polls: Electoral Opera-Bouffe (see Theatre de l'Epee de
    Bois)
At the Shrine (see Young, Stark)
At the Wakehouse (see O'Donovan, Michael)
At War with the Mongols (see Heide, Robert)
Athaliah (see Racine, Jean Baptiste)
ATHERTON, Camille Skrivanek
    Chit-Chat on a Rat
        (In First Stage, Vol. 2, Winter 1962-63)
ATLAS, Leopold
    The Story of G. I. Joe, by Leopold Atlas and Guy Endore, based
    on the books "Here Is Your War" and "Brave Men" by Ernie
    Pyle; screenplay directed by William A. Wellman

(In Theatre Arts, Vol. 29, Sept. 1945, excerpt)
(In Best Film Plays, 1945, Vol. 2)
Atomic Bombs   (see Hursley, Frank)
The Atonement of Pan   (see Redding, Joseph D.)
Atsumori at Ikuta (Ikuta Atsumori)   (see Motoyasu, Komparn Zembo)
Au Biseau des Baisers   (see Gilles, Guy)
The Au Pair Man   (see Leonard, Hugh)
Au Restaurant   (see Barrier, Maurice)
AUB, Max
    Les Hommes de Haute Vertu
        (In Plaisir de France, supplement theatral, no. 329, March
        1966)
Auberge, Maurice, 1913
    Le Passage du Rhin   (see Cayatte, Andre)
AUCHINCLOSS, Louis
    Club Bedroom
        (In Esquire, Vol. 66, Dec. 1966)
AUDEN, Wystan Hugh, 1907-1973
    Caucasian Circle of Chalk   (see Brecht, Bertolt)
    The Dog Beneath the Skin, by W. H. Auden and Christopher
        Isherwood
        (In Best Short Plays of the Social Theatre, 1939)
    For the Time Being
        (In Religious Drama, Vol. 1)
    The Seven Deadly Sins of the Lower Middle Class   (see Brecht,
        Bertolt)
AUDIBERTI, Jacques, 1899-1965
    Coeur a Cuir
        (In Plaisir de France, supplement theatral, no. 349, Nov.
        1967)
    La Logeuse
        (In L'Avant-Scene du Theatre, no. 473, June 1, 1971)
    Le Mal Court
        (In L'Avant-Scene du Theatre, Oct. 1956)
    Quoat-Quoat
        (In Plaisir de France, supplement theatral, no. 357, July
        1968)
The Audience   (see Garcia Lorca, Federico)
Audioplay 1: Voices   (see Lind, Jakov)
Audioplay 2: Safe   (see Lind, Jakov)
Due Aufgeregten von Goethe   (see Muschg, Adolf)
Aufstieg von Edith Eiserbeck   (see Gozell, Rolf)
August Heat   (see Richards, Stanley)
Augustus   (see Anouilh, Jean)
Augustus, Gaius Julius Caesar Octavius, 63 B.C.-14 A.D.
    *Gloriana; or, The Court of Augustus Caesar   (see Lee,
        Nathaniel)
AULETTA, Robert
    Red Mountain High
        (In Yale Theatre, Vol. 2, no. 3, Winter 1969)
The Aulis Difficulty   (see Baring, Maurice)
Auntie Mame   (see Lawrence, Jerome)
The Aunt's Sake (Obaga Sake)   (see Sakanishi, Shio)

AUREL, Jean, 1925-
   L'Affaire Manet
     (In L'Avant-Scene du Cinema, no. 77, Jan. 1968)
Aurelia (see Dastree, Anne)
Aurelius Antoninus, Marcus, Emperor of Rome, 121-180
   *Faustine, Ritual Tragedy (see Goodman, Paul)
AURENCHE, Jean, 1904-
   Augustus (see Anouilh, Jean)
   Jeux Interdits (see Clement, Rene)
   Special Friendships (Les Amities Particulieres)
   screenplay of the French film.
     (In Show, Vol. 4, Sept. 1964)
Aurevilly, Jules Amedee Barbey d' (see Barbey d'Aurevilly,
   Jules Amedee)
AURTHUR, Robert Alan
   Man on the Mountaintop
     (In Best Television Plays)
Austerlitz; or, The Soldier's Bride (see Haines, John Thomas)
AUSTIN, Mary Hunter, 1868-1934
   Sekala Ka'ajma; an Interpretive Dance-Drama of the Southwest
     (In Theatre Arts, Vol. 13, April 1929)
AUTANT-LARA, Claude, 1903-
   La Traversee de Paris, d'apres la nouvelle de Marcel Ayme
     (In L'Avant-Scene du Cinema, no. 66, 1967)
O Auto da Cobica (see Alencar Pimentel, Altimar de)
The Autocrat of the Coffee Stall (see Chapin, Harold)
Auto-Da-Fe (see Williams, Tennessee)
Autoportrait d'un Pornographe (see Swain, Robert)
Autumn Crocus (see Smith, Dorothy Gladys)
Autumn Fires (see Weid, Gustau Johannes)
The Autumn Garden (see Hellman, Lillian)
Avarice and Ostentation (see Goldoni, Carlo)
The Avenue (see Merrill, Fenimore)
AVERMAETE, Roger
   Les Papiers
     (In L'Avant-Scene du Theatre, no. 473, June 1, 1971)
L'Aveugle et le Paralytique (see Pathiraja, Dharmasena)
L'Avventura (see Antonioni, Michelangelo)
Awake and Sing! (see Odets, Clifford)
The Awakening (see Subert, Frantisek Adolf)
AXEL, Gabriel
   Danish Blue
     (A Black Cat Screenplay, Grove Pr., 1970)
AXELROD, George, 1922-
   The Seven Year Itch
     (In Theatre Arts, Vol. 38, Jan. 1954)
     (In Best American Plays, Fourth Series)
   Will Success Spoil Rock Hunter?
     (A Random House Play, 1956)
AYCHBOURN, Alan
   Pantoufle
     (In Plaisir de France, no. 386)
     (In L'Avant-Scene du Theatre, no. 462)

Aye, Aye, Sir! (see Ellicott, John Morris)
AYLEN, Elise
    The Holy Crown
        (In Best One-Act Plays of 1937, London)
AYME, Marcel, 1902-1967
  **La Traversee de Paris (see Autant-Lara, Claude)
    Clerambard, adapted by Norman Denny and Alvin Sapinsley
        (In Theatre Arts, Vol. 42, June 1958)
    Les Oiseaux de Lune
        (In L'Avant-Scene du Theatre, Sept. 1956)
AYTON, Richard, 1786-1823
    The Rendezvous
        (In Cumberland's British Theatre, Vol. 6, no. 6)
AZEVEDO, Arthur
    Amor por Anexins
        (In Revista de Teatro, no. 316)
    A Capital Federal
        (In Revista de Teatro, no. 298)
    O Cordao
        (In Revista de Teatro, no. 305)
    O Genro de Muitas Sogras, de Arthur Azevedo e Moreira
    Sampaio
        (In Revista de Teatro, no. 291)
    O Mambembe, de Arthur Azevedo e Jose Piza
        (In Revista de Teatro, no. 317)

Baal (see Brecht, Bertolt)
BABEL, Isaac
    Marya
        (In Plays of the Year, 1967-68)
Le Babour (see Marceau, Felicien)
Baby (see Saroyan, William)
The Baby Carriage (see Crocker, Bosworth)
Baby Doll (see Williams, Tennessee)
La Baby-Sitter (see Obaldia, Rene de)
The Bacchae (see Euripides)
Bachelor Mother (see Krasna, Norman)
The Bachelor Party (see Chayefsky, Paddy)
Back Home (see Gunn, Neil M.)
Back to Adam (see Brighouse, Harold)
Bacon, Sir Francis, Viscount St. Albans, 1561-1626
    *Sweet England's Pride (see Rodger, Ian)
    *The Tree (see Arlett, Vers Isabel)
    *The Truth About Shakespeare (see Box, Sydney)
Bacon, Frank, 1864-1922
    Lightnin' (see Smith, Winchell)
BACON, Jean
    La Colombe a Deux Têtes
        (In L'Avant Scene du Theatre, no. 482, Nov. 1, 1971)
BACON, Josephine Dodge Daskam, 1876-1961
    The Twilight of the Gods
        (In Forum, Vol. 53, Jan. 1915)

Bad, Bad Jo-Jo (see Herlihy, James Leo)
A Bad Play for an Old Lady (see Johnson, Elizabeth)
The Bad Seed (see Anderson, Maxwell)
Baden Lehrstück (see Brecht, Bertolt)
The Bachelor Party (see Chayefsky, Paddy)
The Bag O'Dreams (see Scott, Margaretta)
The Bag of Parting (see Sakanishi, Shio)
A Bag of Tangerines (Koj-dawara) (see Sakanishi, Shio)
BAGG, Robert
     The Pope's Right Knee
          (In Massachusetts Review, Vol. 10, Summer 1969)
Baggy Breeks; or, The Wisest Fool in Christendom (see Sims,
     Alan)
The Bagman; or, The Impromptu of Muswell Hill (see Arden, John)
BAGNOLD, Enid
     Call Me Jacky
          (In Plays of the Year, 1967-68, Vol. 34)
BAIERL, Helmut
     Schlag Dreizehn
          (In Theater der Zeit, no. 8, 1971)
BAILEY, Anne Howard
     The Narrow Man
          (In Television Plays for Writers, 1957)
BAILEY, Loretto (Carroll) 1908-
     Job's Kinfolks, a Play of the Mill People
          (In Carolina Folk-Plays)
Les Bains (see Troilet, Elsa)
BAIRD, George M. P.
     The Waiting Room
          (In Drama, Vol. 15, Oct. 1924)
The Bait (see Merrill, James)
BAKER, Elizabeth (Fulton), 1810-1892
     Faithful Admirer
          (In 50 More Contemporary One-Act Plays)
     Miss Fassey
          (In Representative One-Act Plays by British and Irish Authors)
BAKER, Elliott
     The Delinquent, the Hipster, the Square
          (In The Delinquent, the Hipster, the Square, and the Sandpile
     Series)
BAKER, Fred
     Events, 1968-1969; scenario of the film.
          (An Evergreen Black Cat Screenplay, Grove Pr., 1970)
Les Bal des Cuisinieres (see Da Costa, Bernard)
BALACHOVA, Tania
     Lady Macbeth
          (In Plaisir de France, supplement theatral, no. 360, Oct.
     1968)
La Balance d'Eros (see Vazart, Claude)
The Balcony (see Genet, Jean)
The Bald Prima Donna (see Ionesco, Eugene)
The Bald Soprano (see Ionesco, Eugene)

BALDERSTON, John Lloyd, 1889-
  Berkeley Square
    (In 25 Best Plays of the Modern American Theatre, Early
    Series, 1916-1929)
  A Morality Play for the Leisured Class
    (In 50 More Contemporary One-Act Plays)
BALDI, Gian Vittorio, 1930-
  Fiammetta
    (In L'Avant-Scene du Cinema, no. 91, Apr. 1969)
BALDUCCI, Alfredo, 1920-
  Don Juan at the Stake; both French and English texts are given.
    (In Italian Theatre Review, Vol. 17, Jan./Mar. 1968)
BALDWIN, James, 1924-
  Blues for Mister Charlie
    (In Best American Plays, Sixth Series, 1963-67)
BALE, John, bp. of Ossory, 1495-1563
  God's Promises
    (In Dodsley's A Select Collection of Old English Plays, Vol.
    1)
    (In Dodsley's A Select Collection of Old Plays, Vol. 1)
BALL, David
  Assassin!
    (In Playwrights for Tomorrow, Vol. 7)
BALL, Edmund, fl. 1778
  Father and Son; or, The Rock of Charbonniere
    (In Cumberland's British Theatre, Vol. 1, no. 6)
Ballad of Youth (see Kreymborg, Alfred)
La Ballade du Soldat (Ballada o Soldate) (see Tchoukhri, Grigory)
La Balle au Chausseur (see Suffran, Michel)
Ballesteros, Antonio Martinez (see Martinez Ballesteros, Antonio)
The Balloon (see Kenan, Amos)
Balls (see Foster, Paul)
The Ballygombeen Bequest (see Arden, John)
Balo (see Toomer, Jean)
Balzac, Honore de, 1799-1850
  **La Fille Aux Yeux d'Or, d'apres la nouvelle d'Honore de Balzac
    (see Albicocco, Jean-Gabriel)
  **Monsieur Vautrin (see Charpak, Andre)
The Bank Note (see Macready, William)
Bankhead, Tallulah, 1903-1968
  *The Milk Train Doesn't Stop Here Anymore (fiction) (see
    Williams, Tennessee)
Bankruptcy Jazz, a Film Script, 1919 (see Van Ostaijen, Paul)
BANKS, John, fl. 1696
  The Albion Queen; or, The Death of Mary Queen of Scots
    (In Bell's British Theatre, Vol. 22, 1797)
The Banks of the Hudson; or, The Congress Trooper (see Dibdin,
    Thomas Frognall)
The Banquet (see Phillips, Louis)
O Banquete do Prefeito (see Santos, Miguel)
The Baptism (see Jones, Lerio)
BARASCH, Norman, 1922-
  Make a Million, by Norman Barasch and Carroll Moore

(In Theatre Arts, Vol. 43, no. 6, June 1959)
Send Me No Flowers, by Norman Barasch and Carroll Moore
(In Theatre Arts, Vol. 45, June 1961)
BARATIER, Jacques, 1918-
La Desordre a Vingt Ans
(In L'Avant-Scene du Cinema, no. 75, 1967)
Barbarossa (see Brown, John)
Barber, Philip
I, Elizabeth Otis, Being of Sound Mind
(In Playwrights for Tomorrow, Vol. 3)
BARBER, Samuel, 1910-
Vanessa; an opera in four acts by Gian-Carlo Menotti and
music by Samuel Barber.
(In Esquire, Vol. 48, Dec. 1957)
The Barber of Seville (see Beaumarchais, Pierre Augustin Caron
de)
Barbey d'Aurevilly, Jules Amedee, 1808-1889
**Le Rideau Cramoisi (see Astruc, Alexandre)
Le Barbier de Seville (see Beaumarchais, Pierre Augustin Caron
de)
Barca, Pedro Calderon de la (see Calderon de la Barca, Pedro)
BARCLAY, James M.
"My Friend Thompson!"
(In Cumberland's British Theatre, Vol. 32, no. 4)
Barclay, Sir William (see Berkeley, Sir William)
BARDEM, Juan Antonio, 1922-
Mort d'un Cycliste, by Juan Antonio Bardem, d'apres une
nouvelle de Luis F. De Igoa. Titre original: "Muerte de
un Ciclista."
(In L'Avant-Scene du Cinema, no. 34, 1964)
Barefoot in Athens (see Anderson, Maxwell)
Barefoot in the Park (see Simon, Neil)
Barer, Marshall, 1923-
Once Upon a Mattress (see Rodgers, Mary)
The Bargain (see Gilbert, Michael)
BARILLET, Pierre, 1923-
Les Choutes, Barillet and Gredy
(In L'Avant Scene du Theatre, no. 274, Oct. 1962)
Revised:
(In L'Avant Scene du Theatre, no. 322, Nov. 1964)
Fleur de Cactus, by Barillet and Gredy
(In L'Avant Scene du Theatre, no. 322, Nov. 1964)
Folle Amanda, by Barillet and Gredy
(In L'Avant Scene du Theatre, no. 482, Nov. 1, 1971)
4 Pieces sur Jardin, by Barillet and J. P. Gredy
(In Plaisir de France, supplement theatral, no. 370, Sept.
1969)
L'Or et la Paille, by Barillet and Gredy
(In L'Avant Scene du Theatre, no. 142)
La Reine Blanche, by Barillet and Gredy
(In L'Avant Scene du Theatre, no. 87)
BARING, Maurice, 1874-1945
After Euripides' "Electra"

(In Diminutive Dramas)
Ariadne in Naxos
(In Diminutive Dramas)
The Aulis Difficulty
(In Diminutive Dramas)
The Blue Harlequin (with Apologies to Mr. Maeterlinck)
(In Diminutive Dramas)
Caligula's Picnic
(In Diminutive Dramas)
Calpurnia's Dinner-Party
(In Diminutive Dramas)
Catherine Parr; or, Alexander's Horse
(In Diminutive Dramas)
The Death of Alexander
(In Diminutive Dramas)
Don Juan's Failure
(In Diminutive Dramas)
The Drawback
(In Diminutive Dramas)
The Fatal Rubber
(In Diminutive Dramas)
The Greek Vase
(In Diminutive Dramas)
Jason and Medea
(In Diminutive Dramas)
King Alfred and the Neat-Herd
(In Diminutive Dramas)
Lucullus's Dinner-Party
(In Diminutive Dramas)
The Member for Literature
(In Diminutive Dramas)
Pious Aeneas
(In Diminutive Dramas)
The Rehearsal
(In Diminutive Dramas)
Rosamund and Eleanor
(In Diminutive Dramas)
The Stoic's Daughter
(In Diminutive Dramas)
Velasquez and the "Venus"
(In Diminutive Dramas)
Xantippe and Socrates
(In Diminutive Dramas)
BARJOL, Jean-Michel, 1935-
Santo-Pietro
(In L'Avant-Scene du Cinema, no. 108, Nov. 1970)
BARKER, James Nelson, 1784-1858
Superstition
(In Best Plays of the Early American Theatre, from the
beginning to 1916)
BARLOW, Anna Marie
Mr. Biggs
(In New American Plays, Vol. 1)

Barn Burning   (see Vidal, Gore)
BARNEVELDT, Sir Jan Van Olden, 1547-1619 (Anon.)
    *The Tragedy of Sir John Van Olden Barnavelt
        (In A Collection of Old English Plays, Vol. 2)
BARNOUW, Eric, 1908-
    Sink or Swim; or, Harry Raymond's Resolve   (see O'Malley,
        Neill)
    The Story They'll Never Print
        (In Radio's Best Plays, 1947)
Barnstone, Willis
    The Outrageous Saint   (see Vega Carpio, Lope Felix de)
Barnum, Phineas Taylor, 1810-1891
    *The Mighty Barnum   (see Fowler, Gene)
The Baron   (see Moratin, Leandro Fernandes de)
BARR, Betty
    The Good and Obedient Young Man; play in the Japanese manner,
        by Betty Barr and Gould Stevens. Suggested by Grace James'
        story "Reflection," from Green Willow and Other Japanese
        Stories.
        (In Theatre Arts, Vol. 15, Feb. 1931)
BARRAL, Jean, 1930-
    La Belle Saison est Proche; film en Souvenir du Poete Robert
        Desnos
        (In L'Avant-Scene du Cinema, no. 22, Jan. 15, 1963)
Barranca Abajo   (see Sanchez, Florencio)
BARRAS, Charles M., 1820?-1873
    The Black Crook
        (In The Black Crook & Other 19th Century American Plays)
BARRETO, Paulo, 1878-
    Eva
        (In Revista de Teatro, nos. 359-360)
    Que Pena Ser So Ladrao
        (In Revista de Teatro, no. 353)
    Ultima Noite
        (In Revista de Teatro, no. 321)
The Barretts of Wimpole Street (see Besier, Rudolph)
BARRIE, Sir James Matthew, bart., 1860-1937
    The Twelve-Pound Look
        (In Contemporary One-Act Plays, 1922)
        (In 30 Famous One-Act Plays)
    What Every Woman Knows
        (In 16 Famous British Plays)
    The Will
        (In Reading Drama)
BARRIER, Maurice
    Au Restaurant
        (In Plaisir de France, supplement theatral, no. 374, Jan.
        1970)
    L'Explication
        (In L'Avant-Scene du Theatre, no. 441, Jan. 15, 1970)
Barrow, Clyde, 1906-1934
    *Bonnie and Clyde   (see Newman, David)
Barry, David Lord   (see Barry, Lording)

Barry, Lodowich (see Barry, Lording)
BARRY, Lording, 1580?-1629
    Ram-Alley; or, Merrie Trickes
        (In Dodsley's A Select Collection of Old Plays, Vol. 5)
        (In Dodsley's A Select Collection of Old English Plays, Vol.
        10)
Barry, Maurice, 1910-
    Mina de Vanghel (see Clavel, Maurice)
BARRY, Philip, 1896-1949
    The Animal Kingdom
        (In 20 Best Plays of the Modern American Theatre, Vol. 1)
    Here Come the Clowns
        (In Best American Plays, Supp. Vol.)
    Hotel Universe
        (In Theatre Guild Anthology)
    Paris Bound
        (In 25 Best Plays of the Modern American Theatre, Early
        Series, 1916-1929)
    The Philadelphia Story
        (In Best Plays of the Modern American Theatre, Second
        Series)
    Second Threshold
        (In Theatre Arts, Vol. 35, Dec. 1951)
BARRY, S.
    The Dutchman's Ghost; or, All Right
        (In 26 Short & Amusing Plays, 1871)
BARSACQ, Andre
    L'Idiot, adapted from the work of Dostoevskii
        (In Plaisir de France, supplement theatral, no. 337, Nov.
        1966)
BARTH, Ruth
    Red Death
        (In Plays from Radio, 1948)
BARZMAN, Ben, 1910-
    "Give Us This Day"; screenplay, text in French
        (In Cahiers du Cinema, Vol. 1, no. 1, April 1951)
The Basement (see Pinter, Harold)
The Basement (see Schisgal, Murray)
The Basic Training of Pavlo Hummel (see Rabe, David)
BASSHE, Emanuel Jo
    The Turbulent Waters
        (In One-Act Play Magazine, 1937-38 Anthology)
The Bat (see Rinehart, Mary Roberts)
BATE, Lucy
    The Great Silkie of Sule Skerry
        (In Scripts, Vol. 1, no. 8, June 1972)
BATES, William O.
    Asaph
        (In Drama, Vol. 10, Mar. /Apr. 1920)
    In the Light of the Manger
        (In Drama, Vol. 11, Dec. 1920)
    Merry Mount

(In Drama, Vol. 10, Jul. /Sept. 1920)
The Bath Road (see Neilson, Francis)
Bathsheba, 2nd Wife of David and Mother of Solomon
    *David and Bathsheba (see Cornish: The Legend of the Rood II)
The Battle at Yashima (see Zeami Motokiyo)
The Battle of Elderbush Gulch (see Niver, Kemp R.)
The Battle of Hexham; or, Days of Old (see Colman, George, the
    Younger)
The Battle of Sedgemoor; or, The Days of Kirk and Monmouth
    (see Almar, George)
The Battle of the Warsaw Ghetto (see Wishengrad, Morton)
The Battles of Coxinga (Kokusenyo Kassen) (see Chikamatsu
    Monzaemon)
Battleship Bismarck (see Valency, Maurice)
BAUER, Wolfgang
    Change
    (In Theater Heute, Vol. 19, no. 11, Nov. 1969)
BAUM, Vicki, 1888-1960
    Grand Hotel
    (In 16 Famous European Plays)
BAX, Clifford, 1886-
    The Rose Without a Thorn
    (In Famous Plays of Today, 1932)
BAXTER, David
    Will Somebody Please Say Something
    (In Plays and Players, Vol. 14, Apr. 1967)
La Baye (see Adrien, Philippe)
BAYLEY, Jefferson
    Olympus Farewell
    (In First Stage, Vol. 2, Fall 1963)
BAYLEY, Peter, 1778?-1823
    Orestes in Argos
    (In Cumberland's British Theatre, Vol. 3, no. 1)
BAYLY, John Ward
    The Maker of Laws
    (In Best One-Act Plays of 1937, N.Y.)
    Never No Third Degree
    (In Best One-Act Plays of 1938, N.Y.)
Bea, Frank, Richie & Joan (see Taylor, Renee)
BEACH, Lewis, 1891-
    Brothers
    (In 50 Contemporary One-Act Plays)
    The Clod
    (In 30 Famous One-Act Plays)
    (In 25 Best Plays of the Modern American Theatre, Early
    Series, 1916-1929)
Beams of Our House (see Apstein, Theodore Emanuel)
Bean, Roy, c.1825-1903
    *The Life and Times of Judge Roy Bean (see Milius, John)
The Beard (see McClure, Michael)
The Bearded Virgin and the Blind God (see Fiedler, Leslie)
The Bear's Nest (see Donahue, Patricia M.)

The Beast (see Agoston, Gerty)
The Best Man (see Vidal, Gore)
BEAUMARCHAIS, Pierre-Augustin Caron de, 1732-1799
    The Barber of Seville
        (In Genius of the French Theater)
        (In Chief European Dramatists)
        (In World Drama, Vol. 2)
        (In Cumberland's British Theatre, Vol. 12, no. 1)
    Le Barbier de Seville
        (In L'Avant Scene du Theatre, no. 457, Oct. 1, 1970)
    Figaro's Marriage
        (In The Classic Theatre, ed. by Eric Bentley)
BEAUMONT, Francis, 1584-1616
    Bonduca, by Beaumont and Fletcher, adapted by George Colman
        (In Bell's British Theatre, 1797, Vol. 33)
    The Chances, by Beaumont and Fletcher, adapted by the Duke
      of Buckingham
        (In Bell's British Theatre, 1797, Vol. 11)
        (In Great English Plays)
        Lawrence Olivier's version in Plays of the Year, 1961-62,
        Vol. 25)
    The Knight of the Burning Pestle, by Francis Beaumont and
      John Fletcher
        (In Masterworks of World Drama, Vol. 3)
    The Maid's Tragedy, by Beaumont and Fletcher
        (In Great English Plays)
    Philaster, by Beaumont and Fletcher
        (In Bell's British Theatre, 1797, Vol. 18)
    Rule a Wife and Have a Wife, by Beaumont and Fletcher
        (In Cumberland's British Theatre, Vol. 18, no. 2)
        (In Bell's British Theatre, 1797, Vol. 8)
Beauregard, Georges de
    Lola (see Demy, Jacques)
La Beaute du Diable (see Clair, Rene)
Beauty and the Beast (see Cocteau, Jean)
Beauty and the Jacobin (see Tarkington, Booth)
The Beauty Part (see Perelman, Sidney Joseph)
The Beaux' Stratagem (see Farquhar, George)
BEBNONE, Palou
    Kaltouma
        (In Plaisir de France, supplement theatral, no. 317, March
        1965)
Beck, Beatrix
    **Lone Morin Pretre (see Melville, Jean-Pierre)
Beck, Reginald
    Henvy V. (see Olivier, Sir Laurence)
BECKER, Jacques, 1906-1960
    Casque d'Or
        (In L'Avant-Scene du Cinema, no. 43, Dec. 1, 1964)
    Le Trou, by Jacques Becker et Jose Giovanni, d'apres le
      roman de Jose Giovanni.
        (In L'Avant-Scene du Cinema, no. 13, Mar. 1962)

Becket; or, The Honor of God   (see Anouilh, Jean)
Beckett, Gilbert Abbott à   (see A Beckett, Gilbert Abbott)
BECKETT, Samuel, 1906-
    Act Without Words I & II
      (In Evergreen Playscript Series)
    All That Fall
      (In Evergreen Playscript Series)
    Cascando
      (In Evergreen Playscript Series)
      (In Evergreen Review, Vol. 7, no. 30, 1963)
    Eh Joe
      (In Evergreen Review, Vol. 13, no. 62, Jan. 1969)
    Embers
      (In Evergreen Playscript Series)
      (In Evergreen Review, Vol. 3, no. 10, 1959)
    Endgame
      (In Evergreen Playscript Series)
      (In Modern Theatre, ed. by R. W. Corrigan)
    Film
      (In Evergreen Filmscript Series, E-502)
    Happy Days
      (In L'Avant-Scene du Theatre, no. 313, June 15, 1964)
      (In Evergreen Playscript Series)
    Krapp's Last Tape
      (In Evergreen Playscript Series)
      (In Evergreen Review, Vol. 2, no. 5, 1958)
**The Old Tune   (see Pinget, Robert)
    Play
      (In Evergreen Playscript Series)
      (In Evergreen Review, Vol. 8, no. 34, 1964)
    Waiting for Godot.   Originally performed as "En Attendant
    Godot. "
      (In Theatre Arts, Vol. 40, Aug. 1956)
      (In 7 Plays of the Modern Theatre)
    Words and Music
      (In Evergreen Playscript Series)
      (In Evergreen Review, Vol. 6, no. 27, 1962)
Beckett, Thomas A.   (see Thomas à Beckit, Saint, Abp. of Canterbury)
Becky Sharp   (see Mitchell, Langdon Elwyn)
BECQUE, Henri, 1837-1899
    Les Corbeaux
      (In Chief French Plays of the 19th Century)
    La Parisienne
      (In From the Modern Repertoire, Series One)
    Woman of Paris
      (In The Modern Theatre, ed. by Eric Bentley, Vol. 1)
The Bed   (see Adler, Jack)
A Bed with the Others   (see Williamson, Scott Graham)
Bedlam Galore for Two or More   (see Ionesco, Eugene)
Bedtime Story   (see O'Casey, Sean)
The Bee   (see Saunders, Lilian)
BEEBE, Ted, 1899-
    The Eagle; a television script

(In Best One-Act Plays of 1946/47, N. Y.)
Beeding, Francis
**Spellbound (see Hecht, Ben)
The Bee-Hive (see Millingen, T. V.)
BEERBOHM, Max, 1872-1956
    A Social Success
        (In The Modern Theatre, ed. by Eric Bentley, Vol. 6)
Before the Bullfight (see Apstein, Theodore)
Before the Flood (see Milne, Alan Alexander)
The Beggar and the King (see Parkhurst, Winthrop)
Beggar on Horseback (see Kaufman, George Simon)
Beggar, or, The Dead Dog (see Brecht, Bertolt)
The Beggars (see Ruibal, Jose)
The Beggars (see Saroyan, William)
The Beggars' Opera (see Gay, John)
BEHAN, Brendan, 1923-1964
    The Big House
        (In Evergreen Review, Vol. 5, Sept. /Oct. 1961)
    The Hostage
        (In The Quare Fellow & The Hostage, Evergreen Playscript
        Series)
        (In Theatre Arts, Vol. 46, Nov. 1962)
        (In New British Drama)
    The Quare Fellow
        (In 7 Plays of the Modern Theatre)
        (In The Quare Fellow & The Hostage, Evergreen Playscript
        Series)
Behold, We Live (see Van Druten, John)
BEHRMAN, Samuel Nathaniel, 1893-
    Biography
        (In Best American Plays, Supp. Vol.)
        (In 16 Famous American Plays)
    End of Summer
        (In 20 Best Plays of the Modern American Theatre, Vol. 1)
    **Jacobowsky and the Colonel (see Werfel, Franz V.)
    Rain from Heaven
        (In Theatre Guild Anthology)
    The Second Man
        (In 25 Best Plays of the Modern American Theatre, Early
        Series, 1916-1929)
BEIER, Carl
    The Sunny Side of the Atom, by Carl Beier and Ruth Ashton
        (In Best One-Act Plays of 1947/48, N. Y.)
Le Bel Indifferent (see Cocteau, Jean)
BELA, Nicholas, 1900-
    Safecracker's Pride
        (In Best One-Act Plays, 1951/52, N. Y.)
    Silver Nails
        (In Best One-Act Plays of 1945, N. Y.)
    Skeletons
        (In Best One-Act Plays of 1946/47, N. Y.)
    Suffer the Little Children
        (In Best One-Act Plays of 1947/48, N. Y.)

Belcher's Luck (see Mercer, David)
La Belette (see Valdrac, Charles)
Bell, Book, and Candle (see Van Druten, John)
BELL, J. W.
    Symphony in Illusion
        (In Best One-Act Plays of 1932, London)
BELL, Neal
    Play
        (In Yale Literary Magazine, Vol. 140, no. 3, 1971)
    Warren
        (In Yale Literary Magazine, Vol. 140, no. 1, 1970)
Bellak, George, 1919-
    Open Secret (see Adler, Robert)
Bellavita (see Pirandello, Luigi)
Belle de Jour (see Buñuel, Luis)
La Belle Saison est Proche (see Barral, Jean)
The Belle's Stratagem (see Cowley, Mrs. Hannah Parkhouse)
Les Belles-de-Nuit (see Claire, Rene)
BELLIDO CORMENZANA, Jose Maria, 1922-
    The Interrogation
        (In Drama and Theatre, Vol. 9, no. 3, Spring 1971)
    Madam Takes a Bath
        (In First Stage, Vol. 5, no. 4, Winter 1966-67)
    Train to H...
        (In Modern International Drama, Vol. 1, no. 2, Mar. 1968)
BELLOCCHIO, Marco, 1940-
    China is Near; screenplay, trans. from the Italian by Judith
    Green
        (In Grossman Library of Film Classics, 1969)
BELLON, Yannick
    Goemons
        (In L'Avant-Scene du Cinema, no. 85, Oct. 1968)
Bellour, Raymond, 1939-
    San Fermin (see Destanque, Robert)
    Satan Mon Prochain (see Lacassin, Francis)
BELLOW, Saul, 1915-
    Humanities
        (In Partisan Review, Vol. 29, Summer 1962)
    The Last Analysis
        (In Best American Plays, Sixth Series, 1963-67)
        (In Broadway's Beautiful Losers)
    Orange Souffle
        (In Esquire, Vol. 64, Oct. 1965)
    Wen
        (In Esquire, Vol. 63, Jan. 1965)
The Bells (see Lewis, Leopold David)
Bells are Ringing (see Styne, Jule)
BELMONT, Charles, 1936-
    RAK
        (In L'Avant-Scene du Cinema, no. 126, June 1972)
Bemelmans, Ludwig, 1898-1962
    **Now I Lay Me Down to Sleep (see Ryan, Elaine)

Ben Franklin in Paris   (see Sandrich, Mark)
BENAVENTE Y MARTINEZ, Jacinto, 1866-1954
   His Widow's Husband
      (In 50 Contemporary One-Act Plays)
   The Passion Flower
      (In 20 Best European Plays on the American Stage)
BENET, Stephen Vincent, 1898-1943
   **All That Money Can Buy   (see Totheroh, Dan)
   A Child is Born
      (In Radio Drama in Action, 1945)
   The Devil and Daniel Webster
      (In Plays as Experience)
      (In 15 American One-Act Plays)
      (In 24 Favorite One-Act Plays)
   The Devil and Daniel Webster (Adapted for radio by Charles
      Jackson)
      (In Plays From Radio, 1948)
   **The Last Speech   (see Cooper, Lou)
   Scratch   (see MacLeish, Archibald)
   They Burned the Books
      (In Best One-Act Plays of 1942, N.Y.)
   Western Star
      (In Radio's Best Plays, 1947)
BENET, William Rose, 1886-1950
   Day's End
      (In Best One-Act Plays of 1939, N.Y.)
BENGAL, Ben
   "All Aboard!"
      (In Theatre Arts, Vol. 28, Sept. 1944)
   Plant in the Sun
      (In Best Short Plays of the Social Theatre, 1939)
Benito Cereno   (see Lowell, Robert)
Benkei on the Bridge (Hashi-Benkei)   (see Hiyoshi Sa-ami Yasukiyo)
BENNER, Richard V.
   The Last of the Order
      (In Drama at Calgary, Vol. 4, no. 1)
BENNETT, Alan
   Getting On
      (In Plays and Players, Vol. 19, no. 4, Jan. 1972)
BENNETT, Arnold, 1867-1931
   Flora
      (In Five Three-Act Plays.   Strand, 1933)
   A Good Woman
      (In 50 Contemporary One-Act Plays)
   Milestones, by Arnold Bennett and Edward Knoblock
      (In Dramas by Present-Day Writers)
      (In Modern Plays, London, 1937)
      (In 16 Famous British Plays)
   The Stepmother
      (In Representative One-Act Plays by British and Irish
         Authors)
Benten the Thief (Aoto Zoshi Hana no Nishikie, or Shiranami Gonin
   Otoko)

(In Three Japanese Plays from the Traditional Theatre)
BENTLEY, Eric Russell, 1916-
**The Forced Marriage (see Moliere, Jean Baptiste Poquelin)
Larry Parks' Day in Court
   (In Scripts, Vol. 1, no. 5, Mar. 1972)
A Time to Live
   (In Best Short Plays, 1969)
BEOLCO, Angelo, c. 1502-1542
Bilora
   (In Masterworks of World Drama, Vol. 3)
Ruzzante Returns from the Wars
   (In The Classic Theatre, ed. by Eric Bentley, Vol. 1)
A Bequest to the Nation (see Rattigan, Terence)
Berenice (see Racine, Jean Baptiste)
BERG, Gertrude, 1899-
The Goldbergs
   (In Best Television Plays of the Year, 1949)
The Goldbergs (Rosie's Hair)
   (In Best Television Plays of the Year, 1950/51)
BERGEN, Candice
The Freezer
   (In Best Short Plays, 1968)
BERGMAN, Ingmar, 1918-
The Communicants (Winter Light)
   (In A Film Trilogy)
Une Passion
   (In L'Avant-Scene du Cinema, no. 109, Dec. 1970)
Persona
   (In Bergman: Persona and Shame)
   (In L'Avant-Scene du Cinema, no. 85, Oct. 1968)
The Seventh Seal
   (Modern Film Scripts Series)
Shame
   (In Bergman: Persona and Shame)
Le Silence. Titre original: "Tystnaden."
   (In L'Avant-Scene du Cinema, no. 37, 1964)
The Silence
   (In A Film Trilogy)
Smiles of a Summer Night
   (In Modern Film Scripts)
Through a Glass Darkly
   (In A Film Trilogy)
Wild Strawberries
   (In Modern Film Scripts)
Wood Painting
   (In Tulane Drama Review, Vol. 6, Nov. 1961)
   (In Film Focus Series: Focus on "The Seventh Seal")
BERKELEY, Reginald Cheyne, 1890-
The Lady with the Lamp
   (In Famous Plays of Today, 1929)
BERKELEY, Sir William, 1608?-1677
The Lost Lady
   (In Dodsley's A Select Collection of Old English Plays, Vol.
   12)

Berkeley Square (see Balderston, John Lloyd)
Berkey, Ralph
   Time Limit! (see Denker, Henry)
BERMEL, Albert
   The Mountain Chorus
      (In Best Short Plays, 1968)
   One Leg Over the Wrong Wall
      (In Drama & Theatre, Vol. 8, no. 3, Spring 1970)
Bernanos, Georges, 1888-1948
   **Mouchette, d'apres l'oeuvre de Georges Bernanos (see Bres-
      son, Robert)
BERNARD, Kenneth
   Goodbye, Dan Bailey
      (In Drama and Theatre, Vol. 9, no. 3, Spring 1971)
   Marko's: A Vegetarian Fantasy
      (In Massachusetts Review, Vol. 19, Summer 1969)
BERNARD, William Baile, 1807-1875
   The Old Regimentals
      (In Cumberland's British Theatre, Vol. 28, no. 2)
Bernardine (see Chase, Mary)
BERNHARD, Thomas
   Ein Fest Für Boris
      (In Theater Heute, Jan. 1970)
   Der Ignorant und der Wahsinnige
      (In Theater Heute, no. 9, Sept. 1972)
Bernice (see Glaspell, Susan)
BERNSTEIN, Leonard, 1918-
   West Side Story; a musical, based on a conception of Jerome
      Robbins; book by Arthur Laurents; lyrics by Stephen Sondheim.
      (In Theatre Arts, Vol. 43, no. 10, Oct. 1959)
BERRETTA, Alfio, 1897-
   The Turks Toss for Her; both French and English texts are
      included.
      (In Italian Theatre Review, Vol. 11, Jan./Mar. 1962)
Bertha (see Koch, Kenneth)
BERTIN, Charles
   Christopher Columbus
      (In Two Plays)
   Don Juan
      (In Two Plays)
Bertoldo at Court (see Dursi, Massimo)
BERTOLUCCI, Bernardo, 1940-
   Prima Della Rivoluzione
      (In L'Avant-Scene du Cinema, no. 82, June 1968)
Bertran de Born (see Lunts, Lev)
BESIER, Rudolph, 1878-1942
   The Barretts of Wimpole Street
      (In Famous Plays of Today, 1931)
      (In 16 Famous British Plays)
BESOYAN, Rick, 1924-
   Little Mary Sunshine; book, music and lyrics by Rick Besoyan.
      (In Theatre Arts, Vol. 44, no. 12, Dec. 1960)
The Bespoke Overcoat (see Mankowitz, Wolf)

The Best Man (see Vidal, Gore)
The Best of All Possible Worlds (see Martinez Ballerteros, Antonio)
BETHENCOURT, Joao
  Como Matar um Playboy
    (In Revista de Teatro, no. 372, Nov./Dec. 1969)
  Frank Sinatra 4815
    (In Revista de Teatro, no. 383, Sept./Oct. 1971)
The Betrayal (see Colum, Padraic)
Betrayals (see Fratti, Mario)
Better Than Average (see Kikuchi Kwan)
BETTI, Ugo, 1892-1953
  Corruption in the Palace of Justice
    (In New Theatre of Europe, 1962)
    (In Tragedy: Texts and Commentary)
  The Queen and the Rebels
    (In Makers of the Modern Theater, 1961)
    (In The Modern Theatre, ed. by R.W. Corrigan)
Between Two Moons (see Mungo, Raymond)
BEVAN, Donald, 1920-
  Stalag 17, by Donald Bevan and Edmund Trazcinski
    (In Theatre Arts, Vol. 37, Feb. 1953)
Beware of the Dog (see Arout, Gabriel)
BEYE, Holly
  It's All (Y)ours!
    (In Quarterly Review of Literature, Vol. 11, no. 1, 1961)
  Th(us)
    (In Quarterly Review of Literature, Vol. 11, no. 1, 1961)
Beyond (see Ustinov, Peter)
Beyond the Horizon (see O'Neill, Eugene Gladstone)
Bhasa (Sanskrit) c. 3rd century
  **The Toy Cart (Krichchakatika) (see Shudraka, King)
BIBERMAN, Herbert J., 1900-1971
  Le Sel de la Terre; titre original "Salt of the Earth."
    (In L'Avant-Scene du Cinema, no. 115, June 1971)
The Bible Salesman (see Double Entry)
BICKERSTAFF, Isaac, 1735?-1812?
  The Hypocrite
    (In Cumberland's British Theatre, Vol. 15, no. 2)
    (In Bell's British Theatre, 1797, Vol. 21)
  Love in a Village
    (In Cumberland's British Theatre, Vol. 17, no. 3)
    (In Bell's British Theatre, 1797, Vol. 13)
  The Maid of the Mill
    (In Cumberland's British Theatre, Vol. 32, no. 5)
    (In Bell's British Theatre, 1797, Vol. 8)
  The Padlock
    (In Cumberland's British Theatre, Vol. 16, no. 7)
  The School for Fathers; or, Lionel and Clarissa
    (In Bell's British Theatre, 1797, Vol. 21)
The Bicycle Thief (see De Sica, Vittorio)
Il Bidone (see Fellini, Federico)

BIEL, Nicholas J.
  The Devil's Foot
    (In Best One-Act Plays of 1945, N. Y.)
  Sound on the Goose
    (In First Stage, Vol. 3, Winter 1963-64)
BIERCE, Ambrose, 1842-1914?
  **La Riviere du Hibou, d'apres la nouvelle Americaine (see
    Enrice, Robert)
  A Strained Relation
    (In Cosmopolitan, Vol. 42, Mar. 1907)
BIERSTADT, Edward Hale
  The Fifth Commandment
    (In Drama, Vol. 10, May 1920)
The Big and the Little Maneuver (see Adamov, Arthur)
Big-Ben (see Gourgue, Jean)
The Big Deal (see Chayefsky, Paddy)
Big Fish, Little Fish (see Wheeler, Hugh)
The Big House (see Behan, Brendan)
The Big Killing (see Mackie, Philip)
The Big Knife (see Odets, Clifford)
The Big Road (see Rosten, Norman)
The Big Sleep (see Faulkner, William)
Bigelow, Franklyn
  Let It Burn (see Van der Veer, Ethel)
Biggers, Earl Derr, 1884-1933
  **Seven Keys to Baldpate (see Cohan, George Michael)
The Biggest Thief in Town (see Trumbo, Dalton)
A Bill of Divorcement (see Ashton, Winifred)
BILLETDOUX, Francois, 1927-
  Femmes Paralleles
    (In L'Avant Scene du Theatre, no. 469-470, April 1-15, 1971)
  Pour Finalie
    (In Plaisir de France, supplemental theatral, no. 293, Mar.
    1963)
Billy Budd (see Coxe, Louis Osborne)
Billy Jack (see Christina, Frank)
Billy Liar (see Waterhouse, Keith)
Billy Taylor; or, The Gay Young Fellow (see Buckstone, John
  Baldwin)
Billy the Kid (see Bonney, William H.)
Bilora (see Beolco, Angelo)
Biografie (see Frisch, Max)
Biography (see Behrman, Samuel Nathaniel)
BIRAGHI, Guglielmo, 1927-
  The Sun and the Moon; both French and English texts are given.
    (In Italian Theatre Review, Vol. 15, Apr. /June 1966)
BIRCH, Samuel, 1757-1841
  The Adopted Child
    (In Cumberland's British Theatre, Vol. 24, no. 8)
    (In The London Stage, Vol. 1)
The Bird Child (see White, Lucy)
Birdbath (see Melfi, Leonard)

The Birdcatcher (see O'Brien, Seumas)
The Bird-Catcher in Hades (see Sakanishi, Shio)
The Birds (see Aristophanes)
Birds of a Feather (see Francis, James Oswald)
Birds of Sorrow (see Seami Motokiyo)
Birger, Jarl, d. 1266
    *Earl Birger of Bjälbo (see Strindberg, August)
BIRIMISA, George, 1924-
    Porgie Georgie
        (In More Plays From Off Off Broadway)
BIRNKRANT, Oscar
    A Whisper in God's Ear
        (In Drama & Theatre, Vol. 8, no. 3, Spring 1970)
BIRO, Lajos, 1880-1950
    The Grandmother
        (In 50 Contemporary One-Act Plays)
The Birth of Christ (see York Tile-Thatchers' Play)
The Birthday (see Goodman, Paul)
The Birthday Party (see Pinter, Harold)
Bishop, Sir Henry Rowley, 1786-1855
    **Clari; or, The Maid of Milan (see Payne, John Howard)
Bissell, Richard Pike
    **The Pajama Game (see Abbott, George)
BIVAR, Antonio
    Abre a Janela e Deixa Entrar o Ar Puro e o Sol da Manha
        (In Revista de Teatro, no. 367, Jan. /Feb. 1969)
Black Comedy (see Shaffer, Peter)
The Black Crook (see Barras, Charles M.)
Black Mass (see Bond, Edward)
A Black Mass (see Jones, LeRoi)
The Black President (see Schevill, James Erwin)
"Black Sheep" (see Simpson, J. Palgrave)
The Black Swan Winter (see Hale, John)
The Black Terror (see Wesley, Richard)
The Blacks (see Genet, Jean)
BLAKE, Thomas G.
    A Spanking Legacy; or, The Corsican Vendetta
        (In 26 Short & Amusing Plays, 1871)
Blake's Design (see Brown, Kenneth H.)
BLAND, Margaret
    Lighted Candles
        (In Carolina Folkplays)
BLANKENSHIP, Catherine
    Murder is Fun!
        (In Best One-Act Plays of 1943, N. Y.)
Bleiwe Losse (see Deichsel, Wolfgang)
Blessed Above Women (see Godefroy, Vincent)
The Blind Bargain; or, Hear It Out (see Reynolds, Frederick)
The Blind Boy (see Kenney, James)
The Blind Goddess (see Toller, Ernst)
Bliss Apocalypse (see Moore, Daniel)
BLITZSTEIN, Marc, 1905-1964
    The Airborne

(In Radio's Best Plays, 1947)
The Cradle Will Rock
    (In Best Short Plays of the Social Theatre, 1939)
Blobo's Boy (see Zuckerman, Albert J.)
BLOCH, Pedro
    Amor a Oito Maos
        (In Revista de Teatro, no. 344)
    Brasileiros em Nova Iorque
        (In Revista de Teatro, no. 325)
    O Contrato Azul
        (In Revista de Teatro, no. 384, Nov. /Dec. 1971)
    Dona Xepa
        (In Revista de Teatro, no. 303)
    Uma Flauta Para o Negro
        (In Revista de Teatro, no. 314)
    LSD
        (In Revista de Teatro, no. 384, Nov. /Dec. 1971)
    Miquelina
        (In Revista de Teatro, no. 318)
    Morre um Gato na China
        (In Revista de Teatro, no. 354)
    Os Inimigos Nao Mandam Flores
        (In Revista de Teatro, Mar. /Apr. 1970)
    Os Pais Abstratos
        (In Revista de Teatro, no. 368, Mar. /Apr. 1969)
    Roleta Paulista
        (In Revista de Teatro, no. 335)
Blockade (see Dunbar, Olivia Howard)
Blood Money (see Jasudowicz, Dennis)
The Blood of a Poet (see Cocteau, Jean)
Blood of the Bambergs (see Osborne, John)
Blood of the Martyrs (see Wilde, Percival)
Blood-Photo (see Friedman, Edward)
Blood Wedding (see Garcia Lorca, Federico)
The Bloody Tenet (see Schevill, James Erwin)
The Blue Angel (see Von Sternberg, Joseph)
Blue Beard (see Colman, George, the Younger)
Bluebeard (see Ludlam, Charles)
Blue Blood (see Johnson, Mrs. Georgia Douglas Camp)
Blue Concerto (see Seiger, Marvin L.)
Blue Denim (see Herlihy, James Leo)
Blue Devils (see Colman, George)
The Blue Harlequin (see Baring, Maurice)
The Blue Hotel (see Agee, James)
Blue Jeans (see O'Glor, Michele)
The Blue Sphere (see Dreiser, Theodore)
Blues for Mister Charlie (see Baldwin, James)
BOADEN, Caroline
    Fatality
        (In Cumberland's British Theatre, Vol. 4, no. 6)
    The First of April
        (In Cumberland's British Theatre, Vol. 29, no. 5)

William Thomson; or, Which is He?
   (In Cumberland's British Theatre, Vol. 11, no. 7)
Boadicea, Queen of the Iceni, d. 62 A.D.
   *Boadicea (see Glover, Richard)
   *Caesar Aderat Forte; or, Brutus Adsum Jam (see Sims, Alan)
BOBB, Ralph
   A Late Spring. Based on Henry James' "The Wings of the
   Dove. "
   (In First Stage, Vol. 2, Summer 1963)
Bobrick, Sam
   Get Smart, a television filmscript (see Idelson, Bill)
Bobrowski, Johannes
   Levins Mühle, Oper in Neun Bildern (see Zimmerman, Udo)
BOCAYUVA, Quintino
   A Familia
   (In Revista de Teatro, no. 294)
Boccaccio '70 (see The Temptation of Dr. Antonio)
Boccaccio's Untold Tale (see Kemp, Harry Hibbard)
BOCK, Jerry
   The Diary of Adam and Eve, by Jerry Bock and Sheldon Har-
   nick
   (In Modern Short Comedies from Broadway & London)
   Fiddler on the Roof; a musical comedy by Joseph Stein, based
   on Sholom Aleichem's stories, with music by Jerry Bock and
   lyrics by Sheldon Harnick.
   (In Best American Plays, Sixth Series, 1963-67)
   Fiorello! Book by Jerome Weidman and George Abbott. Music
   by Jerry Bock and lyrics by Sheldon Harnick.
   (In Theatre Arts, Vol. 45, Nov. 1961)
La Boheme (see Dietz, Howard)
The "Boise" (see MacDougall, Ranald)
BOKER, George Henry, 1823-1890
   Francesca da Rimini
   (In The Black Crook & Other 19th Century American Plays)
BOLAND, Bridget, 1913-
   Gordon
   (In Plays of the Year, Vol. 25, 1961-62)
A Bold Stroke for a Husband (see Cowley, Mrs. Hannah Parkhouse)
A Bold Stroke for a Wife (see Centlivre, Mrs. Susanna)
Boleyn, Anne, Consort of Henry VIII, King of England, 1401-1437
   *Ann Boleyn (see McCarty, Nick)
   *Anne of the Thousand Days (see Anderson, Maxwell)
Bologna, Joseph
   Bea, Frank, Richie & Joan (see Taylor, Renee)
Bolschewiki (see Schatrow, Michail)
BOLT, Robert, 1924-
   A Man for All Seasons
   (In New Theatre of Europe, 1962)
   (In Plays of Our Time)
   (In Theatre Arts, Vol. 47, May 1963)
Bolton, Guy, 1884-
   **Anastasia (see Marcelle-Maurette)

Bombastes Furioso (see Rhodes, William Barnes)
BOND, Edward, 1934-
   Black Mass
      (In Best Short Plays, 1972)
   Die Hochzeit des Papstes (The Pope's Wedding)
      (In Theatre Heute, Special Edition, 1970)
   Narrow Road to the Deep North
      (In Plays and Players, Vol. 15, Sept. 1968)
   Passion
      (In Plays and Players, Vol. 18, no. 9)
   The Pope's Wedding
      (In Plays and Players, Vol. 16, no. 7, Apr. 1969)
   Saved
      (In Plays and Players, Vol. 13, Jan. 1966)
   Trauer zu Früh
      (In Theatre Heute, Vol. 10, no. 5, May 1969)
BOND, Nelson, 1908-
   Mr. Mergenthwirker's Lobblies, by Nelson Bond and David
   Kent
      (In Theatre Arts, Vol. 35, July 1951)
A Bond Honoured (see Osborne, John)
The Bondman (see Massinger, Philip)
Bonduca (see Beaumont, Francis)
Le Bonheur (see Medvedkine, Alexandre)
"Bonjour Rodolphe... Adieu Gilbert!" (see Paquin, Dorian)
Les Bonnes Soirees de Madame France (see Gesbert, Bernard)
Bonney, William H., 1859-1881
   *The Death of Billy the Kid (see Vidal, Gore)
Bonnie and Clyde (see Newman, David)
Les Bonshommes (see Dorin, Francoise)
Booker T. Washington in Atlanta (see Hughes, Langston)
Books for the Dead (see Skidmore, Hobart)
The Boor (see Chekhov, Anton Pavlovich)
BORDEAUX, Henri
   Shattered
      (In Best One-Act Plays of 1933, London)
Borderline of Fear (see Roos, Joanna)
BOREL, Jacques
   Tate, Ou de l'Education
      (In L'Avant-Scene du Theatre, no. 491, Mar. 15, 1972)
BORETZ, Alvin
   The Trial of Poznan
      (In Best Television Plays of the Year, 1957)
BORETZ, Nick
   Shelter Area
      (In Playwrights for Tomorrow, Vol. 2)
Borges, Jose Carlos Cavalcanti (see Cavalcanti Borges, Jose
   Carlos)
Borgia, Caesar, 1476-1507
   *Caesar Borgia (see Lee, Nathaniel)
Borgia, Lucrezia, 1480-1519
   *Lucrezia Borgia's Little Party (see Talbot, A. J.)

Boris Godunov (see Musorgskii, Modest Petrovich)
Born Yesterday (see Kanin, Garson)
BORNSTEAD, Beulah
    The Diabolical Circle
      (In Contemporary One-Act Plays, 1922)
The Bosom of the Family (see O'Neill, Michael)
Bost, Pierre, 1901-
    Jeux Interdits (see Clement, Rene)
BOSWORTH, Raymond F.
    Happy the Bride
      (In Bread Loaf Book of Plays)
Both Your Houses (see Anderson, Maxwell)
Bottled In Bond (see Hughes, Glenn)
BOTTOMLEY, Gordon, 1874-1948
    Culbin Sands
      (In 24 One-Act Plays. Revised edition, 1954)
    Gruach
      (In Bread Loaf Book of Plays)
    The Riding to Lithend
      (In Atlantic Book of Modern Plays, 1921)
BOUCICAULT, Dion, 1820-1890
    The Octoroon; or, Life in Louisiana
      (In Best Plays of the Early American Theatre, from the be-
      ginning to 1916)
      (In The Black Crook & Other 19th Century American Plays)
      (In Six Early American Plays, 1798-1890)
Boulanger, Daniel, 1932-
    La Vie de Chateau (see Rappeneau, Jean-Paul)
Boulevard Durand (see Salacrow, Armand)
BOULLE, Pierre
    William Conrad
      (In Plaisir de France, supplement theatral, no. 280, Feb.
      1962)
Bound 'Prentice to a Waterman; or, The Flower of Woolwich (see
    Campbell, L. L. V.)
BOURNE, John
    The Second Visit
      (In Best One-Act Plays of 1932, London)
BOVASSO, Julie
    Schubert's Last Serenade
      (In Best Short Plays, 1972)
BOWEN, John, 1924-
    Trevor
      (In Best Short Plays, 1970)
      (In Modern Short Comedies from Broadway & London)
The Bowlers (see Grecco, Stephen)
Bow Wow; a skit from the Paper Bag play "Dandelion" (see Martin,
    Judith)
Box (see Albee, Edward)
The Box (see also The Sandbox)
BOX, Sidney, 1907-
    "Bring Me My Bow"
      (In Best One-Act Plays of 1937, London)

The Truth About Shakespeare
  (In Best One-Act Plays of 1939, London)
Self-Made Man
  (In Best One-Act Plays of 1934, London)
Waiter!
  (In Best One-Act Plays of 1935, London)
The Box-Lobby Challenge (see Cumberland, Richard)
The Boy in the Basement (see Inge, William Motter)
Boy Meets Girl (see Spewack, Bella Cohen)
The Boy: What Will He Become? (see Brighouse, Harold)
BOYCE, Neith "Mrs. Hutchins Hapgood, 1872-
Winter's Night
  (In 50 More Contemporary One-Act Plays)
BOYER, Francois, 1920-
Dieu Aboie-t-il?
  (In L'Avant-Scene du Cinema, no. 498, July 1, 1972)
BRACKETT, Charles, 1892-1969
  The Lost Weekend, a screenplay by Charles Brackett and Billy
  Wilder, based on the book by Charles Jackson; directed by
  Billy Wilder.
  (In Best Film Plays, 1945)
  Ninotchka, screenplay by Charles Brackett, Billy Wilder, and
  Walter Reisch; story by Melchior Lengyel; directed by
  Ernst Lubitsch.
  (In Best Pictures, 1939-40)
  (In MGM Library of Film Scripts Series)
BRADBURY, Ray, 1920-
The Meadow
  (In Best One-Act Plays of 1947/48, N.Y.)
BRADFORD, Benjamin, 1925-
Where Are You Going, Hollis Jay?
  (In Best Short Plays, 1970)
Braganza (see Jephson, Robert)
BRANCATI, Vitaliano, 1907-1954
Don Giovanni Involontario
  (In Teatro, Opere Complete di Vitaliano Brancati, Vol. 5)
Una Donna di Casa
  (In Teatro, Opere Complete di Vitaliano Brancati, Vol. 5)
La Governante
  (In Teatro, Opere Complete di Vitaliano Brancati, Vol. 5)
Questo Matrimonio si Deve Fare
  (In Teatro, Opere Complete di Vitaliano Brancati, Vol. 5)
Raffaele
  (In Teatro, Opere Complete di Vitaliano Brancati, Vol. 5)
Le Trombe d'Eustachio
  (In Teatro, Opere Complete di Vitaliano Brancati, Vol. 5)
Brand, Max, pseud. (see Faust, Fredrick)
Brasileiros em Nova Iorque (see Bloch, Pedro)
The Brass Butterfly (see Golding, William Gerald)
Le Brave Soldat Sveik (see Kepel, Milan)
Bread (see Eastman, Fred)
Bread and Butter (see Taylor, Cecil P.)

Bread & Puppet Theater
Love and Marriage of the River Winooski and Lake Champlain
(In Scripts, Vol. 1, no. 10, Oct. 1972)
The Bread of Affliction (see Greenbaum, Avrom)
Breaking Point (see Time Limit!)
BREAL, Pierre-Aristide
La Grande Oreille
(In Plaisir de France, supplement theatral, no. 292, Feb.
1963)
Jules
(In L'Avant-Scene du Theatre, Apr. 1956)
Les Suisses
(In Plaisir de France, supplement theatral, no. 353, Mar.
1968)
BRECHT, Bertolt, 1898-1956
Baal
(In Evergreen Playscript Series)
Baden Lehrstück
(In Tulane Drama Review, Vol. 4, May 1960)
Beggar; or, The Dead Dog
(In TDR/The Drama Review, Vol. 12, Winter 1968)
The Caucasian Chalk Circle
(In Genius of the German Theater)
The Caucasian Chalk Circle; based on a 14th Century play "The
Story of the Circle of Chalk," by Hui-lan-ki
(In The Modern Theatre, ed. by R. W. Corrigan)
Caucasian Circle of Chalk, translated by James Stern and W. H.
Auden
(In Kenyon Review, Vol. 8, no. 2, Spring 1946)
The Days of the Commune, translated by Leonard Lehrman
(In Massachusetts Review, Vol. 12, Summer 1971)
Drums in the Night
(In Evergreen Playscript Series)
The Elephant Calf
(In Evergreen Playscript Series)
The Elephant Calf; English version by Eric Bentley
(In Evergreen Review, Vol. 7, no. 29, 1963)
Galileo, translated by Charles Laughton
(In From the Modern Repertoire, Series Two)
In Search of Justice
(In Evergreen Playscript Series)
In the Jungle of Cities
(In Theatre Arts, Vol. 46, Aug. 1961)
The Informers
(In Evergreen Playscript Series)
The Jewish Wife
(In Evergreen Playscript Series)
Jungle of Cities
(In Evergreen Playscript Series)
Life of Confucius
(In Kenyon Review, Vol. 8, no. 2, Spring 1958)
Macbeth: Murder at the Gate-Keeper's House; Estranging
Shakespeare

(In TDR/Drama Review, Vol. 12, Fall 1967)
**Mahagonny (see Weill, Kurt)
A Man's A Man
    (In Evergreen Playscript Series)
The Measures Taken
    (In Evergreen Playscript Series)
    (In The Modern Theatre, ed. by Eric Bentley, Vol. 6)
Mother Courage
    (In The Modern Theatre, ed. by Eric Bentley, Vol. 2)
    (In New Theatre of Europe, 1962)
Romeo and Juliet: The Servants; Estranging Shakespeare; to be
played between scenes i and ii of Act II.
    (In TDR/Drama Review, Vol. 12, Fall 1967)
Roundheads and Peakheads
    (In Evergreen Playscript Series)
Saint Joan of the Stockyards
    (In From the Modern Repertoire, Series Three)
Salzburg Dance of Death
    (In Evergreen Playscript Series)
The Seven Deadly Sins of the Lower Middle Class, translated
by W. H. Auden and Chester Kallman
    (In Tulane Drama Review, Vol. 6, Sept. 1961)
The Threepenny Opera; adaptation of "The Beggar's Opera" by
John Gay
    (In From the Modern Repertoire, Series One)
    (In The Modern Theatre, ed. by Eric Bentley, Vol. 1)
**The Three-Penny Opera; screenplay (see Lania, Leo)
Yes, I'm Going Away
    (In Living Age, Vol. 356, May 1939)
Breit, Harvey
The Disenchanted (see Schulberg, Budd)
BRENNER, Alfred
Survival
    (In Best Television Plays of the Year, 1957)
BRENTON, Howard
Lay By, by Howard Brenton, Brian Clark, Trevor Griffiths,
David Hare, Steven Poliakoff, Hugh Stoddart, Snoo Wilson.
    (In Plays and Players, Vol. 19, no. 2, Nov. 1971)
BRESSON, Robert
Mouchette, d'apres l'oeuvre de Georges Bernanos
    (In L'Avant-Scene du Cinema, no. 80, Apr. 1968)
Bretherton, Vivien R.
**Love Finds Andy Hardy (see Ludwig, William)
Bretton Woods (see Lyon, Peter)
Brewsie and Willie (see Stein, Gertrude)
Bricaire, Jean-Jacques
Lolie Douce de Jean-Jacques Bricaire (see Maurice Lasaygues)
The Bridal Dinner (see Gurney, A. R. , Jr.)
The Bridal Night (see Mayer, Paul A.)
The Bride (see Jennings, Gertrude)
The Bride (see Nabbes, Thomas)
The Bride Comes to Yellow Sky (see Agee, James)

The Bride of Ludgate (see Jerrold, Douglas)
The Bridegroom Waits (see Hayes, Marijane)
Bride-Ship (see Jacobs, Jack)
The Bridge (see Corrie, Joe)
BRIDGEMAN, J. V.
    The Rifle and How to Use It
       (In Lacy's Acting Plays, Vol. 14)
Bridie, James, pseud. (see Mavor, Osborne Henry)
Brief Encounter (see Coward, Noel Pierce)
BRIEUX, Eugene, 1858-1932
    La Robe Rouge
       (In Chief French Plays of the 19th Century)
The Brig (see Brown, Kenneth H.)
Brigadoon (see Lerner, Alan Jay)
The Brigand (see Planche, James Robinson)
BRIGHOUSE, Harold, 1882-1958
    Above Rubies
       (In Best One-Act Plays, 1952-53, London)
    Albert Gates
       (In Best One-Act Plays of 1937, London)
    Back to Adam
       (In Best One-Act Plays of 1935, London)
    The Boy: What Will He Become?
       (In Best One-Act Plays of 1934, London)
    The Bureaucrats, by Olive Conway (pseud.)
       (In Best One-Act Plays of 1934, London)
    The Desperationist, by Olive Conway (pseud.)
       (In Best One-Act Plays of 1933, London)
    Dux, by Olive Conway (pseud.)
       (In Best One-Act Plays of 1936, London)
    Exhibit C
       (In Best One-Act Plays of 1933, London)
    Followers, based on "Cranford" by Elizabeth Gaskell
       (In 24 One-Act Plays, Revised edition, 1954)
    Inner Man
       (In Best One-Act Plays of 1942/43, London)
    Let's Live in England
       (In Best One-Act Plays of 1944/45, London)
    London Front
       (In Best One-Act Plays of 1940, London)
    Lonesome-like
       (In Representative One-Act Plays by British and Irish
         Authors, 1921)
       (In Atlantic Book of Modern Plays, 1921)
    The Man Who Ignored the War
       (In Best One-Act Plays of 1940, London)
**The Murder Scream (see Aklom, Mikhail)
    New Leisure
       (In Best One-Act Plays of 1936, London)
    The Romany Road
       (In Best One-Act Plays of 1932, London)
    Smoke Screens
       (In Best One-Act Plays of 1931, London)

Tip and Run, by Olive Conway (pseud.)
   (In One-Act Theatre, Vol. 2)
When the Bells Rang, by Olive Conway (pseud.)
   (In Best One-Act Plays of 1935, London)
Wireless Can't Lie, by Olive Conway (pseud.)
   (In Best One-Act Plays of 1932, London)
The Wish Shop
   (In New Plays for Women & Girls, 1932)
Women Do Things Like That, by Olive Conway (pseud.)
   (In Best One-Act Plays of 1931, London)
Bringing It All Back Home (see McNally, Terrence)
"Bringing Me My Bow" (see Box, Sidney)
BRISTOL, George Digby, 2d Earl of, 1612-1677
   Elvira; or, The Worst Not Always True
   (In Dodsley's A Select Collection of Old English Plays, Vol.
   15)
   (In Dodsley's A Select Collection of Old Plays, Vol. 12)
Britannia's Honor (see Dekker, Thomas)
Britannicus (see Racine, Jean Baptiste)
Broadway (see Dunning, Philip Hart)
BRODSKY, Ruth
   No Hats, No Banquets
   (In First Stage, Vol. 2, no. 2, Spring 1963)
BRODY, Alter
   Rapunzel
   (In Theatre Arts, Vol. 9, April 1925)
The Broken Banjo (see Richardson, Willis)
The Broken Jug (see Kleist, Heinrich von)
BROME, Richard, d. 1652?
   The Jovial Crew; or, The Merry Beggars
   (In Dodsley's A Select Collection of Old Plays, Vol. 10)
   The Sparagus Garden
   (In The City and the Court)
BROME Manuscript
   The Sacrifice of Isaac
   (In Religious Drama, Vol. 2)
BRONSON, Howard, 1842-1906
   Shenandoah, a Military Comedy
   (In The Black Crook & Other 19th Century American Plays)
   (In Six Early American Plays, 1798-1890)
Brontë, Charlotte, 1816-1855
   *Patrick Brontë and the Saint (see Packer, Barbara)
   *Wild Decembers (see Ashton, Winifred)
Brontë, Emily Jane, 1818-1848
   *Wild Decembers (see Ashton, Winifred)
   **Wuthering Heights (see Hecht, Ben)
The Bronx Is Next (see Sanchez, Sonia)
Brooke, Eleanor
   King of Hearts (see Kerr, Jean)
BROOKE, Mrs. Frances Moore, 1724-1789
   Rosina
   (In Cumberland's British Theatre, Vol. 3, no. 7)
   (In The London Stage, Vol. 2)

BROOKE, Henry, 1703-1783
    Gustavus Vasa, the Deliverer of His Country
      (In Bell's British Theatre, 1797, Vol. 32)
BROOKE, Rupert
    Lithuania
      (In 30 Famous One-Act Plays)
BROOME, D. M.
    The Moon
      (In Best One-Act Plays of 1932, London)
BROPHY, Brigid
    The Waste Disposal Unit
      (In Best Short Plays of the World Theatre, 1958-67)
BROPHY, Edmund
    Nothin' to Nothin'
      (In Best Short Plays, 1960/61, N. Y.)
BROSSA, Joan
    Ten Accio-Spectacles
      (In Chicago Review, Vol. 18, nos. 3/4, 1966)
Brother Bill, a Little Play from Harlem (see Kreymborg, Alfred)
Brother Sun (see Housman, Laurence)
Brother to Dragons (see Warren, Robert Penn)
Brothers (see Beach, Lewis)
Brothers (see Castro, Edward)
The Brothers (see Cumberland, Richard)
Brothers (see Reisin, Abraham)
The Brothers (see Young, Edward)
BROUGH, William
    A Comical Countess
      (In Lacy's Plays)
    Dinorah Under Difficulties
      (In Lacy's Acting Plays, Vol. 81)
BROUGHTON, James
    The Last Word
      (In Religious Drama, Vol. 3)
    The Playground
      (In Theatre Arts, Vol. 30, Aug. 1946)
    Summer Fury
      (In Best One-Act Plays of 1945, N. Y.)
      (In Best Short Plays, 1956/57)
BROUN, Heywood Campbell, 1888-1939
    Death Says It Isn't So
      (In 50 More Contemporary One-Act Plays)
BROWN, Beverly S.
    Snake Chief
      (In Negro History Bulletin, Vol. 34, Mar. 1971)
BROWN, Ivor John Carnegie, 1891-
    Pictures on the Wall
      (In Best One-Act Plays, 1952-53, London)
BROWN, John, 1715-1766
    Barbarossa
      (In Cumberland's British Theatre, Vol. 13, no. 1)
      (In Bell's British Theatre, 1797, Vol. 26)
      (In The London Stage, Vol. 2)

BROWN, John Mason, 1900-1969
Many a Watchful Night, by John Mason Brown and Howard M.
Teichmann
(In Plays from Radio, 1948)
(In Radio's Best Plays, 1947)
**Pageant of the Shearmen and Tailors (see Pageant of the
Shearmen and Tailors: a miracle play adapted by John
Mason Brown)
BROWN, Kenneth H., 1936-
Blake's Design
(In Best Short Plays, 1969)
The Brig
(In Tulane Drama Review, Vol. 8, Spring 1964)
BROWN, Laura Norton
Kissing Goes By Favor
(In Drama, Vol. 16, Oct. 1925)
BROWN, Lennox
I Have to Call my Father
(In Drama & Theatre, Vol. 8, no. 3, Spring 1970)
BROWN, Sonia
Strange Rain
(In Best One-Act Plays of 1944, N.Y.)
BROWN, Stewart Pierce
Operation Coral
(In Best Television Plays of the Year, 1949)
Browning, Elizabeth Barrett, 1806-1861
*The Barretts of Wimpole Street (see Besier, Rudolf)
Browning, Robert, 1812-1889
*The Barretts of Wimpole Street (see Besier, Rudolf)
The Browning Version (see Rattigan, Terence)
BRUCE, Richard
Sahdji, an African Ballet
(In Plays of Negro Life)
La Brulure de Mille Soleils (see Kast, Pierre)
BRUNE, Jean
Maitre Francois est Mort
(In L'Avant-Scene du Theatre, no. 142)
BRUNIUS, Jacques B.
Violons d'Ingres
(In L'Avant-Scene du Cinema, no. 67, 1967)
BRUNO, Giordano, 1548-1600
Candle Bearer
(In Genius of the Italian Theater)
BRUNO, Pierrette
Pepsie, by Pierre-Edmond Victor (pseud.)
(In Plaisir de France, supplement theatral, no. 333, July
1966)
BRUSATI, Franco
The Other Face of November; both French and English versions
are included.
(In Italian Theatre Review, Vol. 15, Jan./Mar. 1966)
The Troublesome One; both French and English versions are
included.

(In Italian Theatre Review, Vol. 12, Apr./June 1963)
Brutus, Lucius Junius, fl. 500 B.C.
  *Brutus; or, The Fall of Tarquin (see Payne, John Howard)
  *Lucius Junius Brutus, Father of His Country (see Lee, Nathaniel)
Bryan, William Jennings, 1860-1925
  *Inherit the Wind (see Lawrence, Jerome)
Buaku (see Sakanishi, Shio)
The Buccaneer (see Mayer, Edwin Justus)
BUCHMAN, Sidney, 1902-
  Here Comes Mr. Jordan, a screenplay by Sidney Buchman
    and Seton I. Miller, based on the play "Heaven Can Wait" by
    Harry Segall.
    (In Twenty Best Film Plays)
  Mr. Smith Goes to Washington; screenplay by Sidney Buchman;
    original story by Lewis R. Foster
    (In Best Pictures, 1939-40)
    (In Twenty Best Film Plays)
  Over Twenty-One, by Sidney Buchman, adapted from the play
    by Ruth Gordon; directed by Charles Vidor)
    (In Best Film Plays, 1945, Vol. 2)
Buck, Pearl Sydenstricker, 1892-1973
  **Dragon Seed (see Roberts, Marguerite)
  **The Good Earth (see Jennings, Talbot)
  Will This Earth Hold?
    (In Radio Drama in Action, 1945)
    (In Asia and the Americas, Vol. 44, Nov. 1944)
BUCKINGHAM, George Villiers, 2d Duke of, 1626-1687
  The Rehearsal, by George Villiers, Duke of Buckingham
    (In Bell's British Theatre, 1797, Vol. 29)
    (The Burlesque Plays of the 18th Century)
BUCKSTONE, John Baldwin, 1802-1879
  Billy Taylor; or, The Gay Young Fellow
    (In Cumberland's British Theatre, Vol. 36, no. 3)
  Damon and Pythias
    (In Cumberland's British Theatre, Vol. 40, no. 6)
  Happiest Day of My Life
    (In Cumberland's British Theatre, Vol. 10, no. 4)
  A Husband At Sight
    (In Cumberland's British Theatre, Vol. 43, no. 4)
  The Ice Witch; or, The Frozen Hand
    (In Cumberland's British Theatre, Vol. 23, no. 8)
  Luke the Labourer
    (In Cumberland's British Theatre, Vol. 13, no. 3)
  Mischief-Making
    (In Cumberland's British Theatre, Vol. 13, no. 7)
  Open House; or, The Twin Sisters
    (In Cumberland's British Theatre, Vol. 37, no. 7)
  Popping the Question
    (In Cumberland's British Theatre, Vol. 22, no. 8)
  Snakes in the Grass
    (In Cumberland's British Theatre, Vol. 18, no. 6)
  23 John Street, Adelphi
    (In Cumberland's British Theatre, Vol. 28, no. 3)

A Budapest Salesman Should Not Read French Illustrated Magazines
    (see Szenes, Bela)
Buddha (see Gautama Buddha)
BÜCHNER, George, 1813-1837
    Danton's Death
        (In From the Modern Repertoire, Series One)
        (In Masterworks of World Drama, Vol. 6)
        (In The Modern Theatre, ed. by Eric Bentley, Vol. 5)
    Leonce and Lena
        (In Genius of the German Theater)
        (In From the Modern Repertoire, Series Three)
    Woyzeck
        (In The Modern Theatre, ed. by Eric Bentley, Vol. 1)
        (In The Modern Theatre, ed. by R. W. Corrigan)
BUENAVENTURA, Enrique, 1925-
    In the Right Hand of God the Father
        (In Voices of Change in the Spanish American Theater)
    The Twisted State
        (In TDR, The Drama Review, Vol. 14, no. 2, Winter 1970)
BUERMANN, Howard, 1908-
    Debt Takes a Holiday
        (In Best One-Act Plays of 1937, N. Y.)
BUFANO, Remo
    Orlando Furioso
        (In 50 More Contemporary One-Act Plays)
Buffalmacco's Jest (see Jagendorf, M.)
The Buggbears (see Jeffere, John)
The Bull-Fighter; or, The Bridal Ring (see Almar, George)
BULLINS, Ed, 1936-
    Clara's Ole Man
        (In Best Short Plays, 1969)
        (In TDR, The Drama Review, Vol. 12, Summer 1968)
    The Electronic Nigger
        (In New American Plays, Vol. 3)
    The Fabulous Miss Marie
        (In Scripts, Vol. 1, no. 4, Feb. 1972)
    The Gentleman Caller
        (In Best Short Plays, 1970)
    Goin'a Buffalo
        (In New Black Playwrights)
Bumbo the Clown (see Gibson, Lawrence)
Bumplepuppy; a Comedy of Climate (see Rogers, John Williams,
    Jr.)
BUNJE, Emil T. H.
    Yat Pak or The Hundredth Notch
        (In The Banner Anthology of One-Act Plays by American
        Authors)
BUÑUEL, Luis, 1900-
    L'Age d'Or, by Luis Buñuel et Salvador Dali
        (In L'Avant-Scene du Cinema, no. 27-28, June 15-July 15,
        1963)
    L'Age d'Or and Un Chien Andalou, filmscripts by Luis Buñuel
    and Salvador Dali.

(In Classic Film Scripts Series, no. 12)
L'Ange Exterminateur, by Luis Buñuel, d'apres le cine-drame
de Luis Alcoriza et Luis Buñuel "Les Naufrages de la Rue de
la Province."
   (In L'Avant-Scene du Cinema, no. 27-28, June 15-July 15,
   1963)
Belle de Jour
   (In Modern Film Scripts Series)
Un Chien Andalou, by Luis Buñuel et Salvador Dali
   (In L'Avant-Scene du Cinema, no. 27-28, June 15-July 15,
   1963)
The Exterminating Angel
   (In Three Screenplays)
Las Hurdes (Terre Sans Pain)
   (In L'Avant-Scene du Cinema, no. 36, 1964)
Le Journal d'Une Femme de Chambre, by Luis Buñuel et Jean-
Claude Carriere, d'apres le roman d'Octave Mirabeau.
   (In L'Avant-Scene du Cinema, no. 36, 1964)
Nazarin, by Luis Buñuel et Julio Alejandro, d'apres la nouvelle
originale de Benito Perez Galdos.
   (In L'Avant-Scene du Cinema, no. 89, 1969)
Simon du Desert. Titre original: "Simon del Desierto."
   (In L'Avant-Scene du Cinema, no. 94-95, July-Sept. 1969)
Simon of the Desert
   (In Three Screenplays)
Tristana
   (In Modern Film Scripts)
Tristana; un film de Luis Buñuel d'apres la nouvelle de Benito
Perez Galdos.
   (In L'Avant-Scene du Cinema, no. 110, Jan. 1971)
Viridiana
   (In Three Screenplays)
La Voie Lactee
   (In L'Avant Scene du Cinema, no. 94-95, July-Sept. 1969)
A Bunyan Yarn (see Young, Stanley)
The Bureaucrats (see Brighouse, Harold)
BURGES, Sir James Bland, bart, 1752-1824
   Riches; or, The Wife and Brother; founded on Massinger's
   "City Madam"
   (In Cumberland's British Theatre, Vol. 10, no. 3)
   (In Old Plays, 1810)
BURGESS, Jackson
   Dyer Day
   (In First Stage, Vol. 4, Winter 1965/66)
The Burgomaster (see Hofmann, Gert)
BURGOYNE, John, 1722-1792
   The Lord of the Manor
   (In Cumberland's British Theatre, Vol. 30, no. 7)
The Burial Committee (see Crochett, Otway)
BURNAND, F. C.
   Villikins and His Dinah
   (In Lacy's Acting Plays, Vol. 14)

Burnett, Murray
  **Casablanca (see Epstein, Julius J.)
Burnett, William Riley, 1899-
  **Little Caesar (see Faragoh, Francis Edwards)
Burnside, Norman
  **Dr. Ehrlich's Magic Bullet (see Huston, John)
The Burosaurs (see Ambrogi, Silvano)
BURTON, Richard, 1861-1940
    Tatters
        (In Drama, Vol. 12, March 1922)
BURTT, Theodore C., Jr.
    The Interview
        (In Drama & Theatre, Vol. 8, no. 3, Spring 1970)
Bury the Dead (see Shaw, Irwin)
Bus Riley's Back in Town (see Inge, William Motter)
Bus Stop (see Inge, William Motter)
Busch, Niven, 1903-
  **In Old Chicago (see Trotti, Lamar)
BUSH, Josef, 1933-
    French Gray
        (In New American Plays, Vol. 2)
Busiris, King of Egypt (see Young, Edward)
Busu, Literate Highwayman (Fumi Yamadachi) . (see Sakanishi,
    Shio)
The Busy Body (see Centlivre, Mrs. Susanna)
The Busy Martyr (see Hitchcock, George)
But Fred Freud is Dead (see Terson, Peter)
Butch Cassidy and the Sundance Kid (see Goldman, William)
BUTLER, Frank
    Going My Way, by Frank Butler and Frank Cavett, based on a
    story by and directed by Leo McCarey
        (In Best Film Plays, 1943/44, Vol. 1)
    A Medal for Benny, by Frank Butler, with additional dialogue
    by Jack Wagner, based on a story by John Steinbeck and Jack
    Wagner; directed by Irving Pichel
        (In Best Film Plays, 1945, Vol. 2)
BUTLER, Hugh
    The Southerner, by Hugh Butler, from the novel "Hold Autumn
    in Your Hand" by George Sessions Perry; directed by Jean
    Renoir
        (In Best Film Plays, 1945, Vol. 2)
Butley (see Gray, Simon)
BUTTERFIELD, Walton
    Tea for Six
        (In Drama, Vol. 16, Jan. 1926)
BUTTITTA, Anthony
    Singing Piedmont
        (In One-Act Play Magazine, 1937/38 Anthology)
By Ourselves (see Fulda, Ludwig)
BYRON, George Gordon Noël Byron, 6th Baron, 1788-1824
    Cain: A Mystery
        (In Genius of the Later English Theater)

(In The Poems and Plays of Lord Byron)
The Deformed Transformed
(In The Poems and Plays of Lord Byron)
Heaven and Earth: A Mystery
(In The Poems and Plays of Lord Byron)
*Lord Byron's Love Letter (see Williams, Tennessee)
Manfred
(In The Poems and Plays of Lord Byron)
**Man-Fred: A Burlesque Ballet Opera (see A Beckett, Gilbert
Abbott)
Marino Faliero, Doge of Venice
(In The Poems and Plays of Lord Byron)
Sardanapalus: A Tragedy
(In The Poems and Plays of Lord Byron)
The Two Foscari: An Historical Tragedy
(In The Poems and Plays of Lord Byron)
Werner; or, The Inheritance
(In The Poems and Plays of Lord Byron)
BYRON, Henry James, 1835-1884
Der Freischutz; or, The Bill! the Belle!! and the Bullet!!!
(In Lacy's Acting Plays, Vol. 81)
Robinson Crusoe; or, Harlequin Friday and the King of the
Caribee Islands!
(In Lacy's Acting Plays, Vol. 14)

A Cabin by the Lake (see Waldau, Roy S.)
The Cabinet (see Dibdin, Thomas)
The Cabinet of Dr. Caligari (see Wiene, Robert)
La Cachette d'Harpagon (see Camp, Andre)
CADY, Jerome
The Purple Heart, screenplay; directed by Lewis Milestone
(In Best Film Plays, Vol. 1, 1943-44)
Caesar, Caius Julius, 100-44 B.C.
*Caesar Aderat Forte; or Brutus Adsum Jam (see Sims, Alan)
*Caesar and Cleopatra (see Shaw, George Bernard)
*Calpurnia's Dinner-Party (see Baring, Maurice)
*Jules Cesar (text in French) (see Shakespeare, William)
Caesar Borgia (see Lee, Nathaniel)
Cafeteria Style (see Lichter, Morton)
Os Caftens (see Lopes Cardoso, A.)
The Cage (see Fratti, Mario)
La Cage de Pierre (see Zucca, Pierre)
The Cages (see Arrabal, Fernando)
CAILLOL, Pierrette
L'Home qui se Taisait
(In Plaisir de France, supplement theatral, no. 291, Jan.
1963)
Cain, James Mallahan, 1892-
**Algiers (see Lawson, John Howard)
**Double Indemnity (see Wilder, Billy)
Cain (see Nemerov, Howard)

Cain: A Mystery (see Byron, George Gordon Nöel, 6th Baron)
The Caine Mutiny Court-Martial (see Wouk, Herman)
Caius Gracchus (see Knowles, James Sheridan)
Calculated Risk (see Hayes, Joseph)
CALDERON, George, 1868-1915
    The Little Stone House
    (In 50 Contemporary One-Act Plays)
CALDERON de la Barca, Pedro, 1600-1681
    L'Alcade de Zalamea
    (In L'Avant-Scene du Theatre, no. 263, April 15, 1962)
**Elvira; or, The Worst Not Always True (see Bristol, George
    Digby, 2d Earl of)
    Fortune Mends, translated by Fanny Holcroft.
    (In Theatrical Recorder, ed. by Thomas Holcroft, Vol. 2,
        no. 8, July 1805)
    From Bad to Worse, translated by Fanny Holcroft
    (In Theatrical Recorder, ed. by Thomas Holcroft, Vol. 1,
        no. 4, Mar. 1805)
    A House with Two Doors is Difficult to Guard
    (In Tulane Drama Review, Vol. 8, Fall 1963)
    Life is a Dream
    (In The Classic Theatre, Vol. 3)
    Love After Death
    (In The Classic Theatre, Vol. 3)
    La Vie est un Songe
    (In Plaisir de France, supplement theatral, no. 280, Feb.
        1962)
    (In L'Avant-Scene du Theatre, no. 258, Feb. 1, 1962)
CALDWELL, Ben
    The Job
    (In TDR/The Drama Review, Vol. 12, Summer 1968)
    Mission Accomplished
    (In TDR/The Drama Review, Vol. 12, Summer 1968)
    Riot Sale; or Drellar Psyche Fake Out
    (In TDR/The Drama Review, Vol. 12, Summer 1968)
    Top Secret, or A Few Million After B.C.
    (In TDR/The Drama Review, Vol. 12, Summer 1968)
    The Wall
    (In Scripts, Vol. 1, no. 7, May 1972)
Caldwell, Erskine, 1903-
    **Tobacco Road (see Kirkland, Jack)
Caleb Stove's Death Watch (see Flavin, Martin A.)
Caligula, Emperor of Rome (Gaius Caesar) 12 A.D.-41 A.D.
    *Caligula (see Camus, Albert)
    *Caligula's Picnic (see Baring, Maurice)
The Call (see Inge, William)
Call Me a Liar (see Mortimer, John)
Call Me Jacky (see Bagnold, Enid)
CALLADO, Antonio
    Pedro Mico
    (In Revista de Teatro, no. 326)
    O Tesouro de Chica da Silva
    (In Revista de Teatro, no. 325)

Callicachus   (see Hrotsvit, of Gandersheim)
Calling for Help   (see Handke, Peter)
Calm Down Mother   (see Terry, Megan)
Calpurnia, Wife of Julius Caesar
   *Calpurnia's Dinner-Party   (see Baring, Maurice)
Calypso   (see Kemp, Harry Hibbard)
CAMARGO, Joracy
   Deus Lhe Pague
      (In Revista de Teatro, no. 302)
   Juizo Final
      (In Revista de Teatro, no. 348)
   Mocinha
      (In Revista de Teatro, no. 338)
Cambyses   (see Preston, Thomas)
The Camel and I   (see Wishengrad, Morton)
Le Cameleon   (see Praga, Andre)
CAMERON, Kenneth, 1931-
   The Hundred and First
      (In New American Plays, Vol. 1)
CAMERON, Margaret (Mrs. Harrison Case Lewis), 1867-
   One of These Days
      (In New Plays for Women & Girls, 1932)
Camino Real   (see Williams, Tennessee)
Les Camisards   (see Allio, Rene)
CAMOLETTI, Marc
   Secretissimo
      (In Plaisir de France, supplement theatral, no. 326, Dec.
      1965)
The Camp   (see Gambaro, Griselda)
CAMP, Andre
   La Cachette d'Harpagon
      (In Plaisir de France, supplement theatral, no. 313, Nov.
      1964)
CAMPBELL, Andrew Leonard Voullaire, 1789-1870
   Bound 'Prentice to a Waterman; or, The Flower of Woolwich
      (In Cumberland's British Theatre, Vol. 33, no. 9)
   Tom Bowling
      (In Cumberland's British Theatre, Vol. 11, no. 5)
CAMPBELL, J. Gounod
   Summit Conference
      (In Best Short Plays, 1960/61, N. Y.)
CAMPBELL, Lawton
   The Girl Who Slipped
      (In Drama, Vol. 17, Apr. 1927)
CAMPBELL, M.
   The Forest Oracle; or, The Bridge of Tresino
      (In Cumberland's British Theatre, Vol. 24, no. 5)
Campbell, William Edward March, 1894-1954
   **The Bad Seed   (see Anderson, Maxwell)
CAMUS, Albert, 1913-1960
   Caligula
      (In Caligula and Three Other Plays)

The Just Assassins
   (In Caligula and Three Other Plays)
The Misunderstanding
   (In Caligula and Three Other Plays)
*Presence d'Albert Camus   (see Regnier, Georges)
State of Siege
   (In Caligula and Three Other Plays)
"... Can Die but Once?"   (see Dawson, N.)
Le Canard a l'Orange   (see Home, William Douglas)
The Canavans   (see Gregory, Isabella Augusta (Persse) Lady)
Cancao Dentro de Pao   (see Magalhaes Junior, Raymundo)
Cancer   (see Weller, Michael)
Candaules, Commissioner   (see Gerould, Daniel C.)
Candidat   (see Prin, Claude)
Candle Bearer   (see Bruno, Giordano)
CANDONI, Luigi, 1921-
   Saturday Night Desire; both French and English texts are in-
   cluded.
   (In Italian Theatre Review, Vol. 11, Apr./June 1962)
CANFIELD, Mary Cass
   The Duchess Says Her Prayers
   (In 50 More Contemporary One-Act Plays)
CANGIULLO, Francesco
   Detonation; a synthesis of all modern theatre
   (In TDR/The Drama Review, Vol. 15, Fall 1970)
   There is No Dog
   (In TDR/The Drama Review, Vol. 15, Fall 1970)
CANNAN, Gilbert, 1884-
   Gloves, a Fragment of the Eternal Duet
   (In Theatre Arts, Vol. 4, 1920)
   James and John
   (In Representative One-Act Plays by British and Irish Authors)
   Mary's Wedding
   (In 50 Contemporary One-Act Plays)
CANNING, George, 1770-1827
   The Rovers, by George Canning, John Hookham Frere, and
   George Ellis.
   (In Burlesque Plays of the 18th Century)
CAPEK, Josef, 1887-1945
   The World We Live In (The Insect Comedy), by Josef and Karl
   Capek, adapted by Owen Davis
   (In 20 Best European Plays on the American Stage)
CAPEK, Karl, 1890-1938
   R. U. R.
   (In 16 Famous European Plays)
   The World We Live In (The Insect Comedy) (see Capek, Josef)
A Capital Federal   (see Azevedo, Arthur)
CAPOTE, Truman, 1924-
   The Grass Harp.   Based on his novel.
   (In Theatre Arts, Vol. 36, Sept. 1952)
CAPPELLI, Salvato, 1911-
   Two Hundred Thousand and One; both French and English texts
   are included.

(In Italian Theatre Review, Vol. 15, Oct./Dec. 1966)
CAPRA, Frank, 1897-
   It Happened One Night (see Riskin, Robert)
   Lady for a Day (see Riskin, Robert)
   Mr. Smith Goes to Washington (see Buchman, Sidney)
   You Can't Take It with You (see Riskin, Robert)
CAPRON, Marcelle
   Le Tabique Taboque
      (In Plaisir de France, supplement theatral, no. 318, April
      1965)
Captain Jack's Revenge (see Smith, Michael)
Captain Jinks of the Horse Marines (see Fitch, Clyde)
The Captain of the Gate (see Dix, Beulah Marie)
"The Captains and the Kings" (see Pollock, Channing)
The Captives (see Plautus, Titus Maccius)
The Captives; or, A Comicall Historie (see Heywood, Thomas)
The Capture (see Howard, F. Morton)
The Car Lover (see Friedman, Bruce Jay)
Caractacus (see Mason, William)
Caram, Populo! (see Strindberg, August)
CARBALLIDO, Emilio
   The Day They Let the Lions Loose
      (In Voices of Change in the Spanish American Theater)
   I Too Speak of the Rose, translated by William I. Oliver
      (In Drama & Theatre, Vol. 8, no. 1)
      (In Modern Stage in Latin America, 1971)
The Cardinal of Spain (see Montherlant, Henry de)
Cardinal's Learning (see Williamson, Hugh Ross)
Career (see Lee, James)
The Caretaker (see Pinter, Harold)
CAREY, Henry, d. 1743
   The Dragon of Wantley
      (In The London Stage, Vol. 1)
      (In Burlesque Plays of the 18th Century)
   Chrononhotonthologos
      (In Burlesque Plays of the 18th Century)
CARLE, Gilles, 1929-
   La Vraie Nature de Bernadette
      (In L'Avant-Scene du Cinema, no. 130, Nov. 1972)
The Carmelite (see Cumberland, Richard)
Carmer, Carl Lamson, 1893-
   The Last Speech (see Cooper, Lou)
CARMONTELLE, Louis Carrogis, known as, 1717-1806
   False Indifference
      (In Theatrical Recorder, Vol. 2, Suppl., Dec. 1805)
   The Opera Dancer
      (In Theatrical Recorder, ed. by Thomas Holcroft, Vol. 1,
      no. 5, Apr. 1805)
   The Portrait
      (In Theatrical Recorder, Thomas Holcroft, editor, Vol. 2,
      no. 11, Oct. 1805)
   The Pullet
      (In Theatrical Recorder, Thomas Holcroft, editor, Vol. 2,

no. 9, Aug. 1805)
CARNE, Marcel, 1909-
  Children of Paradise
  (Classic Film Scripts Series)
  Drole de Drame, by Marcel Carne et Jacques Prevert, d'apres
  "His First Offence" by Storer Clouston.
  (In L'Avant-Scene du Cinema, no. 90, 1969)
  Les Enfants du Paradis (see Prevert, Jacques)
  Les Jeunes Loups
  (In L'Avant-Scene du Cinema, no. 81, May 1968)
  Le Jour se Leve, by Marcel Carne et Jacques Prevert
  (In L'Avant-Scene du Cinema, no. 53, 1965)
  Le Jour se Leve (text in English) (see Prevert, Jacques)
  Les Visiteurs du Soir (see Prevert, Jacques)
Carnival Saturday (see Arrafat, A.)
Carola ou les Cabotins (see Renoir, Jean)
CARRICK, Pat
  "3"
  (In Story, the Yearbook of Discovery, 3d Series, 1970)
CARRIERE, Albert
  Danbury Fair
  (In Best One-Act Plays of 1940, N.Y.)
CARRIERE, Jean-Claude
  Le Journal d'une Femme de Chambre (see Buñuel, Luis)
  La Pince a Ongles
  (In L'Avant-Scene du Cinema, no. 110, Jan. 1971)
  Viva Maria (see Malle, Louis)
Carriere, John
  Taking Off (see Forman, Milos)
Carrington, V.C. (see Christie, Dorothy)
CARROLL, Paul Vincent, 1900-1968
  Shadow and Substance
  (In 16 Famous European Plays)
CARSON, Julia Brainard
  The Monster
  (In Best Short Plays, 1960/61, N.Y.)
CARSON, L.M. Kit
  David Holzman's Diary, a screenplay from Jim McBride's film
  (Farrar, Straus & Giroux Screenplays)
CARSWELL, Donald, 1882-
  Count Albany
  (In 24 One-Act Plays, Rev. ed., 1954)
CARTER, Conrad C.
  And Now--The Journey
  (In Best One-Act Plays of 1935, London)
CARTER, Lonnie
  Is She Izzy or Iz He Ain'tzy or Iz They Both, with music by
  Robert Montgomery
  (In Scripts, Vol. 1, no. 7, May 1972)
CARTWRIGHT, William, 1611-1643
  The Ordinary
  (In Dodsley's A Select Collection of Old English Plays, Vol.
  12)

(In Dodsley's A Select Collection of Old Plays, Vol. 10)
CARVALHO, Helio
    Joaozinho e Maria. Musica de Diana Franco e Lauro Gomes
        (In Revista de Teatro, no. 390, Nov./Dec. 1972)
Casablanca (see Epstein, Julius J.)
Cascando (see Beckett, Samuel)
The Case of Mrs. Kantsey Know (see Jarrell, Myra Williams)
The Case of the Crushed Petunias (see Williams, Tennessee)
Cash--$2,000 (see Chatterton, Nathan G.)
Casina (see Plautus, Titus Maccius)
CASONA, Alejandro
    Ines de Portugal
        (In Plaisir de France, supplement theatral, no. 325, Nov.
        1965)
Casque d'Or (see Becker, Jacques)
Cassandra Singing (see Madden, David)
CASSAVETES, John
    Faces
        (New American Library Screenplays, 1970)
Cassilis Engagement (see Hankin, St. John)
O Castagnaro de Festa (see Viana, Oduvaldo Filho)
The Castle and the Plain (see Sanchez Paredes, Pedro)
Castle in the Village (see Woskoff, Verna)
The Castle of Andalusia (see O'Keeffe, John)
The Castle of Sorrento; or, The Prisoner of Rochelle (see Haetwell,
    Henry)
The Castle Spectre (see Lewis, M.G.)
CASTRO, Edward, 1920-
    Brothers
        (In Best One-Act Plays, 1950/51, N.Y.)
CASTRO, Juan Antonio
    Only a Man in Black
        (In Modern International Drama, Vol. 6, no. 1, Fall 1972)
    The Visit
        (In Modern International Drama, Vol. 5, no. 1, Fall 1971)
The Cat and the Canary (see Willard, John)
Cat on a Hot Tin Roof (see Williams, Tennessee)
Catch as Catch Can (see Anouilh, Jean)
Catherine de Medici, 1519-1589
    *La Princesse de Cleves (see Dorfmann, Robert)
    *Shadow in the Sun (see Mitchell, Julian)
Catherine Howard (see Cross, Beverley)
Catherine of Aragon, 1st wife of Henry VIII, king of England, 1485-
    1536
    *Catherine of Aragon (see Sisson, Rosemary Anne)
Catherine of Valois, consort of Henry V, king of England, 1401-1437
    *Henry V (see Olivier, Sir Laurence)
    *The Queen and the Welshman (see Sisson, Rosemary Anne)
Catherine Parr (see Prebble, John)
Catherine Parr; or, Alexander's Horse (see Baring, Maurice)
Catherine II, Empress of Russia, 1729-1796
    *Great Catherine (see Shaw, George Bernard)
Cathleen ni Houlihan (see Yeats, William Butler)

Catiline, Lucius Sergius Catilina, 108?-62 B.C.
*The Conspiracy (see Prosperi, Giorgio)
Cato, Marcus Porcius Uticenois (the Younger), 95-46 B.C.
*Cato (see Addison, Joseph)
Cato Street (see Shaw, Robert)
Catullus, Gaius Valerius, 84?-54 B.C.
  *The Vengeance of Catullus (see Frida, Emil Bohslav)
Cau, Jean
  L'Insoumis (see Cavalier, Alain)
The Caucasian Chalk Circle (see Brecht, Bertolt)
Caught by the Cuff (see Hay, Frederic)
Cavalcade (see Coward, Noël Pierce)
CAVALCANTI BORGES, Jose Carlos
  A Flor e o Fruto; segundo "Dom Casmurro," de Machado de
  Assis
    (In Revista de Teatro, no. 385, Jan. /Feb. 1972)
CAVALIER, Alain
  L'Insoumis, by Alain Cavalier et Jean Cau
    (In L'Avant-Scene du Cinema, no. 41, 1964)
Cavalleria Rusticana (see Verga, Giovanni)
CAVANDER, Kenneth
  Godbug
    (In First Stage, Vol. 6, Winter 1967-68)
The Cave (see Hennefeld, Edmund B.)
The Cave Dwellers (see Saroyan, William)
The Cave Man (see Field, Charles K.)
Cavett, Frank
  Going My Way (see Butler, Frank)
Caviar ou Lentilles (see Scarnicci, Giulio)
CAYATTE, Andre, 1904-
  Le Passage du Rhin, filmscript by Andre Cayatee and Maurice
  Auberge
    (In L'Avant-Scene du Cinema, no. 1, Feb. 15, 1961)
CAYROL, Jean, 1911-
  Madame se Meurt, by Jean Cayrol et Claude Durand.
    (In L'Avant-Scene du Cinema, no. 14, Apr. 15, 1962)
  Night and Fog (Nuit et Brouillard); the script for Alain Res-
  nais' film
    (In Evergreen Filmscript Series, Book 2)
    (In Film: Book 2, 1962)
    (In L'Avant-Scene du Cinema, no. 1, Feb. 15, 1961)
  On Vous Parle, by Jean Cayrol et Claude Durand.
    (In L'Avant-Scene du Cinema, no. 5, Jun. 15, 1961)
Ce Soir ou Jamais (see Deville, Michele)
Cecile; or, The School for Fathers (see Anouilh, Jean)
The Cedar Chest; or, The Lord Mayor's Daughter; to which is
  added, The Silver Palace (see Almar, George)
Celenio, Inarco, pseud. (see Moratin, Leandro Fernandes de)
Celestina (see Rojas, Fernando de)
Celles Qu'on Prend dans Ses Bras (see Montherlant, Henry de)
Les Cenci (see Artaud, Antonin)
The Cenci (see Shelley, Percy Bysshe)

Cendres et Diamant   (see Wajda, Andrzej)
Le Centenaire   (see Kerautem, Louis de)
CENTILIVRE, Susanna, 1667?-1723
    A Bold Stroke for a Wife
        (In Bell's British Theatre, 1797, Vol. 12)
        (In Cumberland's British Theatre, Vol. 17, no. 1)
        (In The London Stage, Vol. 1)
    The Busy Body
        (In Bell's British Theatre, 1797, Vol. 16)
        (In Cumberland's British Theatre, Vol. 19, no. 5)
        (In The London Stage, Vol. 2)
    The Wonder: A Woman Keeps a Secret
        (In Bell's British Theatre, 1797, Vol. 21)
        (In The London Stage, Vol. 1)
        (In Cumberland's British Theatre, Vol. 23, no. 7)
CEPELOS, Batista
    Maria Madelena
        (In Revista de Teatro, no. 304)
Ceremonie Secrete   (see Losey, Joseph)
Ceremonies in Dark Old Men   (see Elder, Lonne)
CERVANTES, Saavedra, Miguel de, 1574-1616
    **Don Quichott, based on Cervantes' work   (see Jamaique, Yves)
    Le Retable des Mervilles, adapted by Paul Delon
        (In L'Avant-Scene du Theatre, no. 146)
    The Siege of Numanta
        (In The Classic Theatre, ed. by Eric Bentley, Vol. 3)
Cesar et Rosalie   (see Sautet, Claude)
Cet Animal Etrange   (see Arout, Gabriel)
Cette Sacree Force   (see Medvedkine, Alexandre)
CHABANNES, Jacques
    Monsieur et Madame Moliere
        (In Plaisir de France, supplement theatral, no. 360, Oct.
        1968)
CHABROL, Claude, 1930-
    Les Cousins, by Claude Chabrol et Paul Gregauff
        (In Cahiers du Cinema, Vol. 14, no. 90, Dec. 1958)
    La Femme Infidele
        (In L'Avant-Scene du Cinema, no. 92, May 1969)
    La Muette, sketch du film "Paris vu par..."
        (In L'Avant-Scene du Cinema, no. 92, May 1969)
Le Chagrin et la Pitie   (see Ophuls, Marcel)
The Chain of Guilt; or, The Inn on the Heath   (see Taylor, Thomas
    Proclus)
The Chairs   (see Ionesco, Eugene)
Chamber Music   (see Kopit, Arthur L.)
Chambre 29   (see Verdot, Guy)
Champignol Wider Willen (Champignol Malgre Lui)   (see Feydeau,
    Georges)
Champion North   (see Wilson, Theodora Wilson)
The Chances   (see Beaumont, Francis)
Chandler, Raymond, 1888-1959
    **The Big Sleep   (see Faulkner, William)

**Double Indemnity (see Wilder, Billy)
Change (see Bauer, Wolfgang)
A Change of Heart (see James, Henry)
Changeling (see Middleton, Thomas)
The Changeling (see Stephens, Peter John)
Changing of the Guard (see Ruiz, Raul)
Le Chant du Styrwne (see Queneau, Georges)
Chapetuba, Futebol Clube (see Viana, Oduvaldo Filho)
CHAPIN, Harold, 1886-1915
   The Autocrat of the Coffee Stall
    (In Theatre Arts, Vol. 5, 1921)
   It's the Poor that 'elps the Poor
    (In 24 One-Act Plays, Rev. ed., 1954)
   The Philosopher of Butterbiggens
    (In Atlantic Book of Modern Plays, 1921)
CHAPLIN, Charles, 1889-
   The Gold Rush, filmscript compiled from the Chaplin film by
    Timothy J. Lyons
    (In Cinema, Vol. 4, no. 2, Summer 1968)
CHAPMAN, George, 1559?-1634
   All Fools
    (In Dodsley's A Select Collection of Old Plays, Vol. 4)
   Eastward Hoe, by George Chapman, John Marston, and Ben
    Jonson
    (In Great English Plays)
    (In Dodsley's A Select Collection of Old Plays, Vol. 4)
    (In The City and the Court)
   The Widow's Tears
    (In Dodsley's A Select Collection of Old Plays, Vol. 6)
The Chapter of Accidents (see Lee, Sophia)
The Charcoal Burner; or, The Dropping Well of Knaresborough
   (see Almar, George)
Charivari (see Stephens, Nan Badby)
Charles Mort ou Vif (see Tanner, Alain)
Charles I, king of Great Britain, 1600-1649
   *Charles the First (see Shelley, Percy Bysshe)
   *King Charles I (see Havard, William)
Charles II, king of Great Britain, 1660-1685
   *Charles the Second (see Payne, John Howard)
   *Mistress Nell (see Hazelton, George Cochrane)
   *Peveril of the Peak; or, The Days of King Charles II
Charles VI, king of France, called "the Foolish," 1368-1422
   *The Fatal Rubber (see Baring, Maurice)
Charles IX, king of France, 1550-1574
   *The Massacre of Paris (see Lee, Nathaniel)
Charles XII, king of Sweden, 1682-1718
   *Charles the XII (see Planche, James Robinson)
   *Charles XII (see Strindberg, August)
Charlie (see Morzek, Slawomir)
Charlie Barringer (see Martin, John Joseph)
Charlie McDeath (see Forsell, Lars)
Charlotte et son Jules (see Godard, Jean-Luc)

CHARPAK, Andre
  La Femme d'un Autre... Ou le Mari sous le Lit, based on a
    story by Dostoevski
      (In Plaisir de France, supplement theatral, no. 301, Nov.
      1963)
  Monsieur Vautrin, based on the book by Balzac
      (In Plaisir de France, supplement theatral, no. 301, Nov.
      1963)
CHARRAS, Charles
  Onze Degres d'Aptitude
      (In L'Avant-Scene du Theatre, no. 489, Feb. 15, 1972)
  Trois Cents Metres d'Elevation
      (In L'Avant Scene du Theatre, Jan. 1, 1969)
The Chartist (see Schofield, Stephen)
CHARVET, Philippe
  L'Ecole des Morts
      (In Plaisir de France, supplement Theatral, no. 308, June
      1964)
CHASE, Mary (Coyle), 1907-
  Bernardine
      (In Theatre Arts, Vol. 38, Mar. 1954)
  Harvey
      (In Best American Plays, Supp. Vol.)
La Chasse au Lion a l'Arc (see Rouch, Jean)
Un Chat est un Chat (see Worms, Jeannine)
Les Chats (see Durand, Philippe)
CHATTERTON, Nathan G.
  Cash--$2,000
      (In Drama, Vol. 15, Jan. 1925)
Chatterton (see Vigny, Alfred de)
Chaucer, Geoffrey, d. 1400
  **The Pardoner's Tale (see Mavor, Osborne Henry)
CHAYEFSKY, Paddy, 1923-
  The Bachelor Party
      (In Television Plays, 1955)
  The Bachelor Party, screenplay by Paddy Chayefsky, based on
    his teleplay.
      (In New American Library Screenplays)
  The Big Deal
      (In Television Plays, 1955)
  Gideon
      (In Esquire, Vol. 56, Dec. 1961)
      (In Best American Plays, Fifth Series, 1957-63)
  The Goddess
      (In Esquire, Vol. 49, Mar. 1958, Supp. sec.)
  Holiday Song
      (In Television Plays, 1955)
  The Latent Heterosexual
      (In Esquire, Vol. 68, Aug. 1967)
  Marty
      (In Television Plays, 1955)
  Middle of the Night
      (Random House Play, 1957)

The Mother
    (In Television Plays, 1955)
    (In Best Television Plays)
Printer's Measure
    (In Television Plays, 1955)
The Tenth Man
    (In Theatre Arts, Vol. 45, no. 1, Jan. 1961)
    (In 6 American Plays for Today, edited by Bennett Cerf,
       New York Modern Library, 1961)
A Cheap Bunch of Nice Flowers (see O'Brien, Edna)
Checkmate (see Halliday, Andrew)
CHEDID, Andree
  Le Montreur
    (In L'Avant Scene du Theatre, no. 469-470, Apr. 1-15, 1971)
  Le Personnage
    (In L'Avant-Scene du Theatre, no. 401, Apr. 15, 1968)
CHEKHOV, Anton Pavlovich, 1860-1904
  The Boor
    (In Contemporary One-Act Plays, 1922)
    (In Plays as Experience)
    (In 50 Contemporary One-Act Plays)
    (In 30 Famous One-Act Plays)
**Cet Animal Etrange (see Arout, Gabriel)
  The Cherry Orchard
    (In Introduction to Literature: Plays)
    (In The Modern Theatre, ed. by R.W. Corrigan)
**The Chorus Girl (see Stone, John A.)
**La Contrebasse (see Fasquel, Maurice)
**La Dame au Petit Chien (see Kobrynski, Lazare)
**Le Garde-Chasse (see Kobrynski, Lazare)
  Ivanov
    (In Makers of the Modern Theatre, 1961)
  A Marriage Proposal
    (In 24 Favorite One-Act Plays)
  L'Ours
    (In Plaisir de France, supplement theatral, no. 302, Dec.
      1963)
  The Proposal
    (In Acting is Believing)
  The Sea Gull, translated by Stark Young
    (In 16 Famous European Plays)
    (In 20 Best European Plays on the American Stage)
**The Shoemaker and the Devil (see Ginsbury, Norman)
  Summer in the Country. English version by Eric Bentley.
    (In Tulane Drama Review, Vol. 2, Feb. 1958)
  The Swan Song
    (In Short Plays by Representative Authors, 1920)
  The Three Sisters
    (In Tragedy: Texts and Commentary, 1969)
  The Tobacco Evil
    (In Theatre Arts, Vol. 7, 1923)
  Uncle Vanya
    (In The Modern Theatre, ed. by R.W. Corrigan)

Der Waldschrat
  (In Theater Heute, no. 5, May 1972)
A Wedding
  (In Four Continental Plays, 1964)
CHELTNAM, Charles Smith
  Fireside Diplomacy
  (In 26 Short & Amusing Plays, 1871)
La Chemise de Nylon (see Madern, Jose-Maria)
Cher Antoine (see Anouilh, Jean)
CHERRY, Andrew
  The Soldier's Daughter
  (In Cumberland's British Theatre, Vol. 25, no. 2)
The Cherry Orchard (see Chekhov, Anton Pavlovich)
CHESTER Pageant of the Water-Leaders and Drawers in Dee
  Noah's Flood
  (In Religious Drama, Vol. 2)
CHETHAM-STRODE, Warren
  Sometimes Even Now
  (In Famous Plays of Today, 1933)
Chettle, Henry, d. 1607?
  The Death of Robert Earl of Huntington, otherwise called Robin
    Hood of Merrie Sherwodde (see Munday, Anthony
  The Downfall of Robert Earl of Huntington (see Munday,
    Anthony)
  Patient Grissil (see Dekker, Thomas)
Le Cheval Evanoui (see Sagan, Francoise)
Les Chevaliers de la Table Ronde (see Cocteau, Jean)
La Chevauchee Fantastique (see Nichols, Dudley)
La Chevelure (see Kyrou, Ado)
CHEVIGNY, Hector, 1904-
  Radioman Jack Cooper
  (In Radio Drama in Action, 1945)
CHIANG, Ching
  Red Detachment of Women
  (In Chinese Literature, no. 5, 1969)
Chicago (see Shepard, Sam)
Chichevache and Bycorne (see Lydgate, John)
The Chicken Made of Rags (see Serrano, Nina)
Chicken Soup with Barley (see Wesker, Arnold)
Un Chien Andalou (see Buñuel, Luis)
Chi-Fu (see Justima, William, Jr.)
CHIKAMATSU Monzaemon
  The Battles of Coxinga (Kokusenyo Kassen)
  (In Major Plays of Chikamatsu)
  (In Four Major Plays)
  The Courier for Hell (Meido no Hikyaku)
  (In Genius of the Oriental Theater)
  The Drum of the Waves of Horikawa (Horikawa Nami no Tsuzumi)
  (In Major Plays of Chikamatsu)
  The Girl from Kakata, or Love at Sea (Hakata Kojoro Namima-
    kura)
  (In Major Plays of Chikamatsu)

Gonza the Lancer (Yari no Gonza)
    (In Major Plays of Chikamatsu)
The Love Suicides at Amijima (Shinja Ten no Amijima)
    (In Four Major Plays)
    (In Major Plays of Chikamatsu)
The Love Suicides at Sonezaki (Sonezaki Shinju)
    (In Four Major Plays)
    (In Major Plays of Chikamatsu)
The Love Suicides in the Women's Temple (Shinju Mannenso)
    (In Major Plays of Chikamatsu)
The Uprooted Pine (Nebiki no Kadomatsu)
    (In Major Plays of Chikamatsu)
    (In Four Major Plays)
The Woman-Killer and the Hell of Oil (Onnagoroshi Abura
    Jigoku)
    (In Major Plays of Chikamatsu)
Yosaku from Tamba (Tamba Yosaku)
    (In Major Plays of Chikamatsu)
A Child is Born (see Benet, Stephen Vincent)
The Child of Nature (see Inchbald, Mrs. Elizabeth Simpson)
Childhood (see Wilder, Thornton)
The Children (see Ruthenburg, G. Hutchinson)
The Children and the Evangelists (see Tomes, Margaret Otey)
The Children in the Wood (see Morton, Thomas)
Children in Uniform (see Winsloe, Christa)
Children is All (see Purdy, James)
Children of Darkness (see Corrie, Joe)
Children of Darkness (see Mayer, Edwin Justus)
Children of Paradise (see Carne, Marcel)
The Children's Hour (see Hellman, Lillian)
CHILDRESS, Alice
    Wine in the Wilderness
        (In Best Short Plays, 1972)
CHINA. People's Republic. Cultural Ensemble of the Political
Department of the Navy.
    Sea Battle at Night
        (In Chinese Literature, nos. 3, 4, 1968)
China is Near (see Bellocchio, Marco)
CHINA Peking Opera Troupe
    On the Docks
        (In Chinese Literature, no. 1, 1969)
    The Red Lantern
        (In Chinese Literature, no. 8, 1970)
        (In TDR/The Drama Review, Vol. 13, no. 4, Summer 1969)
        (Revised in TDR/The Drama Review, Vol. 15, no. 2,
        Spring 1971)
    Schachiapang
        (In Chinese Literature, no. 11, 1967)
        (Revised version in Chinese Literature, no. 11, 1970)
        (In TDR/The Drama Review, Vol. 15, no. 2, Spring 1971)
    Spark Among the Reeds
        (In Chinese Literature, Sept. 1964)

Taking the Bandit's Stronghold
  (In Chinese Literature, no. 8, 1967)
CHINA Peking Opera Troupe of Shanghai
  On the Docks; revised script 1972
    (In Chinese Literature, no. 5, 1972)
  Song of the Dragon River; revised
    (In Chinese Literature, no. 7, 1972)
  Taking Tiger Mountain by Strategy; a revised version of "Taking
  the Bandit's Stronghold"
    (In Chinese Literature, no. 1, 1970)
CHINA Shantung Provincial Peking Opera Troupe
  Raid on the White Tiger Regiment
    (In Chinese Literature, no. 10, 1967)
The Chinese Wall (see Frisch, Max)
The Chinese Water Wheel (see Strachan, Edna Higgins)
Chinese White (see Gielgud, Val Henry)
Les Chinois (see Schisgal, Murray)
La Chinoise (see Goddard, Jean-Luc)
The Chip Woman's Fortune (see Richardson, Willis)
Chips with Everything (see Wesker, Arnold)
Chit-Chat on a Rat (see Athetton, Camille Skrivanek)
CHLUMBERG, Hans von, 1897-1930
  Miracle at Verdun
    (In Famous Plays of Today, 1932-33)
CHODOROV, Edward, 1904-
  Kind Lady
    (In 13 Famous Plays of Crime and Detection)
  Yellow Jack, screenplay; based on the play by Sidney Howard
  in collaboration with Paul de Kruif, with contributions to the
  treatment by Dan Totheroh, directed by George B. Seitz.
    (In Twenty Best Film Plays)
CHODOROV, Jerome
  Anniversary Waltz
    (In Theatre Arts, Vol. 39, Feb. 1955)
The Choephori (see Aeschylus, 525-456 B. C.)
The Chorus Girl (see Stone, John A.)
CHOSE, Raymond
  La Farce de L'Auberge Rouge
    (In Plaisir de France, supplement theatral, no. 368, June
    1969)
  La Farce Rouge ou le Dernier Vivant
    (In Plaisir de France, supplement theatral, no. 295, May
    1963)
Les Choses de la Vie (see Sauet, Claude)
Les Choutes (see Barillet, Pierre)
CHOWN, Patricia
  Sea-Shell
    (In Best One-Act Plays of 1944/45, London)
Chpalikov, Guennady (see Khoutziev, Marlen)
Chris Sick, or Happy New Year Anyway (see Saroyan, William)
Christ (see Jesus Christ)
Christ (see Hartmann, Sadakichi)

The Christening (see Jennings, Gertrude)
CHRISTIE, Agatha (Miller) 1891-
    Witness for the Prosecution
        (In Famous Plays of Today, 1954)
CHRISTIE, Dorothy
    Carrington, V. C., by Dorothy and Campbell Christie
        (In Famous Plays of Today, 1954)
CHRISTINA, Frank
    Billy Jack, screenplay by Frank and Theresa Christina, di-
    rected by Tom Laughlin.
        (Avon Books Screenplays, 1973)
Christina's World (see Ravel, Ronald)
A Christmas Carol (see Agenoux, Soren)
A Christmas Carol (see Kaufman, George Simon)
Christmas in Las Vegas (see Richardson, Jack)
The Christmas Tree (see Housman, Laurence)
Christopher Columbus (see Bertin, Charles)
Christopher Columbus (see Ghelderode, Michel de)
The Chronicle of Edward the First (see Peele, George)
Chrononhotonthologos (see Carey, Henry)
Chukrai, Grigori (see Tchoukhri, Grigory)
CHURCH, Virginia
    Very Social Service
        (In Drama, Vol. 15, Dec. 1924)
    What Men Live By
        (In Drama, Vol. 12, Oct.-Nov. 1921)
CIBBER, Colley, 1671-1757
    The Careless Husband
        (In Bell's British Theatre, 1797, Vol. 8)
    The Double Gallant
        (In Bell's British Theatre, 1797, Vol. 10)
    The Lady's Last Stake; or, The Wife's Resentment
        (In Bell's British Theatre, 1797, Vol. 24)
    Love Makes a Man; or, The Fop's Fortune
        (In Bell's British Theatre, 1797, Vol. 7)
    The Provoked Husband; or, A Journey to London (see Van-
    brugh, Sir John)
    The Refusal; or, The Ladies' Philosophy
        (In Bell's British Theatre, 1797, Vol. 2)
    She Wou'd and She Wou'd Not; or, The Kind Impostor
        (In Bell's British Theatre, 1797, Vol. 5)
    Ximena; or, The Heroic Daughter
        (In Bell's British Theatre, 1797, Vol. 15)
        (In Cumberland's British Theatre, Vol. 36, no. 2)
Cicero, Marcus Tullius, 106-43 B. C.
    *The Conspiracy (see Prosperi, Giorgio)
Cid, El, Campeador, 1043-1099
    *The Cid (see Corneille, Pierre)
CID Perez, Jose
    The Comedy of the Dead (La Comedia de los Muertos)
        (In First Stage, Vol. 6, no. 1, Spring 1967)
Le Ciel de Lit (see Hartog, Jan de)
Cigalon (see Pagnol, Marcel)

Cinderella Married (see Field, Rachel Lyman)
The Circle (see Maugham, William Somerset)
Circumstances Alter Cases (see Yaltsev, P.)
Circumventin' Saady (see MacDonald, Zillah K.)
The Citadel (see Dalrymple, Ian)
The Citizen (see Murphy, Arthur)
Citizen Kane (see Welles, Orson)
The City Madam (see Massinger, Philip)
City Madam (see also Riches)
The City Match (see Mayne, Jasper)
City Match (see also The Merchant's Wedding)
The City Night-Cap; or, Crede Quod Habes and Habes (see Davenport, Robert)
City Symphony (see Jones, Barbara Elgin)
The City Wives Confederacy (see Vanbrugh, John)
CLAIR, Rene, 1898-
    La Beaute du Diable
        (In Clair, Four Screenplays)
        (In Comedies et Commentaires)
    Les Belles-de-Nuit
        (In Clair, Four Screenplays)
        (In Comedies et Commentaires)
    Entre'acte
        (In L'Avant-Scene du Cinema, no. 86, Nov. 1968)
        (In A Nous La Liberte, Classic Film Scripts)
    Les Grandes Manoeuvres
        (In Clair, Four Screenplays)
        (In Comedies et Commentaires)
    A Nous la Liberte
        (In Classic Film Scripts)
        (In L'Avant-Scene du Cinema, no. 86, Nov. 1968)
    Porte des Lilas
        (In Comedies et Commentaires)
    Le Silence est d'Or
        (In Clair, Four Screenplays)
        (In Comedies et Commentaires)
Claire's Knee (see Rohmer, Eric)
The Clandestine Marriage (see Colman, George)
Clara's Ole Man (see Bullins, Ed.)
Clarence (see Tarkington, Booth)
Clari; or, The Maid of Milan (see Payne, John Howard)
CLARK, China
    Perfection in Black
        (In Scripts, Vol. 1, no. 7, May 1972)
CLARK, John Pepper, 1935-
    Song of the Goat
        (In Plays From Black Africa)
CLARK, T. E. B.
    Encore. Scripts for the film by T. E. B. Clark, Arthur Macrae, and Eric Ambler, based on three short stories by Somerset Maugham.
        (In Encore, Doubleday, 1952)

Clark, Walter Van Tilburg, 1909-
**The Ox-Bow Incident (see Trotti, Lamar)
CLARKE, Sebastian
Helliocentric World
(In Scripts, Vol. 1, no. 7, May 1972)
The Classic Dancing School (see Duncan, Winifred)
Claude De Lyon (see Husson, Albert)
Claudius, Appius, 451-450 B. C.
*Virginius (see Knowles, James Sheridan)
CLAUS, Hugo
Friday
(In Plays and Players, Vol. 19, no. 5, Feb. 1972)
CLAVEL, Maurice
Mina de Vanghel, by Maurice Clavel et Maurice Barry
(In L'Avant-Scene du Cinema, no. 15, May 15, 1962)
CLEMENT, Rene, 1913-
Jeux Interdits, by Rene Clement, Jean Aurenche, et Pierre Bost
(In L'Avant-Scene du Cinema, no. 15, May 15, 1962)
Monsieur Ripois, by Rene Clement et Hugh Mills, d'apres le
roman de Louis Hemon "Monsieur Ripois et la Nemesis."
(In L'Avant-Scene du Cinema, no. 55, 1966)
CLEMENTS, Claudine E.
A Troubadour's Dream
(In Drama, Vol. 16, Nov. 1925)
CLEMENTS, Colin Campbell, 1894-
Across the Border
(In 50 More Contemporary One-Act Plays)
Farewell to Love (see Ryerson, Florence)
On the Lot (see Ryerson, Florence)
That's Hollywood (see Ryerson, Florence)
Clements, Samuel Langhorne, 1835-1910
**The King and the Duke (see Fergusson, Francis)
Cleo and Max (see Marcus, Frank)
Cleone (see Dodsley, Robert)
Cleonice, Princess of Bithynia (see Hoole, John)
Cleopatra, Queen of Egypt, 69-30 B. C.
*Caesar and Cleopatra (see Shaw, George Bernard)
*Lucullus's Dinner-Party (see Baring, Maurice)
Clerambard (see Ayme, Marcel)
CLERQUE, Lucien, 1934-
Delta de Sel
(In L'Avant-Scene du Cinema, no. 123, Mar. 1972)
CLEUGH, Dennis
The Violet Under the Snow
(In Drama, Vol. 13, Nov. 1922)
CLEVEL, Maurice
Saint Euloge de Cordoue
(In Plaisir de France, supplement theatral, no. 330, April
1966)
Une Cliente Perdue (see Vandenberghe, Paul)
CLIFFORD, Lucy (Lane) "Mrs. W. K. Clifford"
The Likeness of the Night
(In Anglo Saxon Review, Vol. 4, Mar. 1900)

Clifford, Mrs. William Kingdon (see Clifford, Lucy Lane)
The Climate of Eden (see Hart, Moss)
Climb the Greased Pole (see Longhi, Vincent)
Cline, Edward, 1892-1961
     Never Give a Sucker an Even Break (see Neville, John T.)
The Clinic (see Key, Ted)
Clive, Robert, baron Clive of Plassey, 1725-1774
     *Clive of India (see Lipscomb, William Percy)
The Clock Shop (see Golden, John)
The Clock Strikes Ten (see Hickey, D.E.)
The Clockwork Orange (see Kubrick, Stanley)
The Clod (see Beach, Lewis)
Close, Upton, pseud. (see Hall, Josef Washington)
Close Quarters (see Somin, W.O.)
Closely Watched Trains (see Menzel, Jiri)
The Closing Door (see Knox, Alexander)
Cloud Over Breakshin (see Stone, Weldon)
The Clouds (see Aristophanes)
The Clouds (see Gale, Zona (Breese))
Clouston, Storer
     **Drole de Drame (see Carne, Marcel)
CLOUZOT, Henri-Georges, 1907-
     Quai des Orfevres, by Henri-Georges et Jean Ferry
          (In L'Avant-Scene du Cinema, no. 29, Sept. 15, 1963)
     Le Salaire de la Peur, by Henri-Georges Clouzot et Jerome
     Geronimi, d'Apres le Roman de Georges Arnaud.
          (In L'Avant-Scene du Cinema, no. 17, July 15, 1962)
Club Bedroom (see Auchincloss, Louis)
Coast to Coast Big Mouth (see Bersky, Bill)
COBB, James, 1756-1818
     The Doctor and the Apothecary
          (In The London Stage, Vol. 2, 1824-27)
     The Haunted Tower
          (In Cumberland's British Theatre, Vol. 39, no. 5)
          (In The London Stage, Vol. 2)
     Paul and Virginia
          (In Cumberland's British Theatre, Vol. 38, no. 6)
     Ramah Droog
          (In Modern Theatre, 1811, Vol. 6)
     The Siege of Belgrade
          (In Cumberland's British Theatre, Vol. 4, no. 1)
     The Wife of Two Husbands
          (In Modern Theatre, 1811, Vol. 6)
A Cock Crows at Midnight (A Puppet Film Scenario)
          (In Chinese Literature, no. 4, 1970)
Cockade (see Wood, Charles)
Cock-A-Doodle (see O'Casey, Sean)
The Cocktail Party (see Eliot, Thomas Stearns)
COCTEAU, Jean, 1889-1963
     Antigone
          (In his Five Plays)
          (In Oeuvres Completes de Jean Cocteau, Vol. 5)

Beauty and the Beast
   (In Three Screenplays)
Le Bel Indifferent
   (In Nouveau Theatre de Poche)
The Blood of a Poet
   (In Two Screenplays)
Les Chevaliers de la Table Ronde
   (In Oeuvres Completes de Jean Cocteau, Vol. 6)
The Eagle with Two Heads
   (In his Five Plays)
L'Ecole des Veuves, d'apres le Conte de Petrone, "La Matrone
   d'Ephese"
   (In Nouveau Theatre de Poche)
   (In Oeuvres Completes de Jean Cocteau, Vol. 8)
L'Epouse Injustement Soupconnee
   (In Nouveau Theatre de Poche)
The Eternal Return
   (In Three Screenplays)
The Holy Terrors
   (In his Five Plays)
The Infernal Machine
   (In From the Modern Repertoire, Series One)
Intimate Relations
   (In From the Modern Repertoire, Series Three)
   (In his Five Plays)
La Machine a Ecrire
   (In Oeuvres Completes de Jean Cocteau, Vol. 8)
La Machine Infernale
   (In Oeuvres Completes de Jean Cocteau, Vol. 5)
Les Maries de la Tour Eiffel
   (In Oeuvres Completes de Jean Cocteau, Vol. 7)
Les Monstres Sacres
   (In Oeuvres Completes de Jean Cocteau, Vol. 8)
Oedipe Roi
   (In Oeuvres Completes de Jean Cocteau, Vol. 5)
Orphee
   (In his Five Plays)
   (In Oeuvres Completes de Jean Cocteau, Vol. 5)
Orpheus
   (In Three Screenplays)
Le Pauvre Matelot
   (In Nouveau Theatre de Poche)
Les Parents Terribles
   (In Oeuvres Completes de Jean Cocteau, Vol. 7)
La Princess de Cleves (see Dorfmann, Robert)
Renaud et Armide
   (In Oeuvres Completes de Jean Cocteau, Vol. 6)
Romeo and Juliet (d'apres William Shakespeare)
   (In Oeuvres Completes de Jean Cocteau, Vol. 6)
Le Rossignol de l'Empereur de Chine (see Trinka, Jiri)
The Testament of Orpheus
   (In Two Screenplays)

La Voix Humaine
(In Oeuvres Completes de Jean Cocteau, Vol. 7)
The Codfish (El Bacalao) (see Ruibal, Jose)
COE, Fred
Something in the Wind
(In Best Television Plays of the Year, 1949)
O Coelhinhi Pitomba (see Luiz, Milton de)
Coeur a Cuir (see Audiberti, Jacques)
Coeur a Deux (see Foissy, Guy)
COFFEY, Charles, d. 1747
The Devil to Pay; or, The Wives Metamorphosed
(In The London Stage, Vol. 1, 1824/27)
COFFIN, Gertrude Wilson
A Shotgun Splicin'
(In Carolina Folkplays, 1928)
COHAN, George Michael, 1878-1942
Seven Keys to Baldpate, based on the novel by Earl Derr Biggers
(In 13 Famous Plays of Crime and Detection)
COLEMAN, Lonnie
Hot Spell; the film based on the play "Next of Kin"
(In Avon Plays Publications, 1958)
Colette, Sidonie Gabrielle, 1875-1954
**Le Ciel de Lit (see Hartog, Jan de)
**Gigi (see Loos, Anita)
Collect Your Hand Baggage (see Mortimer, John)
The Collection (see Pinter, Harold)
La Collectionneuse (see Rohmer, Eric)
Collectionneuse (see Rohmer, Eric)
A Collier's Friday Night (see Lawrence, David Herbert)
Collings, Pierre
The Story of Louis Pasteur (see Gibney, Sheridan)
COLLON, Robert
Trencavel
(In Plaisir de France, supplement theatral, no. 300, Oct.
1963)
COLMAN, George, 1732-1794
Bonduca (see Beaumont, Francis)
The Clandescent Marriage
(In Cumberland's British Theatre, Vol. 4, no. 3)
(In Bell's British Theatre, 1797, Vol. 14)
The Connoisseur
(In Harrison's British Classicks, Vol. 6)
The Jealous Wife
(In Bell's British Theatre, 1797, Vol. 20)
(In Cumberland's British Theatre, Vol. 6, no. 3)
(In The London Stage, Vol. 1)
COLMAN, George (the Younger), 1762-1836
The Battle of Hexham; or, Days of Old
(In Cumberland's British Theatre, Vol. 36, no. 9)
Blue Beard
(In Cumberland's British Theatre, Vol. 39, no. 4)

Blue Devils
   (In Lacy's Plays)
The English Merchant
   (In Modern Theatre, 1811, Vol. 9)
The Heir at Law
   (In Cumberland's British Theatre, Vol. 43, no. 1)
Inkle and Yarico
   (In Cumberland's British Theatre, Vol. 26, no. 3)
John Bull; or, The Englishman's Fireside
   (In Cumberland's British Theatre, Vol. 41, no. 6)
Love Laughs at Locksmiths
   (In Cumberland's British Theatre, Vol. 41, no. 8)
The Mountaineers
   (In Cumberland's British Theatre, Vol. 41, no. 10)
Polly Honeycombe
   (In The London Stage, Vol. 2)
The Review; or, The Wags of Windsor
   (In Cumberland's British Theatre, Vol. 41, no. 2)
The Surrender of Calais
   (In Cumberland's British Theatre, Vol. 44, no. 5)
Who Wants a Guinea?
   (In Cumberland's British Theatre, Vol. 27, no. 2)
   (In Modern Theatre, 1811, Vol. 3)
X. Y. Z.
   (In Cumberland's British Theatre, Vol. 10, no. 7)
La Colombe a Deux Tetes (see Bacon, Jean)
La Colonie (see Marivaux, Pierre Carlet de Chamblain de)
The Colonnade (see Young, Stark)
The Color of Our Skin (see Gorostiza, Celestino)
Color Scheme (see Serling, Rod)
Colors (see Depero, Francesco)
Colour-Blind: A Comedy of Twenty Minutes (see Aide, Hamilton)
COLTON, John, 1889-1946
   Rain, founded on William Somerset Maugham's story "Miss
   Thompson"
   (In Best American Plays, Supp. Vol.)
COLUM, Padraic, 1881-
   The Betrayal
   (In Drama, Vol. 11, Oct. 1920)
   Miracle of the Corn
   (In Theatre Arts, Vol. 5, 1921)
Columbine in Business (see Field, Rachel Lyman)
Columbus, Christopher, 1451-1506
   *Christopher Columbus, a dramatic fairy tale (see Ghelderode,
   Michel de)
   *Columbus Day (see Welles, Orson)
La Combinaison (see Paquin, Dorian)
COMDEN, Betty, 1919-
   Bells are Ringing (see Styne, Jule)
   Singin' in the Rain, film script by Betty Comden and Adolph
   Green, directed by Gene Kelly and Stanley Donen.
   (In MGM Library of Film Scripts Series)

Come Back, Little Sheba (see Inge, William Motter)
Come Blow Your Horn (see Simon, Neil)
Come into the Garden, Maude (see Coward, Noel)
A Comedia Atomica (see Muniz, Lauro Cesar)
The Comedy of Asses (see Plautus, Titus Maccius)
A Comedy of Danger (see Hughes, Richard Arthur Warren)
The Comedy of the Dead (La Comedia de los Muertos) (see Cid
     Perez, Jose)
Comes the Dreamer (see Wexley, John)
Comfortable Lodgings; or, Paris in 1750 (see Peake, Richard
     Brinsley)
"Comic Strip" (see King of Hearts)
A Comical Countess (see Brough, William)
Command Decision (see Haines, William Wister)
Le Commandant Watrin (see Lenoux, Armand)
Comme au Theatre (see Dorin, Francoise)
Comme avant, Mieux qu'avant (see Pirandello, Luigi)
Comme la Pierre (see Weingarten, Romain)
Comme les Chats (see Silvain, Jean)
Comme un Oiseau (see Millar, Ronald and Nigel Balchin)
COMMEDIA dell'Arte
     The Scenario of the Impostor Prince
        (In Masterworks of World Drama, Vol. 3)
The Committee (see Howard, Sir Robert)
Commodus (see Wallace, Lewis)
A Common for All Saints (see Ziegelmaier, Gregory)
Common Man (see Prelovsky, Anatoly)
La Commune de Paris (see Menegoz, Robert)
The Communicants (Winter Light) (see Bergman, Ingmar)
"Como Matar um Playboy" (see Bethencourt, Joao)
Como Se Frazia um Deputado (see Junior, Franca)
The Compromise (see Jaeger, C. Stephen)
Compton-Burnett, Ivy, 1892-
     A Heritage--and Its History (see Mitchell, Julian)
Le Comte Oderland (see Frisch, Max)
La Comtesse aux Pieds Nus (see Mankiewicz, Joseph Leo)
Comus (see Milton, John)
The Conceited Count (see Destouches, Phillipe Nericault)
Concerning the Red Army (see Rosten, Norman)
The Concert at Saint Ovide (see Vallejo, Antonio Buero)
Concerto de l'Aube (see Prigent, Yves)
The Condemned Squad (see Sastre, Alfonso)
Conditioned Reflex (see Zahn, Curtis)
CONDROYER, Philippe, 1927-
     Une Lettre
        (In L'Avant-Scene du Cinema, no. 53, 1965)
Confessional (see Wilde, Percival)
The Confidant (see Fabbi, Diego)
The Confidential Clerk (see Eliot, Thomas Stearns)
Confidenze a Pagamento (see Fratti, Mario)
The CONFLICT of Conscience (Anon.)
        (In Dodsley's A Select Collection of Old English Plays, Vol.
     6)

Confrontation (see Fortuno, Claude)
Confucius (K'ung Fu-tzu) c. 551-479 B. C.
   *Confucius (see Hartmann, Sadakichi)
   *Life of Confucius (see Brecht, Bertolt)
Congresswoman (see Aristophanes)
CONGREVE, William, 1670-1729
   The Double Dealer
      (In Bell's British Theatre, 1797, Vol. 28)
   Love for Love
      (In Masterworks of World Drama, Vol. 4)
      (In Bell's British Theatre, 1797, Vol. 1)
      (In Cumberland's British Theatre, Vol. 19, no. 2)
   The Mourning Bride
      (In Bell's British Theatre, 1797, Vol. 19)
   The Old Batchelor
      (In Bell's British Theatre, 1797, Vol. 28)
   The Way of the World
      (In Genius of the Later English Theater)
      (In Bell's British Theatre, 1797, Vol. 33)
      (In Great English Plays)
CONKLE, Ellsworth Prouty, 1899-
   Abbie, the Bug Boy
      (In Best One-Act Plays, 1952/53, N. Y.)
   Gold Is Where You Don't Find It
      (In Best One-Act Plays of 1938, N. Y.)
   Hawk A-Flyin'
      (In Best One-Act Plays of 1938, N. Y.)
   Heaven is a Long Time to Wait
      (In Best Short Plays, 1958/59)
   The Last One
      (In Best One-Act Plays, 1951/52, N. Y.)
   Minnie Field
      (In 25 Best Plays of the Modern American Theatre, Early
      Series, 1916-29)
   Muletail Prime
      (In Best One-Act Plays, 1950/51, N. Y.)
   Prologue to Glory
      (In Three Distinctive Plays about Abraham Lincoln)
The Connection (see Gelber, Jack)
CONNELLY, Marcus Cook, 1890-
   Beggar on Horseback (see Kaufman, George Simon)
   A Christmas Carol (see Kaufman, George Simon)
   Ex Cathedra; a monophonic pantomine, by Marc Connelly)
      (In Theatre Arts, Vol. 10, Dec. 1926)
   The Good Earth (see Jennings, Talbot)
   Green Pastures
      (In 16 Famous American Plays)
      (In 20 Best Plays of the Modern American Theatre, Vol. 1)
   The Green Pastures
      (In Pulitzer Prize Plays)
   Little David
      (In Best One-Act Plays of 1937, London)

Merton of the Movies (see Kaufman, George Simon)
The Traveler, by Marc Connelly
    (In 24 Favorite One-Act Plays)
Connie und der Löwe (see Zimmerman, Rolf)
The Connoisseur (see Colman, George)
The Conqueror (see Wincelberg, Simon)
The Conquest of Everest (see Kopit, Arthur)
La Conquete de l'Everest (see Kopit, Arthur)
CONRAD, Joseph, 1857-1924
    One Day More
    (In The Modern Theatre, ed. by Eric Bentley, Vol. 3)
Considine, Robert
    Thirty Seconds over Tokyo (see Trombo, Dalton)
The Conspiracy (see Prosperi, Giorgio)
The Conspiracy of Feelings (see Olyesha, Yurii)
The Conspirators (see Merimee, Prosper)
The Constant Lover (see Hankin, St. John Emile Clavering)
Constantine I, called the Great (Flavius Valerius Aureleus Con-
    stantinus), c. 274-337
    *Constantine the Great (see Lee, Nathaniel)
Constantinople Smith (see Mee, Charles L., Jr.)
A Construcao (see Pimental, Altimar)
CONTI, Antonio, 1897-
    Useless Oedipus; both French and English texts are included.
    (In Italian Theatre Review, Vol. 13, July/Sept. 1964)
The Contractor (see Storey, David)
The Constant Prince (see Waldman, Max)
The Construction of Boston (see Koch, Kenneth)
CONTENTION between Liberality and Prodigality (Anon.)
    (In Dodsley's A Select Collection of Old English Plays, Vol.
    8)
The Contrast (see Tyler, Royall)
O Contrato Azul (see Bloch, Pedro)
La Contrebasse (see Fasquel, Maurice)
Contribution (see Shine, Ted)
Conversation Piece (see Coward, Noel Pierce)
Conway, Jack, 1887-1952
    Dragon Seed (see Roberts, Marguerite)
Conway, Olive; pseud. (see Brighouse, Harold)
COOK, Albert
    The Death of Trotsky
    (In Drama & Theatre, Vol. 9, no. 1, Fall 1970)
COOK, Richard
    The Inheritors
    (In Drama & Theatre, Vol. 7, no. 2, Winter 1968/69)
Cookbook (see Parsons, M.R.)
COOKE, John, fl. 1600
    Green's Tu Quoque; or, The City Gallant
    (In Dodsley's A Select Collection of Old English Plays, Vol.
    11)
    (In Dodsley's A Select Collection of Old Plays, Vol. 7)
COOKE, Joshua
    How a Man May Choose a Good Wife From a Bad

(In Dodsley's A Select Collection of Old English Plays, Vol.
  9)
COOKSEY, Curtis
  Mountain Laurel
    (In 50 More Contemporary One-Act Plays)
COONEY, Ray
  Le Saut du Lit, de Ray Cooney et John Chapman
    (In L'Avant-Scene du Theatre, no. 506, Nov. 15, 1972)
COOPER, Frederick Fox, 1806-1879
  The Spare Bed; or, The Shower Bath
    (In Cumberland's British Theatre, Vol. 43, No. 5)
COOPER, Giles
  Happy Family
    (In Plays and Players, Vol. 14, May 1967)
  Out of the Crocodile
    (In Plays of the Year, Vol. 27, 1962-63)
Cooper, James Fenimore, 1789-1851
  **The Pilot (see Fitz-Ball, Edward)
COOPER, Lou
  The Last Speech, a cantata with music by Lou Cooper and
    words by Carl Carmer, Stephen Vincent Benet, and Franklin
    Delano Roosevelt.
    (In Radio's Best Plays, 1947)
Cop and Blow (see Harris, Neil)
COPEAU, Jacques, 1879-1945
  Les Freres Karamazov, by Jacques Copeau and Jean Croue,
    based on the novel by Dostoevskii.
    (In L'Avant-Scene du Theatre, no. 481, Oct. 15, 1971)
  The House into Which We are Born
    (In Theatre Arts, Vol. 8, July 1924)
Cophetua (see Drinkwater, John)
The Copped Coup (see Sudekum, Fred)
O Coracao Nao Envelhece (see Magalhaes, Paulo de)
Les Corbeaux (see Becque, Henri)
O Cordao (see Azevedo, Arthur)
O Cordao Umbilical (see Prata, Mario)
Corfe Gate (see Foy, Helen)
CORKERY, Daniel, 1878-1965
  Resurrection
    (In Theatre Arts, Vol. 8, Apr. 1924)
CORLETT, William
  Tinker's Curse
    (In Plays of the Year, Vol. 34, 1967-68)
Cormack, Bartlett
  Fury (see Lang, Fritz)
Cormanzana, Jose Maria Bellido (see Bellido Cormanzana, Jose
  Maria)
Cormon, Eugene, 1811-1908
  The Two Oephans (see Dennery, Adolphe Philippe)
The Corn is Green (see Williams, Emlyn)
CORNEAU, Perry Boyer
  Masks
    (In Drama, Vol. 12, Apr. 1922)

CORNEILLE, Pierre, 1606-1684
  The Cid
    (In The Classic Theatre, ed. by Eric Bentley, Vol. 4)
    (In Masterworks of World Drama, Vol. 4)
  **The Roman Father (see Whitehead, William)
Cornelia (see Garnier, Robert)
The Corner (see Freda, Frank)
CORNISH, Roger N.
  Open Twenty-Four Hours
    (In Drama & Theatre, Vol. 7, no. 1, Fall 1968)
CORNISH Cycle
  The Three Maries
    (In Religious Drama, Vol. 2)
CORNISH: The Legend of the Rood
  I. David Takes the Shoots to Jerusalem
    (In Religious Drama, Vol. 2)
  II. David and Bathsheba
    (In Religious Drama, Vol. 2)
The Coronation (see Forssell, Lars)
Corpo A Corpo (see Viana Filho, Oduvaldo)
CORRA, Bruno
  Grey Red Violet Orange, A Net of Sensations (see Settimelli,
    Emilio)
  Hands: A Showcase, by Bruno Corra and F. T. Marinetti
    (In TDR/The Drama Review, Vol. 15, Fall 1970)
  Negative Acts, by Bruno Corra and Emilio Settimelli
    (In TDR/The Drama Review, Vol. 15, Fall 1970)
CORREA, Viriato
  Jariti
    (In Revista de Teatro, no. 329)
  Mauricio de Nassau
    (In Revista de Teatro, no. 357)
CORRIE, Joe
  The Bridge
    (In Best One-Act Plays of 1940, London)
  Children of Darkness
    (In Best One-Act Plays of 1936, London)
  The Failure
    (In Best One-Act Plays of 1944/45, London)
  Hewers of Coal
    (In 24 One-Act Plays, Revised edition, 1954)
  The Hoose O' The Hill
    (In Best One-Act Plays of 1931, London)
  Litchen Fair
    (In Best One-Act Plays of 1942/43, London)
  The Maid of Domremy
    (In Best One-Act Plays of 1935, London)
  Tell It Not in Gath
    (In Best One-Act Plays of 1948/49, London)
  There is No Glory
    (In Best One-Act Plays of 1937, London)
The Corrupters (see Samuels, Gertrude)

Corruption in the Palace of Justice (see Betti, Ugo)
Corry, Will
    Two Lane Blacktop (see Wurlitzer, Rudolph)
CORSO, Gregory
    Standing on a Street Corner
        (In Evergreen Review, Vol. 6, no. 23, 1961)
CORWIN, Norman Lewis, 1910-
    Daybreak
        (In Radio's Best Plays, 1947)
    London by Clipper
        (In Radio Drama in Action, 1945)
    My Client, Curley, by Norman Corwin and Lucille Fletcher
        (In Plays from Radio, 1948)
    On a Note of Triumph
        (In Best One-Act Plays of 1945, N.Y.)
    Samson
        (In Theatre Arts, Vol. 26, Sept. 1942)
    We Hold These Truths
        (In Best One-Act Plays of 1942, N.Y.)
Cosi fan tutte (see Mozart, Johann Chrysostom Wolfgang Amadeus)
Le Cosmonaute Agricole (see Obaldia, Rene de)
COSTA-Gavras, 1933-
    Z; or, L'Anatomie d'un Assassinat Politique
        (In L'Avant-Scene du Cinema, no. 96, Oct. 1969)
COSTELLO, Ward
    A Wake for Me and Thee
        (In Best One-Act Plays of 1948/49, N.Y.)
The COSTLIE Whore, A Comicall Historie (Anon.)
        (In A Collection of Old English Plays, Vol. 4)
Counsel Retained (see Mackay, Constance D'Arcy)
Counsellor-At-Law (see Rice, Elmer L.)
Count Albany (see Carswell, Donald)
The Count of Monte Cristo (see Fechter, Charles)
The Countess of Salisbury (see Hartson, Hall)
Country Dance (see Kennaway, James)
The Country Girl (see Garrick, David)
The Country Girl (see Odets, Clifford)
The Country Wife (see Wycherley, William)
Un Coup de Soleil (see Vandenberghe, Paul)
Der Coup Von Trafalgar (see Vitrac, Roger)
Les Coups de Theatre (see Mithois, Marcel)
The Courier for Hell (Meido No Hikyaku) (see Chikamatsu Mon-
    zaemon)
COURTELINE, George
    A Rule is a Rule. Translated by Jacques Barzun
        (In Tulane Drama Review, Vol. 3, Oct. 1958)
The Courtesan (Kagotsurube) (see Kawatake, Shinichi)
The Courting of Marie Jenvrin (see Ringwood, Gwen Pharis)
COURTNEY, John, 1804-1865
    Old Joe and Young Joe
        (In Lacy's Acting Plays, Vol. 14)
COURTENY, William Leonard, 1850-1928
    Gaston Bonnier; or, Times Revenges

(In <u>Anglo Saxon Review</u>, Vol. 8, Mar. 1901)
COUSIN, Gabriel
  La Descente sur Recife
    (In <u>L'Avant-Scene du Theatre</u>, no. 469-470, Apr. 1-15, 1971)
Cousin Tom (see Roberts, George)
Les Cousins (see Chabrol, Claude)
Le Couteau (see Perret, Jacques)
Covent Garden: A Pleasant Comedie (see Nabbes, Thomas)
The Covent-Garden Tragedy (see Fielding, Henry)
The Covent-Garden Tragedy (see also, The Distrest Mother;
  Andromaque)
COVENTRY Shearmen and Tailors' Play
  Herod and the Kings
    (In <u>Religious Drama</u>, Vol. 2)
COWAN, Sada
  In the Morgue
    (In <u>50 Contemporary One-Act Plays</u>)
COWARD, Noël Pierce, 1899-1973
  The Astonished Heart
    (In <u>Curtain Calls</u>)
    (In <u>Tonight at 8:30</u>)
  Brief Encounter
    (In <u>Three British Screenplays</u>)
  Cavalcade
    (In <u>16 Famous British Plays</u>)
  Come into the Garden, Maude
    (In <u>Best Short Plays of the World Theatre</u>, 1958-67)
  Conversation Piece
    (In <u>Curtain Calls</u>)
  Easy Virtue
    (In <u>Curtain Calls</u>)
  Family Album
    (In <u>Curtain Calls</u>)
    (In <u>Tonight at 8:30</u>)
  Fumed Oak
    (In <u>Best One-Act Plays of 1936</u>, London)
    (In <u>30 Famous One-Act Plays</u>)
    (In <u>Curtain Calls</u>)
    (In <u>Tonight at 8:30</u>)
  Hands Across the Sea
    (In <u>24 Favorite One-Act Plays</u>)
    (In <u>Curtain Calls</u>)
    (In <u>Tonight at 8:30</u>)
    (In <u>24 One-Act Plays</u>, Revised edition, 1954)
  Hay Fever
    (In <u>Modern Plays</u>, 1937, London)
  Point Valaine
    (In <u>Curtain Calls</u>)
  Present Laughter
    (In <u>Theatre Arts</u>, Vol. 33, July 1949)
  "Red Peppers"
    (In <u>Curtain Calls</u>)
    (In <u>Tonight at 8:30</u>)

Shadow Play
  (In Curtain Calls)
  (In Tonight at 8:30)
Shadows of the Evening
  (In Modern Short Comedies from Broadway & London)
Still Life
  (In Curtain Calls)
  (In Tonight at 8:30)
"This was a Man"
  (In Curtain Calls)
Tonight at 8:30
  (In Curtain Calls)
Ways and Means
  (In Curtain Calls)
  (In Tonight at 8:30)
We Were Dancing
  (In Curtain Calls)
  (In Tonight at 8:30)
The Cow-Catcher on the Caboose (see Devany, Edward H.)
The Cow-Herd and the Weaving Maid (see Shen, Hung)
COWLEY, Mrs. Hannah (Parkhouse), 1743-1809)
  Albina, Countess Raimond
    (In Bell's British Theatre, 1797, Vol. 29)
  The Belle's Stratagem
    (In Cumberland's British Theatre, Vol. 7, no. 3)
    (In The London Stage, Vol. 1)
  A Bold Stroke for a Husband
    (In Cumberland's British Theatre, Vol. 43, no. 10)
  Which is the Man?
    (In The London Stage, Vol. 2)
    (In Modern Theatre, 1811, Vol. 10)
  Who's the Dupe?
    (In The London Stage, Vol. 1)
COX, Nancy Burney
  Tugging
    (In Drama, Vol. 15, Feb. 1925)
COX, William Norment
  The Scuffletown Outlaws, A Tragedy of the Lowrie Gang
    (In Carolina Folkplays)
COXE, Louis Osborn, 1918-
  Billy Budd, by Louis Coxe and Robert Chapman, based on the
    novel by Herman Melville
    (In Theatre Arts, Vol. 36, Feb. 1952)
    (In Religious Drama, Vol. 3)
    (In Best American Plays, Third Series)
COYNE, Joseph Stirling, 1803-1868
  A Terrible Secret
    (In 26 Short & Amusing Plays, 1871)
  The Woman of the World
    (In Lacy's Acting Plays, Vol. 81)
Crabbed Youth and Age (see Robinson, Lennox)
Crabs, Cross-Country (see Ordway, Sally)

Crac!...Dans le Sac (see Gripari, Pierre)
A Crack in the Universe (see Olson, Elder)
The Cracked Teapot (see Dobie, Charles Caldwell)
Cracker Money (see Gethers, Steven)
The Cradle Song (see Martinez Sierra, Gregorio)
The Cradle will Rock (see Blitzstein, Marc)
CRAIGIE, Mrs. Pearl Teresa (Richards), 1867-1906
     Osbern and Ursyne, by John Oliver Hobbes, pseud.
        (In Anglo Saxon Review, Vol. 1, June 1899)
Craig's Wife (see Kelly, George Edward)
Cranmer, Thomas, Abp. of Canterbury, 1489-1556
     *Thomas Cranmer of Canterbury (see Williams, Charles)
CRAVEN, Henry Thornton, 1818-1905
     Dove Brown
        (In Lacy's Acting Plays, Vol. 81)
Crawling Arnold (see Feiffer, Jules)
Crazy Jane (see Somerset, Charles A.)
The Crazy Locomotive (see Witkiewicz, Stanislaw Ignacy)
The Creation of Man (see York Cardmakers' Play)
The Creation of the Heavenly Beings: The Fall of Lucifer (see
     York Tanners' Play)
O Credito (see Alencar, Jose de)
The Creditor (see Strindberg, August)
Creeds (see Healey, Frances)
The Creeper (see Macaulay, Pauline)
Creighton, Anthony
     Epitaph for George Dillon (see Osborne, John)
The Cresta Run (see Simpson, Norman Frederick)
The Cretan Woman (see Jeffers, Robinson)
Creusa, Queen of Athens (see Whitehead, William)
Crime in the Streets (see Rose, Reginald)
Crimes and Crimes (see Strindberg, August)
The Criminals (see Triana, Jose)
The Critic; or, A Tragedy Rehearsed (see Sheridan, Richard
     Brinsley)
The Critic as Artist (see Marowitz, Charles)
CROCKER, Bosworth
     The Baby Carriage
        (In 50 Contemporary One-Act Plays)
     The Last Straw
        (In Contemporary One-Act Plays, 1922)
CROCKETT, Otway
     The Burial Committee
        (In First Stage, Vol. 5, no. 4, Winter 1966-67)
Les Crocodiles (see Matsas, Nestor)
CROMMELYNCK, Fernand
     Les Amants Puerils
        (In L'Avant-Scene du Theatre, July/Aug. 1956)
CROMWELL, John, 1888-
     **Algiers (see Lawson, John Howard)
     Opening Night
        (In Best Short Plays, 1968)

CRONYN, George William, 1888-
   A Death in Fever Flat
      (In 50 Contemporary One-Act Plays)
   A Lady and the Law
      (In 50 More Contemporary One-Act Plays)
Croque-Monsieur (see Mithois, Marcel)
CROSS, Beverley
   Catherine Howard; a television script in the series "The Six
   Wives of Henry VIII"
      (In Plays of the Year Special, 1972)
   The Mines of Sulphur
      (In Plays of the Year, Vol. 30, 1965)
Cross Purposes (see O'Brien, William)
Crouse, Russel, 1893-1966
   The Great Sebastians (see Lindsay, Howard)
   Life with Father (see Lindsay, Howard)
   State of the Union (see Lindsay, Howard)
The Crowded Bedroom (see Sassoon, R. L.)
The Crown of Life (see Yamamoto Yuzo)
The Crown of St. Felice (see Sladen-Smith, Francis)
A Crowne for a Conquerour (see Davenport, Robert)
The Crucible (see Miller, Arthur)
The Crucifixion (see York Butchers' Play)
Cruelle Galejade (see Mithois, Marcel)
'Cruiter (see Matheur, John)
Cuba Si (see Marker, Chris)
The Cuban Thing (see Gelber, Jack)
Le Cuirasse Potemkine (see Eisenstein, Sergei-Mikailovitch)
La Cuisine (see Wesker, Arnold)
Cukor, George, 1899-
   Adam's Rib (see Gordon, Ruth)
   Little Women (see Mason, Sarah Y.)
   The Women (see Loos, Anita)
CULBERTSON, Ernest Howard
   Across the Jordan
      (In Theatre Arts, Vol. 13, Dec. 1929)
   The End of the Trail
      (In Theatre Arts, Vol. 8, May 1924)
   Rackey
      (In Plays of Negro Life)
Culbin Sands (see Bottomley, Gordon)
CULLEN, Countee
   The Third Fourth of July, by Countee Cullen and Owen Dodson
      (In Theatre Arts, Vol. 30, Aug. 1946)
CUMBERLAND, Richard, 1732-1811
   The Battle of Hastings
      (In Bell's British Theatre, 1797, Vol. 6)
   The Box-Lobby Challenge
      (In Modern Theatre, 1811, Vol. 5)
   The Brothers
      (In Bell's British Theatre, 1797, Vol. 12)
      (In The London Stage, Vol. 2)

The Carmelite
   (In Bell's British Theatre, 1797, Vol. 16)
   (In Modern Theatre, 1811, Vol. 5)
The Cholerie Man
   (In Bell's British Theatre, 1797, Vol. 4)
False Impressions
   (In Modern Theatre, 1811, Vol. 5)
The Fashionable Lover
   (In Bell's British Theatre, 1797, Vol. 18)
The Imposters
   (In Modern Theatre, 1811, Vol. 6)
The Mysterious Husband
   (In Modern Theatre, 1811, Vol. 5)
The Natural Son
   (In Modern Theatre, 1811, Vol. 5)
   (In Cumberland's British Theatre, Vol. 38, no. 9)
   (In Bell's British Theatre, 1797, Vol. 20)
The West Indian
   (In Cumberland's British Theatre, Vol. 30, no. 3)
   (In The London Stage, Vol. 1)
   (In Bell's British Theatre, 1797, Vol. 19)
CUMMINGS, Edward Estlin, 1894-1962
   Him
     (In From the Modern Repertoire, Series Two)
   Santa Claus, A Morality
     (In Theatre Experiment)
     (In Religious Drama, Vol. 3)
Cunningham, John M.
   **High Noon (see Foreman, Carl)
Cupium (see Wanderley, Jose)
Curcio, Louis L.
   Neighbors (see Gorostiza, Carlos)
Curculio (see Plautus, Titus Maccius)
A Cure for the Heartache (see Morton, Thomas)
The Curmudgeon (see Menander)
CURNIEU, Georges de, 1860-1917
   Monsieur Lamblin, by Georges Ancey, pseud.
     (In 50 Contemporary One-Act Plays)
The Curse of Mammon (see Reynoldson, Thomas H.)
The Curtain (see Flanagan, Hallie F.)
Curtain Call, Mr. Aldridge, Sir (see Davis, Ossie)
Curtiz, Michael, 1888-1962
   Casablanca (see Epstein, Julius J.)
Curtmantle (see Fry, Christopher)
Cuvelier, Marcel (see Oblomov)
The Cyclops (see Euripides)
Cymon (see Garrick, David)
Cyrano de Bergerac (see Rostand, Edmond)
Cyrus (see Hoole, John)
CZECHOWSKI, Heinz
   Konig Drosselbart
     (In Theater der Zeit, Vol. 24, no. 7, 1969)

Rumpelstilzchen, Märchen frei nach den Gebrüdern Grimm
(In Theater der Zeit, no. 8, 1972)

DABRIL, Lucien
  L'Honneur des Dupont
    (In L'Avant Scene du Theatre, no. 445, Mar. 15, 1970)
DACE, Wallace
  We Commit This Body
    (In Best Short Plays, 1959/60)
DA COSTA, Bernard
  Le Bal des Cuisinieres
    (In L'Avant-Scene du Theatre, no. 507, Dec. 1, 1972)
Les Dactylos (see Schisgal, Murray)
DADIE, Bernard
  Assemien Dehyle
    (In Plaisir de France, supplement theatral, no. 325, Nov.
    1965)
Daft Dream Adyin' (see Grainger, Tom)
DAGGETT, James L., 1908-
  Goodnight Please!
    (In Best One-Act Plays of 1937, N.Y.)
Daisy Miller (see James, Henry)
DALBRAY, Muse
  Tragedie de L'Absence
    (In Plaisir de France, supplement theatral, no. 314, Dec.
    1964)
Dali, Salvador, 1904-
  L'Age d'Or (see Buñuel, Luis)
  L'Age d'Or and Un Chien Andalou; filmscripts (see Buñuel,
    Luis)
  Un Chien Andalou (see Buñuel, Luis)
DALRYMPLE, Ian, 1903-
  The Citadel; screenplay by Ian Dalrymple, Frank Wead and
    Elizabeth Hill, with additional dialogue by Emlyn Williams
    (In Foremost Films of 1938)
DALRYMPLE, J. S.
  Lurline; or, The Revolt of the Naiades
    (In Cumberland's British Theatre, Vol. 38, no. 8)
DALY, Augustin, 1838-1899
  Under the Gaslight; or, Life and Love in These Times
    (In Hiss the Villain)
    (In Lacy's Acting Plays, Vol. 81)
The Damask Drum (see Hiraoka, Kimitake)
La Dame au Petit Chien (see Kobryski, Lazare)
La Dame aux Camelias (see Dumas, Alexandre (Fils))
Damn Yankees (see Abbott, George)
Damon and Pithias (see Edwards, Richard)
Damon and Pythias (see Buckstone, John Baldwin)
DANA, Robert Patrick
  Trunk
    (In North American Review (n. s.), Vol. 4, Mar. 1967)

Danbury Fair (see Carriere, Albert)
Dance, George
    Telemachus; or, The Island of Calypso (see Planche, James
    Robinson)
The Dance Below (see Strode, Hudson)
La Dance de Mort (see Strindberg, August)
The Dance of Death (see Strindberg, August)
The Dancers (see Foote, Horton)
Dane, Clemence; pseud. (see Ashton, Winifred)
DANE, Essex
    The Workers at the Loom
       (In Ten Fantasies for Stage and Study, 1932)
Dangerous Corner (see Priestley, John Boynton)
DANIEL, George, 1789-1864
    The Disagreeable Surprise
       (In Cumberland's British Theatre, Vol. 5, no. 1)
    Doctor Bolus
       (In Cumberland's British Theatre, Vol. 25, no. 3)
    "Sworn at Highgate!"
       (In Cumberland's British Theatre, Vol. 35, no. 6)
Danish Blue (see Axel, Gabriel)
Danse Calindo (see Torrence, Frederic Ridgely)
Danton, Georges Jacques, 1759-1794
    *Danton's Death (see Büchner, Georg)
Da Ponte, Lorenzo, 1749-1838
    Cosi Fan Tutti (see Mozart, Johann Chrysostom Wolfgang
    Amadeus)
The Dark at the Top of the Stairs (see Inge, William Motter)
Dark Brown (see Johnson, Philip)
Dark Possession (see Vidal, Gore)
The Dark Room (see Williams, Tennessee)
The Dark Tower (see MacNeice, Louis)
Darkness at Noon (see Kingsley, Sidney)
DARMADY, J.
    The Annual Jumble Sale
       (In Best One-Act Plays of 1931, London)
DA ROCHA MIRANDA, Edgard
    And The Wind Blows
       (In Best Short Plays, 1972)
Darrow, Clarence Seward, 1857-1938
    *Inherit the Wind (see Lawrence, Jerome)
DARYL, Sidney
    His First Brief
       (In 26 Short & Amusing Plays, 1871)
"Das Hemd eines Glüchlichen" (see Wagner, Bernd)
DASTREE, Anne
    Aurelia
       (In L'Avant-Scene du Cinema, no. 38, 1964)
DATTA, Jyotirmoy
    Dramatist Digested
       (In TDR/The Drama Review, Vol. 15, Spring 1971)
A Daughter to Marry (see My Daughter, Sir!)

The Daughter-in-Law (see Lawrence, David Herbert)
D'AVENENT, Sir William, 1606-1668
    The Wits
        (In Dodsley's A Select Collection of Old Plays, Vol. 8)
DAVENPORT, E. V.
    An Interlude in Porcelain
        (In Best One-Act Plays of 1935, London)
    The Map, by E. V. Davenport and Dorothy Margaret Stuart
        (In Best One-Act Plays of 1934, London)
DAVENPORT, Robert, fl. 1623
    The City-Night-Cap; or, Crede Quod Habes & Habes
        (In A Collection of Old English Plays (n. s.), Vol. 3)
        (In Dodsley's A Select Collection of Old English Plays, Vol.
        13)
        (In Dodsley's A Select Collection of Old Plays, Vol. 11)
    A Crowne for a Conquerour
        (In A Collection of Old English Plays (n. s.), Vol. 3)
    King John and Matilda
        (In A Collection of Old English Plays (n. s.), Vol. 3)
    A New Tricke to Cheat the Divell
        (In A Collection of Old English Plays (n. s.), Vol. 3)
    A Survey of the Sciences
        (In A Collection of Old English Plays (n. s.), Vol. 3)
    Too Late to call Backe Yesterday and To-morrow Comes Not
    Yet
        (In A Collection of Old English Plays (n. s.), Vol. 3)
DAVEY, Kathleen
    Unnatural Scene
        (In 24 One-Act Plays, Revised edition, 1954)
David and Broccoli (see Mortimer, John)
David Holzman's Diary (see Carson, L. M. Kit)
David, King of Judah & Israel, d. 973 B. C.
    *David (see Lawrence, David Herbert)
    *David and Bathsheba (see Cornish: The Legend of the Rood:
    II)
    *David Takes the Shoots to Jerusalem (see Cornish: The Legend
    of the Rood: I)
David, la Nuit Tombe (see Kops, Bernard)
DAVIDSON, Madeline
    Finally I Am Born
        (In First Stage, Vol. 1, no. 2, Spring 1962)
DAVIES, Hubert Henry, 1869-1917
    The Mollusc
        (In Late Victorian Plays)
DAVIES, Mary Carolyn
    The Slave With Two Faces
        (In 50 Contemporary One-Act Plays)
        (In Dramas by Present-Day Writers)
Daviot, Gordon, pseud. (see Mackintosh, Elizabeth)
Davis, Donald
    Ethan Frome (see Davis, Owen)
DAVIS, Luther
    Run For Your Life: "The Committee For the 25th. " A

    television filmscript.
    (In Writing For Television)
DAVIS, Ossie, 1917-
    Curtain Call, Mr. Aldridge, Sir
    (In The Black Teacher and the Dramatic Arts)
DAVIS, Owen, 1874-1956
    Ethan Frome, by Owen and Donald Davis
    (In Best American Plays, Suppl. Vol.)
    Icebound
    (In Pulitzer Prize Plays)
    The World We Live In (The Insect Comedy)   (see Capek, Josef)
Davor (see Grass, Günter)
DAWSON, Jessie
    Tables Turned
    (In The Banner Anthology of One-Act Plays by American
    Authors)
DAWSON, N.
    "...Can Die but Once?"
    (In Best One-Act Plays of 1944/45, London)
DAY, Frederic Lansing
    The Fall of the House of Usher, based on the story by Edgar
    Allan Poe
    (In Bread Loaf Book of Plays)
    The Slump
    (In 50 Contemporary One-Act Plays)
DAY, John, 1574-1640?
    Humour Out of Breath, edited by Arthur Symons
    (In Best Plays of the Old Dramatists: Nero & Other Plays)
    Lust's Dominion; or, The Lascivious Queen (see Marlowe,
    Christopher)
    The Parliament of Bees, edited by Arthur Symons
    (In Best Plays of the Old Dramatists: Nero & Other Plays)
A Day After the Fair (see Somerset, C.A.)
The Day After the Wedding; or, A Wife's First Lesson (see Kemble,
    Marie-Therese)
The Day After Tomorrow (see Lonsdale, Frederick)
A Day at the Races (see Pirosh, Robert)
Day Before Yesterday (see Holland, Norman)
A Day by the Sea (see Hunter, Norman Charles)
A Day for Surprises (see Guare, John)
Day of Absence (see Ward, Douglas Turner)
Day of Wrath (see Dreyer, Carl Theodore)
The Day the Whores Came Out to Play Tennis (see Kopit, Arthur
    L.)
The Day They Let the Lions Loose (see Carballido, Emilio)
Daybreak (see Corwin, Norman Lewis)
Day's End (see Benet, William Rose)
Days in the Trees (see Duras, Marguerite)
The Days of the Commune (see Brecht, Bertolt)
Days on a Cloud (see Abell, Kjeld)
Days to Come (see Hellman, Lillian)
The Deacon and the Jewess (see Rubenstein, Harold Frederick)

The Deacon's Hat   (see Marks, Jeannette Augustus)
Dead End   (see Kingsley, Sidney)
The Dead Saint   (see Hadges, Bertha)
A Dead Secret   (see Ackland, Rodney)
Deaf and Dumb; or, The Orphan Protected   (see Holcroft, Thomas)
DE ALMEIDA, Lyad
    Apolonio I, O Astronauta
        (In Revista de Teatro, no. 383, Sept./Oct. 1971)
DEAN, Alexander
    Just Neighborly
        (In Drama, Vol. 12, Oct./Nov. 1921)
Dear Delinquent   (see Popplewell, Jack)
The Dear Departed   (see Houghton, Stanley)
The Death and Life of Sneaky Fitch   (see Rosenberg, James L.)
The Death Dance   (see Duncan, Thelma)
A Death in Fever Flat   (see Cronyn, George W.)
Death Knocks   (see Allen, Woody)
The Death of a Kinsman   (see Taylor, Peter)
Death of a Salesman   (see Miller, Arthur)
The Death of Alexander   (see Baring, Maurice)
The Death of Aunt Aggie   (see MacDougall, Ranald)
The Death of Bessie Smith   (see Albee, Edward)
The Death of Billy the Kid   (see Vidal, Gore)
The Death of Clytemnestra   (see Lytton, Edward George Earle
    Lytton Bulwer-Lytton, 1st Baron)
The Death of Columbine   (see Vail, Walter J.)
The Death of Good Fortune   (see Williams, Charles)
Death of Mohammed   (see El-Hakin, T.)
The Death of Nero   (see Gorman, Herbert Sherman)
The Death of Robert Earl of Huntington   (see Munday, Anthony)
The Death of Satan   (see Duncan, Ronald Frederick Henry)
Death of Seneca   (see Hine, Daryl)
The Death of the Old Man   (see Foote, Horton)
The Death of Trotsky   (see Cook, Albert)
Death of Wallenstein   (see Schiller, Johann Christoph Friedrich von)
Death Says It Isn't So   (see Broun, Heywood Campbell)
Death-Trap   (see Munro, Hector Hugh)
Deathwatch   (see Genet, Jean)
Debit and Credit   (see Strindberg, August)
Debt Takes a Holiday   (see Buerman, Howard)
DE BURCA, Seamus
    Limpid River
        (In First Stage, Vol. 5, Spring 1966)
DE CASTRO, Consuelo, 1946-
    A Flor da Pele
        (In Revista de Teatro, no. 382, July/Aug. 1971)
DECAUX, Alain
    Les Rosenberg ne Doivent pas Mourir
        (In L'Avant Scene du Theatre, no. 411, Oct. 1, 1968)
The DECEIVED (Anon.)
        (In Genius of the Italian Theater)
DECKELMAN, Ethel
    Helen Keller

(In Radio's Best Plays, 1947)
The Decoy (see Slade, Philip)
The Deep Blue Sea (see Rattigan, Terence)
The Deer Park (see Mailer, Norman)
DEEVY, Teresa
    The King of Spain's Daughter
      (In Theatre Arts, Vol. 19, June 1935)
DEFELICE, James
    The Elixir
      (In First Stage, Vol. 3, Winter 1963-64)
The Defiant Ones (see Douglas, Nathan E.)
De Filippo, Eduardo (see Filippo, Edwardo de)
Defoe, Daniel, 1661?-1731
    **Robinson Crusoe; or, The Bold Buccaniers (see Pocock, Isaac)
The Deformed Transformed (see Byron, George Gordon Noël Byron,
    6th Baron)
DE GRAZIA, Edward
    The Swings
      (In Evergreen Review, Vol. 6, no. 26, 1962)
DEICHSEL, Wolfgang
    Bleiwe Losse
      (In Theater Heute, no. 12, Dec. 1971)
De Igoa, Luis F.
    **Mort d'un Cycliste (see Bardem, Juan Antonio)
Deirdre (see Yeats, William Butler)
Deirdre of the Sorrows (see Synge, John Millington)
DEKKER, Thomas, 1570?-1641
    Britannia's Honor
      (In Dramatic Works, Vol. 4)
    The Honest Whore, Part 1, by Thomas Dekker and Thomas Mid-
    dleton
      (In Dramatic Works, Vol. 2)
    The Honest Whore, Part 2
      (In Dramatic Works, Vol. 2)
    The Honest Whore, Parts 1-2
      (In Dodsley's A Select Collection of Old Plays, Vol. 3)
    If This be not a Good Play, the Devil is in It
      (In Dramatic Works, Vol. 3)
    London's Tempe
      (In Dramatic Works, Vol. 4)
    Lust's Dominion; or, The Lascivious Queen (see Marlowe,
    Christopher)
    The Magnificent Entertainment given to King James
      (In Dramatic Works, Vol. 2)
    Match Me in London
      (In Dramatic Works, Vol. 3)
    The Noble Spanish Soldier (see Rowley, Samuel)
    Northward Ho, by Thomas Dekker and John Webster
      (In Dramatic Works, Vol. 2)
    Old Fortunatus
      (In Dramatic Works, Vol. 1)
    Patient Grissil, by Thomas Dekker, Henry Chettle and William

Haughton
(In Dramatic Works, Vol. 1)
The Roaring Girl; or, Moll Cut-Purse (see Middleton, Thomas)
Satiromastix, based on Ben Jonson's "Poetaster"
(In Dramatic Works, Vol. 1)
The Shoemaker's Holiday
(In Dramatic Works, Vol. 1)
(In Great English Plays)
The Sun's Darling, by Thomas Dekker and John Ford
(In Dramatic Works, Vol. 4)
Sir Thomas Wyatt, by Thomas Dekker and John Webster
(In Dramatic Works, Vol. 1)
Tria-Nova Triumphans
(In Dramatic Works, Vol. 3)
The Virgin Martyr (see Massinger, Philip)
The Welsh Embassador
(In Dramatic Works, Vol. 4)
Westward Ho, by Thomas Dekker and John Webster
(In Dramatic Works, Vol. 2)
The Whore of Babylon
(In Dramatic Works, Vol. 2)
The Witch of Edmonton (see Rowley, William)
The Wonder of a Kingdom
(In Dramatic Works, Vol. 3)
De Kruif, Paul Henry, 1890-1971
**The Fight for Life (see Lorentz, Pare)
**Yellow Jack (see Chodorov, Edward)
De la Barca, Calderon (see Calderon de la Barca, Pedro)
Delacour, Alfred Charlemagne Lartigue, known as, 1817-1883
Pots of Money (see Labiche, Eugene Marin)
Delafield, E.M., pseud. (see De La Pasture, Emee Elizabeth
Monica)
DELANEY, Shelagh, 1939-
A Taste of Honey
(In Theatre Arts, Jan. 1963)
(In New British Drama)
(In 7 Plays of the Modern Theatre)
DE LA PASTURE, Emee Elizabeth Monica, 1890-
To See Ourselves, by E.M. Delafield, pseud.
(In Famous Plays of Today, 1931)
De l'Eau Sous les Ponts (see Silvain, Jean)
DELGADO, Ramon, 1937-
Omega's Nineth
(In First Stage, Vol. 3, Winter 1963-64)
Once Below a Lighthouse
(In Best Short Plays, 1972)
Delicate Balance (see Albee, Edward)
The Delinquent (see Reynolds, Frederick)
The Delinquent, the Hipster, the Square (see Baker, Elliott)
DELL, Jeffrey
Payment Deferred
(In 13 Famous Plays of Crime and Detection)

DELMAR, Vina, 1905-
Make Way for Tomorrow; a screenplay based on the novel
"Years Are So Long" by Josephine Lawrence, and a play by
Helen and Nolan Leary, directed by Leo McCarey.
(In Twenty Best Film Plays)
Delon, Paul Le Retable des Mervilles (see Cervantes Saavedra,
Miguel de)
DELOUCHE, Dominique, 1931-
Aquarelle
(In L'Avant-Scene du Cinema, no. 80, Apr. 1968)
Edith Stein
(In L'Avant-Scene du Cinema, no. 44, 1964)
Delphica (see Korber, Serge)
Demain, une Fenetre sur Rue (see Grumberg, Jean-Claude)
The Demands of Society (see Harper, Harold)
The Demands of Society (see Hartleben, Otto Erich)
La Demangeaison (see Spiraux, Alain)
Les Demi-Fous (see Gouin, Ollivier Mercier)
De Mille, Cecil Blount, 1881-1959
The Buccaneer (see Mayer, Edwin Justus)
DE MILLE, William Churchill, 1878-1955
The Warrens of Virginia
(In Monte Cristo and Other Plays)
The Demolition Downtown (see Williams, Tennessee)
Demos and Dionysus (see Robinson, Edwin Arlington)
DEMPSEY, David
It Ain't Brooklyn
(In Best One-Act Plays of 1944, N.Y.)
DEMY, Jacques, 1931-
Lola, by Jacques Demy and Georges de Beauregard. Music by
Michel Legrand
(In L'Avant-Scene Du Cinema, no. 4, May 15, 1961)
DENISON, Merrill, 1893-
Haven of the Spirit
(In Plays as Experience)
The Weather Breeder
(In 50 More Contemporary One-Act Plays)
DENKER, Henry
Time Limit! by Henry Denker and Ralph Berkey, original
title "Breaking Point"
(In Theatre Arts, Vol. 41, April 1957)
DENNERY, Adolphe Philippe, 1811-1899
The Two Orphans, by Adolphe d'Ennery and Eugene Cormon
(In S.R.O., the Most Successful Plays...)
Dennis, Patrick; pseud. (see Tanner, Edward Everett)
DENNISON, George
The Operation
(In Scripts, Vol. 1, no. 10, Oct. 1972)
The Service for Joseph Axminster
(In Scripts, Vol. 1, no. 7, May 1972)
Denon, Dominique Vivant, baron, 1747-1825
**Les Amants (see Malle, Louis)

Dentist and Patient (see Saroyan, William)
The Departing (see Snyder, William H., Jr.)
DEPERO, Fortunato
    Colors; an abstract theatrical synthesis
      (In TDR/The Drama Review, Vol. 15, Fall 1970)
DePurey, Marianne
    Viet Rock (see Terry, Megan)
The Deputy (see Hochhuth, Rolf)
Los Derechos de la Salud (see Sanchez, Florencio)
Les Derniers Jours de Solitude de Robinson Crusoë (see Savary,
    Jerome)
El Desalojo (see Sanchez, Florencio)
La Descente sur Recife (see Cousin, Gabriel)
Le Desert Rouge (Il Deserto Rosso) (see Antonioni, Michelangelo)
The Deserter (see Abercrombie, Lascelles)
DE SICA, Vittorio, 1901-
    The Bicycle Thief
      (In Modern Film Scripts)
    Miracle in Milan
      (In Grossman Library of Film Classics, 1968)
      (In Cahiers du Cinema, Vol. 2, no. 7, Dec. 1951)
    Le Voleur de Bicyclette. Titre original: "Ladri di Biciclette"
      (In L'Avant-Scene du Cinema, no. 76, Dec. 1967)
Le Desir Attrape par la Queue (see Picasso, Pablo)
Desire Under the Elms (see O'Neill, Eugene Gladstone)
Desnos, Robert
    *La Belle Saison est Proche (see Barral, Jean)
La Desordre a Vingt Ans (see Baratier, Jacques)
The Desperationist (see Brihouse, Harold)
DESSAU, Paul
    Lanzelot
      (In Theater der Zeit, Vol. 25, March 1970)
DESTANQUE, Robert, 1931-
    San Fermin, by Robert Destanque et Raymond Bellour
      (In L'Avant-Scene du Cinema, no. 49, 1965)
DESTOUCHES, Phillipe Nericault, 1680-1754
    The Conceited Count
      (In French Comedies of the 18th Century)
Destry Rides Again (see Jackson, Felix)
Detective Story (see Kingsley, Sidney)
Detonation (see Cangiullo, Francesco)
DE TRUEBA COSIO, Don T.
    Mr. and Mrs. Pringle
      (In Cumberland's British Theatre, Vol. 21, no. 5)
Deus Lhe Pague (see Camargo, Joracy)
DEUTSCH, Leon
    Le Soleil et les Parapluies...
      (In L'Avant-Scene du Theatre, no. 143)
    Les Vagues Etaient Trop Fortes...
      (In Plaisir de France, supplement theatral, no. 337, Nov.
    1966)
Les Deux Anglaises et le Continent (see Truffaut, Francois)

Deux Chats et...un Souris (see Thomas, Robert)
Deux Femmes pour un Fantome (see Obaldia, Rene de)
2 ou 3 Choses Que Je Said d'Elle (see Godard, Jean-Luc)
Le Deuxieme Coup de Feu (see Thomas, Robert)
The Deva King (Niwo) (see Sakanishi, Shio)
DEVAL, Jacques, 1894-
    Tovarich
       (In 16 Famous European Plays)
    La Venus de Milo
       (In Plaisir de France, supplement theatral, no. 295, May 1963)
DEVAL, Patrick, 1944-
    Heraclite l'Obscur
       (In L'Avant-Scene du Cinema, no. 93, June 1969)
DEVANY, Edward H.
    The Cow-Catcher on the Caboose
       (In Best Short Plays, 1958/59)
    The Red and Yellow Ark
       (In Best Short Plays, 1958/59)
The Devil and Daniel Webster (see Benet, Stephen Vincent)
The Devil Comes to Alcaraz (see Fulham, William H.)
The Devil is a Good Man (see Kozlenko, William)
Devil Take a Whittler (see Stone, Weldon)
The Devil to Pay; or, The Wives Metamorphosed (see Coffee,
    Charles)
DEVILLE, Michel, 1931-
    Ce Soir ou Jamais
       (In L'Avant-Scene du Cinema, no. 9, Nov. 15, 1961)
Devils and Angels (see Eberhart, Richard)
The Devil's Ducat; or, The Gift of Mammon (see Jerrold, Douglas)
The Devil's Elixir; or, The Shadowless Man (see Fitz-Ball, Edward)
The Devil's Foot (see Biel, Nicholas J.)
DEVOS, Raymond
    Extra-Muros
       (In L'Avant Scene du Theatre, no. 392, Dec. 1, 1967)
Dewar, James, 1793-1846
    Peveril of the Peak; or, The Days of King Charles II (see
    Fitz-Ball, Edward)
DEWHURST, Keith
    Rafferty's Chant
       (In Plays of the Year, Vol. 33, 1967)
DEY, James Paul, 1930
    Passacaglia
       (In New American Plays, Vol. 2)
    What Did You Say "What" For?
       (In Players Magazine, Vol. 40, no. 1, Oct. 1963)
D'Hele, Thomas (see Hele, Thomas d')
Un Dia de Guerra (see Valle-Inclan, Ramon del)
Le Diable en Ete (see Faure, Michel)
The Diabolical Circle (see Bornstead, Beulah)
Dial "M" for Murder (see Knott, Frederick)
Dialog (see Dunster, Mark)
Dialogue des Inconnus (see George-Schreiber, Isabelle)

Diamond, I. A. L.
  The Apartment (see Wilder, Billy)
  The Fortune Cookie (see Wilder, Billy)
  Some Like It Hot (see Wilder, Billy)
Diane de Poitiers, mistress of Henri II of France, 1499-1566
  *La Princesse de Cleves (see Dorfmann, Robert)
The Diary of a Scoundrel (see Ostrovskii, Aleksandr Nikolaevich)
The Diary of Adam and Eve (see Bock, Jerry)
The Diary of Anne Frank (see Goodrich, Frances)
DIAS, Goncalves
  Leonor de Mendonca
    (In Revista de Teatro, no. 340)
DIAZ, Jorge
  Man does not Die by Bread Alone
    (In TDR/The Drama Review, Vol. 14, no. 2, Winter 1970)
DIAZ, Jose
  The Place where the Mannals Die
    (In Modern Stage in Latin America, 1971)
DIBDIN, Charles, 1745-1814
  The Great Devil; or, The Robber of Genoa
    (In Cumberland's British Theatre, Vol. 43, no. 3)
  The Lord of the Manor
    (In The London Stage, Vol. 2)
  The Quaker
    (In Cumberland's British Theatre, Vol. 29, no. 4)
    (In The London Stage, Vol. 1)
  The Waterman; or, The First of August
    (In Cumberland's British Theatre, Vol. 22, no. 2)
  The Wild Man
    (In Cumberland's British Theatre, Vol. 31, no. 9)
DIBDIN, Thomas Frognall, 1776-1847
  The Banks of the Hudson; or, The Congress Trooper
    (In Cumberland's British Theatre, Vol. 21, no. 4)
  The Cabinet
    (In Cumberland's British Theatre, Vol. 30, no. 1)
  Don Giovanni; or, A Spectre on Horseback
    (In Cumberland's British Theatre, Vol. 40, no. 1)
  The English Fleet in 1342
    (In Cumberland's British Theatre, Vol. 43, no. 6)
  The Heart of Mid-Lothian
    (In Cumberland's British Theatre, Vol. 4, no. 5)
  Humphrey Clinker
    (In Cumberland's British Theatre, Vol. 25, no. 1)
  Ivanhoe; or, The Jew's Daughter; adapted from the novel by Sir
    Walter Scott
    (In Cumberland's British Theatre, Vol. 9, no. 5)
  The Jew and the Doctor
    (In Cumberland's British Theatre, Vol. 43, no. 9)
  Kenilworth; adapted from the work of Sir Walter Scott
    (In Cumberland's British Theatre, Vol. 36, no. 7)
  The Lady of the Lake; adapted from the work of Sir Walter
    Scott

(In Cumberland's British Theatre, Vol. 19, no. 5)
Paul Jones
    (In Cumberland's British Theatre, Vol. 12, no. 2)
The Ruffian Boy
    (In Cumberland's British Theatre, Vol. 30, no. 9)
St. David's Day; or, The Honest Welshman
    (In Cumberland's British Theatre, Vol. 40, no. 9)
The School for Prejudice
    (In Modern Theatre, 1811, Vol. 4)
The Sixes; or, The Devil's in the Dice
    (In Cumberland's British Theatre, Vol. 41, no. 7)
Suil Dhuv the Coiner
    (In Cumberland's British Theatre, Vol. 5, no. 7)
The Two Gregories; or Where Did the Money come From?
    (In Cumberland's British Theatre, Vol. 12, no. 6)
Valentine and Orson
    (In Cumberland's British Theatre, Vol. 14, no. 7)
Dick Van Dyke Show (see Coast to Coast Big Mouth)
DICKE of Devonshire (Anon.)
    (In A Collection of Old English Plays, Vol. 2)
DICKENS, Charles, 1812-1870
A Christmas Carol (see Agenoux, Soren)
A Christmas Carol (see Kaufman, George Simon)
Is She His Wife? or, Something Singular!
    (In Works, Vol. 18)
The Lamplighter
    (In Works, Vol. 18)
Mr. Nightingale's Diary
    (In Works, Vol. 18)
No Thoroughfare
    (In Works, Vol. 18)
The Signal Man; adapted for radio by Charles Tazewell)
    (In Plays From Radio, 1948)
The Strange Gentleman
    (In Works, Vol. 18)
The Village Coquettes
    (In Works, Vol. 18)
DICKINSON, Thorold
Secret People, screenplay by Thorold Dickinson and Wolfgang
    Wilhelm, directed by Lindsay Anderson
    (In In Making a Film)
DICKSON, Lee
Whose Money? by Lee Dickson and Leslie M. Hickson
    (In 50 More Contemporary One-Act Plays)
DIDIER, Pierre
Le Francais tel Qu'on le Parle
    (In Plaisir de France, supplement theatral, no. 366)
Louis Pasteur; text in French
    (In Plaisir de France, supplement theatral, no. 345, July
    1967)
Le Retour de Lumiere
    (In L'Avant-Scene du Theatre, no. 443, Feb. 15, 1970)

DI DONATO, Pietro, 1911-
  The Love of Annunziata
    (In Best One-Act Plays of 1941, N.Y.)
Dies Irae (see Dreyer, Carl Theodor)
Diese Geschichte von Ihnen (see Hopkins, John)
Dieterle, William, 1893-
  All That Money Can Buy (see Totheroh, Dan)
  Dr. Ehrlich's Magic Bullet (see Huston, John)
  Juarez (see Reinhardt, Wolfgang)
  The Life of Emile Zola (see Herald, Heinz)
  The Story of Louis Pasteur (see Gibney, Sheridan)
DIETZ, Howard
  La Boheme; English adaptation by Howard Dietz of Puccini's
    "La Boheme"
    (In Theatre Arts, Vol. 37, Dec. 1953)
Dieu Aboie-t-il? (see Boyer, Francois)
DIEZ, Bernard
  Amphitryon 1968
    (In Plaisir de France, supplement theatral, no. 353, Mar.
    1968)
Difference of Opinion (see Ross, George)
The Difficult Hour (see Lagerkvist, Pär)
Digby, George (see Bristol, George Digby, 2d earl of)
DIGHTON, John
  Who Goes There!
    (In Plays of the Year, Vol. 6, 1951)
Dija (see White, Edgar
DILL, Jack
  The Duel
    (In Plays and Players, Vol. 15, June 1968)
DILLON, Thomas Patrick
  The Doctor from Dunmore, by Thomas Patrick Dillon and Nolan
    Leary
    (In Best One-Act Plays of 1941, N.Y.)
DI MATTIA, Vincenzo, 1932-
  The Landsknecht Girl; both French and English texts are in-
    cluded
    (In Italian Theatre Review, Vol. 13, Apr./June, 1964)
Dimitrii the Impostor; A Tragedy (see Sumarokov, Aleksandr
  Petrovich)
DIMOND, William, fl. 1800-1830
  The Foundling of the Forest
    (In Cumberland's British Theatre, Vol. 40, no. 8)
  The Hunter of the Alps
    (In Cumberland's British Theatre, Vol. 41, no. 5)
  The Young Hussar
    (In Cumberland's British Theatre, Vol. 41, no. 3)
  Youth, Love, and Folly; or, The Little Jockey
    (In Cumberland's British Theatre, Vol. 44, no. 9)
Dingo (see Wood, Charles)
DINNER, William
  Mr. Fothergill joins the Angels
    (In Best One-Act Plays of 1942/43, London)

Dinny and the Witches (see Gibson, William)
Dino (see Rose, Reginald)
Dinorah under Difficulties (see Brough, William)
Diocletian (Gaius Aurelius Valerius Dioclelianus), Emperor of
Rome, 245-313
*The Virgin Martyr (see Massinger, Philip)
Dirty Hearts (see Sanchez, Sonia)
Dis May (see Theatre de L'Epee de Bois)
Disabled (see Ransley, Peter)
The Disagreeable Surprise (see Daniel, George)
The Discontented Man (see Le Brun, M.)
Le Discours du Pere (see Foissy, Guy)
The Disenchanted (see Schulberg, Budd)
DISNEY, Walt, 1901-1966
    Snow White and the Seven Dwarfs; adapted from Grimm's Fairy
    Tale by Ted Sears, Otto Englander, Earl Hurd, Dorothy Ann
    Blank, Richard Creedon, Dick Rickard, Merrill De Maris,
    Webb Smith.
        (In Foremost Films of 1938)
The Disobedient Child (see Ingelend, Thomas)
The Disposal (see Inge, William)
The Distaff Side (see Van Druten, John)
Distress upon Distress (see Stevens, George Alexander)
The Distrest Mother (see Philips, Ambrose)
The Distrest Mother (see also The Covent-Garden Tragedy; Andro-
    maque)
District of Columbia (see Richards, Stanley)
DITT, Jean Bruller
    Zoo, or L'Assassin Philanthrope, by Vercors, pseud.
        (In Plaisir de France, supplement theatral, no. 311, Sept.
        1964)
Divorciados (see Silva, Eurico)
DIX, Beulah Marie, 1876-
    The Captain of the Gate
        (In Atlantic Book of Modern Plays, 1921)
Dix Mille Soleils (see Kosa, Ferenc)
Do You Know the Milky Way? (see Wittlinger, Karl)
DOBIE, Charles Caldwell
    The Cracked Teapot
        (In The Banner Anthology of One-Act Plays by American
        Authors)
    The Immortals
        (In The Banner Anthology of One-Act Plays by American
        Authors)
DOBIE, Laurence
    The Tinker, by Dobie Laurence and Robert Sloman
        (In Plays of the Year, Vol. 24, 1961)
The Dock Brief (see Mortimer, John Clifford)
Docteur Jerry et Mister Love (see Lewis, Jerry)
The Doctor and the Apothecary (see Cobb, James)
The Doctor and the Devils (see Thomas, Dylan)
The Doctor and the Patient (see Saroyan, William)

Doctor Bolus (see Daniel, George)
Dr. Ehrlich's Magic Bullet (see Huston, John)
Doctor Faustus (see Marlowe, Christopher)
Doctor Faustus Lights the Lights (see Stein, Gertrude)
The Doctor from Dunmore (see Dillon, Thomas Patrick)
Dr. Kheal (see Fornes, Maria Irene)
Dr. Knock (see Romains, Jules)
Dr. McGrath (see Wilson, Edmund)
"Dod Gast Ye Both!" (see Heffner, Hubert Crouse)
DODSLEY, Robert, 1703-1764
      Cleone
          (In Bell's British Theatre, 1797, Vol. 5)
          (In Cumberland's British Theatre, Vol. 33, no. 3)
DODSON, Owen, 1914-
      Everybody Join Hands
          (In Theatre Arts, Vol. 27, Aug. 1943)
      The Third Fourth of July (see Cullen, Countee)
Dödsdansen (see Strindberg, August)
The Dog Beneath the Skin (see Auden, Wystan Hugh)
The Dogs or the Paris Comedy (see Saroyan, William)
La Dolce Vita (see Fellini, Federico)
A Dollar (see Pinski, David)
Dolls (see Armstrong, Mrs. Louise (Van Voorhis))
Doll's House 1970 (see Luce, Clare Boothe)
A Doll's House 1970 (see also Slam the Door Softly)
DOMINGUEZ, Franklin
      Un Portrait sur les Bras
          (In L'Avant Scene du Theatre, no. 444, Mar. 1, 1970)
          (In Plaisir de France, supplement theatral, no. 377, Apr.
          1970)
Don Carlos (see Schiller, Johann Christoph Friedrich von)
Don Giovanni; or, A Spectre on Horseback (see Dibdin, Thomas)
Don Giovanni Involontario (see Brancati, Vitaliano)
Don Juan (see Bertin, Charles)
Don Juan at the Stake (see Balducci, Alfredo)
Don Juan in Hell (see Shaw, George Bernard)
Don Juan in the Garden (see Kemp, Harry Hibbard)
Don Juan Malgre Lui (see Turpin, Francois)
Don Juan, or The Love of Geometry (see Frisch, Max)
Don Juan's Christmas Eve (see Kemp, Harry Hibbard)
Don Juan's Failure (see Baring, Maurice)
Don Quichotte (see Jamiaque, Yves)
Don Quixote in England (see Fielding, Henry)
Dona Patinha Vai Ser Miss (see Maia, Arthur)
Dona Xepa (see Bloch, Pedro)
DONAHUE, Patricia M.
      The Bear's Nest
          (In Best One-Act Plays of 1937, London)
Donato, Pietro, 1911- (see Di Donato, Pietro)
DONIOL-Valcroze, Jacques, 1920-
      La Maison des Bories
          (In L'Avant-Scene du Cinema, no. 118, Oct. 1971)

Una Donna di Casa   (see Brancati, Vitaliano)
DONNER, Clive, 1927-
   Quoi de Neuf, Pussycat? by Clive Donner et Woody Allen.
   Titre original: "What's New, Pussycat?"
      (In L'Avant-Scene du Cinema, no. 59, 1966)
Don't Know Sic'em From Sooey (see Jacobs, Fred Rue)
Don't Let Summer Come (see Feely, Terence)
The Door (see Stuart, Jeb)
A Door Should Be Either Open or Shut (see Musset, Alfred de)
Dope (see Lee, Maryat)
DORFMANN, Robert
   La Princesse de Cleves, by Robert Dorfmann, adapted by
   Jean Cocteau.
      (In L'Avant-Scene du Cinema, no. 3, Apr. 15, 1961)
DORIN, Francoise
   Les Bonshommes
      (In L'Avant-Scene du Theatre, no. 459, Nov. 1, 1970)
      (In Plaisir de France, supplement theatral, no. 385)
   Comme au Theatre
      (In L'Avant Scene du Theatre, no. 446, Apr. 1, 1970)
   Un Sale Egoiste
      (In L'Avant Scene du Theatre, no. 446, Apr. 1, 1970)
Dormer Windows (see Raphael, Alice)
Dorothea of Cappadocia (St. Dorothea)
   *The Virgin Martyr (see Massinger, Philip)
Dorset, Thomas Sackville, 1st earl of, 1536-1608
   Ferrex and Porrex (see Norton, Thomas)
DORST, Tankred, 1925-
   Kleiner Mann, Was Nun? Eine Revue von Tankred Dorst und
   Peter Zadek.
      (In Theater Heute, no. 11, Nov. 1972)
DOS PASSOS, John Roderigo, 1896-1970
   U.S.A., dramatized by John Dos Passos and Paul Shyre from
   selections of John Dos Passos' "U.S.A. Trilogy."
      (In Theatre Arts, Vol. 44, no. 6, June 1960)
Dostoevskii, Fedor Mikhailovich, 1821-1881
   **La Femme d'un Autre... or Le Mari sous le Lit (see Charpak,
   Andre)
   **Les Freres Karamazov (see Copeau, Jacques)
   **L'Idiot (see Barsacq, Andre)
The Double Dealer (see Congreve, William)
Double Dealing; or, The Rifle Volunteer (see Suter, W. E.)
The Double Deceit; or, A Cure for Jealousy (see Popple, William)
Double Entry (see Thompson, Jay)
Double Indemnity (see Wilder, Billy)
Double Jeu (see Thomas, Robert)
Douglas (see Home , John)
DOUGLAS, Nathan E.
   The Defiant Ones, by Nathan E. Douglas and Harold Jacob
   Smith, based on "The Long Road," by the authors.
      (In Film Scripts Two)
Les Doulos (see Melville, Jean Pierre)

Dove Brown (see Craven, H. T.)
The Dover Road (see Milne, Alan Alexander)
DOVIZI, Bernardo, da Bibbiena, cardinal, 1470-1520
    Follies of Calandro
    (In Genius of the Italian Theater)
DOVZHENKO, Oleksandr Petrovych, 1894-1956
    Earth
    (In Classic Film Scripts)
DOWN, Oliphant, 1885-1917
    The Maker of Dreams
    (In Representative One-Act Plays by British and Irish
    Authors)
    (In 24 Favorite One-Act Plays)
The Downfall of Robert Earl of Huntington (see Munday, Anthony)
DOWSON, Ernest Christopher, 1867-1900
    The Pierrot of the Minute
    (In 50 Contemporary One-Act Plays)
Doyle, Sir Arthur Conan, 1859-1930
    Sherlock Holmes (see Gillette, William Hooker)
DOZER, David
    Ol-Dopt; or, The Adventures of Charles and Emily Ann Andrews.
    A radio serial.
    (In Scripts, Vol. 1, no. 8, June 1972)
DOZIER, Robert
    A Real Fine Cutting Edge
    (In Television Plays for Writers, 1957)
DRACH, Michel, 1930-
    Amelie ou le Temps d'Aimer; d'apres le roman de Michele
    Angot "Amelie Boule. "
    (In L'Avant-Scene du Cinema, no. 8, Oct. 15, 1961)
The Dragon of Wantley (see Carey, Henry)
Dragon Seed (see Roberts, Marguerite)
The Dragon's Head (see Valle-Inclan, Ramon Maria del)
Dragon's Mouth (see Priestley, John Boynton)
DRAGUN, Osvaldo
    And They Told Us We Were Immortal
    (In Modern Stage in Latin America, 1971)
DRAIN, Richard
    The Tiger in the Rockery
    (In First Stage, Vol. 6, Winter 1967-68)
Drake, Sir Francis, c. 1540-1596
    *The Enterprise of England (see Prebble, John)
    *A Word with Sir Francis Drake During His Last Night in
    London
    (In Atlantic, Vol. 208, July 1961)
Dramatist Digested (see Datta, Jyotirmoy)
Draw the Fires! (see Toller, Ernst)
The Drawback (see Baring, Maurice)
The Dream (see Dreiser, Theodore)
Dream Girl (see Rice, Elmer)
The Dream Maker (see Thompson, Blanche Jeening)
Dream On, Soldier (see Hart, Moss)

The Dreaming of the Bones   (see Yeats, William Butler)
Dreams   (see Günter, Eich)
The Dreamy Kid   (see O'Neill, Eugene)
DREISER, Theodore, 1871-1945
    The Blue Sphere
        (In Plays of the Natural and the Supernatural)
    The Dream
        (In Seven Arts, Vol. 2, July 1917)
    The Girl in the Coffin
        (In Plays of the Natural and the Supernatural)
    In The Dark
        (In Plays of the Natural and the Supernatural)
    Laughing Gas
        (In Plays of the Natural and the Supernatural)
    The Light in the Window
        (In Plays of the Natural and the Supernatural)
    La Mort de Roberta   (see Eisenstein, Sergei-Mikailovitch)
    "Old Ragpicker"
        (In Plays of the Natural and the Supernatural)
    The Spring Recital
        (In Little Review, Vol. 2, Dec. 1915)
        (In Plays of the Natural and the Supernatural)
DREXLER, Rosalyn
    Hot Buttered Roll
        (In Theatre Experiment)
DREYER, Carl Theodor, 1889-1968
    Day of Wrath
        (In Four Screenplays by Carl Theodor Dreyer)
    Dies Irae, d'apres la piese Norvegienne "Anne Pegersdotter"
        de Johanssen Wiers-Jensen. Titre original: "Vredens Dag."
        (In L'Avant-Scene du Cinema, no. 100, Feb. 1970)
    Jesus
        (A Dial Press Screenplay, 1972)
    The Passion of Joan of Arc
        (In Four Screenplays by Carl Theodor Dreyer)
    Vampire
        (In Four Screenplays by Carl Theodor Dreyer)
    The Word
        (In Four Screenplays by Carl Theodor Dreyer)
Dreyfus, Alfred, c.1859-1935
    *The Life of Emile Zola   (see Herald, Heinz)
Drieu La Rochelle, Pierre-Eugene, 1893-1945
    **Le Feu Follet   (see Malle, Louis)
DRINKWATER, John, 1882-1937
    Abraham Lincoln
        (In Three Distinctive Plays About Abraham Lincoln)
    Cophetua
        (In Dramas by Present-Day Writers)
    The Storm
        (In Theatre Arts, Vol. 4, 1920)
Drive-In   (see Kranes, David)
Drole de Couple   (see Simon, Neil)

Drole de Drama (see Carne, Marcel)
The Drum of the Waves of Horikawa (Horikawa Nami no Tsuzumi)
    (see Chikamatsu Monzaemon)
The Drummer; or, The Haunted House (see Addison, Joseph)
Drums in the Night (see Brecht, Bertolt)
The Drums of Father Ned (see O'Casey, Sean)
The Drums of Oude (see Strong, Austin)
Drunken Sisters (see Wilder, Thornton)
Druten, John van (see Van Druten, John)
DRYDEN, John, 1631-1700
    All for Love; or, The World Well Lost
        (In Bell's British Theatre, 1797, Vol. 16)
        (In Tragedy: Texts and Commentary, 1969)
        (In Masterworks of World Drama, Vol. 4)
    Amphitryon; or, The Two Sosias
        (In Bell's British Theatre, 1797, Vol. 21)
    The Duke of Guise, by John Dryden and Nathaniel Lee
        (In Works of Nathaniel Lee, Vol. 2)
    Oedipus, by John Dryden and Nathaniel Lee
        (In Bell's British Theatre, 1797, Vol. 15)
        (In Works of Nathaniel Lee, Vol. 1)
    The Spanish Fryar
        (In Bell's British Theatre, 1797, Vol. 2)
DRYER, Bernard Victor
    Typhus
        (In Radio Drama in Action, 1945)
Du Vent dans les Branches de Sassafras (see Obaldia, Rene de)
DUBERMAN, Martin B. , 1930-
    History
        (In Evergreen Review, Vol. 13, no. 65, April 1969)
    In White America
        (In Best American Plays, Sixth series, 1963-67)
    The Recorder: A History
        (In Best Short Plays, 1970)
DUBILLARD, Roland
    Naives Hirondelles
        (In Evergreen Playscript Series, no. 18)
    Si Camille Me Voyait
        (In L'Avant Scene du Theatre, no. 469-470, Apr. 1-15, 1971)
The Duchess of Mansfeldt (see Souvestre, Emile)
The Duchess Says Her Prayers (see Canfield, Mary Cass)
Duck Soup (see Marx Brothers)
Dudley, Robert, 1st earl of Leicester, 1532?-1588
    *The Enterprise of England (see Prebble, John)
    *The Marriage Game (see Sisson, Rosemary Anne)
    *Shadow in the Sun (see Mitchell, Julian)
The Duel (see Dill, Jack)
The Duel; or, My Two Nephews (see Peake, R.B.)
The Duenna (see Sheridan, Richard Brinsley)
DÜRRENMATT, Friedrich, 1921-
    An Angel Comes to Babylon
        (In Evergreen Playscript Series)

Frank V
(In Plaisir de France, supplement theatral, no. 294, April
1963)
The Marriage of Mr. Mississippi
(In Evergreen Playscript Series)
The Physicists
(In Evergreen Playscript Series)
Romulus le Grand
(In Plaisir de France, supplement theatral, no. 313, Nov.
1964)
Rumulus the Great
(In Evergreen Playscript Series)
The Visit; adapted from "Der Besuch der Alten Dame, " by
Maurice Valency
(In Theatre Arts, Vol. 43, Dec. 1959)
(In The Modern Theatre, ed. by R. W. Corrigan)
Duet for Cannibals (see Sontag, Susan)
DUFFIELD, Brainerd
The Lottery, adapted from a story by Shirley Jackson.
(In 15 American One-Act Plays)
DUFFY, Maureen
Rites
(In Plays and Players, Vol. 17, no. 1, Oct. 1969)
DUGAN, Lawrence Joseph
Hospital Scene
(In Best One-Act Plays of 1939, N.Y.)
DUHIG, D. E.
The Ruling Passion
(In Best One-Act Plays of 1935, London)
The Duke of Guise (see Dryden, John)
DUKES, Ashley, 1885-1959
From Morn to Midnight (see Kaiser, Georg)
The Mask of Virtue (see Sternheim, Carl)
The Players' Dressing Room
(In Theatre Arts, Vol. 20, June 1936)
Such Men are Dangerous
(In Famous Plays of Today, 1929)
Tyl Ulenspiegel, or, The Song of Drums
(In Theatre Arts, Vol. 19, Apr. /July, 1926)
DUMAS, Alexandre (Pere), 1802-1870
The Count of Monte Cristo (see Fechter, Charles)
Henri III et Sa Cour
(In Chief French Plays of the 19th Century)
Mademoiselle de Belle Isle
(In Plays, by Frances Anne Kemble)
Monte Cristo (see Fechter, Charles Albert)
DUMAS, Alexandre (Fils), 1824-1895
La Dame aux Camelias
(In Chief French Plays of the 19th Century)
Du Maurier, Daphne, 1907-
**Rebecca (see Sherwood, Robert Emmet)
The Dumb Knight (see Machin, Lewis)

The Dumb Lady (see Lacy, John)
The Dumb Waiter (see Pinter, Harold)
DUNBAR, Olivia Howard
    Blockade
        (In Theatre Arts, Vol. 7, 1923)
DUNCAN, Ronald Frederick Henry, 1914-
    The Death of Satan
        (In Satan, Socialites, and Solly Gold)
DUNCAN, Thelma
    The Death Dance
        (In Plays of Negro Life)
DUNCAN, Winifred
    The Classic Dancing School
        (In Dramas, Vol. 17, May 1927)
DUNLAP, William, 1766-1839
    Andre
        (In Six Early American Plays, 1798-1890)
DUNNE, Philip, 1908-
    How Green Was My Valley; a screenplay based on the novel by
    Richard Llewellyn. Directed by John Ford.
        (In Twenty Best Film Plays)
DUNNING, Philip Hart, 1892-
    Broadway, by Philip H. Dunning and George Abbott.
        (In 13 Famous Plays of Crime and Detection)
        (In 25 Best Plays of the Modern American Theatre, Early
        Series, 1916-1929)
DUNSANY, Edward John Moreton Drax Plunkett, 18th baron, 1878-
1957
    Fame and the Poet
        (In Atlantic Book of Modern Plays, 1921)
    The Golden Doom
        (In Representative One-Act Plays by British and Irish Authors)
    A Night at the Inn
        (In 24 One-Act Plays, Revised edition, 1954)
        (In Thirty Famous One-Act Plays)
        (In Plays as Experience)
        (In Dramas by Present-Day Writers)
    The Jest of Hahalaba
        (In Twenty-Four Favorite One-Act Plays)
Dunsany, Lord (see Dunsany, Edward John Moreton Drax Plunkett,
    18th Baron)
DUNSTER, Mark
    Dialog
        (In Drama & Theatre, Vol. 9, no. 2, Winter 1970/71)
    Skelton
        (In Drama and Theatre, Vol. 7, no. 2, Winter 1968/69)
Dupin, Jean Henri, 1791-1887
    **Love in Humble Life (see Payne, John Howard)
Duplicity (see Holcroft, Thomas)
DU PONT, Lawrence
    No Shoes
        (In Best Television Plays of the Year, 1949)

Durand, Claude, 1938-
   Madame se Meurt (see Cayrol, Jean)
   On Vous Parle (see Cayrol, Jean)
DURAND, Philippe, 1932-
   Les Chats
     (In L'Avant-Scene du Cinema, no. 101, Mar. 1970)
DURAS, Marguerite, 1914-
   L'Amante Anglaise
     (In Plaisir de France, supplement theatral, no. 368, June
     1969)
   Days in the Trees
     (In Plays and Players, Vol. 14, Nov. 1966)
   Hiroshima Mon Amour, by Marguerite Duras et Alain Resnais
     (In L'Avant-Scene du Cinema, no. 61-62, July/Sept. 1966)
     (In Evergreen Filmscript Series)
DURRELL, Lawrence, 1912-
   Acte
     (In Show (New York), Vol. 1, Dec. 1961)
DURSI, Massimo
   Bertoldo at Court; both French and English texts are included.
     (In Italian Theatre Review, Vol. 1, Apr. /June 1961)
   Stefano Pelloni, called the Ferryman; both French and English
   texts are included.
     (In Italian Theatre Review, Vol. 13, Oct. /Dec. 1964)
     (In Drama and Theatre, Vol. 8, no. 1, 1969)
D'Usseau, Armand, 1916-
   Tomorrow the World (see Gow, James)
Dust (see Muldrow, Edna)
Dust of the Road (see Goodman, Kenneth Sawyer)
Dutchman (see Jones, Leroi)
The Dutchman's Ghost; or, All Right (see Barry, S.)
DUTOURD, Jean
   L'Arbre
     (In L'Avant-Scene du Theatre, no. 145)
DUVAL, M.
   Marriage Projects
     (In Theatrical Recorder, Vol. 2, Suppl. , Dec. 1805)
Dux (see Brighouse, Harold)
The Dwarfs (see Pinter, Harold)
The Dybbuk (see Rappoport, Solomon)
DYER, Charles
   Rattle of a Simple Man
     (In Plays of the Year, Vol. 26, 1962/63)
   Staircase
     (In Plays and Players, Vol. 14, January 1967)
Dyer Day (see Burgess, Jackson)
Dyscolus (see Menander)
Dyskolos (see Menander)

E. Kology (see Koch, Kenneth)
Each His Own Wilderness (see Lessing, Doris)

The Eagle (see Beebe, Ted)
The Eagle with Two Heads (see Cocteau, Jean)
Earl Birger of Bjälbo (see Strindberg, August)
The Earl of Essex (see Jones, Henry)
The Earl of Poverty; or, The Old Wooden House of London Wall
    (see Almar, George)
The Earl of Warwick (see Francklin, Thomas)
Early Snow (Hatsuyuki) (see Motoyasu, Komparn Zembo)
Earth (see Dovzhenko, Oleksandr Petrovych)
The Earth Is Ours (see Kozlenko, William)
The Easiest Way (see Walter, Eugene)
East Lynn (see Wood, Ellen Price, Mrs. Henry Wood)
Easter Eve (see Trevisan, Anna F.)
EASTMAN, Charles
    Little Fauss and Big Halsey
    (A Pocket Books Noonday Original Screenplay, 1970)
EASTMAN, Fred, 1886-
    Bread
    (In Plays as Experience)
Eastward Hoe (see Chapman, George)
Easy Money (see Ostrovskii, Alexsandr Nikolaevich)
Easy Money (see Poverman, Helen)
Easy Rider (see Fonda, Peter)
Easy Virtue (see Coward, Noel Pierce)
EATON, Walter Prichard
    Period House
    (In Best One-Act Plays of 1949/50, N.Y.)
EBERHART, Richard, 1904-
    Devils and Angels
    (In Tulane Drama Review, Vol. 6, June 1962)
    The Mad Musicians
    (In Tulane Drama Review, Vol. 6, June 1962)
Eboli, Ana de Mendoza y la Cerda, Princes de, 1540-1592
    *That Lady (see O'Brien, Kate)
EBSWORTH, Joseph, 1788-1868
    The Rival Valets
    (In Cumberland's British Theatre, Vol. 29, no. 3)
The Ecclesiazusae (see Aristophanes)
ECKART, Walter
    Les Femmes de Kalatas
    (In Plaisir de France, supplement theatral, no. 307, May
    1964)
L'Eclisse (see Antonioni, Michelangelo)
L'Ecole des Autres (see Roussin, Andre)
L'Ecole des Morts (see Charvet, Philippe)
L'Ecole des Veuves (see Cocteau, Jean)
Ecrit sur le Sable (see Vallejo, Antonio Buero)
Eddie Lechner's Trip to Paradise (see Soyfer, Jura)
Eddy, Mary Morse Baker, 1821-1910
    *Mary Baker Eddy (see Toller, Ernest)
The Eddystone Elf (see Pitt, George Dibdin)
The Edge of the Wood (see Roof, Katherine Metcalf)

Edith Stein (see Delouche, Dominique)
EDSON, Eric
  The Reign of the Wooden Horse
    (In Story, the Yearbook of Discovery, 3rd series, 1970)
EDSON, Russell
  The Falling Sickness
    (In Theatre Experiment)
Education (see Morton, Thomas)
Edufa (see Sutherland, Efua T.)
Edward I, King of England, 1239-1307
  *The Chronicle of Edward I (see Peele, George)
Edward II, King of England, 1284-1327
  *Edward II (see Marlowe, Christopher)
Edward VI, King of England and Ireland, 1537-1553
  *The Lion's Cub (see Hale, John)
Edward and Eleonora (see Thomson, James)
Edward, My Son (see Morley, Robert)
Edward the Black Prince, 1330-1376
  *Edward the Black Prince; or, The Battle of Poictiers (see
    Shirley, William)
The Edwardians (see Gow, Ronald)
EDWARDS, Richard, 1523?-1566
  Damon and Pithias
    (In Dodsley's A Select Collection of Old English Plays, Vol.
    4)
    (In Dodsley's A Select Collection of Old Plays, Vol. 1)
The Effect of Gamma Rays on Man-in-the-Moon Marigolds (see
    Zindel, Paul)
Egmont (see Goethe, Johann Wolfgang von)
Eh Joe (see Beckett, Samuel)
EHLERT, Fay
  The Undercurrent
    (In Drama, Vol. 18, Jan. 1928)
    (In 15 American One-Act Plays)
EHNI, Rene
  Que Ferez-vous en Novembre?
    (In L'Avant-Scene du Theatre, no. 412, Oct. 15, 1968)
EHRLICH, Mrs. Ida Lublenski, 1886-
  Peace-Makers
    (In The One-Act Theatre, Vol. 1)
  Winners All
    (In 50 More Contemporary One-Act Plays)
Ehrlich, Paul, 1854-1915
  *Die Ehrlich's Magic Bullet (see Huston, John)
Die Eigene Insel (see Kaugver, Raimond)
Eisenhower, Dwight David, pres. U.S., 1890-1969
  *The Election (political satire) (see Koch, Kenneth)
EISENSTEIN, Mark
  The Fighter
    (In Four New Yale Playwrights)
EISENSTEIN, Sergei-Mikailovitch, 1898-1948
  Le Cuirasse Potemkine
    (In L'Avant-Scene du Cinema, no. 11, Jan. 1962)

Ivan le Terrible, I, II, III; text in French
    (In L'Avant-Scene du Cinema, nos. 50-51, 1965)
Ivan the Terrible
    (In Classic Film Scripts)
La Mort de Roberta; extrait de l'adaptation de "An American
Tragedy" by Theodore Dreiser
    (In Cahiers du Cinema, Vol. 1, no. 5, Sept. 1951)
Octobre (Oktiabr)
    (In L'Avant-Scene du Cinema, no. 74, Oct. 1967)
Potemkin
    (In Classic Film Scripts)
Potemkin; a shot-by-shot re-creation of the film by David Mayer
    (Grossman Library of Film Classics)
Que Viva Mexico!; outline script for the film released as
"Thunder Over Mexico"
    (In Que Viva Mexico!, Vision Pr., London, 1952)
Eisenwicher (see Henkel, Heinrich)
ELDER, Eleanor
    Official Announcement
    (In Best One-Act Plays of 1935, London)
ELDER, Lonne
    Ceremonies in Dark Old Men
    (In New Black Playwrights)
The Elder Statesman (see Eliot, Thomas Stearns)
ELDRIDGE, Paul
    The Loser
    (In Drama, Vol. 11, Feb. 1921)
Eleanor of Aquitaine, Consort of Henry II, 1122?-1204
    *Curtmantle (see Fry, Christopher)
    *Lion in Winter (see Goldman, James)
The Election (see Koch, Kenneth)
Electra (see Euripides)
Electra (see Giraudoux, Jean)
Electra (see Hofmannsthal, Hugo von Hofmann, Elder von)
Electra (see Sophocles)
The Electronic Nigger (see Bullins, Ed)
Elegie (see Huszarik, Zoltan)
The Elephant Calf (see Brecht, Bertolt)
Eles Nao Usam Black-Tie (see Guarnieri, Gianfrancesco)
Elevan A.M. (See Reid-Jamieson, Marion)
Elfrida (see Mason, William)
EL-HAKIM, T.
    Death of Mohammed
    (In Atlantic Monthly, Vol. 198, Oct. 1956)
Eli and Emily (see Levoy, Myron)
An Eligible Situation (see Archer, Thomas)
ELINSON, Jack
    Gomer Pyle, a television filmscript
    (In Writing for Television)
ELIOT, Thomas Stearns, 1888-1965
    The Cocktail Party
    (In Complete Plays)

The Confidential Clerk
(In Complete Plays)
The Elder Statesman
(In Complete Plays)
The Family Reunion
(In Complete Plays)
Murder in the Cathedral
(In Complete Plays)
(In The Modern Theatre, ed. by R. W. Corrigan)
Sweeney Agonistes
(In From the Modern Repertoire, Series One)
(In 24 One-Act Plays, Revised edition, 1954)
Eliphant & Flamingo Vaudeville (see Harkin, Eleanor)
Elisabeth Est Morte (see Mithois, Marcel)
The Elixir (see DeFelice, James)
Elizabeth I, Queen of England, 1533-1603
    *Elizabeth the Queen (see Anderson, Maxwell)
    *The Enterprise of England (see Prebble, John)
    *Horrible Conspiracies (see Whitmore, Hugh)
    *The Lion's Cub (see Hale, John)
    *The Marriage Game (see Sisson, Rosemary Anne)
    *Mary of Scotland (see Anderson, Maxwell)
    *The Queen Waits (see Pemberton, Madge)
    *The Queen's Shift (see Ingersoll, James H.)
    *Shadow in the Sun (see Mitchell, Julian)
    *Sweet England's Pride (see Rodger, Ian)
    *Till Time Shall End (see Ashton, Winifred)
    *The Whore of Babylon (see Dekker, Thomas)
Elka (see Kerautem, Louis de)
ELKIN, Stanley
    The Six-Year-Old Man. A screenplay
        (In Esquire, Vol. 70, Dec. 1968)
Ella Rosenberg (see Kenney, James)
Elle Etait Rousse (see Roudy, Pierre)
Ellen (see Ransley, Peter)
ELLICOTT, John Morris
    Aye, Aye, Sir!
        (In The Banner Anthology of One-Act Plays by American
        Authors)
ELLIS, Edith M. O. Lees
    The Subjection of Kezia, by Mrs. Havelock Ellis
        (In 50 Contemporary One-Act Plays)
Ellis, George, 1753-1815
    The Rovers (see Canning, George)
Ellis, Havelock, 1859-1939
    The Two Angry Women (see Porter, Henry)
Elopements While You Wait (see Stevens, Caroline D.)
ELSE, George
    Joey
        (In Best Short Plays, 1960/61, N. Y.)
Elvira, or, The Worst Not Always True (see Bristol, George Digby,
    2d earl of)

Em Moeda Corrente do Pais (see Almeida, Abilio Pereira de)
Embers (see Beckett, Samuel)
Emilia Galotti (see Lessing, Gotthold Ephraim)
Emperor (see Pirandello, Luigi)
The Emperor (Enrico IV) (see also Henry IV)
The Emperor (Enrico IV) (see Pirandello, Luigi)
The Emperor Jones (see O'Neill, Eugene)
The Empire Builders (see Vian, Boris)
The Empty Noose (see Perl, Arnold)
En Familia (see Sanchez, Florencio)
En Fiacre (see Adamov, Arthur)
En Regardant Tomber les Murs (see Foissy, Guy)
The Enchanted (see Giraudoux, Jean)
Enchanted Night (see Mrozek, Slawomir)
L'Enclos (O Grada) (see Gateschi, Rossana)
Encore (see Clark, T. E. B.)
Encounter (see Fayans, B.)
The End (see Wiener, Joel)
End of Summer (see Behrman, Samuel Nathaniel)
The End of the Trail (see Culbertson, Ernest Howard)
The End of the World (Weltuntergang) (see Soyfer, Jura)
The End of the World; or, Fragments from a Work in Progress
    (see Neilson, Keith)
Endgame (see Beckett, Samuel)
Endore, Guy (see Endore, S.)
Endore, S. Guy, 1901-
    The Story of G. I. Joe (see Atlas, Leopold)
Enemy (see Alexander, I. J.)
Enemy! (see Maugham, Robin)
L'Enfant Sauvage (see Truffaut, Francois)
Les Enfants du Paradis (see Prevert, Jacques)
Engagement (see Ottey, M. E.)
ENGEL, Johann Jakob, 1741-1802
    The Affectionate Son
        (In Theatrical Recorder, Vol. 3, no. 9, Aug. 1805)
England, Preserved (see Watson, George)
The English Fleet in 1342 (see Dibdin, Thomas)
The English Merchant (see Colman, George, the Younger)
An English Tragedy (see Kemble, Frances Anne)
English-Men for My Money; or, A Woman Will Have Her Will (see
    Haughton, Wm.)
L'Enlevement (see Veber, Francis)
The Enlightenment of Others by Will Skuffel (see Smith, Peter J.)
Les Ennemis (see Gor'kii, Maksim)
Ennery, Adolphe d' (see Dennery, Adolphe Philippe)
Enquette sur un Citoyen Au-Dessus de Tout Soupcon (see Petri,
    Elio)
ENRICO, Robert, 1931-
    La Riviere du Hibou, d'apres la nouvelle Americaine, "An
    Occurrence at Owl Creek Bridge" d'Ambrose Bierce.
        (In L'Avant-Scene du Cinema, no. 10, Dec. 1961)
ENSANA, Joel A.
    Please, No Flowers

(In First Stage, Vol. 5, Spring 1966)
(In Best Short Plays, 1969)
Enter Solly Gold (see Kops, Bernard)
Enter the Hero (see Helburn, Theresa)
The Enterprise of England (see Prebble, John)
L'Enterrement (see Monnier, Henry)
The Entertainer (see Osborne, John)
Entr'acte (see Clair, Rene)
Entre Medina et Olmedo (see Arauz, Alvaro)
Ephraim (see Knee, Allan)
Ephron, Henry, 1912-
    Take Her, She's Mine (see Ephron, Phoebe)
EPHRON, Phoebe, 1916-
    Take Her, She's Mine, by Phoebe and Henry Ephron.
        (In Theatre Arts, Vol. 47, July 1963)
Epidicus (see Plautus, Titus Maccius)
Episode from an Author's Life (see Anouilh, Jean)
Episode in the Life of an Author (see Anouilh, Jean)
Episodes from the Fighting in the East (see Howard, Roger)
Epitaph for George Dillon (see Osborne, John)
Epitelioma (see Hamou, Rene)
L'Epouse Injustement Soupconnee (see Cocteau, Jean)
EPSTEIN, David
    They Told Me That You Came This Way
        (In Yale/Theatre, Vol. 2, no. 2, Summer 1969)
    Trip-Tych
        (In Yale/Theatre, Vol. 3, no. 1, Fall 1970)
EPSTEIN, Julius J., 1909-
    Casablanca, a filmscript by Julius J. and Philip G. Epstein and
    Howard Koch, based on the play "Everybody Comes to Rick's"
    by Murray Burnett and Joan Alison, directed by Michael Curtiz
        (In Best Film Plays, 1943/44, Vol. 1)
EPSTEIN, Paul
    Intersections 7
        (In Scripts, Vol. 1, no. 2, Dec. 1971)
Epstein, Philip G., 1910-1952
    Casablanca (see Epstein, Julius J.)
Equals (see Strindberg, August)
L'Equarrissage pour Tous (see Vian, Boris)
Equinox (see Sundgaard, Arnold)
ERDMAN, Nikolai
    Der Selbstmorder
        (In Theater Heute, Vol. 11, no. 7, July 1970)
L'Ere Quaternaire (see Le Bihan, Michel)
Eric XIV, King of Sweden, 1533-1577
    *Erik XIV (see Strindberg, August)
The Ermine (see Anouilh, Jean)
ERNST, Alice Henson
    Spring Sluicing
        (In Theatre Arts, Vol. 12, Feb. 1928)
    The Valley of Lost Men
        (In Theatre Arts, Vol. 14, May 1930)

Erschwerte Möglichkeit der Konzentration   (see Havel, Vaclav)
ERVINE, St. John Greer, 1883-1971
    John Ferguson
        (In Theatre Guild Anthology)
    The Magnanimous Lover
        (In Representative One-Act Plays by British and Irish Authors)
    Progress
        (In 24 One-Act Plays, Revised edition, 1954)
Escape   (see Pratt, Theodore)
The Escape Route   (see Serling, Rod)
Escurial   (see Ghelderode, Michel de)
Esker Mike and His Wife, Agiluk   (see Hardin, Herschel)
L'Espace Vital   (see Leconte, Patrice)
Essex, Robert Devereux, Earl of, 1566-1601
    *The Earl of Essex   (see Jones, Henry)
    *Elizabeth the Queen   (see Anderson, Maxwell)
    *The Enterprise of England   (see Prebble, John)
    *Sweet England's Pride   (see Rodger, Ian)
Este Ovo e um Galo   (see Muniz, Lauro Cesar)
A Estoria da Rosa Principe   (see Rodrigues, Elza Correa)
ESTRIN, Marc
    An American Playground Sampler
        (In New American Plays, Vol. 3)
    Four Infiltration Pieces
        (In Scripts, Vol. 1, no. 5, Mar. 1972)
Et... Dieu Crea la Femme   (see Vadim, Roger)
L'Ete   (see Weingarten, Romain)
Ethan Frome   (see Davis, Owen)
ETHERIDGE, Vere
    The Modern Masterpiece
        (In The One-Act Theatre, Vol. 1)
Ethiopia   (see Arent, Arthur)
ETHRIDGE, Ken
    Folly of Seithenyn
        (In Best One-Act Plays of 1944/45, London)
ETIENNE, Charles Guillaume, 1771-1845
    The Mothers
        (In Theatrical Recorder, Vol. 1, no. 5, Apr. 1805)
L'Etoile au Front   (see Roussel, Raymond)
Ett Dromspel   (see Le Songe)
ETTLINGER, Karl, Ritter von, 1874-1938
    Altruism
        (In 50 Contemporary One-Act Plays)
Eufemia   (see Rueda, Lope de)
Eugene Aram; or, Saint Robert's Cave   (see Moncrieff, William
    Thomas)
The Eumenides   (see Aeschylus)
The Eunuch   (see Terence; Publius Terentius Afer)
Eunuchs of the Forbidden City   (see Ludlam, Charles)
Eunuchus 232-291   (see Terence; Publius Terentius Afer)
EURIPIDES, 480 or 484 B.C.-406 B.C.
    **African Medea   (see Magnuson, Jim)

**After Euripides' Electra   (see Baring, Maurice)
Andromache
   (In Complete Greek Drama)
The Bacchae
   (In Masterworks of World Drama, Vol. 1)
**The Cretan Woman (see Jeffers, Robinson)
**Creusa, Queen of Athens (see Whitehead, William)
The Cyclops
   (In Complete Greek Drama, Vol. 2)
Electra
   (In Complete Greek Drama, Vol. 2)
Hecuba
   (In Complete Greek Drama, Vol. 1)
Helen
   (In Complete Greek Drama, Vol. 2)
Helena, de Euripedes, Traducao de Lopes Goncalves
   (In Revista de Teatro, no. 292)
The Heracleidae
   (In Complete Greek Drama, Vol. 1)
Heracles
   (In Complete Greek Drama, Vol. 1)
Hippolytus
   (In Complete Greek Drama, Vol. 1)
Ion
   (In Complete Greek Drama, Vol. 1)
Iphigenia in Aulis
   (In Complete Greek Drama, Vol. 2)
Iphigenia in Tauris
   (In Complete Greek Drama, Vol. 1)
**Jason and Medea (see Baring, Maurice)
Medea
   (In Tragedy: Texts and Commentary, 1969)
   (In Complete Greek Drama, Vol. 1)
**Medea (see Anouilh, Jean)
**Medea (see Jeffers, Robinson)
Orestes
   (In Complete Greek Drama, Vol. 2)
The Phoenissae
   (In Complete Greek Drama, Vol. 2)
Rhesus
   (In Complete Greek Drama, Vol. 2)
The Suppliants
   (In Complete Greek Drama, Vol. 2)
The Trojan Women
   (In Masterworks of World Drama, Vol. 1)
   (In Complete Greek Drama, Vol. 1)
Europort: Rotterdam (see Ivens, Joris)
Eurydice (see Mallet, David)
Eurydice (see Fielding, Henry)
Eurydice Hiss'd; or, A Word to the Wise (see Fielding, Henry)
Eurydice (Legend of Lovers) (see Anouilh, Jean)
Eva (see Barreto, Paulo)

Evariste Galois   (see Astruc, Alexandre)
Evarts, John
    Play, Life, Illusion   (see Schawinsky, Xanti)
The Eve in Evelyn   (see Hughes, Glenn)
EVELING, Stanley
    Oh Starlings!
        (In Plays and Players, Vol. 19, Mar. 1971)
    Sweet Alice
        (In Plays and Players, Vol. 19, Mar. 1971)
An Evening in an Important Asylum   (see Stettner, Louis)
Events, 1968-1969   (see Baker, Fred)
Events while Guarding the Bofors Gun   (see McGrath, John)
Ever Young   (see Gerstenberg, Alice)
Everie Woman in Her Humor (Anon.)
        (In A Collection of Old English Plays, Vol. 4)
Every Man in His Humour   (see Jonson, Ben)
Every Number Wins   (see Almaz, Michael)
Everybody Join Hands   (see Dodson, Owen)
Everybody's Husband   (see Ryan, Richard)
Everyman (Anon.)
        (In Genius of the Early English Theater)
        (In Dodsley's A Select Collection of Old English Plays, Vol.
        1)
        (In Masterworks of World Drama, 1968)
        (In Great English Plays)
        (In Introduction to Literature: Plays)
        (In Tragedy: Texts and Commentary, 1969)
        (In Religious Drama, Vol. 2)
Everyone Has His Fault (see Inchbald, Mrs. Elizabeth Simpson)
Ex Cathedra   (see Connelly, Marcus Cook)
The Exception and the Rule   (see Brecht, Bertolt)
The Exchange   (see Thurston, Althea)
Exchange No Robbery   (see Hook, Theodore Edward)
Exhibit C   (see Brighouse, Harold)
The Exile (Anon.)
        (In Old Plays, 1810)
The Exile; or, The Deserts of Siberia   (see Reynolds, Frederick)
The Exiles   (see Vodanovic, Sergio)
Exit   (see Roberts, Cyril)
Exit the King   (see Ionesco, Eugene)
Ex-Miss Copper Queen on a Set of Pills   (see Terry, Megan)
Exodus   (see Robinson, Marvin W.)
Expectant Relations   (see Foote, Horton)
Experiment   (see Parkington, Mary)
Experimental Death Unit #1   (see Jones, LeRoi)
L'Explication   (see Barrier, Maurice)
Explosion   (see Gerould, Daniel C.)
Express for Santiago   (see Aguiree, Isidora)
The Exterminating Angel   (see Buñuel, Luis)
EXTON, Clive
    Have You Any Dirty Washing, Mother Dear?
        (In Plays of the Year, Vol. 37, 1969-70)
        (In Plays and Players, Vol. 16, no. 8, May 1969)

Extra-Muros   (see Devos, Raymond)
EYEN, Tom
    Grand Tenement and November 22
       (In More Plays From Off Off Broadway)
    The White Whore and the Bit Player
       (In New American Plays, Vol. 2)
Eyes   (see Serling, Rod)

FABBRI, Diego
    The Confidant; both French and English texts are included.
       (In Italian Theatre Review, Vol. 14, Jan./Mar. 1965)
    Le Seducteur
       (In L'Avant-Scene du Theatre, Mar. 1956)
A Fable   (see Scholl, Ralph)
The Fabulous Miss Marie   (see Bullins, Ed)
A Fabulous Tale   (see Stockton, Richard F.)
The Face   (see Laurents, Arthur)
A Face in the Crowd   (see Schulberg, Budd)
Faces   (see Cassavetes, John)
FAGAN, James Bernard, 1873-1933
    The Improper Duchess
       (In Famous Plays of Today, 1931)
The Failure   (see Corrie, Joe)
A Faint Heart Which Did Win a Fair Lady   (see Wooler, John Pratt)
Fair Beckoning One   (see Koebnick, Sarah Monson)
The Fair Penitent   (see Rowe, Nicholas)
FAIRCHILD, William
    The Sound of Murder
       (In Plays of the Year, Vol. 20, 1959)
Fairly Taken In   (see Kemble, Mrs. Charles)
Fairly Taken In   (see also Personation; or, Fairly Taken In)
Faith of Our Fathers   (see Marble, Annie)
Faithful Admirer   (see Baker, Elizabeth Fulton)
A Falecida   (see Rodrigues, Nelson)
Faliero, Marino, Doge of Venice, c.1274-1355
    *Marino Faliero, Doge of Venice   (see Byron, George Gordon
    Nöel)
FALKLAND, Henry Cary, 4th viscount, 1634-1663
    The Marriage Night, by Lord Viscount Falkland
       (In Dodsley's A Select Collection of Old English Plays, Vol.
    15)
The Fall of Algiers (Anon.)
       (In Cumberland's British Theatre, Vol. 42, no. 3)
The Fall of Man   (see York Cowpers' Play)
The Fall of the City   (see MacLeish, Archibald)
The Fall of the House of Usher   (see Day, Frederic Lansing)
The Fall of Ug   (see Steele, Rufus)
The Falling Sickness   (see Edson, Russell)
The Falls of Clyde   (see Soane, George)
The False Confessions   (see Marivaux, Pierre Carlet de Chamblain
de)

False Delicacy (see Kelly, Hugh)
False Impressions (see Cumberland, Richard)
False Indifference (see Carmontelle, Louis Carrogis, known as)
Falstaff's Wedding (see Kenrick, William)
Fame (see Miller, Arthur)
Fame and the Poet (see Dunsany, Edward John Moreton Drax
    Plunkett, 18th Baron)
A Familia (see Bocayuva, Quintino)
Family Album (see Coward, Noel Pierce)
Family Meeting (see Mackey, William Wellington)
The Family Quarrel (Mizu-ron Muko) (see Sakanishi, Shio)
The Family Reunion (see Eliot, Thomas Stearns)
Fan Tan (see Finn, John, Jr.)
The Fan Windows (see Marques, Rene)
Fancy Free (see Houghton, Stanley)
Fanghorn (see Pinner, David)
Fantasia Is an Old Familiar Theme (see Lanzl, Frank)
Fantasio (see Musset, Alfred de)
The Fantastic Impromptu (see Ivan, Rosalind)
The Fantasticks (see Schmidt, Harvey L.)
The Far Distant Shore (see Finch, Robert)
FARAGOH, Francis Edwards
    Little Caesar; a screenplay based on the novel by W. R. Burnett,
    directed by Mervyn Le Roy.
    (In Twenty Best Film Plays)
The Far-Away Princess (see Sudermann, Hermann)
La Farce de l'Auberge Rouge (see Chose, Raymond)
La Farce Rouge ou le Dernier Vivant (see Chose, Raymond)
Farewell Appearance (see Holland, Norman)
A Farewell Supper (see Schnitzler, Arthur)
Farewell to Altamount (see Lomax, Elizabeth)
Farewell to Love (see Ryerson, Florence)
FARJEON, Eleanor, 1881-
    The Two Bouquets, by Eleanor and Herbert Farjeon.
    (In Famous Plays of Today, 1936)
Farjeon, Herbert
    The Two Bouquets (see Farjeon, Eleanor)
The Farm House (see Kemble, John Philip)
The Farmer (see O'Keeffe, John)
Farmer Brown's Pig (see Young, Stanley)
FARQUHAR, George, 1677?-1707
    The Beaux' Stratagem
        (In Bell's British Theatre, Vol. 10, 1797)
        (In Cumberland's British Theatre, Vol. 7, no. 2)
        (In The London Stage, Vol. 2)
        (In Masterworks of World Drama, Vol. 5)
    The Constant Couple; or, A Trip to the Jubilee
        (In Bell's British Theatre, Vol. 16, 1797)
    The Inconstant; or, The Way to Win Him
        (In Bell's British Theatre, Vol. 32, 1797)
        (In Cumberland's British Theatre, Vol. 11, no. 3)
        (In The London Stage, Vol. 1)

The Recruiting Officer
(In Bell's British Theatre, Vol. 13, 1797)
(In Cumberland's British Theatre, Vol. 32, no. 2)
(In Great English Plays)
(In The London Stage, Vol. 1)
Sir Harry Wildair, being the sequel of The Trip to Jubilee
(In Bell's British Theatre, Vol. 31, 1797)
The Twin Rivals
(In Bell's British Theatre, Vol. 32, 1797)
FARRELL, James Thomas, 1904-
A Lesson in History
(In Quarterly Review of Literature, Vol. 2, no. 2, 1944)
A Farsa da Esposa Perfeita (see Lima, Edy)
Farther Off from Heaven (see The Dark at the Top of the Stairs)
The Fascinating Mr. Denby (see Sage, Selwin)
Fashion; or, Life in New York (see Mowatt, Anna Cora Ritchie)
Fashionable Levities (see Macnally, Leonard)
The Fashionable Lover (see Cumberland, Richard)
FASQUEL, Maurice, 1931-
La Contrebasse; d'apres la nouvelle "Le Roman de la Contre-
basse, " d'Anton Tchekhov.
(In L'Avant-Scene du Cinema, no. 34, 1964)
FASSBINDER, Rainer Werner
Das Kaffeehaus
(In Theatre Heute, Vol. 10, Oct. 1969)
The Fatal Curiosity (see Lillo, George)
The Fatal Dowry (see Massinger, Philip)
The Fatal French Dentist (see Mandel, Oscar)
The Fatal Rubber (see Baring, Maurice)
Fatality (see Boaden, Caroline)
The Father (see Strindberg, August)
Father and Son; or, The Rock of Charbonniere (see Ball, Edmund)
The Father Out of the Machine (see Simpson, Louis M.)
The Father Outwitted (see Vega Carpio, Lope Felix de)
The Father Returns (see Kikuchi Kwan)
Father Uxbridge Wants to Marry (see Gagliano, Frank)
Fauchois, Rene, 1882-
**The Late Christopher Bean (see Howard, Sidney Coe)
**The Late Christopher Bean (see Williams, Emlyn)
FAULK, John
Fourth of July Picnic
(In Radio's Best Plays, 1947)
FAULKNER, William, 1897-1962
**Barn Burning (see Vidal, Gore)
The Big Sleep, screenplay by William Faulkner, Leigh Brackett
and Jules Furthman, based on "The Big Sleep" by Raymond
Chandler
(In Film Scripts One)
**The Old Man (see Foote, Horton)
**Smoke (see Vidal, Gore)
**Tomorrow (see Foote, Horton)
FAURE, Michel
Le Diable en Ete

(In L'Avant Scene du Theatre, No. 450, June 1, 1970)
Faust, Frederick, 1892-1944
**Destry Rides Again (see Jackson, Felix)
Faust, Part 1 (see Goethe, Johann Wolfgang von)
Faustina, Ritual Tragedy (see Goodman, Paul)
Faustus (see Norman, Charles)
Faustus (see Soane, George)
Fawcett, John, 1768-1837
    The Barber of Seville (see Beaumarchais, Pierre Augustin
    Caron de)
The Fawn (see Flexner, Hortense)
FAYAD, Samy, 1925-
    How to Rob a Bank; both French and English texts are included.
    (In Italian Theatre Review, Vol. 15, July/Sept. 1966)
FAYANS, B.
    Encounter
    (In Soviet One-Act Plays)
The Feast of Ortolans (see Anderson, Maxwell)
Feat Accomplished and a Hero Completely Defeated (see Mrwebi,
    Gwigwi)
Feathertop (see Valency, Maurice Jacques)
FECHTER, Charles Albert, 1824-1879
    The Count of Monte Cristo, based on the novel by Alexandre
    Dumas
        (In Best Plays of the Early American Theatre, from the
        beginning to 1916)
    Monte Cristo; the James O'Neill version, based on the novel
    "The Count of Monte Cristo" by Alexandre Dumas
        (In Monte Cristo and Other Plays)
FEELY, Terence
    Don't Let Summer Come
        (In Plays of the Year, 1964/65, Vol. 29)
Feet (see Marinetti, Filippo Tommaso)
Fegefeuer in Ingolstadt (see Fleisser, Marieluise)
FEIFFER, Jules, 1929-
    Crawling Arnold
        (In Horizon, Vol. 4, Nov. 1961)
        (In Best Short Plays of the World Theatre, 1958/67)
    God Bless
        (In Plays and Players, Vol. 16, no. 4, Jan. 1969)
FELDHAUS-WEBER, Mary
    The World Tipped Over, and Laying on Its Side
        (In Playwrights for Tomorrow, Vol. 4)
FELLINI, Federico, 1920-
    Il Bidone
        (In Three Screenplays, 1970)
    La Dolce Vita
        (Ballantine Screenplay Series, 1961)
    Fellini-Roma
        (In L'Avant-Scene du Cinema, no. 129, Oct. 1972)
    Fellini's Satyricon
        (A Ballantine Screenplay Series, 1970)

Huit et Demi
   (In L'Avant-Scene du Cinema, no. 63, 1966)
Juliet of the Spirits
   (Orion Press Filmscript)
Rome, Ville Ouverte (Roma, Citta Aperta) by Federico Fellini
   et Roberto Rossellini d'apres un sujet de Sergio Amidei
   (In L'Avant-Scene du Cinema, no. 71, 1967)
La Strada
   (In L'Avant-Scene du Cinema, no. 102, Apr. 1970)
The Temptation of Dr. Antonio
   (In Three Screenplays, 1970)
Variety Lights
   (In Early Screenplays)
I Vitelloni
   (In Three Screenplays, 1970)
The White Sheik
   (In Early Screenplays)
Fellini-Roma (see Fellini, Federico)
Fellini's Satyricon (see Fellini, Federico)
FELLOWS, Malcolm Stuart
   Ou Vivrez-vous Demain?
   (In Plaisir de France, supplement theatral, no. 372, Nov.
   1969)
FELTON, Keith Spencer
   The Last Lost Weekend of Missionary Peale
   (In Story, the Yearbook of Discovery, 1968)
The Feminine Touch (see Kvasnitsky, V.)
La Femme du Boulanger (see Giono, Jean)
La Femme d'un Autre...Ou le Mari Sous le Lit (see Charpak,
   Andre)
La Femme Infidele (see Chabrol, Claude)
Une Femme Mariee (La Femme Mariee) (see Godard, Jean-Luc)
Les Femmes de Kalatas (see Eckart, Walter)
Les Femmes de Stermetz (see Grospierre, Louis)
Femmes Paralleles (see Billetdoux, Francois)
FENN, Frederick
   'Op-o-me-thumb
   (In Representative One-Act Plays by British and Irish Authors)
FENTON, Elijah, 1683-1730
   Marianne
   (In Bell's British Theatre, 1797, Vol. 26)
FERBER, Edna, 1887-1968
   Stage Door, by Edna Ferber and George S. Kaufman
   (In Nine Modern American Plays)
   (In 20 Best Plays of the Modern American Theatre, Vol. 1)
Ferdinand V, King of Spain, 1452-1516
   *Fuente Ovejuna (see Vega Carpio, Lope Felix de)
FERGUSSON, Francis
   The King and the Duke; a melodramatic farce from "Huckleberry
   Finn"
   (In From the Modern Repertoire, Series Two)
FERREIRE, Helvecio

A Historia do Grito
    (In Revista de Teatro, no. 389, Sept. /Oct. 1972)
Ferret, Roger, 1932-
    Concerto de l'Aube (see Prigent, Yves)
Ferrex and Porrex (see Norton, Thomas)
FERRINI, Vincent
    Innermost I Land
        (In Best One-Act Plays, 1952/53, N.Y.)
    Telling of the North Star
        (In Best Short Plays, 1953/54)
Ferry, Jean, 1906-
    Quai des Orfevres (see Clouzot, Henri-Georges)
Ein Fest Für Boris (see Bernhard, Thomas)
Le Feu Follet (see Malle, Louis)
A Few Words Beforehand (see Kemp, Harry Hibbard)
FEYDEAU, Georges, 1862-1921
    Champignol Wider Willen (Champignol Malgre Lui)
        (In Theatre Heute, no. 11, Nov. 1971)
    Going to Pot
        (In Tulane Drama Review, Vol. 5, Sept. 1950)
Feyder, Jacques, 1887-1948
    La Kermesse Heroique (see Spaak, Charles)
Fiammetta (see Baldi, Gian Vittorio)
Fiddler on the Roof (see Bock, Jerry)
FIEDLER, Leslie Aaron, 1917-
    The Bearded Virgin and the Blind God
        (In Kenyon Review, Vol. 25, no. 4, Autumn 1963)
FIELD, Charles K.
    The Cave Man
        (In The Grove Plays of the Bohemian Club, Vol. 2)
    The Man in the Forest
        (In The Grove Plays of the Bohemian Club, Vol. 1)
    The Owl and Care
        (In The Grove Plays of the Bohemian Club, Vol. 1)
FIELD, Nathan, 1587-1620?
    Amends for Ladies
        (In Best Plays of the Old Dramatists: Nero and Other Plays)
        (In Dodsley's A Select Collection of Old English Plays, Vol.
        11)
    A Woman Is a Weather-Cock
        (In Best Plays of the Old Dramatists: Nero and Other Plays)
        (In Dodsley's A Select Collection of Old English Plays, Vol.
        11)
Field, Nathaniel (see Field, Nathan)
FIELD, Rachel Lyman, 1894-1942
    Cinderella Married
        (In Six Plays)
    Columbine in Business
        (In Six Plays)
    The Fifteenth Candle
        (In Plays as Experience)
    The Patchwork Quilt
        (In Six Plays)

Theories and Thumbs
(In Six Plays)
Three Pills in a Bottle
(In Six Plays)
Wisdom Teeth
(In Six Plays)
FIELDING, Henry, 1707-1754
The Covent-Garden Tragedy
(In Burlesque Plays of the 18th Century)
Don Quixote in England
(In his Works: Plays, Vol. 3)
Eurydice
(In his Works: Plays, Vol. 3)
Eurydice Hiss'd; or, A Word to the Wise
(In his Works: Plays, Vol. 3)
The Historical Register for the Year 1736
(In his Works: Plays, Vol. 3)
The Miser
(In Bell's British Theatre, 1797, Vol. 11)
(In Cumberland's British Theatre, Vol. 31, no. 3)
Miss Lucy in Town. A sequel to The Virgin Unmask'd
(In his Works: Plays, Vol. 3)
The Mock Doctor; or, The Dumb Lady Cured
(In The London Stage, Vol. 2)
The Old Man Taught Wisdom; or, The Virgin Unmask'd
(In his Works: Plays, Vol. 3)
Pasquin: A Dramatic Satire on the Times
(In his Works: Plays, Vol. 3)
**Tom Jones (see Osborne, John)
Tom Thumb, altered by Kane O'Hara.
(In Cumberland's British Theatre, Vol. 44, no. 4)
(In The London Stage, Vol. 2)
Tom Thumb, by Scriblerus Secundus (pseud.)
(In Burlesque Plays of the 18th Century)
Tumble-Down Dick; or, Phaeton in the Suds
(In his Works: Plays, Vol. 3)
The Universal Gallant; or, The Different Husbands
(In his Works: Plays, Vol. 3)
The Wedding Day
(In his Works: Plays, Vol. 3)
Fields, Joseph
Anniversary Waltz (see Chodorov, Jerome)
Fields, W. C. (William Claude Dunkinfield), 1879-1946
**Never Give a Sucker an Even Break (see Neville, John T.)
The Fifth Commandment (see Bierstadt, Edward Hale)
The Fifth Season (see Regan, Sylvia Ellstein)
FIFE, Evelyn Henderson
We Are Three
(In Drama, Vol. 16, Oct. 1925)
The Fifteenth Candle (see Field, Rachel Lyman)
Figaro's Marriage (see Beaumarchais, Pierre Augustin Caron de)
The Fight for Barbara (see Lawrence, David Herbert)

The Fight for Life (see Lorentz, Pare)
The Fighter (see Eisenstein, Mark)
The Fighting Cock (see Anouilh, Jean)
FIGUEIREDO, Guilherme
    O Asilado
        (In Revista de Teatro, no. 328)
Filigrane (see Fortuno, Claude)
FILIPPO, Edward de, 1900-
    Filumena Marturano
        (In Genius of the Italian Theatre)
    Oh, These Ghosts! based on "Questi Fantasmi!" translated by
    Louise H. Warner and Marguerita Carra
        (In Tulane Drama Review, Vol. 8, Spring 1964)
FILIPPONE, Vincenzo
    Ichheit on a Holiday
        (In Drama & Theatre, Vol. 7, no. 3)
La Fille Aux Yeux d'Or (see Albicocco, Jean-Gabriel)
La Fille Bien Gardee (see Labiche, Eugene)
Une Fille Dans Ma Soupe (see Frisby, Terence)
FILLIA
    Mechanical Sensuality
        (In TDR/The Drama Review, Vol. 15, Fall 1970)
Film (see Beckett, Samuel)
Film und Frau; Shakespeare the Sadist (see Nyssen, Ute)
Un Fils Unique (see Polac, Michel)
Filumena Marturano (see Filippo, Edward de)
Fin de Carnaval (see Topol, Josef)
Finally I am Born (see Davidson, Madeline)
FINCH, Robert, 1900-
    The Far Distant Shore, by Robert Finch and Betty Smith
        (In Best One-Act Plays of 1945, N.Y.)
    Summer Comes to the Diamond O, by Robert Finch and Betty
    Smith
        (In Best One-Act Plays of 1940, N.Y.)
    Western Night (see Smith, Betty)
Find Your Way Home (see Hopkins, John)
FINE, Sylvia (Mrs. Danny Kaye), 1913-
    Local Board Makes Good, by Sylvia Fine and Max Liebman
        (In Theatre Arts, Vol. 26, Sept. 1942)
The Finger of God (see Wilde, Percival)
Finian's Rainbow (see Kushner, Morris Hyman)
FINKEL, Donald
    The Jar
        (In Quarterly Review of Literature, Vol. 12, no. 1-2, 1962)
FINN, John, Jr.
    Fan Tan
        (In The Banner Anthology of One-Act Plays by American
        Authors)
Finnegans Wake (see Joyce, James)
Fiorello! (see Bock, Jerry)
The Firebugs (see Frisch, Max)
The Firefly (see Yirenchi, Emmanuel)

The Fireman's Ball (see Forman, Milos)
Fireside Diplomacy (see Cheltnam, Charles Smith)
FIRKINS, Oscar W., 1864-1932
    After Twenty-Five Years
        (In Drama, Vol. 15, Feb. 1925)
    The Looking-Glass
        (In Drama, Vol. 16, Feb. 1926)
    The Reference
        (In Drama, Vol. 14, Mar./Apr. 1924)
    The Reticent Convict
        (In Drama, Vol. 18, Feb. 1928)
    Two Passengers for Chelsea
        (In 50 More Contemporary One-Act Plays)
The First of April (see Boaden, Caroline)
The First White Woman (see Hughes, Babette Piechner)
The Firstborn (see Fry, Christopher)
FISCHBORN, Gottfried
    Mildernde Umstände Keine
        (In Theater der Zeit, no. 2, 1972)
FISHER, David
    Music Hath Charms
        (In Lacy's Plays)
FISHER, Jasper, fl. 1639
    Fuimus Troes: The True Trojans
        (In Dodsley's A Select Collection of Old English Plays, Vol.
        12)
        (In Dodsley's A Select Collection of Old Plays, Vol. 7)
The Fisherman (see Tree, Jonathan)
Fit as a Fiddle (see Hughes, Babette)
FITCH, Clyde, 1865-1909
    Captain Jinks of the Horse Marines
        (In The Modern Theatre, ed. by Eric Bentley, Vol. 4)
    The Truth
        (In Best Plays of the Early American Theatre, from the
        beginning to 1916)
FITZ-BALL, Edward, 1792-1873
    The Devil's Elixir; or, The Shadowless Man, founded on Hoff-
    man's "Die Elixiere des Teufels."
        (In Cumberland's British Theatre, Vol. 7, no. 6)
    The Floating Beacon
        (In Cumberland's British Theatre, Vol. 10, no. 6)
    The Flying Dutchman; or, The Phantom Ship; with music by
    G. H. Rodwell
        (In Cumberland's British Theatre, Vol. 16, no. 3)
    The Fortunes of Nigel
        (In Cumberland's British Theatre, Vol. 26, no. 7)
    Hofer, the Tale of the Tyrol
        (In Cumberland's British Theatre, Vol. 23, no. 1)
    The Inchcape Bell; with music by G. H. Rodwell
        (In Cumberland's British Theatre, Vol. 6, no. 7)
    The Innkeeper of Abbeville
        (In Cumberland's British Theatre, Vol. 17, no. 6)

Joan of Arc; or, The Maid of Orleans
(In Cumberland's British Theatre, Vol. 30, no. 6)
Koeuba; or, The Pirate Vessel
(In Cumberland's British Theatre, Vol. 40, no. 2)
Mary Glastonbury; or, The Dream Girl of the Devil-Holl
(In Cumberland's British Theatre, Vol. 34, no. 7)
Peveril of the Peak; or, The Days of King Charles II; founded
upon the celebrated romance of the same name of Sir Walter
Scott; music by James Dewar and William Ware.
(In Cumberland's British Theatre, Vol. 25, no. 5)
The Pilot; taken from the well-known tale of James Fenimore
Cooper
(In Cumberland's British Theatre, Vol. 7, no. 1)
Robin Hood; or, The Merry Outlaws of Sherwood
(In Lacy's Acting Plays, Vol. 14)
Thalaba, the Destroyer
(In Cumberland's British Theatre, Vol. 42, no. 9)
Wardock Kennilson; or, The Wild Woman of the Village
(In Cumberland's British Theatre, Vol. 45, no. 5)
FITZGERALD, Francis Scott Key, 1896-1940
*The Disenchanted (fiction) (see Schulberg, Budd)
*An Interview with F. Scott Fitzgerald (see Hunter, Paul)
"Send Me In, Coach"
(In Esquire, Vol. 6, Nov. 1936)
Five Days (see Zeiger, Henry)
The Five Dollar Bill (see Mosel, Tad)
Five Easy Payments (see Lewin, John)
Five Finger Exercise (see Shaffer, Peter)
Five Minutes (see Slade, Philip)
Flagrantes do Rio (see Sampaio, Silveira)
FLANAGAN, Hallie F.
The Curtain
(In Drama, Vol. 13, Feb. 1923)
FLANNER, Hildegarde
Mansions
(In 50 Contemporary One-Act Plays)
Flare Path (see Rattigan, Terence)
Flash-Back (see Aklom, Mikhail)
The Flattering Word (see Kelly, George)
Uma Flauta Para o Negro (see Bloch, Pedro)
FLAVIN, Martin A.
Caleb Stove's Death Watch
(In Drama, Vol. 14, Jan. 1924)
FLEISSER, Marieluise
Fegefeuer in Ingolstadt
(In Theater Heute, Jan. 1972)
FLEMING, Berry
The Acrobats
(In First Stage, Vol. 1, no. 1, Winter 1961/62)
Fletcher, John, 1579-1625
Bonduca (see Beaumont, Francis)
The Chances (see Beaumont, Francis)

The Knight of the Burning Pestle (see Beaumont, Francis)
The Maid's Tragedy (see Beaumont, Francis)
Philaster (see Beaumont, Francis)
Rule a Wife and Have a Wife (see Beaumont, Francis)
The Widow (see Jonson, Ben)
FLETCHER, Lucille (Mrs. J. D. Wallop III), 1912-
  The Hitch Hiker
    (In Radio's Best Plays, 1947)
  My Client, Curley (see Corwin, Norman Lewis)
  Sorry, Wrong Number
    (In Plays from Radio, 1948)
    (In 15 American One-Act Plays)
    (In 24 Favorite One-Act Plays)
Fleur de Cactus (see Barillet, Pierre)
FLEXNER, Hortense
  The Fawn
    (In Drama, Vol. 11, June 1921)
Flight (see Foote, Horton)
Flight Cage (see Hadler, Walter)
Flight from Destiny (see Stevenson, Dorothy)
Flight of the Dove (see Wilson, Donald)
The Flight of the Herons (see Kennard, Marietta C.)
The Flight of the Natives (see Richardson, Willis)
Flight of the Sea Warriors (see Johnson, Wallace)
Flittermouse (see Reely, Mary Katherine)
The Floating Beacon (see Fitz-Ball, Edward)
Flood (see Grass, Günter)
The Floor (see Swenson, May)
A Flor da Pele (see De Castro, Consuelo)
A Flor e o Fruto (see Cavalcanti Borges, Jose Carlos)
Flora (see Bennett, Arnold)
A Florentine Tragedy (see Wilde, Oscar)
FLORESS, Isadora
  Helene et l'Amour, ou La Verite d'Aphrodite
    (In Plaisir de France, supplement theatral, no. 349, Nov.
    1967)
FLORIN, Peter
  There's Money Coming to You
    (In The One-Act Theatre, Vol. 1)
Flower (see Whiteman, Robert)
FLOWER, Pat
  The Tape Recorder
    (In Best Short Plays, 1969)
FLOYD, Carlisle
  Susannah; a musical drama in two acts
    (In Theatre Arts, Vol. 42, Jan. 1958)
Fly Blackbird (see Jackson, C. B.)
The Flying Dutchman; or, The Phantom Ship (see Fitz-Ball, Edward)
The Flying Nun (see Slade, Bernard)
Une Fois par Semaine (see Resnik, Muriel)
FOISSY, Guy
  Coeur a Deux

(In L'Avant-Scene du Theatre, no. 469-470, April 1-15, 1971)
Le Discours du Pere
   (In L'Avant Scene du Theatre, no. 480, Oct. 1, 1971)
En Regardant Tomber les Murs
   (In Plaisir de France, supplement theatral, no. 328, Feb.
   1966)
Zanet Kloubu (L'Arthrite)
   (In Divaldo, January 1970)
Folle Amanda (see Barillet, P.)
Follies of Calandro (see Dovizi, Bernardo, da Bibbiene, cardinal)
Followers (see Brighouse, Harold)
Folly As It Flies (see Reynolds, Frederick)
Folly of Seithenyn (see Ethridge, Ken)
FONDA, Peter
   Easy Rider, filmscript by Peter Fonda, Dennis Hopper and
   Terry Southern
   (New American Library Screenplays)
   Easy Rider; scenario et dialogue Peter Fonda, Dennis Hopper,
   Terry Southern; text in French
   (In L'Avant-Scene du Cinema, no. 117, Sept. 1971)
Fontainbleau (see O'Keeffe, John)
Football (see Swan, Jon)
FOOTE, Horton
   The Dancers
   (In Harrison, Texas: 8 Television Plays)
   The Death of the Old Man
   (In Harrison, Texas: 8 Television Plays)
   Expectant Relations
   (In Harrison, Texas: 8 Television Plays)
   Flight
   (In Television Plays for Writers, 1957)
   John Turner Davis
   (In Best Short Plays, 1953/54)
   (In Harrison, Texas: 8 Television Plays)
   The Midnight Caller
   (In Harrison, Texas: 8 Television Plays)
   The Old Man, adapted from a story by William Faulkner
   (In Three Plays)
   Roots in a Parched Garden
   (In Three Plays)
   Screenplay of To Kill a Mockingbird, based on the novel by
   Harper Lee.
   (Harcourt, Brace & World Screenplay)
   The Tears of My Sister
   (In Harrison, Texas: 8 Television Plays)
   Tomorrow, adapted from a story by William Faulkner
   (In Three Plays)
   The Trip to Bountiful
   (In Harrison, Texas: 8 Television Plays)
   A Young Lady of Property
   (In Best Television Plays)
   (In Harrison, Texas: 8 Television Plays)

FOOTE, Samuel, 1720-1777
    The Liar
      (In The London Stage, Vol. 1)
    The Mayor of Garratt
      (In Cumberland's British Theatre, Vol. 23, no. 2)
    The Minor
      (In Bell's British Theatre, 1797, Vol. 2)
The Footsteps of Doves (see You Know I Can't Hear You When the
    Water's Running)
For a Maiden Whom Nobody Pities (see Mainardi, Renato)
For All Time (see Wellman, Rita)
For Each Man Kills (see Agoston, Gerty)
For England, Ho! (see Pocock, Isaac)
For Services Rendered (see Maugham, William Somerset)
For the Love of Michael (see Hughes, Glenn)
For the Time Being (see Auden, Wystan Hugh)
The Forced Marriage (see Moliere, Jean Baptiste Poquelin)
FORD, John, 1586?-ca. 1640
    The Sun's Darling (see Dekker, Thomas)
    'Tis a Pity She's a Whore
      (In Great English Plays)
    The Witch of Edmonton (see Rowley, William)
Ford, John, 1895-1973
    The Grapes of Wrath (see Johnson, Nunnally)
    How Green Was My Valley (see Dunne, Philip)
    The Informer (see Nichols, Dudley)
    Stagecoach (see Nichols, Dudley)
The Foreign Girl (La Gringa) (see Sahcnez, Florencio)
FOREMAN, Carl
    High Noon; filmscript based on "The Tin Star" by John M.
    Cunningham
      (In Film Scripts Two)
FOREMAN, Stephen H.
    The Resolution of Mossie Wax
      (In Scripts, Vol. 1, no. 8, June 1972)
Forensic and the Navigators (see Shepard, Sam)
The Forest Oracle; or, The Bridge of Tresino (see Campbell, M.)
La Foret (see Ostrovskii, Alexsandr Nikolaevich)
The Forgotten Land (see Hoffman, Leo Calvin)
Forgotten Souls (see Pinski, David)
FORLANI, Remo
    Le Mystere de l'Atelier Quinze; court metrage d'Alain Resnais
    et Andre Heinrich. Scenario original Remo Forlani.
      (In L'Avant-Scene du Cinema, no. 61-62, July/Sept. 1966)
FORMAN, Milos
    Les Amours d'une Blonde. Titre original: "Lasky Jedne
    Plavovlasky."
      (In L'Avant-Scene du Cinema, no. 60, 1966)
    The Fireman's Ball
      (In Modern Filmscripts Series)
    Loves of a Blonde
      (In Modern Filmscripts Series)

Taking Off, screenplay by Milos Forman, John Carriere and
John Klein.
    (New American Library Screenplays)
The Formation Dancers (see Marcus, Frank)
FORNES, Maria Irene
    Dr. Kheal
        (In The Best of Off Off Broadway)
        (In Yale/Theatre, Vol. 1, no. 3, Winter 1968)
    The Successful Life of Three: A Skit for Vaudeville
        (In Playwrights for Tomorrow, Vol. 2)
        (In Eight Plays from Off-Off Broadway)
    Tango Palace
        (In Playwrights for Tomorrow, Vol. 2)
Forrobodo (see Peixoto, Luiz)
FORSELL, Lars
    Charlie McDeath
        (In Literary Review, Vol. 9, Winter 1965/66)
    The Coronation
        (In Players Magazine, Vol. 40, no. 2, Nov. 1963)
Forster, Edward Morgan, 1879-1950
    **A Passage to India (see Rau, Santha Rama)
FORSYTH, James, 1913-
    Heloise
        (In Theatre Arts, Vol. 43, Jan. 1959)
Fortunata Writes a Letter (see Apstein, Theodore)
Fortune and Men's Eyes (see Herbert, John)
The Fortune Cookie (see Wilder, Billy)
Fortune Mends (see Calderon de la Barca, Pedro)
Fortune's Fool (see Reynolds, Frederick)
Fortune's Frolic (see Allingham, John Till)
The Fortunes of Nigel (see Fitz-Ball, Edward)
FORTUNO, Claude
    Confrontation
        (In L'Avant Scene du Theatre, no. 451, June 15, 1970)
    Filigrane
        (In L'Avant-Scene du Theatre, no. 507, Dec. 1, 1972)
    La Victime
        (In Plaisir de France, supplement theatral, no. 368, June
        1969)
The Forty Thieves (Anon.)
        (In Cumberland's British Theatre, Vol. 40, no. 5)
The Forty-Seven Ronin (Chushingura) (see Takeda, Izumo)
Foscari, Francesco, c. 1370-1457
    *Foscari (see Mitford, Mary Russell)
    *The Two Foscari: An Historical Tragedy (see Byron, George
        Gordon Noël Byron, 6th baron)
Foster, Lewis R.
    Mr. Smith Goes to Washington (see Buchman, Sidney)
FOSTER, Paul, 1931-
    Balls
        (In Eight Plays from Off-Off Broadway)
    Tom Paine
        (In Evergreen Playscript Series, no. 21)

The Foundling (see Mapes, Victor)
The Foundling of the Forest (see Dimond, William)
The 400 Blows (see Truffaut, Francois)
Four Infiltration Pieces (see Estrin, Marc)
4 Pieces sur Jardin (see Barillet, P.)
The Four P's (see Heyward, John)
The Foure Prentises of London (see Heywood, Thomas)
The Fourposter (see Hartog, Jan de)
Foursome (see Ionesco, Eugene)
Fourteen (see Gerstenberg, Alice)
Fourth of July Picnic (see Faulk, John)
Les Fous de la Mer (see Helias, Pierre Jakez)
FOWLER, Gene, 1891-1960
    The Mighty Barnum; a screenplay by Gene Fowler and Bess
    Meredyth, directed by Walter Lang.
        (A Covici-Friede Screenplay, 1934)
The Fox Mound (Kutsune-zuka) (see Sakanishi, Shio)
FOY, Helen
    Corfe Gate
        (In Best One-Act Plays of 1942/43, London)
    "Poor Caro!"
        (In Best One-Act Plays of 1949, London)
Fragments (see Schisgal, Murray)
Le Francais Tel Qu'on le Parle (see Didier, Pierre)
FRANCE, Anatole, 1844-1924
    **"Das Hemd Eines Gluchlichen" (see Wagner, Bernd)
    The Man Who Married a Dumb Wife
        (In 30 Famous One-Act Plays)
Francesca da Rimini, d. 1285?
    *Francesca da Rimini (see Boker, George Henry)
FRANCIS, James Oswald, 1882-
    Birds of a Feather
        (In 24 One-Act Plays, Revised edition, 1954)
    The Poacher
        (In Theatre Arts, Vol. 9, May 1925)
FRANCIS, William
    Portrait of a Queen
        (In Plays of the Year, Vol. 30, 1965)
FRANCKLIN, Thomas, 1721-1784
    The Earl of Warwick, adapted from "The Grecian" by La Harpe
        (In Bell's British Theatre, 1797, Vol. 17)
Francois II, Dauphin puis, King of France, 1544-1560
    *La Princesse de Cleves (see Dorfmann, Robert)
Francoise' Luck (see Porto-Riche, Georges de)
FRANJU, Georges, 1912-
    Hotel des Invalides
        (In L'Avant-Scene du Cinema, no. 38, 1964)
    Le Sang des Betes
        (In L'Avant-Scene du Cinema, no. 41, 1964)
Frank, Anne, 1929-1944
    Diary of Anne Frank (see Goodrich, Frances)
FRANK, Mrs. Florence Kiper

The Home for the Friendly
  (In 50 More Contemporary One-Act Plays)
Over the Hills and Far Away
  (In Drama, Vol. 11, Dec. 1920)
The Return of Proserpine
  (In Drama, Vol. 11, Aug./Sept. 1921)
The Three Spinners
  (In Drama, Vol. 16, Feb. 1926)
Frank Sinatra 4815 (see Bethencourt, Joao)
Frank V (see Dürrenmatt, Friedrich)
FRANKEL, Doris
  Journey for an Unknown Soldier
  (In Best One-Act Plays of 1943, N.Y.)
FRANKEL, Marvin
  The Ventriloquist
  (In Chicago Review, Vol. 22, Jan./Feb. 1971)
Frankie and Albert (see Hughes, Elizabeth Wilson)
Franklin, Benjamin, 1706-1790
  *Ben Franklin in Paris (see Sandrich, Mark)
Franklin, Sidney, 1893
  The Good Earth (see Jennings, Talbot)
Franziska Lesser (see Müller, Armin)
Il Frate (see Grazzini, Antonio Francesco, called Il Lasca)
FRATTI, Mario, 1927-
  L'Academia; both French and English texts are included.
  (In Italian Theatre Review, Vol. 13, Jan./Mar. 1964)
  (In Best Short Plays of the World Theatre, 1958/67)
  Betrayals
  (In Drama & Theatre, Vol. 7, no. 3, 1969)
  The Cage
  (In New Theatre of Europe, 1962)
  Confidenze a Pagamento; both French and English texts are
  included.
  (In Italian Theatre Review, Vol. 13, Jan./Mar. 1964)
  In Altesa; both French and English texts are included
  (In Italian Theatre Review, Vol. 13, Jan./Mar. 1964)
  The Refrigerators
  (In Modern International Drama, Vol. 3, no. 1, 1969)
  Il Ritorno; both French and English texts are included.
  (In Italian Theatre Review, Vol. 13, Jan./Mar. 1964)
  The Suicide
  (In New Theatre of Europe, 1962)
  La Telefonta; both French and English texts are included.
  (In Italian Theatre Review, Vol. 13, Jan./Mar. 1964)
  The Third Daughter
  (In First Stage, Vol. 5, Fall 1966)
Frazier, Charles
  Gas (see Kaprow, Allan)
FREDA, Frank
  The Corner
  (In Drama & Theatre, Vol. 7, no. 3)
Freddie the Pigeon (see Leichman, Seymour)

Freddy (see Southgate, Patsy)
Freddy (see Thomas, Robert)
Frederick II, Known as Prince of Homburg, 1633-1708
    *Prince Frederick of Homburg (see Kleist, Heinrich von)
Frederick II, the Great, 1712-1786
    *Frederick the Great (see Maddox, Frederick More)
FREDERICKS, Claude, 1923-
    A Summer Ghost
        (In New American Plays, Vol. 1)
The Free Knights (see Reynolds, Frederick)
Free This Day; A Trial in Seven Exhibits (see Novas, Himilce)
Freedom (see Reed, John)
Freedom Left Out in the Rain (see Mazzucco, Roberto)
The Freezer (see Bergen, Candice)
Freight (see White, Kenneth)
Der Freischutz; or, The Bill! the Belle!! and the Bullet!!! (see
    Byron, Henry James)
Der Freischutz; or, The Seventh Bullet (see Weber, Carl Maria
    von)
French Gray (see Bush, Josef)
French Without Tears (see Rattigan, Terence)
Frenzy for Two or More (see Ionesco, Eugene)
Frere, John Hookham, 1769-1846
    The Rovers (see Canning, George)
Les Freres (see Praga, Andre)
Les Freres Karamazov (see Copeau, Jacques)
Friar Bacon and Friar Bungay (see Greene, Robert)
FRIDA, Emil Bohslav, 1853-1912
    At the Chasm
        (In Poet Lore, Vol. 24, Autumn 1913)
    The Vengeance of Catullus
        (In Poet Lore, Vol. 25, Winter 1914)
    The Witness
        (In Poet Lore, Vol. 25, Winter 1914)
Friday (see Claus, Hugo)
Das Friedensfest (see Hauptmann, Gerhart Johann Robert)
FRIEDMAN, Bruce Jay, 1930-
    The Car Lover
        (In Esquire, Vol. 69, June 1968)
Friedman, Charles
    My Darlin' Aida (see Verdi, Giuseppe)
FRIEDMAN, Edward, 1933-
    Blood-Photo
        (In Best Short Plays, 1969)
FRIEL, Brian
    Losers
        (In Modern Short Comedies from Broadway & London)
The Friends (see Wesker, Arnold)
FRINGS, Ketti
    Look Homeward Angel, based on the book by Thomas Wolfe
        (In Best American Plays, Fifth series, 1957-63)
FRINK, Charles

The Human Accident
    (In First Stage, Vol. 1, no. 3, Summer 1962)
FRISBY, Terence
    There's a Girl in My Soup
    (In Plays of the Year, 1966, Vol. 32)
    (In Plays and Players, Vol. 13, Sept. 1966)
    Une Fille Mans Ma Soupe
    (In L'Avant Scene du Theatre, no. 464, Jan. 15, 1971)
FRISCH, Max, 1911-
    Biografie
    (In Atlas, Vol. 15, May 1968)
    The Chinese Wall
    (In Theatre Arts, Vol. 47, No. 8/9, Aug./Sept. 1963)
    (In Modern Theatre, ed. by R.W. Corrigan)
    Le Comte Oederland; musique de Jean-Claude Petit
    (In L'Avant-Scene du Theatre, no. 493, Apr. 15, 1972)
    Don Juan, or, The Love of Geometry
    (In his Three Plays)
    The Firebugs
    (In Best Short Plays of the World Theatre, 1958/67)
    The Great Rage of Philip Hotz
    (In his Three Plays)
    Philip Hotz's Fury
    (In Esquire, Vol. 58, Oct. 1962)
    When the War Was Over
    (In his Three Plays)
Des Frites, des Frites, des Frites... (see Wesker, Arnold)
The Frogs (see Aristophanes)
From Bad to Worse (see Calderon de la Barca, Pedro)
From Morn to Midnight (see Kaiser, Georg)
From 7:15 to 8:00, the Entrance is Through the Hoop (see Alvarado,
    Rafael)
The Front Page (see Hecht, Ben)
The Front Porch (see Miles, Nadine)
FROST, Robert, 1875-1963
    A Masque of Mercy
    (In Atlantic, Vol. 180, Nov. 1947)
    A Way Out
    (In Seven Arts, Vol. 1, Feb. 1917)
FRY, Christopher, 1907-
    Curtmantle
    (In Oxford University Press Plays of Fry)
    The Firstborn
    (In Religious Drama, Vol. 1)
    The Lady's Not for Burning; text in French
    (In L'Avant Scene du Theatre, no. 301, Dec. 15, 1963)
    A Phoenix Too Frequent
    (In English One-Act Plays of Today)
    (In Hudson Review, Vol. 3, Summer 1950)
    A Sleep of Prisoners
    (In The Modern Theatre, ed. by R.W. Corrigan)
Fuente Ovejuna (see Vega Carpio, Lope Felix de)

Fugir, Casar ou Morrer (see Magalhaes Junior, Raymundo)
The Fugitive (see Reynolds, Frederick)
The Fugitive Kind (see Orpheus Descending)
Fuimus Troes: The True Trojans (see Fisher, Jasper)
FULDA, Ludwig, 1862-1939
    By Ourselves
    (In Short Plays by Representative Authors, 1920)
FULHAM, William Henry
    The Devil Comes to Alcaraz
    (In Theatre Arts, Vol. 14, Sept. 1930)
Full Circle (see Pedrolo, Manuel de)
A Full Moon in March (see Yeats, William Butler)
Fuller, Dean
    Once Upon a Mattress (see Rodgers, Mary)
FULLER, Samuel, 1911-
    Shock Corridor
    (In L'Avant-Scene du Cinema, no. 54, 1965)
Fumed Oak (see Coward, Noël Pierce)
The Funeral; or, Grief Alamode (see Steele, Richard)
Funnyhouse of a Negro (see Kennedy, Adrienne)
Furie (see Lang, Fritz)
Furnished Apartments (see H. A. Y, pseud.)
Furthman, Jules, 1888-1966
    The Good Earth (see Jennings, Talbot)
    Morocco (see Von Sternberg, Josef)
    Shanghai Express (see Von Sternberg, Josef)
Fury (see Lang, Fritz)
The Future Is In Eggs; or, It Takes All Sorts to Make a World
    (see Ionesco, Eugene)
Futz (see Owens, Rochelle)
FYLEMAN, Rose, 1877-1957
    In Arcady
    (In Ten Fantasies for Stage and Study, 1932)

Le Gage (see Larger, Pierre)
GAGLIANO, Frank
    Father Uxbridge Wants to Marry
    (In Showcase 1)
GAINES, Frederick
    The New Chautauqua
    (In Playwrights for Tomorrow, Vol. 5)
GAINFORT, John
    Going Home
    (In Best One-Act Plays of 1949/50, N. Y.)
Galdos, Benito Perez (see Perez Galdos, Benito)
GALE, Zona (Breese), 1874-1938
    The Clouds
    (In New Plays for Women & Girls, 1932)
    Miss Lulu Bett
    (In The Pulitzer Prize Plays)
    The Neighbors
    (In 15 American One-Act Plays)

Galilei, Galileo, 1564-1642
*Galileo (see Brecht, Bertolt)
Gallathea (see Lyly, John)
Gallicanus (see Hrotsvit, of Gandersheim)
Gallo, Daniel
   Comme Les Chats (see Silvain, Jean)
Gallows Humor (see Richardson, Jack)
GALSWORTHY, John, 1867-1933
   Hall-Marked
      (In Atlantic, Vol. 113, June 1914)
   Justice
      (In Late Victorian Plays)
   The Little Dream
      (In Scribner's, Vol. 49, May 1911)
   The Little Man
      (In 30 Famous One-Act Plays)
   Loyalties
      (In Dramas by Present-Day Writers)
      (In Everybody's Magazine, Vol. 48, Feb. 1923)
      (In 16 Famous British Plays)
   Sekhet: A Dream
      (In Scribner's, Vol. 65, May 1919)
   The Sun
      (In Atlantic Book of Modern Plays, 1921)
GAMA, Jota
   Loucuras de Mamae
      (In Revista de Teatro, no. 299)
GAMBARO, Griselda
   The Camp
      (In Voices of Change in the Spanish American Theater)
The Gamblers (see Gogol, Nikolai Vasil'evich)
The Gambler's Fate; or, A Lapse of Twenty Years (see Thompson,
   Charles)
The Game Called Kiss (see Kemp, Harry Hibbard)
The Game of Chess (see Goodman, Kenneth Sawyer)
The Game of Love and Chance (see Marivaux, Pierre Carlet de
   Chamblain de)
The Gamester (see Moore, Edward)
The Gamesters (see Shirley, William)
Gammer Gurton's Needle (see Still, John)
The Gang's All Here (see Lawrence, Jerome)
Gap (see Ionesco, Eugene)
GARCIA Lorca, Federico, 1899-1936
   The Audience
      (In Evergreen Review, Vol. 2, no. 6, 1958)
   Blood Wedding
      (In Introduction to Literature: Plays)
   The House of Bernarda Alba
      (In Theatre Arts, Vol. 36, Mar. 1952)
   The Love of Don Perlimplin and Belisa in the Garden
      (In From the Modern Repertoire, Series One)
   La Maison de Bernarda Alba

(In L'Avant-Scene du Theatre, no. 452-453, July 1-15, 1970)
Mariana Pineda
    (In Tulane Drama Review, Vol. 7, Winter 1962)
    (In Chicago Review, Vol. 16, no. 4, 1964)
Le Petit Retable de Don Cristobal
    (In L'Avant-Scene du Theatre, no. 452-453, July 1-15, 1970)
Yerma
    (In Makers of the Modern Theatre, 1961)
    (In The Modern Theatre, ed. by R.W. Corrigan)
    (In Tragedy: Texts and Commentary, 1969)
Le Garde-Chasse (see Kobrynski, Lazare)
The Garden of Eden (see York Fullers' Play)
Garden Party (see Havel, Vaclay)
Le Gardien (see Pinter, Harold)
GARDNER, Gary
    Just Like in the Movies
    (In Story, the Yearbook of Discovery, 1968)
    A Train Going Somewhere
    (In Best Short Plays, 1968)
GARDNER, Herb, 1936
    A Thousand Clowns
    (In Theatre Arts, Vol. 48, Jan. 1964)
    Who is Harry Kellerman and Why Is He Saying Those Terrible
    Things About Me?
    (New American Library Screenplays, 1967)
Gargoyle (Oni-gawara) (see Sakanishi, Shio)
GARNETT, Louise Ayres, d. 1937
    Hilltop
    (In Drama, Vol. 11, May 1921)
    The Pig Prince
    (In Drama, Vol. 12, Apr. 1922)
GARNETT, Porter
    The Green Knight
    (In The Grove Plays of the Bohemian Club, Vol. 2)
GARNIER, Robert, 1534-1590
    Cornelia, by Robert Garnier, translated by Thomas Kyd
    (In Dodsley's A Select Collection of Old English Plays, Vol.
    5)
    (In Dodsley's A Select Collection of Old Plays, Vol. 2)
GARNUNG, Francis
    Les Membres de la Famille
    (In L'Avant-Scene du Theatre, no. 488, Feb. 1, 1972)
GARRETT, Jimmy
    And We Own the Night; a Play of Blackness
    (In TDR/The Drama Review, Vol. 12, Summer 1968)
GARRICK, David, 1717-1779, joint author
    The Clandestine Marriage, by George Colman & David Garrick
    (In Cumberland's British Theatre, Vol. 4, no. 3)
    (In Bell's British Theatre, 1797, Vol. 14)
    The Country Girl
    (In Cumberland's British Theatre, Vol. 23, no. 3)
    Cymon, adapted by Mr. Arne

(In Bell's British Theatre, 1797, Vol. 23)
Every Man in His Humor
   (In Bell's British Theatre, 1797, Vol. 4)
The Gamesters (see Shirley, William)
The Lying Valet
   (In The London Stage, Vol. 1)
Rule a Wife and Have a Wife (see Beaumont, Francis)
GARRO, Elena
   A Solid House
      (In Evergreen Review, Vol. 2, no. 7, 1959)
GARSON, Barbara
   MacBird
      (In Ramparts, Vol. 5, Dec. 1966)
      (An Evergreen Black Cat Play, 1967)
Gas (see Kaprow, Allen)
Gas I (see Kaiser, Georg)
The Gas Tank (see Smith, Peter J.)
The Gas-Burning Heart (see Tzara, Tristan)
Gascoigne, George, 1542?-1577
   Supposes (see Aristo, Lodovico)
Gaskell, Elizabeth Cleghorn Stevenson, 1810-1865
   **Followers (see Brighouse, Harold)
Gaston, Bonnier; or, Times Revenges (see Courtner, William
   Leonard)
GATESCHI, Rossana, 1924-
   Antigone lo Cassio; text in both French and English
      (In Italian Theatre Review, Vol. 12, July/Sept. 1963)
   L'Enclos (O Grada) by Armand Gratti, pseud.
      (In L'Avant-Scene du Cinema, no. 5, June 15, 1961)
   The Owl, by Armand Gatti (pseud.)
      (In Yale/Theatre, no. 2, Summer 1968)
   Le Vie Imaginaire de l'Eboueur Auguste Geai
      (In L'Avant Scene du Theatre, No. 272
O Gato Playboy (see Pinheiro, Jair)
Gatti, Guilio, pseud. (see Gateschi, Rossana)
Gautama Buddha (Prince Siddhartha), 568? B.C.-?483 B.C.
   *Buddha (see Hartmann, Sadakichi)
GAY, John, 1685-1732
   The Beggar's Opera
      (In Bell's British Theatre, 1797, Vol. 11)
      (In Cumberland's British Theatre, Vol. 15, no. 6)
   Three Hours after Marriage, by John Gay, Alexander Pope, and
   John Arbuthnot
      (In Burlesque Plays of the 18th Century)
   The Threepenny Opera (see Brecht, Bertolt)
   The What D'Ye Call It
      (In Burlesque Plays of the 18th Century)
The Gazing Globe (see Pillot, Joseph Eugene)
GAZZO, Michael Vincente, 1923-
   A Hatful of Rain
      (In Theatre Arts, Vol. 40, December 1956)
      (In Best American Plays, Fourth Series)

GEAR, Brian, 1936-
   A Pretty Row of Pretty Ribbons
     (In Best Short Plays, 1970)
   The Sky is Green
     (In Plays of the Year, Vol. 27, 1962/63)
GEHAN, Brendan
   The New House
     (In Best Short Plays of the World Theatre, 1958-67)
GEIGER, Milton
   One Special for Doc
     (In Plays From Radio, 1948)
Geist von Cranitz (see Köhler, Erich)
GELBER, Jack
   The Apple
     (In Evergreen Original Playscripts, E-291)
   The Connection
     (In 7 Plays of the Modern Theatre)
     (In Evergreen Original Playscripts, E-223)
   The Cuban Thing
     (In Evergreen Playscript Series)
   Square in the Eye
     (In Evergreen Original Playscripts, E-394)
GELLERT, Christian Fürchtegott, 1715-1769
   The Tender Sisters
     (In Theatrical Recorder, Vol. 1, no. 1, Dec. 1804)
Le Gelosia (see Grazzini, Antonio Francesco, called Il Lasca)
Le Gendre de M. Porrier (see Angier, Emile)
General Audax (see Mandel, Oscar)
Le General Inconnu (see Obaldia, Rene de)
The General Returns from One Place to Another (see O'Hara,
   Frank)
The General's Tea Party (see Vian, Boris)
Generation (see Wajda, Andrzej)
GENET, Jean, 1910-
   The Balcony
     (In Evergreen Playscript Series)
     (In 7 Plays of the Modern Theatre)
   The Blacks
     (In Evergreen Playscript Series)
   Deathwatch
     (In Evergreen Playscript Series)
     (In The Modern Theatre, ed. by R. W. Corrigan)
   The Maids
     (In Evergreen Playscript Series)
   The Screens
     (In Evergreen Playscript Series)
O Genro de Muitas Sogras (see Azevedo, Arthur)
Gentle Like a Dove (see Mackie, Albert)
The Gentle Shepherd (see Ramsay, Allan)
The Gentleman Caller (see Bullins, Ed.)
GENTLEMAN, Francis, 1728-1784

The Tobacconist
(In The London Stage, Vol. 2)
George a Greene, the Pinner of Wakefield (Anon.)
(In Dodsley's A Select Collection of Old Plays, Vol. 3)
George Barnwell (see Lillo, George)
George Dandin (see Moliere, Jean Baptists Poquelin)
George Washington Crossing the Delaware (see Koch, Kenneth)
George's Room (see Owen, Alun)
GEORGE-Schreiber, Isabelle
    Dialogue des Inconnus
        (In Plaisir de France, supplement theatral, no. 310, Aug.
        1964)
GERLACH, Friedrich
    Die Herren des Strandes
        (In Theater der Zeit, Nov. 1970)
GERMOZ, Alain
    Le Temoin
        (In Plaisir de France, supplement theatral, no. 298, Aug.
        1963)
Germs (see Sharp, H. Sutton)
GEROULD, Daniel C.
    Candaules, Commissioner
        (In First Stage, Vol. 4, Fall 1965)
    Explosion; an overpopulation farce for two actors and percussion
        (In Drama and Theatre, Vol. 9, no. 3, Spring 1971)
GERSHWIN, George, 1898-1937
    Of Thee I Sing, a musical comedy by George S. Kaufman and
        Morrie Riskind, with Music by George Gershwin and lyrics by
        Ira Gershwin
        (In Pulitzer Prize Plays)
        (In Famous Plays of Today, 1933)
Gershwin, Ira, 1896-
    Of Thee I Sing (see Gershwin, George)
GERSTENBERG, Alice
    Ever Young
        (In Drama, Vol. 12, Feb. 1922)
    Fourteen
        (In Drama, Vol. 10, Feb. 1920)
    Overtones
        (In 30 Famous One-Act Plays)
    The Pot Boiler
        (In 50 Contemporary One-Act Plays)
GESBERT, Bernard, 1932-
    Les Bonnes Soirees de Madame France
        (In L'Avant-Scene du Cinema, no. 126, June 1972)
GETHERS, Steven
    Cracker Money
        (In Best Television Plays of the Year, 1957)
    The Sandpile: Human Relations, God and Prayer, Death
        (In The Delinquent, the Hipster, the Square, and the Sandpile
        Series, ed. by Cox)

Getting Married (see Shaw, George Bernard)
Getting On (see Bennett, Alan)
Gettysburg (see Mackaye, Percy)
GEVEL, Claude
  Mon Mari s'Endort
    (In L'Avant-Scene du Theatre, no. 141)
  Va-t'en
    (In Plaisir de France, supplement theatral, no. 341, Mar.
    1967)
GHELDERODE, Michel de, 1898-1962
  Christopher Columbus, a dramatic fairy tale.
    (In Tulane Drama Review, Vol. 3, Mar. 1959)
  Escurial
    (In The Modern Theatre, ed. Eric Bentley, Vol. 5)
  Pantagleize
    (In New Theatre of Europe, 1962)
    (In Theatre Arts, Vol. 47, Aug. 1962)
The Ghost of Benjamin Sweet (see Gilsdorf, Frederick & Pauline)
The Ghost Sonata (see Strindberg, August)
Ghosts (see Ibsen, Jenrik Johan)
GIACOSA, Guiseppe, 1847-1906
  The Rights of the Soul
    (In 50 Contemporary One-Act Plays)
The Giant's Stair (see Steele, Wilbur Daniel)
GIBBS, Wolcott, 1902-1958
  Season in the Sun
    (In Theatre Arts, Vol. 35, June 1951)
GIBNEY, Sheridan
  The Story of Louis Pasteur, a screenplay by Sheridan Gibney
    and Pierre Collings, directed by William Dieterle
    (In Four-Star Scripts)
GIBSON, Lawrence
  Bumbo the Clown
    (In 50 More Contemporary One-Act Plays)
GIBSON, William, 1914-
  Dinny and the Witches
    (In Dinny and the Witches: Two Plays)
  Miracle en Alabama
    (In Plaisir de France, supplement theatral, no. 291, Jan.
    1963)
  The Miracle Worker
    (In Dinny and the Witches: Two Plays)
  The Miracle Worker; text in French
    (In L'Avant-Scene du Theatre, no. 279, Jan. 1, 1963)
  Two for the Seesaw
    (In Best American Plays, Fifth Series, 1957-63)
Gideon (see Chayefsky, Paddy)
GIELGUD, Val Henry, 1900-
  Chinese White
    (In Five Three-Act Plays, Strand, 1933)
GIFFORDS, Franklin Rent
  All or None
    (In Drama, Vol. 16, Mar. 1926)

Gigi (see Loos, Anita)
Gil Blas; or, The Boy of Santillane (see Macfarren, George)
Gilan, Yvonne, 1935-
    Les Peches (The Peaches) (see Gill, Michael)
GILBERT, Christie
    The Stocking
        (In Best One-Act Plays of 1932, London)
Gilbert, Marie Dolores Eliza Rosanna (see Montez, Lola)
GILBERT, Michael
    The Bargain
        (In Plays of the Year, Vol. 23, 1960/61)
GILBERT, William Schwenck, 1836-1911
    A Medical Man
        (In 26 Short & Amusing Plays, 1871)
GILL, Michael, 1927-
    Les Peches (The Peaches) by Michael Gill et Yvonne Gilan
        (In L'Avant-Scene du Cinema, no. 59, 1966)
GILL, Peter
    Over Gardens Out
        (In Plays and Players, Vol. 17, no. 4, Jan. 1970)
    The Sleepers Den
        (In Plays and Players, Vol. 17, no. 4, Jan. 1970)
GILLES, Ange
    Il y a une Vertu dans le Soleil
        (In L'Avant-Scene du Theatre, no. 468, Mar. 15, 1971)
        (In Plaisir de France, supplement theatral, no. 390)
GILLES, Guy, 1940-
    Au Biseau des Baisers
        (In L'Avant-Scene du Cinema, no. 19, Oct. 15, 1962)
GILLETTE, William Hooker, 1855-1937
    Secret Service
        (In Best Plays of the Early American Theatre, from the be-
        ginning to 1916)
    Sherlock Holmes, based on stories by Sir Arthur Conan Doyle
        (In 13 Famous Plays of Crime and Detection)
GILLIATT, Penelope
    Property
        (In The New Yorker, Vol. 46, May 2, 1970)
    Sunday Bloody Sunday
        (Viking Press Screenplays, 1972)
GILLMAN, Jonathan
    The Marriage Test
        (In Playwrights for Tomorrow, Vol. 6)
GILLOIS, Andre
    Monsieur Gogo
        (In Plaisir de France, supplement theatral, no. 348, Oct.
        1967)
GILROY, Frank D., 1925-
    The Subject Was Roses
        (In Best American Plays, Sixth series, 1963-67)
GILSDORF, Frederick & Pauline
    The Ghost of Benjamin Sweet
        (In Plays From Radio, 1948)

"Gimba, o Presidente dos Valentes" (see Guarnieri, Gianfrancesco)
Gin and Bitterness (see Richards, Stanley)
Ginger Anne (see Washburn, Deric)
GINSBURY, Norman
    The Shoemaker and the Devil; based on the story by Anton
    Chekhov
      (In Best Short Plays, 1968)
GINZBURG, Natalia
    Teresa
      (In L'Avant Scene du Theatre, no. 444, Mar. 1, 1970)
      (In Plaisir de France, Supplemental theatral, no. 377, Apr.
      1970)
The Gioconda Smile (see Huxley, Aldous Leonard)
GIONO, Jean, 1895-
    La Femme du Boulanger
      (In Plaisir de France, supplement theatral, no. 375, Feb.
      1970)
GIORLOFF, Ruth
    "Lavender and Red Pepper"
      (In New Plays for Women & Girls, 1932)
Giovanni, Jose, 1923-
    Le Trou (see Becker, Jacques)
Giovanni in London; or, The Libertine Reclaimed (see Moncrieff,
    William Thomas)
GIRARDEAU, Claude M.
    The God of the Wood
      (In Drama, Vol. 10, May 1920)
GIRAUDOUX, Jean, 1882-1944
    Amphitryon 38
      (In 16 Famous European Plays)
      (In his Three Plays, Vol. 2)
    The Apollo of Bellac
      (In 24 Favorite One-Act Plays)
      (In his Four Plays, Vol. 1)
    Electra
      (In The Modern Theatre, ed. by R. W. Corrigan)
      (In The Modern Theatre, Vol. 1, ed. by Eric Bentley)
      (In his Three Plays, Vol. 2)
    The Enchanted, adapted by Maurice Valency from Giraudoux's
    "Intermezzo"
      (The Theatre Arts, Vol. 34, Oct. 1950)
      (In his Four Plays, Vol. 1)
    La Guerre de Troie n'Aura Pas Lieu
      (In L'Avant Scene du Theatre, no. 479, Sept. 15, 1971)
    Judith
      (In The Modern Theatre, ed. by Eric Bentley, Vol. 3)
    The Madwoman of Chaillot, adapted by Maurice Valency
      (In Theatre Arts, Vol. 33, Nov. 1949)
      (In 20 Best European Plays of the American Stage)
      (In his Four Plays, Vol. 1)
    Ondine, adapted by Maurice Valency
      (In Theatre Arts, Vol. 38, Dec. 1954)

(In 20 Best European Plays on the American Stage)
(In his Four Plays, Vol. 1)
Paris Impromptu
   (In Theatre Arts, Vol. 22, Mar. 1938)
Siegfried
   (In his Three Plays, Vol. 2)
Sodom and Gomorrah
   (In Makers of the Modern Theater, 1961)
Song of Songs
   (In Tulane Drama Review, Vol. 3, May 1959)
   (In Makers of the Modern Theater, 1961)
   (In Genius of the French Theater)
Tiger at the Gates
   (In 20 Best European Plays on the American Stage)
A Girl for Buddy (see Saul, Milton)
The Girl from Kakata, or Love at Sea (Hakata Kojoro Namimakura)
   (see Chikamatsu Monzaemon)
The Girl from Samos (see Menander)
The Girl from Stockholm (see Leto, Alfonso)
The Girl in the Coffin (see Dreiser, Theodore)
The Girl Who Slipped (see Campbell, Lawton)
Give All Thy Terrors to the Wind (see Sifton, Claire)
"Give Us This Day" (see Barzman, Ben)
GLADKOV, Alexander
   The Unknown Sailor
      (In Soviet One-Act Plays)
Glanz und Tod Joaquin Murietas (see Neruda, Pablo)
GLAPTHORNE, Henry, fl. 1635-1643
   The Lady Mother
      (In A Collection of Old English Plays, Vol. 2)
GLASPELL, Susan, 1882-1948
   Allison's House
      (In Pulitzer Prize Plays)
   Bernice
      (In Theatre Arts, Vol. 3, 1919)
   Suppressed Desires
      (In 30 Famous One-Act Plays)
   Trifles
      (In Dramas by Present-Day Writers)
      (In 15 American One-Act Plays)
      (In 24 Favorite One-Act Plays)
      (In 50 Contemporary One-Act Plays)
      (In English One-Act Plays of Today)
      (In 25 Best Plays of the Modern American Theatre, Early
      series, 1916-1929)
The Glass Menagerie (see Williams, Tennessee)
GLICK, Carl
   Ten Days Later
      (In Drama, Vol. 11, Feb. 1921)
Glickman, Will, 1910-
   Plain and Fancy (see Hague, Albert Martin)
Gloriana; or, The Court of Augustus Caesar (see Lee, Nathaniel)

Glory Day (see Lake, Goldie)
Glory in the Flower (see Inge, William)
GLOVER, Richard, 1712-1785
    Boadicea
      (In Bell's British Theatre, 1797, Vol. 2)
      (In Cumberland's British Theatre, Vol. 34, no. 6)
    Medea (see Seneca)
Gloves, a Fragment of the Eternal Duet (see Cannan, Gilbert)
Gnädiges Fräulein (see Williams, Tennessee)
The Goal (see Jones, Henry Arthur)
Goat Song (see Werfel, Franz V.)
The Go-Between (see Pinter, Harold)
The Goblins (see Suckling, Sir John)
God and Texas (see Ardrey, Robert)
God Bless (see Feiffer, Jules)
God Bless Us, Everyone (see Mel, Charles L., Jr.)
The God of the Wood (see Girardeau, Claude M.)
GODARD, Jean-Luc, 1930-
    Alphaville
      (In Modern Film Scripts Series)
    A Bout de Souffle, d'apres un sujet de Francois Truffaut
      (In L'Avant-Scene du Cinema, no. 79, Mar. 1968)
    Charlotte et Son Jules
      (In L'Avant-Scene du Cinema, no. 5, Jan. 15, 1961)
    La Chinoise
      (In L'Avant-Scene du Cinema, no. 114, May 1971)
    Une Femme Mariee (La Femme Mariee)
      (In L'Avant-Scene du Cinema, no. 46, 1965)
    El Grand Escroc
      (In L'Avant-Scene du Cinema, no. 46, 1965)
    Une Histoire d'Eau (see Truffaut, Francois)
    Le Petit Soldat
      (In Modern Film Scripts Series)
      (In Cahiers du Cinema, Vol. 20, nos. 119, 120, May, June
        1961)
    Pierro Le Fou
      (In Modern Film Scripts Series)
    2 ou 3 Choses que Je Sais d'Elle
      (In L'Avant-Scene du Cinema, no. 70, 1967)
    Vivre Sa Vie, Film en Douze Tableaux
      (In L'Avant-Scene du Cinema, no. 19, Oct. 15, 1962)
    Weekend
      (In Modern Film Scripts Series)
    Wind from the East
      (In Modern Film Scripts Series)
Godbug (see Cavander, Kenneth)
The Goddess (see Chayefsky, Paddy)
GODEFROY, Vincent
    Blessed Above Women
      (In Best One-Act Plays of 1937, London)
Godiva, Lady, d. 1080
    *Peeping Tom of Coventry (see O'Keeffe, John)

*Scandal at Coventry (see Ashton, Winifred)
Gods of the Lightning (see Anderson, Maxwell)
God's Promises (see Bale, John, bp of Ossory)
GODSEY, Townsend
    A Meeting in the Woods
        (In Players Magazine, Vol. 38, no. 6, Mar. 1962)
Goemons (see Bellon, Yannick)
GÖREY, Gabor, 1902-
    Afternoon Tea
        (In Modern International Drama, Vol. 2, no. 2, 1968)
GOERING, Reinhard, 1887-1936
    Naval Engagement (Seeschlacht)
        (In Drama & Theatre, Vol. 10, no. 1, Fall 1971)
GOETHE, Johann Wolfgang von, 1749-1832
    *Die Aufgeregten Von Goethe (see Muschg, Adolf)
    Egmont
        (In The Classic Theatre, ed. by Eric Bentley, Vol. 2)
    Faust, part 1
        (In Genius of the German Theater)
    **Ironhand (see Arden, John)
GOGGAN, John Patrick, 1907-
    The Hasty Heart, by John Patrick, pseud.
        (In Best Plays of the Modern American Theatre, Second
        series)
    The Teahouse of the August Moon, by John Patrick, pseud.
        (In Best American Plays, Supp. Vol.)
        (In Theatre Arts, Vol. 39, June 1955)
Gogh, Vincent van, 1853-1890
    *Vincent van Gogh (see Hays, Hoffman R.)
    *Van Gogh; Court Metrage d'Alain Resnais (see Hessens,
        Robert)
GOGOL, Nikalai Vasil'evich, 1809-1952
    After the Play, translated by David Magarshack
        (In Tulane Drama Review, Vol. 4, Dec. 1959)
    Gamblers
        (In The Modern Theatre, ed. by Eric Bentley, Vol. 3)
        (In Collected Tales and Plays)
        (In Tulane Drama Review, Vol. 2, Nov. 1957)
    The Inspector General
        (In Masterworks of World Drama, Vol. 6)
        (In Collected Tales and Plays)
    The Marriage
        (In The Modern Theatre, ed. by Eric Bentley, Vol. 5)
        (In Collected Tales and Plays)
    Le Revizor
        (In L'Avant-Scene du Theatre, no. 398, Mar. 1, 1968)
Goin'a Buffalo (see Bullins, Ed)
GOING, Charles Buxton, 1863-
    Twilight of the Moon
        (In Ten Fantasies for Stage and Study, 1932)
Going Home (see Gainfort, John)
Going My Way (see Butler, Frank)

Going to Pot (see Feydeau, Georges)
Gold (see Myrtle, Frederick S.)
Gold Is Where You Don't Find It (see Conkle, Ellsworth Prouty)
The Gold Rush (see Chaplin, Charles)
The Gold Standard (see Koch, Kenneth)
The Goldbergs (see Berg, Gertrude)
GOLDEN, John, 1874-1955
    The Clock Shop; including musical score by John Golden
        (In Three John Golden Plays)
    The Robe of Wood
        (In Three John Golden Plays)
    The Vanishing Princess
        (In Three John Golden Plays)
        (In 50 More Contemporary One-Act Plays)
The Golden Arrow (see Webber, James Plaisted)
The Golden Axe (see Scholl, Ralph)
Golden Boy (see Odets, Clifford)
The Golden Bull of Boredom (see Yerby, Lorees)
The Golden Calf (see Jerrold, Douglas)
The Golden Circle (see Patrick, Robert)
The Golden Doom (see Dunsany, Lord)
The Golden Eagle Child (see Lobner, Joyce E.)
The Golden Farmer; or, The Last Crime (see Webster, Benjamin)
The Golden Fleece (see Grillparzer, Franz)
The Golden Fleece (see Gurney, A.R., Jr.)
Goldfish (see Andrews, Isobel)
GOLDING, William Gerald, 1911-
    The Brass Butterfly
        (In Genius of the Later English Theater)
GOLDMAN, James, 1927-
    Lion in Winter
        (In Best American Plays, Sixth series, 1963-67)
GOLDMAN, Paul
    Mermaid Avenue Is the World
        (In Best Short Plays, 1959/60)
GOLDMAN, William
    Butch Cassidy and the Sundance Kid
        (Bantam Books Noonday Original Screenplays)
GOLDONI, Carlo, 1707-1793
    Avarice and Ostentation
        (In Theatrical Recorder, Vol. 1, no. 3, Feb. 1805)
    The King Stag
        (In The Classic Theatre, ed. by Eric Bentley, Vol. 1)
    Le Menteur
        (In L'Avant-Scene du Theatre, no. 451, June 15, 1970)
        (In Plaisir de France, supplement theatral, no. 381, Aug.
        1970)
    The Servant of Two Masters
        (In Plays of the Year, Vol. 36, 1968/69)
        (In The Classic Theatre, ed. by Eric Bentley, Vol. 1)
GOLDSCHMIDT, Walter
    A Word in Your Ear
        (In Best Short Plays, 1953/54)

GOLDSMITH, Oliver, 1728-1774
   The Good Natured Man
      (In Bell's British Theatre, 1797, Vol. 17)
      (In Cumberland's British Theatre, Vol. 13, no. 2)
      (In The London Stage, Vol. 2)
   She Stoops to Conquer; or, The Mistakes of a Night
      (In Genius of the Later English Theater)
      (In Bell's British Theatre, 1797, Vol. 9)
      (In Cumberland's British Theatre, Vol. 11, no. 1)
      (In Great English Plays)
GOLL, Yvan
   Methusalem, or, The Eternal Bourgeois
      (In Plays for a New Theatre)
GOMBROWITZ, Witold
   Operette
      (In L'Avant-Scene du Theatre, no. 449, May 15, 1970)
      (In Theater Heute, Vol. 11, no. 2, Feb. 1970)
Gomer Pyle (see Elinson, Jack)
GOMES, Alfredo Dias
   Journey to Bahia, adapted from the Brazilian play "O Pagador
      de Promessas" by Stanley Richards
      (In Players Magazine, Vol. 49, no. 4, Jan. 1964)
   Payment as Pledged
      (In Modern Stage in Latin America, 1971)
GONCHAROV, Y.
   The Marksman
      (In Soviet One-Act Plays)
Gone Tomorrow (see Harrity, Richard)
GONTHIE, Max H.
   Maria et les Isles
      (In Plaisir de France, supplement theatral, no. 311, Sept.
      1964)
Gonza the Lancer (Yari no Gonza) (see Chikamatsu Monzaemon)
Gonzalo Sent la Violette (see Vattier, Robert)
The Good and Obedient Young Man (see Barr, Betty)
The Good Earth (see Jennings, Talbot)
The Good Hope (see Heijermans, Herman)
The Good Lieutenant (see Murray, Robert Bruce)
Good Night (see Smith, Marian Spencer)
Good Night, Caroline (see Seiler, Conrad)
A Good Shot (see Housman, Laurence)
A Good Woman (see Bennett, Arnold)
Goodbye, Dan Bailey (see Bernard, Kenneth)
Goodbye, Mr. Chips (see Sherriff, R. C.)
Goodbye to the Clown (see Kinoy, Ernest)
The Good-Looking Fellow; or, The Roman Nose (see Almar,
      George)
GOODMAN, Kenneth Sawyer
   Dust of the Road
      (In 15 American One-Act Plays)
   The Game of Chess
      (In 30 Famous One-Act Plays)

GOODMAN, Paul, 1911-
The Birthday
(In Theatre Experiment)
Faustina, Ritual Tragedy
(In Quarterly Review of Literature, Vol. 11, no. 2/3, 1961)
Theory of Tragedy
(In Quarterly Review of Literature, Vol. 5, no. 4, 1950)
The Good-Natured Man (see Goldsmith, Oliver)
Goodnight Please! (see Daggett, James L.)
GOODRICH, Frances
The Diary of Anne Frank, by Frances Goodrich and Albert
Hackett
(In Best American Plays, Supp. Vol.)
Diary of Anne Frank, by Frances Goodrich and Albert Hackett.
Text in French.
(In L'Avant-Scene du Theatre, no. 192, Mar. 1, 1959)
The Gooseberry Mandarin (see Ruthenburg, Grace Dorcus)
Gooseberry Tarts (see Lowe, Charles F.)
Gordon (see Boland Briget)
GORDON, Ruth, 1896-
Adam's Rib, film script by Ruth Gordon and Garson Kanin,
directed by George Cukor
(In MGM Library of Film Scripts Series)
The Leading Lady
(In Theatre Arts, Vol. 34, Feb. 1950)
Over Twenty-One (see Buchman, Sidney)
GORDON-Lennox, Cosmo Charles, 1869-
The Impertinence of the Creature
(In Representative One-Act Plays by British and Irish Authors)
Gorgonio (see Pinelli, Tullio)
Gorilla Queen (see Tavel, Ronald)
Gorki, Maxim (see Gor'kii, Maksim)
GOR'KII, Maksim, 1868-1936
Les Ennemis. French text by Francais d'Arthur Adamov, from
Maxime Gorki's play.
(In L'Avant-Scene du Theatre, no. 475, July 1, 1971)
The Lower Depths
(In The Modern Theatre, ed. by R.W. Corrigan)
(In 16 Famous European Plays)
GORMAN, Herbert Sherman, 1893-1954
The Death of Nero
(In Theatre Arts, Vol. 8, Mar. 1924)
(In 50 More Contemporary One-Act Plays)
GOROSTIZA, Carlos
Neighbors, translated and adapted by Louis L. Curcio
(In Drama & Theatre, Vol. 9, no. 2, Winter 1970/71)
GOROSTIZA, Celestino
The Color of Our Skin
(In Drama and Theatre, Vol. 9, no. 3, Spring 1971)
The Gospel Witch (see Phelps, Lyon)
GOTT, Henry
The Wizard of the Moor
(In Cumberland's British Theatre, Vol. 44, no. 8)

GOTTLIEB, Alex, 1906-
   Stud
      (In Best Short Plays, 1969)
GOTTLIEB, Joseph
   The Halls of Congress
      (In Radio Drama in Action, 1945)
GOTTLIEB, Saul
   American Atrocities in Vietnam. Script for the film.
      (In TDR/The Drama Review, Vol. 12, Spring 1968)
GOUIN, Ollivier Mercier, 1928-
   Les Demi-Fous
      (In L'Avant-Scene du Theatre, no. 502, Sept. 15, 1972)
GOURGUE, Jean
   Big-Ben
      (In Plaisir de France, Supplement Theatral, no. 386)
Le Gouter   (see Worms, Jeannine)
La Governante   (see Brancati, Vitaliano)
The Governor's Lady   (see Mercer, David)
GOW, James
   Tomorrow the World, by James Gow and Armand d'Usseau
      (In Best Plays of the Modern American Theatre, Second
      series)
GOW, Ronald
   The Edwardians, based on the novel by V. Sackville-West
      (In Plays of the Year, Vol. 20, 1959)
GOZELL, Rolf
   Aufsteig von Edith Eiserbeck
      (In Theater der Zeit, Oct. 1970)
GOZZI, Carlo, conte, 1722-1806
   Turnandot
      (In Genius of the Italian Theatre)
Grab and Grace; or, It's the Second Step   (see Williams, Charles)
GRABBE, Christian Dietrich, 1801-1836
   Jest, Satire, Irony
      (In From the Modern Repertoire, Series Two)
Gracchus, Caius Sempronius, c. 159-121 B. C.
   *Caius Gracchus   (see Knowles, James Sheridan)
Grace and George and God   (see Hierholzer, Alexander)
Grace Huntley   (see Holl, Henry)
Die Gräfin von Rathenow   (see Lange, Hartmut)
GRAFTON, Edith & Samuel
   Mock Trial
      (In Television Plays for Writers, 1957)
GRAHAM, Mary
   Idyll
      (In Drama, Vol. 16, April 1926)
GRAINGER, Tom, 1921-
   Daft Dream Adyin'
      (In Best Short Plays, 1969)
GRANBERRY, Edwin
   A Trip to Czardis, a television filmscript.
      (In Writing for Television)

El Grand Escroc (see Godard, Jean-Luc)
Grand Hotel (see Baum, Vicki)
Grand Illusion (see Renoir, Jean)
Le Grand Jeu (see Ruinet, Gerard)
Grand Tenement and November 22 (see Eyen, Tom)
La Grande Enquete (see Kulpa, Francois-Felix)
La Grande Illusion (see Renoir, Jean)
Grand Marido (see Silva, Eurico)
La Grande Oreille (see Breal, P. A.)
Les Grandes Manoeuvres (see Clair, Rene)
The Grandmother (see Biro, Lajos)
Grandpa and the Statue (see Miller, Arthur)
GRANICK, Harry
      Witches' Sabbath
            (In First Stage, Vol. 1, no. 1, Winter, 1961/62)
Granite (see Ashton, Winifred)
Granny Boling (see Green, Paul)
Granny Maumee (see Torrence, Frederic Ridgely)
GRANT, Neill
      The Last War
            (In Best One-Act Plays of 1933, London)
      On Dartmoor
            (In Best One-Act Plays of 1932, London)
      A Spot of Lunch
            (In The One-Act Theatre, Vol. 1)
GRANVILLE-Barker, Harley Granville, 1877-1946
      Rococo
            (In Representative One-Act Plays by British and Irish Authors)
      The Voysey Inheritance
            (In Late Victorian Plays)
The Grapes of Wrath (see Johnson, Nunnally)
GRASS, Günter, 1927-
      Davor
            (In Theater Heute, Vol. 19, no. 4, Apr. 1969)
      Flood
            (In Four Plays)
      Mister, Mister
            (In Four Plays)
      Only Ten Minutes to Buffalo
            (In Four Plays)
      The Wicked Cooks
            (In New Theatre of Europe, 1962)
            (In Four Plays)
The Grass Grows Red (see Wright, Ethan Armstrong)
The Grass Harp (see Capote, Truman)
The Grass Is Greener (see Williams, Hugh and Margaret)
GRASSIAN, Dolores
      La Surface Perdue
            (In L'Avant-Scene du Cinema, no. 57, 1966)
The Grass's Springing (see Labrenz, Theodore)
GRATZIK, Paul
      "Umwege"
            (In Theater der Zeit, no. 2, 1971)

GRAVES, Robert, 1895-
  I Claudius (see Mortimer, John)
Gray (see Orlovitz, Gil)
GRAY, Simon, 1936-
  Butley
    (In Plays and Players, Vol. 19, no. 11, Aug. 1972)
  Wise Child
    (In Plays and Players, Vol. 15, Dec. 1967)
GRAZIANI, Henri, 1930-
  Anatol
    (In L'Avant-Scene du Cinema, no. 43, Dec. 1, 1964)
  Le Temps d'Apprendre a Vivre
    (In L'Avant-Scene du Cinema, no. 54, 1965)
GRAZZINI, Antonio Francesco, called Il Lasca, 1503-1584
  L'Arzigogolo
    (In Scrittori d'Italia)
  Il Frate
    (In Scrittori d'Italia)
  La Gelosia
    (In Scrittori d'Italia)
  I Parentadi
    (In Scrittori d'Italia)
  La Pinzochers
    (In Scrittori d'Italia)
  Prologo alla Monica
    (In Scrittori d'Italia)
  La Sibilla
    (In Scrittori d'Italia)
  La Spiritata
    (In Scrittori d'Italia)
  La Strega
    (In Scrittori d'Italia)
The Great American Desert (see Oppenheimer, Joel)
The Great American Light War (see Melmoth, D.)
Great Catherine (see Shaw, George Bernard)
The Great Dark (see Totheroh, Dan)
The Great Devil; or, The Robber of Genoa (see Dibdin, Charles)
The Great Divide (see Moody, William Vaughn)
The Great Exhibition (see Hare, David)
The Great Git-Away (see Muller, Romeo)
Great Goodness of Life (see Jones, Le Roi)
The Great Nebula of Orion (see Wilson, Lanford)
The Great Noontide (see Kearney, Patrick)
The Great Rage of Philip Holz (see Frisch, Max)
The Great Rage of Philip Holz (see also Phillip Holtz's Fury)
The Great Sebastians (see Lindsay, Howard)
The Great Silkie of Sule Skerry (see Bate, Lucy)
Great Wig (see Karvas, Peter)
GRECCO, Stephen
  The Bowlers
    (In Yale/Theatre, no. 3, Winter 1968)
  The Orientals
    (In Playwrights for Tomorrow, Vol. 7)

The Grecian Daughter (see Murphy, Arthur)
Gredy, Jean-Pierre, 1920-
  Les Choutes (see Barillet, Pierre)
  Fleur de Cactus (see Barillet, Pierre)
  Folle Amanda (see Barillet, Pierre)
  4 Pieces sur Jardin (see Barillet, Pierre)
  L'Or et la Paille (see Barillet, Pierre)
  La Reine Blanche (see Barillet, Pierre)
Greed (see Von Stroheim, Erich)
The Greek Vase (see Baring, Maurice)
Green, Adolph, 1915-
  Bells Are Ringing (see Styne, Jule)
  Singin' in the Rain (see Comden, Betty)
GREEN, Carolyn
  Janus
    (In Theatre Arts, Vol. 41, Oct. 1957)
GREEN, Frederick Lawrence, 1902-
  Odd Man Out
    (In Three British Screenplays, 1950)
Green, Julien, 1900-
  Leviathan (see Keigel, Leonard)
GREEN, Paul, 1894-1947
  Alma Mater
    (In Best One-Act Plays of 1938, N.Y.)
  Granny Boling
    (In Drama, Vol. 11, Aug./Sept. 1921)
  The House of Connelly
    (In Best American Plays, Supp. Vol.)
  Hymn to the Rising Sun
    (In Best Short Plays of the Social Theatre, 1939)
  In Abraham's Bosom
    (In Plays of Negro Life)
    (In Best Short Plays, 1956/57)
    (In Pulitzer Prize Plays)
  Johnny Johnson; music by Kurt Weill
    (In 20 Best Plays of the Modern American Theatre, Vol. 1)
  The Last of the Lowries
    (In Carolina Folkplays)
    (In Plays as Experience)
  The Man Who Died at Twelve O'Clock
    (In 15 American One-Act Plays)
  The No 'count Boy
    (In Theatre Arts, Vol. 8, Nov. 1924)
    (In Plays of Negro Life)
  Quare Medicine
    (In Carolina Folkplays)
    (In 50 More Contemporary One-Act Plays)
  White Dresses
    (In 25 Best Plays of the Modern American Theatre, Early
      Series, 1916-1929)
    (In Plays of Negro Life)
    (In Contemporary One-Act Plays, 1922)

The Green Bay Tree   (see Shairp, Mordaunt)
The Green Cockatoo   (see Schnitzler, Arthur)
The Green-eyed Monster   (see Planche, James Robinson)
Green Eyes from Romany   (see Kirkpatrick, John Alexander)
The Green Goddess   (see Archer, William)
Green Grow the Lilacs   (see Riggs, Lynn)
Green Julia   (see Ableman, Paul)
The Green Knight   (see Garnett, Porter)
Green Pastures   (see Connelly, Marcus Cook)
Green Veil Passes   (see Ames, G.)
GREENBAUM, Avrom
     The Bread of Affliction
         (In Best One-Act Plays of 1937, London)
GREENE, Graham, 1904-
     The Potting Shed
         (In Theatre Arts, Vol. 42, Mar. 1958)
     The Third Man, filmscript by Graham Greene and Carol Reed.
         (Modern Film Scripts Series)
GREENE, Robert, 1558-1592
     Friar Bacon and Friar Bungay
         (In Dodsley's A Select Collection of Old Plays, Vol. 8)
Greene's tu Quoque; or, The City Gallant   (see Cooke, John)
GREENWOOD, Thomas
     Jack Sheppard; or, The House-Breaker of the Last Century
         (In Cumberland's British Theatre, Vol. 40, no. 10)
Gregauff, Paul
     Les Cousins   (see Chabrol, Claude)
GREGORY, Isabella Augusta (Persse) lady, 1859-1932
     The Canavans
         (In Genius of the Irish Theater)
     Hyacinth Halvey
         (In Contemporary One-Act Plays, 1922)
     The Rising of the Moon
         (In Three Anglo-Irish Plays)
         (In Thirty Famous One-Act Plays)
         (In 24 One-Act Plays)
     Spreading the News
         (In Atlantic Book of Modern Plays, 1921)
         (In Short Plays by Representative Authors, 1920)
         (In Plays as Experience)
         (In Representative One-Act Plays by British and Irish Authors)
         (In Twenty-Four Favorite One-Act Plays)
         (In Dramas by Present-Day Writers)
     The Workhouse Ward, by Lady Gregory
         (In 50 Contemporary One-Act Plays)
Gregory, Lady   (see Gregory, Isabella Augusta (Persse) lady,
     1859-1932)
Greichische Hochzeit   (see Hanell, Robert)
GREMILLON, Jean, 1901-
     Andre Masson et les Quatre Elements
         (In L'Avant-Scene du Cinema, no. 18, Sept. 15, 1962)
GREPPI, Antonio, 1894-

Passengers; both French and English texts are included
(In Italian Theatre Review, Vol. 11, July/Sept. 1962)
GRESSIEKER, Hermann, 1903-
Royla Gambit, by Hermann Gressieker, translated and adapted
by George White
(In Theatre Arts, Vol. 43, no. 7, July 1959)
Grey, Jane, lady, 1537-1554
*Lady Jane Grey (see Rome, Nicholas)
*The Lion's Cub (see Hale, John)
Grey Red Violet Orange (see Settimelli, Emilio)
Gribble, Harry Wagstaff (see Juliet and Romeo)
Il Grido (see Antonioni, Michelangelo)
Grief Goes Over (see Hodge, Merton)
GRIFFI, Guiseppe Patroni
Say, One Evening at Dinner; both French and English texts are
included
(In Italian Theatre Review, Vol. 16, Jan./Mar. 1967)
Griffith, David Wark, 1875-1948
D.W. Griffith's "The Battle of Elderbush Gulch" (see Niver,
Kemp R.)
Intolerance
(In Classic Film Scripts)
Intolerance; description plan par plan, texte etabli par P. Baudry
(In Cahiers du Cinema, nos. 231-235, Aug. 1971-Jan. 1972)
GRIFFITH, Elizabeth (Griffith), 1720?-1793
The School for Rakes
(In Bell's British Theatre, 1797, Vol. 30)
(In Cumberland's British Theatre, Vol. 33, no. 4)
Griffith, Hubert
Youth at the Helm (see Vulpius, Paul)
Griffiths, Elizabeth (see Griffith, Elizabeth (Griffith))
GRIFFITHS, Glyn
My Hills, My Home
(In Best One-Act Plays, London, 1952/53)
GRIFFITHS, Trevor
Sam, Sam
(In Plays and Players, Vol. 19, no. 7, Apr. 1972)
GRILLPARZER, Franz, 1791-1872
The Golden Fleece: I. The Guest; II. The Argonauts; III. Medea
(In Plays on Classic Themes)
Sappho
(In Plays on Classic Themes)
The Waves of Sea and Love
(In Plays on Classic Themes)
Grim, the Collier of Croyden; or, The Devil and the Dame (Anon.)
(In Dodsley's A Select Collection of Old English Plays, Vol.
8)
(In Dodsley's A Select Collection of Old Plays, Vol. 11)
Grimm, Jakob Ludwig Karl, 1785-1863
**Rumpelstilzchen (see Czechowski, Heinz)
**Snow White and the Seven Dwarfs (see Disney, Walt)
Grimm, Wilkelm Karl, 1786-1859

**Rumpelstilzchen (see Czechowski, Heinz)
**Snow White and the Seven Dwarfs (see Disney, Walt)
La Gringa (see Sanchez, Florencio)
GRIPARI, Pierre
    Crac!... Dans le Sac
        (In Plaisir de France, supplement theatral, no. 323, Sept.
        1965)
Un Gros Gateau (see Worms, Jeannine de)
GROSPIERRE, Louis, 1927-
    Les Femmes de Stermetz
        (In L'Avant-Scene du Cinema, no. 23, Feb. 15, 1963)
GROTOWSKI, Jerzy
    Der Standhafte Prinz
        (In Theater Heute, Aug. 1971)
The Grouch (Dyskolos) (see Menander)
The Groupuscule of My Heart (see Arrabal, Fernando)
GROVER, Harry Greenwood
    What's in a Name?
        (In The One-Act Theatre, Vol. 2)
The Growl (see McClure, Michael)
Gruach (see Bottomley, Gordon)
Gruault, Jean
    Les Deux Anglaise et le Continent (see Truffaut, Francois)
    Jules et Jim (see Truffaut, Francois)
    Paris Nous Appartient (see Rivette, Jacques)
GRUMBERG, Jean-Claude
    Demain, une Fenetre sur Rue
        (In Plaisir de France, supplement theatral, no. 358, Aug.
        1968)
    Rixe
        (In L'Avant-Scene du Theatre, no. 469-470, April 1-15, 1971)
GUARE, John, 1939-
    A Day for Surprises
        (In Best Short Plays, 1970)
    Muzeeka
        (In Showcase 1)
GUARNIERI, Gianfrancesco
    Arena Conta Zumbi
        (In Revista de Teatro, no. 378, Nov. /Dec. 1970)
    Eles Nao Usam Black-Tie
        (In Revista de Teatro, no. 307-309)
    "Gimba, O Presidente dos Valentes"
        (In Revista de Teatro, no. 307-309)
GÜNTER, Eich
    Dreams
        (In Evergreen Review, Vol. 5, no. 21, 1961)
Le Guepard (see Visconti, Luchino)
Guernica (see Resnais, Alain)
GUERRA, Ruy, 1931-
    Tendres Chasseurs; title anglais: "Sweet Hunters"; titres prevus
        puis abondonnes "Jailbird"
        (In L'Avant-Scène du Cinema, no. 112, Mar. 1971)

La Guerre de Trois n'Aura Pas Lieu (see Giradoux, Jean)
La Guerre Est Finie (see Semprun, Jorge)
GUILBAND, Pierre, 1925-
   Les Primitifs du XIIIe, by Pierre Guilband and Jacques Prevert
     (In L'Avant-Scene du Cinema, no. 2, Mar. 15, 1961)
Guilty Party (see Ross, George)
GUIMARAES, Pinheiro
   Historia de uma Rica
     (In Revista de Teatro, no. 297)
Guimard, Paul
   **Les Choses de la Vie (see Sauet, Claude)
Guinevere; or, The Death of the Kangaroo (see Koch, Kenneth)
Guiscard, Robert, 1015?-1085
   *Robert Guiscard (see Kleist, Heinrich von)
Guise, Henry, 3rd Duke, "LaBalafre," 1550-1588
   *The Duke of Guise (see Dryden, John)
GUNN, Bill
   Johannas
     (In TDR/The Drama Review, Vol. 12, Summer 1968)
GUNN, Neil M.
   Back Home
     (In Best One-Act Plays of 1931, London)
Gunpowder, Treason and Plot (see Williamson, Hugh Ross)
The Gun-Site (see Weiss, Vsevolod)
GURNEY, A.R., Jr.
   The Bridal Dinner
     (In First Stage, Vol. 4, Spring 1965)
   The Golden Fleece
     (In Best Short Plays, 1969)
   The Love Course
     (In Best Short Plays, 1970)
   Three People
     (In Best Short Plays, 1955/56)
   Turn of the Century
     (In Best Short Plays, 1958/59)
Gustaf I, Vasa, King of Sweden, 1496-1560
   *Gustavus Vasa, the Deliverer of His Country (see Brooke,
     Henry)
   *The Regent (see Strindberg, August)
Gustaf III, King of Sweden, 1746-1792
   *Gustav III (see Strindberg, August)
GUSTAFSSON, Lars
   Die Nachtliche Huldigung
     (In Theatre Heute, Vol. 11, no. 6, June 1970)
Guthrie, Arlo
   **Alice's Restaurant (see Herndon, Venable)
Gutman, John
   Arabella (see Strauss, Richard)
   Boris Godunov (see Musorgskii, Modest Petrovich)
Guy Faux; or, The Gunpowder Treason (see Macfarren, George)
Guys and Dolls (see Swerling, Jo)
Gwyn, Eleanor, known as Nell, 1650-1687

*Mistress Nell (see Hazelton, George Cochrane)
Gypsy (see Styne, Jule)

H. A. Y. (see Furnished Apartments)
HAAVIKKO, Paavo
    Superintendent
        (In Literary Review, Vol. 14, Fall 1970)
HABINGTON, William, 1605-1654
    The Queen of Arragon
        (In Dodsley's A Select Collection of Old English Plays, Vol.
        13)
        (In Dodsley's A Select Collection of old Plays, Vol.
        9)
Hackett, Albert, 1900-
    The Diary of Anne Frank (see Goodrich, Frances)
HACKETT, Francis
    Nan Bullen
        (In Show, N. Y., Vol. 4, Oct. 1964)
HACKS, Peter
    Adam und Eva
        (In Theater Heute, no. 12, Dec. 1972)
    Noch Einen Löffel Gift, Liebling? (see Matthus, Sieg-
    fried)
    Omphale
        (In Theater Heute, Vol. 11, no. 5, May 1970)
    Opening of the Indian Era
        (In Modern International Drama, Vol. 4, Fall 1970)
HADLER, Walter
    Flight Cage
        (In More Plays From Off Off Broadway)
Hadrian the Seventh (see Luke, Peter)
Hadrien VII (see Luke, Peter)
HAGUE, Albert Martin
    Plain and Fancy, by Joseph Stein and Will Glickman. Lyrics
    by Arnold B. Horwitt. Music by Albert Hague.
        (In Theatre Arts, Vol. 40, July 1956)
The Ha-Ha Play (see Yankowitz, Susan)
Hail the Conquering Hero (see Sturges, Preston)
HAILEY, Oliver, 1932-
    Hey You, Light Man!
        (In Players Magazine, Vol. 38, Oct. 1961)
        (In 3 Plays From the Yale School of Drama)
    Who's Happy Now?
        (In Showcase 1)
HAINES, John Thomas, 1799?-1843
    Austerlitz; or, The Soldier's Bride
        (In Cumberland's British Theatre, Vol. 28, no. 4)
    My Poll and My Partner Joe
        (In Cumberland's British Theatre, Vol. 39, no. 2)
        (In Hiss the Villain)
    The Ocean of Life; or, "Every Inch a Sailor!"

(In Cumberland's British Theatre, Vol. 34, no. 5)
Richard Plantagenet
   (In Cumberland's British Theatre, Vol. 46, no. 1)
HAINES, William Wister, 1908-
   Command Decision; based on his Book
     (In Theatre Arts, Vol. 32, Summer 1948)
     (In Nine Modern American Plays)
Hair (see MacDermot, Galt)
HAIRE, Wilson John
   Within Two Shadows
     (In Scripts, Vol. 1, no. 9, Sept. 1972)
     (In Plays and Players, Vol. 19, no. 9, June 1972)
The Hairy Ape (see O'Neill, Eugene)
Haku Rakuten (see Zeami Motokiyo)
HALE, John
   The Black Swan Winter
     (In Plays and Players, Vol. 16, no. 10, July 1969)
     (In Plays of the Year, Vol. 37, 1969/70)
   The Lion's Cub
     (In Plays of the Year Special, 1972)
   Spithead
     (In Plays of the Year, Vol. 38, 1969/70)
HALET, Pierre
   Votre Silence, Cooper?
     (In Plaisir de France, supplement theatral, no. 358, Aug.
     1968)
Half a Loaf (see Let Them Eat Cake)
Half-Hour, Please (see Richards, Stanley)
Hall, Adam, pseud. (see Trevor, Elleston)
Hall, Alexander, 1894-1968
   Here Comes Mr. Jordan (see Buchman, Sidney)
Hall, Holworthy, pseud. (see Porter, Harold Everett)
HALL, Josef Washington, 1894-1960
   The Joy Lady, by Upton Close, pseud.
     (In Drama, Vol. 18, May 1928)
HALL, Willis, 1929-
   Air Mail from Cyprus
     (In Television Playwright: 10 Plays for BBC)
   Billy Liar (see Waterhouse, Keith)
   The Sponge Room (see Waterhouse, Keith)
Hallelujah les Collines (see Mekas, Adolfas)
HALLIDAY, Andrew, 1830-1877
   Checkmate
     (In Lacy's Plays)
HALLIWILL, David
   Little Malcolm and His Struggle Against the Eunuchs
     (In Plays and Players, Vol. 13, April 1966)
Hall-Marked (see Galsworthy, John)
The Halls of Congress (see Gottlieb, Joseph)
HALMAN, Doris
   The Rocking Horse
     (In Best Television Plays of the Year, 1950/51)

HALPERN, Martin
  Mrs. Middleman's Descent
    (In First Stage, Vol. 5, Fall 1966)
  Reservations
    (In First Stage, Vol. 5, no. 4, Winter 1966-67)
The Hamaadryads (see Irwin, Will)
The Hamburger King (see Smith, Marian Spencer)
HAMER, Robert, 1911-
  Noblesse Oblige, by Robert Hamer et John Dighton, d'apres le
    roman de Roy Horniman. Titre original: "Kind Hearts and
    Coronets."
    (In L'Avant-Scene du Cinema, no. 18, Sept. 15, 1962)
HAMILTON, Cicely Mary, 1875-
  Jack and Jill and a Friend
    (In 50 More Contemporary One-Act Plays)
Hamilton, Edith, 1867-1963
  Prometheus Bound (see Aeschylus)
HAMILTON, Patrick, 1904-1962
  Angel Street
    (In 13 Famous Plays of Crime and Detection)
Hamlet: A Tragedy (see Sumarokov, Aleksandr Petrovich)
The Hamlet of Stepney Green (see Kops, Bernard)
Hammerstein, Oscar, 1895-1960
  Oklahoma! (see Rodgers, Richard)
HAMMETT, Dashiell, 1894-1961
  Watch on the Rhine; screenplay by Dashill Hammett, based on
    the play by Lillian Hellman
    (In Best Film Plays, 1943/44, Vol. 1)
HAMMOND, Virginia Maye
  It's All a Matter of Dress
    (In The Banner Anthology of One-Act Plays by American
    Authors)
HAMOU, Rene
  Epitelioma
    (In L'Avant-Scene du Theatre, no. 508, Dec. 15, 1972)
HAMPTON, Christopher
  Der Menschen-Freund
    (In Theater Heute, no. 2, Feb. 1971)
  When Did You Last See My Mother?
    (In Evergreen Playscript Series)
HANDKE, Peter
  Calling for Help
    (In TDR/The Drama Review, Vol. 15, Fall 1970)
  Kaspar
    (In Kaspar and Other Plays)
  Das Mündel Will Vormund sein
    (In Theater Heute, Vol. 10, no. 2, Feb. 1969)
  My Foot My Tutor
    (In TDR/The Drama Review, Vol. 15, Fall 1970)
  Offending the Audience
    (In Kaspar and Other Plays)
  The Ride Across Lake Constance

(In Scripts, Vol. 1, no. 5, Mar. 1972)
Der Ritt über den Bodensee
     (In Theater Heute, Oct. 1970)
Self-Accusation
     (In Kaspar and Other Plays)
Handkerchief of Clouds (see Tzara, Tristan)
Hands: A Showcase (see Corra, Bruno)
Hands Across the Sea (see Coward, Noel Pierce)
The Handshakers (see Saroyan, William)
HANELL, Robert
     Greichische Hochzeit
     (In Theater der Zeit, Vol. 24, no. 1, 1969)
Hang By Their Shoelaces (see Tunberg, Karl A.)
Hangs Over Thy Head (see Purkey, Ruth Angell)
Hanjo (see Hiraoke, Kimitake)
HANKIN, St. John Emile Clavering, 1869-1909
     The Cassilis Engagement
     (In Late Victorian Plays)
     The Constant Lover
     (In 50 Contemporary One-Act Plays)
     (In Theatre Arts, Vol. 3, 1919)
HANLEY, James
     Say Nothing
     (In Plays of the Year, Vol. 27, 1962/63)
HANLEY, William, 1931-
     Slow Dance on the Killing Ground
     (In Best American Plays, Sixth series, 1963-67)
HANNA, Tacie May
     The House Beautiful
     (In Drama, Vol. 15, Feb. 1925)
     Hyacinthis
     (In Drama, Vol. 12, Sept. 1922)
     Upon the Waters
     (In Drama, Vol. 14, Nov. 1923)
Hannele (see Hauptman, Gerhart)
Hannibal, "the grace of Baal," 247-182 B.C.
     *Hannibal and Scipio: an Historical Tragedy (see Nabbes,
          Thomas)
     *Sophonisba; or, Hannibal's Overthrow (see Lee, Nathaniel)
HANSBERRY, Lorraine, 1930-1965
     A Raisin in the Sun
     (New American Library Screenplays)
     (In Theatre Arts, Vol. 44, no. 10, Oct. 1960)
     (In 6 American Plays for Today, ed. by Bennett Cerf, N.Y.
          Mod. Library, 1961)
     (In Plays of Our Time)
     The Sign in Sidney Brustein's Window
     (In Show, Vol. 5, Jan. 1965)
     (In Best American Plays, Sixth series, 1963-67)
Happiest Day of My Life (see Buckstone, John Baldwin)
The Happy Apple (see Pulman, Jack)
Happy Days (see Beckett, Samuel)

Happy Ending   (see Ward, Douglas Turner)
Happy Family   (see Cooper, Giles)
The Happy Haven   (see Arden, John)
Happy House Wife   (see Rosten, Hedda)
The Happy Journey   (see Wilder, Thornton)
The Happy Journey to Trenton and Camden   (see Wilder, Thornton)
Happy the Bride   (see Bosworth, Raymond F.)
The Happy Time   (see Taylor, Samuel)
Harburg, E. Y., 1898-
     Finian's Rainbow   (see Kushner, Morris Hyman)
Hard Core   (see Lineberger, James)
A Hard Struggle   (see Marston, John Westland)
HARDIN, Herschel
     Esker Mike and His Wife, Agiluk
          (In TDR/Drama Review, Vol. 14, Fall 1969)
Hardy Perennials   (see Meeker, Arthur, Jr.)
HARE, David
     The Great Exhibition
          (In Plays and Players, Vol. 19, no. 8, May 1972)
     Slag
          (In Plays and Players, Vol. 17, no. 9, June 1970)
HARKIN, Eleanor
     Eliphant & Flamingo Vaudeville
          (In Scripts, Vol. 1, no. 10, Oct. 1972)
Harlequin Bridge   (see Sladen-Smith, Francis)
Harlequinade   (see Rattigan, Terence)
Harnick, Sheldon
     The Diary of Adam and Eve   (see Bock, Jerry)
     Fiddler on the Roof   (see Bock, Jerry)
     Fiorello!   (see Bock, Jerry)
HARNWELL, Anne
     Sojourners, by Anne Harnwell and Isabelle Meeker
          (In Drama, Vol. 19, Jul. /Sept. 1920)
HARPER, Harold
     The Demands of Society
          (In The One-Act Theatre, Vol. 2)
     My Taylor
          (In The One-Act Theatre, Vol. 1)
HARRINGTON, Edward, 1845-1911
     Squatter Sovereignty (abridged)
          (In Theatre Arts, Vol. 19, Mar. 1926)
HARRIS, Augustus Glossip, 1825-1873
     Thom Thrasher
          (In Lacy's Acting Plays, Vol. 81)
HARRIS, Claudia Lucas
     It's Spring
          (In Drama, Vol. 11, Apr. 1921)
     Young Mr. Santa Claus
          (In Drama, Vol. 12, Oct. /Nov. 1921)
HARRIS, Neil
     Cop and Blow
          (In Scripts, Vol. 1, no. 7, May 1972)

HARRIS, Richard W.
  The Spineless Drudge
    (In First Stage, Vol. 2, Winter 1962/63)
HARRIS, Tom
  Always with Love
    (In New American Plays, Vol. 3)
HARRIS, W. Eric
  Twenty-Five Cents
    (In Best One-Act Plays of 1937, N.Y.)
HARRISON, John
  Knight in Four Acts
    (In Plays of the Year, Vol. 38, 1969/70)
HARRITY, Richard, 1907-
  Gone Tomorrow
    (In Theatre Arts, Vol. 30, Aug. 1946)
  Hope is a Thing with Feathers
    (In Theatre Arts, Vol. 29, Sept. 1945)
The Harrowing of Hell (see York Saddlers' Play)
Harry Amses of Buffalo (see Lovejoy, Tim)
Hart, Elisabeth
  A Trip to Czardis (see Hart, James)
HART, James
  A Trip to Czardis, by James and Elisabeth Hart
    (In Plays From Radio, 1948)
HART, Moss, 1904-1961
  The Climate of Eden
    (In Theatre Arts, Vol. 38, May 1954)
  Dream On, Soldier, by Moss Hart and George S. Kaufman
    (In Theatre Arts, Vol. 27, Sept. 1943)
  Light Up the Sky
    (In Theatre Arts, Vol. 33, Sept. 1949)
  The Man Who Came to Dinner, by Moss Hart and George S.
    Kaufman
    (In 16 Famous American Plays)
    (In Best Plays of the Modern American Theatre, Second
    Series)
  Once in a Lifetime, by Moss Hart and George S. Kaufman
    (In Famous Plays of Today, 1932)
  You Can't Take It with You, by Moss Hart and George S.
    Kaufman
    (In Nine Modern American Plays)
    (In 20 Best Plays of the Modern American Theatre, Vol. 1)
    (In Pulitzer Prize Plays)
  You Can't Take It With You; screenplay (see Riskin, Robert)
Hartford Bridge; or, The Skirts of the Camp (see Pearce, William)
HARTLEBEN, Otto Erich, 1864-1905
  The Demands of Society
    (In 50 More Contemporary One-Act Plays)
Hartley, Leslie Poles
  The Go-Between (see Pinter, Harold)
HARTMANN, Sadakichi, 1867-1944
  Buddha

(In Buddha, Confucius, Christ: Three Prophetic Plays)
Christ
(In Buddha, Confucius, Christ: Three Prophetic Plays)
Confucius
(In Buddha, Confucius, Christ: Three Prophetic Plays)
HARTOG, Jan de, 1914-
Le Ciel de Lit, based on the work of Colette
(In L'Avant-Scene du Theatre, no. 477, Aug. 1, 1971)
The Fourposter
(In Best American Plays, Fourth Series)
HARTSON, Hall, d. 1773
The Countess of Salisbury
(In Bell's British Theatre, 1797, Vol. 18)
HARTWEG, Norman
The Pit
(In Tulane Drama Review, Vol. 9, Spring 1965)
HARTWELL, Henry
The Castle of Sorrento; or, The Prisoner of Rochelle
(In Cumberland's British Theatre, Vol. 38, no. 2)
HARVEIS, Lionel
The Rose of Persia
(In Drama, Vol. 11, Mar. 1921)
Harvey (see Chase, Mary Coyle)
The Hasty Heart (see Goggan, John Patrick)
The Hat Rack (see Herman, George)
Hatch, Eric
My Man Godfrey (see Ryskind, Morrie)
Hatch, James
Fly Blackbird (see Jackson, C.B.)
Hatchfeld, Rainer
Stokkerlok und Millipilli (see Ludwig, Volker)
A Hatful of Rain (see Gazzo, Michael Vincente)
The Hatmaker (Eboshi-Ori) (see Miyamasu)
Hatton, Sir Christopher, 1540-1591
Tancred and Gismunda (see Wilmot, Robert)
HAUDIQUET, Philippe, 1937-
Trente-Six Heures
(In L'Avant-Scene du Cinema, no. 111, Feb. 1971)
HAUGHTON, William, fl. 1598
English-Men for My Money; or, A Woman Will Have Her Will
(In Dodsley's A Select Collection of Old English Plays, Vol. 10)
Lust's Dominion; or, The Lascivious Queen (see Marlowe,
Christopher)
Patient Grissil (see Dekker, Thomas)
The Haunted Inn (see Peake, Richard Brinsley)
The Haunted Tower (see Cobb, James)
Haunted Water (see Kreymborg, Alfred)
HAUPTMANN, Gerhart Johann Robert, 1862-1946
Das Friedensfest
(In Das Deutsche Drama, 1880-1933, Vol. 1)
Hannele
(In Makers of the Modern Drama)
The Weavers

(In 16 Famous European Plays)
(In Modern Theatre, ed. by R. W. Corrigan)
Haut Oder Hemd (see Neutsch, Erik)
HAVARD, William, 1710?-1778
King Charles I; written in imitation of Shakespeare
(In Bell's British Theatre, 1797, Vol. 19)
Have You Any Dirty Washing, Mother Dear? (see Exton, Clive)
HAVEL, Vaclav, 1936-
Erschwerte Möglichkeit der Konzentration
(In Theater Heute, Vol. 10, no. 1, Jan. 1969)
Garden Party
(In Literary Review, Vol. 13, Fall 1969)
The Memorandum, translated by Vera Blackwell
(In Three East European Plays)
The Memorandum
(In Tulane Drama Review, Vol. 11, Spring 1967)
(In Evergreen Playscript Series, no. 6)
Le Rapport Dont Vous Etes l'Objet, piece de Vaclav; adaptation
de Milan Kepel
(In L'Avant-Scene du Theatre, no. 486, Jan. 1972)
Haven of the Spirit (see Denison, Merril)
"Having Wonderful Time" (see Kober, Arthur)
Hawk A-Flyin' (see Conkle, Ellsworth Prouty)
Hawkes, Jacquetta
Dragon's Mouth (see Priestley, John Boynton)
HAWKES, John
The Wax Museum
(In Plays for a New Theatre)
HAWLEY, Esther M.
On the Way Home
(In Best One-Act Plays of 1944, N. Y.)
HAWORTH, Don
A Hearts and Minds Job
(In Plays and Players, Vol. 18, no. 11, Aug. 1971)
Hawthorne, Nathaniel, 1804-1864
**Feathertop (see Valency, Maurice Jacques)
HAY, Frederic
Caught by the Cuff
(In Lacy's Acting Plays, Vol. 14)
A Sudden Arrival
(In 26 Short & Amusing Plays, 1871)
HAY, Gyula
Mithridates
(In Literary Review, Vol. 9, Spring 1966)
HAY, Julius, 1900-
The Horse, translated by Peter Hay
(In Three East European Plays)
Hay Fever (see Coward, Noel Pierce)
Haycox, Ernest, 1899-1950
**La Chevauchee Fantastique (see Nichols, Dudley)
**Stagecoach (see Nichols, Dudley)
HAYES, Joseph, 1918-
The Bridegroom Waits (see Hayes, Marrijane)

Calculated Risk
   (In Theatre Arts, Vol. 47, Dec. 1963)
Silver Key
   (In Best One-Act Plays of 1948/49, London)
A Woman's Privilege (see Hayes, Marrijane)
HAYES, Marrijane
   The Bridegroom Waits, by Marrijane and Joseph Hayes
   (In Best One-Act Plays of 1943, N. Y.)
   A Woman's Privilege, by Marrijane and Joseph Hayes
   (In Best One-Act Plays of 1947/48, N. Y.)
HAYN, Annette
   Hollowishes
   (In Scripts, Vol. 1, no. 10, Oct. 1972)
   Tyrone and the Robbers
   (In Scripts, Vol. 1, no. 10, Oct. 1972)
HAYS, Hoffman R.
   Vincent Van Gogh
   (In Best Television Plays of the Year, 1950/51)
HAZELTON, George Cochrane, 1868-1921
   Mistress Nell
   (In Monte Cristo and Other Plays)
He Left Home (see Rosewichy, Tadeusz)
He Wants Shih (see Owens, Rochelle)
He Was Born Gay (see Williams, Emlyn)
He Who Gets Slapped (see Andreev, Leonid Nikolaevich)
He Would Be a Soldier (see Philon, Frederic)
HEAD, Robert
   Kill Viet Cong, by Hed (pseud.)
   (In Tulane Drama Review, Vol. 10, Summer 1966)
   Sancticity
   (In Tulane Drama Review, Vol. 8, Winter 1963)
HEALEY, Frances
   Creeds
   (In 50 More Contemporary One-Act Plays)
Hearst, William Randolph, 1863-1951
   *Citizen Kane (fiction) (see Welles, Orson)
Heart of Bruce (see Williamson, Hugh Ross)
The Heart of Mid-Lothian (see Dibdin, Thomas)
The Heart of Pierrot (see Scott, Margaretta)
Heart to Heart (see Rattigan, Terence)
A Hearts and Minds Job (see Haworth, Don)
Heat Wave (see Pertwee, Roland)
HEATH, Crosby
   The Unruly Member
   (In 50 More Contemporary One-Act Plays)
Heaven and Earth: A Mystery (see Byron, George Gordon Noël
   Byron, 6th Baron)
Heaven Is a Long Time to Wait (see Conkle, Ellsworth Prouty)
Heaven on Earth (see Johnson, Philip)
HEBBEL, Friedrich, 1813-1863
   Agnes Bernauer
   (In Plaisir de France, supplement theatral, no. 336, Oct.
   1966)

Maria Magdalena
    (In The Modern Theatre, ed. by R. W. Corrigan)
HECHT, Ben, 1893-1964
    The Front Page, by Ben Hecht and Charles MacArthur
      (In 16 Famous American Plays)
      (In 25 Best Plays of the Modern American Theatre, Early
      Series, 1916-1929)
    It's Fun to Be Free, by Ben Hecht and Charles MacArthur
      (In Best One-Act Plays of 1941, N. Y.)
    Miracle on the Pullman
      (In Best One-Act Plays of 1944, N. Y.)
    Spellbound, by Ben Hecht, suggested by the novel "The House of
    Dr. Edwardes" by Francis Beeding, directed by Alfred Hitch-
    cock
      (In Best Film Plays, 1945, Vol. 2)
    A Tribute to Gallantry
      (In Best One-Act Plays of 1943, N. Y.)
    Winkelberg
      (In A Treasury of Ben Hecht)
    Wuthering Heights, a screenplay based on the novel by Emily
    Bronte, by Ben Hecht and Charles MacArthur, directed by
    William Wyler
      (In 20 Best Film Plays)
Hecuba (see Euripides)
Hed (pseud.) (see Head, Robert)
Hedda Gabler (see Ibsen, Henrik)
HEDGES, Bertha
    The Dead Saint
      (In Drama, Vol. 12, June-Aug. 1922)
Heerman, Victor
    Little Women (see Mason, Sarah Y.)
HEFFNER, Hubert Crouse, 1901-
    "Dod Gast Ye Both!"
      (In Carolina Folkplays)
Hegge Cycle
    The Parliament of Heaven: The Annunciation and Conception
      (In Religious Drama, Vol. 2)
    The Woman Taken in Adultry
      (In Religious Drama, Vol. 2)
Hegge Manuscript
    The Mystery of the Redemption
      (In Representative Medieval & Tudor Plays)
HEGGEN, Thomas Orlo, 1919-1949
    Mister Roberts, by Thomas O. Heggen and Joshua Logan, based
    on the novel by Thomas O. Heggen
      (In Theatre Arts, Vol. 34, March 1950)
      (In Plays of Our Time)
HEIDE, Robert
    At War with the Mongols
      (In New American Plays, Vol. 4)
    Moon
      (In Best of Off Off Broadway)

HEIJERMANS, Herman, 1864-1924
  Ahasverus
    (In Drama, Vol. 19, Feb. 1929)
  The Good Hope
    (In 20 Best European Plays on the American Stage)
  Jubilee
    (In Drama, Vol. 13, July 1923)
  Saltimbank
    (In Drama, Vol. 13, Aug./Sept. 1923)
Heinrich aus Andernach (see Unruh, Fritz von)
The Heir (see May, Thomas)
The Heir at Law (see Colman, George; the Younger)
HELBURN, Theresa
  Enter the Hero
    (In 50 Contemporary One-Act Plays)
HELE, Thomas d', 1740?-1780
  Unforeseen Events
    (In Theatrical Recorder, ed. by Thomas Holcroft, Vol. 2,
      Suppl., Dec. 1805)
Helen (see Euripides)
Helen Keller (see Deckelman, Ethel)
Helena (see Euripides)
Helena's Husband (see Moeller, Philip)
Helene et l'Amour ou la Verite d'Aphrodite (see Floress, Isadora)
HELIAS, Pierre Jakez
  Les Fous de la Mer
    (In Plaisir de France, supplement theatral, no. 322, Aug.
      1965)
Hellas (see Shelley, Percy Bysshe)
Hellas (see Strindberg, August)
Hell-Bent fer Heaven (see Hughes, Hatcher)
Helliocentric World (see Clarke, Sebastian)
HELLMAN, Lillian, 1905-
  Another Part of the Forest
    (In Six Plays by Lillian Hellman)
  The Autumn Garden
    (In Best American Plays, Third Series)
    (In Theatre Arts, Vol. 35, Sept./Nov. 1951)
    (In Six Plays by Lillian Hellman)
  The Children's Hour
    (In Theatre Arts, Vol. 37, May 1953)
    (In Six Plays by Lillian Hellman)
  Days to Come
    (In Six Plays by Lillian Hellman)
  The Lark (see Jean Anouilh)
  The Little Foxes
    (In Six Plays by Lillian Hellman)
    (In 16 Famous American Plays)
    (In The Modern Theatre, ed. by R. W. Corrigan)
  North Star; a motion picture about some Russian people, di-
  rected
    (A Viking Press Master Script, 1943)

Toys in the Attic
(In Theatre Arts, Vol. 45, October 1961)
(In 6 American Plays for Today, ed. by Bennett Cerf, N. Y.
   Modern Library, 1961)
Watch on the Rhine
(In Six Plays by Lillian Hellman)
(In Best Plays of the Modern American Theatre, Second
   Series)
**Watch on the Rhine; screenplay (see Hammett, Dashiell)
Hello, Dolly! (see Herman, Jerry)
Hello from Bertha (see Williams, Tennessee)
Hello Out There (see Saroyan, William)
Hell's Pavement (see Levi, Paolo)
Heloise (see Forsythe, James)
Helpless Herberts (see Kreymborg, Alfred)
Hemon, Louis, 1880-1913
**Monsieur Ripois (see Clement, Rene)
HENDERSON, B. J.
There's Some Milk in the Ice Box
(In Mademoiselle, Vol. 62, Nov. 1965)
HENKEL, Heinrich
Eisenwichser
(In Theater Heute, Sept. 1970)
HENNEFELD, Edmund B.
The Cave
(In First Stage, Vol. 4, Summer 1965)
Henri II, King of France, 1519-1559
*La Princesse de Cleves (see Dorfmann, Robert)
Henri III, King of France, 1551-1589
*Henri III et sa Cour (see Dumas, Alexandre, Pere)
Henry II, King of England, 1133-1189
*Becket; or, The Honor of God (see Anouilh, Jean)
*Curtmantle (see Fry, Christopher)
*Henry II; or, The Fall of Rosamond (see Hull, Thomas)
*Lion in Winter (see Goldman, James)
*Murder in the Cathedral (see Eliot, Thomas Stearns)
Henry IV, German Holy Roman Emperor, 1050-1106
*Henry IV (see Pirandello, Luigi)
Henry V, king of Great Britain, 1387-1422
*Henry V (see Olivier, Sir Laurence)
Henry VIII, king of England, 1491-1547
*Anne Boleyn (see McCarty, Nick)
*Anne of Cleves (see Morris, Jean)
*Anne of the Thousand Days (see Anderson, Maxwell)
*Catherine Howard (see Cross, Beverley)
*Catherine of Aragon (see Sisson, Rosemary Anne)
*Catherine Parr (see Prebble, John)
*Catherine Parr; or, Alexander's Horse (see Baring, Maurice)
*Jane Seymour (see Thorne, Ian)
HENSHAW, James Ene
The Jewels of the Shrine
(In Plays From Black Africa)

The Heracleidae (see Euripides)
Heracles (see Euripides)
Heraclite l'Obscur (see Deval, Patrick)
HERALD, Heinz
    The Life of Emile Zola, a screenplay by Heinz Herald and
    Geza Herczeg, directed by William Dieterle
    (In 20 Best Film Plays)
HERBERT, Frederick Hugh, 1897-
    La Lune Etait Bleue; extracts from the screenplay directed by
    Otto Preminger; text in French
    (In Cahiers du Cinema, Vol. 5, no. 28, Nov. 1953)
    The Moon Is Blue
    (In Theatre Arts, Vol. 36, Jan. 1952)
    (In Best American Plays, Third Series)
    That Certain Age (see Manning, Bruce)
HERBERT, John
    Fortune and Men's Eyes
    (In Evergreen Playscript Series)
Hercules on Oeta (see Seneca, Lucius Annaeus)
Herczeg, Geza
    The Life of Emile Zola (see Herald, Heinz)
Here Come the Clowns (see Barry, Philip)
Here Comes Mr. Jordan (see Buchman, Sidney)
Here Comes Santa Claus (see Oliansky, Joel)
Here Comes the Best Part (see Kaminsky, Stuart M.)
Here We Are (see Parker, Dorothy)
A Heritage--and Its History (see Mitchell, Julian)
HERLIHY, James Leo
    Bad, Bad Jo-Jo
    (In Stop You're Killing Me)
    Blue Denim, by James Leo Herlihy and William Noble. Original
    title: "The Sleepwalker's Children"
    (Random House Play, 1958)
    Laughs, etc.
    (In Stop You're Killing Me)
    Terrible Jim Fitch
    (In Stop You're Killing Me)
HERMAN, George
    The Hat Rack
    (In First Stage, Vol. 1, no. 4, Fall 1962)
HERMAN, Jean, 1933-
    Actua Tilt
    (In L'Avant-Scene du Cinema, no. 8, Oct. 1961)
HERMAN, Jerry
    Hello, Dolly! Book by Michael Stewart; music and lyrics by
    Jerry Herman; based on the play "The Matchmaker" by
    Thornton Wilder.
    (New American Library Screenplays)
L'Hermine (see Anouilh, Jean)
Herminie (see Nagnier, Claude)
HERNANDEZ, Luisa Josefina, 1928-
    The Mulatto's Orgy
    (In Voices of Change in the Spanish American Theater)

Hernani (see Hugo, Victor)
HERNDON, Venable
  Alice's Restaurant, by Venable Herndon and Arthur Penn, based
  on Arlo Guthrie's "The Alice's Restaurant Massacree"
  (A Doubleday Screenplay, 1970)
  Until the Monkey Comes
  (In New American Plays, Vol. 2)
HERNE, James A., 1839-1901
  Margaret Fleming
  (In The Black Crook & Other 19th Century American Plays)
  (In Six Early American Plays, 1798-1890)
  Shore Acres
  (In American Drama)
The Hero (see Kopit, Arthur L.)
Herod Antipas, d. after 40 A.D.
  *Herod and the Kings (see Coventry Shearmen and Tailors'
  Play)
The Heroes (see Ashbery, John)
Der Herr Schmidt (see Rücker, Günther)
Die Herren des Strandes (see Gerlach, Friedrich)
HERVIEU, Paul Ernest, 1857-1915
  Modesty
  (In Contemporary One-Act Plays, 1922)
He's Much to Blame (Anon.)
  (In Modern Theatre, 1811, Vol. 4)
HESSENS, Robert
  Le Petit Forain
  (In L'Avant-Scene du Cinema, no. 40, 1964)
  Statues d'Epouvante
  (In L'Avant-Scene du Cinema, no. 19, Oct. 15, 1962)
  Van Gogh; Court Metrage d'Alain Resnais.   Conception et
  scenario Robert Hessens et Gaston Dielh
  (In L'Avant-Scene du Cinema, no. 61-62, July/Sept. 1966)
Une Heure pour Dejeumer (see Mortimer, John)
Hewers of Coal (see Corris, Joe)
Hey You, Light Man! (see Hailey, Oliver)
Heyward, Dorothy Hartzell (Kuhns), 1890-1961
  Porgy (see Heyward, Dubose)
HEYWARD, Dubose, 1885-1940
  Porgy, by Dubose and Dorothy Heyward, from the novel by
  Dubose Heyward
  (In Theatre Arts, Vol. 39, Oct. 1955)
  (In Theatre Guild Anthology)
HEYWOOD, John, 1497?-1580?
  The Four P's
  (In Dodsley's A Select Collection of Old English Plays, Vol.
  1)
  (In Dodsley's A Select Collection of Old Plays, Vol. 1)
  John, Tyb, and Sir John
  (In Great English Plays)
  (In Representative Medieval & Tudor Plays)
  The Pardoner and the Friar

(In Dodsley's A Select Collection of Old English Plays, Vol.
1)
(In Representative Medieval and Tudor Plays)
HEYWOOD, Thomas, d. 1641
The Captives; or, A Comicall Historie
(In A Collection of Old English Plays, Vol. 4)
The Foure Prentises of London
(In Dodsley's A Select Collection of Old Plays, Vol. 6)
A Woman Killed by Kindness
(In Dodsley's A Select Collection of Old Plays, Vol. 7)
HICKENLOOPER, Margaret
"St. Anselm Only Carved One Soul"
(In Ten Fantasies for Stage and Study, 1932)
Hickerson, Harold
Gods of the Lightning (see Anderson, Maxwell)
HICKEY, D. E.
The Clock Strikes Ten, by D. E. Hickey and A. G. Prys-Jones
(In Best One-Act Plays of 1935, London)
HICKEY, E. and D. E.
Over the Top
(In Best One-Act Plays of 1934, London)
Hickscorner (Anon.)
(In Dodsley's A Select Collection of Old English Plays, Vol.
1)
HICKSON, Leslie M.
A Leap-Year Bride
(In 50 More Contemporary One-Act Plays)
Whose Money? (see Dickson, Lee)
Hide and Seek (see Lunn, Joseph)
HIERHOLZER, Alexander
Grace and George and God
(In Playwrights for Tomorrow, Vol. 7)
The High Heart (see Rowell, Adelaide C.)
High Life Below Stairs (see Townley, James)
High Noon (see Foreman, Carl)
The High School (see Perl, Arnold)
High Tea (see Miller, Hugh)
High Tor (see Anderson, Maxwell)
High Ways and By Ways (see Webster, Benjamin)
The Highland Reel (see O'Keefe, John)
HIGUERA, Pablo de la, 1932-
Le Miroir
(In L'Avant-Scene du Theatre, no. 498, July 1, 1972)
Les Trois Musiciens
(In Plaisir de France, supplement theatral, no. 324, Oct.
1965)
HILARIUS, Saint, bp. of Poitiers, d. 367?
The Miracle of Saint Nicholas and the Image
(In Representative Medieval & Tudor Plays)
HILDESHEIMER, Wolfgang, 1916-
Mary Stuart
(In Scripts, Vol. 1, no. 3, Jan. 1972)

The Sacrifice of Helen (Das Opfer Helena)
   (In Modern International Drama, Vol. 2, no. 1, Sept. 1968)
HILL, Aaron, 1685-1750
   Alzira
   (In Bell's British Theatre, 1797, Vol. 7)
   Merope
   (In Bell's British Theatre, 1797, Vol. 23)
   Zara
   (In Bell's British Theatre, 1797, Vol. 17)
   (In Cumberland's British Theatre, Vol. 35, no. 10)
HILL, Errol
   Man Better Man
   (In 3 Plays From the Yale School of Drama)
HILL, James
   Matched Pair, a filmscript
   (In Story: The Yearbook of Discovery, 1969)
   Miguelito, a filmscript
   (In Story: The Yearbook of Discovery, 1969)
Hiller, Lejaren, Jr.
   The Man with the Oboe (see Smalley, Webster)
HILTON, James, 1900-1954
   **Goodbye, Mr. Chips; screenplay (see Sherriff, R. C.)
   Mrs. Miniver, a screenplay by James Hilton and Arthur Wim-
    peris
   (In 20 Best Film Plays)
Hilltop (see Garnett, Louise Ayres)
Him (see Cummings, Edward Estlin)
"Himmelfahrt zur Erde" (see Stolper, Armin)
Hindle Wakes (see Houghton, Stanley)
HINE, Daryl
   Death of Seneca
   (In Chicago Review, Vol. 22, Autumn 1970)
HINES, Leonard
   Vindication, by Leonard Hines and Frank King
   (In Best One-Act Plays of 1931, London)
Hinkemann (see Toller, Ernst)
Hippolytus (see Euripides)
Hippolytus (see Howe, Julia Ward)
HIRAOKA, Kimitake
   The Damask Drum, by Yukio Mishima (pseud.)
   (In Five Modern No Plays)
   Hanjo, by Yukio Mishima (pseud.)
   (In Five Modern No Plays)
   Kantan, by Yukio Mishima (pseud.)
   (In Five Modern No Plays)
   The Lady Aoi, by Yukio Mishima (pseud.)
   (In Five Modern No Plays)
   Madame de Sade, by Yukio Mishima (pseud.)
   (Evergreen Playscript Series)
   Sotaba Komachi, by Yukio Mishima (pseud.)
   (In Five Modern No Plays)
   (In Virginia Quarterly Review, Vol. 33, Spring 1957)
   (In Anthology of Japanese Literature)

Hiroshima mon Amour   (see Duras, Marguerite)
His First Brief (see Daryl, Sidney)
His Widow's Husband   (see Benavente y Martinez, Jacinto)
HISAMATSU, Issei
    Takatsuki
    (In Six Kabuki Plays)
Une Histoire d'Eau (see Truffaut, Francois)
Histoire d'une Chemise et d'un Violon (see Praga, Andre)
Historia de uma Rica (see Guimaraes, Pinheiro)
Historia Histrionica: a Dialogue of Plays and Players (see Wright,
    James)
The Historical Register for the Year 1736 (see Fielding, Henry)
A Historis do Grito (see Ferreire, Helvecio)
History (see Duberman, Martin)
The History of Jacob and Esau (Anon.)
    (In Dodsley's A Select Collection of Old English Plays, Vol.
    2)
The History of the Tryall of Chevalry (Anon.)
    (In A Collection of Old English Plays, Vol. 3)
Hit or Miss (see Pocok, Isaac)
The Hitch Hiker (see Fletcher, Lucille)
Hitchcock, Alfred, 1899-
    North by Northwest (see Lehman, Ernest)
    Rebecca (see Sherwood, Robert Emmet)
    Spellbound (see Hecht, Ben)
HITCHCOCK, George
    The Busy Martyr
    (In First Stage, Vol. 2, Winter, 1962/63)
    Upward, Upward
    (In First Stage, Vol. 3, Summer-Fall 1964)
HIVNOR, Robert
    The Assault upon Charles Sumner
    (In Plays for a New Theatre)
HIYOSHI Sa-ami Yasukiyo, 15th cent. ?
    Benkei on the Bridge (Hashi-Benkei)
    (In Genius of the Oriental Theater)
HOADLY, Benjamin, 1706-1757
    The Suspicious Husband
    (In Cumberland's British Theatre, Vol. 3, no. 4)
    (In Bell's British Theatre, 1797, Vol. 4)
    (In The London Stage, Vol. 2)
HOARE, Prince, 1755-1834
    Lock and Key
    (In Cumberland's British Theatre, Vol. 35, no. 5)
    My Grandmother
    (In Cumberland's British Theatre, Vol. 35, no. 3)
    No Song, No Supper
    (In Cumberland's British Theatre, Vol. 35, no. 2)
    The Prize; or, 2, 5, 3, 8
    (In Cumberland's British Theatre, Vol. 35, no. 4)
    The Three and the Deuce; or, Which is Which?
    (In Cumberland's British Theatre, Vol. 44, no. 6)
Hobbes, John Oliver, pseud. (see Craigie, Mrs. P. T. Richards)

HOCHHUTH, Rolf, 1933-
   The Deputy
      (In Evergreen Playscript Series)
   Soldiers
      (In Evergreen Playscript Series)
HOCHWALDER, Fritz, 1911-
   L'Accusateur Public
      (In Plaisir de France, supplement theatral, no. 319, May 1965)
   The Order
      (In Modern International Drama, Vol. 3, no. 2, 1969)
   The Public Prosecutor
      (In Plays of the Year, Vol. 16, 1956/57)
Die Hochzeit des Papstes (see Bond, Edward)
HODGE, Merton, 1903-
   Grief Goes Over
      (In Famous Plays of Today, 1935)
   The Wind and the Rain
      (In Famous Plays of Today, 1933/34)
Hölderlin (see Weiss, Peter)
Hofer, the Tale of the Tyrol (see Fitz-Ball, Edward)
HOFFE, Monckton, 1881-
   Many Waters
      (In Famous Plays of Today, 1929)
HOFFMAN, Byrd
   The King of Spain
      (In New American Plays, Vol. 3)
Hoffman, Ernst Theodor Amadeus, 1776-1822
   **The Devil's Elixir; or, The Shadowless Man (see Fitz-Ball, Edward)
HOFFMAN, Leo Calvin
   The Forgotten Land, by John Sheffield, pseud.
      (In Best Short Plays, 1953/54)
   Imploring Flame, by John Sheffield, pseud.
      (In Best One-Act Plays, 1952/53, N.Y.)
HOFFMAN, M.
   The Sage and His Father
      (In Theatrical Recorder, Vol. 1, no. 5, April 1805)
HOFFMAN, Phoebe, 1894-
   The Man of the Moment
      (In Ten Fantasies for Stage and Study, 1932)
   Mrs. Leicester's School
      (In New Plays for Women & Girls, 1932)
   The Turn of a Hair
      (In Drama, Vol. 15, Jan. 1925)
HOFFMAN, William M.
   Thank You, Miss Victoria
      (In New American Plays, Vol. 3)
      x x
   x   x
      x
      x   [sic]
      (In More Plays From Off Off Broadway)
HOFMANN, Gert

The Burgomaster
  (In Evergreen Playscript Series, no. 12)
Our Man in Madras
  (In Evergreen Review, Vol. 13, no. 63, Feb. 1969)
HOFMANNSTHAL, Hugo von Hoffmann, Elder von, 1874-1929
  Anatol (see Schnitzler, Arthur)
  Arabella (see Strauss, Richard)
  Electra
    (In Modern Theatre, ed. by R. W. Corrigan)
  Madonna Dianora
    (In 50 Contemporary One-Act Plays)
  Der Tor und der Tod
    (In Das Deutsch Drama, 1880-1933, Vol. 1)
The Hog Hath Lost His Pearl (see The Hogge Hath Loste His
  Pearle)
Hogan's Goat (see Alfred, William)
Hogan's Successor (see Spiers, Russell)
HOGARTH, William, 1697-1764
  **The Curse of Mammon
    (In Cumberland's British Theatre, Vol. 46, no. 6)
The Hogge Hath Lost His Pearle (see Tailor, Robert)
HOLBERG, Ludvig von, baron, 1684-1754
  Jeppe of the Hill
    (In Genius of the Scandinavian Theater)
Holcroft, Fanny
  The Baron (see Moratin, Leonard Ferendes de)
  Emilia Galotti (see Lessing, Gotthold Ephraim)
  Fortune Mends (see Calderon de la Barca, Pedro)
  From Bad to Worse (see Calderon de la Barca, Pedro)
  Minna von Barnhelm (see Lessing, Gotthold Ephraim)
  Philip the Second (see Alfieri, Vittoro)
  Rosamond (see Weisse, Christian Felix)
HOLCROFT, Thomas, 1745-1809
  Deaf and Dumb; or, The Orphan Protected
    (In Cumberland's British Theatre, Vol. 6, No. 5)
    (In The London Stage, Vol. 1)
  Duplicity
    (In Modern Theatre, 1811, Vol. 4)
  The Road to Ruin
    (In Cumberland's British Theatre, Vol. 29, no. 2)
  The School for Arrogance
    (In Modern Theatre, 1811, Vol. 4)
  Seduction
    (In Modern Theatre, 1811, Vol. 4)
  A Tale of Mystery
    (In Cumberland's British Theatre, Vol. 18, no. 7)
    (In The London Stage, Vol. 1)
HOLDEN, Joan
  The Independent Female; or, A Man Has His Pride
    (In Ramparts, Dec. 1970)
The Holiday (see Mazaud, Emile)
Holiday Song (see Chayefsky, Paddy)

HOLL, Henry
    Grace Huntley
      (In Cumberland's British Theatre, Vol. 38, no. 1)
HOLLAND, Anthony
    Lekythos
      (In Mademoiselle, Vol. 72, Nov. 1970)
HOLLAND, Norman
    Day Before Yesterday
      (In Best One-Act Plays of 1949/50, N. Y.)
    Farewell Appearance, by Norman Holland the Stanley Richards
      (In Best One-Act Plays, 1950/51, N. Y.)
    Leopard's Spots
      (In Best One-Act Plays of 1944/45, London)
    One Hour Alone
      (In Best One-Act Plays of 1942/43, London)
    The Small, Private World of Michael Marston
      (In Best Short Plays, 1968)
    Tea With a Legend
      (In Best One-Act Plays of 1948/49, London)
    Wages of Sin
      (In Best One-Act Plays, 1960/61, N. Y.)
Hollowishes (see Hayn, Annette)
HOLM, John Cecil
    Quiet--Facing the Park
      (In Best One-Act Plays of 1943, N. Y.)
    Three Men on a Horse (see Abbott, George)
HOLMAN, Joseph George, 1764-1817
    The Votary of Wealth
      (In Modern Theatre, 1811, Vol. 3)
HOLME, Constance
    The Home of Vision
      (In Best One-Act Plays of 1932, London)
    "I Want!"
      (In Five Three-Act Plays, Strand, 1933)
The Holy Crown (see Aylen, Elise)
The Holy Terrors (see Cocteau, Jean)
Home (see Storey, David)
HOME, John, 1722-1808
    Douglas
      (In Cumberland's British Theatre, Vol. 6, no. 2)
      (In Bell's British Theatre, 1797, Vol. 3)
HOME, William Douglas, 1912-
    Le Canard a l'Orange
      (In L'Avant Scene du Theatre, no. 480, Oct. 1, 1971)
    The Queen's Highland Servant
      (In Plays of the Year, Vol. 35, 1967/68)
    The Reluctant Debutante
      (In Theatre Arts, Vol. 41, May 1957)
    The Secretary Bird
      (In Plays of the Year, Vol. 36, 1968/69)
    Yes, M'Lord
      (In Theatre Arts, Vol. 34, Apr. 1950)

The Home for the Friendly (see Frank, Mrs. Florence Kiper)
Home of the Brave (see Laurents, Arthur)
The Home of Vision (see Holme, Constance)
Home on the Range (see Jones, Leroi)
Home, Sweet Home (song) (see Clari; or, The Maid of Milan)
The Homecoming (see Pinter, Harold)
O Homem que Fica (see Magalhaes Jor, Raymundo)
L'Homme Couche (see Maura, Carlos Semprun)
Un Homme dans la Foule (see Schulberg, Budd)
L'Homme de Rangoon (see Abecassis, Guy)
Un Homme et une Femme (see Lelouch, Claude)
L'Homme Qui se Taisait (see Caillol, Pierrette)
Les Hommes de Haute Vertu (see Aub, Max)
Les Hommes de la Baleine (see Ruspoli, Mario)
The Honest Thieves (see Knight, Thomas)
Honest Urubamba (see Mandel, Oscar)
The Honest Whore (see Dekker, Thomas)
The Honey Moon (see Tobin, John)
Honeymoon in Haiti (see Kleb, William E.)
L'Honneur des Dupont (see Dabril, Lucien)
Honor (see Vidal, Gore)
Honorable Togo (see McInroy, Harl)
HOOK, Theodore Edward, 1788-1841
    Exchange No Robbery
        (In Cumberland's British Theatre, Vol. 32, no. 8)
    Killing No Murder
        (In Cumberland's British Theatre, Vol. 36, no. 1)
    Tekeli; or, The Siege of Montgatz
        (In Cumberland's British Theatre, Vol. 22, no. 3)
HOOLE, John, 1727-1803
    Cleonice, Princess of Bithynia
        (In Bell's British Theatre, 1797, Vol. 24)
        (In Cumberland's British Theatre, Vol. 34, no. 3)
    Cyrus
        (In Bell's British Theatre, 1797, Vol. 24)
    Timanthes
        (In Bell's British Theatre, 1797, Vol. 34)
Hoopla! Such Is Life (see Toller, Ernst)
The Hoose o' the Hill (see Corrie, Joe)
Hope Is a Thing with Feathers (see Harrity, Richard)
HOPKINS, Arthur Melancthon, 1878-1950
    Moonshine
        (In Theatre Arts, Vol. 3, 1919)
        (In Contemporary One-Act Plays, 1922)
HOPKINS, John
    Diese Geschichte von Ihnen
        (In Theater Heute, Vol. 10, no. 7, July 1969)
    Find Your Way Home
        (In Plays and Players, Vol. 17, no. 10, July 1970)
    This Story of Yours
        (In Plays and Players, Vol. 16, no. 5, Feb. 1969)
Hopper, Dennis
    Easy Rider (see Fonda, Peter)

Hopwood, Avery, 1884-1928
    The Bat (see Rinehart, Mary Roberts)
Horatti
    *The Roman Father (see Whitehead, William)
Horniman, Roy
    Noblesse Oblige (see Hamer, Robert)
Hornthal, Larry
    The Dance Below (see Strode, Hudson)
HOROVITZ, Israel, 1939-
    Acrobats
        (In Best Short Plays, 1970)
    The Indian Wants the Bronx
        (In Best Short Plays, 1969)
        (In Showcase 1)
Horrible Conspiracies (see Whitemore, Hugh)
The Horse (see Hay, Julius)
Horwitt, Arnold B.
    Plain and Fancy (see Hague, Albert Martin)
Hospital Scene (see Dugan, Lawrence Joseph)
The Hostage (see Behan, Brendan)
Hot Buttered Roll (see Drexler, Rosalyn)
Hot Spell (see Coleman, Lonnie)
Hotel (see Van Itallie, Jean-Claude)
Hotel des Invalides (see Franju, Georges)
Hotel Universe (see Barry, Philip)
HOUGHTON, Stanley, 1881-1913
    The Dear Departed
        (In 30 Famous One-Act Plays)
        (In 24 One-Act Plays, Rev. Ed., 1954)
    Fancy Free
        (In Representative One-Act Plays by British and Irish Authors)
    Hindle Wakes
        (In Late Victorian Plays)
House and Home (see Miles, Josephine)
The House Beautiful (see Hanna, Tacie May)
The House by the Stable (see Williams, Charles)
House Divided (see Neuenberg, Evelyn)
The House I Live In (see Oboler, Arch)
The House into which We Are Born (see Copeau, Jacques)
The House of Bernarda Alba (see Garcia Lorca, Federico)
The House of Connelly (see Green, Paul)
House of Cowards (see Abse, Dannie)
The House of Sugawara (Sugawara Denju Tenarai Kagami) (see
    Takeda Izumo)
The House of the Octopus (see Williams, Charles)
A House with Two Doors Is Difficult to Guard (see Calderon de
    la Barca, Pedro)
A Household Fairy (see Talfourd, Francis)
The Housetop Madman (see Kikuchi Kwan)
HOUSMAN, Laurence, 1865-1959
    Brother Sun
        (In 24 One-Act Plays, Revised edition, 1954)

The Christmas Tree
  (In Drama, Vol. 11, Dec. 1920)
A Good Shot
  (In Best One-Act Plays of 1936, London)
The Revolting Daughter
  (In Palace Plays)
The Snowman
  (In Representative One-Act Plays by British and Irish Authors)
Victoria Regina
  (In 16 Famous British Plays)
The Wicked Uncles; or, Victorious Virtue
  (In Palace Plays)
HOUSTON, Noel
  According to Law
  (In Best One-Act Plays of 1940, N. Y.)
How a Man May Choose a Good Wife from a Bad (see Cooke,
  Joshua)
How Green Was My Valley (see Dunne, Philip)
How They Knocked the Devil Out of Uncle Ezra (see Wishengrad,
  Morton)
How to Grow Rich (see Reynolds, Frederick)
How to Rob a Bank (see Fayad, Samy)
Howard, Catherine, 4th wife of Henry VIII, king of England
  *Catherine Howard (see Cross, Beverly)
HOWARD, F. Morton
  The Capture
  (In The One-Act Theatre, Vol. 2)
HOWARD, James, fl. 1674
  All Mistaken; or, The Mad Couple
  (In Dodsley's A Select Collection of Old English Plays, Vol.
  15)
HOWARD, Sir Robert, 1626-1698
  The Committee
  (In Bell's British Theatre, 1797, Vol. 20)
HOWARD, Roger
  Three Short Plays
  (In Scripts, Vol. 1, no. 4, Feb. 1972)
HOWARD, Sidney Coe, 1891-1939
  The Late Christopher Bean, based on "Prenez Garde a la
  Peinture" by Rene Fauchois
  (In 20 Best European Plays on the American Stage)
  Madam, Will You Walk?
  (In Theatre Arts, Vol. 41, Feb. 1957)
  **The Most Happy Fella (see Loesser, Frank)
  The Silver Cord
  (In Theatre Guild Anthology)
  They Knew What They Wanted
  (In Pulitzer Prize Plays)
  (In 25 Best Plays of the Modern American Theatre, Early
  Series, 1916/29)
  (In 16 Famous American Plays)
  Yellow Jack

(In Best American Plays, Supp. Vol.)
**Yellow Jack; screenplay (see Chodorov, Edward)
HOWARTH, Donald
    Three Months Gone
        (In Plays and Players, Vol. 17, no. 7, April 1970)
HOWE, Carroll V., 1923-
    The Long Fall
        (In Best One-Act Plays of 1949/50, N. Y.)
        (In Best Short Plays, 1956/57)
HOWE, Julia Ward, 1819-1910
    Hippolytus
        (In Monte Cristo and Other Plays)
HOWELL, Florence
    Jane Wogan
        (In Best One-Act Plays of 1934, London)
HOWELLS, William Dean, 1837-1920
    The Mouse-Trap
        (In Best Plays of the Early American Theatre, from the
        beginning to 1916)
How's the World Treating You? (see Milner, Roger)
Hrabal, Bohumil
    Closely Watched Trains (see Menzel, Jiri)
The Hraun Farm (see Sigurjonsson, Johann)
HROTSVIT, of Gandersheim
    Abraham
        (In The Plays of Roswitha)
    Callimachus
        (In The Plays of Roswitha)
    Dulcitius
        (In The Plays of Roswitha)
    Gallicanus
        (In The Plays of Roswitha)
    Paphuntius
        (In The Plays of Roswitha)
    Sapientia
        (In The Plays of Roswitha)
HSIUNG, Cheng-Chin
    The Marvelous Romance of Wen Chun-Chin
        (In Poet Lore, Vol. 35, 1924)
    The Thrice Promised Bride
        (In Theatre Arts, Vol. 7, 1923)
        (In Golden Book, Vol. 2, Aug. 1925)
HUDSON, Holland, 1889-
    Pottery
        (In 50 More Contemporary One-Act Plays)
    The Shepherd in the Distance
        (In 50 Contemporary One-Act Plays)
Hugh of the Glenn & His Clogs Are All One (see Stephens, Peter
    John)
HUGHES, Babette (Piechner), 1906-
    The First White Woman
        (In New Plays for Women & Girls, 1932)

Fit As a Fiddle
  (In The One-Act Theatre, Vol. 2)
If the Shoe Pinches
  (In Best One-Act Plays of 1937, N. Y.)
The Liar and the Unicorn
  (In 50 More Contemporary One-Act Plays)
HUGHES, Elizabeth (Wilson), 1918-
  Frankie and Albert
    (In Best One-Act Plays of 1947/48, N. Y.)
    (In Best Short Plays, 1956/57)
  The Lord and Hawksaw Sadie
    (In Best One-Act Plays of 1946/47, N. Y.)
  Rise of Her Bloom
    (In Best One-Act Plays, 1950/51, N. Y.)
  Wantin' Fever
    (In Best One-Act Plays of 1948/49, N. Y.)
  A Wishful Taw
    (In Best Short Plays, 1953/54)
Hughes, Elwil (pseud.)   (see Hughes, Elizabeth Wilson)
HUGHES, Glenn, 1894-
  Bottled in Bond
    (In Drama, Vol. 13, Feb. 1923)
  The Eve in Evelyn
    (In 50 More Contemporary One-Act Plays)
  For the Love of Michael
    (In New Plays for Woman & Girls, 1932)
  Men Only
    (In The One-Act Theatre, Vol. 1)
  Red Carnations
    (In 15 American One-Act Plays)
HUGHES, Hatcher, 1881-1945
  Hell-Bent fer Heaven
    (In Pulitzer Prize Plays)
HUGHES, John, 1677-1720
  The Siege of Damascus
    (In Bell's British Theatre, 1797, Vol. 12)
HUGHES, Ken
  Sammy
    (In Television Playwright: 10 Plays for BBC, 1960)
HUGHES, Langston, 1902-1967
  Book T. Washington in Atlanta
    (In Radio Drama in Action, 1945)
  The Prodigal Son
    (In Players Magazine, Vol. 43, no. 1, Oct. /Nov. 1967)
HUGHES, Richard Arthur Warren, 1900-
  A Comedy of Danger
    (In 50 More Contemporary One-Act Plays)
Hughes, Rupert, 1872-1956
  Tillie and Gus   (see Martin, Francis)
HUGHES, Thomas, fl. 1587
  The Misfortunes of Arthur
    (In Dodsley's A Select Collection of Old English Plays, Vol.
    4)

Hughie (see O'Neill, Eugene Gladstone)
HUGO, Victor Marie, comte, 1802-1885
   Hernani
     (In Genius of the French Theater)
     (In Chief French Plays of the 19th Century)
  **Les Miserables (see Archard, Paul)
   Ruy Blas
     (In Chief French Plays of the 19th Century)
Hui, Lan-Ki (see Brecht, Bertolt)
Huit et Demi (see Fellini, Federico)
Huit Femmes (see Thomas, Robert)
HULL, Thomas, 1728-1808
   Henry II; or, The Fall of Rosamond
     (In Bell's British Theatre, 1797, Vol. 28)
     (In Modern Theatre, 1811, Vol. 9)
The Human Accident (see Frink, Charles)
Humanities (see Bellow, Saul)
Humour Out of Breath (see Day, John)
The Humpbacked Lover (see Mathews, Charles, Jr.)
Humphrey Clinker (see Dibdin, Thomas)
     (In Cumberland's British Theatre, Vol. 25, no. 1)
Humulus le Muet (see Augustus (English Version))
The Hunchbacks (Anon.)
     (In Cumberland's British Theatre, Vol. 22, no. 9)
The Hundred and First (see Cameron, Kenneth)
The Hundred Pound Note (see Peake, Richard Brinsley)
HUNG, Josephine Huang, adapter
   The Price of Wine (Mei Lung Chen) (Anon.)
     (In Traditional Asian Plays)
Hunger and Thirst (see Ionesco, Eugene)
The Hungerers (see Saroyan, William)
The Hunted (see Senior, Edward)
HUNTER, Norman Charles, 1908
   A Day By the Sea
     (In Famous Plays of Today, 1954)
   Waters of the Moon
     (In Famous Plays of Today, 1953)
HUNTER, Paul, 1933-
   An Interview with F. Scott Fitzgerald
     (In Best Short Plays, 1972)
The Hunter and the Bird (see Van Itallie, Jean-Claude)
The Hunter of the Alps (see Dimond, William)
Las Hurdes (Terre sans Pain) (see Buñuel, Luis)
HURSLEY, Frank
   Atomic Bombs, by Frank and Doris Hursley
     (In Best One-Act Plays of 1945, N.Y.)
A Husband (see Sevo, Italo)
Husband and Wife (see Saroyan, William)
A Husband at Sight (see Buckstone, John Baldwin)
A Husband for Breakfast (see Mitchell, Ronald Elwy)
HUSSON, Albert, 1912-
   Absence of a Cello (see Wallach, Ira)

Claude de Lyon
  (In Plaisir de France, supplement theatral, no. 279, Jan.
  1962)
L'Impromptu des Collines
  (In Plaisir de France, supplement theatral, no. 279, Jan.
  1962)
**My 3 Angels (see Spewack, Samuel)
L'Ombre du Cavalier
  (In L'Avant-Scene du Theatre, May 1956)
Le Systeme Fabrizzi
  (In Plaisir de France, supplement theatral, no. 303, Jan.
  1964)
HUSTER, Francis
  Les Amours de Jacques le Fataliste
  (In L'Avant Scene du Theatre, no. 466, Feb. 15, 1971)
The Hustler (see Rossen, Robert)
HUSTON, John, 1906-
  Dr. Ehrlich's Magic Bullet; original screenplay by John Huston,
  Heinz Herald and Norman Burnside, from an idea by Norman
  Burnside. Directed by William Dieterle.
  (In Best Pictures, 1939/40)
  Juarez (see Reinhardt, Wolfgang)
  Let There Be Light
  (In Film: Book 2, 1962)
  (In Evergreen Filmscript Series: Book 2)
  The Life and Times of Judge Roy Bean (see Milius, John)
HUSZARIK, Zoltan, 1931-
  Elegie
  (In L'Avant-Scene du Cinema, no. 87, Dec. 1968)
HUTCHINSON, Alfred
  The Rain Killers
  (In Plays from Black Africa)
Hutton, Brian G., 1935-
  XY & Zee (see O'Brien, Edna)
HUTTON, Michael Clayton
  Roundabout
  (In Best One-Act Plays, London, 1952/53)
HUXLEY, Aldous Leonard, 1894-1963
  The Gioconda Smile. Original title "Mortal Coils," based on
  his short story "The Gioconda Smile."
  (In Theatre Arts, Vol. 35, May 1951)
Hyacinth Halvey (see Gregory, Isabella Augusta Persse, lady)
Hyacinths (see Hanna, Tacie May)
Hyman, Mac, 1923-1963
  No Time for Sergeants (see Levin, Ira)
Hymn to the Rising Sun (see Green, Paul)
The Hypocrite (see Bickerstaff, Isaac)
L'Hypothese (see Pinget, Robert)

I Am a Camera (see Van Druten, John)
I Am Curious (Blue) (see Sjoman, Vilgot)

I Am Curious (Yellow) (see Sjoman, Vilgot)
I Can't Imagine Tomorrow (see Williams, Tennessee)
I Claudius (see Mortimer, John)
I, Elizabeth Otis, Being of Sound Mind (see Barber, Philip)
I Have to Call My Father (see Brown, Lennox)
I Know George Washington (see Phelps, Pauline)
I Never Sang for My Father (see Anderson, Robert)
I Rise in Flame, Cried the Phoenix (see Williams, Tennessee)
I Spy (see Mortimer, John)
I Too Have Lived in Arcadia (see Lang, V. R.)
I Too Speak to the Rose (see Carballido, Emilio)
"I Want!" (see Holme, Constance)
IBSEN, Henrik Johan, 1828-1906
    Doll's House 1970 (see Luce, Clare Boothe)
    Hedda Gabler
        (In The Modern Theatre, ed. by R. W. Corrigan)
    Hedda Gabler; text in French
        (In L'Avant-Scene du Theatre, no. 143)
    Ghosts
        (In Tragedy: Texts and Commentary, 1969)
        (In Introduction to Literature: Plays)
    John Gabriel Borkman
        (In Makers of the Modern Theater, 1961)
        (In Plays of the Year, Vol. 23, 1960/61)
    Master Builder
        (In Genius of the Scandinavian Theater)
    The Wild Duck
        (In Genius of the Scandinavian Theater)
        (In The Modern Theatre, ed. by R. W. Corrigan)
        (In 16 Famous European Plays)
Icarus (see Rubenstein, Ken)
The Ice Witch; or, The Frozen Land (see Buckstone, John Baldwin)
Icebound (see Davis, Owen)
The Iceman Cometh (see O'Neill, Eugene)
"Ich Spiele dir die Welt durch" (see Schreiter, Helfried)
Ichheit on a Holiday (see Filippone, Vincenzo)
"Icke und die Hexe Yu" (see Medek, Tilo)
IDELSON, Bill
    Get Smart, a television filmscript, by Bill Idelson and Sam
      Bobrick.
        (In Writing for Television)
L'Idiot (see Barsacq, Andre)
Idiot's Delight (see Sherwood, Robert Emmet)
Idyll (see Graham, Mary)
If (see Anderson, Lindsay)
If Men Played Cards as Women Do (see Kaufman, George S.)
If the Shoe Pinches (see Hughes, Babette Piechner)
If This Be Not a Good Play, the Devil Is in It (see Dekker, Thomas)
If This Is a Man (see Levi, Primo)
Der Ignorant und der Wahsinnige (see Bernhard, Thomas)
Ikiru (see Kurosawa, Akira)
Ikkaku Sennin (see Motoyasu, Komparn Zembo)
Il n'y a Pas d'Automne sans Ete (see Ruth, Leon)

INCHBALD, Mrs. Elizabeth (Simpson), 1753-1831
 Animal Magnetism
  (In Cumberland's British Theatre, Vol. 24, no. 7)
 The Child of Nature
  (In Cumberland's British Theatre, Vol. 26, no. 2)
  (In The London Stage, Vol. 2)
 Everyone Has His Fault
  (In Cumberland's British Theatre, Vol. 19, no. 6)
  (In The London Stage, Vol. 2)
 I'll Tell You What
  (In Modern Theatre, 1811, Vol. 7)
 Lovers' Vows; altered from the German of Kotzebue
  (In Cumberland's British Theatre, Vol. 7, no. 5)
 The Midnight Hour
  (In Cumberland's British Theatre, Vol. 12, no. 4)
 Next Door Neighbours
  (In Modern Theatre, 1811, Vol. 7)
 Such Things Are
  (In The London Stage, Vol. 1)
 The Wedding Day
  (In Cumberland's British Theatre, Vol. 42, no. 7)
  (In The London Stage, Vol. 2)
 The Wise Men of the East
  (In Modern Theatre, 1811, Vol. 7)
 Wives As They Were, and Maids As They Are
  (In Cumberland's British Theatre, Vol. 24, no. 6)
The Inchcape Bell (see Fitz-Ball, Edward)
Incident à Vichy (see Miller, Arthur)
Incident at a Grave (see Lake, Goldie)
An Incident at the Standish Arms (see Inge, William Motter)
Un Incompris (see Montherlant, Henry de)
The Inconstant (see Farquhar, George)
The Incredible World of Horace Ford (see Rose, Reginald)
The Independent Female; or, A Man Has His Pride (see Holden, Joan)
The Indian Wants the Bronx (see Horovitz, Israel)
INDICK, Benjamin P.
 Apples
  (In Players Magazine, Vol. 41, no. 7)
Ines de Portugal (see Casona, Alejandro)
"A Infedelidade ao Alcance de Todos" (see Muniz, Laura Cesar)
The Infernal Machine (see Cocteau, Jean)
The Informer (see Nichols, Dudley)
The Informers (see Brecht, Bertolt)
INGE, William Motter, 1913-1973
 The Boy in the Basement
  (In Eleven Short Plays)
 Bus Riley's Back in Town
  (In Eleven Short Plays)
 Bus Stop
  (In Four Plays by Inge)
  (In Theatre Arts, Vol. 40, Oct. 1956)

The Call
  (In Best Short Plays, 1968)
Come Back, Little Sheba
  (In Plays of Our Time)
  (In Four Plays by Inge)
  (In Theatre Arts, Vol. 34, Nov. 1950)
  (In Best American Plays, Third Series)
The Dark at the Top of the Stairs; original title, "Farther Off
  from Heaven"
  (In Four Plays by Inge)
  (In Theatre Arts, Vol. 43, no. 9, Sept. 1959)
  (In 6 American Plays for Today)
  (In Best American Plays, 5th series, 1957-63)
The Disposal
  (In Best Short Plays of the World Theatre, 1958-67)
Glory in the Flower
  (In 24 Favorite One-Act Plays)
An Incident at the Standish Arms
  (In Eleven Short Plays)
A Loss of Roses
  (In Esquire, Vol. 53, Jan. 1960)
A Loss of Roses, filmed as "The Stripper"
  (Random House Play, 1960)
The Mall
  (In Eleven Short Plays)
  (In Esquire, Vol. 51, Jan. 1959)
Memory of Summer
  (In Eleven Short Plays)
Midwestern Manic
  (In Best Short Plays, 1969)
People in the Wind
  (In Eleven Short Plays)
Picnic
  (In Four Plays by Inge)
  (In Theatre Arts, Vol. 38, April 1954)
  (In Best American Plays, Fourth Series)
The Rainy Afternoon
  (In Eleven Short Plays)
A Social Event
  (In Eleven Short Plays)
Splendor in the Grass
  (Bantam Books Screenplays)
The Strains of Triumph
  (In Eleven Short Plays)
The Tiny Closet
  (In Best Short Plays, 1958/59)
  (In Eleven Short Plays)
To Bobolink, for Her Spirit
  (In Eleven Short Plays)
INGELEND, Thomas, fl. 1560
  The Disobedient Child
  (In Dodsley's A Select Collection of Old English Plays, Vol.
  2)

INGERSOLL, James H.
  The Queen's Shift
    (In The Banner Anthology of One-Act Plays by American
    Authors)
INGHAM, Robert E., 1934-
  A Simple Life
    (In Four New Yale Playwrights)
Inherit the Wind (see Lawrence, Jerome)
The Inheritors (see Cook, Richard)
Os Inimigos Nao Mandam Flores (see Bloch, Pedro)
Inkle and Yarico (see Colman, George)
The Ink-Smeared Lady (see Sakanishi, Shio)
Inner Man (see Brighouse, Harold)
Innermost I Land (see Ferrini, Vincent)
The Innkeeper of Abbeville (see Fitz-Ball, Edward)
The Innocents (see Archibald, William)
Inside a Kid's Head (see Lawrence, Jerome)
Insideout (see Norman, Frank)
L'Insoumis (see Cavalier, Alain)
An Inspector Calls (see Priestley, John Boynton)
The Inspector General (see Gogol, Nikolai)
Interior (see Maeterlinck, Maurice)
Interlude (see More, Federico)
An Interlude in Porcelain (see Davenport, E.V.)
Interlude of the Four Elements (Anon.)
    (In Dodsley's A Select Collection of Old English Plays, Vol.
    1)
Interlude of Youth (Anon.)
    (In Dodsley's A Select Collection of Old English Plays, Vol.
    2)
The Interrogation (see Bellido, Jose Maria)
Intersections 7 (see Epstein, Paul)
The Interview (see Burtt, Theodore C., Jr.)
Interview (see Van Itallie, Jean-Claude)
An Interview with F. Scott Fitzgerald (see Hunter, Paul)
Intimate Relations (see Cocteau, Jean)
The Intimate Strangers (see Tarkington, Booth)
Intolerance (see Griffith, David Wark)
The Intriguing Chambermaid (see Fielding, Henry)
The Intruder (see Maeterlinck, Maurice)
The Invasion (L'Invasion) (see Adamov, Arthur)
The Invasion from Mars (see Koch, Howard)
The Investigation (see Weiss, Peter)
The Invincibles (see Morton, Thomas)
Invitation to a March (see Laurents, Arthur)
Ion (see Euripides)
IONESCO, Eugene, 1912-
  Amedee; or, How to Get Rid of It
    (In Evergreen Playscript Series, Vol. 2)
    (In Amedee; The New Tenant; Victims of Duty)
  Anger
    (In Hunger and Thirst and Other Plays)

The Bald Prima Donna
   (In Evergreen Playscript Series, Vol. 1)
The Bald Soprano
   (In Makers of the Modern Theatre, 1961)
   (In Four Plays)
Bedlam Galore for Two or More
   (In Tulane Drama Review, Vol. 7, Spring 1963)
The Chairs
   (In One Act)
   (In Modern Theatre, ed. by R. W. Corrigan)
   (In Introduction to Literature: Plays)
   (In Theatre Arts, Vol. 42, July 1958)
   (In Four Plays)
   (In Evergreen Playscript Series, Vol. 1)
Exit the King
   (In Evergreen Playscript Series, Vol. 5)
Foursome
   (In Evergreen Review, Vol. 4, May/June 1960)
   (In Evergreen Playscript Series, Vol. 5)
Frenzy for Two or More
   (In A Stroll in the Air)
   (In Evergreen Playscript Series, Vol. 6)
   (In Evergreen Review, Vol. 9, no. 36, 1965)
The Future is in Eggs; or, It Takes All Sorts to Make a World
   (In Evergreen Playscript Series, Vol. 4)
Gap
   (In Massachusetts Review, Vol. 10, Winter 1969)
Hunger and Thirst
   (In Hunger and Thirst and Other Plays)
Improvisation; or, The Shepherd's Cameleon
   (In Horizon, Vol. 3, May 1961)
   (In Evergreen Playscript Series, Vol. 3)
   (In The Killer and Other Plays)
Jack, or the Submission
   (In Four Plays)
Jeux de Massacre
   (In L'Avant-Scene du Theatre, no. 472, May 15, 1971)
Jocques, or Obedience
   (In Evergreen Playscript Series, Vol. 1)
The Killer
   (In Evergreen Playscript Series, Vol. 3)
   (In The Killer and Other Plays)
La Lacune
   (In L'Avant-Scene du Theatre, no. 472)
The Leader
   (In Evergreen Playscript Series, Vol. 4)
The Lesson
   (In Theatre Arts, Vol. 42, July 1958)
   (In Four Plays)
   (In Evergreen Playscript Series, Vol. 1)
Macbett; text in French
   (In L'Avant-Scene du Theatre, no. 501, Sept. 1, 1972)

Macbett; text in German
   (In Theater Heute, no. 7, July 1972)
Maid to Marry
   (In Evergreen Playscript Series, Vol. 3)
   (In The Killer and Other Plays)
The Motor Show
   (In Evergreen Playscript Series, Vol. 5)
The New Tenant
   (In Evergreen Playscript Series, Vol. 2)
   (In Amedee; The New Tenant; Victims of Duty)
The Picture
   (In Hunger and Thirst and Other Plays)
Rhinoceros
   (In Theatre Arts, Vol. 46, July 1962)
   (In Evergreen Playscript Series, Vol. 4)
   (In 7 Plays of the Modern Theatre)
Saturations
   (In Hunger and Thirst and Other Plays)
A Stroll in the Air
   (In Evergreen Playscript Series, Vol. 6)
   (In A Stroll in the Air; Frenzy for Two)
Victims of Duty
   (In Evergreen Playscript Series, Vol. 2)
   (In Amedee; The New Tenant; Victims of Duty)
Iphigenia in Aulis   (see Euripides)
Iphigenia in Tauris   (see Euripides)
Ireland--As It Was   (see Amherst, J. A.)
Irene   (see Johnson, Samuel)
The Irishman in London   (see Macready, William)
The Iron Harp   (see O'Conor, Joseph)
Ironhand   (see Arden, John)
The Irregular Verb to Love   (see Williams, Hugh and Margaret)
Irving, Washington, 1783-1859
   Charles the Second   (see Payne, John Howard)
  **Rip Van Winkle   (see Jefferson, Joseph)
IRWIN, Will
   The Hamaadryads
      (In The Grove Plays of the Bohemian Club, Vol. 1)
Is Romance Dead?   (see Wellington, Barbara)
Is She His Wife? or, Something Singular!   (see Dickens, Charles)
Isabella; or, The Fatal Marriage   (see Southern, Thomas)
Isabelle et le General   (see Mithois, Marcel)
Isherwood, Christopher, 1904-
   The Dog Beneath the Skin   (see Auden, Wystan Hugh)
  **I Am a Camera   (see Van Druten, John)
The Island   (see Thon, Frederick)
It Ain't Brooklyn   (see Dempsey, David)
It Happened One Night   (see Riskin, Robert)
It Is So (If You Think So)   (see Pirandello, Luigi)
It Is So (If You Think So!)   (see also, Right You Are (If You
   Think So!))
It Should Happen to a Dog   (see Mankowitz, Wolf)

It Takes a Thief   (see Kozlenko, William)
The Italian Girl (see Murdoch, Iris)
An Italian Straw Hat (see Labiche, Eugene Marin)
Itallie, Jean Claude van (see Van Itallie, Jean-Claude)
Itard, Jean Marc Gaspard, 1775-1838
  **L'Enfant Sauvage (see Truffaut, Francois)
It's a Long Way to St. Louis (see Miller, Adam David)
It's All a Matter of Dress (see Hammond, Virginia Maye)
It's All (Y)ours!
It's Almost Like Being (see Van Itallie, Jean-Claude)
It's Almost Like Being (see also, Almost Like Being)
It's Fun to be Free (see Hecht, Ben)
It's Spring (see Harris, Claudia Lucas)
It's the Poor That 'elps the Poor (see Chapin, Harold)
Ivan IV, called "The Terrible," 1530-1584
  *Ivan the Terrible (see Eisenstein, Sergei Mikhailovich)
  *Ivan the Terrible (see Priestley, Horace)
Ivanhoe; or, The Jew's Daughter (see Dibdin, Thomas Frognall)
Ivanov (see Chekhov, Anton Pavlovich)
IVENS, Joris, 1898-
    Europort: Rotterdam
      (In L'Avant-Scene du Cinema, no. 99, Jan. 1970)
    A Valparaiso
      (In L'Avant-Scene du Cinema, no. 76, Dec. 1967)
Iwasaki Yozan T. (see Nari-Kin)
Iz She Izzy or Is He Ain'tzy or Iz They Both (see Carter, Lonnie)

J.B. (see MacLeish, Archibald)
Jack and Jill and a Friend (see Hamilton, Cicely Mary)
Jack Brag (see A Beckett, Gilbert Abbott)
Jack Juggler (Anon.)
      (In Dodsley's A Select Collection of Old English Plays, Vol.
      2)
Jack of All Trades (Anon.)
      (In 26 Short & Amusing Plays)
Jack; or, The Submission (see Ionesco, Eugene)
Jack Sheppard; or, The House-Breaker of the Last Century (see
    Greenwood, Thomas)
The Jackass (El Asno) (see Ruibal, Jose)
Jackie the Jumper (see Thomas, Gwyn)
JACKSON, C.B.
    Fly Blackbird, by C.B. Jackson and James Hatch
      (In The Black Teacher and the Dramatic Arts)
Jackson, Charles, 1903-1968
  **The Lost Weekend (see Bracket, Charles)
JACKSON, Felix
  **Bachelor Mother (see Krasna, Norman)
    Destry Rides Again; screenplay by Felix Jackson, Gertrude Pur-
    cell and Henry Meyers; based on the novel by Max Brand
    (pseud.). Directed by George Marshall.
      (In Best Pictures, 1939/40)

JACKSON, Shirley, 1920-1965
  The Lottery, a television script based on her story.
    (In Best Television Plays of the Year, 1950/51)
  The Lottery; a one-act play (see Duffield, Brainerd)
Jacobowsky and the Colonel (see Werfel, Franz V.)
JACOBS, Fred Rue
  Don't Know Sic'em from Sooey
    (In Yale/Theatre, Vol. 3, no. 1, Fall 1970)
JACOBS, Jack, 1919-
  Bride-Ship
    (In Best One-Act Plays of 1946/47, N.Y.)
JACOBS, William Wymark, 1863-1943
  A Love Passage
    (In Dramas by Present-Day Writers)
  The Monkey's Paw
    (In 30 Famous One-Act Plays)
JAEGER, C. Stephen
  The Compromise
    (In Drama & Theatre, Vol. 8, no. 3, Spring 1970)
JAGENDORF, M.
  Buffalmacco's Jest
    (In Best One-Act Plays of 1934, London)
J'ai Vingt Ans (Faubourg d'Illytch) (see Khoutziev, Marlen)
Jambinho do Contra (see Leonardos, Stella)
James, Grace
  **The Good and Obedient Young Man (see Barr, Betty)
JAMES, Henry, 1843-1916
  A Change of Heart
    (In Atlantic, Vol. 29, Jan. 1872)
  Daisy Miller
    (In Atlantic, Vol. 51, April /June 1883)
  **The Innocents (see Archibald, William)
  **A Late Spring (see Bobb, Ralph)
  **The Turn of the Screw (see Vidal, Gore)
  **The Wings of the Dove (see Taylor, Christopher)
James and John (see Cannan, Gilbert)
James I, King of Scotland as James VI and of Great Britain as
  James I, 1566-1625
  *The Magnificent Entertainment Given to King James (see Dek-
    ker, Thomas)
  *Baggy Breeks; or, The Wisest Fool in Christendom (see Sims,
    Alan)
JAMIAQUE, Yves
  Don Quichotte (Based on Cervantes' work)
    (In Plaisir de France, supplement theatral, no. 321, July
    1965)
Jane Seymour (see Thorne, Ian)
Jane Shore (see Rowe, Nicholas)
Jane Wogan (see Howell, Florence)
JANNELLI, Guglielmo
  Synthesis of syntheses, by Guglielmo Jannelli and Luciano Ni-
    castro
    (In TDR/The Drama Review, Vol. 15, Fall 1970)

Janowitz, Hans
  The Cabinet of Dr. Caligari   (see Wiene, Robert)
JANOWSKI, Maurycy
  Karambolage
    (In Theatre der Zeit, Vol. 25, Jan. 1970)
Janus (see Green, Carolyn)
Japanese-Americans (see Kleiner, Harry)
Japan's Advance Base: The Bonin Islands (see Marquis, Arnold)
JAQUINE, Jacques
  Raphael...Fais Tourner le Monde
    (In L'Avant-Scene du Theatre, no. 497, June 15, 1972)
The Jar (see Finkel, Donald)
The Jar (see Pirandello, Luigi)
Un Jardin sur la Mer (see Vermorel, Claude)
Jariti (see Correa, Viriato)
JARRELL, Myra Williams
  The Case of Mrs. Kantsey Know
    (In Drama, Vol. 12, March 1922)
Jason and Medea (see Baring, Maurice)
JASUDOWICZ, Dennis, 1940-
  Blood Money
    (In New American Plays, Vol. 1)
  Strumming
    (In Tulane Drama Review, Vol. 9, Winter 1964)
JAVET, Pierre
  Louis XIV
    (In Plaisir de France, supplement theatral, no. 294, April
    1963)
Jazznite (see Jones, Walter)
The Jealous Wife (see Colman, George)
JEFFERE, John, supposed author
  The Buggbears
    (In Early Plays from the Italian)
JEFFERS, Robinson, 1887-1962
  The Cretan Woman
    (In From the Modern Repertoire, Series Three)
  Medea, freely adapted from the "Medea" of Euripides
    (In Theatre Arts, Vol. 32, Fall 1948)
    (In Best American Plays, Third Series)
JEFFERSON, Joseph, 1829-1905
  Rip Van Winkle
    (In The Black Crook & Other 19th Century American Plays)
    (In S.R.O., the Most Successful Plays...)
Jefferson, Thomas, pres. U.S., 1743-1826
  *Brothers to Dragons (see Warren, Robert Penn)
JELLICOE, Ann, 1927-
  Le Knack
    (In L'Avant Scene du Theatre, Nov. 15, 1967)
    (In Plaisir de France, supplement theatral, no. 350, Dec.
    1967)
  The Knack; the Sport of My Mad Mother
    (In Evergreen Playscript Series)

JENNINGS, Gertrude
   The Bride
     (In Best One-Act Plays of 1931, London)
   The Christening
     (In The One-Act Theatre, Vol. 2)
JENNINGS, Talbot
   The Good Earth; a screenplay by Talbot Jennings and Tess
   Slesinger, with additional dialogue by Frances Marion, Marc
   Connelly and Jules Furthman, based on the novel by Pearl
   Buck, directed by Sidney Franklin.
     (In Twenty Best Film Plays)
JEPHSON, Robert, 1736-1803
   Braganza
     (In Modern Theatre, 1811, Vol. 6)
   The Law of Lombardy
     (In Modern Theatre, 1811, Vol. 6)
   Two Strings to Your Bow
     (In Cumberland's British Theatre, Vol. 45, no. 6)
Jeppe of the Hill (see Holberg, Ludvig von, baron)
JERROLD, Douglas
   The Bride of Ludgate
     (In Cumberland's British Theatre, Vol. 21, no. 1)
   The Devil's Ducat; or, The Gift of Mammon
     (In Cumberland's British Theatre, Vol. 22, no. 1)
   The Golden Calf
     (In Cumberland's British Theatre, Vol. 35, no. 9)
   The Mutiny at the Nore
     (In Cumberland's British Theatre, Vol. 21, no. 2)
The Jest of Hahalaba (see Dunsany, Lord)
Jest, Satire, Irony (see Grabbe, Christian Dietrich)
Jesus Christ
   *The Birth of Christ (see York Title-Thatchers' Play)
   *Christ (see Hartmann, Sadakichi)
   *The Crucifixion (see York Butcher's Play)
   *The Harrowing of Hell (York Saddlers' Play)
   *Jesus (see Dreyer, Carl Theodor)
   *Jesus-Fric Supercrack (see Scoff, Alain)
   *The Lamb and the Beast (see Strindberg, August)
   *Palm Sunday (see York Skinners' Play)
   *The Temptation of Christ (see York Locksmiths' Play)
   *The Woman Taken in Adultry (see Hegge Cycle)
Les Jeunes Loups (see Carne, Marcel)
Jeux de Massacre (see Ionesco, Eugene)
Jeux de Nuit (see Zetterling, Mai)
Jeux Interdits (see Clement, Rene)
The Jew and the Doctor (see Dibdin, Thomas)
The Jew of Malta (see Marlowe, Christopher)
The Jewels of the Shrine (see Henshaw, James Ene)
The Jewish Wife (see Brecht, Bertolt)
Jinen the Preacher (see Kannami, Kiyotsugu)
Joan of Arc, St., c. 1412-1431
   *Joan of Arc; or, The Maid of Orleans (see Fitz-Ball, Edward)

*Joan of Lorraine (see Anderson, Maxwell)
*The Lark (see Anouilh, Jean)
*The Maid of Domremy (see Corrie, Joe)
*The Passion of Joan of Arc (see Dreyer, Carl Theodor)
*Saint Joan (see Shaw, George Bernard)
Joao do Rio, pseud. (see Barreto, Paulo)
Joao Farrapo (see Pires, Meira)
Joaozinho e Maria (see Carvalho, Helio)
The Job (see Caldwell, Ben)
The Job (see Visconti, Luchino)
Job's Kinfolks (see Bailey, Loretto Carroll)
JOCKYMAN, Sergio, 1930-
    "La"
        (In Revista de Teatro, no. 381, May 1971)
Jocques, or Obedience (see Ionesco, Eugene)
JODOROWSKY, Alexandro
    The Mole; a filmscript
        (In TDR/The Drama Review, Vol. 14, no. 2, Winter 1970)
    El Topo; screenplay
        (In El Topo, a Book of the Film)
Joey (see Else, George)
John Bull; or, The Englishman's Fireside (see Colman, George,
    the Younger)
John Bull's Other Island (see Shaw, George Bernard)
JOHN, Errol
    Moon on a Rainbow Shawl
        (In Evergreen Playscript Series, no. 1)
JOHN, Evan
    Prelude to Massacre
        (In Best One-Act Plays of 1937, London)
John Ferguson (see Ervine, St. John Greer)
John Gabriel Borkman (see Ibsen, Henrik)
John of Paris (see Pocock, Isaac)
John Turner Davis (see Foote, Horton)
John, Tyb, and Sir John (see Heywood, John)
Johnnas (see Gunn, Bill)
Johnny Johnson (see Green, Paul)
Johnny No-Trump (see Mercier, Mary)
JOHNSON, Charles, 1679-1748
    The Country Lasses; or, The Custom of the Manor
        (In Bell's British Theatre, 1797, Vol. 9)
    The Gamesters (see Shirley, William)
JOHNSON, Elizabeth
    A Bad Play for an Old Lady
        (In Playwrights for Tomorrow, Vol. 1)
JOHNSON, Mrs. Georgia Douglas (Camp), 1886-
    Blue Blood
        (In 50 More Contemporary One-Act Plays)
    Plumes
        (In Plays of Negro Life)
Johnson, Lyndon Baines, pres. U.S., 1908-1973
    *The Election (political satire) (see Koch, Kenneth)

*MacBird (political satire)   (see Garson, Barbara)
JOHNSON, Martyn
    Mr. and Mrs. P. Roe
        (In Drama, Vol. 13, Dec. 1922)
JOHNSON, Nunnally, 1897-
    The Grapes of Wrath, screenplay; based on the book by John
    Steinbeck, directed by John Ford
        (In Twenty Best Film Plays)
JOHNSON, Philip, 1900-
    Dark Brown
        (In Best One-Act Plays of 1944/45, London)
    Heaven on Earth
        (In The One-Act Theatre, Vol. 2)
    In Waltz Time
        (In Best One-Act Plays of 1940, London)
    Orange Blossom
        (In Best One-Act Plays of 1942/43, London)
    Tinsel Duchess
        (In Best One-Act Plays of 1948/49, London)
JOHNSON, Samuel, 1696-1772
    Irene
        (In Bell's British Theatre, 1797, Vol. 25)
JOHNSON, Wallace
    Flight of the Sea Warriors
        (In TDR/Drama Review, Vol. 14, Sept. 1970)
    What Did You Learn in School?
        (In Players Magazine, Vol. 41, no. 4, Jan. 1965)
JOLLY, Andrew
    Quintila
        (In First Stage, Vol. 1, no. 4, Fall 1962)
JONAS, Joan
    Organic Honey's Visual Telepathy
        (In TDR/The Drama Review, Vol. 16, no. 2, June 1972)
JONES, Barbara Elgin
    City Symphony
        (In Best One-Act Plays of 1942, N.Y.)
JONES, David B.
    Neither Here nor There; a filmscript
        (In Story: the Yearbook of Discovery, 1968)
JONES, Henry, 1721-1770
    The Earl of Essex
        (In Bell's British Theatre, 1797, Vol. 6)
        (In Cumberland's British Theatre, Vol. 37, no. 3)
JONES, Henry Arthur, 1851-1929
    The Goal
        (In Representative One-Act Plays by British and Irish Authors)
        (Dramas by Present-Day Writers)
    Judah
        (In Great English Plays)
    The Liars
        (In Late Victorian Plays)
JONES, LeRoi, 1934-

The Baptism
(In Evergreen Playscript Series, no. 10)
A Black Mass
(In Four Black Revolutionary Plays)
Dutchman
(In Evergreen Playscript Series)
Experimental Death Unit #1
(In Four Black Revolutionary Plays)
Great Goodness of Life
(In Best Short Plays of the World Theatre, 1958-1967)
(In Four Black Revolutionary Plays)
Home on the Range
(In TDR/The Drama Review, Vol. 12, Summer 1968)
Madheart
(In Four Black Revolutionary Plays)
Police
(In TDR/The Drama Review, Vol. 12, Summer 1968)
The Slave
(In Evergreen Playscript Series)
The Toilet
(In Best American Plays, Sixth Series, 1963-67)
(In Evergreen Playscript Series, no. 10)
JONES, Pamela
The Schoolhouse Is Burning
(In Yale/Theatre, Vol. 2, no. 2, Summer 1969)
JONES, Peter
The Party Spirit, by Peter Jones and John Jowett
(In Plays of the Year, Vol. 11, 1954)
Jones, Robert Edmond, 1887-1954
The Cenci (see Shelley, Percy Bysshe)
Jones, Tom, 1928-
The Fantasticks (see Schmidt, Harvey L.)
JONES, Walter
Jazznite
(In Scripts, Vol. 1, no. 6, April 1972)
JONSON, Ben, 1573?-1637
The Alchymist
(In Bell's British Theatre, 1797, Vol. 1)
Eastward Hoe (see Chapman, George)
Every Man in His Humour
(In Cumberland's British Theatre, Vol. 9, no. 4)
**Satiormastix (see Dekker, Thomas)
The Silent Woman
(In Great English Plays)
Volpone; or, The Fox, adapted by Stefan Zweig
(In 20 Best European Plays on the American Stage)
(In Genius of the Early English Theater)
(In Masterworks of World Drama, Vol. 3)
The Widow, by Ben Jonson, John Fletcher, and Thomas Middle-
ton
(In Dodsley's A Select Collection of Old Plays, Vol. 12)
Joseph Kilian un Personnage a Soutenir (see Juracek, Pavel)

Un Jour a Paris (see Korber, Serge)
Un Jour dans la Mort de Joe Egg (see Nichols, Peter)
Un Jour de Folie (see Vilalta, Maruxa)
Le Jour se Leve (see Carne, Marcel)
The Journey (see Rondi, Brunello)
Journey for an Unknown Soldier (see Frankel, Doris)
Journey to Bahia (see Gomes, Alfred Dias)
Journey's End (see Sherriff, Robert Cedric)
Le Journal d'une Femme de Chambre (see Buñuel, Luis)
The Jovial Crew; or, The Merry Beggars (see Brome, Richard)
Jowett, John
    The Party Spirit (see Jones, Peter)
The Joy Lady (see Hall, Josef Washington)
JOYCE, James, 1882-1941
    Finnegans Wake; complete dialogue script for the film by Ex-
    panding Cinema
        (In Passages from Joyce's "Finnegans Wake")
Juarez, Benito Pablo, President Mexico, 1806-1872
    *Juarez (see Reinhardt, Wolfgang)
Jubilee (see Heijermans, Herman)
Judah (see Jones, Henry Arthur)
Judas (see Pagnol, Marcel)
Judas No Tribunal (see Tinoco, Godofredo)
Judd for the Defense (see Monash, Paul)
Judge Lynch (see Rogers, John W., Jr.)
Judgement at Chelmsford (see Williams, Charles)
The Judgement of Indra (see Mukerji, Dhan Gopal)
Judith (see Giraudoux, Jean)
Judith (see Kemp, Harry Hibbard)
Juizo Final (see Camargo, Joracy)
Jules (see Breal, Pierre-Aristide)
Jules and Jim (see Truffaut, Francois)
Jules Cesar; text in French (see Shakespeare, William)
Jules et Jim (see Truffaut, Francois)
Julie (see Strindberg, August)
Juliet and Romeo (see Gribble, Harry Wagstaff)
Juliet of the Spirits (see Fellini, Federico)
Jungle of Cities (see Brecht, Bertolt)
Jungle of Cities (see also, In the Jungle of Cities)
JUNIOR, Franca
    Como Se Frazia um Deputado
        (In Revista de Teatro, no. 347)
    Maldita Parentela
        (In Revista de Teatro, no. 300)
Juno und der Pfau (see O'Casey, Sean)
JUPP, Kenneth
    The Socialites
        (In Satan, Socialites, and Solly Gold)
JURACEK, Pavel, 1935-
    Josef Kilian un Personnage a Soutenir (Pastava K. Podpirani)
    by Pavel Juracek et Jan Schmidt.
        (In L'Avant-Scene du Cinema, no. 60, 1966)

JURU Motomasa
     The Sumida River
          (In Plays of Old Japan)
The Just Assassins (see Camus, Albert)
Just Like in the Movies (see Gardner, Gary)
Just Neighborly (see Dean, Alexander)
Just Off Piccadilly (see Parish, James)
Justice (see Galsworthy, John)
JUSTIMA, William, Jr.
     Chi-Fu
          (In Drama, Vol. 13, Aug./Sept. 1923)

Das Kaffeehaus (see Fassbinder, Rainer Werner)
Kafka, Franz, 1883-1924
     **Le Proces (see Welles, Orson)
     **The Trial (see Welles, Orson)
KAFKA, Sherry
     The Man Who Loved God
          (In Best Short Plays, 1968)
Kagekiyo (see Zeami Motokiyo)
KAHLAU, Heinz
     Musterschüler
          (In Theater der Zeit, Vol. 24, Dec. 1969)
KAISER, Georg, 1878-1945
     From Morn to Midnight, translated by Ashley Dukes
          (In 20 Best European Plays on the American Stage)
     Gas I
          (In Das Deutsche Drama, 1880-1933, Vol. 2)
     The Protagonist
          (In Tulane Drama Review, Vol. 5, Dec. 1960)
     The Raft of Medusa
          (In First Stage, Vol. 1, no. 2, Spring 1962)
KALCHEIM, Lee H.
     And the Boy Who Came to Leave
          (In Playwrights for Tomorrow, Vol. 2)
KALIDASA
     Shahuntala and the Ring of Recognition
          (In Genius of the Oriental Theater)
Kaltouma (see Bebnone, Palou)
KAMINSKY, Stuart M.
     Here Comes the Best Part
          (In First Stage, Vol. 6, Fall 1967)
Der Kammersanger (see Wedekind, Frank)
Kanal (see Wajda, Andrzej)
KANAMI Kiyotsugu
     Jinen the Preacher
          (In The Old Pine Tree & Other Noh Plays)
     The Maiden's Tomb
          (In Plays of Old Japan)
     Sotoba Komachi
          (In Anthology of Japanese Literature)

KANIN, Garson, 1912-
Adam's Rib (see Gordon, Ruth)
Bachelor Mother (see Krasna, Norman)
Born Yesterday
(In Best Plays of the Modern American Theatre, Second
Series)
Kanjincho (see Kabuki Play, trans. by James R. Brandon and
Tamako Niwa)
Kantan (see Hiraoke, Kimitake)
KANZE Kojiro Nobumitsu
The Maple Viewing (Momijigari)
(In Three Japanese Plays from the Traditional Theatre)
KAPROW, Allan
Gas, by Allan Kaprow and Charles Frazier
(In Theatre Experiment)
Karambolage (see Janowski, Maurycy)
KARCHMER, Sylvan, 1914-
On This Green Bank
(In Best One-Act Plays of 1947/48, N.Y.)
Karin Lenz (see Kochan, Günter)
KARINTHY, Ferenc, 1921-
Steinway Grand (Bösendorfer)
(In Modern International Drama, Vol. 1, no. 2, March 1968)
KARINTHY, Fritz
Refund; translated and adapted by Percival Wilde
(In Best One-Act Plays of 1936, London)
Karl XII, King of Sweden, 1682-1718
*Charles XII (see Strindberg, August)
Karl-Ludwig's Window (see Munro, Hector Hugh)
Karma (see Kocher, Eric)
KARPOWICZ, Tymoteusz
The Strange Passenger
(In Drama & Theatre, Vol. 7, no. 2, Winter 1968/69)
KARVAS, Peter
Great Wig
(In Literary Review, Vol. 13, Fall 1969)
Kaspar (see Handke, Peter)
KAST, Pierre, 1920-
L'Architecte Maudit: Claude-Nicholas Ledoux
(In L'Avant-Scene du Cinema, no. 88, Jan. 1969)
La Brulure de Mille Soleils
(In L'Avant-Scene du Cinema, no. 89, 1969)
Kathleen Listens In (see O'Casey, Sean)
The Kathryn Steffan Story (see Steffan, Kathryn)
KAUFMAN, George Simon, 1889-1961
Beggar on Horseback, by George S. Kaufman and Marc Connelly
(In 25 Best Plays of the Modern American Theatre, Early
Series, 1916-1929)
A Christmas Carol, by George S. Kaufman and Marc Connelly,
based on the story by Charles Dickens.
(In Bookman, Vol. 56, Dec. 1922)
Dream On, Soldier (see Hart, Moss)

If Men Played Cards As Women Do
  (In 30 Famous One-Act Plays)
The Man Who Came to Dinner (see Hart, Moss)
Merton of the Movies, by George S. Kaufman and Marc Con-
  nelly, based on the story by Harry Leon Wilson
  (In Dramas by Present-Day Writers)
A Night at the Opera, film script by George S. Kaufman and
  Morrie Ryskind; story by James Kevin McGuinness; directed
  by Sam Wood
  (In In MGM Library of Film Scripts Series)
Of Thee I Sing (see Gershwin, George)
Once in a Lifetime (see Hart, Moss)
The Social Worker and the Alcoholic
  (In First Stage, Vol. 3, Winter 1963/64)
The Solid Gold Cadillac (see Teichmann, Howard)
Stage Door (see Ferber, Edna)
The Still Alarm
  (In 15 American One-Act Plays)
  (In 24 Favorite One-Act Plays)
You Can't Take It with You (see Hart, Moss)
You Can't Take It with You; screenplay (see Riskin, Robert)
KAUGVER, Raimond
  Die Eigene Insel
  (In Theater der Zeit, no. 10, 1972)
KAWATAKE Mokuami
  Benten the Thief (Aoto Zoshi Hana no Nishikie, or Shiranami
  Gonin Otoko)
  (In Three Japanese Plays from the Traditional Theatre)
KAWATAKE, Shinichi
  The Courtesan (Kagotsurube)
  (In Six Kabuki Plays)
Kazan, Elia, 1909-
  Baby Doll (see Williams, Tennessee)
  A Tree Grows in Brooklyn (see Slesinger, Tess)
KEARNEY, Patrick, 1894-
  The Great Noontide
  (In Drama, Vol. 11, Jan. 1921)
  The Murder of Murat
  (In Drama, Vol. 18, Apr. 1928)
  Tongues of Fire
  (In Drama, Vol. 11, Aug./Sept. 1921)
KEATS, John, 1795-1821
  King Stephen; a dramatic fragment.
  (In Complete Works, Vol. 3)
  Otho the Great; a tragedy in 5 acts
  (In Complete Works, Vol. 3)
KEELER, Charles
  A Pagoda Slave
  (In Drama, Vol. 12, Feb. 1922)
The Keep (see Thomas, Gwyn)
Keep Tightly Closed in a Cool, Dry Place (see Terry, Megan)
KEIGEL, Leonard, 1929-

Keller   206
    Leviathan, by Leonard Keigel et Julien Green
      (In L'Avant-Scene du Cinema, no. 14, Apr. 15, 1962)
Keller, Helen, 1880-1968
    *Helen Keller (see Deckelman, Ethel)
    *The Miracle Worker (see Gibson, William)
    *Miracle en Alabama; French text of "The Miracle Worker"
      (see Gibson, Wm.)
KELLEY, Arthur
    Tour of Duty
      (In Best One-Act Plays, 1951/52, N.Y.)
KELLING, Gerhard
    Arbeitgeber
      (In Theatre Heute, Vol. 10, no. 12, Dec. 1969)
Kelly, Gene, 1912-
    Singin' in the Rain (see Comden, Betty)
KELLY, George Edward, 1887-
    Craig's Wife
      (In Pulitzer Prize Plays)
    The Flattering Word
      (In 24 Favorite One-Act Plays)
    Poor Aubrey
      (In 25 Best Plays of the Modern American Theatre, Early
      Series, 1916-29)
KELLY, Hugh, 1739-1777
    False Delicacy
      (In Bell's British Theatre, 1797, Vol. 30)
    The School for Wives
      (In Bell's British Theatre, 1797, Vol. 7)
    A Word to the Wise
      (In Bell's British Theatre, 1797, Vol. 30)
KELLY, Mary
    The Spell
      (In 24 One-Act Plays, Revised edition, 1954)
KELLY, Terence, 1920-
    Stella
      (In Best Short Plays, 1972)
KEMBLE, Charles, 1715-1854
    The Point of Honour
      (In Cumberland's British Theatre, Vol. 22, no. 5)
Kemble, Mrs. Charles (see Kemble, Mrs. Marie Therese (De
    Camp), 1774-1838)
Kemble, Fanny (see Kemble, Frances Anne, 1809-1893)
KEMBLE, Frances Anne, 1809-1893
    An English Tragedy
      (In Plays, by Frances Anne Kemble)
KEMBLE, John Philip, 1757-1823
    The Farm House
      (In The London Stage, Vol. 1)
    Lodoiska
      (In The London Stage, Vol. 1)
KEMBLE, Mrs. Marie-Therese (De Camp), 1774-1838
    The Day after the Wedding; or, A Wife's First Lesson
      (In Cumberland's British Theatre, Vol. 25, no. 6)

Fairly Taken In
  (In 26 Short & Amusing Plays, 1871)
  Personation; or, Fairly Taken In
  (In Cumberland's British Theatre, Vol. 46, no. 8)
KEMP, Harry Hibbard, 1883-
  Boccaccio's Untold Tale
  (In Boccaccio's Untold Tale)
  (In 50 Contemporary One-Act Plays)
  Calypso
  (In Boccaccio's Untold Tale)
  Don Juan in the Garden
  (In Boccaccio's Untold Tale)
  Don Juan's Christmas Eve
  (In Boccaccio's Untold Tale)
  (In 50 More Contemporary One-Act Plays)
  A Few Words Beforehand
  (In Boccaccio's Untold Tale)
  The Game Called Kiss
  (In Boccaccio's Untold Tale)
  Judith
  (In Boccaccio's Untold Tale)
  The Plays Themselves
  (In Boccaccio's Untold Tale)
  Solomon's Song
  (In Boccaccio's Untold Tale)
  Their Day
  (In Boccaccio's Untold Tale)
  The White Hawk
  (In Boccaccio's Untold Tale)
KENAN, Amos
  The Balloon
  (In First Stage, Vol. 2, Summer 1963)
  The Lion
  (In First Stage, Vol. 4, Spring 1965)
KENDRICK, William, 1735?-1799
  Falstaff's Wedding; written in imitation of Shakespeare
  (In Bell's British Theatre, 1797, Vol. 31)
Kenilworth (see Dibdin, Thomas)
KENNARD, Marietta C.
  The Flight of the Herons
  (In Drama, Vol. 14, Dec. 1923)
KENNAWAY, James
  Country Dance
  (In Plays of the Year, Vol. 33, 1967)
KENNEDY, Adrienne, 1931-
  Funnyhouse of a Negro
  (In Best Short Plays, 1970)
  The Owl Answers
  (In New American Plays, Vol. 2)
  A Rat's Mass
  (In More Plays From Off Off Broadway)
  (In New Black Playwrights)
  Sun

(In Scripts, Vol. 1, no. 1, Nov. 1971)
KENNEDY, James, 1780-1849
The Alcaid; or, The Secrets of Office
   (In Cumberland's British Theatre, Vol. 2, no. 1)
The Blind Boy
   (In Cumberland's British Theatre, Vol. 18, no. 5)
Ella Rosenberg
   (In Cumberland's British Theatre, Vol. 23, no. 6)
The Illustrious Stranger; or, Married and Buried
   (In Cumberland's British Theatre, Vol. 39, no. 3)
Love, Law, and Physic
   (In Cumberland's British Theatre, Vol. 23, no. 5)
Matrimony
   (In Cumberland's British Theatre, Vol. 27, no. 4)
Raising the Wind
   (In Cumberland's British Theatre, Vol. 28, no. 9)
Kennedy, John Fitzgerald, pres. U.S., 1917-1963
   *The Election (political satire) (see Koch, Kenneth)
   *MacBird (political satire) (see Garson, Barbara)
Kent, David
   Mr. Mergenthwirker's Lobblies (see Bond, Nelson)
KEPEL, Milan
   Le Rapport Dont Vous Etes l'Objet (see Havel, Vaclav)
   Le Brave Soldat Sveik
      (In Plaisir de France, supplement theatral, no. 334, Aug.
      1966)
KEPHART, William M.
   All-American Ape
      (In Best One-Act Plays of 1941, N.Y.)
KERAUTEM, Louis de
   Le Centenaire, by Elka (pseud.)
      (In L'Avant-Scene du Theatre, no. 494, May 1972)
   Le Roti de Veau, by Elka (pseud.)
      (In L'Avant-Scene du Theatre, no. 506, Nov. 15, 1972)
La Kermesse Heroique (see Spaak, Charles)
KERNDL, Rainer
   Wann Kommt Ehrlicher?
      (In Theater der Zeit, no. 1, 1972)
   Zweipersonenstück
      (In Theater der Zeit, Dec. 1970)
KERR, Jean (Collins)
   King of Hearts, by Jean Kerr and Eleanor Brooks. (First
   issued under title "Comic Strip")
      (In Theatre Arts, Vol. 39, July 1955, p. 35)
   Mary, Mary
      (In Best American Plays, Fifth Series, 1957-1963)
KESSELRING, Joseph, 1902-
   Arsenic and Old Lace
      (In Best Plays of the Modern American Theatre, Second
      Series)
      (In S.R.O., the Most Successful Plays...)
KESTER, Katherine

Penny a Flower
    (In Drama, Vol. 15, Dec. 1924)
Key, Francis Scott, 1780-1843
    *The Passing of Francis Scott Key (see Markgraf, Bruce)
KEY, Ted
    The Clinic
        (In Plays from Radio, 1948)
The Key (see Sender, Ramon)
Key Largo (see Anderson, Maxwell)
Khorev: A Tragedy (see Sumarokov, Aleksandr Petrovich)
KHOUTZIEV, Marlen
    J'ai Vingt Ans (Faubourg d'Illytch) by Marlen Houtziev et
    Guennady Chpalikov
        (In L'Avant-Scene du Cinema, no. 42, 1964)
KIKUCHI Kwan
    Better than Revenge
        (In Tojuro's Love & Four Other Plays)
    The Father Returns
        (In Tojuro's Love & Four Other Plays)
    The Housetop Madman
        (In Tojuro's Love & Four Other Plays)
    The Madman on the Roof
        (In Three Modern Japanese Plays)
    The Miracle
        (In Tojuro Love & Four Other Plays)
    Tojuro's Love
        (In Tojuro's Love & Four Other Plays)
Kill Viet Cong (see Head, Robert)
The Killer (see Ionesco, Eugene)
KILLIGREW, Thomas, 1612-1683
    The Parson's Wedding
        (In Dodsley's A Select Collection of Old English Plays, Vol.
        14)
        (In Dodsley's A Select Collection of Old Plays, Vol. 11)
Killing No Murder (see Hook, Theodor Edward)
The Killing of Sister George (see Marcus, Frank)
Kills-with-Her-Man (see Alexander, Hartley Burr)
KIMBALL, Kathleen
    The Meat Rack
        (In Scripts, Vol. 1, no. 7, May 1972)
KIMMEL, H. B.
    Radio Felicity
        (In The Literary Review, Vol. 15, no. 1, Fall 1971)
Kind Lady (see Chodorov, Edward)
KING, Grace Elizabeth
    A Splendid Offer
        (In Drama, Vol. 16, Mar. 1926)
King, Henry, 1888 or 1892-
    In Old Chicago (see Trotti, Lamar)
    Wilson (see Trotti, Lamar)
KING, Philip
    Serious Charge
        (In Plays of the Year, Vol. 11, 1954)

King Alfred and the Neat-Herd (see Baring, Maurice)
King Alfred the Cake Burner (see Sims, Alan)
The King and the Duke (see Fergusson, Francis)
King Charles I (see Havard, William)
King Glumpus (see Thackeray, William Makepeace)
King John and Matilda (see Davenport, Robert)
King Nicolo; or, Such Is Life (see Wedekind, Frank)
King of Hearts (see Kerr, Jean)
The King of Spain (see Hoffman, Byrd)
The King of Spain's Daughter (see Deevy, Teresa)
The King Stag (see Goldoni, Carlo)
King Stephen; a Dramatic Fragment (see Keats, John)
Kingdom of Earth (see Williams, Tennessee)
The King's Son, Churl's Son (see Oliver, Margaret Scott)
KINGSLEY, Sidney, 1906-
    Darkness at Noon, based on the novel by Arthur Koestler
        (In Theatre Arts, Vol. 37, April 1953)
        (In Best American Plays, Third Series)
    Dead End
        (In 16 Famous American Plays)
        (In 20 Best Plays of the Modern American Theatre, Vol. 1)
    Detective Story
        (In Best American Plays, Third Series)
    Men in White
        (In Best American Plays, Supp. Vol.)
        (In Pulitzer Prize Plays)
    The Patriots
        (In Best Plays of the Modern American Theatre, Second
        Series)
KINOY, Ernest
    Goodbye to the Clown
        (In Best One-Act Plays, 1950/51, N.Y.)
    Whistle, Daughter, Whistle
        (In Best One-Act Plays of 1948/49, N.Y.)
Kiper, Frances (see Frank, Mrs. Florence (Kiper))
KIRKLAND, Jack, 1901-
    Tobacco Road, by Jack Kirkland and Erskine Caldwell, from
    the novel by Erskine Caldwell
        (In 20 Best Plays of the Modern American Theatre, Vol. 1)
        (In S.R.O., the Most Successful Plays...)
KIRKPATRICK, John Alexander, 1895-
    Green Eyes from Romany
        (In New Plays for Women & Girls, 1932)
    Of Time and the Blizzard
        (In Best One-Act Plays of 1939, N.Y.)
    Sleeping Dogs
        (In Best One-Act Plays of 1940, N.Y.)
    The Strangest Feeling
        (In Best One-Act Plays of 1942, N.Y.)
A Kiss in the Dark (Anon.)
        (In 26 Short & Amusing Plays, 1871)
Kiss Me Kate (see Porter, Cole)

Kissing Goes by Favor (see Brown, Laura Norton)
Kiste; German text of "The Box" (see Albee, Edward)
KITANI, Shigeo
    The Sound of Night
        (In Players Magazine, Vol. 41, no. 1, Oct. 1964)
Kitchenette (see Tavel, Ronald)
Das Klassentreffen (see Rosow, Viktor von)
KLEB, William E., 1939-
    Honeymoon in Haiti
        (In Four New Yale Playwrights)
KLEINER, Harry
    Japanese-Americans
        (In Radio Drama in Action, 1945)
Kleiner Mann, Was Nun? (see Dorst, Tankred)
KLEINSINGER, George
    Archie and Mehitabel, a back-alley opera, based on the vig-
        nettes of Don Marquis
        (In Best Short Plays, 1958/59)
KLEIST, Heinrich von, 1777-1811
    The Broken Jug
        (In Four Continental Plays, 1964)
    L'Ordalie ou la Petit Catherine de Heilbronn
        (In Plaisir de France, supplement theatral, no. 340, Feb.
        1967)
    Panthesilea
        (In The Classic Theatre, Vol. 2)
    Prince Frederick of Homburg
        (In Genius of the German Theater)
        (In Masterworks of World Drama, Vol. 6)
    The Prince of Homburg
        (In The Classic Theatre, Vol. 2)
        (In Plays of the Year, Vol. 36, 1968/69)
    Robert Guiscard
        (In Tulane Drama Review, Vol. 6, Mar. 1962)
Le Knack (see Jellicoe, Ann)
Knackery for All (see Vian, Boris)
The Knave of Hearts (see Saunders, Louise)
KNEALE, Nigel
    Mrs. Wickens in the Fall
        (In Television Playwright: 10 Plays for BBC)
KNEE, Allan
    Ephraim
        (In First Stage, Vol. 5, Spring 1966)
KNIGHT, Thomas, d. 1820
    The Honest Thieves
        (In Cumberland's British Theatre, Vol. 26, no. 8)
    The Turnpike Gate
        (In Cumberland's British Theatre, Vol. 29, no. 8)
Knight in Four Acts (see Harrison, John)
The Knight of the Burning Pestle (see Beaumont, Francis)
The Knights (see Aristophanes)
The Knights of the Cross; or, The Hermit's Prophecy (Anon.)

(In Cumberland's British Theatre, Vol. 46, no. 2)
Knoblock, Edward, 1874-1945
  Milestones (see Bennett, Arnold)
KNOTT, Frederick
  Dial "M" for Murder
    (In Famous Plays of Today, 1953)
    (In Theatre Arts, Vol. 39, Mar. 1955)
Know Your Own Mind (see Murphy, Arthur)
KNOWLES, James Sheridan, 1784-1862
  Caius Gracchus
    (In Cumberland's British Theatre, Vol. 1, no. 5)
  Virginius
    (In Cumberland's British Theatre, Vol. 1, no. 4)
  William Tell
    (In Cumberland's British Theatre, Vol. 4, no. 5)
Knowlton, Beatrice
  The Way the Noise Began (see Knowlton, Don)
KNOWLTON, Don
  The Way the Noise Began, by Don and Beatrice Knowlton
    (In Drama, Vol. 12, Oct./Nov. 1921)
KNOX, Alexander, 1907-
  The Closing Door
    (In Theatre Arts, Vol. 34, May 1950)
KOBER, Arthur, 1900-
  "Having Wonderful Time"
    (In 16 Famous American Plays)
KOBRYNSKI, Lazare
  La Dame au Petit Chien; based on a story by Tchekhov
    (In Plaisir de France, supplement theatral, no. 347, Sept.
    1967)
  Le Garde-Chasse; based on a story by Tchekov
    (In Plaisir de France, supplement theatral, no. 321, July
    1965)
KOCH, Howard, 1902-
  Casablanca (see Epstein, Julius J.)
  The Invasion from Mars; script from the Orson Welles broad-
    cast, based on "War of the Worlds" by H.G. Wells
    (In Invasion From Mars; a Study in the Psychology of Panic)
KOCH, Kenneth, 1925-
  Bertha
    (In Evergreen Playscript Series)
    (In A Change of Hearts)
  The Construction of Boston
    (In Evergreen Playscript Series)
    (In A Change of Hearts)
  E. Kology
    (In A Change of Hearts)
  The Election
    (In A Change of Hearts)
  George Washington Crossing the Delaware
    (In Theatre Experiment)
    (In Evergreen Playscript Series)
    (In A Change of Hearts)

The Gold Standard
  (In A Change of Hearts)
Guinevere; or, The Death of the Kangaroo
  (In Evergreen Playscript Series)
  (In A Change of Hearts)
The Moon Balloon
  (In A Change of Hearts)
The Tinguely Machine Mystery; or, The Love Suicides at Kaluka
  (In A Change of Hearts)
KOCHAN, Günter
  Karin Lenz, Oper in zehn Bildern. Libretto: Erik Neutsch;
  Music: Günter Kochan
    (In Theater der Zeig, no. 11, 1971)
KOCHER, Eric, 1912-
  Karma
    (In Best Short Plays, 1953/54)
  A Medal for Julien
    (In Best Short Plays, 1954/55)
  Shadow of the Cathedral
    (In Best One-Act Plays, 1951/52, N.Y.)
KOCOURKOVA, Marketa
  O Pravde-Podobnosti a Bicovani
    (In Divaldo, Jan. 1970)
KOEBNICK, Sarah Monson
  Fair Beckoning One
    (In Playwrights for Tomorrow, Vol. 5)
KÖHLER, Erich
  Geist von Cranitz
    (In Theater der Zeit, no. 7, 1972)
Koestler, Arthur, 1905-
  Darkness at Noon (see Kingsley, Sidney)
The Koeuba; or, The Private Vessel (see Fitz-Ball, Edward)
KOKOSCHKA, Oskar, 1886-
  Murder, The Women's Hope
    (In Tulane Drama Review, Vol. 2, May 1958)
Komparu Zenpo Motoyasu (see Motoyasu, Komparn Zembo)
Konig Drosselbart (see Czechowski, Heinz)
Kontraption (see Owens, Rochelle)
KOPIT, Arthur L., 1937-
  Chamber Music
    (In Kopit, The Day the Whores Came Out to Play Tennis)
  The Conquest of Everest
    (In Kopit, The Day the Whores Came Out to Play Tennis)
  La Conquete de L'Everest
    (In Plaisir de France, supplement theatral, no. 357, July
    1968)
  The Day the Whores Came Out to Play Tennis
    (In Kopit, The Day the Whores Came Out to Play Tennis
    and Other Plays)
  The Hero
    (In Kopit, The Day the Whores Came Out to Play Tennis)
  Oh, Dad, Poor Dad, Mamma's Hung You in the Closet and
  I'm Feelin' So Sad

(In Plays and Players, Vol. 13, Nov. /Dec. 1965)
(In Best American Plays, Fifth Series, 1957-63)
The Questioning of Nick
(In Kopit, The Day the Whores Came Out to Play Tennis)
Sing to Me Through Open Windows
(In Kopit, The Day the Whores Came Out to Play Tennis)
KOPS, Bernard, 1926-
David, la Nuit Tombe
(In L'Avant-Scene du Theatre, no. 454, Aug. 1, 1970)
(In Plaisir de France, supplement theatral, no. 382, Oct. 1970)
Enter Solly Gold
(In Satan, Socialites, and Solly Gold)
The Hamlet of Stepney Green
(In New English Dramatists, 1959)
KORBER, Serge, 1936-
Delphica
(In L'Avant-Scene du Cinema, no. 30, Oct. 15, 1963)
Un Jour a Paris
(In L'Avant-Scene du Cinema, no. 56, 1966)
KOSA, Ferenc, 1937-
Dix Mille Soleils
(In L'Avant-Scene du Cinema, no. 87, Dec. 1968)
KOTZEBUE, August Friedrich Ferdinand von, 1761-1819
Lovers' Vows; altered from the German by Mrs. Inchbald
(In Cumberland's British Theatre, Vol. 7, no. 5)
KOUTOUKAS, H. M.
Tidy Passions; or, Kill, Kaleidoscope, Kill
(In More Plays From Off Off Broadway)
KOZLENKO, William
The Devil Is a Good Man
(In Best One-Act Plays of 1939, N. Y.)
The Earth Is Ours
(In Best One-Act Plays of 1937, N. Y.)
It Takes a Thief
(In First Stage, Vol. 4, Winter 1965/66)
The Street Attends a Funeral
(In One-Act Play Magazine, 1937/38 Anthology)
This Earth Is Ours
(In Best Short Plays of the Social Theatre)
KRANES, David
Drive-In
(In Playwrights for Tomorrow, Vol. 7)
Krapp's Last Tape (see Beckett, Samuel)
KRASNA, Norman, 1909-
Bachelor Mother; screenplay, from a story by Felix Jackson, directed by Garson Kanin
(In Best Pictures, 1939-40)
Fury (see Lang, Fritz)
KRAUSS, Ruth
Poem-Plays: A Beautiful Day; In a Bull's Eye; Pineapple Play; There's a Little Ambiguity Over There among the Bluebells;

The 50,000 Dogwood Trees at Valley Forge
  (In Theatre Experiment)
KREYMBORG, Alfred, 1883-1966
  Ballad of Youth
    (In Best One-Act Plays of 1938, N.Y.)
  Brother Bill, a little play from Harlem
    (In Theatre Arts, Vol. 11, April 1927)
  Haunted Water
    (In Best One-Act Plays of 1939, N.Y.)
  Helpless Herberts; a mask comedy
    (In Theatre Arts, Vol. 8, Feb. 1924)
  I'm Not Complaining; a Kaffeeklatsch
    (In Theatre Arts, Vol. 15, June 1931)
  Manikin and Minikin
    (In Contemporary One-Act Plays, 1922)
  Monday
    (In Drama, Vol. 10, May 1920)
  No More War; an Ode to Peace
    (In Esquire, Vol. 29, Feb. 1948)
  Pianissimo
    (In Poetry, Vol. 20, July 1922)
  Privilege and Privation
    (In One-Act Play Magazine, 1937-38 Anthology)
  Show Blue
    (In Poetry, Vol. 54, July 1939)
  Trap Doors
    (In Theatre Arts, Vol. 9, Nov. 1925)
  When the Willow Nods
    (In Poetry, Vol. 11, Mar. 1918)
Kristina, Queen of Sweden, 1626-1689
  *Queen Christina (see Strindberg, August)
KROETZ, Franz Xaver
  Stallerhof
    (In Theater Heute, Special Issue, 1971)
KRUCHENYKH, Alexei
  Victory Over the Sun
    (In TDR/The Drama Review, Vol. 15, no. 4, Fall 1971)
KUBRICK, Stanley
  A Clockwork Orange
    (A Ballantine Books Screen Play)
KULPA, Francois-Felix
  La Grande Enquete
    (In L'Avant-Scene du Theatre, no. 460, Nov. 15, 1970)
KUNAD, Rainer
  Maitre Pathelin
    (In Theater der Zeit, Vol. 24, no. 8, 1969)
KURNITZ, Harry, 1908-
  The Reclining Figure
    (In Theatre Arts, Vol. 40, June 1956)
KUROSAWA, Akira, 1910-
  Ikiru
    (Modern Film Scripts Series)

Rashomon, filmscript by Akira Kurosaw and Shinobu Hashimoto
   (Evergreen Black Cat Series)
   Les Sept Samourais; title original "Schichinin no Samurai"
   (In L'Avant-Scene du Cinema, no. 113, Apr. 1971)
   The Seven Samurai
   (In Modern Filmscripts)
KUSHNER, Morris Hyman, 1912-
   Finian's Rainbow, by Fred Saidy and E. Y. Harburg.   Music
   composed by Burton Land (pseud.)
   (In Theatre Arts, Vol. 33, Jan. 1949)
KVARES, Donald
   Mushrooms
   (In The Best of Off Off Broadway)
KVASNITSKY, V.
   The Feminine Touch
   (In Soviet One-Act Plays)
KYD, Thomas, 1558-1594
   Cornelia (see Garnier, Robert)
   The Spanish Tragedy
   (In Great English Plays)
   The Spanish Tragedy; or, The First Part of Jeronimo (Hieron-
   imo)
   (In Dodsley's A Select Collection of Old English Plays, Vol.
   4)
   (In Dodsley's A Select Collection of Old Plays, Vol. 3)
   The Spanish Tragedy; or, The Second Part of Jeronimo (Hieron-
   imo Is Mad Again)
   (In Dodsley's A Select Collection of Old English Plays, Vol.
   5)
   (In Dodsley's A Select Collection of Old Plays, Vol. 3)
KYROU, Ado, 1923-
   La Chevelure, d'apres une nouvelle de Guy de Maupassant
   (In L'Avant-Scene du Cinema, no. 9, Nov. 15, 1961)

LSD (see Bloch, Pedro)
"La" (see Jockyman, Sergio)
La La Noo (see Yeats, Jack Butler)
LA BARGE, Bernadette
   La Visiteuse
   (In Plaisir de France, supplement theatral, no. 339, Jan.
   1967)
La Barthe, Henri
   **Algiers (see Lawson, John Howard)
LABICHE, Eugene Marin, 1815-1888
   La Fille Bien Gardee d'Eugene Labiche et Marc-Michel
   (In L'Avant-Scene du Theatre, no. 503, Oct. 1, 1972)
   An Italian Straw Hat
   (In The Modern Theatre, ed. by Eric Bentley, Vol. 3)
   The Man Who Set Fire to a Lady
   (In Tulane Drama Review, Vol. 4, Dec. 1959)
   Pots of Money, by Eugene Labiche and Alfred Delacour

(In Genius of the French Theater)
La Station Champbaudet d'Eugene Labiche et Marc-Michel
(In L'Avant-Scene du Theatre, no. 503, Oct. 1, 1972)
LABRENZ, Theodore
The Grass's Springing
(In First Stage, Vol. 2, Fall 1963)
LACASSIN, Francis, 1932-
Satan Mon Prochain, by Francis Lacassin et Raymond Bellour
(In L'Avant-Scene du Cinema, no. 16, June 15, 1962)
La Cava, Gregory, 1892-1949
My Man Godfrey (see Ryskind, Morris)
LACHENAY, Robert, 1930-
Le Scarabee d'Or, by Robert Lachenay, d'apres une histoire
extraordinaire d'Edgar Poë
(In L'Avant-Scene du Cinema, no. 35, 1964)
La Lacune (see Ionesco, Eugene)
LACY, John, d. 1681
The Dumb Lady
(In Dramatic Works of John Lacy)
The Old Troop
(In Dramatic Works of John Lacy)
Sauny the Scot
(In Dramatic Works of John Lacy)
Sir Hercules Buffoon
(In Dramatic Works of John Lacy)
LACY, Michael Rophino, 1795-1867
The Maid of Judah; or, The Knights Templars
(In Cumberland's British Theatre, Vol. 17, no. 4)
The Two Friends
(In Cumberland's British Theatre, Vol. 11, no. 6)
LADER, Lawrence
Pacific Task Force
(In Radio Drama in Action, 1945)
Ladies in Waiting (see Maule, Wendy St. John)
Lady Alamony; or, The Alamony Lady (Anon.)
(In Dodsley's A Select Collection of Old English Plays, Vol. 14)
A Lady and the Law (see Cronyn, George William)
The Lady Aoi (see Hiraoke, Kimitake)
Lady for a Day (see Riskin, Robert)
Lady Jemima's Weekly Thought (see White, Leonard)
Lady Luck (see Short, Marion)
Lady Macbeth (see Balachova, Tania)
The Lady Mother (see Glapthorne, Henry)
A Lady of Eternal Springtime (see Sabath, Bernard)
The Lady of Larkspur Lotion (see Williams, Tennessee)
The Lady of Pleasure (see Shirley, James)
The Lady of the Lake (see Dibdin, Thomas Frognall)
Lady Windermere's Fan (see Wilde, Oscar)
The Lady with the Lamp (see Berkeley, Reginald Cheyne)
The Lady's Last Stake; or, The Wife's Resentment (see Cibber, Colley)
The Lady's Not for Burning (see Fry, Christopher)

La Fayette, Comtessee de, nee Marie Madeleine Pioche de La
Vergne, 1634-1693
　*La Princess de Cleves (see Dorfmann, Robert)
Lafayette, Marie Joseph Paul Yves Roch Gilbert Motier, Marquis
de, 1757-1834
　*Valley Forge (see Anderson, Maxwell)
Laferriere, Adolph, d. 1877
　　Two Can Play at That Game (see Pierron, Eugene Athanase)
Laffite, Jean, c. 1780-c. 1826
　*The Buccaneer (see Mayer, Edwin Justus)
Lafont, Joseph de, 1686-1725
　**Cross Purposes (see O'Brien, William)
Lagerfeuer (see Wolf, Klaus)
LAGERKVIST, Pär Fabian, 1891-
　　The Difficult Hour
　　　(In Tulane Drama Review, Vol. 6, Nov. 1961)
　　Let Man Live
　　　(In Religious Drama, Vol. 3)
Lago, Mario
　　Amanha e' Dia de Pecar (see Wanderley, Jose)
LA GUMA, Alex
　　The Man in the Tree
　　　(In The Literary Review, Vol. 15, no. 1, Fall 1971)
La Harpe, Jean Francois de, 1739-1803
　　The Earl of Warwick (see Francklin, Thomas)
LAKE, Goldie, 1916-
　　Glory Day
　　　(In Best One-Act Plays, 1951/52, N. Y.)
　　Incident at a Grave
　　　(In Best One-Act Plays, 1952/53, N. Y.)
Lake, Stuart N.
　　Wells Fargo (see Schofield, Paul)
LALOUX, Rene, 1929-
　　Les Temps Morts
　　　(In L'Avant-Scene du Cinema, no. 116, July 1971)
The Lamb and the Beast (see Strindberg, August)
LAMOUREUX, Robert
　　La Soupiere
　　　(In L'Avant-Scene du Theatre, no. 504, Oct. 15, 1972)
LAMPELL, Millard, 1919-
　　The Lonesome Train, by Millard Lampell with music by Earl
　　Robinson
　　　(In Radio Drama in Action, 1945)
　　October Morning
　　　(In Radio's Best Plays, 1947)
The Lamplighter (see Dickens, Charles)
The Lancers (see Payne, John Howard)
The Land beyond the River (see Mitchell, Loften)
The Land of Happiness (see Redding, Joseph D.)
The Land of Heart's Desire (see Yeats, William Butler)
Landscape (see Pinter, Harold)
The Landsknecht Girl (see Di Mattia, Vincenzo)

Lane, Burton, pseud.   (see Kushner, Morris Hyman)
LANG, Fritz, 1890-
    Furie.   Titre original: "Fury"
        (In L'Avant-Scene du Cinema, no. 78, Feb. 1968)
    Fury, a screenplay by Fritz Lang and Bartlett Cormack, based
        on a story by Norman Krasna
        (In Twenty Best Film Plays)
    M
        (Classic Film Scripts Series)
    "M" Le Maudit
        (In L'Avant-Scene du Cinema, no. 39, 1964)
LANG, Michel, 1939-
    Un Tout Autre Visage
        (In L'Avant-Scene du Cinema, no. 45, 1965)
LANG, V. R.
    I too Have Lived in Arcadia
        (In Poetry, Vol. 86, April 1955)
Lang, Walter, 1896-
    The Mighty Barnum (see Fowler, Gene)
LANGE, Hartmut
    Die Gräfin von Rathenow
        (In Theater Heute, Vol. 10, no. 9, 1969)
    Trotzki in Coyocan
        (In Theater Heute, no. 3, March 1972)
Langley, Noel, 1911-
    Edward, My Son (see Morley, Robert)
    Trio (see Sherriff, Robert Cedric)
LANGNER, Lawrence, 1890-
    Another Way Out
        (In 50 Contemporary One-Act Plays)
        (In 30 Famous One-Act Plays)
Langtry, Lillie (Emilie Charlotte LeBreton), 1853-1929
    *The Life and Times of Judge Roy Bean (see Milius, John)
The Language of Love (see Percy, Edward)
LANIA, Leo
    The three-penny opera; screenplay by Leo Lania, Ladislas
        Vajda and Bela Balazs; based on John Gay's "Beggar's Opera";
        adapted from the play by Bertolt Brecht; music by Kurt Weill;
        directed by G. W. Pabst
        (In Classic Film Scripts)
Lannox, Gilbert
    Close Quarters (see Somin, W. O.)
Lanzelot (see Dessau, Paul)
LANZL, Frank, 1925-
    Fantasia on an Old Familiar Theme
        (In Best One-Act Plays of 1949/50, N.Y.)
LAPENA, Amelia L.
    Sepang Loca
        (In Literary Review, Vol. 3, Summer 1960)
The Larboard Fin; or, Twelve Months since Wills (see Wills,
    William Gorman)
LARDNER, Ring Wilmer, 1885-1933

Abend di Anni Nouveau
  (In Theatre Experiment)
The Tridget of Greva, translated from the Squinch
  (In Theatre Experiment)
  (In Twenty-Four Favorite One-Act Plays)
Zone of Quiet, adapted by David Shaw
  (In Best Television Plays of the Year, 1949)
LARGER, Pierre
  La Gage
    (In Plaisir de France, supplement theatral, no. 371, Oct.
    1969)
The Lark (see Anouilh, Jean)
Larnin' (see Webb, Alla)
Larry Parks' Day in Court (see Bentley, Eric Russell)
Lasayques, Maurice
  Lolie Douce (see Bricaire, Jean-Jacques)
LASCELLES, Kendrew, 1935-
  The Trophy Hunters
    (In Best Short Plays, 1970)
The Last Analysis (see Bellow, Saul)
The Last Day of the War (see Laurents, Arthur)
The Last Days of Lincoln (see Van Doren, Mark)
The Last Frontier (see Rowell, Adelaide C.)
The Last Inca (see Wishengrad, Morton)
The Last Judgment (see York Mercers' Play)
The Last Lost Weekend of Missionary Peal (see Felton, Keith
  Spencer)
The Last of My Solid Gold Watches (see Williams, Tennessee)
The Last of the Knights (see Strindberg, August)
The Last of the Lowries (see Green, Paul)
The Last of the Order (see Benner, Richard V.)
Last of the Red Hot Lovers (see Simon, Neil)
The Last One (see Conkle, Ellsworth Prouty)
The Last Speech (see Cooper, Lou)
The Last Straw (see Crocker, Bosworth)
The Last War (see Grant, Neil)
The Last Word (see Broughton, James)
Last Year at Marienbad (see Robbe-Grillet, Alain)
The Late Christopher Bean (see Howard, Sidney Coe)
The Late Christopher Bean (see Williams, Emlyn)
The Late Spring (see Robb, Ralph)
The Latent Heterosexual (see Chayefsky, Paddy)
Laugh When You Can (see Reynolds, Frederick)
Laughing Gas (see Dreiser, Theodore)
The Laughing Woman (see Mackintosh, Elizabeth)
Laughlin, Tom
  Billy Jack (see Christina, Frank)
Laughs, Etc. (see Herlihy, James Lee)
Laughton, Charles, 1899-1962
  Galileo (see Brecht, Bertolt)
Laure et les Jacques (see Arout, Gabriel)
Laurent, Cecil Saint, pseud. (see Laurent, Jacques)

Laurent, Jacques, 1919-
**Lola Montes (see Ophuls, Max)
LAURENTS, Arthur, 1918-
   The Face
     (In Best One-Act Plays of 1945, N.Y.)
     (In Radio's Best Plays, 1947)
   Gypsy (see Styne, Jule)
   Home of the Brave
     (In Best Plays of the Modern American Theatre, Second
     Series)
   Invitation to a March
     (In Theater Arts, Vol. 46, Jan. 1962)
   The Last Day of the War
     (In Radio Drama in Action, 1945)
   The Time of the Cuckoo
     (In Theatre Arts, Vol. 37, Nov. 1953)
   West Side Story (see Bernstein, Leonard)
"Lavender and Red Pepper" (see Giorloff, Ruth)
The Law of Lombardy (see Jephson, Robert)
LAWLER, Ray, 1921-
   Summer of the Seventeenth Doll
     (In Theater Arts, Vol. 43, no. 8, Aug. 1959)
LAWRENCE, David Herbert, 1885-1933
   Altitude
     (In Complete Plays of Lawrence)
   A Collier's Friday Night
     (In Complete Plays of Lawrence)
   The Daughter-in-Law
     (In Complete Plays of Lawrence)
     (In Plays and Players, Vol. 14, June 1967)
   David
     (In Complete Plays of Lawrence)
     (In Religious Drama, Vol. 1)
   The Fight for Barbara
     (In Complete Plays of Lawrence)
  *I Rise in Flame, Cried the Phoenix (see Williams, Tennessee)
   The Married Man
     (In Complete Plays of Lawrence)
     (In Virginia Quarterly Review, Vol. 16, Autumn 1940)
   The Merry-Go-Round
     (In Complete Plays of Lawrence)
     (In Virginia Quarterly Review, Vol. 17, Winter 1941, suppl.)
   Noah's Flood
     (In Complete Plays of Lawrence)
   Touch and Go
     (In Complete Plays of Lawrence)
   The Widowing of Mrs. Holroyd
     (In Complete Plays of Lawrence)
LAWRENCE, Jerome, 1915-
   Auntie Mame, by Jerome Lawrence and Robert E. Lee. Based
   on the novel by Patrick Dennis.
     (In Theatre Arts, Vol. 42, Nov. 1958)

The Gang's All Here, by Jerome Lawrence and Robert E. Lee
  (In Theatre Arts, Vol. 144, no. 11, Nov. 1960)
Inherit the Wind, by Jerome Lawrence and Robert E. Lee
  (In Theatre Arts, Vol. 41, Aug. 1957)
  (In Best American Plays, Fourth Series)
Inside a Kid's Head, by Jerome Lawrence and Robert E. Lee
  (In Radio Drama in Action, 1945)
Live Spelled Backwards
  (In Best Short Plays, 1972)
Lawrence, Josephine
  Make Way for Tomorrow (see Delmar, Vina)
LAWSON, John Howard, 1895-
  Algiers; screenplay by John Howard Lawson, with additional
  dialogue by James M. Cain, from the story "Pepe le Moko,"
  by Detective Ashelbe (pseud.). Directed by John Cromwell.
  (In Foremost Films of 1938)
Lawson, Ted. W.
  Thirty Seconds over Tokyo (see Trombo, Dalton)
LAWSON, Wayne
  Reflections
  (In Hudson Review, Vol. 8, Fall 1955)
LAY, Elizabeth A.
  When Witches Ride
  (In Carolina Folkplays)
Lay By (see Brenton, Howard)
The Lay-Figure (see Van Der Veer, Ethel)
LEACOCK, Stephen, 1869-1944
  The Two Milords; or, The Blow of Thunder
  (In Atlantic, Vol. 159, May 1937)
The Leader (see Ionesco, Eugene)
The Leading Lady (see Gordon, Ruth)
A Leap-Year Bride (see Hickson, Leslie M.)
Leary, Helen
  **Make Way for Tomorrow (see Delmar, Vina)
Leary, Nolan
  The Doctor from Dunmore (see Dillon, Thomas Patrick)
Lebendige Stunden (see Schnitzler, Arthur)
LEBESQUE, Morvan
  La Nouvelle
  (In L'Avant-Scene du Theatre, no. 145)
LE BIHAN, Michel
  L'Ere Quaternaire
  (In L'Avant-Scene du Theatre, no. 488, Feb. 1, 1972)
  Square X
  (In L'Avant-Scene du Theatre, no. 488, Feb. 1, 1972)
LE BRUN, M.
  The Discontented Man
  (In Theatrical Recorder, Vol. 2, no. 9, Aug. 1805)
LECONTE, Patrice, 1947-
  L'Espace Vital
  (In L'Avant-Scene du Cinema, no. 125, May 1972)
LEDOUX, Claude-Nicholas, 1736-1806

*L'Architecte Maudit: Claude-Nicholas Ledoux
    (In L'Avant-Scene du Cinema, no. 88, Jan. 1969)
Lee, Charles (see Lee, James Charles)
Lee, Gypsy Rose, 1914-1970
    *Gypsy (see Styne, Jule)
Lee, Harper
    To Kill a Mockingbird; screenplay (see Foote, Horton)
LEE, James, 1923-
    Career
        (In Theatre Arts, Vol. 41, Nov. 1957)
LEE, James Charles, 1870-
    Mr. Sampson, by Charles Lee
        (In 24 One-Act Plays, Revised edition, 1954)
LEE, Maryat
    Dope
        (In Best One-Act Plays, 1952/53, N. Y.)
LEE, Nathaniel, 1653-1692
    Alexander the Great
        (In The London Stage, Vol. 1)
    Caesar Borgia
        (In Works, Vol. 2)
    Constantine the Great
        (In Works, Vol. 2)
    The Duke of Guise (see Dryden, John)
    Gloriana; or, The Court of Augustus Caesar
        (In Works, Vol. 1)
    Lucius Junius Brutus, Father of His Country
        (In Works, Vol. 2)
        (In Bell's British Theatre, 1797, Vol. 31)
    The Massacre of Paris
        (In Works, Vol. 2)
    Mithridates, King of Pontus
        (In Works, Vol. 1)
    Oedipus (see Dryden, John)
    The Princess of Cleve
        (In Works, Vol. 2)
    The Rival Queens; or, The Death of Alexander the Great
        (In Works, Vol. 1)
        (In Cumberland's British Theatre, Vol. 36, no. 5)
        (In Bell's British Theatre, 1797, Vol. 1)
    Sophonisba; or, Hannibal's Overthrow
        (In Works, Vol. 1)
    Theodosius; or, The Force of Love
        (In Works, Vol. 2)
        (In Bell's British Theatre, 1797, Vol. 10)
    The Tragedy of Nero, Emperour of Rome
        (In Works, Vol. 1)
        (In A Collection of Old English Plays, Vol. 1)
Lee, Robert Edward, 1807-1870
    *Lee at Gettysburg (see Sapinsley, Alvin)
Lee, Robert Edwin, 1918-
    Auntie Mame (see Lawrence, Jerome)
    The Gang's All Here (see Lawrence, Jerome)

Inherit the Wind (see Lawrence, Jerome)
Inside a Kid's Head (see Lawrence, Jerome)
LEE, Sophia, 1750-1824
   The Chapter of Accidents
     (In Bell's British Theatre, 1797, Vol. 34)
     (In The London Stage, Vol. 2)
     (In Modern Theatre, 1811, Vol. 9)
Lee at Gettysburg (see Sapinsley, Alvin)
LEFEVRE, Raymond, 1927-
   Petite Fleur de Megeve de Raymond Lefevre et Robert Tourbe
     (In L'Avant-Scene du Cinema, no. 115, June 1971)
LEFFERTS, George
   The Nantucket Legend
     (In Best Television Plays of the Year, 1949)
Left-Handed Liberty (see Arden, John)
The Legacy of Cain (see Living Theater)
LEHMAN, Ernest, 1920-
   North by Northwest; screenplay of the film directed by Alfred Hitchcock
     (In MGM Library of Film Scripts Series)
LEHMAN, Leo
   Thirty Pieces of Silver
     (In Television Playwright: 10 Plays for BBC)
Leicester, Robert Dudley, Earl of, c. 1532-1588
   *Till Time Shall End (see Ashton, Winifred)
LEICHMAN, Seymour
   Freddie the Pigeon
     (In Playwrights for Tomorrow, Vol. 7)
Lekythos (see Holland, Anthony)
LELAND, Oliver Shepard, 1833-1870
   The Rights of Man
     (In Lacy's Plays)
LELOUCH, Claude, 1937-
   Un Homme et une Femme
     (In L'Avant-Scene du Cinema, no. 65, 1966)
   A Man and a Woman
     (In Modern Film Scripts Series)
Lengyel, Melchior
   **Ninorchka (see Brackett, Charles)
LENOUX, Armand
   Le Commandant Watrin
     (In Plaisir de France, supplement theatral, no. 320, June 1965)
LENZ, Siegfried, 1926-
   Time of Innocence
     (In Modern International Drama, Vol. 5, Spring 1971)
Leon Morin Pretree (see Melville, Jean-Pierre)
Leon, Ou la Bonne Formule (see Magnier, Claude)
LEONARD, Hugh
   The Au Pair Man
     (In Plays and Players, Vol. 16, Dec. 1968)
   Mick and Mick

(In Plays and Players, Vol. 14, Dec. 1966)
The Patrick Pearse Motel
(In Plays of the Year, Vol. 41, 1971/72)
(In Plays and Players, May 1971)
The Poker Session
(In Plays of the Year, Vol. 28, 1963/64)
LEONARDOS, Stella, 1923-
Jambinho do Contra
(In Revista de Teatro, no. 381, May 1971)
Leonce and Lena (see Büchner, Georg)
LEONHARDT, Arne
"Der Abiturmann"
(In Theater der Zeit, Vol. 24, no. 5, 1969)
Leonor de Mendonca (see Dias, Goncalves)
Leopard's Spots (see Holland, Norman)
LERNER, Alan Jay, 1918-
Brigadoon, by Alan Jay Lerner and Frederick Loewe
(In Theatre Arts, Vol. 36, Aug. 1952)
Paint Your Wagon
(In Theatre Arts, Vol. 36, Dec. 1952)
Le Roy, Mervyn, 1900-
Little Caesar (see Faragoh, Francis Edwards)
Thirty Seconds over Tokyo (see Trumbo, Dalton)
LE SAGE, Alain-Rene, 1668-1747
**Gil Blas (see Macfarren, George)
The Rival of His Master
(In Tulane Drama Review, Vol. 6, June 1962)
Turcaret; or, The Financier
(In The Classic Theatre, Vol. 4)
(In French Comedies of the 18th Century)
LESLIE, Henry
Time and Tide; a Tale of the Thames!
(In Lacy's Acting Plays, Vol. 81)
Lesou, Pierre G.
Le Doulos (see Melville, Jean-Pierre)
LESSING, Doris, 1921-
Each His Own Wilderness
(In New English Dramatists, 1959)
LESSING, Gotthold Ephraim, 1729-1781
Emilia Galotti, translated by Fanny Holcroft
(In Theatrical Recorder, Vol. 1, no. 6, May 1805)
(In Old Plays, 1810)
Emilia Galotti
(In Genius of the German Theater)
Minna von Barnheim, trans. by Fanny Holcroft
(In Theatrical Recorder, Vol. 2, no. 10, Sept. 1805)
Miss Sara Sampson
(In Masterworks of World Drama, Vol. 5)
The Lesson (see Ionesco, Eugene)
A Lesson in History (see Farrell, James Thomas)
Lestocq; or, The Fete at the Hermitage (see Macfarren, George)
Let It Burn (see Van der Veer, Ethel)

Let Man Live				226

Let Man Live   (see Lagerkvist, Pär Fabian)
Let Them Eat Cake   (see Lonsdale, Frederick)
Let There Be Farce   (see Walsh, Norman)
Let There Be Light   (see Huston, John)
LETHBRIDGE, Nemone
    The Portsmouth Defence
        (In Plays of the Year, Vol. 32, 1966)
LETO, Alfonso, 1920-
    The Girl from Stockholm; both French and English texts are
    included.
        (In Italian Theatre Review, Vol. 16, Oct./Dec. 1967)
Let's Get a Divorce!   (see Sardou, Victorien)
Let's Get Out of Here   (see Welch, Rae)
Let's Live in England   (see Brighouse, Harold)
The Letter "I" (I-moji)   (see Sakanishi, Shio)
Letter to Jackie   (see Anderson, Maxwell)
Letters   (see Ryerson, Florence)
The Letters   (see Tomplins, Frank Gerow)
Une Lettre   (see Condroyer, Philippe)
Lettre de Siberie   (see Marker, Chris)
LEVI, Paolo, 1919-
    Hell's Pavement; both French and English texts are included
        (In Italian Theatre Review, Vol. 19, July/Sept. 1961)
    If This Is a Man; both French and English texts are included
        (In Italian Theatre Review, Vol. 16, Apr./June, 1967)
Leviathan   (see Keigel, Leonard)
LEVIN, Ira
    No Time for Sergeants, by Ira Levin and Mac Hyman
        (In Best American Plays, Fourth Series)
LEVINGER, Elma Ehrlich
    The Tenth Man
        (In Drama, Vol. 19, April 1929)
        (In Best One-Act Plays of 1934, London)
Levins Mühle   (see Zimmerman, Udo)
LEVINSON, Alfred
    Socrates Wounded
        (In New American Plays, Vol. 1)
LEVITT, Saul
    The Andersonville Trial
        (In Theatre Arts, Vol. 45, no. 5, May 1961)
LEVOY, Myron
    Eli and Emily
        (In North American Review (n.s.), Vol. 2, July 1965)
LEVY, Benn Wolf, 1900-
    The Member for Gaza
        (In Plays of the Year, Vol. 32, 1966)
    Mrs. Moonlight
        (In Famous Plays of Today, 1929)
    The Rape of the Belt
        (In Theatre Arts, Vol. 46, no. 3, March 1961)
LEWIN, John
    Five Easy Payments
        (In Playwrights for Tomorrow, Vol. 3)

LEWIS, Jerry, 1926-
   Docteur Jerry et Mister Love, by Jerry Lewis. Titre original:
   "The Nutty Professor."
   (In L'Avant-Scene du Cinema, no. 35, 1964)
LEWIS, Leopold David, 1828-1890
   The Bells
   (In Hiss the Villain)
LEWIS, Matthew Gregory, 1775-1818
   Adelgitha; or, The Fruits of a Single Error
   (In Cumberland's British Theatre, Vol. 45, no. 7)
   Alfonso, King of Castile
   (In Old Plays, 1810)
   The Castle Spectre
   (In Cumberland's British Theatre, Vol. 9, no. 6)
   One O'Clock! or, The Knight and the Wooden Demon
   (In Cumberland's British Theatre, Vol. 22, no. 7)
   Raymond and Agnes; the Travellers Benighted; or, The Bleeding
   Nun of Lindenberg
   (In Cumberland's British Theatre, Vol. 32, no. 7)
   Rugantino; or, The Bravo of Venice
   (In Cumberland's British Theatre, Vol. 44, no. 7)
   Timour the Tartar
   (In Cumberland's British Theatre, Vol. 40, no. 4)
   Venoni; or, The Novice of St. Mark's
   (In Old Plays, 1810)
   (In Cumberland's British Theatre, Vol. 39, no. 6)
The Liar (see Foote, Samuel)
The Liar and the Unicorn (see Hughes, Babette Piechner)
The Liars (see Jones, Henry Arthur)
Liars (see Rabinowitz, Shalom)
Liberty Comes to Krahwenkel (see Nestroy, Johann)
The Library (see Maggi, Carlos)
LICHTER, Morton
   Cafeteria Style
   (In Yale/Theatre, Vol. 2, no. 2, Summer 1969)
Lie of a Day (see O'Keeffe, John)
LIEBERMAN, Herbert Henry, 1933-
   Matty, the Moron and the Madonna
   (In Chicago Review, Vol. 16, Autumn 1963)
Liebman, Max, 1902-
   Local Board Makes Good (see Fine, Sylvia)
Liebmann, Robert
   The Blue Angel (see Von Sternberg, Josef)
Lien de Sang (see Valle-Inclan, Ramon Maria del)
LIFCHITZ, Philippe
   X. Y. Z.
   (In L'Avant-Scene du Cinema, no. 2, Mar. 15, 1961)
Life (see Reynolds, Frederick)
Life and Death of Jack Straw (Anon.)
   (In Dodsley's A Select Collection of Old English Plays, Vol. 5)
Life and Letters (see Saroyan, William)

The Life and Times of J. Walter Smintheus (see White, Edgar)
The Life and Times of Judge Roy Bean (see Milius, John)
Life Begins at 84! (see White, Bessie F.)
Life Is a Dream (see Calderon de la Barca, Pedro)
Life of Confucius (see Brecht, Bertolt)
The Life of Emile Zola (see Herald, Heinz)
Life Price (see O'Neill, Michael)
Life with Father (see Lindsay, Howard)
The Lifeness of the Night (see Clifford, Lucy Lane, "Mrs. W. K.
    Clifford")
The Light in the Window (see Dreiser, Theodore)
The Light of Heart (see Williams, Emlyn)
Light-O-Love (see Schnitzler, Arthur)
Light Up the Sky (see Hart, Moss)
Lighted Candles (see Bland, Margaret)
Lightnin' (see Smith, Winchell)
Lights of Bohemia (see Valle-Inclan, Ramon Maria del)
Like Father Like Son (see Wilson, Leila Weekes)
Like Will to Like (Anon.)
    (In Dodsley's A Select Collection of Old English Plays, Vol.
    3)
Liliom (see Molnar, Ferenc)
Lilith (see Rossen, Robert)
LILLO, George, 1693-1739
    The Fatal Curiosity
    (In Bell's British Theatre, 1797, Vol. 23)
    George Barnwell
    (In Bell's British Theatre, 1797, Vol. 14)
    (In Cumberland's British Theatre, Vol. 19, no. 3)
    (In The London Stage, Vol. 1)
LIMA, Edy
    A Farsa da Esposa Perfeita
    (In Revista de Teatro, no. 315)
Limpid River (see De Burca, Seamus)
Lincoln, Abraham, pres. U.S., 1809-1865
    *Abe Lincoln in Illinois (see Sherwood, Robert Emmet)
    *Abraham Lincoln (see Drinkwater, John)
    *The Last Days of Lincoln (see Van Doren, Mark)
    *Lincoln Reckons Up (see Stevens, Henry Bailey)
    *Prologue to Glory (see Conkle, Ellsworth Prouty)
Lincoln, Richard, 1925-
    The Soldier Who Became a Great Dane (see Shore, Joseph)
LIND, Jakov
    Audioplay 1: Voices
    (In Scripts, Vol. 1, no. 4, Feb. 1972)
    Audioplay 2: Safe
    (In Scripts, Vol. 1, no. 8, June 1972)
LINDENBERGER, Herbert
    Victims
    (In Players Magazine, Vol. 42, no. 2-4, Nov. 1965-Spring
    Summer 1966)
LINDSAY, Howard, 1889-1968

The Great Sebastians, by Howard Lindsay and Russel Crouse
   (In Theatre Arts, Vol. 41, July 1957)
Life with Father, by Howard Lindsay and Russel Crouse
   (In S. R. O., the Most Successful Plays...)
   (In 16 Famous American Plays)
   (In Best Plays of the Modern American Theatre, Second
   Series)
State of the Union, by Howard Lindsay and Russel Crouse
   (In Best American Plays, Third Series)
LINEBERGER, James
   Hard Core
      (In TDR/Drama Review, Vol. 14, Fall 1969)
   A Song for All Saints
      (In Tulane Drama Review, Vol. 9, Fall 1964)
Lingua; or, The Combat of the Tongue and the Five Senses (see
   Tomkis, Thomas)
LINS, Osman
   Lisbela e o Prisioneiro
      (In Revista de Teatro, no. 334)
The Lion (see Kenan, Amos)
Lion in Winter (see Goldman, James)
The Lion's Cub (see Hale, John)
LIPSCOMB, William Percy, 1887-
   Clive of India, by W. P. Lipscomb and R. J. Minney
      (In Famous Plays of Today, 1933/34)
Lisbela e o Prisioneiro (see Lins, Osman)
LISS, Joseph
   Rebirth of Barrows Inlet
      (In Theatre Arts, Vol. 30, Aug. 1946)
      (In Radio's Best Plays, 1947)
Litchen Fair (see Corrie, Joe)
The Literary Society (see Ofori, Henry)
Literature (see Schnitzler, Arthur)
Lithuania (see Brooke, Rupert)
Little Annie's Birthday (see Suter, William E.)
Little Caesar (see Faragoh, Francis Edwards)
The Little Clay Cart (Mrcchakatika) (Anon.)
   (In Plays of the Year, Vol. 29, 1964/65)
   (In Two Plays From Ancient India)
   (In Genius of the Oriental Theater)
Little David (see Connelly, Marcus Cook)
Little David and His Struggle against the Eunuchs (see Halliwill,
   David)
The Little Dream (see Galsworthy, John)
Little Fauss and Big Halsey (see Eastman, Charles)
Little Fish (see Samble, Hazel V.)
The Little Flaw of Ernesto Lippi (see Schaefer, Lee)
The Little Fool (see Meyer, Adolph E.)
The Little Foxes (see Hellman, Lillian)
The Little Glass Clock (see Mills, Hugh)
The Little Hut (see Roussin, Andre)
Little Johnny Appleseed (see Schoenfeld, Bernard)

The Little Man (see Galsworthy, John)
Little Mary Sunshine (see Besoyan, Rick)
The Little One (see Morgan, Al)
The Little Stone House (see Calderon, George)
The Little Taylor (see Arnold, Paul)
Little Toddlekins (see Mathews, Charles)
Little Women (see Mason, Sarah Y.)
Live Like Pigs (see Arden, John)
Live Spelled Backwards (see Lawrence, Jerome)
Lives of the Magicians (see Silk, Dennis)
The Living and the Dead (see Saroyan, William)
Living Room with 6 Oppressions (see Mandel, Oscar)
Living Theater
     The Legacy of Cain
          (In Scripts, Vol. 1, no. 1, Nov. 1971)
LIVIUS, Charles Barham, d. 1865
     Maid or Wife; or, The Deceiver Deceived
          (In Cumberland's British Theatre, Vol. 39, no. 1)
Llewellyn, Richard, 1907?-
     **How Green Was My Valley (see Dunne, Philip)
     **None but the Lonely Heart (see Odets, Clifford)
Lloyd, Frank, 1888-1960
     Wells Fargo (see Schofield, Paul)
The Loan of a Lover (see Planche, James Robinson)
LOBNER, Joyce E.
     The Golden Eagle Child
          (In The Banner Anthology of One-Act Plays by American
          Authors)
Local Board Makes Good (see Fine, Sylvia)
Le Locataire (see Orton, Joe)
Lock and Key (see Hoare, Prince)
The Locked Chest (see Masefield, John)
LODGE, Thomas, 1558?-1625
     The Wounds of Civil War
          (In Dodsley's A Select Collection of Old English Plays, Vol.
          7)
          (In Dodsley's A Select Collection of Old Plays, Vol. 8)
Lodoiska (see Kemble, John Phillip)
LOESSER, Frank, 1910-
     The Most Happy Fella, music, lyrics and libretto by Frank
     Loesser. Based on Sidney Howard's "They Knew What They
     Wanted."
          (In Theatre Arts, Vol. 42, Oct. 1958)
Loewe, Frederick, 1901-
     Brigadoon (see Lerner, Alan Jay)
Lofty Projects; or, Arts in an Attic (see Lunn, Joseph)
Logan, Joshua, 1908-
     Mister Roberts (see Heggen, Thomas Orlo)
La Logeuse (see Audiberti, Jacques)
The Logical Stigmatic (see Williams, Heathcote)
Lola (see Demy, Jacques)
Lola Montes (see Ophuls, Max)

Lolie Douce (see Bricaire, Jean-Jacques)
LOMAX, Alan, 1915-
    Mister Ledford and the TVA
        (In Radio Drama in Action, 1945)
LOMAX, Elizabeth
    Farewell to Altamount, adapted from the novel "Look Homeward,
    Angel, " by Thomas Wolfe
        (In Radio's Best Plays, 1947)
London by Clipper (see Corwin, Norman Lewis)
The London Chaunticleers (Anon.)
        (In Dodsley's A Select Collection of Old English Plays, Vol.
    12)
London Frolics in 1638 (see The Merchant's Wedding)
London Wall (see Van Druten, John)
London's Tempe (see Dekker, Thomas)
The Lonely (see Serling, Rod)
Lonesome-like (see Brighouse, Harold)
The Lonesome Train (see Lampell, Millard)
Long, Huey Pierce, 1893-1935
    *All the King's Men; play (fiction) (see Warren, Robert Penn)
    *All the King's Men; screenplay (fiction) (see Rossen, Robert)
The Long Box (see MacDonald, Zillah K.)
The Long Christmas Dinner (see Wilder, Thornton Niven)
The Long Fall (see Howe, Carroll V.)
The Long Goodbye (see Williams, Tennessee)
The Long Night of Medea (see Alvaro, Corrado)
The Long Stay Cut Short (see also The Unsatisfactory Supper)
The Long Stay Cut Short; or, The Unsatisfactory Supper (see
    Williams, Tennessee)
The Long Voyage Home (see O'Neill, Eugene Gladstone)
The Long War (see O'Morrison, Kevin)
LONGHI, Vincent
    Climb the Greased Pole
        (In Plays and Players, Vol. 15, Feb. 1968)
LONSDALE, Frederick, 1881-1954
    The Day after Tomorrow
        (In Theatre Arts, Vol. 35, Apr. 1951)
    Let Them Eat Cake
        (In Plays of the Year, Vol. 19, 1958/59)
Look About You (Anon.)
        (In Dodsley's A Select Collection of Old English Plays, Vol.
    7)
Look Back in Anger (see Osborne, John)
Look Homeward Angel (see Frings, Ketti)
Look Up and Live; television series (see The Delinquent, the Hip-
    ster, the Square, and the Sandpile series)
Look, We've Come Through (see Wheeler, Hugh)
The Looking Glass (see Firkins, Oscar W.)
LOOS, Anita, 1894-
    Gigi, based on the novel by Colette
        (In Theatre Arts, Vol. 36, July 1952)
    The Women, a screenplay by Anita Loos and Jane Murfin,

based on the play of the same name by Clare Luce Boothe,
directed by George Cukor.
(In 20 Best Film Plays)
Loot (see Orton, Joe)
Lope de Rueda (see Rueda, Lope de)
Lope de Vega, Felix (see Vega Carpio, Lope Felix de)
LOPES Cardoso, A.
Os Caftens
(In Revista de Teatro, no. 310)
LOPEZ Mozo, Jeronimo
The Testament
(In Modern International Drama, Vol. 4, Fall 1970)
Lorca, Federico Garcia (see Garcia Lorca, Federico)
The Lord and Hawksaw Sadie (see Hughes, Elizabeth Wilson)
Lord Byron's Love Letter (see Williams, Tennessee)
The Lord of the Manor (see Burgoyne, John)
The Lord of the Manor (see Dibdin, Charles)
LORENTZ, Pare
The Fight for Life; screenplay based on the book by Paul de
Kruif, and directed by Pare Lorentz.
(In Twenty Best Film Plays)
Lorenzaccio (see Musset, Alfred de)
The Loser (see Eldridge, Paul)
Losers (see Friel, Brian)
LOSEY, Joseph, 1909-
Ceremonie Secrete. Titre original: "Secret Ceremony"
(In L'Avant-Scene du Cinema, no. 93, June 1969)
A Loss of Roses (see Inge, William)
Lost in London (see Phillips, Watts)
Lost in the Stars (see Anderson, Maxwell)
The Lost Lady (see Berkeley, Sir William)
The Lost Princess (see Totheroh, Dan)
The Lost Weekend (see Brackett, Charles)
The Lottery (see Jackson, Shirley)
The Lottery (see Duffield, Brainerd)
The Lottery Ticket; or, The Lawyer's Clerk (Anon.)
(In Cumberland's British Theatre, Vol. 37, no. 6)
Loucuras de Mamae (see Gama, Jota)
Louis XIV, King of France, 1638-1715
*Louis XIV (see Javet, Pierre)
Louis XVI, King of France, 1754-1793
*Ben Franklin in Paris (see Sandrich, Mark)
Louis XVII, King of France, known as Charles de France, 1785-
1795
*He Was Born Gay (see Williams, Emlyn)
Louis XVIII, King of France, called Louis le Desire, 1755-1824
*Catch As Catch Can (see Anouilh, Jean)
Louis Pasteur (see Didier, Pierre)
Louise (see Speenhoff, J. H.)
LOURENCO, Pasqual
O Sorriso do Palhaco
(In Revista de Teatro, no. 388, July/Aug. 1972)

La Louve (see Verga, Giovanni)
Love (see Schisgal, Murray)
Love After Death (see Calderon de la Barca, Pedro)
Love, and How to Cure It (see Wilder, Thornton)
Love and Marriage of the River Winooski and Lake Champlain (see
     Bread & Puppet Theatre)
The Love Course (see Gurney, A. R., Jr.)
Love Finds Andy Hardy (see Ludwig, William)
Love for Love (see Congreve, William)
Love in a Village (see Bickerstaff, Isaac)
Love in Humble Life (see Payne, John Howard)
Love in Idleness (see Rattigan, Terence)
Love in the Ape-House (see Sladen-Smith, Francis)
Love Laughs at Locksmiths (see Colman, George, the Younger)
Love, Law, and Physic (Kenney, James)
The Love of Annunziata (see Di Donato, Pietro)
The Love of Don Perlimplin and Belisa in the Garden (see Garcia
     Lorca, Federico)
Love of Four Colonels (see Ustinov, Peter)
Love of Life (see Shaw, Robert J.)
Love of One's Neighbor (see Andreyev, Leonid Nikolaevich)
A Love Passage (see Jacobs, William Wymark)
The Love Suicides at Amijima (Shinja Ten no Amijima) (see
     Chikamatsu Monzaemon)
The Love Suicides at Sonezaki (Sonezaki Shinju) (see Chikamatsu
     Monzaemon)
The Love Suicides in the Women's Temple (Shinju Mannenso)
     (see Chikamatsu Monzaemon)
LOVEJOY, Tim
     Harry Amses of Buffalo
          (In Yale Literary Magazine, Vol. 134, Nov. 1965)
LOVELL, Caroline C.
     The War Woman
          (In Drama, Vol. 13, Oct. 1922)
The Lover (see Pinter, Harold)
Lovers' Vows (see Kotzebue, August Friedrich Ferdinand von)
Loves of a Blonde (see Forman, Milos)
LOWE, Charles F.
     Gooseberry Tarts
          (In Best One-Act Plays, N. Y., 1950-51)
LOWELL, Robert, 1917-
     Benito Cereno, based on a novella by Herman Melville
          (In Theatre Experiment)
          (In Best American Plays, Sixth series, 1963-67)
          (In Show, Vol. 4, Aug. 1964)
          (In Best Short Plays of the World Theatre, 1958-67)
     My Kinsman, Major Molineux
          (In Partisan Review, Vol. 31, Fall 1964)
The Lower Depths (see Gor'kii, Maksim)
Loyalties (see Galsworthy, John)
Lubitsch, Ernst, 1892-1947
     Ninotchka (see Brackett, Charles)

LUBTCHANSKY, Jean-Claude
    Ourane
        (In L'Avant-Scene du Cinema, no. 17, July 15, 1962)
LUCE, Clare (Boothe), 1903-
    Doll's House 1970. A modern version of Ibsen's play. Pub-
    lished separately as "Slam the Door Softly."
        (In Life, Vol. 69, Oct. 16, 1970)
    Slam the Door Softly
        (In Best Short Plays, 1972)
    The Women
        (In 16 Famous American Plays)
        (In 20 Best Plays of the Modern American Theatre, Vol. 1)
    The Women; a screenplay (see Loos, Anita)
Lucian, c. 117-180 A.D.
    *Lucian; the Mark Twain of Antiquity (see Yliruusi, Tauno)
Lucius Junius Brutus, Father of His Country (see Lee, Nathaniel)
Lucrezia Borgia's Little Party (see Talbot, A.J.)
Lucullus, Lucius Licinus, c. 110-57 B.C.
    *Lucullus's Dinner-Party (see Baring, Maurice)
LUDLAM, Charles
    Bluebeard
        (In More Plays From Off Off Broadway)
    Eunuchs of the Forbidden City
        (In Scripts, Vol. 1, no. 6, April 1972)
    Turds in Hell
        (In TDR/Drama Review, Vol. 14, Sept. 1970)
Ludwig, Edward, c. 1900-
    That Certain Age (see Manning, Bruce)
LUDWIG, Volker
    Stokkerlok und Millipilli, by Volker Ludwig and Rainer Hatch-
    feld
        (In Theatre Heute, April 1970)
LUDWIG, William
    Love Finds Andy Hardy; screenplay from a story by Vivien R.
    Bretherton, based on characters created in the play "Skidding,"
    by Aurania Rouverol, directed by George B. Seitz.
        (In Foremost Films of 1938)
LUIZ, Milton de
    O Coelinho Pitomba
        (In Revista de Teatro, no. 378, Nov./Dec. 1970)
LUKE, Peter
    Hadrian the Seventh
        (In Plays and Players, Vol. 15, May 1968)
        (In Plays of the Year, Vol. 33, 1967)
    Hadrien VII
        (In L'Avant-Scene du Theatre, no. 471, May 1971)
Luke the Labourer (see Buckstone, John Baldwin
Lumieres de Boheme (see Valle-Inclan, Ramon Maria del)
Lunch Hour (see Mortimer, John)
La Lune Etait Bleue (see Herbert, Frederick Hugh)
Lune ou l'Autre (see Screiber, Isabelle Georges)
LUNN, Joseph, 1784-1863
    Hide and Seek

(In Cumberland's British Theatre, Vol. 18, no. 3)
Lofty Projects; or, Arts in an Attic
    (In Cumberland's British Theatre, Vol. 25, no. 8)
Management; or, The Prompter Puzzled
    (In Cumberland's British Theatre, Vol. 42, no. 6)
Roses and Thorns; or, Two Houses Under One Roof
    (In Cumberland's British Theatre, Vol. 26, no. 6)
The Shepherd of Derwent Vale
    (In Cumberland's British Theatre, Vol. 14, no. 5)
LUNTS, Lev.
    Bertran De Born
    (In Drama & Theatre, Vol. 9, no. 1, Fall 1970)
LUONGO, Guiseppe
    Adonai; both French and English texts are included
    (In Italian Theatre Review, Vol. 12, Jan./Mar. 1962)
Lurline; or, The Revolt of the Naiades (see Dalrymple, J. S.)
Lust's Dominion; or, The Lascivious Queen (see Marlowe,
    Christopher)
Lusty Juventus, a Morality (Anon.)
    (In Dodsley's A Select Collection of Old English Plays, Vol.
    2)
LUTHER, Martin, 1483-1546
    *Luther (see Osborne, John)
    The Nightingale of Wittenberg
    (In World Historical Plays)
Luv (see Schisgal, Murray)
LYDGATE, John, 1370?-1451?
    Chichevache and Bycorne
    (In Dodsley's A Select Collection of Old Plays, Vol. 12)
The Lying Valet (see Carrick, David)
LYLY, John, 1554?-1606
    Alexander and Campaspe
    (In Dodsley's A Select Collection of Old Plays, Vol. 2, 1703-
    1764)
    Gallathea
    (In Regents Renaissance Drama Series)
    Midas
    (In Regents Renaissance Drama Series)
LYON, Peter, 1915-
    Bretton Woods
    (In Radio Drama in Action, 1945)
Lysistrata (see Aristophanes)
LYTTON, Edward George Earle Lytton Bulwer-Lytton, 1st baron,
    1803-1873
    The Death of Clytemnestra
    (In Living Age, Vol. 3, Dec. 1844)
    The Rightful Heir
    (In Harper's, Vol. 38, Dec. 1868)
    Walpole; or, Every Man Has His Price
    (In Harper's, Vol. 40, Feb. 1870)

M (see Lang, Fritz)

"M" Le Maudit (see Lang, Fritz)
Ma Nuit Chez Maud (see Rohmer, Eric)
Maastricht Play; A Christmas Miracle, adapted by Donald Fay
    Robinson
        (In Theatre Arts, Vol. 11, Dec. 1927)
MacArthur, Charles, 1895-1956
    The Front Page (see Hecht, Ben)
    It's Fun to Be Free (see Hecht, Ben)
    Wuthering Heights (see Hecht, Ben)
MACAULAY, Pauline
    The Creeper
        (In Plays of the Year, Vol. 29, 1964/65)
Macbeth (see Müller, Heiner)
Macbeth (see Shakespeare, William)
Macbeth: Murder at the Gate-Keeper's House (see Brecht, Bertolt)
Macbett; text in French (see Ionesco, Eugene)
Macbett; text in German (see Ionesco, Eugene)
MacBird (see Garson, Barbara)
McBride, Jim
    David Holzman's Diary (see Carson, L. M. Kit)
MCCABE, Hazel G.
    The Path Between
        (In The Banner Anthology of One-Act Plays by American
        Authors)
McCarey, Leo, 1898-1969
    Going My Way (see Butler, Frank)
    Make Way for Tomorrow (see Delmar, Vina)
McCarty, E. Clayton
    Three's a Crowd (see McCarty, Sara Sloane)
MCCARTY, Nick
    Anne Boleyn; a television script in the Series "The Six Wives of
    Henry VIII"
        (In Plays of the Year Special, 1972)
MCCARTY, Sara (Sloane), 1905-
    Three's a Crowd, by Sara Sloane McCarty and E. Clayton Mc-
    Carty
        (In Plays as Experience)
MCCAULEY, Clarice Vallette
    The Queen's Hour
        (In Drama, Vol. 10, May 1920)
    The Threshold
        (In 50 More Contemporary One-Act Plays)
MCCLURE, Michael
    The Beard
        (In Evergreen Review, Vol. 11, no. 49, 1967)
        (In Evergreen Playscript Series)
    The Growl
        (In Evergreen Review, Vol. 8, no. 32, 1964)
MACCORMICK, Iain
    The Small Victory
        (In Television Playwright: 10 Plays for BBC)
McCoy, Horace, 1897-

**They Shoot Horses, Don't They? (see Poe, James)
MCCRACKEN, Wycliffe
    Vengeance in Leka
        (In One-Act Play Magazine, 1937/38 Anthology)
MCCULLERS, Mrs. Carson (Smith), 1917-1967
    The Member of the Wedding
        (In Best American Plays, Third Series)
MACDERMOT, Galt
    Hair; the American tribal love-rock musical. Music by Galt
    MacDermot; book and lyrics by Gerome Ragni and James Rado.
        (In Pocket Books Scripts Series)
MACDONALD, Zillah K., 1885-
    Circumventin' Saandy
        (In Drama, Vol. 16, May 1926; rev. ed. in Drama, Vol. 17,
        Feb. 1927)
    The Long Box
        (In Drama, Vol. 14, Feb. 1924)
MACDOUGALL, Ranald, 1915-
    The "Boise"
        (In Radio Drama in Action, 1945)
    The Death of Aung Aggie
        (In Best One-Act Plays of 1943, N.Y.)
        (In Theatre Arts, Vol. 27, Sept. 1943)
MACEDO, Joaquim Manuel de, 1820-1882
    O Macaco da Vizinha
        (In Revista de Teatro, no. 312)
    A Moreninha
        (In Revista de Teatro, no. 312)
    O Novo Otelo
        (In Revista de Teatro, no. 366, Nov./Dec. 1968)
    Uma Pupila Rica
        (In Revista de Teatro, no. 380, Mar./Apr. 1971)
    Remissao Dos Pecados
        (In Revista de Teatro, no. 301)
O Macedo da Vizinha (see Macedo, Joaquim Manuel de)
MCENROE, Robert Edward
    The Silver Whistle
        (In Theatre Arts, Vol. 33, June 1949)
MACFARREN, George, 1788-1843
    Gil Blas; or, The Boy of Santillane. (Founded upon "Gil Blas
    de Santillane," by Alain-Rene LeSage)
        (In Cumberland's British Theatre, Vol. 31, no. 8)
    Guy Faux; or, The Gunpowder Treason
        (In Cumberland's British Theatre, Vol. 26, no. 4)
    Lestocq; or, The Fete at the Hermitage
        (In Cumberland's British Theatre, Vol. 40, no. 7)
    Malvina
        (In Cumberland's British Theatre, Vol. 34, no. 2)
    "My Old Woman"
        (In Cumberland's British Theatre, Vol. 37, no. 2)
    Winning a Husband; or, Seven's the Main
        (In Cumberland's British Theatre, Vol. 31, no. 7)

MCGRATH, John
    Events While Guarding the Bofors Gun
        (In Plays and Players, Vol. 13, June 1966)
    Plugged In
        (In Plays and Players, Vol. 20, Nov. 1972)
Macgregor, Robert, known as Rob Roy, 1671-1734
    *Rob Roy (see Soane, George)
McGuinness, James Kevin
    **A Night at the Opera (see Kaufman, George Simon)
MCGUIRE, Harry
    When the Ship Goes Down
        (In Drama, Vol. 18, Dec. 1927)
Machado de Assis, Joaquin Maria, 1839-1908
    A Flor e o Fruto (see Cavalcanti Borges, Jose Carlos)
MACHIAVELLI, Niccolo, 1469-1527
    The Mandrake
        (In The Classic Theatre, ed. by Eric Bentley, Vol. 1)
        (In Masterworks of World Drama, Vol. 3)
Machin, Lewes (see Machin, Lewis)
MACHIN, Lewis, fl. 1608
    The Dumb Knight, by Lewes Machin and Gervase Markham
        (In Dodsley's A Select Collection of Old English Plays, Vol. 10)
        (In Dodsley's A Select Collection of Old Plays, Vol. 4)
Machinal (see Treadwell, Sophie)
The Machine (see Sinclair, Upton)
La Machine a Ecrire (see Cocteau, Jean)
La Machine Infernale (see Cocteau, Jean)
La Machine a Parler d'Amour (see Rossi, Jean-Baptiste)
The Machine Wreckers (see Toller, Ernst)
MACILWRAITH, Bill
    The Anniversary
        (In Plays of the Year, Vol. 31, 1965/66)
MACINNIS, Charles Patterson
    Immortality
        (In Drama, Vol. 16, April 1926)
MCINROY, Hal
    Honorable Togo
        (In Drama, Vol. 11, Aug./Sept. 1921)
MACKAY, Constance D'Arcy
    Counsel Retained
        (In Dramas by Present-Day Writers)
    The Silver Lining
        (In Short Plays by Representative Authors, 1920)
MACKAYE, Percy, 1875-1956
    Gettysburg
        (In Atlantic Book of Modern Plays, 1921)
    Sam Average
        (In Contemporary One-Act Plays, 1922)
    The Scarecrow
        (In Best Plays of the Early American Theatre, from the beginning to 1916)

MACKAYE, Robert Keith
    The Swamp
        (In Drama, Vol. 21, Mar. 1931)
MACKENZIE, Ronald
    Musical Chairs
        (In Famous Plays of Today, 1932)
MACKEY, William Wellington
    Family Meeting
        (In New Black Playwrights)
MACKIE, Albert
    Gentle Like a Dove
        (In Best One-Act Plays, London, 1952/53)
MACKIE, Philip
    The Big Killing
        (In Plays of the Year, Vol. 25, 1961/62)
MACKINTOSH, Elizabeth, 1896-1952
    The Laughing Woman, by Gordon Daviot, pseud.
        (In Famous Plays of Today, 1933/34)
    The Pen of My Aunt, by Gordon Daviot, pseud.
        (In English One-Act Plays of Today)
    Richard of Bordeaux, by Gordon Daviot, pseud.
        (In Famous Plays of Today, 1933)
MACKLIN, Charles, 1697?-1797
    The Man of the World
        (In The London Stage, Vol. 1)
        (In Bell's British Theatre, 1797, Vol. 27)
        (In Cumberland's British Theatre, Vol. 13, no. 5)
MACLEISH, Archibald, 1892-
    The Admiral
        (In Best One-Act Plays of 1944, N.Y.)
    Air Raid
        (In Best One-Act Plays of 1939, N.Y.)
    The Fall of the City
        (In Radio's Best Plays, 1947)
        (In Best Short Plays, 1956/57)
        (In 20 Best Plays of the Modern American Theatre, Vol. 1)
        (In Best One-Act Plays of 1937, N.Y.)
    J.B.
        (In Theatre Arts, Vol. 44, no. 2, Feb. 1960)
        (In Best American Plays, Fifth series, 1957-63)
    J.B.; Prologue to the Play
        (In Saturday Review, Vol. 39, Sept. 1, 1956)
    Scratch, a new play suggested by Stephen Vincent Benet's story
    "The Devil and Daniel Webster."
        (An H.M. Gousha Co. Play, 1971. San Jose, Calif. and
        Dramatic Publishing Co. Series)
    The States Talking
        (In Best One-Act Plays of 1941, N.Y.)
    This Music Crept by Me upon the Waters
        (In One Act)
        (In Best Short Plays, 1955/56)
MACMILLAN, Dougald

Off Nags Head
(In Carolina Folkplays)
MACMILLAN, Mary Louise, 1870-
The Shadowed Star
(In 50 Contemporary One-Act Plays)
(In Short Plays by Representative Authors, 1920)
MACNALLY, Leonard, 1752-1820
Fashionable Levities
(In Modern Theatre, 1811, Vol. 10)
MCNALLY, Terrence
And Things that Go Bump in the Night
(In Playwrights for Tomorrow, Vol. 1)
Bringing It All Back Home
(In Best Short Plays, 1969)
Next
(In Best Short Plays, 1970)
Noon
(In Modern Short Comedies from Broadway & London)
Sweet Eros
(In Yale/Theatre, no. 3, Winter 1968)
MACNEICE, Louis, 1907-1963
The Dark Tower
(In From the Modern Repertoire, Series Two)
One for the Grave
(In Massachusetts Review, Vol. 8, Winter 1967)
MACQUEEN, Lawrence I.
Sacrifice
(In Drama, Vol. 11, Mar. 1921)
MACRAE, Arthur
Encore (see Clark, T. E. B.)
MACREADY, William, 1755?-1829
The Bank Note
(In Modern Theatre, 1811, Vol. 9)
The Irishman in London
(In Cumberland's British Theatre, Vol. 9, no. 1)
Macrunis Guevara (see Spurling, John)
Mad Hercules (see Seneca, Lucius Annaeus, Seneca the Younger)
The Mad Musicians (see Eberhart, Richard)
A Mad World, My Masters (see Middleton, Thomas)
Madam Takes a Bath (see Bellido, Jose Maria)
Madam Will You Walk? (see Howard, Sidney Coe)
Madame de... (see Anouilh, Jean)
Madame de Sade (see Hiraoke, Kimitake)
Madame La Defunte (see Mithois, Marcel)
Madame se Meurt (see Cayrol, Jean)
MADDEN, David
Cassandra Singing
(In First Stage, Vol. 2, no. 2, Spring 1963)
In My Father's House
(In First Stage, Vol. 5, Summer 1966)
MADDOX, Frederick More
Frederick the Great
(In Cumberland's British Theatre, Vol. 38, no. 7)

Mademoiselle Colombe (see Anouilh, Jean)
Mademoiselle de Belle Isle (see Dumas, Alexander)
MADERN, Jose-Maria
   La Chemise de Nylon
     (In L'Avant-Scene du Theatre, no. 486, Jan. 1972)
Madheart (see Jones, LeRoi)
Madly in Love (see Ableman, Paul)
The Madman and the Nun   (see Witkiewicz, Stanislaw Ignacz)
The Madman on the Roof (see Kikuchi Kwan)
Madonna Dianora (see Hofmannsthal, Hugo Hofmann von)
The Madness of Lady Bright (see Wilson, Lanford)
The Madwoman of Chaillot (see Giraudoux, Jean)
Märchen vom Alten Arbat (see Abrusow, Alexej)
MAETERLINCK, Maurice, 1862-1949
  **The Bee (see Saunders, Lilian)
  **The Blue Harlequin; with apologies to Mr. Maeterlinck (see
     Baring, Maurice)
   Interior
     (In A Miracle of Saint Antony)
   The Intruder
     (In A Miracle of Saint Antony)
     (In 50 Contemporary One-Act Plays)
   A Miracle of St. Antony
     (In A Miracle of Saint Antony)
     (In 30 Famous One-Act Plays)
   Sister Beatrice
     (In Anglo-Saxon Review, Vol. 6, Sept. 1900)
MAGALHAES Junior, Raymundo
   Cancao Dentro de Pao
     (In Revista de Teatro, no. 332)
   Fugir, Casar ou Morrer
     (In Revista de Teatro, no. 315)
   O Homem que Fica
     (In Revista de Teatro, no. 376, July/Aug. 1970)
   O Imperador Galante
     (In Revista de Teatro, no. 388, July/Aug. 1972)
MAGALHAES, Paulo de
   O Coracao Nao Envelhece
     (In Revista de Teatro, no. 333)
   A Princesinha de Ouro
     (In Revista de Teatro, no. 310)
MAGGI, Carlos
   The Library
     (In Voices of Change in the Spanish American Theater)
The Magic Mallet of the Devil (Onino Tsuchi) (see Sakanishi, Shio)
The Magic Realists (see Terry, Megan)
The Magistrate (see Pinero, Arthur Wing)
MAGNAN, Jean-Marie
   Le Songe de la Nuit d'un Couple
     (In L'Avant-Scene du Theatre, no. 400, Apr. 1, 1968)
The Magnanimous Lover (see Ervine, St. John Greer)

MAGNIER, Claude
  Herminie
    (In L'Avant-Scene du Theatre, no. 448, May 1, 1970)
    (In Plaisir de France, supplement theatral, no. 379, Mar.
    7, 1970)
  Leon, ou la Bonne Formule
    (In L'Avant-Scene du Theatre, no. 448, May 1, 1970)
    (In Plaisir de France, supplement theatral, no. 379)
  Monsieur Masure
    (In L'Avant-Scene du Theatre, no. 490, Mar. 1, 1972)
  Oscar
    (In L'Avant-Scene du Theatre, no. 490, Mar. 1, 1972)
The Magnificent Entertainment Given to King James (see Dekker, T.)
MAGNUSON, Jim
  African Medea
    (In New American Plays, Vol. 4)
The Magpie, or the Maid? (see Pocock, Isaac)
Mahagonny (see Weill, Kurt)
Mahomet (see Miller, James)
MAI, Fabiene
  Volodia
    (In L'Avant-Scene du Theatre, no. 499, July 15, 1972)
MAIA, Arthur
  Dona Patinha Vai Ser Miss
    (In Revista de Teatro, no. 355)
The Maid of Domremy (see Corrie, Joe)
The Maid of Honour (see Massinger, Philip)
The Maid of Judah; or, The Knights Templars (see Lacy, Michael
  Rophino)
The Maid of the Mill (see Bickerstaff, Isaac)
Maid or Wife; or, The Deceiver Deceived (see Livius, Barham)
Maid to Marry (see Ionesco, Eugene)
The Maid Who Wouldn't be Proper (see Mick, Hettie Louise)
The Maiden's Tomb (see Kanami Kiyotsugu)
The Maids (see Genet, Jean)
The Maid's Tragedy (see Beaumont, Francis)
Maidstone (see Mailer, Norman)
MAILER, Norman, 1923-
  The Deer Park
    (In Partisan Review, Vol. 26, Fall 1959)
  Maidstone
    (In New American Library Screenplays, 1971)
MAINARDI, Renato, 1931-
  For a Maiden Whom Nobody Pities. Both French and English
    versions are included.
    (In Italian Theatre Review, Vol. 14, Oct.-Dec. 1965)
La Maison de Bernarda Alba (see Garcia Lorca, Federico)
La Maison des Bories (see Doniol-Valcroze, Jacques)
Maitre Francois est Mort (see Brune, Jean)
Maitre Pathelin (see Kunad, Rainer)
Major Barbara (see Shaw, George Bernard)
Major Barbara; text in French (see Shaw, George Bernard)

A Majority of One   (see Spigelgass, Leonard)
Make a Million   (see Barasch, Norman)
Make Way for Tomorrow   (see Delmar, Vina)
Make Your Wills   (see Mayhew, Edward)
The Maker of Dreams   (see Down, Oliphant)
The Maker of Laws   (see Bayly, John Ward)
Makeshifts   (see Robins, Gertrude)
Making Money, and Nineteen Other Short Plays   (see Saroyan,
   William)
Making the Bear   (see Apstein, Theodore)
MAKOWSKY, Lucile
   The New World
      (In Best Short Plays, 1958/59)
Le Mal Court   (see Audiberti, Jacques)
Le Mal de Test   (see Wallach, Ira)
MALAMUD, Bernard
   Suppose a Wedding
      (In New Statesman, Vol. 65, Feb. 8, 1963)
Malatesta   (see Montherlant, Henry de)
The Malcontent   (see Marston, John)
Maldita Parentela   (see Junior, Franca)
The Male Animal   (see Thurber, James)
MALES, U. Harold
   The Professional Attitude
      (In First Stage, Vol. 1, no. 4, Fall 1962)
MALJEAN, Jean Raymond
   A Message from Cougar
      (In New American Plays, Vol. 2)
The Mall   (see Inge, William Motter)
MALLE, Louis, 1932-
   Les Amants, by Louis Malle and Louise de Vilmorin, based
      on "Point de Lendemain" by Dominique Vivant, Baron de
      Denon.
      (In L'Avant-Scene du Cinema, no. 2, Mar. 15, 1961)
      (In Cahiers du Cinema, Vol. 14, no. 90, Dec. 1958)
   Le Feu Follet, d'apres le roman de Drieu la Rochelle
      (In L'Avant-Scene du Cinema, no. 30, Oct. 15, 1963)
   Viva Maria, by Louis Malle et Jean-Claude Carriere
      (In L'Avant-Scene du Cinema, no. 56, 1966)
   Zazie dans le Metro, d'apres le roman de Raymond Queneau
      (In L'Avant-Scene du Cinema, no. 104, June 1970)
Malleson, Miles, 1888-
   The Imaginary Invalid   (see Moliere, Jean Baptiste Poquelin)
   The Misanthrope   (see Moliere, Jean Baptiste Poquelin)
   The Prodigious Snob   (see Moliere, Jean Baptiste Poquelin)
   Sganarelle   (see Moliere, Jean Baptiste Poquelin)
MALLET, David, 1705?-1765
   Eurydice
      (In Bell's British Theatre, 1797, Vol. 26)
MALTZ, Albert, 1908-
   Private Hicks
      (In Best Short Plays of the Social Theatre, 1939)

O Maluco da Familia (see Wanderley, Jose)
Malvina (see Macfarren, George)
O Mambembe (see Azevedo, Arthur)
A Man and a Woman (see Lelouch, Claude)
Man and Wife (see Arnold, Samuel James)
Man Better Man (see Hill, Errol)
Man Does Not Die by Bread Alone (see Diaz, Jorge)
A Man for All Seasons (see Bolt, Robert)
The Man from Home (see Tarkington, Booth)
The Man in the Forest (see Field, Charles K.)
The Man in the Glass Booth (see Shaw, Robert)
The Man in the Stalls (see Sutro, Alfred)
The Man in the Street (see Thorburn, John)
The Man in the Tree (see La Guma, Alex)
The Man of the Moment (see Hoffman, Phoebe)
The Man of the World (see Macklin, Charles)
The Man on the Kerb (see Sutro, Alfred)
Man on the Mountaintop (see Aurthur, Robert Alan)
The Man Who Came to Dinner (see Hart, Moss)
The Man Who Died at Twelve O'clock (see Green, Paul)
The Man Who Ignored the War (see Brighouse, Harold)
The Man Who Loved God (see Kafka, Sherry)
The Man Who Married a Dumb Wife (see France, Anatole)
The Man Who Set Fire to a Lady (see Labiche, Eugene)
The Man Who Wouldn't Go to Heaven (see Sladen-Smith, Francis)
The Man With the Carpet Bag (see A Beckett, Gilbert Abbott)
The Man with the Flower in His Mouth (see Pirandello, Luigi)
The Man with the Heart in the Highlands (see Saroyan, William)
The Man with the Oboe (see Smalley, Webster)
The Man without a Face (das Verlorene Gasicht) (see Weisenborn,
    Günther)
Management; or, The Prompter Puzzled (see Lunn, Joseph)
Manana Bandits (see Smith, Betty)
The Mandarin Coat (see Riley, Mrs. Alice Cushing (Donaldson))
MANDEL, Oscar, 1926-
    The Fatal French Dentist
        (In First Stage, Vol. 4, Summer 1965)
    General Audax
        (In First Stage, Vol. 6, Fall 1967)
    Honest Urubamba
        (In Literary Review, Vol. 9, Autumn 1965)
    Living Room with 6 Oppressions
        (In Drama & Theatre, Vol. 8, no. 3, Spring 1970)
    The Monk Who Wouldn't
        (In First Stage, Vol. 1, no. 3, Summer 1962)
    Professor Snaffle's Polypon
        (In First Stage, Vol. 5, Summer 1966)
The Mandrake (see Machiavelli, Niccolo)
Manet, Edouard, 1832-1883
    *L'Affaire Manet (see Aurel, Jean)
Manfred (see Byron, George Gordon Noël Byron, 6th baron)
Man-Fred (see A Beckett, Gilbert Abbott)

Manhas de Sol   (see Viana, Odulvaldo Filho)
MANHOFF, Bill, 1919-
    The Own and the Pussycat
        (In Best American Plays, Sixth series, 1963-67)
Manikin and Minikin   (see Kreymborg, Alfred)
Mankiewicz, Herman J., 1897-1953
    Citizen Kane   (see Welles, Orson)
MANKIEWICZ, Joseph Leo, 1909-
    La Comtesse aux Pieds Nus.   Titre original: "The Barefoot
    Contessa. "
        (In L'Avant-Scene du Cinema, no. 68, 1967)
MANKOWITZ, Wolf, 1924-
    The Bespoke Overcoat
        (In 24 One-Act Plays, Rev. edition, 1954)
        (In English One-Act Plays of Today)
        (In Best One-Act Plays, London, 1953/53)
    It Should Happen to a Dog
        (In Religious Drama, Vol. 3)
Mann, Heinrich, 1871-1950
    **L'Ange Bleu (Der Blaue Engel)   (see Von Sternberg, Josef)
    **The Blue Angel; screenplay (see Von Sternberg, Josef)
MANNERS, John Hartley, 1870-1827
    Peg O' My Heart
        (In S. R. O., the Most Successful Plays...)
MANNING, Bruce
    That Certain Age; screenplay from an original story by F. Hugh
    Herbert, directed by Edward Ludwig.
        (In Foremost Films of 1938)
Manny   (see Vail, Walter J.)
Manohra   (see Thai Lakon Jatri)
A Man's a Man   (see Brecht, Bertolt)
Mansions   (see Flanner, Hildegarde)
The Mantle of the Virgin   (see Sutton, Vida Ravenscroft)
Manuel de Macedo, Joaquim   (see Macedo, Joaquim Manuel de)
Many a Watchful Night   (see Brown, John Mason)
Many Loves   (see Williams, William Carlos)
Many Waters   (see Hoffe, Monckton)
MANZARI, Nicola, 1909-
    Salud; both French and English versions are included
        (In Italian Theatre Review, Vol. 14, July/Sept. 1965)
Mao Tse-Tung, 1893-
    *Quotations from Chairman Mao Tse-Tung   (see Albee, Edward)
The Map   (see Davenport, E. V.)
MAPES, Victor
    The Foundling
        (In Best One-Act Plays of 1937, N. Y.)
The Maple Viewing (Momijigari)   (see Kanze Kojiro Nobumitsu)
Marat, Jean Paul, 1743-1793
    *The Murder of Marat   (see Kearney, Patrick)
    The Persecution and Assassination of Jean-Paul Marat   (see
        Weiss, Peter)
Marat/Sade   (see The Persecution and Assassination of Jean-Paul

Marat as performed by the inmates of the Asylum of Charenton
under the direction of the Marquis de Sade.)
MARBLE, Annie
    Faith of Our Fathers
       (In Drama, Vol. 10, July/Sept. 1920)
MARCEAU, Felicien
    Le Babour
       (In L'Avant-Scene du Theatre, no. 445, Mar. 15, 1970)
MARCEL, Gabriel, 1887-
    Ariadne
       (In Makers of the Modern Theatre, 1961)
MARCELLE-Maurette, 1903-
    Anastasia, adapted by Guy Bolton
       (In Theatre Arts, Vol. 40, May 1956)
    La Nuit de Feu
       (In Plaisir de France, supplement theatral, no. 304, Feb.
       1964)
March, William (see Campbell, William Edward March)
MARCHOU, Pierre
    Project Orfee
       (In L'Avant-Scene du Cinema, no. 112, Mar. 1971)
Marco Polo (see Polo, Marco)
MARCUS, Frank
    Cleo and Max
       (In London Magazine, n.s., Vol. 5, Feb. 1966)
    The Formation Dancers
       (In Plays of the Year, Vol. 28, 1963/64)
    The Killing of Sister George
       (In Esquire, Vol. 66, Nov. 1966)
       (In Plays of the Year, Vol. 31, 1965/66)
    Mrs. Mouse, Are You Within?
       (In Plays and Players, Vol. 15, July 1968)
    Notes on a Love Affair
       (In Plays and Players, Vol. 19, no. 10, July 1972)
    The Window
       (In Best Short Plays of the World Theatre, 1958-67)
Margaret Fleming (see Herne, James A.)
Margaret of Inner Austria, Queen of Spain, wife of Philip III, 1584-
1611
    *Lust's Dominion; or, The Lascivious Queen (see Marlowe,
      Christopher)
Maria (see Salynski, Afanassi)
Maria et les Isles (see Gonthie, Max H.)
Maria Madelena (see Cepelos, Batista)
Maria Magdalena (see Hebbel, Friedrich)
Mariana Pineda (see Garcia Lorca, Federico)
Marianne (see Fenton, Elijah)
MARIE, Andre
    Tartuffe--Acte VI
       (In L'Avant-Scene du Theatre, no. 290, June 15, 1963)
       (In Plaisir de France, supplement theatral, no. 297, July
       1963)

Marie Stuart; text in French   (see Schiller, Johann Christoph Fried-
   rich von)
Les Maries de la Tour Eiffel   (see Cocteau, Jean)
Les Marines   (see Reichenbach, Francois)
MARINETTI, Filippo Tommaso
   Feet
      (In TDR/The Drama Review, Vol. 15, Fall 1970)
   Hands: A Showcase   (see Corra, Bruno)
Marino Faliero, Doge of Venice   (see Byron, George Gordon Noël
   Byron, 6th baron)
Marion, Frances, 1890-
   The Good Earth   (see Jennings, Talbot)
MARIVAUX, Pierre Carlet de Chamblain de, 1688-1793
   La Colonie
      (In L'Avant-Scene du Theatre, no. 269, July 15, 1962)
   The False Confessions
      (In The Classic Theatre, ed. by Eric Bentley, Vol. 4)
   The Game of Love and Chance
      (In French Comedies of the 18th Century)
      (In Masterworks of World Drama, Vol. 5)
   The Test
      (In Poet Lore, Vol. 35, 1924)
   Les Serments Indiscrets
      (In L'Avant-Scene du Theatre, no. 133)
MARK, Francis
   Tarakin
      (In Best One-Act Plays of 1932, London)
MARKER, Chris, 1921-
   Cuba Si
      (In L'Avant-Scene du Cinema, no. 6, July 15, 1961)
   Lettre de Siberie
      (In Cahiers du Cinema, Vol. 14, no. 90, Dec. 1958)
MARKGRAF, Bruce
   Passing of Francis Scott Key
      (In TDR/Drama Review, Vol. 14, Sept. 1970)
Markham, Gervase, 1568?-1637
   The Dumb Knight   (see Machin, Lewis)
MARKLE, Fletcher
   Sometime Every Summertime
      (In Radio's Best Plays, 1947)
Marko's: A Vegetarian Fantasy   (see Bernard, Kenneth)
MARKS, Jeannette Augustus, 1875-1964
   The Deacon's Hat
      (In Contemporary One-Act Plays, 1922)
   The Merry Merry Cuckoo
      (In Short Plays by Representative Authors, 1920)
The Marksman   (see Goncharov, Y.)
MARLOWE, Christopher, 1564-1593
   Doctor Faustus
      (In Genius of the Early English Theater)
      (In Great English Plays)
   Edward II

(In Dodsley's A Select Collection of Old Plays, Vol. 2)
The Jew of Malta
    (In Dodsley's A Select Collection of Old Plays, Vol. 8)
Lust's Dominion; or, The Lascivious Queen, by Christopher
Marlowe, Thomas Dekker, William Haughton, and John Day.
    (In Dodsley's A Select Collection of Old English Plays, Vol.
    14)
    (In Dramatic Works of Dekker, Vol. 4)
The Tragical History of Doctor Faustus
    (In Masterworks of World Drama, Vol. 3)
    (In Tragedy: Texts and Commentary, 1969)
MARMION, Shakerley, 1603-1639
    The Antiquary
    (In Dodsley's A Select Collection of Old English Plays, Vol.
    13)
    (In Dodsley's A Select Collection of Old Plays, Vol. 10)
MAROWITZ, Charles
    The Critic as Artist, adapted from the essay by Oscar Wilde
    (In Plays and Players, Vol. 19, Oct. 1971)
Marquand, John Phillips, 1893-1960
    **Point of No Return (see Osborn, Paul)
MARQUES, Rene
    The Fan Windows
    (In Modern Stage in Latin America, 1971)
MARQUIS, Arnold
    Japan's Advance Base: the Bonin Islands
    (In Radio Drama in Action, 1945)
    Transition In India
    (In Best One-Act Plays of 1946/47, N.Y.)
Marquis, Don, 1878-1937
    **Archie and Mehitabel (see Kleinsinger, George)
The Marquis of Keith (see Wedekind, Frank)
The Marriage (see Gogol, Nikolai Vasil'evich)
The Marriage Game (see Sisson, Rosemary Anne)
A Marriage Has Been Arranged... (see Sutro, Alfred)
The Marriage Night (see Falkland, Henry Cary, 4th Viscount)
The Marriage of Little Eva (see Nicholson, Kenyon)
The Marriage of Mr. Mississippi (see Dürrenmatt, Friedrich)
The Marriage of Wit and Science (Anon.)
    (In Dodsley's A Select Collection of Old English Plays, Vol.
    2)
Marriage Projects (see DuVal, M.)
A Marriage Proposal (see Chekhov, Anton)
The Marriage Test (see Gillman, Jonathan)
The Married Man (see Lawrence, David Herbert)
Marshall, George, 1891-
    Destry Rides Again (see Jackson, Felix)
MARSHALL, Laura
    Winter Sunshine
    (In The Banner Anthology of One-Act Plays by American
    Authors)
MARSTON, John, 1575?-1634

Eastward Hoe   (see Chapman, George)
The Malcontent
   (In Dodsley's A Select Collection of Old Plays, Vol. 4)
MARSTON, John Westland, 1819-1890
A Hard Struggle
   (In Living Age, Vol. 51, April 17, 1858)
Marthe   (see Armstrong, Noel)
MARTIN, Francis
Tillie and Gus; screenplay and direction by Francis Martin
   with Walter Deleon, based on a story by Rupert Hughes
   (In Classic Filmscripts Series)
MARTIN, Jacqueline
La Quintaine
   (In Plaisir de France, supplement theatral, no. 346, Aug.
   1967)
MARTIN, John Joseph, 1893-
Charlie Barringer
   (In Theatre Arts, Vol. 5, 1921)
MARTIN, Judith
Bow Wow; a skit from the Paper Bag play "Dandelion"
   (In Scripts, Vol. 1, no. 10, Oct. 1972)
MARTINEZ Ballesteros, Antonio
The Best of All Possible Worlds
   (In First Stage, Vol. 5, Fall 1966)
The Position
   (In Modern International Drama, Vol. 5, Spring 1971)
The Straw Men (Los Peletes)
   (In Modern International Drama, Vol. 3, no. 1, 1969)
MARTINEZ Sierra, Gregorio, 1881-1947
The Cradle Song
   (In 16 Famous European Plays)
Poor John, translated by John Garrett Underhill
   (In Drama, Vol. 10, Feb. 1920)
Martin's Life   (see Menotti, Gian-Carlo)
Marty   (see Chayefsky, Paddy)
The Martyr'd Souldier   (see Shirley, Henry)
The Martyrdom of Peter Chey   (see Mrozek, Slawomir)
The Marvelous Romance of Wen Chun-Chin   (see Hsiungm Chen-
   Chin)
MARVIN X
Take Care of Business
   (In TDR/Drama Review, Vol. 12, Summer 1968)
Marx Brothers
Chico, 1891-1961
Harpo, 1893-1964
Groucho, 1895-
A Day at the Races   (see Pirosh, Robert)
Monkey Business and Duck Soup
   (In Classic Filmscript Series)
A Night at the Opera   (see Kaufman, George Simon)
Mary Baker Eddy   (see Toller, Ernest)
Mary Glastonbury; or, The Dream Girl of the Devil-Holl   (see
   Fitz-Ball, Edward)

Mary, Mary (see Kerr, Jean Collins)
Mary I, Mary Tudor (Bloody Mary) Queen of England and Ireland,
  1516-1558
  *The Lion's Cub (see Hale, John)
Mary Queen of Scots, 1542-1587
  *The Albion Queen; or, The Death of Mary Queen of Scots (see
    Banks, John)
  *Horrible Conspiracies (see Whitemore, Hugh)
  *Marie Stuart (see Schiller, Joahann Christoph Friedrich von)
  *Mary of Scotland (see Anderson, Maxwell)
  *Mary Queen of Scots (see St. John, John)
  *Mary Stuart (see Hildesheimer, Wolfgang)
  *Mary Stuart (see Schiller, Johann Christoph Friedrich von)
  *La Princesse de Cleves (see Dorfmann, Robert)
Marya (see Babel, Isaac)
Mary's Wedding (see Cannan, Gilbert)
MARZ, Roy
    After Closing
      (In First Stage, Vol. 1, no. 3, Summer 1962)
    O'Fallon's Cup
      (In First Stage, Vol. 5, Summer 1966)
MASEFIELD, John, 1878-1967
    The Locked Chest
      (In Short Plays by Representative Authors, 1920)
    A Word with Sir Francis Drake during His Last Night in London
      (In Atlantic, Vol. 208, July 1961)
The Mask of Virtue (see Sternheim, Carl)
Masks (see Corneau, Perry Boyer)
Masks of Angels (see Peryalis, Notis)
MASON, Sarah Y.
    Little Women, a screenplay based on the novel by Louisa May
      Alcott, by Sarah Y. Mason and Victor Heerman, directed by
      George Cukor
      (In Four-Star Scripts)
MASON, William
    Caractacus
      (In Bell's British Theatre, 1797, Vol. 31)
    Elfrida
      (In Bell's British Theatre, 1797, Vol. 34)
The Mason of Buda (see Planche, James Robinson)
The Masque of Kings (see Anderson, Maxwell)
The Masque of Mercy (see Frost, Robert)
The Massacre of Paris (see Lee, Nathaniel)
Massaroni, Alessandro (the Italian Robin Hood)
    *The Brigand (see Planche, James Robinson)
Masse Mensch (see Toller, Ernst)
Masses and Man (see Toller, Ernst)
MASSINGER, Philip, 1583-1640
    The Bondman
      (In Great English Plays)
      (In Old Plays, 1810)
    The City Madam

(In Plays of the Year, Vol. 28, 1963/64)
(In The City and the Court)
The Fatal Dowry
  (In Cumberland's British Theatre, Vol. 15, no. 1)
  (In Old Plays, 1810)
The Maid of Honour
  (In Cumberland's British Theatre, Vol. 26, no. 1)
  (In Old Plays, 1810)
A New Way to Pay Old Debts
  (In Cumberland's British Theatre, Vol. 6, no. 1)
  (In Great English Plays)
  (In The London Stage, Vol. 2)
  (In Old Plays, 1810)
**Riches; or, The Wife and Brother (see Burges, Sir James
    Bland)
The Virgin Martyr, by Philip Massinger and Thomas Dekker
  (In Dramatic Works of Dekker, Vol. 3)
The Master (see Schevill, James Erwin)
Master Builder (see Ibsen, Henrik)
Master Jones's Birthday (see Morton, John Maddison)
The Master of Santiago (see Montherlant, Henry de)
Master's Rival; or, A Day at Boulogne (see Peake, Richard
    Brinsley)
Matador (see Viana, Oduvaldo Filho)
A Match at Mid-night (see Rowley, William)
Match at Midnight (see also The Merchant's Wedding)
Match Me in London (see Dekker, Thomas)
Matched Pair, a Filmscript (see Hill, James)
The Matchmaker (see Wilder, Thornton Niven)
MATHEUS, John
  'Cruiter
    (In Plays of Negro Life)
MATHEWS, Charles James, 1803-1878
  The Humpbacked Lover
    (In Cumberland's British Theatre, Vol. 41, no. 1)
  Little Toddlekins
    (In Lacy's Plays)
Matilda (Anon.)
    (In Modern Theatre, 1811, Vol. 8)
Matisse, Henri, 1869-1954
  *Matisse, ou le Talent du Bonheur (see Ophuls, Marcel)
Matrimony (see Kenney, James)
Matrimony Up-to-Date (see Tucker, Charles Davis)
Matron of Ephesus (see Sion, Georges)
MATSAS, Nestor
  Les Crocodiles
    (In L'Avant-Scene du Theatre, no. 504, Oct. 15, 1972)
MATTHUS, Siegfried
  Noch einen Löffel Gift, Liebling? Musik von Siegfried Matthus;
    Libretto von Peter Hacks nach der Komödie "Risky Marriage"
    von Saul O'Hara
    (In Theater der Zeit, no. 3, 1972)

Matty, the Moron and the Madonna   (see Lieberman, Herbert
    Henry)
MAUGHAM, Robin, 1916-
    Enemy!
        (In Plays and Players, Vol. 17, no. 6, Mar. 1970)
    The Servant (see Pinter, Harold)
MAUGHAM, William Somerset, 1874-1965
    The Circle
        (In 16 Famous British Plays)
    **Encore (see Clark, T. E. B.)
    For Services Rendered
        (In Modern Plays, London, 1937)
    The Perfect Gentleman (see Moliere, Jean Baptiste Poquelin)
    **Quartet (see Sherriff, Robert Cedric)
    Rain (see Colton, John)
    **Trio (see Sherriff, Robert Cedric)
MAULE, Wendy St. John
    Ladies in Waiting
        (In Best One-Act Plays of 1935, London)
MAULNIER, Thierry, 1909-
    Le Soir du Conquerant
        (In L'Avant-Scene du Theatre, no. 467, Mar. 1, 1971)
        (In Plaisir de France, supplement theatral, no. 389, May
        1971)
MAUPASSANT, Guy de, 1850-1893
    L'Amour Quelquefois
        (In L'Avant Scene du Theatre, no. 418, Jan. 15, 1969)
    **La Chevelure, d'apres une nouvelle de Guy de Maupassant (see
        Kyrou, Ado)
    **Une Partie de Campagne (see Renoir, Jean)
MAURA, Carlos Semprun
    L'Homme Couche
        (In L'Avant-Scene du Theatre, no. 474, June 15, 1971)
MAURIAC, Francois, 1885-
    Asmodee
        (In L'Avant-Scene du Theatre, no. 247, Aug. 1, 1961)
Mauricio de Nassau (see Correa, Viriato)
MAUROC, Daniel
    Sand in My Uniform
        (In First Stage, Vol. 3, Summer/Fall 1964)
Mauvaise Semence (see Vandenberghe, Paul)
Mauvaises Rencontres (see Astruc, Alexandre)
MAVOR, Osborne Henry, 1888-1951
    The Pardoner's Tale, adapted from a story by Geoffrey Chaucer,
        by James Bridie (pseud.)
        (In 24 One-Act Plays, Revised edition, 1954)
MAY, Elaine
    Not Enough Rope
        (In Mademoiselle, Vol. 66, Nov. 1967)
MAY, Thomas, 1595-1650
    The Heir
        (In Dodsley's A Select Collection of Old English Plays, Vol.
        11)

(In Dodsley's A Select Collection of Old Plays, Vol. 8)
The Old Couple
   (In Dodsley's A Select Collection of Old English Plays, Vol.
   12)
   (In Dodsley's A Select Collection of Old Plays, Vol. 8)
MAYAKOVSKY, Vladimir Vladimirovich, 1893-1930
   Vladimir Mayakovsky, a tragedy translated by Pierre Sokolsky
   (In Chicago Review, Vol. 20, no. 4, May 1969)
The Mayde's Metamorphosis (Anon.)
   (In A Collection of Old English Plays, Vol. 1)
Mayer, Carl, 1894-1944
   The Cabinet of Dr. Caligari (see Wiene, Robert)
Mayer, David
   Potemkin (see Eisenstein, Sergei Makhailovich)
MAYER, Edwin Justus
   The Buccaneer; screenplay by Edwin Justus Mayer; Harold Lamb,
   and C. Gardner Sullivan, based on an adaptation by Jeanie
   Macpherson of Lyle Saxon's book "Lafitte the Pirate." Di-
   rected by Cecil B. DeMille.
   (In Foremost Films of 1938)
   Children of Darkness
   (In Best American Plays, Supp. Vol.)
MAYER, Paul A.
   The Bridal Night, based on a story by Frank O'Connor
   (In Best Short Plays, 1968)
MAYHEW, Edward, 1813-1868
   Make Your Wills, by Edward Mayhew and G. Smith
   (In Cumberland's British Theatre, Vol. 46, no. 9)
MAYNE, Jasper, 1604-1672
   The City-Match
   (In Dodsley's A Select Collection of Old English Plays, Vol.
   13)
   (In Dodsley's A Select Collection of Old Plays, Vol. 9)
**The Merchant's Wedding; or, London Frolics in 1638 (see
   Planche, James Robinson)
Mayo, Archie, 1891-1968
   The Adventures of Marco Polo (see Sherwood, Robert Emmet)
The Mayor of Garratt (see Foote, Samuel)
The Mayor of Quinborough (see Middleton, Thomas)
MAYSLES, Albert
   Salesman, screenplay by Albert and David Maysles and Charlotte
   Zwerin
   (New American Library Screenplays, 1969)
MAZAUD, Emile
   The Holiday, based on "La Folle Journee," translated by Ralph
   Roeder
   (In Theatre Arts, Vol. 6, 1922)
Mazeppa (see Milner, Henry M.)
MAZZUCCO, Roberto
   Freedom Left Out in the Rain
   (In Drama & Theatre, Vol. 7, no. 3)
MEADE, Walter

Scott of the Antarctic
    (In Three British Screenplays, 1950)
The Meadow (see Bradbury, Ray)
A Measure of Cruelty (see Passeur, Steve)
The Measures Taken (see Brecht, Bertolt)
Meat Joy (see Schneemann, Carolee)
The Meat Rack (see Kimball, Kathleen)
Mechanical Sensuality (see Fillia)
A Medal for Benny (see Butler, Frank)
A Medal for Julien (see Kocher, Eric)
Medea (see Anouilh, Jean)
Medea (see Euripides)
Medea (see Jeffers, Robinson)
Medea (see Seneca, Lucius Annaeus)
MEDEK, Tilo
    "Icke und die Hexe Yu, " by Manfred Streubel and music by Tilo
    Medek
        (In Theater der Zeit, no. 5, 1971)
A Medical Man (see Gilbert, William Schwenck)
The Medicine Show (see Walker, Stuart)
MEDVEDKINE, Alexandre
    Le Bonheur
        (In L'Avant-Scene du Cinema, no. 120, Dec. 1971)
    Cette Sacree Force
        (In L'Avant-Scene du Cinema, no. 120, Dec. 1971)
MEE, Charles L. , Jr.
    Constantinople Smith
        (In New American Plays, Vol. 1)
MEEKER, Arthur, Jr.
    Hardy Perennials
        (In Drama, Vol. 13, May/June 1923)
Meeker, Isabelle
    Sojourners (see Harnwell, Anne)
Meeting at the Well (see Alexander, Hartley Burr)
A Meeting in the Woods (see Godsey, Townsend)
MEGRUE, Roi Cooper, 1883-
    Under Cover
        (In 13 Famous Plays of Crime and Detection)
Mei Lung Chen (see The Price of Wine)
MEKAS, Adolfas
    Hallelujah les Collines
        (In L'Avant-Scene du Cinema, no. 64, 1966)
MEL, Charles L. , Jr.
    God Bless Us, Everyone
        (In Tulane Drama Review, Vol. 10, Fall 1965)
MELFI, Leonard
    Birdbath
        (In Best Short Plays of the World Theatre, 1958-67)
MELMOTH, D.
    The Great American Light Year
        (In TDR/The Drama Review, Vol. 12, Winter 1968)
The Melon Thief (Uri Nusubito) (see Sakanishi, Shio)

MELVILLE, Alan
    Simon and Laura
       (In Plays of the Year, Vol. 11, 1954)
Melville, Herman, 1819-1861
    **Benito Cereno (see Lowell, Robert)
    **Billy Budd (see Coxe, Louis Osborne)
MELVILLE, Jean-Pierre, 1917-
    Le Coulos, d'apres le roman de Pierre Lesou
       (In L'Avant-Scene du Cinema, no. 24, Mar. 15, 1963)
    Leon Morin Pretre, d'apres le roman de Beatrix Beck
       (In L'Avant-Scene du Cinema, no. 10, Dec. 1961)
MELVILLE, Richard L.
    Pigs Ears and Purses
       (In The Banner Anthology of One-Act Plays by American
       Authors)
The Member for Gaza (see Levy, Benn)
The Member of Literature (see Baring, Maurice)
The Member of the Wedding (see McCullers, Mrs. Carson Smith)
Les Membres de la Famille (see Garnung, Francis)
Memo to Berchtesgaden (see Oboler, Arch)
The Memorandum (see Havel, Vaclav)
Memorial Day (see Schisgal, Murray)
Memory of Summer (see Inge, William Motter)
A Memory of Two Mondays (see Miller, Arthur)
Men in White (see Kingsley, Sidney)
Men Only (see Hughes, Glenn)
MENANDER, c. 342-291 B. C.
    The Arbitration (Epitrepontes)
       (In Complete Greek Drama, Vol. 2)
       (In The Plays of Menander)
    The Curmudgeon
       (In Horizon, Vol. 1, July 1959)
    Dyscolus
       (In Complete Greek Drama, Vol. 2)
    Dyskolos 1-49, 233-426, translated by G. Davenport
       (In Arion, Vol. 6, Summer 1967)
    The Girl From Samos
       (In Complete Greek Drama, Vol. 2)
    The Grouch (Dyskolos)
       (In The Plays of Menander)
    She Who was Shorn (Perikeiromene)
       (In The Plays of Menander)
    The Shield (Aspis)
       (In The Plays of Menander)
    The Woman of Samos (Samia)
       (In The Plays of Menander)
The Mendicant (see A Beckett, Gilbert Abbott)
Mendoza y La Cerda, Ana de, Princess of Eboli (see Eboli, Ana
    de Mendoza y La Cerda, Princes de)
MENEGOZ, Robert, 1923-
    La Commune de Paris
       (In L'Avant-Scene du Cinema, no. 114, May 1971)

MENEZES, Maria Wanderley
   O Amor na Terra do Cangaco
     (In Revista de Teatro, no. 330)
A Menina Que Vendia Flores (see Souto, Alexandrino de)
MENOTTI, Gian-Carlo, 1911-
   Martin's Life
     (In Show, N.Y., Vol. 4, Dec. 1964)
   Vanessa (see Barber, Samuel)
Der Menschen-Freund (see Hampton, Christopher)
Le Menteur (see Goldoni, Carlo)
MENZEL, Kiri
   Closely Watched Trains, a film by Jiri Menzel and Bohumil
     Hrabal
     (In Modern Film Scripts Series)
La Mer et les Jours (see Vogel, Raymond)
MERCER, David
   Belcher's Luck
     (In Plays and Players, Vol. 14, Feb. 1967)
   The Governor's Lady
     (In Best Short Plays of the World Theatre, 1958-67)
   On the Eve of Publication
     (In Scripts, Vol. 1, no. 8, June 1972)
The Merchant of Venice (see Shakespeare, William)
The Merchant of Yonkers (see The Matchmaker)
The Merchant's Wedding (see Planche, James Robinson)
MERCIER, Mary
   Johnny No-Trump
     (In Broadway's Beautiful Losers)
MERCIER, Maurice
   Le Reve de l'Infante
     (In Plaisir de France, supplement theatral, no. 319, May
     1965)
The Merciful Soul (see Alma-Tadema, Sir Lawrence)
MEREDITH, George, 1828-1909
   The Sentimentalists; an unfinished comedy
     (In Scribner's, Vol. 48, Aug. 1910)
MERIMEE, Prosper, 1803-1870
   The Conspirators
     (In Golden Book, Vol. 1, April 1925)
Mermaid Avenue Is the World (see Goldman, Paul)
Merope (see Hill, Aaron)
MERRILL, Fenimore
   The Avenue
     (In Drama, Vol. 10, Nov. 1919)
     (In 50 More Contemporary One-Act Plays)
MERRILL, James
   The Bait
     (In Artists Theatre)
MERRITT, Robert
   Togetherness
     (In Tulane Drama Review, Vol. 7, Winter 1962)
The Merry Devill of Edmonton (Anon.)

(In Dodsley's A Select Collection of Old English Plays, Vol.
    10)
The Merry-Go-Round (see Lawrence, David Herbert)
A Merry Knack to Know a Knave (Anon.)
    (In Dodsley's A Select Collection of Old English Plays, Vol.
    6)
The Merry Merry Cuckoo (see Marks, Jeanette Augustus)
Merry Mount (see Bates, William O.)
Merton of the Movies (see Kaufman, George Simon)
A Message from Cougar (see Maljean, Jean Raymond)
Metamora; or, The Last of the Wampanoags (see Stone, John
    Augustus)
Methusalem or the Eternal Bourgeois (see Goll, Yvan)
La Meule (see Allio, Rene)
MEYER, Adolph E.
    The Little Fool
        (In Drama, Vol. 17, Oct. 1926)
M'Hijo el Dotor (see Sanchez, Florencio)
MICHAEL, Harold
    Peace without Honour
        (In Best One-Act Plays of 1933, London)
MICHAEL, Sandra
    Against the Storm
        (In Radio Drama in Action, 1945)
Michaels, Sidney
    Ben Franklin in Paris (see Sandrich, Mark)
MICK, Hettie Louise
    The Maid Who Wouldn't Be Proper
        (In Drama, Vol. 12, Sept. 1922)
Mick and Mick (see Leonard, Hugh)
O Microbio do Amor (see Tigre, Bastos)
Microcosmus, a Morall Maske (see Nabbes, Thomas)
Midas (see Lyly, John)
Midas (see O'Hara, Kane)
Middle of the Night (see Chayefsky, Paddy)
MIDDLEMASS, Robert, 1885-
    The Valiant, by Robert Middlemass and Holworthy Hall (pseud.)
        (In 30 Famous One-Act Plays)
        (In Plays as Experience)
MIDDLETON, George, 1880-
    Tides
        (In Atlantic Book of Modern Plays, 1921)
    Tradition
        (In Contemporary One-Act Plays, 1922)
MIDDLETON, Thomas, 1570?-1627
    Changeling
        (In Theater Heute, Vol. 11, no. 8, Aug. 1970)
    The Honest Whore, Part 1 (see Dekker, Thomas)
    A Mad World, My Masters
        (In Dodsley's A Select Collection of Old Plays, Vol. 5)
    The Roaring Girle; or, Moll-Cut Purse, by Thomas Middleton
        and Thomas Dekker

(In Dodsley's A Select Collection of Old Plays, Vol. 6)
(In Dramatic Works of Dekker, Vol. 3)
A Trick to Catch the Old One
   (In The City and the Court)
The Widow   (see Jonson, Ben)
The Midnight Caller   (see Foote, Horton)
The Midnight Hour   (see Inchbald, Mrs. Elizabeth Simpson)
Mid-passage   (see Sundgaard, Arnold)
Midwestern Manic   (see Inge, William Motter)
The Mighty Barnum   (see Fowler, Gene)
The Mighty Reservoy   (see Terson, Peter)
Miguelito, a filmscript   (see Hill, James)
Mihalakeas, T.
   Mauvaise Semence   (see Vandenberghe, Paul)
Mildernde Umstände keine   (see Fischborn, Gottfried)
MILES, Josephine
   House and Home
   (In First Stage, Vol. 4, Fall 1965)
MILES, Nadine
   The Front Porch
   (In The One-Act Theatre, Vol. 1)
Milestone, Lewis, 1895-
   The Purple Heart   (see Cady, Jerome)
   North Star   (see Hellman, Lillian)
Milestones   (see Bennett, Arnold)
MILIUS, John
   The Life and Times of Judge Roy Bean; a John Huston film
   (A Bantam Books Screenplay, 1973)
The Milk Train Doesn't Stop Here Anymore   (see Williams, Tennessee)
MILLAR, Ronald, 1933-
   The Affair, based on the novel by C. P. Snow
   (In Theatre Arts, Vol. 47, Mar. 1963)
   Comme un Oisseau, by Ronald Millar and Nigel Balchin
   (In Plaisir de France, supplement theatral, no. 318, April
   1965)
MILLAY, Edna St. Vincent, 1892-1950
   Aria da Capo
   (In 25 Best Plays of the Modern American Theatre, Early
   Series, 1916-1929)
   (In 15 American One-Act Plays)
   (In 30 Famous One-Act Plays)
   (In 25 Best Plays, Early Series)
   (In 50 Contemporary One-Act Plays)
MILLER, Adam David
   It's a Long Way to St. Louis
   (In TDR/The Drama Review, Vol. 12, Summer 1968)
MILLER, Arthur, 1915-
   After the Fall
   (In Saturday Evening Post, Vol. 237, Feb. 1, 1964)
   All My Sons
   (In Best American Plays, Third Series)

The Crucible
  (In Theatre Arts, Vol. 37, Oct. 1953)
  (In Best American Plays, Fourth Series)
Death of a Salesman
  (In Theatre Arts, Vol. 35, March 1951)
  (In Best American Plays, Third Series)
  (In Plays of Our Time)
Fame
  (In Yale Literary Magazine, Vol. 140, no. 4, 1971)
Grandpa and the Statue
  (In Radio Drama in Action, 1945)
  (In Plays From Radio, 1948)
Incident a Vichy
  (In L'Avant-Scene du Theatre, 489, Feb. 15, 1972)
A Memory of Two Mondays
  (In One Act)
  (In Twenty-Four Favorite One-Act Plays)
Mort d'un Commis Voyageur; French text of "Death of a Sales-
man"
  (In Plaisir de France, Supplement Theatral, no. 331, May
  1966)
Price
  (In Saturday Evening Post, Vol. 241, Feb. 10, 1968)
The Story of Gus
  (In Radio's Best Plays, 1947)
That They May Win
  (In Best One-Act Plays of 1944, N. Y.)
A View from the Bridge
  (In The Modern Theatre, ed. by R. W. Corrigan)
  (In Makers of the Modern Theater, 1961)
  (In Best American Plays, Fourth Series)
A View from the Bridge, consisting of two one-act plays titled
  "A Memory of Two Mondays," and "A View from the Bridge."
  (In Theatre Arts, Vol. 40, no. 9, Sept. 1956)
MILLER, Hugh
  High Tea
  (In Best One-Act Plays of 1948/49, London)
MILLER, James, 1706-1744
  Mahomet
  (In Bell's British Theatre, 1797, Vol. 23)
MILLER, Paul Vincent
  The Red, the Pink, and the True Blue
  (In First Stage, Vol. 5, Spring 1966)
Miller, Seton I
  Here Comes Mr. Jordan (see Buchman, Sidney)
The Miller and His Men (see Pocock, Isaac)
MILLINGEN, J. V.
  The Bee-Hive
  (In Cumberland's British Theatre, Vol. 22, no. 6)
MILLS, Hugh
  The Little Glass Clock
  (In Plays of the Year, Vol. 11, 1954)

MILNE, Alan Alexander, 1882-1956
   Before the Flood
     (In Best One-Act Plays, London, 1952/53)
   The Dover Road
     (In Modern Plays, London, 1937)
   Mr. Pim Passes By
     (In 16 Famous British Plays)
     (In Theatre Guild Anthology)
   The Ugly Duckling
     (In Best One-Act Plays of 1940, London)
MILNER, Henry M.
   The Hut of the Red Mountain; or, Thirty Years of a Gamester's
   Life
     (In Cumberland's British Theatre, Vol. 42, no. 2)
   Mazeppa
     (In Cumberland's British Theatre, Vol. 26, no. 9)
MILNER, Roger
   How's the World Treating You?
     (In Plays of the Year, Vol. 30, 1965)
     (In Plays and Players, Vol. 13, March 1966)
MILNER, Ronald
   The Monster
     (In TDR/The Drama Review, Vol. 12, Summer 1968)
MILTON, John, 1608-1674
   Comus
     (In Bell's British Theatre, 1797, Vol. 1)
     (In Cumberland's British Theatre, Vol. 46, no. 7)
   Samson Agonistes
     (In Genius of the Early English Theater)
     (In Bell's British Theatre, 1797, Vol. 34)
     (In Tragedy: Texts and Commentary, 1969)
Mina de Vanghel (see Clavel, Maurice)
Mind in the Shadow (see Perl, Arnold)
Minding the Store; a Street Vaudeville (see Nichols, Robert)
The Mines of Sulphur (see Cross, Beverley)
The Minister's Seal (Anon.)
     (In Two Plays From Ancient India)
Minna von Barnhelm (see Lessing, Gotthold Ephraim)
Minney, Rubeigh James, 1895-
   Clive of India (see Lipscomb, William Percy)
Minnie Field (see Conkle, Ellsworth Prouty)
The Minyana's Daughter (see Treitel, Ralph)
Miquelina (see Bloch, Pedro)
Mirabeau, Octave, 1850-1917
   **Le Journal d'une Femme de Chambre (see Buñuel, Luis)
The Miracle (see Kikuchi Kwan)
The Miracle at Tsubosaka (Tsubosaka Reigenki) (see Toyzawa,
   Chika)
Miracle at Verdun (see Chlumberg, Hans)
Miracle en Alabama (see Gibson, William)
Miracle in Milan (see DeSica, Vittorio)
The Miracle of Morgan's Creek (see Sturges, Preston)

A Miracle of St. Antony (see Maeterlinck, Maurice)
The Miracle of Saint Nicholas and the Image (see Hilarius, Saint,
bp. of Poitiers)
The Miracle of Saint Nicholas and the Schoolboys (Anon.)
(In Representative Medieval and Tudor Plays)
The Miracle of Saint Nicholas and the Virgins (Anon.)
(In Representative Medieval and Tudor Plays)
The Miracle of the Blind Man and the Cripple (see Andrieu de la
Vigne)
Miracle of the Corn (see Colum, Padraic)
The Miracle of the Danube (see Anderson, Maxwell)
Miracle on the Pullman (see Hecht, Ben)
The Miracle Worker (see Gibson, William)
The Miracle Worker; text in French (see Gibson, William)
Le Miroir (see Higuera, Pablo de la)
Le Miroir (see Salabrou, Armand)
Mirthful Marionettes (see Totheroh, Dan)
Misalliance (see Shaw, George Bernard)
The Misanthrope (see Moliere, Jean Baptiste Poquelin)
Mischief-Making (see Buckstone, John Baldwin)
The Miser (see Fielding, Henry)
The Miser (see Moliere, Jean Baptiste Poquelin)
Les Miserables (see Archard, Paul)
Misere et Noblesse (see Scrapetta, Eduardo)
The Miseries of Enforced Marriage (see Wilkins, George)
The Misfortunes of Arthur (see Hughes, Thomas)
Mishima, Yukio, pseud. (see Hiraoka, Kimitake)
Misogonus (Anon.)
(In Early Plays from the Italian)
Miss Fassey (see Baker, Elizabeth)
Miss Julie (see Strindberg, August)
Miss Julie (see also Julie)
Miss Lucy in Town (see Fielding, Henry)
Miss Lulu Bett (see Gale, Zona Breese)
Miss Sara Sampson (see Lessing, Gotthold Ephraim)
Mission Accomplished (see Caldwell, Ben)
The Mistake (see Vanbrugh, John)
Mr. and Mrs. Pringle (see De Trueba Cosio, Don T.)
Mr. and Mrs. P. Roe (see Johnson, Martyn)
Mister Antonio (see Tarkington, Booth)
Mr. Biggs (see Barlow, Anna Marie)
Mr. Dumbtaro (Dontaro) (see Sakanishi, Shio)
Mr. F. (see Wilde, Percival)
Mr. Fothergill Joins the Angels (see Dinner, William)
Mr. Kilt and the Great I Am (see Ross, Kenneth)
Mister Ledford and the TVA (see Lomax, Alan)
Mr. Mergenthwirker's Lobblies (see Bond, Nelson)
Mister, Mister (see Grass, Günter)
Mr. Nightingale's Diary (see Dickens, Charles)
Mr. Pim Passes By (see Milne, Alan Alexander)
Mister Roberts (see Heggen, Thomas)
Mr. Sampson (see Lee, James Charles)

Mr. Smith Goes to Washington (see Buchman, Sidney)
Mistletoe and Moonlight (see Wilbur, Elene)
Les Mistons (see Truffaut, Francois)
Mrs. Leicester's School (see Hoffman, Phoebe)
Mrs. Middleman's Descent (see Halpern, Martin)
Mrs. Miniver (see Hilton, James)
Mrs. Moonlight (see Levy, Benn Wolf)
Mrs. Mouse, Are You Within? (see Marcus, Frank)
Mistress Nell (see Hazelton, George Cochrane)
Mrs. Noah Gives the Sign (see Sladen-Smith, Francis)
Mrs. Wickens in the Fall (see Kneale, Nigel)
Mrs. Willis's Will (see Souvestre, Emile)
The Misunderstanding (see Camus, Albert)
MITCHELL, Julian
    A Heritage--and Its History, by Julian Mitchell, adapted from
    the novel by I. Compton-Burnett
        (In Plays of the Year, Vol. 30, 1965)
    Shadow in the Sun
        (In Plays of the Year Special, 1972)
MITCHELL, Langdon Elwyn, 1862-1935
    Becky Sharp; based on the novel "Vanity Fair" by William
    Makepeace Thackeray
        (In Monte Cristo and Other Plays)
    The New York Idea
        (In Best Plays of the Modern American Theatre, from the
        beginning to 1916)
        (In The Modern Theatre, ed. by Eric Bentley, Vol. 4)
MITCHELL, Loften
    A Land beyond the River
        (In The Black Teacher and the Dramatic Arts)
    Tell Pharaoh
        (In The Black Teacher and the Dramatic Arts)
MITCHELL, Ronald Elwy
    A Husband for Breakfast
        (In Best One-Act Plays of 1936, London)
        (In Best One-Act Plays of 1937, N.Y.)
    Resurrection Ezra
        (In Best One-Act Plays of 1938, N.Y.)
MITCHELL, Yvonne
    The Same Sky
        (In Plays of the Year, Vol. 6, 1951)
MITFORD, Mary Russell, 1787-1855
    Foscari
        (In Cumberland's British Theatre, Vol. 46, no. 5)
    Rienzi
        (In Cumberland's British Theatre, Vol. 9, no. 3)
Mitford, Nancy, 1904-
    The Little Hut (see Roussin, Andre)
MITHOIS, Marcel, 1922-
    L'Accompagnateur
        (In L'Avant-Scene du Theatre, no. 231)
    Les Coups de Theatre

(In L'Avant-Scene du Theatre, no. 240, Apr. 1, 1961)
Croque-Monsieur
(In Plaisir de France, supplement theatral, no. 315, Jan.
1965)
(In L'Avant-Scene du Theatre, no. 325, Jan. 1, 1965)
Cruelle Galejade
(In L'Avant-Scene du Theatre, no. 209, Dec. 1, 1959)
Elisabeth est Morte
(In L'Avant-Scene du Theatre, no. 183, Oct. 1, 1958)
Isabelle et le General
(In L'Avant-Scene du Theatre, no. 174, May 15, 1958)
Madame La Defunte
(In L'Avant-Scene du Theatre, Nov. 15, 1967)
(In Plaisir de France, supplement theatral, no. 350, Dec.
1967)
Le Passe-Temps
(In L'Avant-Scene du Theatre, no. 253, Nov. 1961)
La Troisieme Agnes
(In Plaisir de France, supplement theatral, no. 303, Jan.
1964)
(In L'Avant-Scene du Theatre, no. 300, Dec. 1, 1963)
Les Vacances Revees
(In Plaisir de France, supplement theatral, no. 315, Jan.
1965)
(In L'Avant-Scene du Theatre, no. 325, Jan. 1, 1965)
Mithridates, VI, Eupator, called the Great, c.132-63 B.C.
*Mithridates (see Hay, Gyula)
*Mithridates, King of Pontus (see Lee, Nathaniel)
MIYAMASU, 16th cent.?
The Hatmaker (Eboshi-ori)
(In Genius of the Oriental Theater)
Moby Tick (see Peluso, Emmanuel)
Mocinha (see Camargo, Joracy)
The Mock Doctor; or, The Dumb Lady Cured (see Fielding, Henry)
Mock Trial (see Grafton, Edith & Samuel)
MOCKY, Jean-Pierre
L'Albatros
(In L'Avant-Scene du Cinema, no. 119, Nov. 1971)
Solo
(In L'Avant-Scene du Cinema, no. 103, May 1970)
Modern Antiques; or, The Merry Mourners (see O'Keeffe, John)
The Modern Masterpiece (see Etheridge, Vere)
Modesty (see Hervieu, Paul Ernest)
MOELLER, Philip, 1880-1958
Helena's Husband
(In Thirty Famous One-Act Plays)
(In 50 Contemporary One-Act Plays)
Mohammed (see Muhammad, the Prophet)
Un Mois a la Champagne (see Turgenev, Ivan Sergeyevich)
The Mole (see Jodorowsky, Alexandro)
MOLIERE, Jean Baptiste Poquelin, 1622-1673
George Dandin, or, The Discomfited Husband, translated by
Stark Young

(In Theatre Arts, Vol. 8, Sept. 1924)
The Forced Marriage, edited by Eric Bentley
    (In Tulane Drama Review, Vol. 8, Winter 1963)
The Imaginary Invalid
    (In Genius of the French Theater)
The Imaginary Invalid, adapted by Miles Malleson
    (In Plays of the Year, Vol. 19, 1958/59)
The Misanthrope
    (In Masterworks of World Drama, Vol. 4)
    (In The Classic Theatre, ed. by Eric Bentley, Vol. 4)
The Misanthrope, adapted by Miles Malleson
    (In Plays of the Year, Vol. 11, 1954)
The Miser
    (In Introduction to Literature: Plays)
    (In Masterworks of World Drama, Vol. 4)
*Monsieur et Madame Moliere (see Chabannes, Jacques)
**The Perfect Gentleman, adapted from Moliere's "Le Bourgeois
    Gentilhomme, " by William Somerset Maugham
    (In Theatre Arts, Vol. 39, Nov. 1955)
The Prodigious Snob, translated and adapted from Moliere's "Le
    Bourgeois Gentilhomme, " by Miles Malleson
    (In Plays of the Year, Vol. 6, 1951)
School for Husbands
    (In Dramatic Works, Vol. 1)
School for Wives
    (In Dramatic Works, Vol. 1)
School for Wives Criticized
    (In Dramatic Works, Vol. 1)
Sganarelle, adapted by Miles Malleson
    (In Plays of the Year, Vol. 11, 1954)
**Tartuffe--Acte VI (see Marie, Andre)
Molina, Tirso de (see Tellez, Gabriel)
MOLINARO, Ursule
    The Abstract Wife
        (In New American Plays, Vol. 2)
The Mollusc (see Davies, Hubert Henry)
MOLNAR, Ferenc, 1878-1952
    Liliom
        (In 16 Famous European Plays)
        (In Theatre Guild Anthology)
    The Play's the Thing
        (In Theatre Arts, Vol. 33, Feb. 1949)
    The Play's the Thing, adapted by Pelham Granville Wodehouse
        (In 20 Best European Plays on the American Stage)
    The Putty Club
        (In Theatre Arts, Vol. 7, 1923)
Mon Mari s'Endort (see Gevel, Claude)
MONASH, Paul
    Judd for the Defense, a television filmscript
        (In Writing for Television)
MONCRIEFF, William Thomas, 1794-1857
    All at Coventry; or, Love and Laugh

(In Cumberland's British Theatre, Vol. 45, no. 1)
Eugene Aram; or, Saint Robert's Cave
(In Cumberland's British Theatre, Vol. 37, no. 4)
Giovanni in London; or, The Libertine Reclaimed
(In Cumberland's British Theatre, Vol. 39, no. 7)
Monsieur Tonson
(In Cumberland's British Theatre, Vol. 27, no. 1)
The Scamps of London; or, The Cross Roads of Life!
(In Lacy's Acting Plays, Vol. 81)
The Somnambulist; or, The Phantom of the Village
(In Cumberland's British Theatre, Vol. 14, no. 3)
The Spectre Bridegroom; or, A Ghost in Spite of Himself
(In Cumberland's British Theatre, Vol. 36, no. 6)
Tom and Jerry; or, Life in London
(In Cumberland's British Theatre, Vol. 28, no. 5)
Monday (see Kreymborg, Alfred)
Le Monde Est Ce Qu'il Est (see Moravia, Alberto)
Moneda Falsa (see Sanchez, Florencio)
Money Makes the Man (see Sketchley, Arthur)
Moneys from Shylock (see Rubinstein, Harold Frederick)
Monica (see Macaulay, Pauline)
The Monk Who Wouldn't (see Mandel, Oscar)
Monkey Business (see Marx Brothers)
The Monkey's Paw (see Jacobs, William Wymark)
A la Monnaie du Pape (see Velle, Louis)
MONNIER, Henry
    L'Enterrement
        (In Plaisir de France, supplement theatral, no. 383, Nov.
        1970)
    Monsieur Prudhomme
        (In Plaisir de France, supplement theatral, no. 383, Nov.
        1970)
Monroe, Marilyn, 1926-1962
    *After the Fall (fiction) (see Miller, Arthur)
Monsieur Beaucaire (see Tarkington, Booth)
Monsieur et Madame Moliere (see Chabannes, Jacques)
Monsieur Gogo (see Gillois, Andre)
Monsieur Lamblin (see Curnieu, Georges de)
Monsieur Masure (see Magnier, Claude)
Monsieur Prudhomme (see Monnier, Henry)
Le Monsieur Qui Attend (see Williams, Emlyn)
Monsieur Ripois (see Clement, Rene)
Monsieur Tonson (see Moncrieff, William Thomas)
Monsieur Vautrin (see Charpak, Andre)
The Monster (see Carson, Julia Brainard)
The Monster (see Milner, Ronald)
Les Monstres Sacres (see Cocteau, Jean)
Monte Cristo (see Fechter, Charles Albert)
MONTEIRO, Jose Maria
    Prima Donna
        (In Revista de Teatro, no. 296)
Montez, Lola, 1818-1861
    *Lola Montes (see Ophuls, Max)

Montezuma (see Robertson, Louis A.)
MONTGOMERY, Robert
Iz She Izzy or Iz He Ain'tzy or Iz They Both (see Carter, Lonnie)
Subject to Fits
(In Scripts, Vol. 1, no. 4, Feb. 1972)
A Month in the Country (see Turgenev, Ivan Sergeyevich)
A Month in the Country; text in French (see Turgenev, Ivan Sergeyevich)
MONTHERLANT, Henry de, 1896-
The Cardinal of Spain
(In Plays of the Year, Vol. 37, 1969/70)
Celles Qu'on Prend dans Ses Bras
(In L'Avant-Scene du Theatre, no. 147)
Un Incompris
(In L'Avant-Scene du Theatre, no. 147)
Malatesta
(In Master of Santiago & Four Other Plays)
The Master of Santiago
(In Makers of the Modern Theatre, 1961)
(In Master of Santiago & Four Other Plays)
No Man's Son; or, More than Blood
(In Master of Santiago & Four Other Plays)
Queen after Death; or, How to Kill Women
(In Master of Santiago & Four Other Plays)
Tomorrow the Dawn
(In Master of Santiago & Four Other Plays)
Le Montreur (see Chedid, Andree)
MOODY, William Vaughn, 1869-1910
The Great Divide
(In American Drama)
(In Best Plays of the Early American Theatre, from the beginning to 1916)
The Moon (see Broome, D. M.)
Moon (Heide, Robert)
The Moon Balloon (see Koch, Kenneth)
A Moon for the Misbegotten (see O'Neill, Eugene)
The Moon is Blue (see Herbert, Frederick Hugh)
The Moon of the Caribbees (see O'Neill, Eugene Gladstone)
Moon on a Rainbow Shawl (see John, Errol)
Moonshine (see Hopkins, Arthur Melancthon)
Moony's Kid Don't Cry (see Williams, Tennessee)
Moore, Carroll, 1913-
Make a Million (see Barasch, Norman)
Send Me No Flowers (see Barasch, Norman)
MOORE, Daniel
Blis Apocalypse
(In TDR/Drama Review, Vol. 14, Sept. 1970)
MOORE, Edward, 1712-1757
The Foundling
(In Bell's British Theatre, 1797, Vol. 11)
The Gamester

(In Bell's British Theatre, 1797, Vol. 10)
(In Cumberland's British Theatre, Vol. 5, no. 2)
MOORE, Hortense
    Noah and His Sons
        (In Bread Loaf Book of Plays)
    Snow
        (In Bread Loaf Book of Plays)
Moral Courage (see Salten, Felix)
Moral em Concordata (see Almeida, Abilio Pereira de)
A Morality Play for the Leisured Class (see Balderston, John
    Lloyd)
MORATIN, Leandro Fernandes de, 1760-1828
    The Baron, translated by Fanny Holcroft, from the Spanish of
        Inarco Celenio, pseud.
        (In Theatrical Recorder, ed. by Thomas Holcroft, Vol. 2,
        no. 11, Oct. 1805)
MORAVIA, Alberto, 1909-
    Le Monde Est Ce Qu'il Est
        (In L'Avant-Scene du Theatre, no. 440, Jan. 1, 1970)
    The World Is what It Is; both French and English texts are
        included
        (In Italian Theatre Review, Vol. 16, July/Sept. 1967)
MORE, Federico, 1889-
    Interlude
        (In 50 Contemporary One-Act Plays)
MORE, Hannah, 1745-1833
    Percy
        (In Modern Theatre, 1811, Vol. 7)
More, Sir Thomas, 1478-1535
    *A Man for All Seasons (see Bolt, Robert)
    *Thomas More, or L'Homme Seul; text in French (see Bolt,
        Robert)
The More the Merrier (see Russel, Robert)
A Moreninha (see Macedo, Joaquim Manuel de)
A Moreninha (see Silveira, Miroel)
MORENO, Virginia R.
    Straw Patriot
        (In Literary Review, Vol. 3, Summer 1960)
MORGAN, Al
    The Little One
        (In Radio's Best Plays, 1947)
MORGAN, Edward J.
    The Return
        (In Drama, Vol. 11, Jan. 1921)
MORGAN, Elaine
    You're a Long Time Dead
        (In Television Playwright: 10 Plays for BBC)
MORLEY, Christopher Darlington, 1890-1957
    Thursday Evening
        (In 15 American One-Act Plays)
        (In Dramas by Present-Day Writers)
MORLEY, Robert, 1908-

Edward, My Son, by Robert Morley and Noel Langley
   (In Theatre Arts, Vol. 33, Aug. 1949)
Morning, Noon, and Night (see Shine, Ted)
Mornings at Seven (see Osborn, Paul)
Morocco (see Von Sternberg, Josef)
Morre um Gato Na China (see Block, Pedro)
MORRIS, Colin
   The Unloved
      (In Television Playwright: 10 Plays for BBC)
MORRIS, Jean
   Anne of Cleves; a television script in the series "The Six
   Wives of Henry VIII"
      (In Plays of the Year Special, 1972)
Morris, Richard
   The Unsinkable Molly Brown (see Willson, Meredith)
MORRIS, Thomas Badden
   Ophelia
      (In Best One-Act Plays of 1948/49, London)
   Renaissance Night
      (In Best One-Act Plays of 1940, London)
   Tudor Thorns
      (In Best One-Act Plays of 1942/43, London)
   Tutankhamon, Son of Ra
      (In Best One-Act Plays, 1952/53, London)
MORSE, Richard M., 1922-
   The Narrowest Street
      (In Theatre Arts, Vol. 29, Sept. 1945)
Mort d'un Cycliste (see Bardem, Juan Antonio)
Mort d'un Voyageur (see Miller, Arthur)
Mortal Coils (see Gioconda Smile)
La Morte de Roberta (see Sergei-Mikailovitch)
MORTIMER, John Clifford, 1923-
   Call Me a Liar
      (In Evergreen Playscript Series)
      (In Television Playwright: 10 Plays for BBC)
   Collect Your Hand Baggage
      (In Evergreen Playscript Series)
   David and Broccoli
      (In Evergreen Playscript Series)
   The Dock Brief
      (In English One-Act Plays of Today)
      (In Evergreen Playscript Series)
   Une Heure pour Dejeuner
      (In L'Avant Scene du Theatre, no. 399, Mar. 15, 1968)
   I Claudius, from the novels "I Claudius" and "Claudius the
   God" by Robert Graves
      (In Plays and Players, Vol. 19, no. 12, Sept. 1972)
   I Spy
      (In Evergreen Playscript Series)
   Lunch Hour
      (In Evergreen Playscript Series)
   Two Stars for Comfort

(In Evergreen Playscript Series)
A Voyage Round My Father
(In Plays and Players, Vol. 18, Feb. 1971)
What Shall We Tell Caroline?
(In Evergreen Playscript Series)
Mortimer, Penelope, 1918-
**The Pumpkin Eater (see Pinter, Harold)
MORTON, John Maddison, 1811-1891
Master Jones's Birthday
(In Lacy's Acting Plays, Vol. 81)
A Most Unwarrantable Intrusion
(In 26 Short & Amusing Plays, 1871)
My Husband's Ghost!
(In Cumberland's British Theatre, Vol. 41, no. 9)
MORTON, Thomas, 1764?-1838
The Children in the Wood
(In Cumberland's British Theatre, Vol. 20, no. 1)
A Cure for the Heartache
(In Cumberland's British Theatre, Vol. 15, no. 4)
Education
(In Cumberland's British Theatre, Vol. 12, no. 5)
The Invincibles
(In Cumberland's British Theatre, Vol. 37, no. 8)
The School of Reform; or, How to Rule a Husband
(In Cumberland's British Theatre, Vol. 14, no. 4)
Secrets Worth Knowing
(In Cumberland's British Theatre, Vol. 11, no. 4)
(In Modern Theatre, 1811, Vol. 3)
Speed the Plough
(In Cumberland's British Theatre, Vol. 5, no. 5)
Town and Country
(In Cumberland's British Theatre, Vol. 9, no. 2)
The Way to Get Married
(In Cumberland's British Theatre, Vol. 3, no. 2)
Zorinski
(In Modern Theater, 1811, Vol. 3)
MOSEL, Tad
All the Way Home, based on the novel "Death in the Family,"
by James Agee
(In Theatre Arts, Vol. 46, Oct. 1962)
(In Best American Plays, Fifth Series, 1957-63)
The Five Dollar Bill
(In Best Television Plays of the Year, 1957)
Impromptu
(In Fifteen American One-Act Plays)
My Lost Saints
(In Best Television Plays
The Out-of-Towners
(In Television Plays for Writers, 1957)
The Presence of the Enemy
(In Best Short Plays, 1958/59)
Moses, 14th-13th cent. B.C.

*Through Deserts to Ancestral Lands (see Strindberg, August)
MOSHER, John Chapin
   The Quay of Magic Things
      (In Drama, Vol. 10, Feb. 1920)
Mosley, Nicholas, 1923-
   **Accident (see Pinter, Harold)
MOSSI, Miguen Angel
   Ollantay
      (In First Stage, Vol. 6, no. 1, Spring 1967)
The Most Happy Fella (see Loesser, Frank)
A Most Unwarrantable Intrusion (see Morton, John Maddison)
The Mother (see Chayefsky, Paddy)
Mother Courage (see Brecht, Bertolt)
The Mother-in-Law (see Terence, Publius Terentius Afer)
The Mothers (see Etienne, Charles Guillaume)
The Mothers and Daughters (see St.-Leger, De M.)
Mother's Day (see Priestley, John Boynton)
Motokiyo, Zeami (see Zeami Motokiyo)
The Motor Show (see Ionesco, Eugene)
MOTOYASU, Komparn Zembo, 1453-1532
   Atsumori at Ikuta (Ikuta Atsumori)
      (In Genius of the Oriental Theater)
   Early Snow (Hatsuyuki)
      (In Genius of the Oriental Theater)
   Ikkaku Sennin; English adaptation by William Packard after
   the original translation by Frank Hoff. Japanese text is
   included.
      (In Players Magazine, Vol. 41, no. 6, Mar. 1965)
Le Mouchard (see Nichols, Dudley)
Mouchette (see Bresson, Robert)
The Mountain Chorus (see Bermel, Albert)
Mountain Laurel (see Cooksey, Curtis)
The Mountaineers (see Colman, George, the Younger)
The Mourning Bride (see Congreve, William)
The Mouse-Trap (see Howells, William Dean)
MOUSSEY, Marcel
   Les Quatre Cents Coups (see Truffaut, Francois)
   Trois Hommes sur un Cheval
      (In Plaisir de France, supplement theatral, no. 371, Oct.
      1969)
MOWATT, Anna Cora (Ritchie), 1819-1870
   Fashion
      (In Best Plays of the Early American Theatre, from the
      beginning to 1916)
   Fashion; or, Life in New York
      (In The Black Crook & Other 19th Century American Plays)
      (In Six Early American Plays, 1798-1890)
Moyes, Patricia
   Time Remembered (see Anouilh, Jean)
MOZART, Johann Chrysostom Wolfgang Amadeus, 1756-1791

Cosi fan tutte. English version of the Lorenzo Da Ponte
  libretto by Ruth & Thomas Martin
  (In Theatre Arts, Vol. 40, Jan. 1956)
*Mozart and Salieri (see Pushkin, Aleksandr Sergeyevich)
*Mozart and the Gray Steward (see Wilder, Thornton Niven)
MROZEK, Slawomir, 1930-
  Charlie
    (In Evergreen Playscript Series)
  Enchanted Night
    (In Evergreen Playscript Series)
  The Martyrdom of Peter Chey
    (In Evergreen Playscript Series)
  Out at Sea
    (In Evergreen Playscript Series)
  The Party
    (In Evergreen Playscript Series)
  The Police
    (In Evergreen Playscript Series)
  Strip-Tease
    (In Tulane Drama Review, Vol. 11, Spring 1967)
  Tango, translated by Nicholas Bethell and Tom Stoppard
    (In Three East European Plays)
MRWEBI, Gwigwi
  Feat Accomplished and a Hero Completely Defeated
    (In The Literary Review, Vol. 15, no. 1, Fall 1971)
The Mud Nest (see Power, Victor)
MÜLLER, Andre
  "Der Spiegelfechter"
    (In Theater der Zeit, no. 11, 1972)
MÜLLER, Armin
  Franziska Lesser
    (In Theater der Zeit, no. 12, 1971)
MÜLLER, Heiner
  Macbeth; nach Shakespeare
    (In Theater Heute, no. 6, 1972)
  "Weiberkomödie"
    (In Theater der Zeit, no. 3, 1971)
Münchner Freiheit (see Sperr, Martin)
Das Mündel Will Vormund sein (see Handke, Peter)
Los Muertos (see Sanchez, Florencio)
La Muette (see Chabrol, Claude)
Muhammad, the prophet, A.D. 570-632
  *Death of Mohammed (see El-Hakim, T.)
MUKERJI, Dhan Gopal, 1890-1936
  The Judgement of Indra
    (In 50 Contemporary One-Act Plays)
The Mulatto's Orgy (see Hernandez, Luisa Josefina)
MULDROW, Edna
  Dust
    (In Best One-Act Plays of 1938, N.Y.)
Mulet, Paul, pseud. (see Rivers, Louis)
Muletail Prime (see Conkle, Ellsworth Prouty)

Mulher Zero Quilometro   (see Alves, Edward G.)
MULLALLY, Donn
   Tarzan and the Creeping Giants, a television filmscript
   (In Writing for Television)
MULLER, Romeo
   The Great Git-Away
   (In Playwrights for Tomorrow, Vol. 3)
MULVEY, Timothy J.
   North Atlantic Testament
   (In Radio Drama in Action, 1945)
The Mummer's Play; restored by J. Kinchin Smith
   (In Theatre Arts, Vol. 7, 1923)
MUNDAY, Anthony, 1553-1601
   The Death of Robert Earl of Huntington, otherwise called
   Robin Hood of Merrie Sherwoode, by Anthony Munday and
   Henry Chettle
   (In Dodsley's A Select Collection of Old English Plays, Vol.
   8)
   The Downfall of Robert Earl of Huntington, afterward called
   Robin Hood of Merrie Sherwoode, by Anthony Munday and
   Henry Chettle
   (In Dodsley's A Select Collection of Old English Plays, Vol.
   8)
MUNGO, Raymond
   Between Two Moons; a technicolor travelogue
   (A Beacon Press Screenplay, 1972)
MUNIZ, Lauro Cesar
   A Comedia Atomica
   (In Revista de Teatro, no. 379, Jan./Feb. 1971)
   Este Ovo e um Galo
   (In Revista de Teatro, no. 363, May/June 1968)
   "A Infidelidade ao Alcance de Todos"
   (In Revista de Teatro, no. 371, Sept./Oct. 1969)
   O Santo Milagroso
   (In Revista de Teatro, no. 356)
MUNK, Andrzej, 1921-
   La Passagere, by Andrezej et Zofia Posmysz. Titre original:
   "Pasazerka"
   (In L'Avant-Scene du Cinema, no. 47, 1965)
MUNRO, Hector Hugh, 1870-1916
   Death-Trap
   (In Novels and Plays of Saki)
   Karl-Ludwig's Window
   (In Novels and Plays of Saki)
   The Watched Pot
   (In Novels and Plays of Saki)
Le Mur (see Roullet, Serge)
Murder in the Cathedral (see Eliot, Thomas Stearns)
Murder is Fun! (see Blankenship, Catherine)
The Murder of Marat (see Kearney, Patrick)
The Murder Scream (see Aklom, Mikhail)
Murderer, the Women's Hope (see Kokoschka, Oskar)

MURDOCH, Iris
    The Italian Girl, by Iris Murdoch and James Saunders)
        (In Plays and Players, Vol. 15, Feb. 1968)
Murfin, Jane
    Dragon Seed (see Roberts, Marguerite)
    The Women (see Loos, Anita)
Murieta, Joaquin (see Murrieta, Joaquin)
MURPHY, Arthur, 1727-1805
    All in the Wrong
        (In Cumberland's British Theatre, Vol. 29, no. 7)
        (In Bell's British Theatre, 1797, Vol. 12)
        (In The London Stage, Vol. 2)
    The Citizen
        (In Cumberland's British Theatre, Vol. 15, no. 7)
    The Grecian Daughter
        (In Cumberland's British Theatre, Vol. 10, no. 1)
        (In Bell's British Theatre, 1797, Vol. 4)
    Know Your Own Mind
        (In Cumberland's British Theatre, Vol. 10, no. 2)
        (In The London Stage, Vol. 2)
    The Orphan of China
        (In Bell's British Theatre, 1797, Vol. 24)
    The School for Guardians
        (In Bell's British Theatre, 1797, Vol. 33)
    The Way to Keep Him
        (In Bell's British Theatre, 1797, Vol. 17)
        (In Cumberland's British Theatre, Vol. 16, no. 6)
    Zenobia
        (In Bell's British Theatre, 1797, Vol. 33)
MURRAY, J.
    Adieu Berthe!
        (In Plaisir de France, supplement theatral, no. 357, July
        1968)
MURRAY, Robert Bruce
    The Good Lieutenant
        (In Four New Yale Playwrights)
Murrieta, Joaquin, 1828/9-1953
    *Glanz und Tod Joaquin Murietas (see Neruda, Pablo)
MUSCHG, Adolf
    Die Aufgeregten von Goethe
        (In Theater Heute, Nov. 1970)
The Muse's Looking-Glass (see Randolph, Thomas)
Mushrooms (see Kvares, Donald)
Music Hath Charms (see Fisher, David)
Musical Chairs (see Mackenzie, Ronald)
MUSORGSKII, Modest Petrovich, 1839-1881
    Boris Gudonov; opera in four acts by Modest Mussorgsky
    from Pushkin's play by the same name. English text by
    John Gutman.
        (In Theatre Arts, Vol. 43, March 1959)
MUSSET, Alfred de, 1810-1857
    A Door Should be either Open or Shut

(In From the Modern Repertoire, Series Three)
Fantasio
(In From the Modern Repertoire, Series One)
(In The Modern Theatre, ed. Eric Bentley, Vol. 2)
Lorenzaccio
(In The Modern Theatre, ed. by Eric Bentley, Vol. 6)
On ne Badine pas avec l'Amour
(In Chief Plays of the 19th Century)
Mussorgsky, Modest Petrowitsch (see Musorgskii, Modest Petro-
vich)
Musterschüler (see Kahlau, Heinz)
The Mute Canary (see Ribemont-Dessaugnes, Georges)
Mutilated (see Williams, Tennessee)
The Mutiny at the Nore (see Jerrold, Douglas)
Muzeeka (see Guare, John)
My Client, Curley (see Corwin, Norman Lewis)
My Darlin' Aida (see Verdi, Giuseppe)
My Daughter, Sir! or A Daughter to Marry (see Planche, James
Robinson)
My Dear! (see O'Connor, Patricia)
My Foot My Tutor (see Handke, Peter)
"My Friend Thompson!" (see Barclay, James M.)
My Grandmother (see Hoare, Prince)
My Hills, My Home (see Griffiths, Glyn)
My Husband's Ghost! (see Morton, John Maddison)
My Kinsman, Major Molineux (see Lowell, Robert)
My Lost Saints (see Mosel, Tad)
My Man Godfrey (see Ryskind, Morris)
My Night at Maude's (see Rohmer, Eric)
"My Old Woman" (see Macfarren, George)
My Pol and My Partner Joe (see Haines, John Thomas)
My Taylor (see Harper, Harold)
My 3 Angels (see Spewack, Samuel)
My Unfinished Portrait (see Voteur, Ferdinand)
MYALL, Charles A.
     Ships on the Sand
        (In Drama, Vol. 12, Feb. 1922)
MYERS, Irvin H.
     Socrates Up-to-Date
        (In Atlantic, Vol. 143, Jan. 1929)
MYRTLE, Frederick S.
     Gold
        (In The Grove Plays of the Bohemian Club, Vol. 3)
Le Mystere de l'Atelier Quinze (see Forlani, Remo)
The Mysterious Husband (see Cumberland, Richard)
The Mystery of Adam (Anon.)
        (In Masterworks of World Drama, Vol. 2)
The Mystery of the Redemption (see Hegge Manuscript)

NABBES, Thomas, fl. 1657
     The Bride

(In A Collection of Old English Plays (n. s.), Vol. 2)
Covent Garden: A Pleasant Comedie
(In A Collection of Old English Plays (n. s.), Vol. 1)
Hannibal and Scipio: An Historical Tragedy
(In A Collection of Old English Plays (n. s.), Vol. 1)
Microcosmus, A Morall Maske
(In Dodsley's A Select Collection of Old Plays, Vol. 9)
(In A Collection of Old English Plays (n. s.), Vol. 2)
The Springs Glory, A Maske
(In A Collection of Old English Plays (n. s.), Vol. 2)
Totenham Court: A Pleasant Comedie
(In A Collection of Old English Plays (n. s.), Vol. 1)
The Unfortunate Mother
(In A Collection of Old English Plays (n. s.), Vol. 2)
Die Nachtliche Huldigung (see Gustafsson, Lars)
Naives Hirondelles (see Dubillard, Roland)
Najac, Emile de, 1828-1889
  Let's Get a Divorce! (see Sardou, Victorien)
NAKAMURA Kichizo, 1877-
  The Razor
    (In 50 More Contemporary One-Act Plays)
    (In Three Modern Japanese Plays)
NAKAZAWA, Ken
  The Persimmon Thief
    (In Drama, Vol. 16, Dec. 1925)
NAMIKI Gohei III, 1789-1855
  The Subscription List (Kanjincho), a Japanese Kabuki play,
  adapted from the Noh play "Ataka."
    (In Genius of the Oriental Theatre)
    (In Traditional Asian Plays)
Nan Bullen (see Hackett, Francis)
Nannie's Night Out (see O'Casey, Sean)
The Nantucket Legend (see Lefferts, George)
Nao Posso Viver Assim (see Santos, Miguel)
Napoleon I (Napoleon Bonaparte), Emperor of the French, 1769-
1821
  *Catch as Catch Can (see Anouilh, Jean)
Nari-kin (see Iwasaki Yozan T.)
The Narrow Man (see Bailey, Anne Howard)
Narrow Road to the Deep North (see Bond, Edward)
The Narrowest Street (see Morse, Richard M.)
NASH, N. Richard, 1913-
  Rouge Atomique
    (In Best Short Plays, 1954/55)
  See the Jaguar
    (In Theatre Arts, Vol. 37, Aug. 1953)
  The Young and Fair
    (In Theatre Arts, Vol. 33, Apr. 1949)
NASH, Thomas, 1567-1601
  Summer's Last Will and Testament
    (In Dodsley's A Select Collection of Old English Plays, Vol.
    8)

(In Dodsley's A Select Collection of Old Plays, Vol. 9)
NATANSON, Jacques
La Ronde, by Jacques Natanson et Max Ophuls, d'apres le
piece d'Arthur Schnitzler, "Der Reigen"
(In L'Avant-Scene du Cinema, no. 25, Apr. 15, 1963)
The National Enquirer (see Whyte, Tom)
The Natural Son (see Cumberland, Richard)
The Naturewoman (see Sinclair, Upton)
Naval Engagement (Seeshlacht) (see Goering, Reinhard)
Nazarin (see Buñuel, Luis)
Ne m'Oubliez Pas (see Nichols, Peter)
Ne Reveillez Pas Madame! (see Anouilh, Jean)
Nec-Natama (see Shiels, J. Wilson)
Negative Act (see Corra, Bruno)
Negerinde! (see Swanson, Walter S. J.)
The Negro Domestic (see Ottley, Roi)
The Neighbors (see Gale, Zona)
Neighbors (see Gorostiza, Carlos)
Neighbors (see Saunders, James)
NEILSON, Francis
The Bath Road
(In Drama, Vol. 13, Feb. , Mar. , April 1923)
NEILSON, Keith
The End of the World; or, Fragments from a Work in Progress
(In Playwrights for Tomorrow, Vol. 6)
Neither Here nor There (see Jones, David B.)
NEMEROV, Howard
Cain
(In Tulane Drama Review, Vol. 4, Dec. 1959)
NEMETH, Laszio
Voyage
(In Literary Review, Vol. 9, Spring 1966)
Nero Claudius Caesar Drusus Germanicus, 37-68 A. D.
*The Death of Nero (see Gorman, Herbert Sherman)
*Nero; a tragedy (Anon.)
(In Best Plays of the Old Dramatists: Nero and Other Plays)
*The Tragedy of Nero, Emperour of Rome (see Lee, Nathaniel)
NERUDA, Pablo
Glanz und Tod Joaquin Murietas
(In Theatre Heute, no. 4, April 1971)
NESSENSON, Elsa Behaïm
In the Secret Places
(In Drama, Vol. 17, Nov. 1926)
NESTROY, Johann
Liberty Comes to Krähwenkel
(In Tulane Drama Review, Vol. 5, June 1961)
Ein Strick mit Linem Ende
(In Theater Heute, Vol. 10, no. 6, June 1969)
Netley Abbey (see Pearce, William)
NETO, Coelho
O Patinho Torto
(In Revista de Teatro, no. 341)

Nettlewig Hall; or, Ten to One (see Westmacott, C.M.)
NETTO, Coelho
    Quebranto
    (In Revista de Teatro, 295)
NEUENBURG, Evelyn
    House Divided
    (In Best One-Act Plays of 1942, N.Y.)
NEUMANN, Sara
    The Old Order
    (In Drama, Vol. 11, Feb. 1921)
NEUTSCH, Erik
    Haut Oder Hemd
    (In Theater der Zeit, no. 4, 1971)
    Karin Lenz, Oper in zehn Bildern (see Kochan, Günter)
Never Give a Sucker an Even Break (see Neville, John T.)
Never No Third Degree (see Bayly, John Ward)
NEVILLE, John T.
    Never Give a Sucker an Even Break; screenplay by John T.
    Neville and Prescott Chaplin, from an original story by Otis
    (W.C. Fields) Criblecoblis, directed by Edward Cline.
    (Classic Filmscripts Series)
The New Chatauqua (see Gaines, Frederick)
New Custome (Anon.)
    (In Dodsley's A Select Collection of Old English Plays, Vol.
    3)
    (In Dodsley's A Select Collection of Old Plays, Vol. 1)
The New House (see Behanm, Brendan)
New Leisure (see Brighouse, Harold)
The New Play (see Saroyan, William)
The New Tenant (see Ionesco, Eugene)
A New Tricke to Cheat the Divell (see Davenport, Robert)
A New Way to Pay Old Debts (see Massinger, Philip)
A New Wonder, a Woman Never Vexed (see Rowley, William)
The New World (see Makowsky, Lucile)
The New York Idea (see Mitchell, Langdon Elwyn)
NEWMAN, David
    Bonnie and Clyde; film script by David Newman and Robert
    Benton, directed by Arthur Penn
    (In The Bonnie and Clyde Book)
Next (see McNally, Terrence)
Next Door Neighbours (see Inchbald, Mrs. Elizabeth Simpson)
Next of Kin (see Hot Spell)
The Next Thing (see Smith, Michael)
Next-to-Last Rites (see Thomas, Dorothy)
Nicastro, Luciano
    Synthesis of Syntheses (see Jannelli, Guglielmo)
NICCODEMI, Dario
    The Poet
    (In Four Continental Plays, 1964)
Nice Wanton (Anon.)
    (In Dodsley's A Select Collection of Old English Plays, Vol.
    2)

NICHOLS, Anne
   Abie's Irish Rose
     (In S. R. O. , the Most Successful Plays...)
NICHOLS, Dudley, 1895-
   La Chevauchee Fantastique, by Dudley Nichols, d'apres "Etape
   a Lordsburg" de Ernest Haycox. Titre original: "Stagecoach, "
   directed by John Ford.
     (In L'Avant-Scene du Cinema, no. 22, Jan. 15, 1963)
   The Informer, a screenplay based on the novel by Liam
   O'Flaherty, directed by John Ford.
     (In Theatre Arts, Vol. 35, Aug. 1951)
   Le Mouchard, by Dudley Nichols, d'apres le roman de Liam
   O'Flaherty, "The Informer. "
     (In L'Avant-Scene du Cinema, no. 45, 1965)
   Stagecoach, screenplay by Dudley Nichols, directed by John
   Ford, based on the story "Stage to Lordsburg" by Ernest
   Haycox
     (In Twenty Best Film Plays)
     (In Classic Film Scripts)
   This Land Is Mine, screenplay by Dudley Nichols, directed
   by Jean Renoir
     (In Twenty Best Film Plays)
NICHOLS, Peter
   Un Jour dans la Mort de Joe Egg, Francaise de Claude Roy
     (In Plaisir de France, supplement theatral, no. 376, Mar.
     1970)
     (In L'Avant-Scene du Theatre, no. 442, Feb. 1, 1970)
   Ne m'Oubliez Pas, adapted by Claude Roy from the English
   play
     (In L'Avant-Scene, no. 497, June 15, 1972)
NICHOLS, Robert
   Minding the Story; a Street Vaudeville
     (In Scripts, Vol. 1, no. 10, Oct. 1972)
   The Wax Engine
     (In Scripts, Vol. 1, no. 5, Mar. 1972)
NICHOLSON, Kenyon, 1894-
   The Marriage of Little Eva
     (In 50 More Contemporary One-Act Plays)
NIGGLI, Josephina
   Soldadera
     (In Best One-Act Plays of 1937, N. Y.)
   This Is Villa
     (In Best One-Act Plays of 1938, N. Y.)
Night (see Asch, Shalom)
Night and Fog (Nuit et Brouillard) (see Cayrol, Jean)
A Night at the Inn (see Dunsany, Edward John Moreton Drax
   Plunkett, 18th Baron)
A Night at the Opera (see Kaufman, George Simon)
Night Brings a Counselor (see Saunders, Lilian)
The Night Club Girl (see Phelps, Pauline)
Night Must Fall (see Williams, Emlyn)
The Night Nurse (see Wittlenger, Karl)

The Night of the Hunter   (see Agee, James)
The Night of the Iguana   (see Williams, Tennessee)
A Night Out (see Pinter, Harold)
Night over Taos (see Anderson, Maxwell)
Night School (see Pinter, Harold)
The Night They Made a Bum out of Helen Hayes   (see Rose, Billy)
Night Train (see Reinecker, Herbert)
Night with Guests (see Weiss, Peter)
Nightingale, Florence, 1820-1910
    *The Lady with the Lamp (see Berkeley, Reginald Cheyne)
The Nightingale of Wittenberg (see Strindberg, August)
Nil Medium (see Parkington, Mary)
Ninotchka (see Brackett, Charles)
Nishikigi (see Seami Motokiyo)
NIVER, Kemp R.
    D. W. Griffith's "The Battle of Elderbush Gulch"
        (Reconstructed screenplay, Locare Research Group, Los
        Angeles, 1972)
Nixon, Richard Milhous, pres. U. S. , 1913-
    *The Election (political satire) (see Koch, Kenneth)
NKOSI, Louis
    The Rhythm of Violence
        (In Plays From Black Africa)
"No!" (see Reynolds, Francis)
The No 'count Boy (see Green, Paul)
No Exit (see Sartre, Jean-Paul)
No Hats, No Banquets (see Brodsky, Ruth)
No Man's Son; or, More than Blood (see Montherlant, Henry de)
No More War; an Ode to Peace (see Kreymborg, Alfred)
No Shoes (see Du Pont, Lawrence)
No Song, No Supper (see Hoare, Prince)
No Thoroughfare (see Dickens, Charles)
No Time for Sergeants (see Levin, Ira)
Noa Noa (see Agee, James)
Noah (see Obey, Andre)
Noah and His Sons (see Moore, Hortense)
Noah's Flood (see Chester Pageant of the Water-Leaders and
    Drawers in Dee)
Noah's Flood (see Lawrence, David Herbert)
The Noble Souldier; or, A Contract Broken, Justly Reveng'd (see
    Rowley, Samuel)
The Noble Spanish Soldier (see Rowley, Samuel)
Noble, William
    Blue Denim (see Herlihy, James Leo)
Noblesse Oblige (Hamer, Robert)
Noch einen Löffel Gift, Liebling? (see Matthus, Siegfried)
Noel, Henry, d. 1597
    Tancred and Gismunda (see Wilmot, Robert)
Non Nobis (see Aske, Lake)
None but the Lonely Heart (see Odets, Clifford)
Noon (see McNally, Terrence)
Noon on Doomsday (see Serling, Rod)

NORMAN, Charles, 1904-
  Faustus
    (In Theatre Arts, Vol. 13, April 1930)
  Telemachus
    (In Theatre Arts, Vol. 12, Dec. 1928)
NORMAN, Frank
  Insideout
    (In Plays and Players, Vol. 17, no. 5, Feb. 1970)
Norris, Frank, 1870-1902
  **Greed (see Von Stroheim, Erich)
  **Les Rapaces (see Von Stroheim)
North Atlantic Testament (see Mulvey, Timothy J.)
North by Northwest (see Lehman, Ernest)
North Star (see Hellman, Lillian)
Northward Ho (see Dekker, Thomas)
NORTON, Thomas, 1532-1584
  Ferrex and Porrex, by Thomas Norton and Thomas Sackville
    (In Dodsley's A Select Collection of Old Plays, Vol. 1)
The Nose (see Stove, John A.)
Not Enough Rope (see May, Elaine)
Notes on a Love Affair (see Marcus, Frank)
Nothin' to Nothin' (see Brophy, Edmund)
Nothing Very Much Thank You (see O'Connor, Patrick)
Notoriety (see Reynolds, Frederick)
La Notte (see Antonioni, Michelangelo)
La Nouvelle (see Lebesque, Morvan)
NOVAC, Anna
  Un Peu de Tendressee ou le Complexe de la Soupe
    (In L'Avant-Scene du Theatre, no. 442, Feb. 1, 1970)
    (In Plaisir de France, supplement theatral, no. 376, March
    1970)
NOVAS, Himilce
  Free This Day: a Trial in Seven Exhibits
    (In Scripts, Vol. 1, no. 6, April 1972)
November Afternoon (see Pelissier, Anthony)
O Novo Otelo (see Macedo, Joaquim Manoel de)
Now I Lay Me Down to Sleep (see Ryan, Elaine)
Nude Washing Dishes (see Seiler, Conrad)
Nuestros Hijos (see Sanchez, Florencio)
Nugent, Elliott, 1900-
  The Male Animal (see Thurber, James)
La Nuit d'Avril (see Roussin, Andre)
La Nuit de Feu (see Marcelle-Mauritte)
Nuit et Brouillard (see Cayrol, Jean)
Le Numero (see Roidy, Pierre)
The Nursery Maid of Heaven (see Stevens, Thomas Wood)
NUSBAUM, N. Richard
  Parting at Imsdorf
    (In Best One-Act Plays of 1940, N.Y.)
NYSSEN, Ute
  Film und Frau (Shakespeare the sadist)
    (In Theater Heute, May 5, 1971)

O Bright Flame Lifted! (see Ruthenburg, Grace Dorcas)
O Distant Land (see Richards, Stanley)
OATES, Joyce Carol
    Ontological Proof of My Existence
        (In Partisan Review, Vol. 37, no. 4, 1970)
OBALDIA, Rene de
    La Baby-Sitter
        (In L'Avant-Scene du Theatre, no. 487, Jan. 15, 1972)
    Le Cosmonaute Agricole
        (In L'Avant-Scene du Theatre, no. 418, Jan. 15, 1969)
    Deux Femmes pour un Fantome
        (In L'Avant-Scene du Theatre, no. 487, Jan. 15, 1972)
    Du Vent dans les Branches de Sassafras
        (In Plaisir de France, supplement theatral, no. 328, Feb.
        1966)
    Le General Inconnu
        (In L'Avant-Scene du Theatre, no. 469-470)
    Petite Suite Poetique Resolument Optimiste
        (In L'Avant-Scene du Theatre, no. 487, Jan. 15, 1972)
    The Unknown General
        (In Best Short Plays, 1972)
    Wind in the Branches of the Sassafras
        (In Modern International Drama, Vol. 1, no. 2, 1967)
Oberon; or, The Charmed Horn (Anon.)
        (In Cumberland's British Theatre, Vol. 18, no. 1)
OBEY, Andre, 1892-
    Noah, adapted by Arthur Wilmurt
        (In 20 Best European Plays on the American Stage)
L'Objet (see Presles, Claude des)
        (In L'Avant-Scene du Theatre, no. 503, Oct. 1, 1972)
Oblomov (see Cuvelier, Marcel)
OBOLER, Arch, 1907-
    The House I Live In
        (In Radio Drama in Action, 1945)
    Memo to Berchtesgaden
        (In Best One-Act Plays of 1942, N.Y.)
    Suffer the Little Children
        (In Plays as Experience)
O'BRIEN, Edna
    A Cheap Bunch of Nice Flowers
        (In Plays of the Year, Vol. 26, 1962/63)
    XY & Zee; from the original screenplay, directed by Brian G.
    Hutton
        (Lancer Books, N.Y. , 1971)
O'BRIEN, Howard Vincent
    So Long, Son
        (In Best One-Act Plays of 1942, N.Y.)
O'BRIEN, Kate, 1898-
    That Lady; dramatization of the author's novel "For One Sweet
    Grape"
        (In Theatre Arts, Vol. 34, June 1950)
O'BRIEN, Liam, 1913-

The Remarkable Mr. Pennypacker
   (In Theatre Arts, Vol. 39, April 1955)
O'BRIEN, Seumas, 1880-
The Birdcatcher
   (In 50 More Contemporary One-Act Plays)
O'BRIEN, William, d. 1815
Cross Purposes, an adaptation of Lafont's "Les Trois Freres
   Rivaux"
   (In The London Stage, Vol. 2)
O'CASEY, Sean, 1880-1964
Bedtime Story
   (In One Act)
Cock-a-Doodle
   (In The Modern Theatre, ed. by Eric Bentley, Vol. 5)
The Drums of Father Ned
   (In Theatre Arts, Vol. 44, May 1960)
The Drums of Father Ned (the suppressed parts)
   (In Esquire, Vol. 52, Dec. 1959)
Juno und der Pfau, German version of "Juno and the Paycock"
   (In Theater der Zeit, Vol. 25, June 1970)
Kathleen Listens In
   (In Tulane Drama Review, Vol. 5, Jun. 1961)
Nannie's Night Out
   (In Best Short Plays of the World Theatre, 1958-67)
The Plough and the Stars
   (In The Modern Theatre, ed. by R. W. Corrigan)
A Pound on Demand
   (In 24 One-Act Plays, Revised edition, 1954)
Purple Dust
   (In Genius of the Irish Theater)
   (In Makers of the Modern Theatre, 1961)
The Ocean (see Yaltsev, P.)
The Ocean of Life; or, "Every Inch a Sailor!" (see Haines, John
   Thomas)
O'Connor, Frank, pseud. (see O'Donovan, Michael)
O'CONNOR, Patricia
My Dear!
   (In Drama, Vol. 14, Feb. 1924)
O'CONNOR, Patrick
Nothing Very Much Thank You
   (In First Stage, Vol. 6, Winter 1967/68)
The Wooden Box
   (In Best Short Plays, 1968)
   (In First Stage, Vol. 4, Spring 1965)
O'CONOR, Joseph
The Iron Harp
   (In Plays of the Year, Vol. 16, 1956/57)
Octavia (see Seneca, Lucius Annaeus; Seneca the Younger)
October Morning (see Lampell, Millard)
Octobre (Oktiabr) (see Eisenstein, Sergei Mikhailovitch)
The Octoroon; or, Life in Louisiana (see Boucicault, Dion)
The Odd Couple (see Simon, Neil)

Odd Man Out (see Green, Frederick Lawrence)
O'DEA, John B.
    Where E're We Go
        (In Best One-Act Plays of 1943, N.Y.)
ODEA, Mark Leland Hill
    Shivaree
        (In Drama, Vol. 11, Oct. 1920)
    The Song of Solomon
        (In Drama, Vol. 11, Feb. 1921)
ODETS, Clifford, 1906-1963
    Awake and Sing!
        (In Best American Plays, Supp. Vol.)
    The Big Knife
        (In Famous Plays of Today, 1954)
    The Country Girl
        (In Theatre Arts, Vol. 36, May 1952)
    Golden Boy
        (In 20 Best Plays of the Modern American Theatre, Vol. 1)
    None but the Lonely Heart, by Clifford Odets from the novel
        by Richard Llewellyn
        (In Best Film Plays, 1945, Vol. 2)
    Till the Day I Die
        (In Famous Plays of Today, 1936)
    Waiting for Lefty
        (In Modern American Plays)
        (In Best Short Plays of the Social Theatre, 1939)
        (In 30 Famous One-Act Plays)
        (In 16 Famous American Plays)
O'DONOGHUE, Michael
    The Twilight Maelstrom of Cookie La Vagetto
        (In Evergreen Review, Vol. 9, no. 35, 1965)
O'DONOVAN, Michael, 1903-1966
    At the Wakehouse, by Frank O'Connor (pseud.)
        (In Theatre Arts, Vol. 10, June 1926)
    **The Bridal Night (see Mayer, Paul A.)
    In the Train, by Frank O'Connor (pseud.)
        (In Genius of the Irish Theater)
Oedipe Roi (see Cocteau, Jean)
Oedipe Roi (see Pasolini, Pier Paolo)
Oedipus (see Dryden, John)
Oedipus (see Perreault, John)
Oedipus (see Seneca, Lucius Annaeus)
Oedipus at Colonus (see Sophocles)
Oedipus Rex (see Sophocles)
Oedipus the King (see Sophocles)
Oedipus Tyrannus; or, Swellfoot the Tyrant (see Shelley,
    Percy Bysshe)
Of Mice and Men (see Steinbeck, John)
Of Social Significance (see Aklom, Mikhail)
Of Thee I Sing (see Gershwin, George)
Of Time and the Blizzard (see Kirkpatrick, John Alexander)
O'Fallon's Cup (see Marz, Roy)

Off Nags Head   (see MacMillan, Dougald)
Offending the Audience   (see Handke, Peter)
Official Announcement   (see Elder, Eleanor)
O'Flaherty, Liam, 1897-
**The Informer   (see Nichols, Dudley)
**Le Mouchard   (see Nichols, Dudley)
OFORI, Henry
    The Literary Society
        (In Plays From Black Africa)
Oft in the Stilly Night   (see Smith, Marion Spencer)
OGLESBEE, Delle Houghton
    The Ten Fingers of Francois
        (In Drama, Vol. 13, Nov. 1923)
O'GLOR, Michele
    Adieu Philippine, by Michele O'Glor et Jacques Rozier
        (In L'Avant-Scene du Cinema, no. 31, Nov. 15, 1963)
    Blue Jeans, by Michele O'Glor et Jacques Rozier
        (In L'Avant-Scene du Cinema, no. 31, Nov. 15, 1963)
Oh! Calcutta   (see Rynan, Kenneth)
Oh, Dad, Poor Dad, Mama's Hung You in the Closet and I'm
    Feelin' So Sad   (see Kopit, Arthur)
Oh Starlings!   (see Eveling, Stanley)
Oh These Ghosts!   (see Filippo, Edwardo de)
O'HARA, Frank, 1926-
    The General Returns from One Place to Another
        (In Eight Plays From Off-Off Broadway)
    Try! Try! Try!
        (In Artists Theatre)
O'HARA, Kane, 1714?-1782
    Midas
        (In Cumberland's British Theatre, Vol. 45, no. 4)
        (In The London Stage, Vol. 1)
    Tom Thumb   (see Fielding, Henry)
O'Hara, Saul
    **Noch einen Löffel Gift, Liebling?   (see Matthus, Siegfried)
Les Oiseaux de Lune   (see Ayme, Marcel)
OKAMURA Shiko
    The Zen Substitute (Migawarizazen), a Japanese Kabuki farce,
    adapted from the kyogen comedy "Hanako."
        (In Traditional Asian Plays)
O'KEEFFE, A.A.
    Ship Ahoy!
        (In Best One-Act Plays of 1944, N.Y.)
O'KEEFFE, John, 1747-1833
    The Agreeable Surprise
        (In Cumberland's British Theatre, Vol. 46, no. 3)
    The Castle of Andalusia
        (In Cumberland's British Theatre, Vol. 44, no. 10)
    The Farmer
        (In Cumberland's British Theatre, Vol. 24, no. 3)
    Fontainbleau
        (In Cumberland's British Theatre, Vol. 38, no. 3)

The Highland Reel
    (In Cumberland's British Theatre, Vol. 19, no. 1)
Lie of a Day
    (In Modern Theatre, 1811, Vol. 10)
Modern Antiques; or, The Merry Mourners
    (In Cumberland's British Theatre, Vol. 24, no. 4)
Peeping Tom of Coventry
    (In Cumberland's British Theatre, Vol. 43, no. 2)
The Poor Soldier
    (In Cumberland's British Theatre, Vol. 45, no. 3)
The Prisoner at Large
    (In Cumberland's British Theatre, Vol. 45, no. 2)
The Son-in-Law
    (In Cumberland's British Theatre, Vol. 41, no. 4)
Wild Oats; or, The Strolling Gentleman
    (In Cumberland's British Theatre, Vol. 31, no. 2)
The Young Quaker
    (In Cumberland's British Theatre, Vol. 34, no. 9)
Oklahoma! (see Rodgers, Richard)
OKLAM, Mikhail
    Apprehensions
        (In Best One-Act Plays of 1937, London)
Old and Young (Anon.)
        (In Cumberland's British Theatre, Vol. 32, no. 9)
The Old Batchelor (see Congreve, William)
The Old Couple (see May, Thomas)
Old Fortunatus (see Dekker, Thomas)
The Old History Book (see Armstrong, Louise Van Voorhis)
The Old Homestead (see Thompson, Denman)
The Old Jew (see Schisgal, Murray)
Old Joe and Young Joe (see Courtney, John)
Old Judge Moses Is Dead (see White, Joseph)
Old MacDonald Had a Curve (see Serling, Rod)
The Old Man (see Foote, Horton)
The Old Man Taught Wisdom; or, The Virgin Unmask'd (see Fielding,
    Henry)
The Old Ones (see Wesker, Arnold)
The Old Order (see Neumann, Sara)
The Old Pine Tree (see Zeami Motokiyo)
Old Ragpicker (see Dreiser, Theodore)
The Old Regimentals (see Bernard, William Baile)
The Old Troop (see Lacy, John)
The Old Tune (see Pinget, Robert)
The Old Wives Tale (see Peele, George)
The Oldest Trick in the World (see Double Entry)
Ol-Dopt; or, The Adventures of Charles and Emily Ann Andrews
    (see Dozer, David)
OLIANSKY, Joel
    Here Comes Santa Claus
        (In 3 Plays From the Yale School of Drama)
OLIVER, Margaret Scott
    The King's Son, Churl's Son
        (In Drama, Vol. 16, May 1926)

OLIVER, William I.
   The Stallion
      (In Best Short Plays, 1956/57)
OLIVIER, Sir Laurence, 1907-
   Henry V, screenplay by Laurence Olivier and Reginald Beck,
   based on Shakespeare's play.
      (In Film Scripts One)
Ollantay (see Mossi, Miguel Angel)
OLSON, Elder
   The Abstract Tragedy; a Comedy of Masks
      (In First Stage, Vol. 2, Summer 1963)
   A Crack in the Universe
      (In First Stage, Vol. 1, no. 2, Spring 1962)
OLYESHA, Yurii
   The Conspiracy of Feelings
      (In Drama & Theatre, Vol. 7, no. 1, Fall 1968)
Olympus Farewell (see Bayley, Jefferson)
O'MALLEY, Neill
   Sink or Swim; or, Harry Raymond's Resolve, a radio sketch
   by Neill O'Malley and Eric Barnouw, based on the novel of
   Horatio Alger, Jr.
      (In Handbook of Radio Production)
L'Ombre du Cavalier (see Husson, Albert)
Omega's Nineth (see Delgado, Ramon)
O'MORRISON, Kevin
   The Long War
      (In Playwrights for Tomorrow, Vol. 4)
Omphale (see Hacks, Peter)
On a Note of Triumph (see Corwin, Norman Lewis)
On a Vole la Mer (see Salvy, Jean)
On Baile's Strand (see Yeats, William Butler)
On Borrowed Time (see Osborn, Paul)
On Dartmoor (see Grant, Neil)
On Finit Quelquefois par ou l'on Devrait Toujours Commencer (see
   Turpin, Francois)
On ne' Badine Pas avec l'Amour (see Musset, Alfred de)
On ne Sait Jamais (see Roussin, Andre)
On the Docks (see China Peking Opera Troupe)
On the Docks; revised script 1972 (see China Peking Opera Troupe
   of Shanghai)
On the Eve of Publication (see Mercer, David)
On the Lot (see Ryerson, Florence)
On the March to the Sea (see Vidal, Gore)
On the Way Home (see Hawley, Esther M.)
On This Green Bank (see Karchmer, Sylvan)
On Trial (see Rice, Elmer L.)
On Vous Parle (see Cayrol, Jean)
Once a Thief (see Perrini, Alberto)
Once Below a Lighthouse (see Delgado, Ramon)
Once in a Lifetime (see Hart, Moss)
Once Is Enough (see Let Them Eat Cake)
Once Upon a Mattress (see Rodgers, Mary)

Ondine (see Giraudoux, Jean)
One Day More (see Conrad, Joseph)
One for the Grave (see MacNeice, Louis)
One Hour Alone (see Holland, Norman)
One Leg over the Wrong Wall (see Bermel, Albert)
One May Spin a Thread Too Finely (see Turgenev, Ivan Sergieevich)
One O'Clock! or, The Knight and the Wooden Demon (see Lewis,
    Matthew Gregory)
One of These Days (see Cameron, Margaret, Mrs. Harrison Case
    Lewis)
One Special for Doc (see Geiger, Milton)
One, Two, Three, Four, Five; by Advertisement (Anon.)
        (In Cumberland's British Theatre, Vol. 21, no. 7)
One Way Pendulum (see Simpson, Norman Frederick)
One-Car Wedding (see Schochen, Seyril)
O'NEILL, Eugene Gladstone, 1888-1953
    Ah, Wilderness!
        (In 16 Famous American Plays)
    "Anna Christie"
        (In Pulitzer Prize Plays)
    Beyond the Horizon
        (In Reading Drama)
        (In The Pulitzer Prize Plays)
    Desire Under the Elms
        (In 25 Best Plays of the Modern American Theatre, Early
        Series, 1916-1929)
        (In The Modern Theatre, ed. by R. W. Corrigan)
        (In Tragedy: Texts and Commentary, 1969)
        (In Introduction to Literature: Plays)
    The Dreamy Kid
        (In Theatre Arts, Vol. 4, 1920)
        (In Plays of Negro Life)
    The Emperor Jones
        (In Theatre Arts, Vol. 5, 1921)
        (In Plays of Negro Life)
    "The Hairy Ape"
        (In 25 Best Plays of the Modern American Theatre, Early
        Series, 1916-1929)
        (In Nine Modern American Plays)
        (In American Drama)
    Hughie
        (In Best American Plays, Sixth Series, 1963-67)
    The Iceman Cometh
        (In Best American Plays, Third Series)
        (In Plays of Our Time)
    Ile
        (In 25 Best Plays of the Modern American Theatre, Early
        Series, 1916-1929)
        (In Dramas by Present-Day Writers)
        (In 50 Contemporary One-Act Plays)
        (In Atlantic Book of Modern Plays, 1921)
    In the Zone

(In Best Short Plays, 1956/57)
(In Thirty Famous One-Act Plays)
The Long Voyage Home
(In Makers of the Modern Theater, 1961)
A Moon for the Misbegotten
(In Best American Plays, Fourth Series)
A Moon of the Caribbees
(In 24 Favorite One-Act Plays)
(In Famous American Plays of the 1920's)
(In 50 More Contemporary One-Act Plays)
Strange Interlude
(In Theatre Guild Anthology)
(In Pulitzer Prize Plays)
A Touch of the Poet
(In Best American Plays, Fifth Series, 1957-63)
O'Neill, James, 1847-1920
Monte Cristo (see Fechter, Charles Albert)
O'NEILL, Michael
The Bosom of the Family, by Michael O'Neill and Jeremy
Seabrook
(In Plays and Players, Vol. 18, Sept. 1971)
Life Price, by Michael O'Neill and Jeremy Seabrook
(In Plays and Players, Vol. 16, no. 6, Mar. 1969)
Only a Man in Black (see Castro, Juan Antonio)
Only Ten Minutes to Buffalo (see Grass, Günter)
Ontological Proof of My Existence (see Oates, Joyce Carol)
Onze Degrcs d'Aptitude (see Charras, Charles)
Open House; or, The Twin Sisters (see Buckstone, John Baldwin)
Open Letter on Race Hatred (see Robson, William Northrop)
Open Secret (see Adler, Robert)
The Open Theater (see Yankowitz, Susan)
Open Twenty-Four Hours (see Cornish, Roger N.)
Opening Night (see Cromwell, John)
Opening of the Indian Era (see Hacks, Peter)
The Opera Dancer (see Carmontelle, Louis Carrogis, known as)
The Operation (see Dennison, George)
Operation Coral (see Brown, Stewart Pierce)
Operation Sidewinder (see Shepard, Sam)
Operette (see Gombrowitz, Witold)
Ophelia (see Morris, Thomas Badden)
OPHULS, Marcel, 1927-
Le Chagrin et la Pitie
(In L'Avant-Scene du Cinema, no. 127/128)
Matisse, ou le Talent du Bonheur
(In L'Avant-Scene du Cinema, no. 72/73, July-Sept. 1967)
The Sorrow and the Pity (Le Chagrin et la Pitie). Filmscript
translated by Mireille Johnston.
(An Outerbridge & Lazard Film Play)
OPHULS, Max, 1902-
Lola Montes, by Max Ophuls, d'apres le roman de Cecil-Saint-
Laurent, "La Vie Extraordinaire de Lola Montes."
(In L'Avant-Scene du Cinema, no. 88, Jan. 1969)

'Op-O-Me-Thumb (see Fenn, Frederick)
OPPENHEIMER, Joel, 1930-
The Great American Desert
(In Eight Plays From Off-Off Broadway)
(In Evergreen Playscript Series, no. 3)
L'Or et la Paille (see Barillet, Pierre)
Orange Blossoms (see Johnson, Philip)
Orange Blossoms (see Wooler, John Pratt)
Orange Souffle (see Bellow, Saul)
The Orchestra (see Anouilh, Jean)
L'Ordalie ou la Petite Catherine de Heilbronn (see Kleist, Heinrich
von)
The Order (see Hochwalder, Fritz)
The Ordinary (see Cartwright, William)
ORDWAY, Sally
Crabs, Cross-Country
(In Scripts, Vol. 1, no. 2, Dec. 1971)
There's a Wall between Us, Darling
(In Yale/Theatre, no. 2, Summer 1968)
The Oresteia: Agememnon; The Choephoroe; The Eumenides (see
Aeschylus)
Orestes (see Euripides)
Orestes in Argos (see Bayley, Peter)
Organic Honey's Visual Telepathy (see Jonas, Joan)
The Orientals (see Grecco, Stephen)
Orlando Furioso (see Bufano, Remo)
ORLOVITZ, Gil
Gray
(In Literary Review, Vol. 2, Winter 1958/59)
Oroonoko (see Southerne, Thomas)
The Orphan of China (see Murphy, Arthur)
Orphee (see Cocteau, Jean)
Orpheus (see Cocteau, Jean)
Orpheus Descending (see Williams, Tennessee)
ORTON, Joe
Le Locataire
(In L'Avant-Scene du Theatre, no. 483, Nov. 15, 1971)
Loot
(In Evergreen Playscript Series)
The Ruffian on the Stair
(In Best Short Plays, 1970)
Until She Screams
(In Evergreen Review, no. 78, May 1970)
Osbern and Ursyne (see Craigie, Mrs. Pearl Teresa Richards)
OSBORN, Paul, 1901-
Mornings at Seven
(In Best American Plays, Supp. Vol.)
On Borrowed Time
(In Best American Plays, Supp. Vol.)
Point of No Return, based on the novel by John P. Marquand
(In Theatre Arts, Vol. 37, Mar. 1953)
The Young in Heart; screenplay adapted by Paul Osborn and

Charles Bennett from the serial "The Gay Banditti" by I. A. R.
Wylie, published in book form as "Young in Heart," directed
by Richard Wallace.
(In Foremost Films of 1938)
OSBORNE, Duffield
Xanthippe on Woman Suffrage
(In Yale Review, Vol. 4, n. s., April 1915)
OSBORNE, John, 1929-
Blood of the Bambergs
(In Evergreen Playscript Series)
A Bond Honoured; adaptation of "La Fianza Satisfecha" by Lope
de Vega
(In Evergreen Playscript Series)
The Entertainer
(Criterion Play, 1958)
(In Evergreen Playscript Series)
Epitaph for George Dillon
(In Theatre Arts, Vol. 46, March 1962)
Inadmissable Evidence
(In Evergreen Playscript Series)
Look Back in Anger
(In Evergreen Playscript Series)
(In Criterion Plays, 1957)
(In Plays of Our Time)
Luther
(In Vogue, Vol. 139, Mar. 1, 1962)
(In Evergreen Playscript Series)
Luther; text in French
(In Plaisir de France, supplement theatral, no. 322, Aug.
1965)
A Patriot for Me
(In Evergreen Playscript Series)
A Subject of Scandal and Concern
(In Best Short Plays of the World Theatre, 1958-67)
Tom Jones; a filmscript, based on Henry Fielding's "The
History of Tom Jones; a Foundling"
(In Evergreen Filmscript Series)
Under Plain Cover
(In Evergreen Playscript Series)
The World of Paul Slickey
(In Evergreen Playscript Series)
Oscar   (see Magnier, Claude)
OSGOOD, Lawrence
Pigeons
(In New American Plays, Vol. 1)
OSTROVSKII, Aleksandr Nikolaevich, 1823-1886
The Diary of a Scoundrel
(In The Modern Theatre, ed. by Eric Bentley, Vol. 2)
Easy Money; a comedy from "The Taming of the Shrew"
(In From the Modern Repertoire, Series Two)
La Foret
(In Plaisir de France, supplement theatral, no. 378, Feb.
18, 1970)

(In L'Avant Scene du Theatre, no. 447, Apr. 15, 1970)
Ostrovsky, Alexander (see Ostrovskii, Alexsandr Nikolaevich)
Oswald, Lee Harvey, 1939-1963
  *The Other Face of November (see Brusati, Franco)
Othello, the Moor of Venice (see Shakespeare, William)
The Other Face of November (see Brusati, Franco)
Otho I, called the Great, King of Germany & Holy Roman Empire,
  912-973
  *Otho the Great; a Tragedy (see Keats, John)
OTTEY, M. E.
  Engagement
    (In Best One-Act Plays, London, 1952/53)
OTTLEY, Roi, 1906-
  The Negro Domestic
    (In Radio Drama in Action, 1945)
OTWAY, Thomas, 1652-1685
  The Orphan; or, The Unhappy Marriage
    (In Bell's British Theatre, 1797, Vol. 9)
  Venice Preserved; or, A Plot Discovered
    (In Cumberland's British Theatre, Vol. 3, no. 5)
    (In Great English Plays)
    (In The London Stage, Vol. 1)
    (In Bell's British Theatre, 1797, Vol. 15)
Ou Vivrez-Vous Demain? (see Fellows, Malcolm Stuart)
OULTON, Walley Chamberlain, 1770?-1820?
  The Sleep-Walker; or, Which is the Lady?
    (In Cumberland's British Theatre, Vol. 28, no. 7)
Our Man in Madras (see Hofmann, Gert)
Our Town (see Wilder, Thornton Niven)
Ourane (see Lubtchansky, Jean Claude)
L'Ours (see Chekhov, Anton Pavlovich)
Out at Sea (see Morzek, Slawomir)
Out of the Crocodile (see Cooper, Giles)
The Outcast (see Strindberg, August)
The Out-of-Towners (see Mosel, Tad)
The Outrageous Saint (see Vega Carpio, Lope Felix de)
Outward Bound (see Vane, Sutton)
Over Gardens Out (see Gill, Peter)
Over the Hills and Far Away (see Frank, Florence Kiper)
Over the Toast (see Strong, Leonard Alfred George)
Over the Top (see Hickey, E. and D. E.)
Over Twenty-One (see Buchman, Sidney)
Overtones (see Gerstenberg, Alice)
OWEN, Alun
  George's Room
    (In Modern Short Comedies From Broadway and London)
OWENS, Rochelle, 1936-
  Futz
    (In New American Plays, Vol. 2)
  He Wants Shih
    (In Yale/Theatre, no. 2, Summer 1968)
  Kontraption

(In Scripts, Vol. 1, no. 2, Dec. 1971)
The Queen of Greece
    (In Yale/Theatre, Vol. 2, Summer 1969)
The Owl (see Gateschi, Rossana)
The Owl and Care (see Field, Charles K.)
The Owl and the Pussycat (see Manhoff, Bill)
The Owl Answers (see Kennedy, Adrienne)
The Ox-Bow Incident (see Trotti, Lamar)

Pabst, George Wilhelm, 1885-
    Pandora's Box (Lulu) (see Vajda, Ladislaus)
Pacific Task Force (see Lader, Lawrence)
PACKER, Barbara
    Patrick Brontë and the Saint
        (In Best One-Act Plays of 1948/49, N.Y.)
PACQUIN, Dorian
    La Combinaison
        (In Plaisir de France, supplement theatral, Dec. 1969)
The Padlock (see Bickerstaff, Isaac)
A Pageant of Spring (see Thurston, Althea)
Pageant of the Shearmen and Tailors; a miracle play adapted by
    John Mason Brown
        (In Theatre Arts, Vol. 9, Dec. 1925)
PAGNOL, Marcel, 1895-
    Cigalon
        (In L'Avant-Scene du Cinema, no. 105/106, July-Sept. 1970)
    Judas
        (In L'Avant-Scene du Theatre, no. 122, Feb. 1956)
    Le Schpountz
        (In L'Avant-Scene du Cinema, no. 105/106, July-Sept. 1970)
A Pagoda Slave (see Keeler, Charles)
Le Pain de Menage (see Renard, Jules)
Paine, Thomas, 1737-1809
    *Tom Paine (see Foster, Paul)
Paint Your Wagon (see Lerner, Alan Jay)
A Pair of Pigeons (see Stirling, Edward)
Os Pais Abstratos (see Bloch, Pedro)
The Pajama Game (see Rosenberg, Jerold)
PALM, Carla L.
    The Perplexing Pirandello
        (In Drama, Vol. 15, Feb. 1925)
    Schnitzleresque
        (In Drama, Vol. 14, Mar./Apr. 1924)
Palm Sunday (see York Skinners' Play)
Pandora's Box (Lulu) (see Vajda, Ladislaus)
Pandora's Box (see Vallance, Rosalind)
PANELLA, Antoinette
    The Red Slippers
        (In Drama, Vol. 16, Dec. 1925)
Pantagleize (see Ghelderode, Michel de)
Pantoufle (see Ayckbourn, Alan)

Papa's Daughter (see Ahmad, Dorothy)
Paphnutius (see Hrotsvit, of Gandersheim)
Les Papiers (see Avermaete, Roger)
PAQUIN, Dorian
    "Bonjour RODOLPHE... Adieu GILBERT!"
    (In Plaisir de France, supplement theatral, no. 360, Oct.
    1968)
Paradise Inn (see Apstein, Theodore Emanuel)
Paradise Regained (see Snell, Beatrice Saxon)
The Pardoner and the Friar (see Heywood, John)
The Pardoner's Tale (see Mavor, Osborne Henry)
Paredes, Pedro Sanchez (see Sanchez Paredes, Pedro)
I Parentadi (see Grazzini, Antonio Francesco, called Il Lasca)
Les Parents Terribles (see Cocteau, Jean)
La Paria (see Strindberg, August)
Paris and London (see Planche, James Robinson)
Paris Bound (see Barry, Philip)
Paris, Impromptu (see Giraudoux, Jean)
Paris la Belle (see Prevert, Pierre)
Paris Nous Appartient (see Rivette, Jacques)
PARISH, James
    Just Off Piccadilly
    (In The One-Act Theatre, Vol. 1)
    St. Michael Comes to Shepherd's Bush
    (In Best One-Act Plays of 1940, London)
La Parisienne (see Becque, Henry)
Parker, Bonnie, 1911-1934
    *Bonnie and Clyde (see Newman, David)
PARKER, Dorothy (Rothschild), 1893-1967
    Here We Are
    (In 24 Favorite One-Act Plays)
Parkhouse, Hannah (see Cowley, Hannah Parkhouse)
PARKHURST, Winthrop
    The Beggar and the King
    (In Atlantic Book of Modern Plays, 1921)
PARKINGTON, Mary
    Experiment
    (In Best One-Act Plays of 1932, London)
    Nil Medium
    (In Best One-Act Plays of 1936, London)
    Poet's Corner
    (In Best One-Act Plays of 1931, London)
PARLAKIAN, Nishan
    Plagiarized
    (In First Stage, Vol. 1, no. 3, Summer 1962)
The Parliament of Bees (see Day, John)
The Parliament of Heaven: The Annunciation and Conception (Hegge
    Cycle)
Parnell, Charles Stewart, 1846-1891
    *Parnell (see Schauffler, Elsie Tough)
Parr, Catherine, 6th wife of Henry VIII, king of England, 1512-
1548

*Catherine Parr; a television script (see Prebble, John)
*Catherine Parr; or, Alexander's Horse (see Baring, Maurice)
*The Lion's Cub (see Hale, John)
PARSONS, M.R.
    Cookbook
        (In Mademoiselle, Vol. 64, Nov. 1966)
The Parson's Wedding (see Killigrew, Thomas)
Une Partie de Campagne (see Renoir, Jean)
Parting at Imsdorf (see Nusbaum, N. Richard)
The Party (see Arden, Jane)
The Party (see Mrozek, Slawomir)
The Party of the Third Part (see Stow, Clara)
The Party Spirit (see Jones, Peter)
Pascuatina (see Souza, Antonio)
PASOLINI, Pier Paolo, 1923-
    Oedipe Roi, inspire de "Oedipe Roi" de Sophocle
        (In L'Avant-Scene du Cinema, no. 97, Nov. 1969)
    Theoreme
        (In L'Avant-Scene du Cinema, no. 97, Nov. 1969)
Pasquin: A Dramatic Satire on the Times (see Fielding, Henry)
Passacaglia (see Dey, James Paul)
Le Passage du Rhin (see Cayatte, Andre)
A Passage to India (see Rau, Santha Rama)
La Passagere (see Munk, Andrzej)
Passengers (see Greppi, Antonio)
The Passer-by (see Afinogenev, A.)
Le Passe-temps (see Mithois, Marcel)
PASSEUR, Steve
    A Measure of Cruelty
        (In Plays of the Year, Vol. 29, 1964/65)
Passing of Francis Scott Key (see Markgraf, Bruce)
Passing of Galatea (see Talbot, Alfred Julian)
Une Passion (see Bergman, Ingmar)
Passion (see Bond, Edward)
The Passion Flower (see Benavente y Martinez, Jacinto)
The Passion of Joan of Arc (see Dreyer, Carl Theodor)
Les Passions Contraires (see Soria, Georges)
Pasteur, Louis, 1822-1895
    *Louis Pasteur; text in French (see Didier, Pierre)
    *The Story of Louis Pasteur (see Gibney, Sheridan)
Pastorale (see Turpin, Francois)
The Pastrybaker (see Vega Carpio, Lope Feliz de)
The Patchwork Quilt (see Field, Rachel Lyman)
The Path Between (see McCabe, Hazel G.)
Pathetic Prologue (see Sastre, Alfonso)
PATHIRAJA, Dharmesena
    L'Aveugle et le Paralytique

        (In L'Avant-Scene du Theatre, no. 477, Aug. 1, 1971)
Patient Grissil (see Dekker, Thomas)

O Patinho Torto (see Neto, Coelho)
Patiomkin (see Potëmkin)
Paton, Alan, 1903-
**Lost in the Stars (see Anderson, Maxwell)
Patrick, John, pseud. (see Goggan, John Patrick)
PATRICK, Robert
    Action
        (In Yale/Theatre, Vol. 2, no. 2, Summer 1969)
    The Golden Circle
        (In New American Plays, Vol. 3)
    See Other Side
        (In Yale/Theatre, Vol. 2, no. 2, Summer 1969)
Patrick Brontë and the Saint (see Packer, Barbara)
The Patrick Pearse Motel (see Leonard, Hugh)
A Patriot for Me (see Osborne, John)
The Patriots (see Kingsley, Sidney)
Patrol (see Shapiro, Steve)
Patterns (see Serling, Rod)
Paul and Virginia (see Cobb, James)
Paul Clifford; the Highwayman of 1770 (see Webster, Benjamin)
Paul Jones (see Dibdin, Thomas)
Paul II, Pope, 1417-1471
    *Malatesta (see Montherlant, Henry de)
Le Pauvre Matelot (see Cocteau, Jean)
PAVIOT, Paul, 1926-
    Saint-Tropez, Devoir de Vacances
        (In L'Avant-Scene du Cinema, no. 58, 1966)
    Torticola Contre Frankenberg
        (In L'Avant-Scene du Cinema, no. 118, Oct. 1971)
Pawns (see Wilde, Percival)
Payment as Pledged (see Gomes, Alfredo Dias)
Payment Deferred (see Dell, Jeffrey)
PAYNE, John Howard, 1791-1852
    Ali Pacha; or, The Signet-Ring
        (In Cumberland's British Theatre, Vol. 2, no. 3)
    Brutus, or, The Fall of Tarquin
        (In Cumberland's British Theatre, Vol. 1, no. 1)
    Charles the Second, by John H. Payne and Washington Irving
        (In Best Plays of the Early American Theatre, from the
        beginning to 1916)
    Charles the Second; or, The Merry Monarch
        (In Cumberland's British Theatre, Vol. 17, no. 5)
    Clari; or, The Maid of Milan, with music by Bishop, containing
    the famous song "Home Sweet Home"
        (In Cumberland's British Theatre, Vol. 20, no. 3)
    The Lancers
        (In Cumberland's British Theatre, Vol. 17, no. 7)
    Love in Humble Life; adapted from Scribe and Dupin's "Michel
    et Christine"
        (In Cumberland's British Theatre, Vol. 27, no. 8)

Therese, the Orphan of Geneva
    (In Cumberland's British Theatre, Vol. 45, no. 9)
The Two Galley Slaves
    (In Cumberland's British Theatre, Vol. 2, no. 7)
Peace (see Aristophanes)
Peace: 289-955 (see Aristophanes)
Peace without Honour (see Michael, Harold)
Peace-Makers (see Ehrlich, Mrs. Ida Lublenski)
PEACH, Lawrence du Garde, 1890-
    Wind O' the Moors
    (In 50 More Contemporary One-Act Plays)
PEAKE, Richard Brinsley, 1792-1847
    Amateurs and Actors
    (In Cumberland's British Theatre, Vol. 15, no. 5)
    Comfortable Lodgings; or, Paris in 1750
    (In Cumberland's British Theatre, Vol. 20, no. 8)
    The Duel; or, My Two Nephews
    (In Cumberland's British Theatre, Vol. 30, no. 4)
    The Haunted Inn
    (In Cumberland's British Theatre, Vol. 21, no. 3)
    The Hundred Pound Note
    (In Cumberland's British Theatre, Vol. 35, no. 1)
    Master's Rival; or, A Day at Boulogne
    (In Cumberland's British Theatre, Vol. 12, no. 7)
PEARCE, William
    Hartford Bridge; or, The Skirts of the Camp
    (In Cumberland's British Theatre, Vol. 21, no. 2)
    Netley Abbey
    (In Cumberland's British Theatre, Vol. 34, no. 8)
Le Peau Douce (see Truffaut, Francois)
PECH, Claude-Henri
    Strange Morning
    (In L'Avant-Scene du Theatre, no. 475, July 1, 1971)
Les Peches (The Peaches) (see Gill, Michael)
Pedlar's Acre; or, The Wife of Seven Husbands (see Almar,
    George)
Pedro Mico (see Callado, Antonio)
PEDROLO, Manuel de, 1918-
    Full Circle
    (In Modern International Drama, Vol. 3, Fall 1970)
    The Room (Tecnica de Cambra)
    (In Modern International Drama, Vol. 5, no. 2, Spring 1972)
PEELE, George, 1558?-1597?
    The Chronicle of Edward the First
    (In Dodsley's A Select Collection of Old Plays, Vol. 11)
    The Old Wives' Tale
    (In Great English Plays)
Peeping Tom of Coventry (see O'Keeffe, John)
Peg O' My Heart (see Manners, John Hartley)
Peggy, A Tragedy of the Tenant Farmer (see Williamson, Harold)
PEIXOTO, Luiz
    Forrobodo, de Luiz Peixoto e Carlos Bettencourt
    (In Revista de Teatro, no. 322)

Le Pelerin Blanc (see Piexerecourt, M.)
The Pelican (see Strindberg, August)
PELISSIER, Anthony
　　November Afternoon
　　　(In The One-Act Theatre, Vol. 2)
PELUSO, Emanuel
　　Moby Tick
　　　(In New American Plays, Vol. 4)
PEMBERTON, Madge
　　The Queen Waits
　　　(In Best One-Act Plays of 1940, London)
The Pen of My Aunt (see Mackintosh, Elizabeth)
PENLEY, Samson
　　The Sleeping-Draught
　　　(In Cumberland's British Theatre, Vol. 24, no. 9)
Penn, Arthur, 1922-
　　Alice's Restaurant (see Herndon, Venable)
　　Bonnie and Clyde (see Newman, David)
Penny a Flower (see Kester, Katherine)
Pense Alto!... (see Silva, Eurico)
Penthesilea (see Kleist, Heinrich von)
People in the Wind (see Inge, William Motter)
People Like Us (see Vodanovic, Sergio)
Pepsie (see Bruno, Pierrette)
PERCY, Edward
　　The Language of Love
　　　(In Best One-Act Plays of 1934, London)
　　Red Wax
　　　(In Best One-Act Plays of 1940, London)
Percy (see More, Hannah)
Pereira de Almeida, Abilio (see Almeida, Abilio Pereira de)
PERELMAN, Sidney Joseph, 1904-
　　The Beauty Part
　　　(In Broadway's Beautiful Losers)
Les Peres Ennemis (see Vildrac, Charles)
Perez, Antonio, d. 1611
　　*That Lady (see O'Brien, Kate)
Perez Galdos, Genito, 1843-1920
　　**Nazarin (see Buñuel, Luis)
Perez, Jose Cid (see Cid Perez, Jose)
The Perfect Gentleman (see Moliere, Jean Baptiste Poquelin)
The Perfect Marriage (see White, Leonard)
Perfection in Black (see Clark, China)
Pericles, Prince of Tyre (see Shakespeare, William)
Period House (see Eaton, Walter Prichard)
Period of Adjustment (see Williams, Tennessee)
PERL, Arnold
　　The Empty Noose
　　　(In Radio's Best Plays, 1947)
　　The High School; from "The World of Sholom Aleichem"
　　　(In Best Short Plays, 1955/56)
　　Mind in the Shadow

(In Best One-Act Plays of 1948/49, N.Y.)
Tevya and the First Daughter; based on the Tevya stories of
Sholom Aleichem
(In Best Short Plays, 1959/60)
The Perplexing Pirandello (see Palm, Carla L.)
PERREAULT, John
Oedipus, a new work based on Sophocles
(In TDR/The Drama Review, Vol. 15, Summer 1971)
PERRET, Jacques, 1901-
Le Couteau
(In L'Avant-Scene du Theatre, no. 341, Sept. 15, 1965)
(In Plaisir de France, supplement theatral, no. 324, Oct.
1965)
PERRINI, Alberto
Once a Thief
(In Best Short Plays, 1955/56)
Sala su Questo Mare; both French and English texts are included
(In Italian Theatre Review, Vol. 12, Oct./Dec. 1963)
La Perruche et le Poulet (see Thomas, Robert)
Perry, George Sessions
The Southerner (see Butler, Hugh)
PERRY, Marjean
A Trap Is a Small Place
(In Best One-Act Plays, 1952/53, N.Y.)
(In Best Short Plays, 1956/57)
Two's Company
(In Best Short Plays, 1959/60)
The Persecution and Assassination of Jean-Paul Marat as Performed
by the Inmates of the Asylum of Charenton under the Direction
of the Marquis of Sade (see Weiss, Peter)
The Persians (see Aeschylus)
The Persimmon Thief (see Nakazawa, Ken)
PERSKY, Bill
The Dick Van Dyke Show: "Coast to Coast Big Mouth." A
television filmscript, by Bill Persky and Sam Denoff.
(In Writing for Television)
The Person in the Chair (see Shaw, Frances)
Persona (see Bergman, Ingmar)
Personation; or, Fairly Taken In (see Kemble, Mrs. Marie
Therese De Camp)
Personation; or, Fairly Taken In (see also Fairly Taken In)
Le Personnage (see Chedid, Andree)
PERTWEE, Roland, 1885-
Heat Wave; from a story by Denise Robins
(In Five Three-Act Plays, Strand, 1933)
PERYALIS, Notis
Masks of Angels
(In New Theatre of Europe, 1962)
PETERSON, Agnes Emelie
In the Light of the Star
(In Drama, Vol. 21, 1930)

The Wind
    (In Drama, Vol. 15, May 1925)
Petit a Petit (see Rouch, Jean)
Un Petit Drame (see Shaw, George Bernard)
Le Petit Forain (see Hessens, Robert)
Le Petit Retable de don Cristobal (see Garcia Lorca, Federico)
Le Petit Soldat (see Godard, Jean-Luc)
Petite Fleur de Megeve (see Lefevre, Raymond)
Petite Suite Poetique Resolument Optimiste (see Obaldia, Rene de)
Petraglia, Claudio
    A Moreninha (see Silveira, Miroel)
PETRESCO, Julia
    Reglement de Comptes
        (In L'Avant-Scene du Theatre, no. 465, Feb. 1, 1971)
        (In Plaisir de France, supplement theatral, no. 388)
PETRI, Elio, 1929-
    Enquete sur un Citoyen Au-dessus de Tout Soupcon
        (In L'Avant-Scene du Cinema, no. 111, Feb. 1971)
The Petrified Forest (see Sherwood, Robert Emmet)
Petronius Arbiter, fl. 1st Cent. A.D., d. 66
    **L'Ecole des Veuves (see Cocteau, Jean)
    **Fellini's Satyricon (see Fellini, Federico)
    **Matron of Ephesus (see Sion, Georges)
    *The Stoic's Daughter (see Baring, Maurice)
Un Peu de Tendresse ou le Complexe de la Soupe (see Novac, Anna)
Peveril of the Peak; or, The Days of King Charles II (see Fitz-
    Ball, Edward)
Peyrou, Pierre
    Le Rendez-vous de Saint-Germain (see Vandenberghe, Paul)
PFAFF, Siegfried
    Regina B. -- Ein Tag in Ihrem Leben
        (In Theatre der Zeit, Vol. 25, 1970)
Phaedra (see Racine, Jean Baptiste)
Phaedra (see Seneca, Lucius Annaeus, Seneca the Younger)
Phaedra and Hippolitus (see Smith, Edmund)
The Pharmacist's Mate (see Schulberg, Budd)
Phedre (see Racine, Jean Baptiste)
PHELPS, Lyon, 1923-
    The Gospel Witch
        (In Religious Drama, Vol. 3)
PHELPS, Pauline
    I Know George Washington
        (In New Plays for Women & Girls, 1932)
    The Night Club Girl, by Pauline Phelps and Marion Short
        (In New Plays for Women & Girls, 1932)
The Philadelphia Story (see Barry, Philip)
Philaster (see Beaumont, Francis)
Philip II, King of France, 1165-1223
    *Lion in Winter (see Goldman, James)
Phillip II, King of Spain, 1527-1598
    *The Enterprise of England (see Prebble, John)
    *The Lion's Cub (see Hale, John)

*Philip the Second (see Alfieri, Vittori)
*That Lady (see O'Brien, Kate)
Philip III, King of Spain, 1578-1621
  *Lust's Dominion; or, The Lascivious Queen (see Marlowe,
    Christopher)
PHILIPS, Ambrose, 1674-1747
  The Distrest Mother, adapted from Andromaque of Racine
    (In Bell's British Theatre, 1797, Vol. 6)
Phillip Holtz's Fury (see Frisch, Max)
PHILLIPS, Louis
  The Banquet
    (In Drama & Theatre, Vol. 9, no. 2, Winter 1970/71)
PHILLIPS, Watts, 1825-1874
  Lost in London
    (In Hiss the Villain)
Philoctetes (see Sophocles)
PHILON, Frederic
  He Would Be a Soldier
    (In Modern Theatre, 1811, Vol. 8)
The Philosopher of Butterbiggens (see Chapin, Harold)
The Philosopher's Stone (see Artaud, Antonin)
The Phoenician Women (see Seneca, Lucius Annaeus)
The Phoenissae (see Euripides)
A Phoenix Too Frequent (see Fry, Christopher)
Phormio (see Terence, Publius Terentius Afer)
The Physicists (see Dürrenmatt, Friedrich)
PIALAT, Maurice, 1925-
  L'Amour Existe
    (In L'Avant-Scene du Cinema, no. 12, Feb. 1962)
Pianissimo (see Kreymborg, Alfred)
PICASSO, Pablo, 1881-1973
  Le Desir Attrape par la Queue
    (In L'Avant-Scene du Theatre, no. 500, Aug. 1972)
  Les Quatres Petites Filles
    (In L'Avant-Scene du Theatre, no. 500, Aug. 1972)
Pichel, Irving, 1891-1954
  A Medal for Benny (see Butler, Frank)
Picnic (see Inge, William Motter)
The Picnic (see Sundgaard, Arnold)
Picnic on the Battlefield (see Arrabal, Fernando)
The Picture (see Ionesco, Eugene)
Pictures on the Wall (see Brown, Ivor John Carnegie)
Piege pour un Homme Seul (see Thomas, Robert)
Pierro Le Fou (see Godard, Jean-Luc)
PIERRON, Eugene Athanase, 1819-1865
  Two Can Play at That Game, by Eugene Pierron and Adolphe
    Laferriere
    (In Lacy's Plays)
The Pierrot of the Minute (see Dowson, Ernest Christopher)
PIETERSON, Freda
  Security
    (In Best One-Act Plays of 1934, London)

PIEXERECOURT, M.
Le Pelerin Blanc; translated and adapted as "The Wandering
Boys"
(In Cumberland's British Theatre, Vol. 30, no. 2)
The Pig Prince (see Garnett, Louise Ayres)
Pigeons (see Osgood, Lawrence)
Pigs Ears and Purses (see Melville, Richard L.)
Pilate, Pontius, 5th Roman procurator of Judaea & Samaria, 1st
half 1st c. A.D.
*The Second Trial Before Pilate: the Scourging and Condemna-
tion (see York Tilemakers' Play)
Pillot, Eugene (see Pillot, Joseph Eugene)
PILLOT, Joseph Eugene
The Gazing Globe
(In Contemporary One-Act Plays, 1922)
The Young Wonder
(In Drama, Vol. 11, Feb. 1921)
The Pilot (see Fitz-Ball, Edward)
PIMENTEL, Altimar
A Construcao
(In Revista de Teatro, no. 373, Jan./Feb. 1970)
La Pince a Ongles (see Carriere, Jean-Claude)
PINELLI, Tullio
Gorgonio
(In L'Avant-Scene du Theatre, no. 241, Apr. 15, 1961)
PINERO, Arthur Wing, 1855-1934
The Magistrate
(In From the Modern Repertoire, Series Three)
(In Plays of the Year, Vol. 38, 1969/70)
The Second Mrs. Tanqueray
(In Introduction to Literature: Plays)
(In Late Victorian Plays)
(In 16 Famous British Plays)
Trelawny (see Slade, Julian)
The Widow of Wasdale Head
(In Representative One-Act Plays by British and Irish
Authors)
PINGET, Robert, 1920-
Architruc
(In L'Avant-Scene du Theatre, no, 469/470, Apr. 1-15, 1971)
L'Hypothese
(In L'Avant-Scene du Theatre, no. 313, June 15, 1964)
The Old Tune
(In Evergreen Review, Vol. 5, Mar./Apr. 1961)
The Ping-Pong Players (see Saroyan, William)
PINHEIRO, Jair
O Gato Playboy
(In Revista de Teatro, no. 377, Sept./Oct. 1970)
PINNER, David
Fanghorn
(In Plays and Players, Vol. 15, Jan. 1968)
Pinocchios Abenteuer (see Schwaen, Kurt)

PINSKI, David, 1872-1959
  A Dollar
    (In Contemporary One-Act Plays, 1922)
  Forgotten Souls
    (In 50 Contemporary One-Act Plays)
PINTER, Harold, 1930-
  Accident; based on the novel by Nicholas Mosley
    (In Five Screenplays of Harold Pinter)
  The Basement
    (In Evergreen Playscript Series)
  The Birthday Party
    (In Evergreen Playscript Series)
    (In 7 Plays of the Modern Theatre)
  The Caretaker
    (In Evergreen Playscript Series)
    (In New British Drama)
  The Collection
    (In Evergreen Playscript Series)
  The Dumb Waiter
    (In Evergreen Playscript Series)
  The Dwarfs
    (In Evergreen Playscript Series)
  Le Gardien
    (In L'Avant-Scene du Theatre, no. 441, Jan. 15, 1970)
  The Go-Between, based on the novel by L. P. Hartley
    (In Five Screenplays by Harold Pinter)
  The Homecoming
    (In Evergreen Playscript Series)
  Landscape
    (In Evergreen Review, Vol. 13, no. 68, July 1969)
  The Lover
    (In Evergreen Playscript Series)
  A Night Out
    (In Early Plays)
  Night School
    (In Early Plays)
  The Pumpkin Eater; based on the novel by Penelope Mortimer
    (In Five Screenplays by Harold Pinter)
  The Quiller Memorandum, based on "The Berlin Memorandum:
    by Adam Hall
    (In Five Screenplays by Harold Pinter)
  Le Retour; French text of "The Homecoming"
    (In Plaisir de France, supplement theatral, no. 343, May
    1967)
  Revue Sketches from the London Revues: "Pieces of Eight"
    and "One to Another"
    (In Early Plays)
  The Room
    (In Evergreen Playscript Series)
  The Servant; based on the novel by Robin Maugham
    (In Five Screenplays by Harold Pinter)
  A Slight Ache

(In Evergreen Playscript Series)
Tea Party
(In Evergreen Playscript Series)
La Pinzochera (see Grazzini, Antonio Francesco, called Il Lasca)
Pious Aeneas (see Baring, Maurice)
PIRANDELLO, Luigi, 1867-1936
As You Desire Me
(In 20 Best European Plays on the American Stage)
Bellavita
(In Best Short Plays of the World Theatre, 1958-67)
Comme avant, Mieux qu-avant
(In L'Avant-Scene du Theatre, June 1956)
Emperor (Enrico IV)
(In Genius of the Italian Theater)
(In The Modern Theatre, ed. by R. W. Rorrigan)
Henry IV
(In Makers of the Modern Theatre, 1961)
(In Tragedy: Texts and Commentary, 1969)
It Is So (If You Think So)
(An Introduction to Literature: Plays)
The Jar
(In Four Continental Plays, 1964)
The Man with the Flower in His Mouth
(In Dial, Vol. 74, Oct. 1923)
(In Tulane Drama Review, Vol. 1, June 1957)
(In One Act)
*The Perplexing Pirandello (see Palm, Carla L.)
Right You Are (If You Think So!)
(In his Three Plays, 1922)
(In Dramas of Modernism, 1931)
The Rules of the Game, adapted by William Murray
(In Theatre Arts, Vol. 45, no. 4, Apr. 1961)
Sicilian Limes, translated by Elizabeth Abbott
(In Theatre Arts, Vol. 6, 1922)
Six Characters in Search of an Author
(In The Modern Theatre, ed. by R. W. Corrigan)
(In 16 Famous European Plays)
PIRES, Meira
Joao Farrapo
(In Revista de Teatro, no. 342)
PIROSH, Robert, 1910-
A Day at the Races, film script by Robert Pirosh, George
Seaton, and George Oppenheimer. Directed by Sam Wood.
(In MGM Library of Film Scripts Series)
The Pit (see Hartweg, Norman)
PITT, George Dibdin, 1799-1855
The Eddystone Elf
(In Cumberland's British Theatre, Vol. 31, no. 6)
PIXLEY, Frank
Apollo
(In The Grove Plays of the Bohemian Club, Vol. 3)
Pizarro (see Sheridan, Richard Brinsley)

The Place Where the Mammals Die   (see Diaz, Jose)
Plagiarized (see Parlakian, Nishan)
Plain and Fancy (see Hague, Albert Martin)
The Plain Dealer (see Wycherley, William)
Le Plaisir de Rompre (see Renard, Jules)
PLANCHE, James Robinson, 1796-1880
    The Brigand, based on "Le Bandit" by Theaulon, Saint-Laurent,
    and Theodore
        (In Cumberland's British Theatre, Vol. 15, no. 3)
    Charles the XII
        (In Cumberland's British Theatre, Vol. 13, no. 4)
    The Green-Eyed Monster, founded in part on "Les Deux Jaloux
    of Vial"
        (In Cumberland's British Theatre, Vol. 3, no. 6)
    The Loan of a Lover
        (In Lacy's Plays)
    The Mason of Buda
        (In Cumberland's British Theatre, Vol. 7, no. 4)
    The Merchant's Wedding; or, London Frolics in 1638, princi-
    pally founded on Jasper Mayne's "City Match" and W. Rowley's
    "Match at Midnight"
        (In Cumberland's British Theatre, Vol. 6, no. 4)
    My Daughter, Sir! or, A Daughter to Marry
        (In Cumberland's British Theatre, Vol. 31, no. 5)
    Paris and London
        (In Cumberland's British Theatre, Vol. 21, no. 8)
    Telemachus; or, The Island of Calypso, by J. R. Planche and
    George Dance
        (In Lacy's Acting Plays, Vol. 14)
    The Vampire; or, The Bride of the Isles
        (In Cumberland's British Theatre, Vol. 13, no. 6)
    A Woman Never Vext; or, The Widow of Cornhill (see Roxley,
    William)
Plant in the Sun (see Bengal, Ben)
PLAUTUS, Titus Maccius, 254?-184 B. C.
    Amphitryon
        (In Complete Roman Drama, Vol. 1)
    The Captives
        (In Complete Roman Drama, Vol. 1)
    Casina
        (In Complete Roman Drama, Vol. 1)
    The Comedy of Asses
        (In Complete Roman Drama, Vol. 1)
    Curculio
        (In Complete Roman Drama, Vol. 1)
    Epidicus
        (In Complete Roman Drama, Vol. 1)
    The Pot of Gold
        (In Complete Roman Drama, Vol. 1)
    Stichus
        (In Complete Roman Drama, Vol. 2)
    The Three Penny Day

(In Complete Roman Drama, Vol. 2)
Truculentus
(In Complete Roman Drama, Vol. 2)
The Twin Menaechmi
(In Complete Roman Drama, Vol. 1)
(In Masterworks of World Drama, Vol. 2)
The Two Bacchides
(In Complete Roman Drama, Vol. 1)
Play (see Beckett, Samuel)
Play (see Bell, Neal)
Play, Life, Illusion (see Schawinsky, Xanti)
The Play of the Shepherds (see Wakefield Cycle: Secunda Pastorum)
The Playboy of the Western World (see Synge, John Millington)
The Players' Dressing Room (see Dukes, Ashley)
The Playground (see Broughton, James)
The Play's the Thing (see Molnar, Ferenc)
The Plays Themselves (see Kemp, Harry Hibbard)
The Playwright and the Public (see Saroyan, William)
Plaza Suite (see Simon, Neil)
Please, No Flowers (see Ensana, Joel A.)
The Pleasure of His Company (see Taylor, Samuel Albert)
PLOCH, Pedro
    Soraia Posto Dois
        (In Revista de Teatro, no. 339)
Plop! Click! (Dobu Kacchiri) (see Sakanishi, Shio)
The Plot in the Palace (see Watson, Robert)
The Plough and the Stars (see O'Casey, Sean)
Plugged In (see McGrath, John)
Plumes (see Johnson, Georgia Douglas)
Le Plus Saisi des Trois (see Richter, Charles de)
Plutus (see Aristophanes)
Po Chü-i, 722-847 A.D.
    *Haku Rakuten (see Zeami Motokiyo)
The Poacher (see Francis, John Oswald)
POCOCK, Isaac, 1782-1835
    For England, Ho!
        (In Cumberland's British Theatre, Vol. 36, no. 4)
    Hit or Miss
        (In Cumberland's British Theatre, Vol. 32, no. 3)
    John of Paris
        (In Cumberland's British Theatre, Vol. 19, no. 7)
    The Magpie, or the Maid?
        (In Cumberland's British Theatre, Vol. 21, no. 6)
    The Miller and His Men
        (In Cumberland's British Theatre, Vol. 20, no. 2)
        (In Hiss the Villain)
    The Robber's Wife
        (In Cumberland's British Theatre, Vol. 32, no. 1)
    Robinson Crusoe; or, The Bold Buccaniers; adapted from the
        work of Daniel De Foe
        (In Cumberland's British Theatre, Vol. 20, no. 5)
Poe, Edgar Allan, 1809-1849

**The Fall of the House of Usher (see Day, Frederic Lansing)
**Le Puits et le Pendule (see Astruc, Alexandre)
**Le Scarabee d'Or (see Lachenay, Robert)
POE, James
    They Shoot Horses, Don't They? Screenplay by James Poe
    and Robert E. Thompson, based on the novel by Horace Mc-
    Coy.
      (Included in published text of the novel, Avon Books, 1969)
Poem-Plays (see Krauss, Ruth)
The Poet (see Niccodemi, Dario)
Poet's Corner (see Parkington, Mary)
The Poet's Papers (see Starkweather, David)
Pogson, N. A.
    The Adventures of Marco Polo (see Sherwood, Robert Emmet)
Poil de Carotte (see Renard, Jules)
The Point of Honour (see Kemble, Charles)
Point of No Return (see Osborn, Paul)
Point Valaine (see Coward, Noel Pierce)
Poisoned (see Amcott, Vincent)
Les Poissons Rouges (see Anouilh, Jean)
The Poker Session (see Leonard, Hugh)
POLAC, Michel, 1930-
    Un Fils Unique
      (In L'Avant-Scene du Cinema, no. 99, Jan. 1970)
Police (see Jones, Leroi)
The Police (see Mrozek, Slawomir)
POLLOCK, Channing, 1880-1946
    "The Captains and the Kings"
      (In Best One-Act Plays of 1939, N.Y.)
Polly Honeycombe (see Colman, George, the Younger)
Polo, Marco, 1254-1323?
    *The Adventures of Marco Polo (see Sherwood, Robert Emmet)
Pomegranate Seed (see Wharton, Edith)
Les Pommes, les Poires (see Worms, Jeannine)
Des Pommes pour Eve (see Arout, Gabriel)
PONGE, Francis
    Soap
      (In Paris Review, Vol. 11, Summer 1968)
PONGETTI, Henrique
    Amanha Se Nao Chover
      (In Revista de Teatro, no. 336)
    Society em Baby Doll
      (In Revista de Teatro, no. 313)
    Zefa Entre os Hommens
      (In Revista de Teatro, no. 331)
Pons, Maurice
    **Les Mistons (see Truffaut, Francois)
Poof (see Salacrou, Armand)
POOLE, John, 1786?-1872
    Tribulation; or, Unwelcome Visitors
      (In Cumberland's British Theatre, Vol. 30, no. 8)
Poor Aubrey (see Kelly, George Edward)

"Poor Caro!" (see Foy, Helen)
Poor John (see Martinez Sierra, Gregorio)
The Poor Little Match Girl (see Williams, Arthur)
The Poor Soldier (see O'Keeffe, John)
Pope, Alexander, 1688-1744
    Three Hours after Marriage (see Gay, John)
The Pope's Right Knee (see Bagg, Robert)
The Pope's Wedding (see Bond, Edward)
POPOVIC, Aleksandar
    Second Door Left
    (In Drama & Theatre, Vol. 8, no. 2, Winter, 1969/70)
Popping the Question (see Buckstone, John Baldwin)
POPPLE, William
    The Double Deceit; or, A Cure for Jealousy
    (In Plays of the Year, Vol. 26, 1962/63)
POPPLEWELL, Jack
    Dear Delinquent
    (In Plays of the Year, Vol. 16, 1956/57)
Porgie Georgie (see Birimisa, George)
Porgy (see Heyward, Dubose)
Porte des Lilas (see Clair, Rene)
PORTER, Cole, 1892-1964
    Kiss Me, Kate. Music and lyrics by Cole Porter, book by
    Sam & Bella Spewack
    (In Theatre Arts, Vol. 39, Jan. 1955)
Porter, Harold Everett, 1887-1936
    The Valiant (see Middlemass, Robert)
PORTER, Henry, fl. 1599
    The Pleasant Comedy of the Two Angry Women of Abington
    (In Dodsley's A Select Collection of Old English Plays, Vol.
    7)
    The Two Angry Women, edited by Havelock Ellis
    (In Best Plays of the Old Dramatists: Nero & Other Plays)
PORTO-RICHE, Georges de, 1849-1930
    Francoise' Luck
    (In 50 Contemporary One-Act Plays)
The Portrait (see Carmontelle, Louis Carrogis, known as)
Portrait of a Madonna (see Williams, Tennessee)
Portrait of a Queen (see Francis, William)
Portrait of Tiero (see Akins, Zoë)
Un Portrait sur les Bras (see Dominguez, Franklin)
The Portsmouth Defence (see Lethbridge, Nemone)
The Position (see Martinez Ballesteros, Antonio)
Posmysz, Zofia
    La Passagere (see Munk, Andrzej)
The Post Office (see Tagore, Sir Rabindranath)
The Pot Boiler (see Gerstenberg, Alice)
The Pot of Gold (see Plautus, Titus Maccius)
Potemkin (see Eisenstein, Sergei Mikhailovich)
Potëmkin, Grigori Aleksandrovich, 1739-1791
    *Great Catherine (see Shaw, George Bernard)
Pots of Money (see Labiche, Eugene Marin)

POTTER, Dan S.
    A Touch of Marble
      (In Best Short Plays, 1958/59)
Pottery (see Hudson, Holland)
The Potting Shed (see Greene, Graham)
POUND, Ezra, 1885-
    An Anacronism at Chinon
      (In Little Review, Vol. 4, June 1917)
    Woman of Trachis (see Sophocles)
A Pound on Demand (see O'Casey, Sean)
Pour Finalie (see Billetdoux, Francois)
POVERMAN, Helen
    Easy Money
      (In Best Short Plays, 1958/59)
POWELL, Arnold
    The Strangler
      (In Playwrights for Tomorrow, Vol. 4)
POWER, Victor
    The Mud Nest, a television script
      (In Story: the Yearbook of Discovery, 1969)
PRAGA, Andre
    Le Cameleon
      (In L'Avant-Scene du Theatre, no. 392, Dec. 1, 1967)
    Les Freres
      (In L'Avant-Scene du Theatre, no. 495, May 15, 1972)
    Histoire d'une Chemise et d'un Violon
      (In Plaisir de France, supplement theatral, no. 300, Oct. 1963)
The Pragmatists (see Witkiewicz, Stanislaw Ignacy)
PRATA, Mario Alberto Campos de Morais, 1946-
    O Cordao Umbilical
      (In Revista de Teatro, no. 390, Nov./Dec. 1972)
PRATT, Theodore, 1901-
    Escape
      (In 50 More Contemporary One-Act Plays)
PRATT, William W.
    Ten Nights in a Bar-Room, based on the novel by Timothy
    Shay Arthur
      (In Hiss the Villain)
O Pravde-Podobnosti a Bicovani (see Kocourkava, Marketa)
PREBBLE, John
    Catherine Parr; a television script in the series "The Six
    Wives of Henry VIII"
      (In Plays of the Year Special, 1972)
    The Enterprise of England
      (In Plays of the Year Special, 1972)
PRELOVSKY, Anatoly
    Common Man
      (In Literary Review, Vol. 13, Spring 1970)
Prelude to Massacre (see John, Evan)
Prelude to Tragedy (see Rubinstein, Harold Frederick)
Preminger, Otto Ludwig, 1906-
    La Lune Etait Bleue (see Herbert, Frederick Hugh)

PRIN, Claude
    Candidat
        (In L'Avant-Scene du Theatre, no. 474, June 15, 1971)
The Prince and the Showgirl (see Rattigan, Terence Mervyn)
Prince Frederick of Homburg (see Kleist, Heinrich von)
Prince Hagen (see Sinclair, Upton)
The Prince of Homburg (see Kleist, Heinrich von)
Princely Fortune (see Alexander, Hartley Burr)
A Princesinha de Ouro (see Magalhaes, Paulo)
The Princess of Cleve (see Lee, Nathaniel)
La Princesse de Cleves (see Dorfmann, Robert)
Printemps Perdus (see Vendenberghe, Paul)
Printer's Measure (see Chayefsky, Paddy)
The Prisoner at Large (see O'Keeffe, John)
PRITCHARD, Barry
    Visions of Sugar Plums
        (In First Stage, Vol. 4, Fall 1965)
        (In Playwrights for Tomorrow, Vol. 4)
Private Hicks (see Maltz, Albert)
Privilege and Privation (see Kreymborg, Alfred)
The Prize; or, 2, 5, 3, 8 (see Hoare, Prince)
Le Proces (see Welles, Orson)
PROCUNIER, Edwin R.
    Two Sides of Darkness
        (In Best Short Plays, 1958/59)
The Prodigal Son (see Hughes, Langston)
The Prodigies (see Vauthier, Jean)
The Prodigious Snob (see Moliere, Jean Baptiste Poquelin)
The Professional Attitude (see Males, U. Harold)
Professor Berkardi (see Schnitzler, Arthur)
Professor Snaffle's Polypon (see Mandel, Oscar)
Progress (see Ervine, St. John Greer)
Project Orfee (see Marchou, Pierre)
Prologo alla Monica (see Grazzini, Antonio Francesco, called Il
    Lasca)
Prologue to Glory (see Conkle, Ellsworth Prouty)
Prometheus Bound (see Aeschylus)
Prometheus Rebound (see Wunderlich, Lawrence)
Prometheus Unbound (see Shelley, Percy Bysshe)
The Promise (see Arbuzor, Aleksir)
Promises, Promises (see Simon, Neil)
Property (see Gilliatt, Penelope)
The Proposal (see Chekhov, Anton Pavlovich)
PROSPERI, Giorgio, 1911
    The Conspiracy; both French and English versions are included.
        (In Italian Theatre Review, Vol. 10, Jan./Mar. 1961)
The Protagonist (see Kaiser, Georg)
The Provoked Husband (see Vanbrugh, Sir John)
The Provoked Wife (see Vanbrugh, Sir John)
A Proxima Vittima (see Rey, Marcos)
Prys-Jones, A. G.
    The Clock Strikes Ten (see Hickey, D. E.)

The Public Prosecutor (see Hochwalder, Fritz)
Public Speech (see Saroyan, William)
Puccini, Giacomo, 1858-1924
**La Boheme (see Dietz, Howard)
Puis-Je Me Permettre de?... (see Worms, Jeannine)
Le Puits et le Pendule (see Astruc, Alexandre)
The Pullet (see Carmontelle, Louis Carrogis, known as)
Pullman Car Hiawatha (see Wilder, Thornton Niven)
PULMAN, Jack
     The Happy Apple
          (In Plays of the Year, 1967/68)
          (In Plays and Players, Vol. 17, May 1970)
PUMPHREY, Byron
     Sadco; adapted from the short story by Curtis Zahn
          (In First Stage, Vol. 6, Fall 1967)
The Pumpkin Eater (see Pinter, Harold)
Uma Pupila Rica (see Macedo, Joaquim Manoel de)
PURDY, James
     Children Is All
          (In Mademoiselle, Vol. 56, Nov. 1962)
Purgatory (see Yeats, William Butler)
The Purification (see Williams, Tennessee)
PURKEY, Ruth Angel
     Hangs Over Thy Head
          (In Best Short Plays, 1955/56)
Purple Dust (see O'Casey, Sean)
The Purple Heart (see Cady, Jerome)
PUSHKIN, Aleksandr Sergeyevich, 1799-1837
     **Boris Godunov (see Musorgskii, Modest Petrovich)
     Mozart and Salieri
          (In Music and Letters, Vol. 38, Oct. 1957)
The Putty Club (see Molnar, Ferenc)
Pyle, Ernie, 1900-1945
     **The Story of G.I. Joe (see Atlas, Leopold)

Quai des Orfevres (see Clouzot, Henri-Georges)
The Quaker (see Dibdin, Charles)
The Quare Fellow (see Behan, Brendan)
Quare Medicine (see Green, Paul)
Quarter, Half, Three-Quarter, and Whole Notes (see Saroyan,
     William)
Quartet (see Sherriff, Robert Cedric)
O Quati Papa-Ovo (see Amado, Joao Jorge)
Les Quatre Cents Coups (see Truffaut, Francois)
Quatre Pieces sur Jardin (see 4 Pieces sur Jardin)
Les Quatre Saisons (see Wesker, Arnold)
Les Quatres Petites Filles (see Picasso, Pablo)
The Quay of Magic Things (see Mosher, John Chapin)
Que Ferez-vous en Novembre? (see Ehni, Rene)
Que Pena Ser So Ladrao (see Barreto, Paulo)
Que Viva Mexico! (see Eisenstein, Sergei-Mikailovitch)

Quebranto (see Netto, Coelho)
Queen after Death; or, How to Kill Women (see Montherlant,
Henry de)
The Queen and the Rebels (see Betti, Ugo)
The Queen and the Welshman (see Sisson, Rosemary Anne)
Queen Christina (see Strindberg, August)
The Queen of Arragon (see Habington, William)
The Queen of Greece (see Owens, Rochelle)
The Queen of Sheba (see Young, Stark)
The Queen Waits (see Pemberton, Madge)
The Queen's Highland Servant (see Home, William Douglas)
The Queen's Hour (see McCauley, Clarice Vallette)
Queens of France (see Wilder, Thornton)
The Queen's Shift (see Ingersoll, James H.)
QUENEAU, Georges
Le Chant du Styrene, by Georges Queneau and Alain Resnais
(In L'Avant-Scene du Cinema, no. 1, Feb. 15, 1961)
Queneau, Raymond
Zazie dans le Metro (see Malle, Louis)
The Quest of the Gorgon (see Tharp, Newton J.)
The Question (see Saroyan, William)
The Questioning of Nick (see Kopit, Arthur L.)
Questo Matrimonio si Deve Fare (see Brancati, Vitaliano)
The Quick and the Dead (see Russell, Eileen)
Quiet at Home (see Ryan, Richard)
Quiet--Facing the Park (see Holm, John Cecil)
The Quiller Memorandum (see Pinter, Harold)
La Quintaine (see Martin, Jacqueline)
Quintero, Serafin Alvarez (see Alvarez Quintero, Serafin)
Quintila (see Jolly, Andrew)
Quoat-Quoat (see Audiberti, Jacques)
Quoi de Neuf, Pussycat? (see Donner, Clive)
Quotations from Chairman Mao Tse-tung (see Albee, Edward)

RAK (see Belmont, Charles)
R. P. M. (see Segal, Erich)
R. U. R. (see Capek, Karel)
RABE, David
The Basic Training of Pavlo Hummel
(In Scripts, Vol. 1, no. 1, Nov. 1971)
RABINOWITZ, Shalom, 1859-1916
**Fiddler on the Roof (see Bock, Jerry)
**The High School (Perl, Arnold)
Liars
(In 50 More Contemporary One-Act Plays)
**Tevya and the First Daughter (see Perl, Arnold)
A Race for a Dinner (see Rodwell, James Thomas Gooderham)
RACINE, Jean, 1639-1699
Andromache
(In Genius of the French Theater)
(In his Five Plays)

Athaliah
    (In his Five Plays)
Berenice
    (In his Five Plays)
Britannicus
    (In his Five Plays)
**The Distrest Mother (see Philips, Ambrose)
Phaedra
    (In Masterworks of World Drama, Vol. 4)
    (In his Five Plays)
    (In Tragedy: Texts and Commentary, 1969)
    (In The Classic Theatre, ed. by Eric Bentley, Vol. 4)
Phedre, translated by R. Lowell
    (In Partisan Review, Vol. 28, Jan. 1961)
Rackey (see Culbertson, Ernest H.)
Radcliffe, Sir Thomas, 3d Earl of Sussex, 1526?-1583
    *The Lion's Cub (see Hale, John)
    *The Marriage Game (see Sisson, Rosemary Anne)
    *Shadow in the Sun (see Mitchell, Julian)
RADDE, Ronald
    "Transe"
    (In Revista de Teatro, no. 389, Sept./Oct., 1972)
Radio Felicity (see Kimmel, H.B.)
Radioman Jack Cooper (see Chevigny, Hector)
Raffaele (see Brancati, Vitaliano)
Rafferty's Chant (see Dewhurst, Keith)
The Raft of Medusa (see Kaiser, Georg)
The Rage (see Reynolds, Frederick)
Ragni, Gerome
    Hair (see MacDermot, Galt)
The Ragpicker of Paris and the Dressmaker of St. Antoine (see
    Stirling, Edward)
Rags (see Walter, Nancy)
Raid on the White Tiger Regiment (see China Shantung Provincial
    Peking Opera Troupe)
Rain (see Colton, John)
Rain from Heaven (see Behrman, Samuel Nathaniel)
The Rain Killers (see Hutchinson, Alfred)
Rainbows in Heaven (see Stone, Weldon)
The Rainmaker (see Nash, N. Richard)
The Rainy Afternoon (see Inge, William Motter)
Os Raios Y (see Santos, Justino dos)
A Raisin in the Sun (see Hansberry, Lorraine)
Raising the Wind (see Kenney, James)
Raizin (see Torahiko, Enomoto)
Raleigh, Sir Walter, 1552-1618
    *Sweet England's Pride (see Rodger, Ian)
Ralph Roister Doister (see Udall, Nicholas)
Ram-Alley; or, Merrie Trickes (see Barry, Lording)
Ramah Droog (see Cobb, James)
RAMSAY, Allan, 1686-1758
    The Gentle Shepherd
    (In Bell's British Theatre, 1797, Vol. 25)

RANDALL, William M. , 1899-
  Tobacco Alley
    (In Best One-Act Plays of 1937, N. Y.)
RANDOLPH, Thomas, 1605-1635
  The Muse's Looking-Glass
    (In Dodsley's A Select Collection of Old Plays, Vol. 9)
RANSLEY, Peter
  Disabled
    (In Plays and Players, Vol. 18, no. 9)
  Ellen
    (In Plays and Players, Vol. 11, April 1971)
Les Rapaces (see Von Stroheim, Erich)
The Rape of the Belt (see Levy, Benn Wolf)
RAPHAEL, Alice
  Dormer Windows
    (In Drama, Vol. 11, Aug. /Sept. 1921)
Raphael... Fais Tourner le Monde (see Jaquine, Jacques)
RAPHAELSON, Samson, 1896-
  Accent on Youth
    (In Famous Plays of Today, 1935)
RAPPAPORT, Solomon, 1863-1920
  The Dybbuk, by S. Ansky (pseud.)
    (In 20 Best European Plays on the American Stage)
    (In 16 Famous European Plays)
RAPPENEAU, Jean-Paul, 1932-
  La Vie de Chateau, by Jean-Paul Rappeneau et Daniel Boulanger
    (In L'Avant-Scene du Cinema, no. 58, 1966)
Le Rapport Dont Vous Etes l'Objet (see Havel, Vaclav)
Rapunzel (see Brody, Alter)
The Rare Triumphs of Love and Fortune (Anon.)
    (In Dodsley's A Select Collection of Old English Plays, Vol.
      6)
Rashomon (see Kurosawa, Akira)
The Rastifarian (see White, Edgar)
RATCLIFF, Nora
  We Got Rhythm
    (In 24 One-Act Plays, Revised edition, 1954)
A Rat's Mass (see Kennedy, Adrienne)
RATTIGAN, Terence Mervyn, 1911-
  Adventure Story
    (In Collected Plays, Vol. 2)
  All on Her Own
    (In Best Short Plays, 1970)
  A Bequest to the Nation
    (In Plays and Players, Jan. 1971)
  The Browning Version
    (In Collected Plays, Vol. 2)
    (In 24 Favorite One-Act Plays)
    (In English One-Act Plays of Today)
  The Deep Blue Sea
    (In Famous Plays of Today, 1953)
    (In Collected Plays, Vol. 2)
    (In Theatre Arts, Vol. 37, July 1953)

Flare Path
  (In Collected Plays, Vol. 1)
French without Tears
  (In Collected Plays, Vol. 1)
Harlequinade
  (In Collected Plays, Vol. 2)
Heart to Heart
  (In Collected Plays, Vol. 3)
Love in Idleness
  (In Collected Plays, Vol. 1)
The Prince and the Showgirl, by Terence Rattigan based on his
  play "The Sleeping Prince"
  (New American Library Screenplays)
Ross
  (In Collected Plays, Vol. 3)
  (In Theatre Arts, Vol. 47, April 1963)
Separate Tables. Two plays: "Table Number Seven, " and
  "Table by the Window"
  (In Collected Plays, Vol. 3)
  (In Theatre Arts, Vol. 42, May 1958)
The Sleeping Prince. (Film adaptation of this play was called
  "The Prince and the Showgirl. ")
  (In Collected Plays, Vol. 3)
  (In Theatre Arts, Vol. 41, Dec. 1957)
Variations on a Theme
  (In Collected Plays, Vol. 3)
While the Sun Shines
  (In Collected Plays, Vol. 1)
Who Is Sylvia?
  (In Collected Plays, Vol. 2)
The Winslow Boy
  (In Collected Plays, Vol. 1)
  (In Theatre Arts, Vol. 32, Oct. 1948)
Rattle of a Simple Man (see Dyer, Charles)
RAU, Santha Rama
  A Passage to India, based on the novel by E. M. Forster
  (In Theatre Arts, Vol. 46, Apr. 1962)
RAWLINS, Thomas, 1620-1670
  The Rebellion
  (In Dodsley's A Select Collection of Old English Plays, Vol.
  14)
Raymond and Agnes; the Travellers Benighted; or, The Bleeding
  Nun of Lindenberg (see Lewis, Matthew Gregory)
The Razor (see Nakamura Kichizo)
A Real Fine Cutting Edge (see Dozier, Robert)
Rebecca (see Sherwood, Robert Emmet)
The Rebellion (see Rawlins, Thomas)
Rebirth in Barrows Inlet (see Liss, Joseph)
The Reclining Figure (see Kurnitz, Harry)
The Recorder: A History (see Duberman, Martin)
The Recruiting Officer (see Farquhar, George)
The Red and Yellow Ark (see Devany, Edward H.)

Red Carnations (see Hughes, Glenn)
Red Death (see Barth, Ruth)
Red Detachment of Women (see Chiang, Ching)
Red Eye of Love (see Weinstein, Arnold)
The Red Lantern (see China Peking Opera Troupe)
Red Mountain High (see Auletta, Robert)
"Red Peppers" (see Coward, Noel Pierce)
The Red Slippers (see Panella, Antoinette)
The Red, the Pink, and the True Blue (see Miller, Paul Vincent)
Red Wax (see Percy, Edward)
REDDING, Joseph D.
    The Atonement of Pan
        (In The Grove Plays of the Bohemian Club, Vol. 2)
    The Land of Happiness
        (In The Grove Plays of the Bohemian Club, Vol. 3)
Redemption (The Living Corpse) (see Tolstoy, Leo)
Reed, Sir Carol, 1906-
    The Third Man (see Greene, Graham)
REED, John
    Freedom
        (In One-Act Play Magazine, 1937/38 Anthology)
REED, Mark White, 1893-
    Yes My Darling Daughter
        (In 20 Best Plays of the Modern American Theatre, Vol. 1)
REELY, Mary Katherine
    Flittermouse
        (In Drama, Vol. 14, Dec. 1923)
The Reference (see Firkins, Oscar W.)
Reflections (see Lawson, Wayne)
The Refrigerators (see Fratti, Mario)
Refund (see Karinthy, Fritz)
REGAN, Sylvia (Ellstein)
    The Fifth Season
        (In Theatre Arts, Vol. 38, July 1954)
The Regent (see Strindberg, August)
Regina B.--Ein Tag in Ihrem Leben (see Pfaff, Siegfried)
La Regle du Jeu (see Renoir, Jean)
Reglement de Comptes (see Petresco, Julia)
REGNARD, Jean Francois
    The Residuary Legate
        (In French Comedies of the XVIIIth Century)
REGNIER, Georges, 1913
    Presence d'Albert Camus
        (In L'Avant-Scene du Cinema, no. 48, 1965)
The Rehearsal (see Anouilh, Jean)
The Rehearsal (see Baring, Maurice)
The Rehearsal (see Buckingham, George Villiers, 2d duke of)
REICHENBACH, Francois, 1922-
    Les Marines
        (In L'Avant-Scene du Cinema, no. 65, 1966)
REID-Jamieson, Marion
    Eleven A.M.
        (In Best One-Act Plays of 1934, London)

The Reign of the Wooden Horse (see Edson, Eric)
La Reine Blanche (see Barillet, Pierre)
REINECKER, Herbert, 1914-
    Night Train
        (In Modern International Drama, Vol. 1, no. 1, Sept. 1967)
REINHARDT, Wolfgang
    Juarez, a filmscript by Wolfgang Reinhardt and John Huston,
        directed by William Dieterle
        (In 20 Best Film Plays)
Reisch, Walter, 1900-
    Ninotchka (see Brackett, Charles)
REISIN, Abraham, 1876-
    Brothers
        (In 50 More Contemporary One-Act Plays)
The Relapse; or, Virtue in Danger (see Vanbrugh, John)
Les Reliques (see Richaud, Andre de)
The Reluctant Debutante (see Home, William Douglas)
The Remarkable Incident at Carson Corners (see Rose, Reginald)
The Remarkable Mr. Pennypacker (see O'Brien, Liam)
Remissao dos Pecados (see Macedo, Joaquim Manuel de)
A Remittance from Spain (see Apstein, Theodore)
Renaissance Night (see Morris, T. B.)
RENARD, Jules, 1864-1910
    Le Pain de Menage
        (In Plaisir de France, supplement theatral, no. 334, June
        1967)
    Le Plaisir de Rompre
        (In Plaisir de France, supplement theatral, no. 344, June
        1967)
    Poil de Carotte
        (In Plaisir de France, supplement theatral, no. 344, June
        1967)
Renaud et Armide (see Cocteau, Jean)
La Rencontre (see Rit, Gaston)
The Rendezvous (see Ayton, Richard)
Le Rendez-vous de Saint-Germain (see Vandenberghe, Paul)
RENOIR, Jean, 1894-
    Carola ou les Cabotins
        (In Cahiers du Cinema, Vol. 13, no. 78, Dec. 1957)
    Grand Illusion
        (In Classic Film Scripts)
    La Grand Illusion
        (In L'Avant-Scene du Cinema, no. 44, 1964)
    Une Partie de Campagne; d'apres Guy de Maupassant
        (In L'Avant-Scene du Cinema, no. 21, Dec. 15, 1962)
    La Regle du Jeu
        (In L'Avant-Scene du Cinema, no. 52, 1965)
    Rules of the Game
        (In Classic Film Scripts)
    The Southerner (see Butler, Hugh)
    Le Testament du Docteur Cordelier
        (In L'Avant-Scene du Cinema, no. 6, July 15, 1961)

This Land Is Mine   (see Nichols, Dudley)
A Rent in the Universe   (see States, Bert O.)
Une Repetition Generale; ou, La Piece a Conviction   (see Vanden-
     berghe, Paul)
The Representation (or Descent) of the Holy Ghost (Anon.)
     (In Theatrical Recorder, Vol. 2, no. 7, June 1805)
Repression   (see Theatre de l'Epee de Bois)
Requiem for a Heavy-Weight   (see Serling, Rod)
Reservations   (see Halpern, Martin)
The Residuary Legate   (see Regnard, Jean Francois)
RESNAIS, Alain, 1922-
     Le Chant du Styrene   (see Georges Queneau and Alain Resnais)
     Guernica, by Alain Resnais et Robert Hessens
        (In L'Avant-Scene du Cinema, no. 38, 1964)
     La Guerre est Finie   (see Semprun, Jorge)
     Hiroshima mon Amour   (see Duras, Marguerite)
     Last Year at Marinbad   (see Robbe-Grillet, Alain)
     Le Mystere de l'Atelier Quinze   (see Forlani, Remo)
     Night and Fog   (see Cayrol, Jean)
     Nuit et Brouillard   (see Cayrol, Jean)
     Le T'Aime, Je T'Aime, by Alain Resnais et Jacques Sternberg
        (In L'Avant-Scene du Cinema, no. 91, Apr. 1969)
     Route la Memoire du Monde
        (In L'Avant-Scene du Cinema, no. 52, 1965)
     Van Gogh   (see Hessens, Robert)
RESNIK, Muriel
     Une Fois par Semaine
        (In Plaisir de France, supplement theatral, no. 339, Jan.
        1967)
The Resolution of Mossie Wax   (see Foreman, Stephen H.)
Resurrection Ezra   (see Mitchell, Ronald Elwy)
Restless Heart   (see Anouilh, Jean)
The Restoration of Arnold Middleton   (see Storey, David)
Resurrection   (see Corkery, Daniel)
Le Retable des Mervilles   (see Cervantes Saavedra, Miguel de)
The Reticent Convict   (see Firkins, Oscar W.)
Le Retour   (see Pinter, Harold)
Le Retour de Cid   (see Arauz, Alvaro)
Le Retour de Lumiere   (see Didier, Pierre)
The Return   (see Morgan, Edward J.)
The Return from Pernassus; or, The Scourge of Simony (Anon.)
     (In Dodsley's A Select Collection of Old English Plays, Vol.
     9)
The Return of Chandra   (see Wilson, Dorothy Clarke)
The Return of Proserpine   (see Frank, Florence Kiper)
Returning to the Capital   (see Howard, Roger)
Reunion   (see Tayleur, W. St. John)
Reunion in Vienna   (see Sherwood, Robert Emmet)
Le Reve de l'Infante   (see Mercier, Maurice)
The Revenge   (see Young, Edward)
The Revenger's Tragedy   (see Tourneur, Cyril)
Rever pour Vivre   (see Worms, Jeannine)

The Review; or, The Wags of Windsor   (see Colman, George, the
   Younger)
Le Rivizor (see Gogol, Nikalai)
The Revolting Daughter (see Housman, Laurence)
Revue Sketches (see Pinter, Harold)
REY, Marcos
   A Proxima Vittima
      (In Revista de Teatro, no. 358, Jul. /Aug. 1967)
REYNOLDS, Francis
   "No!"
      (In Cumberland's British Theatre, Vol. 20, no. 6)
REYNOLDS, Frederick, 1764-1841
   The Blind Bargain; or, Hear It Out
      (In Cumberland's British Theatre, Vol. 27, no. 5)
   The Delinquent
      (In Modern Theatre, 1811, Vol. 2)
   The Exile; or, The Deserts of Siberia
      (In Cumberland's British Theatre, Vol. 23, no. 9)
   Folly as It Flies
      (In Cumberland's British Theatre, Vol. 16, no. 4)
      (In Modern Theatre, 1811, Vol. 2)
   Fortune's Fool
      (In Modern Theatre, 1811, Vol. 2)
   The Free Knights
      (In Old Plays, 1810)
   The Fugitive
      (In Modern Theatre, 1811, Vol. 8)
   How to Grow Rich
      (In Cumberland's British Theatre, Vol. 35, no. 7)
      (In Modern Theatre, 1811, Vol. 1)
   Laugh When You Can
      (In Cumberland's British Theatre, Vol. 12, no. 3)
      (In Modern Theatre, 1811, Vol. 2)
   Life
      (In Modern Theatre, 1811, Vol. 1)
   Notoriety
      (In Cumberland's British Theatre, Vol. 28, no. 1)
      (In Modern Theatre, 1811, Vol. 1)
   The Rage
      (In Modern Theatre, 1811, Vol. 1)
   Speculation
      (In Modern Theatre, 1811, Vol. 2)
   Werter
      (In Modern Theatre, 1811, Vol. 3)
   The Will
      (In Cumberland's British Theatre, Vol. 19, no. 4)
      (In Modern Theatre, 1811, Vol. 1)
REYNOLDS, Rachel
   Until Charlot Comes Home
      (In Best One-Act Plays of 1941, N.Y.)
REYNOLDSON, Thomas H.
   The Curse of Mammon; being a fac-simile embodiment of

Hogarth's "Marriage à-la-mode"
  (In Cumberland's British Theatre, Vol. 46, no. 6)
The Rich Man of Frankfort; or, The Poisoned Crown
  (In Cumberland's British Theatre, Vol. 39, no. 9)
The Venetian; or, The Council of Ten
  (In Cumberland's British Theatre, Vol. 37, no. 5)
Rhesus (see Euripides)
Rhinoceros (see Ionesco, Eugene)
RHODES, William Barnes, 1772-1826
  Bombastes Furioso
    (In Burlesque Plays of the 18th Century)
The Rhythm of Violence (see Nkosi, Louis)
RIBEMONT-Dessaugnes, Georges, 1884-
  The Mute Canary
    (In TDR/The Drama Review, Vol. 16, no. 1, March 1972)
The Ribs and the Cover (Hone-kawa) (see Sakanishi, Shio)
RICE, Elmer L., 1892-1967
  The Adding Machine
    (In Theatre Guild Anthology)
    (In Best American Plays, Supp. Vol.)
  Counsellor-at-Law
    (In Famous Plays of Today, 1932/33)
  Dream Girl
    (In Best Plays of the Modern American Theatre, Second
    Series)
  On Trial
    (In 13 Famous Plays of Crime and Detection)
  See Naples and Die
    (In Famous Plays of Today, 1932)
  Street Scene
    (In Nine Modern American Plays)
    (In 25 Best Plays of the Modern American Theatre, Early
    Series, 1916-1929)
    (In Pulitzer Prize Plays)
The Rich Man of Frankfort; or, The Poisoned Crown (Anon.)
  (In Cumberland's British Theatre, Vol. 39, no. 9)
Richard I (Coeur de Lion), King of England, 1157-1199
  *Lion in Winter (see Goldman, James)
Richard II, King of England, 1367-1400
  *Richard of Bordeaux (see Mackintosh, Elizabeth)
Richard III, King of England, 1452-1485
  *Richard III; text in French (see Shakespeare, William)
Richard of Bordeaux (see Mackintosh, Elizabeth)
Richard Plantagenet (see Haines, John Thomas)
RICHARDS, Stanley, 1918-
  August Heat
    (In Best One-Act Plays of 1949/50, N.Y.)
  District of Columbia
    (In Best One-Act Plays of 1944, N.Y.)
  Farewell Appearance (see Holland, Norman)
  Gin and Bitterness
    (In Best Short Plays, 1958/59)

Half-Hour, Please
(In Best Short Plays, 1954/55)
Journey to Bahia   (see Gomes, Alfred Dias)
O Distant Land
(In Best One-Act Plays of 1948/49, N. Y.)
Sun Deck
(In Best One-Act Plays, 1951/52, N. Y.)
Through a Glass Darkly
(In Best One-Act Plays of 1947/48, N. Y.)
(In Best Short Plays, 1956/57)
Tunnels of Love
(In Best One-Act Plays, 1952/53, N. Y.)
RICHARDSON, Jack, 1935-
Christmas in Las Vegas
(In Broadway's Beautiful Losers)
Gallows Humor
(In Theatre Experiment)
RICHARDSON, Willis, 1889-
The Broken Banjo
(In Plays of Negro Life)
The Chip Woman's Fortune
(In 50 More Contemporary One-Act Plays)
The Flight of the Natives
(In Plays of Negro Life)
RICHAUD, Andre de
Les Reliques
(In L'Avant-Scene du Theatre, no. 505, Nov. 1, 1972)
Riches (see Burges, Sir James Bland)
RICHTER, Charles de
Le Plus Saisi des Trois
(In Plaisir de France, supplement theatral, no. 330, April
1966)
The Ride Across Lake Constance (see Handke, Peter)
Le Rideau Cramoisi (see Astruc, Alexandre)
The Rider of Dreams (see Torrence, Frederic Ridgely)
Riders to the Sea (see Synge, John Millington)
The Riding to Lithend (see Bottomley, Gordon)
Rienzi, Cola di, c. 1313-1354
*Rienzi (see Mitford, Mary Russell)
Rieux, Albert, 1906-
Gonzalo Sent la Violette (see Vattier, Robert)
The Rifle and How to Use It (see Bridgeman, J. W.)
RIGGS, Lynn, 1899-1954
Green Grow the Lilacs
(In Nine Modern American Plays)
(In Best American Plays, Supp. Vol.)
**Oklahoma! (see Rodgers, Richard)
We Speak for Ourselves
(In Theatre Arts, Vol. 27, Dec. 1943)
A World Elsewhere
(In Best One-Act Plays of 1939, N. Y.)
Right You Are (If You Think So!) (see also It Is So (If You Think
So!))

The Rightful Heir   (see Lytton, Edward George Earle Lytton Bulwer-
    Lytton, 1st baron)
The Rights of Man   (see Leland, Oliver Shepard)
The Rights of the Soul   (see Giacosa, Guiseppe)
RILEY, Mrs. Alice Cushing (Donaldson), 1867-
    The Mandarin Coat
        (In Drama, Vol. 13, Jan. 1923)
    Taxi
        (In Drama, Vol. 16, Feb. 1926)
    Their Anniversary
        (In Drama, Vol. 12, Feb. 1922)
    Uplifting Sadie
        (In New Plays for Women & Girls, 1932)
RINEHART, Mary (Roberts), 1876-1958
    The Bat, by Mary Rinehart and Avery Hopwood, based on the
    story "The Circular Staircase" by Mary Rinehart
        (In 13 Famous Plays of Crime and Detection)
        (In S.R.O., the Most Successful Plays...)
RINGWOOD, Gwen Pharis
    The Courting of Marie Jenvrin
        (In Best One-Act Plays of 1942, N.Y.)
O Rio de Janerio (Verso e Reverso)   (see Alencar, Jose de)
Riot Sale, or Drellar Psyche Fake Out   (see Caldwell, Ben)
Rip Van Winkle   (see Jefferson, Joseph)
Rise of Her Bloom   (see Hughes, Elizabeth Wilson)
The Rising of the Moon   (see Gregory, Isabella Augusta Peresse,
    lady)
RISKIN, Robert, 1897-1955
    It Happened One Night, a screenplay; based on the story "Night
    Bus" by Samuel Hopkins Adams, directed by Frank Capra
        (In Twenty Best Film Plays)
        (In Four-Star Scripts)
    Lady for a Day, screenplay; based on the story "Madame La
    Gimp: by Damon Runyon, directed by Frank Capra
        (In Four-Star Scripts)
    You Can't Take It with You; based on the stage play by George
    S. Kaufman and Moss Hart, directed by Frank Capra
        (In Foremost Films of 1938)
Riskind, Morrie, 1895-
    Of Thee I Sing   (see Gershwin, George)
RIT, Gaston
    La Rencontre
        (In Plaisir de France, supplement theatral, no. 359, Sept.
        1968)
Rites   (see Duffy, Maureen)
Il Ritorno   (see Fratti, Mario)
Der Ritt uber den Bodensee   (see Handke, Peter)
The Rival of His Master   (see Le Sage, Alain-Rene)
The Rival Queens; or, The Death of Alexander the Great   (see Lee,
    Nathaniel)
The Rival Valets   (see Ebsworth, Joseph)
The Rivals   (see Sheridan, Richard Brinsley)

RIVERS, Louis
    The Scabs, by Paul Mulet, pseud.
        (In First Stage, Vol. 1, no. 4, Fall 1962)
RIVETTE, Jacques, 1928-
    Paris Nous Appartient, by Jacques Rivette et Jean Gruault
        (In Cahiers du Cinema, Vol. 14, no. 90, Dec. 1958)
La Riviere du Hibou (see Enrico, Robert)
Rixe (see Grumberg, Jean-Claude)
The Road to Rome (see Sherwood, Robert Emmet)
The Road to Ruin (see Holcroft, Thomas)
The Roaring Girle; or, Moll Cut-Purse (see Middleton, Thomas)
Rob Roy (see Soane, George)
Rob Roy (see Macgregor, Robert, known as Rob Roy)
ROBBE-GRILLET, Alain, 1922-
    Last Year at Marienbad; script from the film by Alain Resnais
        (In Evergreen Filmscript Series)
The Robber's Wife (see Pocock, Isaac)
Robbins, Jerome, 1918-
    West Side Story (see Bernstein, Leonard)
La Robe de Valentine (see Sagan, Francoise)
The Robe of Wood (see Golden, John)
La Robe Rouge (see Brieux, Eugene)
Robert Guiscard (see Kleist, Heinrich von)
ROBERTS, Cyril
    Exit
        (In Best One-Act Plays of 1931, London)
ROBERTS, George
    Cousin Tom
        (In Lacy's Plays)
ROBERTS, Marguerite
    Dragon Seed, a screenplay by Marguerite Roberts and Jane
    Murfin, based on the book by Pearl Buck. Directed by Jack
    Conway and Harold S. Bucquet.
        (In Best Film Plays, 1943/44, Vol. 1)
ROBERTSON, Louis A.
    Montezuma
        (In The Grove Plays of the Bohemian Club, Vol. 1)
ROBERTSON, Thomas William, 1829-1871
    Society
        (In Great English Plays)
Robespierre, Maximilien Marie Isidore de, 1758-1794
    *Danton's Death (see Büchner, Georg)
Robin Hood
    *The Death of Robert Earl of Huntington, otherwise called Robin
        Hood of Merrie Sherwodde (see Munday, Anthony)
    *The Downfall of Robert Earl of Huntington (see Munday,
        Anthony)
    *Robin Hood; or, The Merry Outlaws of Sherwood (see Fitzball,
        Edward)
Robins, Denise
    Heat Wave (see Pertwee, Roland)
Robinson, Donald Fay, adapter (see Maastricht Play, a Christmas
    Miracle)

Robinson, Earl
  The Lonesome Train (see Lampell, Millard)
ROBINSON, Edwin Arlington, 1869-1935
  Demos and Dionysus
    (In Theatre Arts, Vol. 9, Jan. 1925)
ROBINSON, Lennox, 1886-1958
  Crabbed Youth and Age
    (In Theatre Arts, Vol. 8, Jan. 1924)
ROBINSON, Marvin W.
  Exodus
    (In Best One-Act Plays of 1949/50, N.Y.)
ROBINSON, T. S.
  The Student's Frolic
    (In 26 Short & Amusing Plays, 1871)
Robinson Crusoe; or, The Bold Buccaniers (see Pocock, Isaac)
Robinson Crusoe; or, Harlequin Friday and the Kind of the Caribee
  Islands! (see Byron, Henry James)
ROBSON, William Northrop, 1906-
  Open Letter on Race Hatred
    (In Radio Drama in Action, 1945)
Rocco and His Brothers (see Visconti, Luchino)
ROCHA, Glauber, 1938-
  Terre en Transe (Terra em Transe)
    (In L'Avant-Scene du Cinema, no. 77, Jan. 1968)
Roche, Henri Pierre, 1879-
  Les Deux Anglaises et le Continent (see Truffaut, Francois)
  **Jules et Jim (see Truffaut, Francois)
The Rock (see Serling, Rod)
The Rock Garden (see Shepard, Sam)
The Rocking Horse (see Halman, Doris)
Rococo (see Granville-Barker, Harley Granville)
RODENBACH, Georges, 1855-1898
  The Veil
    (In 50 More Contemporary One-Act Plays)
RODGER, Ian
  Sweet England's Pride
    (In Plays of the Year Special, 1972)
RODGERS, Mary
  Once Upon a Mattress, by Jay Thompson, Marshall Barer and
    Dean Fuller, with music by Mary Rodgers
    (In Theatre Arts, Vol. 44, July 1960)
RODGERS, Richard, 1902-
  Oklahoma! by Richard Rodgers and Oscar Hammerstein II,
    based on Lynn Riggs' "Green Grow the Lilacs"
    (In S. R. O., the Most Successful Plays...)
RODRIGUES, Elza Correa
  A Estoria da Rosa Principe
    (In Revista de Teatro, no. 387, May/June, 1972)
RODRIGUES, Nelson
  A Falecida
    (In Revista de Teatro, no. 337)
RODWELL, George Herbert Buonaparte, 1800-1852

The Flying Dutchman; or, The Phantom Ship (see Fitz-Ball,
    Edward)
The Inchcape Bell (see Fitz-Ball, Edward)
Teddy the Tiler
    (In Cumberland's British Theatre, Vol. 21, no. 9)
RODWELL, James Thomas Gooderham, d. 1825
A Race for a Dinner
    (In Cumberland's British Theatre, Vol. 32, no. 6)
RODY, Alberto
Tic-Tac
    (In Plaisir de France, supplement theatral, no. 385, 1970)
ROEPKE, Gabriela, 1920-
A White Butterfly
    (In Best Short Plays, 1959/60)
ROGERS, John William, Jr., 1894-
Bumblepuppy; A Comedy of Climate
    (In Theatre Arts, Vol. 11, Sept. 1926)
    (In 50 More Contemporary One-Act Plays)
Judge Lynch
    (In Plays of Negro Life)
ROGNONI, Angelo
Weariness, a physical state written as a script
    (In TDR/The Drama Review, Vol. 15, Fall 1970)
ROHMER, Eric, 1920-
Claire's Knee
    (In Modern Filmscripts Series)
La Collectionneuse
    (In L'Avant-Scene du Cinema, no. 69, 1967)
Collectionneuse
    (In Modern Filmscript Series)
Ma Nuit chez Maud
    (In L'Avant-Scene du Cinema, no. 98, Dec. 1969)
My Night at Maude's
    (In Modern Filmscript Series)
Presentation ou Charlotte et Son Steak
    (In L'Avant-Scene du Cinema, no. 69, 1967)
    (In Cahiers du Cinema, Vol. 2, no. 12, May 1952)
Le Roi Borgne (see Spiraux, Alain)
ROJAS, Fernando de, d. 1541
Celestina
    (In The Modern Theatre, ed. by Eric Bentley, Vol. 3)
Roleta Paulista (see Bloch, Pedro)
Rolfe, Frederick William, Baron Corvo, 1860-1913
    *Hadrian the Seventh (see Luke, Peter)
ROLI, Mino, 1930-
Sacco and Vanzetti, by Mino Roli and Luciano Vincenzoni.
    Both French and English versions are included.
    (In Italian Theatre Review, Vol. 10, Oct./Dec. 1961)
Rollo (see Achard, Marcel)
ROMAINS, Jules, 1885-
Dr. Knock
    (In From the Modern Repertoire, Series Three)

The Roman Father   (see Whitehead, William)
Romanoff and Juliet   (see Ustinov, Peter)
Romanov, Anastasia Nikolaievna, grand duchess, 1901?-1918
    *Anastasia   (see Marcelle-Maurette)
The Romantics   (see Rostand, Edmond)
The Romany Road   (see Brighouse, Harold)
Romao e Julinha   (see Von Pfuhl, Oscar)
ROME, Nicholas
    Lady Jane Grey
        (In Bell's British Theatre, 1797, Vol. 15)
    The Royal Convert
        (In Bell's British Theatre, 1797, Vol. 27)
Rome, Ville Ouverte   (see Fellini, Federico)
Romeo and Jeannette   (see Anouilh, Jean)
Romeo and Juliet   (see Cocteau, Jean)
Romeo and Juliet: The Servants   (see Brecht, Bertolt)
ROMM, Gregory
    The Watchmaker and the Doctor
        (In Soviet One-Act Plays)
The Romp (Anon.)
        (In Cumberland's British Theatre, Vol. 44, no. 3)
Romulus Augustulus, b. 461?
    *Romulus   (see Vidal, Gore)
    *Romulus le Grand   (see Dürrenmatt, Friedrich)
    *Romulus the Great   (see Dürrenmatt, Friedrich)
La Ronde   (see Natanson, Jacques)
La Ronde   (see Schnitzler, Arthur)
RONDI, Brunello, 1924-
    The Journey; both French and English versions are included.
        (In Italian Theatre Review, Vol. 14, Apr. /June 1965)
ROOF, Katherine Metcalf
    The Edge of the Wood
        (In Drama, Vol. 10, Feb. 1920)
The Roof Scrambler   (see A Beckett, Gilbert Abbott)
The Room   (see Pinter, Harold)
The Room (Tecnica de Cambra)   (see Pedrolo, Manuel de)
ROOS, Joanna
    Borderline of Fear
        (In Best Television Plays of the Year, 1950/51)
Roosevelt, Franklin Delano, pres. U. S., 1822-1945
    The Last Speech   (see Cooper, Lou)
    *Sunrise at Campobello   (see Schary, Dore)
Roots   (see Wesker, Arnold)
Roots in a Parched Garden   (see Foote, Horton)
The Rope Dancers   (see Wishengrad, Morton)
Rosamond   (see Weisse, Christian Felix)
Rosamund and Eleanor   (see Baring, Maurice)
ROSE, Billy, 1899-1966
    The Night They Made a Bum Out of Helen Hayes
        (In Best Television Plays of the Year, 1950/51)
ROSE, Reginald, 1920-
    An Almanac of Liberty

(In Rose, Six Television Plays)
Crime in the Streets
   (In Rose, Six Television Plays)
Dino
   (In Best Short Plays, 1955/56)
The Incredible World of Horace Ford
   (In Rose, Six Television Plays)
The Remarkable Incident at Carson Corners
   (In Rose, Six Television Plays)
Thunder on Sycamore Street
   (In Best Television Plays)
   (In Rose, Six Television Plays)
Tragedy in a Temporary Town
   (In Television Plays for Writers, 1957)
Twelve Angry Men
   (In Film Scripts Two)
   (In Rose, Six Television Plays)
The Rose of Persia (see Harveis, Lionel)
The Rose Tattoo (see Williams, Tennessee)
Rose Windows (see Young, Stark)
The Rose without a Thorn (see Bax, Clifford)
ROSENBERG, James L.
   The Death and Life of Sneaky Fitch
   (In New American Plays, Vol. 1)
ROSENBERG, Jerold, 1926-1955
   The Pajama Game, by George Abbott and Richard Bissell,
   with music and lyrics by Richard Adler and Jerry Ross (pseud.).
   Based on the novel "7 1/2 cents" by Richard Bissell.
   (In Theatre Arts, Vol. 39, Sept. 1955)
Les Rosenberg ne Doivent Pas Mourir (see Decaux, Alain)
Rosencrantz and Guildenstern Are Dead (see Stoppard, Tom)
Roses and Thorns; or, Two Houses under One Roof (see Lunn,
   Joseph)
Rosina (see Brooke, Mrs. Frances Moore)
ROSOW, Viktor von
   Das Klassentreffen
   (In Theater der Zeit, Aug. 1970)
Ross (see Rattigan, Terence)
Ross, Frank
   The More the Merrier (see Russel, Robert)
ROSS, George
   Any Other Business, by George Ross and Campbell Singer
   (In Plays of the Year, Vol. 18, 1958)
   Difference of Opinion, by George Ross and Campbell Singer
   (In Plays of the Year, Vol. 27, 1962/63)
   Guilty Party, by George Ross and Campbell Singer
   (In Plays of the Year, Vol. 24, 1961)
   The Sacking of Norman Banks, by George Ross and Campbell
   Singer
   (In Plays of the Year, Vol. 37, 1969/70)
Ross, Jerry (see Rosenberg, Jerold)
ROSS, Kenneth
   Mr. Kilt and the Great I Am

(In Plays and Players, Sept. 1970)
Under the Skin
   (In Plays and Players, Vol. 15, Aug. 1968)
Rossellini, Roberto, 1906-
   Rome, Ville Ouverte (Roma, Citta Aperta)   (see Fellini,
      Federico)
ROSSEN, Robert
   All the King's Men; screenplay
      (In Three Screenplays by Robert Rossen)
   The Hustler; screenplay
      (In Three Screenplays by Robert Rossen)
   Lilith; screenplay
      (In Three Screenplays by Robert Rossen)
ROSSI, Jean-Baptiste, 1931-
   La Machine a Parler d'Amour
      (In L'Avant-Scene du Cinema, no. 66, 1967)
Le Rossignol de l'Empereur de Chine   (see Trinka, Jiri)
ROSTAND, Edmond, 1868-1918
   Cyrano de Bergerac
      (In Chief French Plays of the 19th Century)
      (In 16 Famous European Plays)
 **The Fantasticks   (see Schmidt, Harvey L.)
   The Romantics
      (In Genius of the French Theater)
ROSTEN, Hedda
   Happy House Wife
      (In Best One-Act Plays, 1951/52, N.Y.)
ROSTEN, Norman, 1914-
   The Big Road
      (In Radio's Best Plays, 1947)
   Concerning the Red Army
      (In Best One-Act Plays of 1944, N.Y.)
      (In Radio Drama in Action, 1945)
Roswitha von Gandersheim   (see Hrotsvit, of Gandersheim)
Le Roti de Veau   (see Kerautem, Louis de, by Elka, pseud.)
ROUCH, Jean, 1917-
   La Chasse au Lion a l'Arc
      (In L'Avant-Scene du Cinema, no. 107, Oct. 1970)
   Petit a Petit
      (In L'Avant-Scene du Cinema, no. 123, Mar. 1972)
   Treichville
      (In Cahiers du Cinema, Vol. 14, no. 90, Dec. 1958)
ROUDY, Pierre
   Elle Etait Rousse
      (In L'Avant-Scene du Theatre, no. 491, Mar. 15, 1972)
   Le Numero
      (In L'Avant-Scene du Theatre, no. 412, Oct. 15, 1968)
Rouge Atomique   (see Nash, N. Richard)
ROULLET, Serge, 1926-
   Le Mur, by Serge Roullet et Jean-Paul Sartre
      (In L'Avant-Scene du Cinema, no. 75, 1967)
Round Dance   (see Schnitzler, Arthur)

Roundabout (see Hutton, Michael Clayton)
Roundheads and Peakheads (see Brecht, Bertolt)
ROUSSEL, Raymond
    L'Etoile au Front
        (In L'Avant-Scene du Theatre, no. 476, July 15, 1971)
ROUSSIN, Andre, 1911-
    Un Amour Qui ne Finit Pas
        (In Plaisir de France, supplement theatral, no. 296, June
        1963)
    L'Ecole des Autres
        (In Plaisir de France, supplement theatral, no. 296, June
        1963)
    The Little Hut, adapted by Nancy Mitford
        (In Theatre Arts, Vol. 38, Oct. 1954)
    On ne Sait Jamais
        (In Plaisir de France, supplement theatral, no. 375)
    Le Nuit d'Avril
        (In L'Avant-Scene du Theatre, no. 501, Sept. 1, 1972)
    La Voyante
        (In Plaisir de France, supplement theatral, no. 305, March
        1964)
ROUVEROL, Aurania (Ellerbeck), 1885-
    **Love Finds Andy Hardy (see Ludwig, William)
    The Price of Love
        (In Drama, Vol. 16, Mar. 1926)
The Rovers (see Canning, George)
ROWE, Nicholas, 1674-1718
    The Ambitious Step-Mother
        (In Bell's British Theatre, 1797, Vol. 25)
    The Fair Penitent
        (In Cumberland's British Theatre, Vol. 2, no. 6)
        (In The London Stage, Vol. 2)
        (In Bell's British Theatre, 1797, Vol. 3)
    Jane Shore
        (In Bell's British Theatre, 1797, Vol. 3)
        (In Cumberland's British Theatre, Vol. 4, no. 2)
    Tamerlane
        (In Bell's British Theatre, 1797, Vol. 22)
ROWELL, Adelaide C.
    The High Heart
        (In Drama, Vol. 17, Mar. 1927)
    The Last Frontier
        (In Drama, Vol. 15, Apr. 1925)
    The Silly Ass
        (In Drama, Vol. 12, Sept. 1922)
    Unto the Least of These
        (In Drama, Vol. 18, Nov. 1927)
ROWELL, George
    Sixty Thousand Nights
        (In Plays of the Year, Vol. 31, 1965/66)
ROWLEY, Samuel, d. 1633?
    The Noble Souldier; or, A Contract Broken, Justly Reveng'd

(In A Collection of Old English Plays, Vol. 1)
The Noble Spanish Soldier, by Samuel Rowley and Thomas
Dekker
(In Dramatic Works of Dekker, Vol. 4)
ROWLEY, William, 1585?-1642?
A Match at Mid-Night
(In Dodsley's A Select Collection of Old English Plays, Vol.
13)
(In Dodsley's A Select Collection of Old Plays, Vol. 7)
The Merchant's Wedding (see Planche, James Robinson)
A New Wonder, a Woman Never Vexed
(In Dodsley's A Select Collection of Old English Plays, Vol.
12)
The Witch of Edmonton, by William Rowley, Thomas Dekker,
John Ford
(In Dramatic Works of Dekker, Vol. 3)
A Woman Never Vext; or, The Widow of Cornhill; with alter-
ations and additions by J. R. Planche
(In Cumberland's British Theatre, Vol. 16, no. 2)
Roy, Claude
Un Jour dans la Mort de Joe Egg (see Nichols, Peter)
Miracle in Milan (see DeSica, Vittorio)
Ne m'Oubliez Pas (see Nichols, Peter)
The Royal Convert (see Rome, Nicholas)
Royal Gambit (see Gressieker, Hermann)
ROZEWICY, Tadeusz
He Left Home
(In Tulane Drama Review, Vol. 11, Spring 1967)
Rozier, Jacques, 1926-
Adieu Philippe (see O'Glor, Michele)
Blue Jeans (see O'Glor, Michele)
Rua Sao Luiz, 27-8° (see Almeida, Abilio Pereira de)
RUBENSTEIN, Ken, 1947-
Icarus
(In New American Plays, Vol. 4)
RUBINSTEIN, Harold Frederick, 1891-
All Things Are Possible
(In Best One-Act Plays of 1936, London)
The Deacon and the Jewess
(In Best One-Act Plays of 1935, London)
Moneys from Shylock
(In Best One-Act Plays of 1939, London)
Prelude to Tragedy
(In Best One-Act Plays of 1937, London)
Ruby Red (see Stratton, Clarence)
RUDKIN, David, 1936-
Afore Night Came
(In Evergreen Playscript Series, no. 4)
RÜCKER, Günther
Der Herr Schmidt
(In Theater der Zeit, Vol. 24, no. 2, 1969)
RUEDA, Lope de, d. 1565

Eufemia
  (In Tulane Drama Review, Vol. 3, Dec. 1958)
The Ruffian Boy (see Dibdin, Thomas)
The Ruffian on the Stair (see Orton, Joe)
Rugantino; or, The Bravo of Venice (see Lewis, Matthew Gregory)
RUIBAL, Jose
  The Beggars
    (In Drama & Theatre, Vol. 7, no. 1, Fall 1968)
  The Codfish (El Bacalao)
    (In Modern International Drama, Vol. 5, no. 2, Spring 1972)
  The Jackass (El Asno)
    (In Modern International Drama, Vol. 2, no. 1, Sept. 1968)
  Tails
    (In TDR/Drama Review, Vol. 13, Summer 1969)
RUINET, Gerard
  Le Grand Jeu
    (In L'Avant-Scene, no. 493, Apr. 15, 1972)
RUIZ, Raul
  Changing of the Guard
    (In First Stage, Vol. 5, no. 4, Winter 1966/67)
Ruiz de Alarcon, Juan (see Ruiz de Alarcon y Mendoza, Juan)
Ruiz de Alarcon y Mendoza, Juan, 1581-1639
  The Suspected Truth (La Verdad Sospechosa)
    (In First Stage, Vol. 6, no. 1, Spring 1967)
Rule a Wife and Have a Wife (see Beaumont, Francis)
A Rule Is a Rule (see Courteline, George)
The Rules of the Game (see Pirandello, Luigi)
Rules of the Game (see Renoir, Jean)
The Ruling Class (see Winter, Mary)
The Ruling Passion (see Duhig, D. E.)
Rumpelstilzchen (see Czechowski, Heinz)
Run for Your Life: "The Committee for the 25th" (see Davis,
  Luther)
Running Dogs (see Wexley, John)
Runyon, Damon, 1880-1946
  **Lady for a Day (see Riskin, Robert)
RUSCOLL, Joseph
  The Test
    (In Plays From Radio, 1948)
RUSPOLI, Mario, 1925-
  Les Hommes de la Baleine
    (In L'Avant-Scene du Cinema, no. 24, Mar. 15, 1963)
RUSSEL, Robert
  The More the Merrier, a screenplay by Robert Russel, Frank
    Ross, Richard Flournoy and Lewis Foster, based on a story
    by Robert Russel and Frank Ross, directed by George Stevens
    (In Best Film Plays, 1943/44, Vol. 1)
RUSSELL, Eileen
  The Quick and the Dead
    (In Best One-Act Plays of 1933, London)
RUTH, Leon
  Il n'y a Pas d'Automne sans Ete
    (In L'Avant-Scene du Theatre, no. 144)

RUTHENBURG, G. Hutchinson
    The Children
      (In Drama, Vol. 15, Mar. 1925)
RUTHENBURG, Grace Dorcus
    The Gooseberry Mandarin; a semi-tragedy for puppets
      (In Theatre Arts, Vol. 12, July 1928)
    O Bright Flame Lifted!
      (In New Plays for Women & Girls, 1932)
RUTMAN, Leo
    They Got Jack
      (In Yale/Theatre, Vol. 2, no. 2, Summer 1969)
Ruy Blas (see Hugo, Victor)
Ruzzante Returns from the Wars   (see Beolco, Angelo)
RYAN, Elaine
    Now I Lay Me Down to Sleep, based on the novel by Ludwig
    Bemelmans
      (In Theatre Arts, Vol. 34, July 1950)
RYAN, Richard, 1796-1849
    Everybody's Husband
      (In Cumberland's British Theatre, Vol. 16, no. 5)
    Quiet at Home
      (In Cumberland's British Theatre, Vol. 28, no. 8)
RYERSON, Florence, 1894-
    Farewell to Love, by Florence Ryerson and Colin Clements
      (In Best One-Act Plays of 1938, N.Y.)
    Letters
      (In Drama, Vol. 16, Apr. 1926)
    On the Lot, by Florence Ryerson and Colin Clements
      (In Drama, Vol. 19, Nov. 1928)
    That's Hollywood, by Florence Ryerson and Colin Clements
      (In Best One-Act Plays of 1939, N.Y.)
    The Third Angle
      (In 50 More Contemporary One-Act Plays)
RYSKIND, Morris, 1895 or 1899-
    My Man Godfrey, screenplay by Morris Ryskind and Eric Hatch,
    directed by Gregory La Cava
      (In 20 Best Film Plays)
    A Night at the Opera (see Kaufman, George Simon)

SABATH, Bernard
    A Lady of Eternal Springtime
      (In First Stage, Vol. 2, no. 2, Spring 1963)
Sabrina Fair (see Taylor, Samuel)
Sacco, Nicola, 1891-1927
    *Gods of the Lightning (see Anderson, Maxwell)
    *Sacco and Vanzetti (see Roli, Mino)
    *Winterset (see Anderson, Maxwell)
The Sacking of Norman Banks   (see Ross, George)
Sackville-West, Hon. Victoria Mary, 1892-1962
    **The Edwardians (see Gow, Ronald)
Sackville-West, V. (see Sackville-West, Hon. Victoria Mary)

Sacrifice (see MacQueen, Lawrence)
The Sacrifice of Helen (Das Opfer Helena) (see Hildesheimer,
     Wolfgang)
The Sacrifice of Isaac (see Brome Manuscript)
Sadco (see Pumphrey, Byron)
Sade, Donatein Alphonse Francois, comte, called Marquis de, 1740-
     1814
     *The Persecution and Assassination of Jean-Paul Marat as Per-
     formed by the Inmates of the Asylum of Charenton under the
     Direction of the Marquis de Sade (see Weiss, Peter)
Safecracker's Pride (see Bela, Nicholas)
SAGAN, Francoise
     Le Cheval Evanoui
          (In Plaisir de France, supplement theatral, no. 345, July
          1967)
     La Robe Mauve de Valentine
          (In Plaisir de France, supplement theatral, no. 312, Oct.
          1964)
SAGE, Selwin
     The Fascinating Mr. Denby
          (In Drama, Vol. 14, Feb. 1924)
The Sage and His Father (see Hoffman, M.)
Sahdji, an African Ballet (see Bruce, Richard)
Saidy, Fred, 1907-
     Finian's Rainbow (see Kushner, Morris Hyman)
The Sailor's Wife (see Vicente, Gill)
SAINER, Arthur
     The Thing Itself
          (In Playwrights for Tomorrow, Vol. 6)
"St. Anselm Only Carved One Soul" (see Hickenlooper, Margaret)
St. David's Day; or, The Honest Welshman (see Dibdin, Thomas)
Saint Euloge de Cordoue (see Clavel, Maurice)
Saint Joan (see Shaw, George Bernard)
Saint Joan of the Stockyards (see Brecht, Bertolt)
ST. JOHN, John, 1746-1793
     Mary Queen of Scots
          (In Modern Theatre, 1811, Vol. 10)
ST.-LEGER, De M.
     The Mother and Daughters
          (In Theatrical Recorder, Vol. 2, no. 7, June 1805)
St. Michael Comes to Shepherd's Bush (see Parish, James)
St. Patrick at Tara (see Stephens, H. Morse)
St. Patrick's Day; or, The Scheming Lieutenant (see Sheridan,
     Richard Brinsley)
Saint's Day (see Whiting, John)
Saint-Tropez, Devoir de Vacances (see Paviot, Paul)
Sait-on Jamais! (see Turpin, Francois)
SAKANISHI, Shio
     The Aunt's Sake (Obaga Sake)
          (In The Ink-Smeared Lady & Other Kyogen)
     The Bag of Parting (Itoma-bukuro)
          (In The Ink-Smeared Lady & Other Kyogen)

A Bag of Tangerines (Koj-dawara)
  (In The Ink-Smeared Lady & Other Kyogen)
The Bird-Catcher in Hades
  (In Anthology of Japanese Literature)
  (In The Ink-Smeared Lady & Other Kyogen)
Buaku
  (In The Ink-Smeared Lady & Other Kyogen)
Busu, Literate Highwayman (Fumi Yamadachi)
  (In The Ink-Smeared Lady & Other Kyogen)
  (In Anthology of Japanese Literature)
The Deva King (Niwo)
  (In Anthology of Japanese Literature)
  (In The Ink-Smeared Lady & Other Kyogen)
The Family Quarrel (Mizu-ron Muko)
  (In The Ink-Smeared Lady & Other Kyogen)
The Fox Mound (Kitsune-zuka)
  (In The Ink-Smeared Lady & Other Kyogen)
Gargoyle (Oni-gawara)
  (In The Ink-Smeared Lady & Other Kyogen)
The Ink-Smeared Lady
  (In The Ink-Smeared Lady & Other Kyogen)
The Letter "I" (I-moji)
  (In The Ink-Smeared Lady & Other Kyogen)
The Magic Mallet of the Devil (Onino Tsuchi)
  (In The Ink-Smeared Lady & Other Kyogen)
The Melon Thief (Uri Nusubito)
  (In The Ink-Smeared Lady & Other Kyogen)
Mr. Dumbtaro (Dontaro)
  (In The Ink-Smeared Lady & Other Kyogen)
Plop! Click! (Dobu Kacchiri)
  (In The Ink-Smeared Lady & Other Kyogen)
The Ribs and the Cover (Hone-kawa)
  (In The Ink-Smeared Lady & Other Kyogen)
Seed of Hojo (Hojo no Tane)
  (In The Ink-Smeared Lady & Other Kyogen)
Thunder God (Kaminari)
  (In The Ink-Smeared Lady & Other Kyogen)
An Unfair Exchange (Sarugai Koto)
  (In The Ink-Smeared Lady & Other Kyogen)
The Wounded Highwayman (Teoi Yamadachi)
  (In The Ink-Smeared Lady & Other Kyogen)
Sakazaki, Lord (see Yamamoto Yuzo)
Saki, pseud. (see Munro, Hector Hugh)
Sala su Questo Mare (see Perrini, Alberto)
SALACROU, Armand, 1899-
  Boulevard Durant
    (In Plaisir de France, supplement theatral, no. 279, Jan.
    1962)
  Le Miroir
    (In L'Avant-Scene du Theatre, Nov. 1956)
  Poof
    (In Modern International Drama, Vol. 1, no. 1, Sept. 1967)

Le Salaire de la Peur (see Clouzot, Henri-Georges)
La Salamandre (see Tanner, Alain)
Un Sale Egoiste (see Dorin, Francoise)
Salesman (see Maysles, Albert)
Saliere, Antonio, 1750-1825
    *Mozart and Salieri (see Pushkin, Aleksandr Sergeyevich)
Salome (see Wilde, Oscar)
Salt for Savor (see Wilde, Percival)
SALTEN, Felix, 1869-1945
    Moral Courage
    (In 50 More Contemporary One-Act Plays)
Saltimbank (see Heijermans, Herman)
Salud (see Manzari, Nicola)
Salvage (see Thompson, Doris K.)
Salvation Nell (see Sheldon, Edward)
SALVY, Jean, 1932-
    On a Vole la Mer
    (In L'Avant-Scene du Cinema, no. 29, Sept. 15, 1963)
SALYNSKI, Afanassi
    Maria
    (In Theater der Zeit, no. 12, 1972)
Salzburg Dance of Death (see Brecht, Bertolt)
Sam Average (see Mackaye, Percy)
Sam, Sam (see Griffiths, Trevor)
The Samaritan (see Terson, Peter)
SAMBLE, Hazel V.
    Little Fish
    (In Drama, Vol. 14, Feb. 1924)
The Same Sky (see Mitchell, Yvonne)
Sammy (see Hughes, Ken)
SAMPAIO, Silveria
    Flagrantes do Rio
    (In Revista de Teatro, no. 365, Sept./Oct. 1968)
Samson (see Corwin, Norman)
Samson Agonistes (see Milton, John)
SAMUELS, Gertrude
    The Corrupters
    (In Best Short Plays, 1969)
San Fermin (see Destanque, Robert)
SANCHEZ, Florencio, 1875-1910
    Barranca Abajo
    (In El Teatro Del Uruguayo, Vol. 3)
    (In Teatro de Florencio Sanchez)
    Los Derechos de la Salud
    (In El Teatro Del Uruguayo, Vol. 2)
    (In Teatro de Florencio Sanchez)
    El Desalojo
    (In El Teatro Del Uruguayo, Vol. 3)
    (In Teatro de Florencio Sanchez)
    En Familia
    (In El Teatro Del Uruguayo, Vol. 2)
    (In Teatro de Florencio Sanchez)

The Foreign Girl (La Gringa)
    (In First Stage, Vol. 6, no. 1, Spring 1967)
La Gringa
    (In El Teatro Del Uruguayo, Vol. 3)
    (In Teatro de Florencio Sanchez)
M'Hijo el Dotor
    (In El Teatro Del Uruguayo, Vol. 1)
Moneda Falsa
    (In El Teatro Del Uruguayo, Vol. 1)
    (In Teatro de Florencio Sanchez)
Los Muertos
    (In El Teatro Del Uruguayo, Vol. 1)
Nuestros Hijos
    (In El Teatro Del Uruguayo, Vol. 1)
SANCHEZ, Sonia
    Bronx Is Next
    (In TDR/The Drama Review, Vol. 12, Summer 1968)
    Dirty Hearts
    (In Scripts, Vol. 1, no. 1, Nov. 1971)
SANCHEZ PAREDES, Pedro
    The Castle and the Plain
    (In Drama & Theatre, Vol. 8, no. 3, Spring 1970)
Sancticity (see Head, Robert)
Sand in My Uniform (see Mauroc, Daniel)
Sand in the Mountains (see Taylor, Peter)
The Sandbox (see Albee, Edward)
The Sandbox (see also The Box)
Sandean, Jules, 1811-1833
    Le Gendre de M. Porrier (see Angier, Emile)
The Sandpile: Human Relations, God and Prayer, Death (see
    Gethers, Steven)
SANDRICH, Mark
    Ben Franklin in Paris; play and lyrics by Sidney Michaels;
    music by Mark Sandrich, Jr.
    (A Random House Play, 1965)
Le Sang des Betes (see Franju, Georges)
Santa Claus (see Cummings, Edward Estlin)
O Santo Milagroso (see Muniz, Lauro Cesar)
Santo-Pietro (see Barjol, Jean-Michel)
SANTOS, Justino dos
    Os Raios Y
    (In Revista de Teatro, no. 314)
SANTOS, Miguel
    O Banquete do Prefeito
    (In Revista de Teatro, no. 297)
    Nao Posso Viver Assim
    (In Revista de Teatro, no. 320)
    Uma Visita de Cerimonia
    (In Revista de Teatro, no. 295)
Sapientia (see Hrotsvit, of Gandersheim)
SAPINSLEY, Alvin
    Lee at Gettysburg
    (In Best Television Plays of the Year, 1957)

Sappho (see Grillparzer, Franz)
Sardanapalus: a Tragedy (see Byron, George Gordon Noël Byron, 6th baron)
SARDOU, Victorien, 1831-1889
   Let's Get a Divorce! by Victorien Sardou and Emile de Najac
      (In Plays of the Year, Vol. 31, 1965/66)
SAROYAN, William, 1908-
   Baby
      (In his Three Times Three)
   The Beggars
      (In his Three Times Three)
   The Cave Dwellers
      (In Theatre Arts, Vol. 42, Dec. 1958)
      (In Best American Plays, Fifth series, 1957-63)
   Chris Sick, or Happy New Year Anyway
      (In his Dogs or the Paris Comedy and Two Other Plays)
   Dentist and Patient
      (In Best Short Plays, 1968)
   The Dogs or the Paris Comedy
      (In his Dogs or the Paris Comedy and Two Other Plays)
   Four Plays: "The Playwright and the Public"; "The Hand-
   shakers"; "The Doctor and the Patient"; "This I Believe."
      (In Atlantic, Vol. 211, April 1963)
   Hello Out There
      (In One Act)
      (In Best One-Act Plays of 1941, N.Y.)
      (In 30 Famous One-Act Plays)
   The Hungerers
      (In Best One-Act Plays of 1939, N.Y.)
   Husband and Wife
      (In Best Short Plays, 1968)
   Life and Letters
      (In his Three Times Three)
   The Living and the Dead
      (In his Three Times Three)
   Making Money, and Nineteen Other Short Plays
      (In his Dogs or the Paris Comedy and Two Other Plays)
   The Man with the Heart in the Highlands
      (In his Three Times Three)
      (In Best Short Plays, 1956/57)
      (In The Modern Theatre, ed. by Eric Bentley, Vol. 4)
   The New Play
      (In Best Short Plays, 1970)
   The Ping-Pong Players
      (In Theatre Experiment)
   Public Speech
      (In his Three Times Three)
   Quarter, Half, Three-Quarter, and Whole Notes
      (In his Three Times Three)
   The Question
      (In his Three Times Three)
   The Slaughter of the Innocents

(In Theatre Arts, Vol. 36, Nov. 1952)
Subway Circus
   (In Best One-Act Plays of 1940, N. Y.)
Summertime
   (In his Three Times Three)
The Time of Your Life
   (In Modern Theatre, ed. by R. W. Corrigan)
   (In 16 Famous American Plays)
   (In Best Plays of the Modern American Theatre, Second
     Series)
SARTRE, Jean-Paul, 1905-
Le Mur (see Roullet, Serge)
No Exit
   (In 20 Best European Plays on the American Stage)
The Victors
   (In The Modern Theatre, ed. by R. W. Corrigan)
SASSOON, R. L.
The Crowded Bedroom
   (In Chicago Review, Vol. 16, no. 2, Summer 1963)
Up, by R. L. Sassoon and D. H. Elliott
   (In First Stage, Vol. 2, Fall 1963)
SASTRE, Alfonso, 1926-
Anna Kleiber
   (In New Theatre of Europe, 1962)
   (In Modern Theater, ed. by R. W. Corrigan)
The Condemned Squad
   (In Players Magazine, Vol. 38, no. 2, Nov. 1961)
Pathetic Prologue
   (In Modern International Drama, Vol. 1, no. 2, March
     1968)
Satan Mon Prochain (see Lacassin, Francis)
Satiromastix (see Dekker, Thomas)
Saturations (see Ionesco, Eugene)
Saturday Night Desire (see Candoni, Luigi)
Saturday's Children (see Anderson, Maxwell)
Satyricon (see Fellini's Satyricon)
SAUET, Claude, 1924-
Les Choses de la Vie by Claude Sauet, d'apres le roman de
   Paul Guimard
   (In L'Avant-Scene du Cinema, no. 101, Mar. 1970)
SAUL, Milton
A Girl for Buddy
   (In Drama & Theatre, Vol. 9, Fall 1970)
Saul, Oscar, adapter
A Streetcar Named Desire (see Williams, Tennessee)
SAUNDERS, James
The Italian Girl (see Murdoch, Iris)
Neighbors
   (In Plays and Players, Vol. 14, Sept. 1967)
SAUNDERS, Lilian
The Bee; based on Maeterlinck's "Life of the Bee"
   (In Drama, Vol. 14, Feb. 1924)

Night Brings a Counselor
   (In Drama, Vol. 13, April 1923)
Sob Sister
   (In Drama, Vol. 11, July 1921)
SAUNDERS, Louise
   The Knave of Hearts
      (In Atlantic Book of Modern Plays, 1921)
Sauny the Scot (see Lacy, John)
Le Saut du Lit (see Cooney, Ray)
SAUTET, Claude, 1924-
   Cesar et Rosalie, scenario de Claude Sautet;un film de Claude
   Sautet
      (In L'Avant-Scene du Cinema, no. 131, Dec. 1972)
Ls Sauvage (see Anouilh, Jean)
SAUVAJON, Marc-Gilbert
   Tchao!
      (In Plaisir de France, supplement theatral, no. 372, Nov.
      1969)
SAVARY, Jerome
   Les Derniers jours de Solitude de Robinson Crusoë.
      (In L'Avant-Scene du Theatre, no. 496, June 1, 1972)
   Zartan
      (In TDR/The Drama Review, Vol. 15, Fall 1970)
Saved (see Bond, Edward)
SAVILL, John Faucit
   Wapping Old Stairs
      (In Cumberland's British Theatre, Vol. 31, no. 4)
Savonarole (see Suffran, Michel)
Sawyer, Elizabeth, d. 1621
   *The Witch of Edmonton (see Rowley, William)
Saxon, Lyle, 1891-1946
   **The Buccaneer (see Mayer, Edwin Justus)
Say Nothing (see Hanley, James)
Say, One Evening at Dinner (see Griffi, Guiseppe Patroni)
SAYERS, Dorothy Leigh, 1893-1957
   The Zeal of Thy House
      (In Religious Drama, Vol. 1)
The Scabs (see Rivers, Louis)
The Scamps of London; or, The Cross Roads of Life! (see Mon-
   crieff, William Thomas)
Scandal at Coventry (see Ashton, Winifred)
SCAPARRO, Mario
   Improvised Balloon, a Cinematographic Poem
      (In TDR/The Drama Review, Vol. 15, Fall 1970)
Scapegrace: a Petite Comedy (Anon.)
      (In Cumberland's British Theatre, Vol. 8, no. 7)
Le Scarabee d'Or (see Lachenay, Robert)
The Scarecrow (see Mackay, Percy)
SCARNICCI, Giulio
   Caviar ou Lentilles
      (In Plaisir de France, supplement theatral, no. 327, Jan.
      1966)

SCARPETTA, Eduardo
  Misere et Noblesse
    (In L'Avant-Scene du Theatre, no. 141)
Scenario of the Impostor Prince (see Commedia dell'Arte)
SCHAEFER, Lee
  The Little Flaw of Ernesto Lippi
    (In Best Short Plays, 1953/54)
  Song for a Hero
    (In Best Short Plays, 1954/55)
SCHÄFER, Siegfried
  "Verlieb Dich Nicht in eine Heilige"
    (In Theater der Zeit, Vol. 24, no. 3, 1969)
SCHARY, Dore, 1905-
  Sunrise at Campobello
    (In Theatre Arts, Vol. 43, Nov. 1959)
SCHATROW, Michail
  Bolschewiki
    (In Theater der Zeit, Vol. 24, no. 4, 1969)
SCHAUFFLER, Elsie (Tough), d. 1935
  Parnell
    (In Famous Plays of Today, 1936)
SCHAWINSKY, Xanti
  Play, Life, Illusion, by Xanti Schawinsky with musical scores
  by John Evarts
    (In TDR/The Drama Review, Vol. 15, no. 3a, Summer 1971)
SCHEFFAUER, Herman
  The Sons of Baldur
    (In The Grove Plays of the Bohemian Club, Vol. 1)
SCHEHADE, Georges
  Vasco
    (In New Theatre of Europe, 1962)
  Violets
    (In Modern International Drama, Vol. 3, no. 2, 1969)
SCHEVILL, James Erwin, 1920-
  American Power; two related one-act plays: "The Space Fan"
  and "The Master"
    (In Playwrights for Tomorrow, Vol. 1)
    (In The Black President and Other Plays)
  The Black President
    (In The Black President and Other Plays)
  The Bloody Tenet
    (In Religious Drama, Vol. 1)
    (In The Black President and Other Plays)
  The Master
    (In The Black President and Other Plays)
  The Space Fan
    (In The Black President and Other Plays)
SCHILLER, Johann Christoph Friedrich von, 1759-1805
  Death of Wallenstein
    (In Genius of the German Theater)
    (In Masterworks of World Drama, Vol. 5)
  Don Carlos

(In The Classic Theatre, ed. by Eric Bentley, Vol. 2)
Marie Stuart; text in French
  (In Plaisir de France, supplement theatral, no. 304, Feb.
  1964)
Mary Stuart
  (In The Classic Theatre, Vol. 2)
  (In Plays, ed. by Frances Anne Kemble)
SCHISGAL, Murray, 1929-
  The Basement
    (In Five One-Act Plays)
  Les Chinois
    (In Plaisir de France, supplement theatral, no. 367)
  Les Dactylos
    (In Plaisir de France, supplement theatral, no. 308, June
    1964)
  Fragments
    (In Five One-Act Plays)
  Fragments; text in French
    (In Plaisir de France, supplement theatral, no. 367, May
    1969)
  Love; text in French
    (In Plaisir de France, supplement theatral, no. 338, Dec.
    1966)
  Luv
    (In Plays of Our Time)
    (In Schisgal, Luv and The Typists and The Tiger)
  Memorial Day
    (In Five One-Act Plays)
  The Old Jew
    (In Five One-Act Plays)
  The Tiger
    (In Schisgal, Luv and The Typists and The Tiger)
  Le Tigre; text in French
    (In Plaisir de France, supplement theatral, no. 308, June
    1964)
  The Typists
    (In Schisgal, Luv and The Typists and The Tiger)
    (In Acting Is Believing)
  Windows
    (In Five One-Act Plays)
    (In Show, N.Y., Vol. 5, April 1965)
Schlag Dreizehn (see Baierl, Helmut)
SCHMIDT, Hans-Dieter
  Tinko
    (In Theater der Zeit, no. 7, 1970)
SCHMIDT, Harvey L., 1929-
  The Fantasticks, a musical play by Tom Jones with music by
  Harvey L. Schmidt, suggested by a play called "Les Roman-
  esques" by Edmond Rostand
    (In Best American Plays, Sixth series, 1963-67)
Schmidt, Jan, 1934-
  Josef Kilian un Personnage a Soutenir (Pastava K. Podpirani)
    (see Juracek, Pavel)

SCHNEEMANN, Carolee
    Meat Joy
        (In Theatre Experiment)
SCHNITZLER, Arthur, 1862-1931
    Anatol
        (In 16 Famous European Plays)
    Anatol; with an introductory poem by "Loris," pseud. of Hugo
        von Hofmannsthal
        (In From the Modern Repertoire, Series Three)
    A Farewell Supper
        (In Reading Drama)
    The Green Cockatoo
        (In Thirty Famous One-Act Plays)
    Lebendige Stunden
        (In Das Deutsche Drama, 1880-1933, Vol. 1)
    Light-o'-Love
        (In Drama, Vol. 2, Aug. 1912)
    Literature
        (In 50 Contemporary One-Act Plays)
    Professor Bernkardi
        (In Famous Plays of Today, 1936)
    La Ronde
        (In The Modern Theatre, ed. by Eric Bentley, Vol. 2)
        (In The Modern Theatre, ed. by R. W. Corrigan)
  **La Ronde; screenplay (see Natanson, Jacques)
    Round Dance
        (In From the Modern Repertoire, Series One)
Schnitzleresque (see Palm, Carla L.)
SCHOCHEN, Seyril
    One-Car Wedding
        (In Best One-Act Plays of 1939, N. Y.)
SCHOENFELD, Bernard
    Little Johnny Appleseed
        (In Plays From Radio, 1948)
SCHOFIELD, Paul
    Wells Fargo; screenplay by Paul Schofield, Gerald Geraghty
        and Frederick Jackson, based on a story by Stuart N. Lake,
        directed by Frank Lloyd
        (In Foremost Films of 1938)
SCHOFIELD, Stephen
    The Chartist
        (In Best One-Act Plays of 1936, London)
SCHOLL, Ralph
    A Fable
        (In First Stage, Vol. 6, Fall 1967)
    The Golden Axe
        (In Best Short Plays, 1958/59)
The School for Arrogance (see Holcroft, Thomas)
The School for Fathers; or, Lionel and Clarissa (see Bickerstaff,
    Isaac)
The School for Guardians (see Murphy, Arthur)
School for Husbands (see Moliere, Jean Baptiste Poquelin)

The School for Prejudice (see Dibdin, Thomas Frognall)
The School for Rakes (see Griffith, Elizabeth Griffith)
The School for Scandal (see Sheridan, Richard Brinsley)
The School for Wives (Anon.)
    (In Modern Theatre, 1811, Vol. 9)
School for Wives (see Moliere, Jean Baptiste Poquelin)
School for Wives Criticized (see Moliere, Jean Baptiste Poquelin)
The School of Reform; or, How to Rule a Husband (see Morton,
    Thomas)
The Schoolhouse Is Burning (see Jones, Pamela)
Le Schpountz (see Pagnol, Marcel)
SCHREIBER, Isabelle Georges
    Lune ou l'Autre
        (In Plaisir de France, supplement theatral, no. 292, Feb.
        1963)
SCHREITER, Helfried
    "Ich Spiele dir die Welt durch"
        (In Theater der Zeit, no. 7, 1971)
Schubert, Franz Peter, 1797-1828
    *Schubert's Last Serenade (see Bovasso, Julie)
SCHULBERG, Budd, 1914-
    The Disenchanted, by Budd Schulberg and Harvey Breit, based
    on the novel of the same name by Budd Schulberg
        (In Theatre Arts, Vol. 44, Aug. 1960)
        (A Random House Play, 1959)
    A Face in the Crowd; a play for the screen based on "Your
    Arkansas Traveler" from the author's short story "Some
    Faces in the Crowd"
        (A Random House Play, 1957)
    Un Homme dans la Foule, by Budd Schulberg, d'apres la
    nouvelle "Your Arkansas Traveller" titre de son livre "Some
    Faces in the Crowd"
        (In L'Avant-Scene du Cinema, no. 40, 1964)
    The Pharmacist's Mate
        (In Best Television Plays of the Year, 1950/51)
SCHWAEN Kurt
    "Pinocchios Abenteuer"
        (In Theater der Zeit, no. 1, 1971)
SCHWARTZ, Delmore
    Shenandoah, or, The Naming of a Child
        (In Kenyon Review, Vol. 3, no. 3, Summer 1941)
SCHWARTZ, Esther Dresden
    Three Souls in Search of a Dramatist
        (In Drama, Vol. 16, Apr. 1926)
Schwartz, Jerome Lawrence (see Lawrence, Jerome)
Scipio Aemilianus, Publis Cornelius Africanus Minor, 185-129 B. C.
    *Hannibal and Scipio: an Historical Tragedy (see Nabbes,
    Thomas)
Scobie Betters Himself (see Simpson, Cormac)
SCOFF, Alain
    Jesus-Fric Supercrack; imagine et realise par Alain Scoff;
    musique de Alain Bert
        (In L'Avant-Scene du Theatre, no. 505, Nov. 1, 1972)

Scopes, John Thomas, 1901-
  *Inherit the Wind (see Lawrence, Jerome)
SCOTT, Margaretta
  The Bag o' Dreams
    (In Drama, Vol. 11, Jan. 1921)
  The Heart of Pierrot
    (In Drama, Vol. 10, Feb. 1920)
  Three Kisses
    (In Drama, Vol. 10, Oct. 1919)
  The Tragedy
    (In Poet Lore, Vol. 53, Autumn 1947)
SCOTT, Natalie Vivian
  Zombi
    (In Theatre Arts, Vol. 13, 1929)
Scott, Robert Falcon, 1868-1912
  *Scott of the Antarctic (see Meade, Walter)
SCOTT, Sir Walter, 1771-1832
  The Antiquary; anonymous play based on the work of Sir Walter
    Scott
    (In Cumberland's British Theatre, Vol., no. 8)
  **Ivanhoe; or, The Jew's Daughter (see Dibdin, Thomas Frognall)
  **Kenilworth (see Dibdin, Thomas Frognall)
  The Knights of the Cross; or, The Hermit's Prophecy; anony-
    mously adapted from the work of Sir Walter Scott
    (In Cumberland's British Theatre, Vol. 46, no. 2)
  **The Lady of the Lake (see Dibdin, Thomas Frognall)
  **Peveril of the Peak; or, The Days of King Charles II (see
    Fitz-Ball, Edward)
  **Rob Roy (see Soane, George)
Scott of the Antarctic (see Meade, Walter)
SCRAPETTA, Eduardo
  Misere et Noblesse
    (In L'Avant-Scene du Theatre, no. 141)
Scratch (see MacLeish, Archibald)
The Screens (see Genet, Jean)
Scribe, Augustin Eugene, 1791-1861
  **Love in Humble Life (see Payne, John Howard)
Scriblerus Secundus, pseud. (see Fielding, Henry)
The Scuffletown Outlaws, a Tragedy of the Lowrie Gang (see Cox,
    William Norment)
Sea Battle at Night (see China, People's Republic; cultural en-
    semble of the Political Department of the Navy)
The Sea Gull (see Chekhov, Anton Pavlovich)
SEAMI Motokiyo
  Birds of Sorrow
    (In Anthology of Japanese Literature)
  Nishikigi
    (In Drama Survey, Vol. 4, Summer 1965)
Sears, Ted
  Snow White and the Seven Dwarfs (see Disney, Walt)
Sea-Shell (see Chown, Patricia)
Season in the Sun (see Gibbs, Wolcott)

Seaton, George, 1911-
    A Day at the Races (see Pirosh, Robert)
Second Door Left (see Popovic, Aleksandar)
The Second Maiden's Tragedy (Anon.)
    (In Dodsley's A Select Collection of Old English Plays, Vol.
    10)
The Second Man (see Behrman, Samuel Nathaniel)
The Second Mrs. Tanqueray (see Pinero, Sir Arthur Wing)
Second Overture (see Anderson, Maxwell)
The Second Shepherd's Play (see Wakefield Master)
The Second Shepherd's Play (see Wakefield Mystery Cycle)
The Second-Story Man (see Sinclair, Upton)
Second Threshold (see Barry, Philip)
The Second Trial before Pilate: the Scourging and Condemnation
    (see York Tilemakers' Play)
The Second Visit (see Bourne, John)
The Secret (see Sender, Ramon)
Secret People (see Dickinson, Thorold)
Secret Service (see Gillette, William)
The Secretary Bird (see Home, William Douglas)
Secretissimo (see Camoletti, Marc)
Secrets of the Citizens Correction Committee (see Tavel, Ronald)
Secrets Worth Knowing (see Morton, Thomas)
Security (see Pieterson, Freda)
Le Seducteur (see Fabbri, Diego)
Seduction (see Holcroft, Thomas)
See Naples and Die (see Rice, Elmer L.)
See Other Side (see Patrick, Robert)
See the Jaguar (see Nash, N. Richard)
Seed of Adam (see Williams, Charles)
Seed of Hojo (Hojo no Tane) (see Sakanishi, Shio)
SEGAL, Erich
    R. P. M.
    (In Yale Literature Magazine, Vol. 140, no. 1, 1970)
Segall, Harry, 1897-
    **Here Comes Mr. Jordan (see Buchman, Sidney)
SEIGER, Marvin L.
    Blue Concerto
    (In Best Short Plays, 1955/56)
SEILER, Conrad
    Good Night, Caroline
    (In Best One-Act Plays of 1938, N.Y.)
    Nude Washing Dishes
    (In Best Short Plays, 1959/60)
    Why I Am a Bachelor
    (In One-Act Play Magazine, 1937/38 Anthology)
Seitz, George B., 1888-1944
    Love Finds Andy Hardy (see Ludwig, William)
    Yellow Jack (see Chocorov, Edward)
Sekala Ka'ajma (see Austin, Mary)
Sekhet: A Dream (see Galsworthy, John)
Le Sel de la Terre (see Biberman, Herbert J.)

Der Selbstmorder (see Erdman, Nikolai)
Self-Accusation (see Handke, Peter)
Self-Made Man (see Box, Sydney)
The Self-Tormenter (see Terence, Publius Terentius Afer)
SELLERS, Irma Peixetto
    The Adored One
        (In Drama, Vol. 14, May/June 1924)
Semira: A Tragedy (see Sumarokov, Aleksandr Petrovich)
SEMPRUN, Jorge
    La Guerre Est Finie; script from the film by Alain Resnais
        (In Evergreen Filmscript Series)
"Send Me In, Coach" (see Fitzgerald, Francis Scott Key)
Send Me No Flowers (see Barasch, Norman)
SENDER, Ramon
    The Key
        (In Kenyon Review, Vol. 5, no. 2, Spring 1943)
    The Secret
        (In One-Act Play Magazine, 1937/38 Anthology)
SENECA, Lucius Annaeus, c. 4 B. C. -65 A. D. (Seneca the Younger)
    Agamemnon
        (In The Complete Roman Drama, Vol. 2)
    Death of Seneca (see Hine, Daryl)
    Hercules on Oeta
        (In The Complete Roman Drama, Vol. 2)
    Mad Hercules
        (In The Complete Roman Drama, Vol. 2)
    Medea
        (In The Complete Roman Drama, Vol. 2)
        (In Masterworks of World Drama, Vol. 2)
    Medea, adapted by Richard Glover
        (In Bell's British Theatre, Vol. 6)
    Octavia
        (In The Complete Roman Drama, Vol. 2)
    Oedipus
        (In The Complete Roman Drama, Vol. 2)
    Phaedra
        (In The Complete Roman Drama, Vol. 2)
    The Phoenician Women
        (In The Complete Roman Drama, Vol. 2)
  *The Stoic's Daughter (see Baring, Maurice)
    Thyestes
        (In The Complete Roman Drama, Vol. 2)
    Thyestes 885-1112, translated by D. Parker and D. Armstrong
        (In Arion, Vol. 7, Spring 1968)
    The Trojan Women
        (In The Complete Roman Drama, Vol. 2)
SENGISSEN, Paule, 1930-
    Les Yeux de l'Ete
        (In L'Avant-Scene du Cinema, no. 109, Dec. 1970)
SENIOR, Edward
    The Hunted
        (In Best Short Plays, 1958/59)

A Sense of Justice (see Vidal, Gore)
Senso (see Visconti, Luchino)
The Sentimentalists; an Unfinished Comedy (see Meredith, George)
Sepang Loca (see Lapena, Amelia L.)
Separate Tables (see Rattigan, Terence)
Les Sept Samourais (see Kurosawa, Akira)
The Serenade (see Vicente, Gill)
The Serf (see Talbot, R.)
Serious Charge (see King, Philip)
Serjeant Musgrave's Dance (see Arden, John)
SERLING, Rod, 1924-
    Color Scheme
        (In The Season To Be Wary)
    The Escape Route
        (In The Season To Be Wary)
    Eyes
        (In The Season To Be Wary)
    Noon on Doomsday
        (In Television Plays for Writers, 1957)
    Old MacDonald Had a Curve
        (In Patterns: 4 Television Plays)
    Patterns
        (In Patterns: 4 Television Plays)
    Requiem for a Heavy Weight
        (In Patterns: 4 Television Plays)
        (In Teaching Literature to Adolescents)
        (In Best Television Plays of the Year, 1957)
    The Rock
        (In Patterns: 4 Television Plays)
    The Strike
        (In Best Television Plays)
    The Twilight Zone: the Lonely; a television filmscript
        (In Writing for Television)
Les Serments Indiscrets (see Marivaux, Pierre Carlet de Chamblain de)
SERRANO, Nina
    The Chicken Made of Rags, a film for children by Nina Serrano and Judith Binder
        (In Scripts, Vol. 1, no. 10, Oct. 1972)
The Servant (see Pinter, Harold)
The Servant of Two Masters (see Goldoni, Carlo)
Service (see Smith, Dorothy Gladys)
The Service for Joseph Axminster (see Dennison, George)
The Set Up (see Weiger, Eugene)
SETTIMELLI, Emilio
    Grey Red Violet Orange, a Net of Sensations, by Emilio Settimelli and Bruno Corra
        (In TDR/The Drama Review, Vol. 15, Fall 1970)
    Negative Act (see Corra, Bruno)
Le Seuil du Jardin (see Suffran, Michel)
The Seven Against Thebes (see Aeschylus)
7 1/2 cents (see The Pajama Game)

The Seven Deadly Sins of the Lower Middle Class (see Brecht,
    Bertolt)
Seven Keys to Baldpate (see Cohan, George Michael)
The Seven Samurai (see Kurosawa, Akira)
The Seven Year Itch (see Axelrod, George)
The Seventh Seal (see Bergman, Ingmar)
SEYMOUR, Alan
    L'Unique Jour de l'Annee
        (In Plaisir de France, supplement theatral, no. 335, Sept.
        1966)
Seymour, Jane, 2nd wife of Henry VIII, king of England, 1509?-1536
    *Jane Seymour (see Thorne, Ian)
Sganarelle (see Moliere, Jean Baptiste Poquelin)
SHABER, David
    The Youngest Shall Ask
        (In Best One-Act Plays, 1952/53, N.Y.)
Shachiapang (see China Peking Opera Troupe)
The Shadow! A Mother's Dream (see Almar, George)
Shadow and Substance (see Carroll, Paul Vincent)
Shadow in the Sun (see Mitchell, Julian)
Shadow of the Cathedral (see Kocher, Eric)
Shadow Play (see Coward, Noel Pierce)
The Shadowed Star (see MacMillan, Mary Louise)
Shadows of the Evening (see Coward, Noel Pierce)
SHADWELL, Charles
    The Fair Quaker of Deal; or, The Humours of the Navy
        (In Bell's British Theatre, 1797, Vol. 14)
SHAFFER, Peter, 1926-
    Black Comedy
        (In Plays and Players, Vol. 15, Apr. 1968)
        (In Modern Short Comedies from Broadway & London)
    Five Finger Exercise
        (In Theatre Arts, Vol. 45, no. 2, Feb. 1961)
    The White Liars
        (In Plays and Players, Vol. 15, Apr. 1968)
        (In Best Short Plays of the World Theatre, 1958/67)
Shahuntala and the Ring of Recognition (see Kalidasa)
SHAIRP, Mordaunt, 1887-
    The Green Bay Tree
        (In 16 Famous British Plays)
SHAKESPEARE, William, 1564-1616
    **Easy Money (see Ostrovskii, Alexandr Nikolaevich)
    **Falstaff's Wedding (see Kenrick, William)
    **Gruach (see Bottomley, Gordon)
    **Hamlet: a Tragedy (see Sumarokov, Aleksandr Petrovich)
    **Henry V; screenplay (see Olivier, Sir Laurence)
    Jules Cesar; text in French
        (In L'Avant-Scene du Theatre, no. 323, Dec. 1, 1964)
        (In Plaisir de France, supplement theatral, no. 314, Dec.
        1964)
    **King Charles I (see Havard, William)
    Macbeth

(In Genius of the Early English Theater)
Macbeth; text in German
    (In Theater der Zeit, no. 4, 1972)
**Macbeth: Murder at the Gate-Keeper's House; Estranging
    Shakespeare (see Brecht, Bertolt)
**Macbeth; nach Shakespeare (see Müller, Heiner)
**Macbett; text in French (see Ionesco, Eugene)
**Macbett; text in German (see Ionesco, Eugene)
The Merchant of Venice; text in French
    (In L'Avant-Scene du Theatre, no. 253, Nov. 15, 1961)
**Moneys from Shylock (see Rubinstein, Harold Frederick)
**O Novo Otelo (see Macedo, Joaquim Manoel de)
Othello, the Moor of Venice
    (In Tragedy: Texts and Commentary, 1969)
Pericles, Prince of Tyre
    (In Bell's British Theatre, 1797, Vol. 29)
*The Rehearsal (see Baring, Maurice)
Richard III; text in French
    (In L'Avant-Scene du Theatre, no. 502, Sept. 15, 1972)
**Romao e Julinha (see Von Pfuhl, Oscar)
**Romeo and Juliet (see Cocteau, Jean)
**Romeo and Juliet: The Servants; Estranging Shakespeare (see
    Brecht, Bertolt)
**Rosencrantz and Guildenstern Are Dead (see Stoppard, Tom)
*Shakespeare's Early Days (see Somerset, Charles A.)
*Shakespeare's Funeral (Anon.)
    (In Living Age, Vol. 117, May 1873)
*The Truth About Shakespeare (see Box, Sydney)
Twelfth Night; text in French
    (In L'Avant Scene du Theatre, no. 243, May 15, 1961)
Shakespeare the Sadist (see Film und Frau)
Sham (see Tompkins, Frank G.)
Shame (see Bergman, Ingmar)
SHANE, Maxwell
    We Refuse to Die
        (In Best One-Act Plays of 1942, N. Y.)
Shanghai (see Stuckes, W.)
Shanghai Express (see Von Sternberg, Josef)
SHANNON, Charles
    The Youthful Queen
        (In Cumberland's British Theatre, Vol. 7, no. 7)
Shapiro, Norman R.
    Going to Pot (see Feydeau, Georges)
SHAPIRO, Steve
    Patrol
        (In Writing for Television)
SHARP, H. Sutton
    Germs
        (In Drama, Vol. 16, Feb. 1926)
Shattered (see Bordeaux, Henri)
SHAW, Frances
    The Person in the Chair
        (In Drama, Vol. 11, Feb. 1921)

SHAW, George Bernard, 1856-1950
  Caesar and Cleopatra
    (In Theatre Arts, Vol. 34, Sept. 1950)
  Don Juan in Hell
    (In Theatre Arts, Vol. 36, Apr. 1952)
  Getting Married
    (In Makers of the Modern Theater, 1961)
  Great Catherine
    (In Everybody's Magazine, Vol. 32, Feb. 1915)
  John Bull's Other Island
    (In Genius of the Irish Theater)
  Major Barbara
    (In The Modern Theatre, ed. by R. W. Corrigan)
  Major Barbara; text in French
    (In L'Avant-Scene du Theatre, no. 450, June 1, 1970)
    (In Plaisir de France, supplement theatral, no. 380, July
      1970)
  Misalliance
    (In Theatre Arts, Vol. 37, Sept. 1953)
  Un Petit Drame; text in French and English
    (In Esquire, Vol. 52, Dec. 1959)
  Saint Joan
    (In Theatre Guild Anthology)
  Why She Would Not: a Little Comedy
    (In Theatre Arts, Vol. 40, Aug. 1956)
SHAW, Irwin, 1913-
  Bury the Dead
    (In Famous Plays of Today, 1936)
    (In 30 Famous One-Act Plays)
    (In Best Short Plays of the Social Theatre, 1939)
    (In 20 Best Plays of the Modern American Theatre, Vol. 1)
SHAW, Robert
  Cato Street
    (In Plays and Players, Vol. 19, no. 3, Dec. 1971)
  The Man in the Glass Booth
    (In Plays of the Year, Vol. 34, 1967/68)
    (In Plays and Players, Vol. 15, Nov. 1967)
SHAW, Robert J.
  Love of Life; Episode no. 4,620 Television Filmscript
    (In Writing for Television)
She Stoops to Conquer (see Goldsmith, Oliver)
She Who Was Shorn (Perikeiromene) (see Menander)
Sheffield, John, pseud. (see Hoffman, Leo Calvin)
SHELDON, Edward, 1886-1946
  Salvation Nell
    (In Best Plays of the Early American Theatre, from the
      beginning to 1916)
SHELLEY, Percy Bysshe, 1792-1822
  The Cenci
    (In Complete Works)
    (In Masterworks of World Drama, Vol. 6)
  The Cenci; adapted with settings by Robert Edmond Jones

(In Theatre Arts, Vol. 8, June 1924)
Charles the First
    (In Complete Works)
Hellas
    (In Complete Works)
Oedipus Tyrannus; or, Swellfoot the Tyrant
    (In Complete Works)
Prometheus Unbound
    (In Complete Works)
Shelter Area (Boretz, Nick)
SHEN, Hung
    The Cow-herd and the Weaving Maid
        (In Drama, Vol. 11, Aug. /Sept. 1921)
    The Wedded Husband
        (In Poet Lore, Vol. 32, no. 1, 1921)
Shenandoah (see Bronson, Howard)
Shenandoah, or, The Naming of a Child (see Schwartz, Delmore)
SHEPARD, Sam, 1943-
    Chicago
        (In Eight Plays From Off Off Broadway)
    Forensic and the Navigators
        (In The Best of Off Off Broadway)
    Operation Sidewinder
        (In Esquire, Vol. 71, May 1969)
    The Rock Garden
        (In Scripts, Vol. 1, no. 3, Jan. 1972)
SHEPHERD, Martin
    Ali the Cobbler
        (In Best One-Act Plays of 1932, London)
The Shepherd in the Distance (see Hudson, Holland)
The Shepherd of Derwent Wale (see Lunn, Joseph)
The Shepherd's Holy-Day (Anon.)
        (In Dodsley's A Select Collection of Old English Plays, Vol.
        12)
SHERIDAN, Emma
    The Wind and Lady Moon
        (In Drama, Vol. 12, June /Aug. 1922)
SHERIDAN, Mrs. Frances (Chamberlaine), 1724-1766
    The Discovery
        (In Bell's British Theatre, 1797, Vol. 5)
SHERIDAN, Richard Brinsley, 1751-1816
    The Critic; or, A Tragedy Rehearsed
        (In Cumberland's British Theatre, Vol. 24, no. 1)
        (In The London Stage, Vol. 1)
    The Duenna
        (In Cumberland's British Theatre, Vol. 27, no. 6)
    Pizarro
        (In Cumberland's British Theatre, Vol. 2, no. 4)
    The Rivals
        (In Cumberland's British Theatre, Vol. 14, no. 6)
        (In The London Stage, Vol. 1)
        (In Masterworks of World Drama, Vol. 5)

St. Patrick's Day; or, The Scheming Lieutenant
    (In Cumberland's British Theatre, Vol. 27, no. 9)
The School for Scandal
    (In Cumberland's British Theatre, Vol. 5, no. 3)
    (In Great English Plays)
    (In Introduction to Literature: Plays)
A Trip to Scarborough
    (In Cumberland's British Theatre, Vol. 26, no. 5)
    (In Modern Theatre, 1811, Vol. 7)
    (In The London Stage, Vol. 2)
Sherlock Holmes (see Gillette, William Hooker)
SHERMAN, Martin, 1940-
    Things Went Badly in Westphalia
    (In Best Short Plays, 1970)
SHERRIFF, Robert Cedric, 1896-
    Goodbye, Mr. Chips; screenplay by R. C. Sherriff, Claudine
    West and Eric Maschwitz, from the book by James Hilton,
    directed by Sam Wood
    (In Best Pictures, 1939/40)
    Journey's End
    (In Famous Plays of Today, 1929)
    (In Modern Plays, London, 1937)
    (In 16 Famous British Plays)
    Quartet; four screenplays by R. C. Sherriff, based on short
    stories by Somerset Maugham
    (In Quartet, Doubleday, 1949)
    Trio; three screenplays by W. Somerset Maugham, R. C.
    Sherriff, and Noel Langley, based on short stories by W.
    Somerset Maugham
    (In Trio, Doubleday, 1950)
SHERWIN, David
    If; a filmscript (see Anderson, Lindsay)
    If... de Lindsay Anderson et David Sherwin
    (In L'Avant-Scene du Cinema, no. 119, Nov. 1971)
SHERWOOD, Robert Emmet, 1896-1955
    Abe Lincoln in Illinois
    (In Pulitzer Prize Plays)
    (In Nine Modern American Plays)
    (In Best Plays of the Modern American Theatre, Second
    Series)
    The Adventures of Marco Polo, a screenplay by Robert E.
    Sherwood, based on a story by N. A. Pogson, directed by
    Archie Mayo
    (In How to Write and Sell Film Stories, by Frances Marion,
    1937)
    Idiot's Delight
    (In 20 Best Plays of the Modern American Theatre, Vol. 1)
    (In Pulitzer Prize Plays)
    The Petrified Forest
    (In American Drama)
    (In 16 Famous American Plays)

Rebecca; screenplay by Robert E. Sherwood and Joan Harrison;
adaptation by Philip MacDonald and Michael Hogan; from the
novel by Daphne du Maurier. Directed by Alfred Hitchcock.
(In 20 Best Film Plays)
(In Best Pictures, 1939/40)
Reunion in Vienna
(In Famous Plays of Today, 1933/34)
(In Theatre Guild Anthology)
The Road to Rome
(In 25 Best Plays of the Modern American Theatre, Early
Series, 1916-1929)
Small War on Murray Hill
(In Theatre Arts, Vol. 42, Aug. 1968)
The Shield (Aspis) (see Menander)
(In The Plays of Menander)
SHIELS, J. Wilson
Nec-Natama
(In The Grove Plays of the Bohemian Club, Vol. 3)
SHINE, Ted
Contribution
(In Best Short Plays, 1972)
Morning, Noon, and Night
(In The Black Teacher and the Dramatic Arts)
Ship Ahoy! (see O'Keeffe, A. A.)
Ships on the Sand (see Myall, Charles A.)
SHIRLEY, Henry, d. 1627
The Martyr'd Souldier
(In A Collection of Old English Plays, Vol. 1)
SHIRLEY, James, 1596-1666
The Lady of Pleasure
(In The City and the Court)
SHIRLEY, William, fl. 1739-1780
Edward the Black Prince; or, The Battle of Poictiers
(In Bell's British Theatre, 1797, Vol. 9)
The Gamesters, by William Shirley and Charles Johnson, altered
by David Garrick
(In Bell's British Theatre, 1797, Vol. 6)
Shivaree (see Odea, Mark Leland)
Shock Corridor (see Fuller, Samuel, 1911-
(In L'Avant-Scene du Cinema, no. 54, 1965)
The Shock of Recognition (see Anderson, Robert)
The Shock of Recognition (see also You Know I Can't Hear You
When the Water's Running)
The Shoemaker and the Devil (see Ginsbury, Norman)
The Shoemaker's Holiday (see Dekker, Thomas)
SHORE, Joseph, 1913-
A Bed with the Others (see Williamson, Scott Graham)
The Soldier Who Became a Great Dane, by Joseph Shore and
Richard Lincoln
(In Best One-Act Plays of 1945/47, N.Y.)
(In Best Short Plays, 1956/57)
Who Are the Weavers, by Joseph Shore and Scott Graham

Williamson
(In Best One-Act Plays of 1947/48, N. Y.)
Shore Acres (see Herne, James A.)
SHORT, Marion
Lady Luck
(In New Plays for Women & Girls, 1932)
The Night Club Girl (see Phelps, Pauline)
A Shotgun Splicin' (see Coffin, Gertrude Wilson)
SHOUB, Mac
Thank you, Edmondo
(In Best Television Plays of the Year, 1957)
SHUDRAKA, King (Indian), c. 4th century
The Toy Cart (Mrichchakatika) adapted from Bhasa's "Daridra-
Charudatta" (Poor Charudatta)
(In Traditional Asian Plays)
SHULMAN, Max, 1919-
The Tender Trap, by Max Shulman and Robert Paul Smith
(In Theatre Arts, Vol. 40, Feb. 1956)
Shumlin, Herman, 1898-
Watch on the Rhine (see Hammett, Dashiell)
Shyre, Paul
U. S. A. (see Dos Passos, John)
Si Camille Me Voyait (see Dubillard, Roland)
La Sibilla (see Grazzini, Antonio Francesco, called Il Lasca)
Sicilian Limes (see Pirandello, Luigi)
SIDDONS, Henry, 1774-1815
Time's a Tell-Tale
(In Modern Theatre, 1811, Vol. 10)
Siegfried (see Giraudoux, Jean)
The Siege of Belgrade (see Cobb, James)
The Siege of Numanta (see Cervantes Saavedra, Miguel de)
Sierra, Gregorio Martinez (see Martinez Sierra, Gregorio)
SIFTON, Claire
Give All Thy Terrors to the Wind, by Claire and Paul Sifton
(In Best Short Plays of the Social Theatre, 1939)
A Sight for Sore Thoughts (see Stein, Howard)
A Sign in Sidney Brustein's Window (see Hansberry, Lorraine)
The Signal Man (see Dickens, Charles)
SIGURJONSSON, Johann, 1880-1919
The Hraun Farm
(In Short Plays by Representative Authors, 1920)
The Silence (see Bergman, Ingmar)
La Silence; text in French (see Bergman, Ingmar)
Le Silence Est d'Or (see Clair, Rene)
Silent Night, Lonely Night (see Anderson, Robert)
A Silent Protector (see Williams, Thomas J.)
The Silent Woman (see Jonson, Ben)
SILK, Dennis
Lives of the Magicians
(In Encounter, Vol. 30, Jan. 1968)
The Silly Ass (see Rowell, Adelaide C.)
SILVA, Eurico

Divorciados
    (In Revista de Teatro, no. 364, July/Aug. 1968)
Grande Marido
    (In Revista de Teatro, no. 351)
Pense Alto!...
    (In Revista de Teatro, no. 386, Apr. 1972)
SILVAIN, Jean
    Comme les Chats, by Jean Silvain and Daniel Gallo
        (In L'Avant Scene du Theatre, no. 447, Apr. 15, 1970)
        (In Plaisir de France, supplement theatral, no. 378)
    De l'Eau sous les Ponts
        (In Plaisir de France, supplement theatral, no. 326, Dec.
        1965)
SILVEIRA, Miroel
    A Moreninha, a musical comedy by Miroel Silveira and Claudio
    Petraglia
        (In Revista de Teatro, no. 369, May/June 1969)
The Silver Cord (see Howard, Sidney Coe)
Silver Key (see Hayes, Joseph)
The Silver Lining (see Mackay, Constance D'Arcy)
Silver Nails (see Bela, Nicholas)
The Silver Palace (see Almar, George)
The Silver Whistle (see McEnroe, Robert Edward)
SILVINO, Paulo
    Anjinho Bossa Nova
        (In Revista de Teatro, no. 343)
SIMMONS, Richard Alan
    The Price of Tomatoes
        (In Writing for Television)
Simon (see Strindberg, August)
Simon and Laura (see Melville, Alan)
Simon du Desert (see Buñuel, Luis)
Simon of the Desert (see Buñuel, Luis)
SIMON, Neil, 1927-
    Barefoot in the Park
        (In The Comedy of Neil Simon)
    Come Blow Your Horn
        (In The Comedy of Neil Simon)
    Drole de Couple
        (In Plaisir de France, supplement theatral, no. 356, Aug.
        1967)
    Last of the Red Hot Lovers
        (In The Comedy of Neil Simon)
    The Odd Couple
        (In The Comedy of Neil Simon)
        (In Best American Plays, Sixth Series, 1963-67)
    Plaza Suite
        (In The Comedy of Neil Simon)
    Promises, Promises
        (In The Comedy of Neil Simon)
    The Star-Spangled Girl
        (In The Comedy of Neil Simon)

Singer, Campbell
   Any Other Business (see Ross, George)
   Difference of Opinion (see Ross, George)
   Guilty Party (see Ross, George)
   The Sacking of Norman Banks (see Ross, George)
Singin' in the Rain (see Comden, Betty)
The Singing Girl of Copan (see Alexander, Hartley Burr)
Singing Piedmont (see Buttutta, Anthony)
Sink or Swim; or, Harry Raymond's Resolve (see O'Malley, Neill)
SION, Georges
   Matron of Ephesus, based on the story of Petronius "The
     Widow of Ephesus"
     (In Best One-Act Plays, 1950/51, N.Y.)
Sir Gyles Goosecappe (Anon.)
     (In A Collection of Old English Plays, Vol. 3)
Sir Harry Wildair, being the sequel of, The Trip to the Jubilee
   (see Farquhar, George)
Sir Hercules Buffoon (see Lacy, John)
Sir Thomas Wyatt
   Sir Thomas Wyatt (see Dekker, Thomas)
SISSON, Rosemary Anne, 1923–
   Catherine of Aragon; a television script in the series "The Six
     Wives of Henry VIII"
     (In Plays of the Year Special, 1972)
SISSON, Rosemary Anne
   The Marriage Game
     (In Plays of the Year Special, 1972)
   The Queen and the Welshman
     (In Plays of the Year, Vol. 18, 1958)
   The Splendid Outcasts
     (In Plays of the Year, Vol. 19, 1958/59)
Sister Beatrice (see Maeterlinck, Maurice)
Six Characters in Search of an Author (see Pirandello, Luigi)
Six Who Pass While the Lentils Boil (see Walker, Stuart)
The Sixes; or, The Devil's in the Dice (see Dibdin, Thomas)
Sixteen (see Stuart, Aimee McHardy)
Sixty Thousand Nights (see Rowell, George)
The Six-Year-Old Man (see Elkin, Stanley)
SJÖMAN, Vilgot
   I Am Curious (Blue), complete scenario of the film
     (Evergreen Black Cat Series, 1970)
   I Am Curious (Yellow), complete scenario of the film
     (Evergreen Black Cat Series, 1968)
Skeletons (see Bela, Nicholas)
Skelton (see Dunster, Mark)
SKETCHLEY, Arthur
   Money Makes the Man
     (In 26 Short & Amusing Plays, 1871)
SKIDMORE, Hobart
   Books for the Dead
     (In The One-Act Theatre, Vol. 2)
The Skin of Our Teeth (see Wilder, Thornton Niven)

Skinner, Cornelia Otis, 1901–
    The Pleasure of His Company (see Taylor, Samuel Albert)
The Sky is Green (see Gear, Brian)
SLADE, Bernard
    The Flying Nun, a television filmscript
      (In Writing for Television)
SLADE, Julian
    Trelawny; a musical play adapted from A. W. Pinero's "Tre-
    lawny of the Wells" by Aubrey Woods, book, music and lyrics,
    Julian Slade and George Rowell
      (In Plays of the Year, Vol. 41, 1971/72)
SLADE, Philip
    The Decoy
      (In The One-Act Theatre, Vol. 1)
    Five Minutes
      (In The One-Act Theatre, Vol. 1)
SLADEN-SMITH, Francis, 1886–
    The Crown of St. Felice
      (In Ten Fantasies for Stage and Study, 1932)
    Harlequin Bridge
      (In Best One-Act Plays of 1942/43, London)
    Love in the Ape-House
      (In Best One-Act Plays of 1933, London)
    The Man Who Wouldn't Go to Heaven
      (In 24 One-Act Plays, Revised edition, 1954)
    Mrs. Noah Gives the Sign
      (In Best One-Act Plays of 1931, London)
Slag (see Hare, David)
Slam the Door Softly (see Luce, Clare Boothe)
Slam the Door Softly (see also A Doll's House, 1970)
The Slaughter of the Innocents (see Saroyan, William)
Slaughterhouse Play (see Yankowitz, Susan)
The Slave (see Jones, Leroi)
The Slave with Two Faces (see Davies, Mary Carolyn)
A Sleep of Prisoners (see Fry, Christopher)
The Sleepers Den (see Gill, Peter)
Sleeping Dogs (see Kirkpatrick, John Alexander)
The Sleeping Prince (see Rattigan, Terence)
The Sleeping-Draught (see Penley, Samson)
The Sleep-Walker; or, Which Is the Lady? (see Oulton, Walley
    Chamberlain)
The Sleepwalker's Children (see Blue Denim)
SLESINGER, Tess
    The Good Earth (see Jennings, Talbot)
    A Tree Grows in Brooklyn, by Tess Slesinger and Frank Davis,
    adapted from the novel by Betty Smith
      (In Best Film Plays, 1945, Vol. 2)
A Slight Ache (see Pinter, Harold)
A Slight Mistake; or, A Prize in a German Lottery (see Souvestre,
    Emile)
Slighted Treasures (see Suter, William)
Slocumb, Paul

Next-to-Last Rites (see Thomas, Dorothy)
The Tinker (see Dobie, Laurance)
Slow Blue (see Kreymborg, Alfred)
Slow but Sure (see Smith, Marian Spencer)
Slow Dance on the Killing Ground (see Hanley, William)
The Slump (see Day, Frederic L.)
The Small, Private World of Michael Marston (see Holland,
    Norman)
The Small Victory (see MacCormick, Iain)
Small War on Murray Hill (see Sherwood, Robert Emmet)
SMALLEY, Webster
    The Man with the Oboe. A comic fantasy with music by Le-
    Jaren Hiller, Jr.
    (In Players Magazine, Vol. 14, no. 5, Feb. 1964)
Smiles of a Summer Night (see Bergman, Ingmar)
Smith, Bessie, 1894-1937
    *The Death of Bessie Smith (see Albee, Edward)
SMITH, Betty, 1904-1972
    The Far Distant Shore (see Finch, Robert)
    Manana Bandits, by Betty Smith and Chase Webb
    (In Best One-Act Plays of 1938, N.Y.)
    Summer Comes to the Diamond O (see Finch, Robert)
    A Tree Grows in Brooklyn (see Slesinger, Tess)
    Western Night, by Betty Smith and Robert Finch
    (In Plays as Experience)
SMITH, Del
    They Asked for It
    (In Best One-Act Plays of 1943, N.Y.)
SMITH, Dorothy Gladys, 1896-
    Autumn Crocus, by C.L. Anthony, pseud.
    (In Famous Plays of Today, 1931)
    Service, by C.L. Anthony, pseud.
    (In Famous Plays of Today, 1932/33)
SMITH, Edmund
    Phaedra and Hippolitus
    (In Bell's British Theatre, 1797, Vol. 28)
Smith, Harold Jacob
    The Defiant Ones (see Douglas, Nathan E.)
Smith, J. Kinchin
    Mummer's Play, restored by J. Kinchin Smith
SMITH, Marion Spencer
    Good Night
    (In Drama, Vol. 16, Feb. 1926)
    The Hamburger King
    (In Drama, Vol. 15, Mar. 1925)
    Oft in the Stilly Night
    (In Drama, Vol. 15, Jan. 1925)
    Slow but Sure
    (In Drama, Vol. 17, Feb. 1927)
    The Wedding Anniversary
    (In Drama, Vol. 17, Apr. 1927)
SMITH, Michael
    Captain Jack's Revenge

(In New American Plays, Vol. 4)
    The Next Thing
        (In The Best of Off Off Broadway)
SMITH, N. K.
    They Refuse to be Resurrected
        (In Best One-Act Plays of 1932, London)
SMITH, Peter J.
    The Enlightenment of Others by Will Skuffel
        (In Drama & Theatre, Vol. 8, no. 1, 1969)
    The Gas Tank
        (In First Stage, Vol. 6, Winter 1967/68)
Smit   Robert Paul, 1915-
    The Tender Trap (see Shulman, Max)
SMITH, Winchell, 1871-1933
    Lightnin', by Winchell Smith and Frank Bacon
        (In S. R. O., the Most Successful Plays...)
Smoke (see Vidal, Gore)
Smoke Screens (see Brighouse, Harold)
Snakes in the Grass (see Buckstone, John Baldwin)
Sneider, Vern J.
    The Teahouse of the August Moon (see Goggan, John Patrick)
SNELL, Beatrice Saxon
    Paradise Regained
        (In One-Act Theatre, Vol. 2)
Snipe Hunt (see Williams, George Llyonel)
The Snob (see Sternheim, Carl)
Snow (see Moore, Hortense)
Snow, Sir Charles Percy, Baron Snow, 1905-
    **The Affair (see Millar, Ronald)
The Snow Man (see Housman, Laurence)
Snow White and the Seven Dwarfs (see Disney, Walt)
SNYDER, William Hartwell, Jr.
    Another Summer
        (In Best Short Plays, 1953/54)
    The Departing
        (In Best Short Plays, 1958/59)
So Long, Son (see O'Brien, Howard Vincent)
SOANE, George, 1790-1860
    The Falls of Clyde
        (In Cumberland's British Theatre, Vol. 25, no. 9)
    Faustus
        (In Cumberland's British Theatre, Vol. 29, no. 6)
    Rob Roy; after Sir Walter Scott
        (In Cumberland's British Theatre, Vol. 40, no. 3)
    The Young Reefer
        (In Cumberland's British Theatre, Vol. 36, no. 8)
    Zarah
        (In Cumberland's British Theatre, Vol. 31, no. 1)
Soap (see Ponge, Francis)
Sob Sister (see Saunders, Lillian)
A Social Event (see Inge, William Motter)
A Social Success (see Beerbohm, Max)

The Social Worker and the Alcoholic   (see Kauffman, George Simon)
The Socialites (see Jupp, Kenneth)
Society (see Robertson, Thomas William)
Society em Baby Doll (see Pongetti, Henrique)
Socrates, 469-399 B. C.
    *Barefoot in Athens (see Anderson, Maxwell)
    *Hellas (see Strindberg, August)
    *Socrates Up to Date (see Myers, Irvin H.)
    *Socrates Wounded (see Levinson, Alfred)
    *Xanthippe on Woman Suffrage (see Osborne, Duffield)
    *Xantippe and Socrates (see Baring, Maurice)
Sodom and Gomorrah (see Giradoux, Jean)
Le Soir du Conquerant (see Maulnier, Thierry)
Sojourners (see Harnwell, Anne)
The Solar Spectrum (see Wedekind, Frank)
Soldadera (see Niggli, Josephina)
The Soldier Who Became a Great Dane (see Shore, Joseph)
Soldiers (see Hochhuth, Rolf)
The Soldier's Daughter (see Cherry, Andrew)
Le Soleil et les Parapluies... (see Deutsch, Leon)
Solemn Communion: Panic Ceremony (see Arrabal, Fernando)
The Solid Gold Cadillac (see Teichmann, Howard)
A Solid House (see Garro, Elena)
Soliman and Perseda (Anon.)
    (In Dodsley's A Select Collection of Old English Plays, Vol.
    5)
Solo (see Mocky, Jean-Pierre)
Solomon, King of Israel, c. 1015-977 B. C.
    *Solomon's Song (see Kemp, Harry Hibbard)
    *The Song of Solomon (see Odea, Mark Leland Hill)
Some Like It Hot (see Wilder, Billy)
Some One Waiting (see Williams, Emlyn)
Somebody Knows (see Van Druten, John)
SOMERSET, Charles A.
    Crazy Jane
        (In Cumberland's British Theatre, Vol. 17, no. 2)
    A Day After the Fair
        (In Cumberland's British Theatre, Vol. 30, no. 5)
    Shakespeare's Early Days
        (In Cumberland's British Theatre, Vol. 22, no. 4)
    Sylvana
        (In Cumberland's British Theatre, Vol. 16, no. 1)
    "Yes !"
        (In Cumberland's British Theatre, Vol. 25, no. 7)
Something in the Wind (see Coe, Fred)
Something Unspoken (see Williams, Tennessee)
Sometime Every Summertime (see Markle, Fletcher)
Sometimes Even Now (see Chetham-Strode, Warren)
SOMIN, W. O.
    Close Quarters; English version by Gilbert Lannox
        (In Famous Plays of Today, 1935)
SOMMER, Harald

Ein Unheimlich Starker Abgang
  (In Theater Heute, Dec. 1970)
The Somnambulist; or, The Phantom of the Village (see Moncrieff, William Thomas)
Sondheim, Stephen
  Gypsy (see Styne, Jule)
  West Side Story (see Bernstein, Leonard)
Song for a Hero (see Schaefer, Lee)
A Song for all Saints (see Lineberger, James)
The Song of Solomon (see Odea, Mark Leland Hill)
Song of Songs (see Giraudoux, Jean)
Song of the Dragon River (see China. Peking Opera Troupe of Shanghai)
Song of the Goat (see Clark, John Pepper)
Le Songe (see Strindberg, August)
Le Songe de la Nuit d'un Couple (see Magnan, Jean-Marie)
The Son-in-Law (see O'Keeffe, John)
SONNIER, Georges
  L'Impromptu de Rome
    (In Plaisir de France, supplement theatral, no. 338, Dec. 1966)
The Sons of Baldur (see Scheffauer, Herman)
SONTAG, Susan
  Duet for Cannibals
    (Farrar, Straus & Giroux Screenplays)
SOPHOCLES, 496-401 B.C.
  Antigone
    (In Complete Greek Drama, Vol. 1)
    (In Introduction to Literature: Plays)
    (In Massachusetts Review, Vol. 10, Summer 1969)
  Electra
    (In Complete Greek Drama, Vol. 1)
  **Oedipe Roi (see Pasolini, Pier Paolo)
  **Oedipus; a new work based on Sophocles (see Perreault, John)
  Oedipus at Colonus
    (In Complete Greek Drama, Vol. 1)
  Oedipus Rex
    (In Masterworks of World Drama, Vol. 1)
    (In Tragedy: Texts and Commentary, 1969)
  Oedipus the King
    (In Complete Greek Drama, Vol. 1)
  Oedipus the King, translated by Paul Roche; text used in the Universal film
    (New American Library Screenplays)
  Philoctetes
    (In Masterworks of World Drama, Vol. 1)
    (In Complete Greek Drama, Vol. 1)
  The Trachinae
    (In Complete Greek Drama, Vol. 1)
  Woman of Trachis, translated by Ezra Pound
    (In Hudson Review, Vol. 6, Winter 1954)
Sophonisba; or, Hannibal's Overthrow (see Lee, Nathaniel)

Soraia Posto Dois   (see Ploch, Pedro)
SORIA, Georges
    Les Passions Contraires
        (In Plaisir de France, supplement theatral, no. 310, August
        1964)
O Sorriso do Palhaco   (see Lourenco, Pasqual)
The Sorrow and the Pity (Le Chagrin et la Pitie)   (see Ophuls,
    Marcel)
Sorry, Wrong Number   (see Fletcher, Lucille)
Sotaba Komachi (see Hiraoke, Kimitake)
The Sound of Apples   (see Young, Stanley)
The Sound of Murder   (see Fairchild, William)
The Sound of Night   (see Kitani, Shigeo)
Sound on the Goose   (see Biel, Nicholas)
La Soupiere (see Lamoureux, Robert)
Southern, Terry, 1926-
    Easy Rider (see Fonda, Peter)
    Easy Rider; text in French   (see Fonda, Peter)
Southern, Thomas (see Southerne, Thomas)
SOUTHERNE, Thomas, 1660-1746
    Isabella; or, The Fatal Marriage
        (In Bell's British Theatre, 1797, Vol. 5)
        (In The London Stage, Vol. 2)
        (In Cumberland's British Theatre, Vol. 5, no. 6)
    Oroonoko
        (In The London Stage, Vol. 2)
        (In Bell's British Theatre, 1797, Vol. 19)
        (In Cumberland's British Theatre, Vol. 11, no. 2)
The Southerner (see Butler, Hugh)
SOUTHGATE, Patsy
    Freddy
        (In Evergreen Review, Vol. 6, no. 25, 1962)
SOUTO, Alexandrino de
    A Menina Que Vendia Flores
        (In Revista de Teatro, no. 311)
SOUVESTRE, Emile, 1806-1854
    The Duchess of Mansfeldt
        (In 26 Short & Amusing Plays, 1871)
    Mrs. Willis's Will
        (In 26 Short & Amusing Plays, 1871)
    A Slight Mistake; or, A Prize in a German Lottery
        (In 26 Short & Amusing Plays, 1871)
SOUZA, Antonio
    Pascuatina
        (In Americas, Vol. 9, Dec. 1957)
SOYFER, Jura
    Eddie Lechner's Trip to Paradise
        (In Modern International Drama, Vol. 4, Spring 1971)
    The End of the World (Weltuntergang)
        (In Modern International Drama, Vol. 5, no. 2, Spring 1972)
SOYINKA, Wole, 1934-
    The Strong Breed

(In Three Short Plays)
The Swamp Dwellers
(In Three Short Plays)
The Trials of Brother Jero
(In Three Short Plays)
SPAAK, Charles
La Kermesse Heroique, by Charles Spaak et Jacques Feyder,
d'apres une nouvelle de Charles Spaak.   German Title: "Die
Klugen Frauen. "
(In L'Avant-Scene du Cinema, no. 26, May 15, 1963)
The Space Fan (see Schevill, James Erwin)
The Spanish Tragedy; or, The First Part of Jeronimo (Hieronimo)
(see Kyd, Thomas)
The Spanish Tragedy; or, The Second Part of Jeronimo (Hieronimo
Is Mad Again) (see Kyd, Thomas)
A Spanking Legacy; or, The Corsican Vendetta (see Blake, Thomas
G.)
The Sparagus Garden (see Brome, Richard)
The Spare Bed; or, The Shower Bath (see Cooper, Frederick Fox)
Spark Among the Reeds (see China Peking Opera Troupe)
Special Friendships (see Aurenche, Jean)
The Spectre Bridegroom; or, A Ghost in Spite of Himself (see
Moncrieff, William Thomas)
Speculation (see Reynolds, Frederick)
Speed the Plow (see Morton, Thomas)
SPEENHOFF, J. H.
Louise
(In 50 Contemporary One-Act Plays)
SPEIRE, Russell
Hogan's Successor
(In Drama, Vol. 19, May 1929)
The Spell (see Kelly, Mary)
Spellbound (see Hecht, Ben)
SPENCE, Eulalie
The Starter
(In Plays of Negro Life)
SPENCER, Colin
Spitting Image
(In Plays and Players, Vol. 16, Nov. 1968)
SPERR, Martin
Münchner Freiheit
(In Theater Heute, March 1971)
SPEWACK, Bella (Cohen), 1899-
Boy Meets Girl, by Bella & Samuel Spewack
(In Famous Plays of Today, 1936)
(In 16 Famous American Plays)
(In 20 Best Plays of the Modern American Theatre, Vol. 1)
Kiss Me, Kate (see Porter, Cole)
My 3 Angels (see Spewack, Samuel)
SPEWACK, Samuel, 1899-
Boy Meets Girl (see Spewack, Bella Cohen)
Kiss Me, Kate (see Porter, Cole)

My 3 Angels, by Sam and Bella Spewack, based on "La Cuisine
des Anges" by Albert Husson
    (In Theatre Arts, Vol. 38, June 1954)
    (In 20 Best European Plays on the American Stage)
Two Blind Mice
    (In Theatre Arts, Vol. 33, Nov. 1949)
"Der Spiegelfechter" (see Müller, Andre)
Das Spiel vom Deutschen Bettelmann (see Weichert, Ernst)
SPIGELGASS, Leonard
    A Majority of One
    (In Theatre Arts, Vol. 44, no. 9, Sept. 1960)
The Spineless Drudge (see Harris, Richard W.)
SPIRAUX, Alain
    La Demangeaison
    (In Plaisir de France, supplement theatral, no. 375, Feb.
    1970)
    Le Roi Borgne
    (In L'Avant Scene du Theatre, no. 483, Nov. 15, 1971)
La Spiritata (see Grazzini, Antonio Francesco, called Il Lasca)
Spithead (see Hale, John)
Spitting Image (see Spencer, Colin)
A Splendid Offer (see King, Grace Elizabeth)
The Splendid Outcasts (see Sisson, Rosemary Anne)
Splendor in the Grass (see Inge, William Motter)
The Spoiled Child (Anon.)
    (In Cumberland's British Theatre, Vol. 42, no. 5)
The Sponge Room (see Waterhouse, Keith)
The Sport of My Mad Mother (see Jellicoe, Ann)
A Spot of Lunch (see Grant, Neil)
Spreading the News (see Gregory, Isabella Augusta Persse, lady)
The Spring Recital (see Dreiser, Theodore)
Spring Sluicing (see Ernst, Alice Henson)
Spring-heeled Jack (see Terson, Peter)
Spring's Awakening (see Wedekind, Frank)
The Springs Glory, a Maske (see Nabbes, Thomas)
SPURLING, John
    Macrunis Guevara
    (In Plays and Players, Vol. 16, Sept. 1969)
Spurt of Blood (see Artaud, Antonin)
Square in the Eye (see Gelber, Jack)
Square X (see Le Bihan, Michel)
Squatter Sovereignty (see Harrington, Edward)
Stage Door (see Ferber, Edna)
Stagecoach (see Nichols, Dudley)
The Stage-Struck Clerk; or, The Office in an Uproar (Anon.)
    (In 26 Short & Amusing Plays, 1871)
Staircase (see Dyer, Charles)
Stalag 17 (see Bevan, Donald)
Stallerhof (see Kroetz, Franz Xaver)
STALLINGS, Lawrence, 1894-1968
    What Price Glory? by Lawrence Stallings and Maxwell Anderson
    (In 25 Best Plays of the Modern American Theatre, Early
    Series, 1916-1929)

The Stallion (see Oliver, William I.)
Der Standhafte Prinz (see Grotowshi, Jerzy)
Standing on a Street Corner (see Corso, Gregory)
STARKWEATHER, David
    The Poet's Papers
        (In New American Plays, Vol. 3)
The Star-Spangled Girl (see Simon, Neil)
The Starter (see Spence, Eulalie)
State of Siege (see Camus, Albert)
State of the Union (see Lindsay, Howard)
STATES, Bert O., Jr.
    A Rent in the Universe
        (In First Stage, Vol. 6, Summer 1967)
    The Tall Grass
        (In Best Short Plays, 1959/60)
The States Talking (see MacLeish, Archibald)
La Station Champbaudet (see Labiche, Eugene)
Statues d'Epouvante (see Hessens, Robert)
Stay Where You Are (see Wymark, Olwen)
The Steamer Tenacity (see Vildrac, Charles)
STEELE, Sir Richard, 1672-1729
    The Conscious Lovers
        (In Bell's British Theatre, 1797, Vol. 13)
    The Funeral; or, Grief Alamode
        (In Bell's British Theatre, 1797, Vol. 27)
    The Tender Husband; or, The Accomplished Fools
        (In Bell's British Theatre, 1797, Vol. 20)
STEELE, Rufus
    The Fall of Ug
        (In The Grove Plays of the Bohemian Club, Vol. 3)
STEELE, Wilbur Daniel, 1886-
    The Giant's Stair
        (In 50 More Contemporary One-Act Plays)
Stefano Pelloni, called the Ferryman (see Dursi, Massimo)
STEFFAN, Kathryn
    The Kathryn Steffan Story
        (In Best Television Plays of the Year, 1950/51)
Stein, Edith, 1891-1942
    *Edith Stein (see Delouche, Dominique)
STEIN, Gertrude, 1874-1946
    Brewsie and Willie; a television play, adapted by Ellen Violett
        and Lisbeth Blake
        (In Best Short Plays, 1954/55; 1956/57)
    Doctor Faustus Lights the Lights
        (In Best One-Act Plays of 1949/50, N.Y.)
    What Happened
        (In Theatre Experiment)
STEIN, Howard
    In Darkness
        (In Best One-Act Plays, 1951/52, N.Y.)
    A Sight for Sore Thoughts
        (In Best Short Plays, 1959/60)

Stein, Joseph, 1912-
  Fiddler on the Roof (see Bock, Jerry)
  Plain and Fancy (see Hague, Albert Martin)
STEINBECK, John, 1902-1968
  **The Grapes of Wrath (see Johnson, Nunnally)
  **A Medal for Benny (see Butler, Frank)
  Of Mice and Men
    (In 20 Best Plays of the Modern American Theatre, Vol. 1)
Steinway Grand (Bösendorfer) (see Karinthy, Ferenc)
Stella (see Kelly, Terence)
STEPHENS, H. Morse
  St. Patrick at Tara
    (In The Grove Plays of the Bohemian Club, Vol. 2)
STEPHENS, Nan Badby
  Charivari
    (In Theatre Arts, Vol. 12, Nov. 1928)
STEPHENS, Peter John
  The Changeling
    (In Best One-Act Plays, 1952/53, N. Y.)
  Hugh of the Glen & His Clogs Are All One
    (In Best One-Act Plays, 1951/52, N. Y.)
The Stepmother (see Bennett, Arnold)
STERLING, George
  The Triumph of Bohemia
    (In The Grove Plays of the Bohemian Club, Vol. 1)
Sternberg, Jacques
  Le T'Aime, Je T'Aime (see Resnais, Alain)
STERNHEIM, Carl, 1878-1942
  The Mask of Virtue; English version by Ashley Dukes
    (In Famous Plays of Today, 1935)
  The Snob
    (In From the Modern Repertoire, Series One)
  The Underpants
    (In The Modern Theatre, ed. by Eric Bentley, Vol. 6)
STETTNER, Louis
  An Evening in an Important Asylum
    (In First Stage, Vol. 6, Summer 1967)
STEVENS, Caroline D.
  Elopements While You Wait
    (In Drama, Vol. 13, Feb. 1923)
Stevens, George, 1904-
  The More the Merrier (see Russel, Robert)
STEVENS, George Alexander, 1710-1784
  Distress upon Distress
    (In Burlesque Plays of the 18th Century)
Stevens, Gould
  The Good and Obedient Young Man (see Barr, Betty)
STEVENS, Henry Bailey
  Lincoln Reckons Up
    (In Best One-Act Plays of 1934, London)
STEVENS, Thomas Wood, 1880-1942
  The Nursery Maid of Heaven
    (In 50 Contemporary One-Act Plays)

STEVENS, Wallace, 1879-1955
    Three Travelers Watch a Sunrise
        (In Theatre Experiment)
        (In 50 Contemporary One-Act Plays)
STEVENSON, Dorothy
    Flight from Destiny
        (In Players Magazine, Vol. 42, no. 1, Oct. 1965)
The Steward; or, Fashion and Feeling (Anon.)
        (In Cumberland's British Theatre, Vol. 42, no. 8)
Stichus (see Plautus, Titus Maccius)
STILL, John, bp. 1543-1608, reputed author
    Gammer Gurton's Needle
        (In Dodsley's A Select Collection of Old English Plays, Vol. 3)
        (In Dodsley's A Select Collection of Old Plays, Vol. 2)
The Still Alarm (see Kaufman, George Simon)
Still Life (see Coward, Noel Pierce)
STIRLING, Edward, 1807-1894
    A Pair of Pigeons
        (In 26 Short & Amusing Plays, 1971)
        (In Lacy's Plays)
    The Ragpicker of Paris and the Dressmaker of St. Antoine
        (In Lacy's Acting Plays, Vol. 81)
The Stocking (see Gilbert, Christie)
STOCKTON, Richard F.
    A Fabulous Tale
        (In Best Short Plays, 1958/59)
The Stoic's Daughter (see Baring, Maurice)
STOKES, Herbert
    The Uncle Toms
        (In TDR/The Drama Review, Vol. 12, Summer 1968)
Stokkerlok und Millipilli (see Ludwig, Volker)
The Stolen Prince (see Totheroh, Dan)
STOLPER, Armin
    "Himmelfahrt zur Erde," freely adapted from the story by
        Antonows, "Der Zerrissene Rubel"
        (In Theater der Zeit, no. 6, 1971)
    Zeitgenossen
        (In Theater der Zeit, Vol. 24, no. 11, 1969)
STONE, John A.
    The Chorus Girl; based on the short story of the same title
        by Anton Chekhov
        (In First Stage, Vol. 1, no. 1, Winter 1961/62)
    The Nose
        (In First Stage, Vol. 3, nos. 3/4, Summer/Fall, 1964)
STONE, John Augustus, 1800-1834
    Metamora; or, The Last of the Wampanoags
        (In Six Early American Plays, 1798-1890)
STONE, Weldon
    Cloud over Breakshin
        (In Best One-Act Plays of 1938, N.Y.)
    Devil Take a Whittler

(In Best One-Act Plays of 1937, N. Y.)
(In Best Short Plays, 1956/57)
Rainbows in Heaven
   (In Best One-Act Plays of 1940, N. Y.)
STOPPARD, Tom, 1937-
   Albert's Bridge
      (In Plays and Players, Vol. 15, Oct. 1967)
   Rosencrantz and Guildenstern Are Dead
      (In Evergreen Review, Vol. 12, no. 52, 1968)
      (In Evergreen Playscript Series)
STOREY, David
   In Celebration
      (In Plays and Players, Vol. 16, no. 9, June 1969)
      (In Plays of the Year, Vol. 38, 1969/70)
   The Contractor
      (In Plays and Players, Vol. 17, no. 3, Dec. 1969)
   Home
      (In Plays and Players, Vol. 16, Aug. 1970)
      (In Plays of the Year, Vol. 41, 1971/72)
   The Restoration of Arnold Middleton
      (In Plays of the Year, Vol. 35, 1967/68)
   Touch It Light
      (In Plays of the Year, Vol. 18, 1958)
The Storm (see Drinkwater, John)
The Story of Chink Okichi (see Yamamoto Yuzo)
The Story of G. I. Joe (see Atlas, Leopold)
The Story of Gus (see Miller, Arthur)
The Story of Louis Pasteur (see Gibney, Sheridan)
The Story They'll Never Print (see Barnouw, Erik)
STOUT, Wilbur
   In Dixon's Kitchen
      (In Carolina Folkplays)
STOW, Clara
   The Party of the Third Part
      (In Drama, Vol. 15, Feb. 1925)
Stowe, Harriet Beecher, 1811-1895
   **Uncle Tom's Cabin (see Aiken, George L.)
STRACHAN, Edna Higgins
   The Chinese Water Wheel
      (In Drama, Vol. 21, Oct. 1930)
La Strada (see Fellini, Federico)
A Strained Relation (see Bierce, Ambrose)
The Strains of Triumph (see Inge, William Motter)
STRANACK, John
   With Malice Aforethought
      (In Playwrights for Tomorrow, Vol. 3)
The Strange Gentleman (see Dickens, Charles)
Strange Interlude (see O'Neill, Eugene Gladstone)
Strange Morning (see Pech, Claude-Henri)
Strange Orchestra (see Ackland, Rodney)
The Strange Passenger (see Karpowicz, Tymoteusz)
Strange Rain (see Brown, Sonia)

The Stranger   (see Thompson, Benjamin)
The Strangest Feeling   (see Kirkpatrick, John Alexander)
The Strangest Kind of Romance   (see Williams, Tennessee)
The Strangler   (see Powell, Arnold)
STRATTON, Clarence
    Ruby Red
        (In Drama, Vol. 10, Feb. 1920)
STRAUSS, Richard, 1864-1949
    Arabella.   English version of the Hugo von Hofmannsthal
    libretto by John Gutman
        (In Theatre Arts, Vol. 41, Jan. 1957)
The Straw Man (Los Peletes)   (see Martinez Ballesteros, Antonio)
Straw Patriot   (see Moreno, Virginia R.)
The Street Attends a Funeral   (see Kozlenko, William)
Street Scene   (see Rice, Elmer L.)
A Streetcar Named Desire   (see Williams, Tennessee)
La Strega   (see Grazzini, Antonio Francesco, called Il Lasca)
Streubel, Manfred
    "Icke und die Hexe Yu"   (see Medek, Tilo)
Ein Strick mit Linem Ende   (see Nestroy, J. N.)
Strictly Dishonorable   (see Sturgis, Preston)
The Strike   (see Serling, Rod)
STRINDBERG, August, 1849-1912
    Caram, Populo!
        (In Tulane Drama Review, Vol. 6, Nov. 1961)
    Charles XII
        (In Queen Christina, and Other Historical Plays)
    The Creditor
        (In 50 Contemporary One-Act Plays)
        (In Poet Lore, Vol. 22, Spring 1911)
    Crimes and Crimes
        (In Genius of the Scandinavian Theater)
    La Dance de Mort; adapted by Pierre Laforet
        (In Plaisir de France, supplement theatral, no. 302, Dec.
        1963)
    The Dance of Death
        (In Plays of the Year, Vol. 32, 1966)
    Debit and Credit
        (In Poet Lore, Vol. 17, Autumn 1906)
    Dödsdansen
        (In L'Avant-Scene du Theatre, no. 305, Feb. 15, 1964)
    Earl Birger of Bjälbo
        (In The Last of the Knights, and Other Historical Plays)
    Equals
        (In Golden Book, Vol. 7, Jan. 1928)
    Erik XIV
        (In L'Avant-Scene du Theatre, no. 224)
    The Father
        (In Tragedy: Texts and Commentary, 1969)
    The Ghost Sonata
        (In The Modern Theatre, ed. by R. W. Corrigan)
    Gustav III

(In Queen Christina, and Other Historical Plays)
Hellas (Socrates)
   (In World Historical Plays)
Julie
   (In Poet Lore, Vol. 22, Summer 1911)
The Lamb and the Beast (Christ)
   (In World Historical Plays)
The Last of the Knights
   (In The Last of the Knights, and Other Historical Plays)
Miss Julie
   (In One Act)
   (In Modern Theatre, ed. by R. W. Corrigan)
   (In 30 Famous One-Act Plays)
The Nightingale of Wittenberg (Martin Luther)
   (In World Historical Plays)
The Outcast
   (In Poet Lore, Vol. 17, Autumn 1906)
La Paria
   (In L'Avant-Scene du Theatre, no. 127)
The Pelican
   (In Tulane Drama Review, Vol. 4, March 1960)
Queen Christina
   (In Queen Christina, and Other Historical Plays)
The Regent
   (In The Last of the Knights, and Other Historical Plays)
Simon
   (In Poet Lore, Vol. 17, no. 3, 1906)
Le Songe
   (In L'Avant-Scene du Theatre, no. 465, Feb. 1, 1971)
   (In Plaisir de France, supplement theatral, no. 388, 1971)
The Stronger
   (In Contemporary One-Act Plays, 1922)
   (In Poet Lore, Vol. 17, Spring 1906)
Through Deserts to Ancestral Lands (Moses)
   (In World Historical Plays)
To Damascus
   (In Genius of the Scandinavian Theater)
To Damascus: a Dream Trilogy in 3 parts, 4 acts each
   (In Poet Lore, Vol. 42, Spring 1933, Autumn 1934, Winter
   1935)
To Damascus, Part 1
   (In Makers of the Modern Theater, 1961)
The Stripper (see A Loss of Roses)
Strip-tease (see Mrozek, Slawomir)
Strip-tease of Jealousy (see Arrabal, Fernando)
STRODE, Hudson, 1893-
   The Dance Below, by Hudson Strode and Larry Hornthal
     (In 50 More Contemporary One-Act Plays)
A Stroll in the Air (see Ionesco, Eugene)
STRONG, Austin
   The Drums of Oude
     (In 30 Famous One-Act Plays)

STRONG, Leonard Alfred George, 1896-
    Over the Toast
        (In Esquire, Vol. 2, Sept. 1934)
The Strong Breed (see Soyinka, Wole)
The Stronger (see Strindberg, August)
Strumming (see Jasudowicz, Dennis)
STUART, Aimee (McHardy), 1890-
    Sixteen, by Aimee and Philip Stuart
        (In Famous Plays of Today, 1933/34)
Stuart, Dorothy Margaret
    The Map (see Davenport, E. V.)
STUART, Jeb
    The Door
        (In Best Television Plays of the Year, 1949)
Stuart, Philip
    Sixteen (see Stuart, Aimee McHardy)
STUCKES, W.
    Shanghai
        (In Best One-Act Plays of 1931, London)
Stud (see Gottlieb, Alex)
The Student's Frolic (see Robinson, T. S.)
Sture, Sten Svantesson, c. 1492-1520
    *The Last of the Knights (see Strindberg, August)
STURGES, Preston, 1898-1959
    Hail the Conquering Hero
        (In Best Film Plays, 1943/44)
    The Miracle of Morgan's Creek
        (In Best Film Plays, 1943/44, Vol. 1)
    Strictly Dishonorable
        (In 25 Best Plays of the Modern American Theatre, Early
        Series, 1916-1929)
STYNE, Jule, 1905-
    Bells Are Ringing. Book and lyrics by Betty Comden and
        Adolph Green. Music by Jule Styne.
        (In Theatre Arts, Vol. 43, April 1959)
    Gypsy; a musical suggested by the memoirs of Gypsy Rose Lee.
        Book by Arthur Laurents. Lyrics by Stephen Sondheim.
        (In Theatre Arts, Vol. 46, June 1962)
SUBERT, Frantisek Adolf, 1849-1915
    The Awakening
        (In Poet Lore, Vol. 33, Summer 1922)
A Subject of Scandal and Concern (see Osborne, John)
Subject to Fits (see Montgomery, Robert)
The Subject Was Roses (see Gilroy, Frank D.)
The Subjection of Kezia (see Ellis, Edith M. O. Lees)
The Subscription List (see Namiki Gohei III)
Subway Circus (see Saroyan, William)
Success (see Yaltsev, P.)
The Successful Life of 3 (see Fornes, Maria Irene)
The Successful Life of Three: A Skit for Vaudeville (see Fornes,
    Maria Irene)
Such is Life (see also King Nicolo; or, Such Is Life)

Such Men Are Dangerous (see Dukes, Ashley)
Such Things Are (see Inchbald, Mrs. Elizabeth Simpson)
SUCKLING, Sir John, 1609-1642
    The Goblins
        (In Dodsley's A Select Collection of Old Plays, Vol. 10)
A Sudden Arrival (see Hay, Frederick)
SUDEKUM, Fred
    The Copped Coup
        (In Drama & Theatre, Vol. 10, no. 1, Fall 1971)
SUDERMANN, Hermann, 1857-1828
    The Far-Away Princess
        (In Contemporary One-Act Plays, 1922)
Suffer the Little Children (see Bela, Nicholas)
Suffer the Little Children (see Oboler, Arch)
SUFFRAN, Michel
    Les Approches du Soir
        (In L'Avant-Scene du Theatre, no. 250, Oct. 1, 1961)
    La Balle au Chasseur
        (In L'Avant-Scene du Theatre, no. 463, Jan. 1, 1971)
    Savonarole, ou Le plaisir de Dieu Seul
        (In L'Avant-Scene du Theatre, no. 463, Jan. 1, 1971)
        (In L'Avant-Scene du Theatre, no. 467, Mar. 1, 1971)
    Le Seuil du Jardin
        (In Plaisir de France, supplement theatral, no. 306, April
        1964)
Sugar Cane (see Wilson, Frank H.)
The Suicide (see Fratti, Mario)
Suil Dhuv the Coiner (see Dibdin, Thomas)
Les Suisses (see Breal, P. A.)
SUMAROKOV, Alexsandr Petrovich, 1718-1777
    Dimitrii the Impostor: a Tragedy
        (In Selected Tragedies)
    Hamlet: a Tragedy
        (In Selected Tragedies)
    Khorev: a Tragedy
        (In Selected Tragedies)
    Semira: a Tragedy
        (In Selected Tragedies)
The Sumida River (see Juru Motomasa)
Summer and Smoke (see Williams, Tennessee)
Summer Comes to the Diamond O (see Finch, Robert)
Summer Fury (see Groughton, James)
A Summer Ghost (see Fredericks, Claude)
Summer in the Country (see Chekhov, Anton Pavlovich)
Summer of the Seventeenth Doll (see Lawler, Ray)
Summer Pavilion (see Vidal, Gore)
Summer's Last Will and Testament (see Nash, Thomas)
Summertime (see Saroyan, William)
Summit Conference (see Campbell, J. Gounod)
The Summoning of Everyman (Anon.)
        (In Representative Medieval and Tudor Plays)
The Sun (see Galsworthy, John)

Sun   (see Kennedy, Adrienne)
The Sun and the Moon   (see Biraghi, Guglielmo)
Sun Deck   (see Richards, Stanley)
Sunday Bloody Sunday   (see Gilliatt, Penelope)
SUNDGAARD, Arnold
    Equinox
        (In Best One-Act Plays of 1941, N.Y.)
    Mid-passage
        (In Best One-Act Plays of 1943, N.Y.)
    The Picnic
        (In Best One-Act Plays of 1944, N.Y.)
A Sunny Morning   (see Alvarez Quintero, Serafin)
The Sunny Side of the Atom   (see Beier, Carl)
Sunrise at Campobello   (see Schary, Dore)
The Sun's Darling   (see Dekker, Thomas)
Superintendent   (see Haavikko, Paavo)
Superstition   (see Barker, James Nelson)
The Suppliants   (see Aeschylus)
The Suppliants   (see Euripides)
Suppose a Wedding   (see Malamud, Bernard)
Supposes   (see Aristo, Lodovico)
Suppressed Desires   (see Glaspell, Susan)
La Surface Perdue   (see Grassian, Dolores)
The Surrender of Calais   (see Colman, George, the Younger)
A Survey of the Sciences   (see Davenport, Robert)
Survival   (see Brenner, Alfred)
Susannah   (see Floyd, Carlisle)
SUSSMANN, C. Julien
    Le Voyage
        (In L'Avant-Scene du Theatre, no. 474, June 15, 1971)
The Suspected Truth (La Verdad Sospechosa)   (see Ruiz de Alarcon
    y Mendoza, Juan)
The Suspicious Husband   (see Hoadly, Benjamin)
SUTER, William E., 1811?-1882
    Double Dealing; or, The Rifle Volunteer
        (In Lacy's Acting Plays, Vol. 14)
    Little Annie's Birthday
        (In Lacy's Acting Plays, Vol. 81)
    Slighted Treasures
        (In 26 Short & Amusing Plays, 1871)
    "Wanted, a Young Lady"
        (In 26 Short & Amusing Plays, 1871)
SUTHERLAND, Efua T.
    Edufa
        (In Plays From Black Africa)
SUTRO, Alfred, 1863-1933
    The Man in the Stalls
        (In Representative One-Act Plays by British & Irish Authors)
    The Man on the Kerb
        (In Short Plays by Representative Authors, 1920)
    A Marriage has been Arranged...
        (In Dramas by Present-Day Writers)

SUTTON, Graham
    T' Pup
        (In Best One-Act Plays of 1933, London)
SUTTON, Vida Ravenscroft
    The Mantle of the Virgin
        (In Drama, Vol. 12, Dec. 1921)
SVEVO, Italo
    A Husband
        (In Modern International Drama, Vol. 6, no. 1, Fall 1972)
SWAIN, Robert
    Autoportrait d'un Pornographe, de Robert Swain et Roland Topor
        (In L'Avant-Scene du Cinema, no. 131, Dec. 1972)
The Swamp (see MacKaye, Robert Keith)
The Swamp Dwellers (see Soyinka, Wole)
SWAN, Jon
    Football
        (In Evergreen Review, Vol. 12, no. 59, 1968)
The Swan Song (see Chekhov, Anton Pavlovich)
SWANSON, Walter S. J.
    Negerinde!
        (In Massachusetts Review, Vol. 11, Autumn 1970)
Sweeney Agonistes (see Eliot, Thomas Stearns)
Sweet Alice (see Eveling, Stanley)
Sweet Bird of Youth (see Williams, Tennessee)
Sweet Confessions (see Arnaud, Georges)
Sweet England's Pride (see Rodger, Ian)
Sweet Eros (see McNally, Terrence)
SWENSON, May
    The Floor
        (In First Stage, Vol. 6, Summer 1967)
SWERLING, Jo, 1897-
    Guys and Dolls
        (In The Modern Theatre, ed. by Eric Bentley, Vol. 4)
The Swings (see De Grazia, Edward)
"Sworn at Highgate!" (see Daniel, George)
Sylvana (see Weber, Carl Maria von)
Symons, Arthur, 1865-1945, adapter
    Humour Out of Breath (see Day, John)
    The Parliament of Bees (see Day, John)
Symphony in Illusion (see Bell, J. W.)
SYNGE, John Millington, 1871-1909
    Deirdre of the Sorrows
        (In Genius of the Irish Theater)
        (In Theatre Arts, Vol. 34, Aug. 1950)
    In the Shadow of the Glen
        (In 24 Favorite One-Act Plays)
    The Playboy of the Western World
        (In The Modern Theatre, ed. by R. W. Corrigan)
        (In 16 Famous European Plays)
    Riders to the Sea
        (In Representative One-Act Plays by British and Irish Authors)
        (In Introduction to Literature: Plays)

(In <u>Ten Fantasies for Stage and Study,</u> 1932)
Tarnish
(In <u>Best One-Act Plays of 1937,</u> London)
TALBOT, R.
The Serf
(In <u>Cumberland's British Theatre,</u> Vol. 1, no. 2)
A Tale of Mystery (see Holcroft, Thomas)
TALFOURD, Francis
A Household Fairy
(In <u>26 Short & Amusing Plays,</u> 1871)
Talk to Me Like the Rain (see Williams, Tennessee)
The Tall Grass (see States, Bert O., Jr.)
Tamerlane, also called Timour, 1336?-1405
*Tamerlane (see Rowe, Nicholas)
*Timour the Tartar (see Lewis, Matthew Gregory)
Tamura (see Zeami Motokiyo)
Tancred and Gismunda (see Wilmot, Robert)
Tango (see Mrozek, Slawomir)
Tango Palace (see Fornes, Maria Irene)
TANNER, Alain, 1929-
Charles Mort ou Vif
(In <u>L'Avant-Scene du Cinema,</u> no. 108, Nov. 1970)
La Salamandre
(In <u>L'Avant-Scene du Cinema,</u> no. 125, May 1972)
Tanner, Edward Everett, 1921-
**Auntie Mame (see Lawrence, Jerome)
The Tape Recorder (see Flower, Pat)
Tarakin (see Mark, Francis)
TARKINGTON, Booth, 1869-1946
Beauty and the Jacobin, an Interlude of the French Revolution
(In <u>Harper's,</u> Vol. 125, Aug./Sept. 1912)
Clarence
(In <u>Best American Plays,</u> Supp. Vol.)
The Intimate Strangers
(In <u>Harper's,</u> Vol. 144-45, April-June 1922)
The Man from Home, by Booth Tarkington and H.L. Wilson
(In <u>S.R.O., the Most Successful Plays...</u>)
Mister Antonio
(In <u>Harper's,</u> Vol. 134, Jan./Feb. 1917)
Monsieur Beaucaire
(In <u>Dramas by Present-Day Writers</u>)
The Trysting Place
(In <u>15 American One-Act Plays</u>)
Tarkington, Newton Booth (see Tarkington, Booth)
Tarnish (see Talbot, Alfred Julian)
Tartuffe--Acte VI (see Marie, Andre)
Tarzan and the Creeping Giants (see Mullally, Donn)
TASSO, Torquato, 1544-1595
Amyntas
(In <u>Genius of the Italian Theater</u>)
A Taste of Honey (see Delaney, Shelagh)
Tata, ou de l'Education (see Borel, Jacques)

Tatters (see Burton, Richard)
Der Tausendjährige Krieg (see Arrabal, Fernando)
TAVEL, Ronald
    Christina's World
      (In Chicago Review, Vol. 16, no. 1, Winter-Spring, 1963)
    Gorilla Queen
      (In The Best of Off Off Broadway)
    Kitchenette
      (In Partisan Review, Vol. 34, Spring 1967)
    Secrets of the Citizens Correction Committee
      (In Scripts, Vol. 1, no. 3, Jan. 1972)
    Vinyl Visits an FM Station
      (In TDR/Drama Review, Vol. 14, Sept. 1970)
Taxi (see Riley, Mrs. Alice Cushing Donaldson)
TAYLEUR, W. St. John
    Reunion
      (In Best One-Act Plays of 1948/49, London)
TAYLOR, Cecil P.
    Bread and Butter
      (In Plays and Players, Vol. 14, Oct. 1966)
TAYLOR, Christopher
    The Wings of the Dove, adapted from the novel by Henry James
      (In Plays of the Year, 1963/64)
Taylor, Donald Fraser
    **The Doctor and the Devils (see Thomas, Dylan)
TAYLOR, Peter, 1919-
    The Death of a Kinsman
      (In Sewanee Review, Vol. 57, no. 1, 1968)
    Sand in the Mountains
      (In Kenyon Review, Vol. 30, no. 2, 1968)
    Tennessee Day in St. Louis
      (In Kenyon Review, Vol. 18, Winter 1956)
    Whistler
      (In Virginia Quarterly Review, Vol. 46, Spring 1970)
TAYLOR, Renee
    Bea, Frank, Richie & Joan, by Renee Taylor and Joseph
    Bologna
      (In Modern Short Comedies from Broadway & London)
TAYLOR, Samuel Albert, 1912-
    The Happy Time
      (In Theatre Arts, Vol. 35, Feb. 1951)
    The Pleasure of His Company, by Samuel Taylor and Cornelia
    Otis Skinner
      (In Theatre Arts, Vol. 44, April 1960)
    Sabrina Fair
      (In Theatre Arts, Vol. 38, Nov. 1954)
Taylor, Thomas Proclus (see Taylor, Tom)
TAYLOR, Tom, 1817-1880
    The Chain of Guilt; or, The Inn on the Heath, by Thomas Pro-
    clus Taylor
      (In Cumberland's British Theatre, Vol. 42, no. 4)
Tchao! (see Sauvajon, Marc-Gilbert)

Tchekhov, Anton (see Chekhov, Anton Pavlovich)
TCHOUKHRI, Grigory, 1921-
    La Ballade du Soldat (Ballada o Soldate)
        (In L'Avant-Scene du Cinema, no. 42, 1964)
Tea and Sympathy (see Anderson, Robert)
Tea for Six (see Butterfield, Walton)
Tea Party (see Pinter, Harold)
Tea with a Legend (see Holland, Norman)
The Teahouse of the August Moon (see Goggan, John Patrick)
The Tears of My Sister (see Foote, Horton)
El Teatro Campesino
    Vietnam Campesino
        (In Theatre 3. International Theatre Institute of the U. S.)
Teatro, Representacao Liturgica (see Vincente, Jose)
Teddy the Tiler (see Rodwell, George Herbert Buonaparte)
TEICHMANN, Howard M.
    Many a Watchful Night (see Brown, John Mason)
    The Solid Gold Cadillac, by Howard Teichmann and George S.
    Kaufman
        (In Theatre Arts, Vol. 40, April 1956)
        (In Best American Plays, Fourth Series)
Tekeli; or, The Siege of Montagatz (see Hook, Theodore Edward)
La Telefonta (see Fratti, Mario)
Telemachus (see Norman, Charles)
Telemachus; or, The Island of Calypso (see Planche, James Robin-
    son)
Tell, Wilhelm
    *William Tell (see Knowles, James Sheridan)
Tell It Not in Gath (see Corrie, Joe)
Tell Pharaoh (see Mitchell, Loften)
TELLEZ, Gabriel, 1570?-1648
    Le Timide au Palais, by Tirso de Molina (pseud.)
        (In Plaisir de France, supplement theatral, no. 293, Mar.
        1963)
    The Trickster of Seville, by Tirso de Molina (pseud.)
        (In The Classic Theatre, ed. by Eric Bentley, Vol. 3)
    El Vergonzoso en Palacio, by Tirso de Molina (pseud.)
        (In L'Avant-Scene du Theatre, no. 284, Mar. 15, 1963)
Telling of the North Star (see Ferrini, Vincent)
Le Temoin (see Germoz, Alain)
Le Temps d'Apprendre a Vivre (see Graziani, Henri)
Les Temps Morts (see Laloux, Rene)
The Temptation of Christ (see York Locksmiths' Play)
The Temptation of Dr. Antonio (see Fellini, Federico)
Ten Accio-Spectacles (see Brossa, Joan)
Ten Blocks on the Camino Real (see Williams, Tennessee)
Ten Days Later (see Glick, Carl)
The Ten Fingers of Francois (see Oglesbee, Delle Houghton)
Ten Nights in a Bar-Room (see Pratt, William W.)
Ten P. M. (see Aldis, Mary)
The Tender Husband; or, The Accomplished Fools (see Steele,
    Richard)

The Tender Sisters (see Gellert, Christian Fürchtegott)
The Tender Trap (see Shulman, Max)
Tendres Chasseurs (see Guerra, Ruy)
Ten-Minute Alibi (see Armstrong, Anthony)
Tennessee Day in St. Louis (see Taylor, Peter)
The Tenor (see Wedekind, Frank)
The Tenth Man (see Chayefsky, Paddy)
The Tenth Man (see Levinger, Elma Ehrlich)
TERENCE (Publius Terentius Afer), 185-159 B.C.
    The Brothers
        (In Complete Roman Drama, Vol. 2)
    The Eunuch
        (In Complete Roman Drama, Vol. 2)
    Eunuchus 232-91, translated by D. Parker
        (In Arion, Vol. 6, Summer 1967)
    The Mother-in-Law
        (In Complete Roman Drama, Vol. 2)
    Phormio
        (In Complete Roman Drama, Vol. 2)
    The Self-Tormenter
        (In Complete Roman Drama, Vol. 2)
    The Woman of Andros
        (In Complete Roman Drama, Vol. 2)
Teresa (see Ginzburg, Natalia)
Teresa of Avila (see Williamson, Hugh Ross)
Terminal (see Yankowitz, Susan)
La Terra Trema (see Visconti, Luchino)
Terre en Transe (Terra em Transe) (see Rocha, Glauber)
La Terre Tremble (see Visconti, Luchino)
Terrible Jim Fitch (see Herlihy, James Leo)
A Terrible Secret (see Coyne, J. Stirling)
Terror of Light (see Williams, Charles)
TERRY, Megan, 1932-
    Calm Down Mother
        (In Eight Plays From Off-Off Broadway)
    Ex-Miss Copper Queen on a Set of Pills
        (In Playwrights for Tomorrow, Vol. 1)
    Keep Tightly Closed in a Cool, Dry Place
        (In Tulane Drama Review, Vol. 10, Summer 1966)
    The Magic Realists
        (In Best Short Plays, 1968)
    The Tommy Allen Show
        (In Scripts, Vol. 1, no. 2, Dec. 1971)
    Viet Rock; a folk war movie with musical score by Marianne de
    Purey
TERSON, Peter
    The Apprentices
        (In Plays and Players, Vol. 16, Oct. 1968)
    But Fred Freud is Dead
        (In Plays and Players, Vol. 19, no. 6, Mar. 1972)
    The Mighty Reservoy
        (In Plays and Players, Vol. 14, Aug. 1967)

The Samaritan
   (In Plays and Players, Vol. 18, no. 10, July 1971)
Spring-Heeled Jack
   (In Plays and Players, Vol. 17, Nov. 1970)
O Tesouro de Chica da Silva   (see Callado, Antonio)
The Test   (see Marivaux, Pierre Carlet de Chamblain de)
The Test   (see Ruscoll, Joseph)
The Testament   (see Lopez Mozo, Jeronimo)
Le Testament du Docteur Cordelier   (see Renoir, Jean)
The Testament of Orpheus   (see Cocteau, Jean)
Tevya and the First Daughter   (see Perl, Arnold)
THACKERAY, William Makepeace, 1811-1863
   **Becky Sharp   (see Mitchell, Langdon Elwyn)
   King Glumpus
      (In Bookman, Vol. 8, Dec. 1898)
Thai Lakon Jatri   (see Manohra)
Thalaba, the Destroyer   (see Fitz-Ball, Edward)
Thank You, Edmondo   (see Shoub, Mac)
Thank You, Miss Victoria   (see Hoffman, William M.)
THARP, Newton J.
   The Quest of the Gorgon
      (In The Grove Plays of the Bohemian Club, Vol. 1)
That Certain Age   (see Manning, Bruce)
That Lady   (see O'Brien, Kate)
That They May Win   (see Miller, Arthur)
That's Hollywood   (see Ryerson, Florence)
Theatre de l'Epee de Bois
   Three Street Plays: Dis May; Repression; At the Polls.
   Paris, 1968
      (In TDR/Drama Review, Vol. 13, Summer 1969)
Theaulon de Lambert, Marie Emmanuel Guillaume Marguerite, 1787-
1841
   *The Brigand   (see Planche, James Robinson)
Their Anniversary   (see Riley, Mrs. Alice Cushing Donaldson)
Their Day   (see Kemp, Harry Hibbard)
Their Very Own and Golden City   (see Wesker, Arnold)
Theodat   (see Verdot, Guy)
Theodosius II, Emperor of the East, 401-450
   *Theodosius; or, The Force of Love   (see Lee, Nathaniel)
Theoreme   (see Pasolini, Pier Paolo)
Theories and Thumbs   (see Field, Rachel Lyman)
Theory of Tragedy   (see Goodman, Paul)
There Is No Dog   (see Cangiullo, Francesco)
There Is No Glory   (see Corrie, Joe)
There's a Girl in My Soup   (see Frisby, Terence)
There's a Wall between Us, Darling   (see Ordway, Sally)
There's Always Juliet   (see Van Druten, John)
There's Money Coming to You   (see Florin, Peter)
There's Some Milk in the Ice Box   (see Henderson, B. J.)
Therese Raquin   (see Zola, Emile)
Therese; the Orphan of Geneva   (see Payne, John Howard)
Thersites (Anon.)

(In Dodsley's A Select Collection of Old English Plays, Vol.
    1)
The Thesmophoriazusae (see Aristophanes)
They Asked for It (see Smith, Del)
They Burned the Books (see Benet, Stephen Vincent)
They Got Jack (see Rutman, Leo)
They Knew What They Wanted (see Howard, Sidney Coe)
They Refuse to be Resurrected (see Smith, N. K.)
They Shoot Horses, Don't They? (see Poe, James)
They Told Me That You Came This Way (see Epstein, David)
Thieves' Carnival (see Anouilh, Jean)
The Thing Itself (see Sainer, Arthur)
Things Went Badly in Westphalia (see Sherman, Martin)
The Third Angle (see Ryerson, Florence)
The Third Daughter (see Fratti, Mario)
The Third Fourth of July (see Cullen, Countee)
The Third Man (see Greene, Graham)
The Thirteenth Chair (see Veiller, Bayard)
Thirty Pieces of Silver (see Lehman, Leo)
Thirty Seconds over Tokyo (see Trumbo, Dalton)
This Earth Is Ours (see Kozlenko, William)
This I Believe (see Saroyan, William)
This Is Villa (see Niggli, Josephina)
This Land Is Mine (see Nichols, Dudley)
This Music Crept by Me upon the Waters (see MacLeish, Archibald)
This Property Is Condemned (see Williams, Tennessee)
This Story of Yours (see Hopkins, John)
"This Was a Man!" (see Coward, Noel Pierce)
THOMA, Ludwig, 1867-1921
    When You Are Twenty-One!
    (In One-Act Play Magazine, 1937/38 Anthology)
THOMAS, Augustus, 1857-1934
    The Witching Hour
    (In Best Plays of the Early American Theatre, from the
        beginning to 1916)
THOMAS, Dorothy
    Next-to-Last Rites
    (In Best Short Plays, 1954/55)
THOMAS, Dylan, 1914-1953
    **Adventures in the Skin Trade (see Sinclair, Andrew)
    The Doctor and the Devils; a film scenario from the story by
        Donald Fraser Taylor
    (A New Directions Book, 1953)
    Under Milk Wood
    (In Mademoiselle, Vol. 38, Feb. 1954)
THOMAS, Gwyn
    Jackie the Jumper
    (In Plays of the Year, Vol. 26, 1962/63)
    The Keep
    (In Plays of the Year, Vol. 24, 1961)
THOMAS, Robert, 1930-
    Assassins Associes

(In L'Avant-Scene du Theatre, no. 346, Dec. 1, 1965)
Deux Chats et...un Souris
   (In L'Avant-Scene du Theatre, no. 346, Dec. 1, 1965)
Le Deuxieme Coup de Feu
   (In L'Avant-Scene du Theatre, no. 327, Feb. 1, 1965)
   (In Plaisir de France, supplement theatral, no. 317, Mar.
   1965)
Double Jeu
   (In L'Avant-Scene du Theatre, no. 458, Oct. 15, 1970)
   (In Plaisir de France, supplement Theatral, no. 384, Dec.
   1970)
Freddy
   (In Plaisir de France, supplement theatral, no. 369, July/
   Aug. 1969)
Huit Femmes
   (In L'Avant-Scene du Theatre, no. 268, July 1, 1962)
La Perruche et le Poulet
   (In Plaisir de France, supplement theatral, no. 341, Mar.
   1967)
Piege pour un Homme Seul
   (In L'Avant-Scene du Theatre, no. 231)
Thomas à Becket, Saint, Abp. of Canterbury, 1118?-1170
   *Becket; or, the Honor of God (see Anouilh, Jean)
   *Curtmantle (see Fry, Christopher)
Thomas Cranmer of Canterbury (see Williams, Charles)
Thomas More, ou L'Homme Seul (see Bolt, Robert)
THOMPSON, Benjamin, 1776?-1816
   The Stranger
   (In Cumberland's British Theatre, Vol. 4, no. 4)
THOMPSON, Blanche Jenning
   The Dream Maker
   (In Drama, Vol. 12, Mar. 1922)
THOMPSON, Charles (dramatist)
   The Gambler's Fate; or, A Lapse of Twenty Years
   (In Cumberland's British Theatre, Vol. 2, no. 3)
THOMPSON, Denman, 1833-1911
   The Old Homestead
   (In S. R. O., the Most Successful Plays...)
THOMPSON, Doris K.
   Salvage
   (In Drama, Vol. 21, May 1931)
THOMPSON, Jay
   Double Entry; two musicals: "The Bible Salesman" and "The
   Oldest Trick in the World"
   (In Theatre Arts, Vol. 45, July 1961)
   Once Upon a Mattress (see Rodgers, Mary)
THOMSON, James, 1700-1748
   Edward and Eleanora
   (In Bell's British Theatre, 1797, Vol. 32)
   Tancred and Sigismunda
   (In Bell's British Theatre, 1797, Vol. 14)
   An Uncle Too Many
   (In Cumberland's British Theatre, Vol. 34, no. 4)

THON, Frederick
  The Island
    (In Best Short Plays, 1954/55)
THORNBURN, John
  The Man in the Street
    (In Best One-Act Plays of 1940, London)
THORNE, Ian
  Jane Seymour; a television script in the series "The Six Wives
    of Henry VIII"
    (In Plays of the Year Special, 1972)
A Thousand Clowns (see Gardner, Herb)
"3" (see Carrick, Pat)
The Three and the Duce; or, Which Is Which? (see Hoare, Prince)
The Three Cuckolds (Anon.)
    (In The Classic Theatre, ed. by Eric Bentley, Vol. 1)
Three Hours after Marriage (see Gay, John)
Three Kisses (see Scott, Margaretta)
The Three Ladies of London (Anon.)
    (In Dodsley's A Select Collection of Old English Plays, Vol.
      6)
The Three Maries (see Cornish Cycle)
Three Men on a Horse (see Abbott, George)
Three Months Gone (see Howarth, Donald)
The Three Penny Day (see Plautus, Titus Maccius)
Three People (see Gurney, A.R., Jr.)
Three Persons (see Agoston, Gerty)
Three Pills in a Bottle (see Field, Rachel Lyman)
The Three Sisters (see Chekhov, Anton Pavlovich)
Three Souls in Search of a Dramatist (see Schwartz, Esther Dres-
  den)
The Three Spinners (see Frank, Florence Kiper)
The Three Temptations (see Williams, Charles)
Three Travelers Watch a Sunrise (see Stevens, Wallace)
The Three Wise Men (see Vincente, Gill)
The Threepenny Opera (see Brecht, Bertolt)
The Three-Penny Opera; screenplay (see Lania, Leo)
Three's a Crowd (see McCarty, Sara Sloane)
The Threshold (see McCauley, Clarice Vallette)
The Thrice Promised Bride (see Hsiung, Cheng-Chin)
Through a Glass Darkly (see Bergman, Ingmar)
Through a Glass Darkly (see Richards, Stanley)
Through Deserts to Ancestral Lands (see Strindberg, August)
Thunder God (Kaminari) (see Sakanishi, Shio)
Thunder on Sycamore Street (see Rose, Reginald)
Thunder Over Mexico (see Que Viva Mexico!)
THURBER, James 1894-1961
    The Male Animal, by James Thurber and Elliott Nugent
      (In Best Plays of the Modern American Theatre, Second
        Series)
      (In Stage, Vol. 1, no. 3, Jan. 1941)
Thursday Evening (see Morley, Christopher)
THURSTON, Althea

The Exchange
    (In Contemporary One-Act Plays, 1922)
A Pageant of Spring
    (In Drama, Vol. 12, April 1922)
Th(us) (see Beye, Holly)
Thyestes (see Seneca, Lucius Annaeus, the Younger)
Thyestes 885-1112 (see Seneca, Lucius Annaeus, the Younger)
Tic-Tac (see Rody, Alberto)
Tides (see Middleton, George)
Tidy Passions; or, Kill, Kaleidoscope, Kill (see Koutoukas, H. M.)
The Tiger (see Schisgal, Murray)
Tiger at the Gates (see Giraudoux, Jean)
The Tiger in the Rockery (see Draim, Richard)
Le Tigre (see Schisgal, Murray)
TIGRE, Bastos
    O Microbio do Amor
    (In Revista de Teatro, no. 316)
Till the Day I Die (see Odets, Clifford)
Till Time Shall End (see Ashton, Winifred)
Tillie and Gus (see Martin, Francis)
Timanthes (see Hoole, John)
Time and the Hour (see Simpson, John Palgrave)
Time and Tide; a Tale of the Thames! (see Leslie, Henry)
Time Limit! (see Denker, Henry)
Time of Innocence (see Lenz, Siegfried)
The Time of the Cuckoo (see Laurents, Arthur)
The Time of Your Life (see Saroyan, William)
Time Out for Ginger (see Alexander, Ronald)
Time Remembered (see Anouilh, Jean)
A Time to Live (see Bentley, Eric Russell)
Time's a Tell-Tale (see Siddons, Henry)
Le Timide au Palais (see Tellez, Gabriel)
Timour the Tartar (see Lewis, Matthew Gregory)
The Tinguely Machine Mystery; or, The Love Suicides at Kaluka
    (see Koch, Kenneth)
The Tinker (see Dobie, Laurence)
Tinker's Curse (see Corlett, William)
Tinko (see Schmidt, Hans-Dieter)
TINOCO, Godofredo
    Judas No Tribunal
    (In Revista de Teatro, no. 321)
Tinsel Duchess (see Johnson, Philip)
Tiny Alice (see Albee, Edward)
The Tiny Closet (see Inge, William)
Tip and Run (see Brighouse, Harold)
'Tis a Pity She's a Whore (see Ford, John)
To Bobolink, for Her Spirit (see Inge, William Motter)
To Damascus (see Strindberg, August)
To Kill a Mockingbird (see Foote, Horton)
To See Ourselves (see De La Pasture, Emee Elizabeth Monica)
To the American People (see Wishengrad, Morton)
Tobacco Alley (see Randall, William M.)

The Tobacco Evil (see Chekhov, Anton Pavlovich)
Tobacco Road (see Kirkland, Jack)
The Tobacconist (see Gentleman, Francis)
TOBIN, John, 1770-1804
    The Honey Moon
        (In Cumberland's British Theatre, Vol. 14, no. 2)
Togetherness (see Merritt, Robert)
Toi et Tes Nuages (see Westphal, Eric)
The Toilet (see Jones, LeRoi)
TOJEIRO, Gastao
    O Simpatico Jeremias
        (In Revista de Teatro, no. 350)
Tojuro's Love (see Kikuchi Kwan)
TOLLER, Ernst, 1893-1939
    The Blind Goddess
        (In Seven Plays of Toller)
    Draw the Fires!
        (In Seven Plays of Toller)
    Hinkemann
        (In Seven Plays of Toller)
    Hoopla! Such Is Life
        (In Seven Plays of Toller)
        (In Makers of the Modern Theater, 1961)
    The Machine-Wreckers
        (In Seven Plays of Toller)
    Mary Baker Eddy
        (In Seven Plays of Toller)
    Masse Mensch
        (In Das Deutsche Drama, 1880-1933, Vol. 2)
    Masses and Man
        (In Seven Plays of Toller)
    Transfiguration
        (In Seven Plays of Toller)
Der Tollste Tag (see Turrini, Peter)
TOLSTOY, Leo Nikolayevitch, 1828-1910
    Redemption (The Living Corpse)
        (In 20 Best European Plays on the American Stage)
Tom and Jerry; or, Life in London (see Moncrieff, William
    Thomas)
Tom Bowling (see Campbell, Andrew Leonard Voullaire)
Tom Jones (see Osborne, John)
Tom Paine (see Foster, Paul)
Tom Thrasher (see Harris, Augustus Glossip)
Tom Thumb (see Fielding, Henry)
TOMES, Margaret Otey
    The Children and the Evangelists
        (In Drama, Vol. 11, Nov. 1920)
TOMHOLT, Sydney
    Anoli: The Blind
        (In Best One-Act Plays of 1936, London)
TOMKIS, Thomas, fl. 1604-1615
    Albumazar

(In Dodsley's A Select Collection of Old English Plays, Vol.
   11)
(In Dodsley's A Select Collection of Old Plays, Vol. 7)
Lingua; or, The Combat of the Tongue and the Five Senses
(In Dodsley's A Select Collection of Old English Plays, Vol.
   9)
(In Dodsley's A Select Collection of Old Plays, Vol. 5)
The Tommy Allen Show (see Terry, Megan)
Tomorrow (see Foote, Horton)
Tomorrow the Dawn (see Montherlant, Henry de)
Tomorrow the World (see Gow, James)
TOMPKINS, Frank Gerow, 1879-
   The Letters
      (In 50 More Contemporary One-Act Plays)
   Sham
      (In 50 Contemporary One-Act Plays)
Tongues of Fire (see Kearney, Patrick)
Tonight at 8:30 (see Coward, Noel Pierce)
Too Late to Call Backe Yesterday and To-Morrow Comes Not Yet
   (see Davenport, Robert)
TOOMER, Jean
   Balo
      (In Plays of Negro Life)
Top Secret; or, A Few Million after B.C. (see Caldwell, Ben)
El Topo (see Jodorowsky, Alexandro)
TOPOL, Josef
   Fin de Carnaval
      (In Plaisir de France, supplement theatral, no. 374, Jan.
      1970)
TOPOR, Tom, 1938-
   Answers
      (In Best Short Plays, 1972)
Der Tor und der Tod (see Hofmannsthal, Hugo von)
TORAHIKO, Enomoto
   Raizan
      (In Best One-Act Plays of 1934, London)
TORRENCE, Frederic Ridgely, 1875-1950
   Danse Calindo
      (In Theatre Arts, Vol. 3, 1919)
      (In Plays of Negro Life)
   Granny Maumee
      (In Plays of Negro Life)
   The Rider of Dreams
      (In Short Plays by Representative Authors, 1920)
      (In Plays of Negro Life)
Torrence, Ridgely (see Torrence, Frederic Ridgely)
Torticola contre Frankensberg (see Paviot, Paul)
TOTHEROH, Dan
   All That Money Can Buy, screenplay based on "The Devil and
   Daniel Webster" by Stephen Vincent Benet, directed by William
   Dieterle
      (In 20 Best Film Plays)

The Great Dark
   (In Best One-Act Plays of 1933, London)
   (In Drama, Vol. 21, Feb. 1931)
The Lost Princess
   (In Drama, Vol. 19, Jan. 1929)
Mirthful Marionettes
   (In Drama, Vol. 21, April 1931)
The Stolen Prince
   (In Drama, Vol. 15, Oct. 1924)
A Tune of a Tune
   (In Drama, Vol. 10, Feb. 1920)
The Widdy's Mite
   (In Drama, Vol. 13, Oct. 1922)
   Yellow Jack (see Chodorov, Edward)
Totenham Court: a Pleasant Comedie (see Nabbes, Thomas)
Touch and Go (see Lawrence, David Herbert)
Touch It Light (see Storey, Robert)
A Touch of Marble (see Potter, Dan S.)
A Touch of the Poet (see O'Neill, Eugene)
Tour of Duty (see Kelley, Arthur)
Tourbe, Robert
   Petite Fleur de Mageve (see Lefevre, Raymond)
TOURNEUR, Cyril, 1575?-1626
   The Revenger's Tragedy
      (In Dodsley's A Select Collection of Old English Plays, Vol.
      10)
      (In Dodsley's A Select Collection of Old Plays, Vol. 4)
Tout a l'Heure (see Worms, Jeannine)
Un Tout Autre Visage (see Lang, Michel)
Toute la Memoire du Monde (see Resnais, Alain)
Tovarich (see Deval, Jacques)
The Tower (see Weiss, Peter)
The Tower of Nesle; or, The Chamber of Death (see Almar,
   George)
The Town (see Anagonostaki, Loula)
Town and Country (see Morton, Thomas)
TOWNLEY, James, 1714-1778
   High Life below Stairs
      (In Cumberland's British Theatre, Vol. 25, no. 4)
The Toy Cart (see Shudraka, King)
TOYAZAWA, Chika
   The Miracle at Tsubosaka Temple (Tsubosaka Reigenki)
      (In Six Kabuki Plays)
Toys in the Attic (see Hellman, Lillian)
The Trachinae (see Sophocles)
Tradition (see Middleton, George)
Tragedie de l'Absence (see Dalbray, Muse)
The Tragedy (see Scott, Margaretta)
Tragedy in a Temporary Town (see Rose, Reginald)
The Tragedy of Nero, Emperour of Rome (see Lee, Nathaniel)
The Tragedy of Sir John Van Olden Barnavelt (Anon.)
      (In A Collection of Old English Plays, Vol. 2)

The Tragedy of the Duchess of Malfi (see Webster, John)
The Tragical Comedy of Appius and Virginia (Anon.)
    (In Dodsley's A Select Collection of Old English Plays, Vol.
    4)
    (In Dodsley's A Select Collection of Old Plays, Vol. 12)
The Tragical History of Doctor Faustus (see Marlowe, Christopher)
The Tragi-Comedy of Calisto and Melibaea (Anon.)
    (In Dodsley's A Select Collection of Old English Plays, Vol.
    1)
A Train Going Somewhere (see Gardner, Gary)
Train to H... (see Bellido Cormanzana, Jose Maria)
"Transe" (see Radde, Ronald)
Transfiguration (see Toller, Ernst)
Transition in India (see Marquis, Arnold)
Trap Doors (see Kreymborg, Alfred)
A Trap in a Small Place (see Perry, Marjean)
Trauer zu Früh (see Bond, Edward)
The Traveler (see Connelly, Marc)
Traveller without Luggage (see Anouilh, Jean)
The Travels of Yi Yuk-Sa to the Caves of Yenan (see Howard,
    Roger)
La Traversee de Paris (see Autant-Lara, Claude)
Trazcinski, Edmund, 1921-
    Stalag 17 (see Bevan, Donald)
TREADWELL, Sophie
    Machinal
    (In 25 Best Plays of the Modern American Theatre, Early
    Series, 1916-1929)
TREE, Jonathan
    The Fisherman
    (In Best One-Act Plays of 1945, N.Y.)
    (In Best Short Plays, 1956/57)
The Tree (see Arlett, Vers Isabel)
A Tree Grows in Brooklyn (see Slesinger, Tess)
Treichville (see Rouch, Jean)
TREITEL, Ralph
    The Minyana's Daughter
    (In Drama & Theatre, Vol. 7, no. 2, Winter 1968/69)
Trelawny (see Slade, Julian)
Trencavel (see Collon, Robert)
Trente-six Heures (see Haudiquet, Philippe)
Tres Peraltas na Praca (see Valluzi, Jose)
TREVISAN, Anna F., 1905-
    Easter Eve
    (In Best One-Act Plays of 1947/48, N.Y.)
    Valley of the Shadow
    (In Best One-Act Plays, 1950/51, N.Y.)
Trevor (see Bowen, John)
Trevor, Elleston
    **The Quiller Memorandum (see Pinter, Harold)
The Trial (see Welles, Orson)
The Trial of Joseph and Mary (Anon.)
    (In Masterworks of World Drama, Vol. 2)

The Trial of Poznan (see Boretz, Alvin)
The Trial to Treasure (Anon.)
    (In Dodsley's A Select Collection of Old English Plays, Vol.
    3)
The Trials of Brother Jero (see Soyinka, Wole)
TRIANA, Jose
    The Criminals
        (In Modern Stage in Latin America, 1971)
        (In TDR/The Drama Review, Vol. 14, no. 2, Winter 1970)
Tria-Nova Triumphans (see Dekker, Thomas)
Tribulation; or, Unwelcome Visitors (see Poole, John)
A Tribute to Gallantry (see Hecht, Ben)
A Trick to Catch the Old One (see Middleton, Thomas)
The Trickster of Seville (see Tellez, Gabriel)
The Tridget of Greva (see Lardner, Ring Wilmer)
Trifles (see Glaspell, Susan)
A Trilogy of Dubrovnik (see Vojnovich, Ino)
TRINKA, Jiri, 1912-
    Le Rosignol de l'Empereur de Chine, by Jiri Trinka and Jean
    Cocteau
        (In L'Avant-Scene du Cinema, no. 3, Apr. 15, 1961)
Trio (see Sherriff, Robert Cedric)
TRIOLET, Elsa
    Les Bains
        (In L'Avant-Scene du Theatre, Apr. 15, 1968)
The Trip to Bountiful (see Foote, Horton)
A Trip to Czardis (see Granberry, Edwin)
A Trip to Czardis (see Hart, James & Elizabeth)
A Trip to Scarborough (see Sheridan, Richard Brinsley)
Trip-Tych (see Epstein, David)
Tristana (see Buñuel, Luis)
The Triumph of Bohemia (see Sterling, George)
The Triumph of the Egg (see Anderson, Sherwood)
Trois Cents Metres d'Elevation (see Charras, Charles)
Trois Hommes sur un Cheval (see Moussy, Marcel)
Les Trois Musiciens (see Higuera, Pablo de la)
La Troisieme Agnes (see Mithois, Marcel)
The Trojan Women (see Euripides)
The Trojan Women (see Seneca, Luccius Annaeus, the Younger)
Le Trombe d'Eustachio (see Brancati, Vitaliano)
The Trophy Hunters (see Lascelles, Kendrew)
Trotsky, Leon, 1879-1940
    *The Death of Trotsky (see Cook, Albert)
    *Trotsky in Exile (see Weiss, Peter)
TROTTI, Lamar, 1900-1952
    In Old Chicago; screenplay by Lamar Trotti and Sonya Levien,
    based upon original story by Niven Busch, directed by Henry
    King.
        (In Foremost Films of 1938)
    The Ox-Bow Incident, by Lamar Trotti, based on the novel by
    Walter Van Tilburg Clark, directed by William A. Wellman.
        (In Best Film Plays, 1943/44, Vol. 1)

Wilson; screenplay by Lamar Trotti, directed by Henry King
   (In Best Film Plays, 1943/44, Vol. 1)
Trotzki in Coyoacan (see Lange, Hartmut)
Le Trou (see Becker, Jacques)
A Troubadour's Dream (see Clements, Claudine E.)
The Troublesome One (see Brusati, Franco)
TROUGHTON, Adolphus Charles
   Wooing in Jest and Loving in Earnest
      (In Lacy's Plays)
Truculentus (see Plautus, Titus Maccius)
The True History of Squire Jonathan and His Unfortunate Treasure
   (see Arden, John)
The True Trojans (see Fuimus Troes: The True Trojans)
TRUFFAUT, Francois, 1932-
  **A Bout de Souffle (see Goddard, Jean-Luc)
   Les Deux Anglaises et le Continent, by Francois Truffaut et
   Jean Gruault, d'apres le roman de Henri Pierre Roche
      (In L'Avant-Scene du Cinema, no. 121, Jan. 1972)
   L'Enfant Sauvage, d'apres "Memoire et Rapport sur Victor de
   L'Aveyron" par Jean Itard
      (In L'Avant-Scene du Cinema, no. 107, Oct. 1970)
   The 400 Blows
      (In Evergreen Filmscripts Series)
   Une Histoire d'Eau, by Francois Truffaut and Jean-Luc Godard
      (In L'Avant-Scene du Cinema, no. 7, Sept. 17, 1961)
   Jules and Jim
      (Modern Film Scripts Series)
   Jules et Jim, by Francois Truffaut et Jean Gruault, d'apres le
   roman de Henri-Pierre Roche
      (In L'Avant-Scene du Cinema, no. 16, June 15, 1962)
   Les Mistons, d'apres une nouvelle de Maurice Pons
      (In L'Avant-Scene du Cinema, no. 4, May 15, 1961)
   La Peau Douce
      (In L'Avant-Scene du Cinema, no. 48, 1965)
   Les Quatre Cents Coups, by Francois Truffaut et Marcel
   Moussy
      (In Cahiers du Cinema, Vol. 14, no. 90, Dec. 1958)
TRUMBO, Dalton, 1905-
   The Biggest Thief in Town
      (In Theatre Arts, Vol. 34, Jan. 1950)
   Thirty Seconds over Tokyo, based on the book by Capt. Ted W.
   Lawson and Robert Considine, directed by Mervyn Le Roy
      (In Best Film Plays, 1945, Vol. 2)
Trunk (see Dana, Robert Patrick)
The Truth (see Fitch, Clyde)
The Truth about Shakespeare (see Box, Sydney)
Try It Again (see Priestley, John Boynton)
Try! Try! Try! (see O'Hara, Frank)
The Trysting Place (see Tarkington, Booth)
Tu Etais Si Gentil Quand Tu Etais Petit! (see Anouilh, Jean)
TUCKER, Charles Davis
   Matrimony Up-to-Date

(In The Banner Anthology of One-Act Plays by American
Authors)
Tudor Thorns (see Morris, Thomas Badden)
Tugging (see Cox, Nancy Burney)
TUKE, Sir Samuel, d. 1674
The Adventures of Five Hours
(In Dodsley's A Select Collection of Old English Plays, Vol.
15)
(In Dodsley's A Select Collection of Old Plays, Vol. 12)
Tumble-down Dick; or, Phaeton in the Suds (see Fielding, Henry)
TUNBERG, Karl A.
Hang by Their Shoelaces
(In Drama & Theatre, Vol. 7, no. 1, Fall 1968)
A Tune of a Tune (see Totheroh, Dan W.)
Tunnel of Love (see Richards, Stanley)
The Turbulent Waters (see Basshe, Emjo)
Turcaret; or, The Financier (see Le Sage, Alain-Rene)
Turds in Hell (see Ludlam, Charles)
TURGENEV, Ivan Sergeyevich, 1818-1883
Un Mois a la Champagne
(In Plaisir de France, supplement theatral, no. 306, April
1964)
A Month in the Country, adapted by Emlyn Williams
(In Masterworks of World Drama, Vol. 6)
(In 20 Best European Plays on the American Stage)
A Month in the Country; text in French
(In L'Avant-Scene du Theatre, no. 307, Mar. 15, 1964)
One May Spin a Thread Too Finely
(In Fortnightly, Vol. 91, April 1909)
The Turks Toss for Her (see Berretta, Alfio)
Turlututu (see Archard, Marcel)
The Turn of a Hair (see Hoffman, Phoebe)
Turn of the Century (see Gurney, A.R., Jr.)
The Turn of the Screw (see Vidal, Gore)
Turnandot (see Gozzi, Carlo, conte)
The Turned Head (see A Beckett, Gilbert Abbott)
The Turnpike Gate (see Knight, Thomas)
TURPIN, Francois
Don Juan Malgre Lui
(In Plaisir de France, supplement theatral, no. 370, Sept.
1969)
On Finit Quelquefois par Ou l'On Devrait Toujours Commencer
(In L'Avant-Scene du Theatre, no. 347, Dec. 15, 1965)
(In Plaisir de France, supplement theatral, no. 327, Jan.
1966)
Pastorale
(In L'Avant-Scene du Theatre, no. 467, Mar 1, 1971)
(In Plaisir de France, supplement theatral, no. 389, May
1971)
Sait-on Jamais!
(In L'Avant-Scene du Theatre, no. 190, Feb. 1, 1959)

TURRINI, Peter
    Der Tollste Tag
      (In Theater Heute, no. 4, April 1972)
Tutankhamon, Son of Ra   (see Morris, T. B.)
Twain, Mark, pseud.   (see Clemens, Samuel Langhorne)
Twelfth Night   (see Shakespeare, William)
Twelve Angry Men   (see Rose, Reginald)
The Twelve-Pound Look   (see Barrie, Sir James Matthew)
Twenty-five Cents   (see Harris, W. Eric)
Twenty-seven Wagons Full of Cotton   (see Williams,
    Tennessee)
23 John Street, Adelphi   (see Buckstone, John Baldwin)
The Twilight Maelstrom of Cookie La Vagetto   (see O'Donoghue,
    Michael)
The Twilight of the Gods   (see Bacon, Josephine Dodge
    Daskam)
Twilight of the Moon   (see Going, Charles Buxton)
Twilight Zone: the Lonely   (see Serling, Rod)
The Twin Menaechmi   (see Plautus, Titius Maccius)
The Twin Rivals   (see Farquhar, George)
The Twisted State   (see Buenaventura, Enrique)
The Two Angry Women   (see Porter, Henry)
The Two Angry Women of Abington   (see Porter, Henry)
The Two Bacchides   (see Plautus, Titus Maccius)
Two Blind Mice   (see Spewack, Samuel)
The Two Bouquets   (see Farjeon, Eleanor)
Two Can Play at That Game   (see Pierron, Eugene Athanase)
Two for the Seesaw   (see Gibson, William)
The Two Foscari: an Historical Tragedy   (see Byron, George
    Gordon Noël Byron, 6th Baron)
The Two Friends   (see Lacy, Michael Rophino)
The Two Galley Slaves   (see Payne, John Howard)
Two Gentlemen at Mivart's   (see Simpson, J. Palgrave)
The Two Gregories; or, Where Did the Money Come From?   (see
    Dibdin, Thomas)
Two Hundred Thousand and One   (see Cappelli, Salvato)
Two Lane Blacktop   (see Wurlitzer, Rudolph)
The Two Milords; or, The Blow of Thunder   (see Leacock, Stephen)
The Two Orphans   (see Dennery, Adolphe Philippe)
2 [deux] ou 3 Choses Que Je Said d'Elle   (see Godard, Jean-Luc)
Two Passengers for Chelsea   (see Firkins, Oscar W.)
Two Sides of Darkness   (see Procunier, Edwin R.)
Two Stars for Comfort   (see Mortimer, John)
Two Strings to Your Bow   (see Jephson, Robert)
Two Tragedies in One   (see Yarington, Robert)
Two's Company   (see Perry, Marjean)
Tyl Ulenspiegel   (see Dukes, Ashley)
TYLER, Royall, 1757?-1826
    The Contrast
      (In American Drama)
      (In Best Plays of the Early American Theatre, from the
    beginning to 1916)

TYNAN, Kenneth
    Oh! Calcutta
        (In Evergreen Review, Vol. 13, no. 69, Aug. 1969)
        (In Evergreen Playscript Series)
Typhus (see Dryer, Bernard Victor)
The Typists (see Schisgal, Murray)
Tyrone and the Robbers (see Hayn, Annette)
TZARA, Tristan
    The Gas-burning Heart
        (In Chicago Review, Vol. 29, no. 4, May 1969)
    Handkerchief of Clouds
        (In TDR/Drama Review, Vol. 16, Dec. 1972)

U.S.A. (see Dos Passos, John)
UDALL, Nicholas, 1805-1556
    Ralph Roister Doister
        (In Dodsley's A Select Collection of Old English Plays, Vol.
        3)
The Ugly Duckling (see Milne, Alan Alexander)
La Ultima Letra (see Vilalta, Maruxa)
Ultima Noite (see Barreto, Paulo)
ULYANINSKY, A.
    Uncle Grumpy
        (In Soviet One-Act Plays)
"Umwege" (see Gratzik, Paul)
Uncle Grumpy (see Ulaninsky, A.)
The Uncle Toms (see Stokes, Herbert)
Uncle Tom's Cabin (see Aiken, George L.)
An Uncle Too Many (see Thomson, James)
Uncle Vanya (see Chekhov, Anton Pavlovich)
Under Cover (see Megrue, Roi Cooper)
Under Milk Wood (see Thomas, Dylan)
Under Plain Cover (see Osborne, John)
Under the Gaslight; or, Life and Love in These Times (see Daly,
    Augustin)
Under the Skin (see Ross, Kenneth)
The Undercurrent (see Ehlert, Fay)
The Underpants (see Sternheim, Carl)
Une Vie (see Astruc, Alexandre)
An Unfair Exchange (Saragai Koto) (see Sakanishi, Shio)
Unforeseen Events (see Hele, Thomas d')
The Unfortunate Mother (see Nabbes, Thomas)
Ein Unheimlich Starker Abgang (see Sommer, Harald)
L'Unique Jour de l'Annee (see Seymour, Alan)
The Universal Gallant; or, The Different Husbands (see Fielding,
    Henry)
The Unknown General (see Obaldia, Rene de)
The Unknown Sailor (see Gladkov, Alexander)
The Unknown Soldier and His Wife (see Ustinov, Peter)
The Unloved (see Morris, Colin)
Unnatural Scene (see Davey, Kathleen)

UNRUH, Fritz von, 1885-
Heinrich aus Andernach
(In Das Deutsche Drama, 1880-1933, Vol. 2)
The Unruly Member (see Heath, Crosby)
The Unsatisfactory Supper (see Williams, Tennessee)
The Unsatisfactory Supper (see also The Long Stay Cut Short)
The Unsinkable Molly Brown (see Willson, Meredith)
Until Charlot Comes Home (see Reynolds, Rachel)
Until She Screams (see Orton, Joe)
Until the Monkey Comes (see Herndon, Venable)
Unto the Least of These (see Rowell, Adelaide C.)
Unveiling (see Szabo, Magda)
Up (see Sassoon, R. L.)
Uplifting Sadie (see Riley, Mrs. Alice Cushing Donaldson)
Upon the Waters (see Hanna, Tacie May)
The Uprooted Pine (Nebiki no Kadomatsu) (see Chikamatsu Mon-
zaemon)
Upward, Upward (see Hitchcock, George)
Useless Oedipus (see Conti, Antonio)
USTINOV, Peter, 1921-
Beyond
(In Best One-Act Plays of 1942/43, London)
Love of Four Colonels; text in French
(In L'Avant-Scene du Theatre, no. 155)
Romanoff and Juliet
(In Theatre Arts, Vol. 43, May 1959)
Romanoff and Juliet; text in French
(In L'Avant-Scene du Theatre, no. 169, Mar. 1, 1958)
The Unknown Soldier and His Wife
(In Plays of the Year, Vol. 36, 1968/69)
(In Ramparts, Vol. 6, July 1967)

Les Vacances Revees (see Mithois, Marcel)
VADIM, Roger, 1928-
Et...Dieu Crea la Femme. English title: "And God Created
Woman)
(In L'Avant-Scene du Cinema, no. 20, Nov. 15, 1962)
Les Vagues Etaient Trop Fortes... (see Deutsch, Leon)
VAIL, Walter J.
The Death of Columbine
(In First Stage, Vol. 4, Summer 1965)
Manny
(In First Stage, Vol. 4, no. 1, Spring 1965)
VAJDA, Ladislaus, 1916-
Pandora's Box (Lulu). Screenplay by Ladislaus Vajda, from
two plays by Frank Wedekind: "Erdquest" and "Die Buchse
der Pandora." Directed by G.W. Pabst.
(In Classic Film Scripts)
The Three-Penny Opera; screenplay by Leo Lania, Ladislas
Vajda and Bela Balazs; based on John Gay's "Beggar's Opera";
adapted from the play by Bertolt Brecht; music by Kurt Weill;

directed by G. W. Pabst.
(In Classic Film Scripts)
VALENCY, Maurice Jacques, 1903-
Battleship Bismarck
(In Best Television Plays of the Year, 1949)
The Enchanted (see Giraudoux, Jean)
Feathertop, adapted from a story by Nathaniel Hawthorne
(In 15 American One-Act Plays)
The Madwoman of Chaillot (see Giraudoux, Jean)
Ondine (see Giraudoux, Jean)
The Visit (see Dürrenmatt, Friedrich)
Valentine and Orson (see Dibdin, Thomas)
The Valiant (see Middlemass, Robert)
VALLANCE, Rosalind
Pandora's Box
(In 24 One-Act Plays, Revised edition, 1954)
VALLE-INCLAN, Ramon Maria del, 1870-1936
Un Dia de Guerra
(In Modern Language Notes, Vol. 83, Mar. 1968)
The Dragon's Head
(In Poet Lore, Vol. 29, Winter 1918)
Lein de Sang
(In L'Avant-Scene du Theatre, no. 112)
Lights of Bohemia (Luces de Bohemia)
(In Kenyon Review, Vol. 29, Nov. 1967)
(In Modern International Drama, Vol. 2, no. 2, 1968)
Lumieres de Boheme
(In Plaisir de France, supplement theatral, no. 298, Aug.
1963)
(In L'Avant-Scene du Theatre, no. 292, July 15, 1963)
VALLEJO, Antonio Buero, 1916-
The Concert at Saint Ovide
(In Modern International Drama, Vol. 1, no. 1, Sept. 1967)
Ecrit sur le Sable
(In L'Avant-Scene du Theatre, no. 183, Oct. 15, 1958)
Valley Forge (see Anderson, Maxwell)
The Valley of Lost Men (see Ernst, Alice Henson)
Valley of the Shadow (see Trevisan, Anna F.)
VALLUZI, Jose
Tres Peraltas na Praca
(In Revista de Teatro, no. 384, Nov./Dec. 1971)
Vamos Brincar de Amor em Cabo Frio (see Viotti, Sergio)
Vampire (see Dreyer, Carl Theodor)
The Vampire; or, The Bride of the Isles (see Planche, James
Robinson)
VANBRUGH, Sir John, 1664-1726
The City Wives Confederacy
(In Bell's British Theatre, 1797, Vol. 22)
The Mistake
(In Bell's British Theatre, 1797, Vol. 25)
The Provoked Husband; or, A Journey to London, by Sir John
Vanbrugh and Colly Cibber

(In Bell's British Theatre, 1797, Vol. 18)
(In Cumberland's British Theatre, Vol. 18, no. 4)
(In The London Stage, Vol. 1)
The Provoked Wife
    (In Bell's British Theatre, 1797, Vol. 27)
    (In Great English Plays)
The Relapse; or, Virtue in Danger
    (In Bell's British Theatre, 1797, Vol. 26)
VANDENBERGHE, Paul
    Une Cliente Perdue
    (In L'Avant-Scene du Theatre, no. 180, Sept. 1, 1958)
    Un Coup de Soleil
    (In L'Avant-Scene du Theatre, no. 148)
    Mauvaise Semence, by Paul Vandenberghe and T. Mihalakeas
    (In L'Avant-Scene du Theatre, no. 197, May 15, 1959)
    Printemps Perdus
    (In L'Avant-Scene du Theatre, no. 103)
    Le Rendez-vous de Saint-Germain, by Paul Vandenberghe and
    Pierre Peyrou
    (In Plaisir de France, supplement theatral, no. 334, Aug.
    1966)
    Une Repetition Generale; ou, La Piece a Conviction
    (In L'Avant-Scene du Theatre, no. 264, May 1, 1962)
VAN DER VEER, Ethel
    The Lay-Figure
    (In The One-Act Theatre, Vol. 2)
    Let It Burn, by Ethel Van der Veer and Franklyn Bigelow
    (In New Plays for Women & Girls, 1932)
VAN DOREN, Mark, 1894-
    The Last Days of Lincoln
    (In Three Distinctive Plays About Abraham Lincoln)
VAN DRUTEN, John, 1901-1957
    After All
    (In Famous Plays of Today, 1931)
    Behold, We Live
    (In Famous Plays of Today, 1932/33)
    Bell, Book, and Candle
    (In Theatre Arts, Vol. 36, June 1952)
    (In Best American Plays, Third Series)
    The Distaff Side
    (In Famous Plays of Today, 1933/34)
    I Am a Camera, based on "Berlin Stories" by Christopher
    Isherwood
    (In Theatre Arts, Vol. 37, Jan. 1953)
    (In Best American Plays, Fourth Series)
    (In Famous Plays of Today, 1954)
    London Wall
    (In Famous Plays of Today, 1931)
    Somebody Knows
    (In Famous Plays of Today, 1932)
    There's Always Juliet
    (In Famous Plays of Today, 1932)

Young Woodley
  (In Famous Plays of Today, 1929)
VANE, Sutton, 1888-1963
  Outward Bound
  (In 16 Famous British Plays)
Vanessa (see Barber, Samuel)
Van Gogh, Vincent (see Gogh, Vincent van)
Van Gogh (see Hessens, Robert)
The Vanishing Princess (see Golden, John)
VAN Itallie, Jean-Claude, 1935-
  American Hurrah
    (In Eight Plays From Off-Off Broadway)
    (In American Hurrah: Plays)
  Almost Like Being
    (In War and Four Other Plays)
  Hotel
    (In American Hurrah: Plays)
  The Hunter and the Bird
    (In War and Four Other Plays)
  I'm Really Here
    (In War and Four Other Plays)
  Interview
    (In American Hurrah: Plays)
  It's Almost Like Being
    (In Tulane Drama Review, Vol. 9, Summer 1965)
  TV
    (In American Hurrah: Plays)
  War
    (In War and Four Other Plays)
  Where Is de Queen?
    (In Playwrights for Tomorrow, Vol. 3)
    (In War and Four Other Plays)
VAN Ostaijen, Paul
  Bankruptcy Jazz, a film script, 1919.
    (In TDR/Drama Review, Vol. 14, no. 3, 1970)
Vanzetti, Bartolomeo, 1888-1927
  *Gods of the Lightning (see Anderson, Maxwell)
  *Sacco and Vanzetti (see Roli, Mino)
  *Winterset (see Anderson, Maxwell)
Variations on a Theme (see Rattigan, Terence)
Variety Lights (see Fellini, Federico)
Vasco (see Schehade, Georges)
Va-T'en (see Gevel, Claude)
VATTIER, Robert, 1914-
  Gonzalo Sent la Violette, by Robert Vattier and Albert Rieux
    (In L'Avant-Scene du Theatre, no. 178, July 15, 1958)
Vaughn, Eric
  The Solar Spectrum (see Wedekind, Frank)
VAUTHIER, Jean
  The Prodigies
    (In First Stage, Vol. 4, Winter 1965/66)
VAZART, Claude

La Balance d'Eros
  (In L'Avant Scene du Theatre, no. 411, Oct. 1, 1968)
VEBER, Francis
  L'Enlevement
    (In Plaisir de France, supplement theatral, no. 366)
VEGA CARPIO, Lope Felix de, 1562-1635
  **A Bond Honoured (see Osborne, John)
  The Father Outwitted
    (In Theatrical Recorder, Vol. 2, no. 7, June 1805)
  Fuente Ouejuna
    (In The Classic Theatre, ed. by Eric Bentley)
    (In Masterworks of World Drama, Vol. 3)
  Fuenteovejuna; text in Portuguese
    (In Revista de Teatro, no. 362, Mar./Apr. 1969)
  The Outrageous Saint
    (In Tulane Drama Review, Vol. 7, Fall 1962)
  The Pastrybaker
    (In Theatre Arts, Vol. 19, Sept. 1935)
The Veil (see Rodenbach, Georges)
VEILLER, Bayard
  The Thirteenth Chair
    (In 13 Famous Plays of Crime and Detection)
  Within the Law
    (In 13 Famous Plays of Crime and Detection)
Velasquez, Diego de Silva, 1599-1660
  *Velasquez and the "Venus" (see Baring, Maurice)
VELLE, Louis
  A la Monnaie du Pape
    (In L'Avant-Scene du Theatre, no. 131)
  La Vie Sentimentale
    (In Plaisir de France, supplement theatral, no. 347, Sept.
    1967)
The Venetian; or, The Count of Ten (see Reynoldson, Thomas H.)
Vengeance in Leka (see McCracken, Wycliffe)
The Vengeance of Catullus (see Frida, Emil Bohslav)
Venice Preserved (see Otway, Thomas)
Venoni; or, The Novice of St. Mark's (see Lewis, Matthew Gregory)
The Ventriloquist (see Frankel, Marvin)
La Venus de Milo (see Deval, Jacques)
Vercors; pseud. (see Dit, Jean Bruller)
VERDI, Giuseppe, 1813-1901
  My Darlin' Aida, adapted by Charles Friedman from Verdi's
  Aida
    (In Theatre Arts, Vol. 37, June 1953)
VERDOT, Guy
  Chambre 29
    (In Plaisir de France, supplement theatral, no. 342, April
    1967)
  Theodat, after Remy de Gourmont
    (In L'Avant-Scene du Theatre, no. 476, July 15, 1971)
VERGA, Giovanni, 1840-1922
  Cavalleria Rusticana

(In The Modern Theatre, ed. by Eric Bentley, Vol. 1)
La Louve
    (In Plaisir de France, supplement theatral, no. 323, Sept.
    1965)
El Vergonzoso en Palacio (see Tellez, Gabriel)
Verity, Arthur Wilson, 1863-
    Amends for Ladies (see Field, Nathaniel)
    A Woman is a Weathercock (see Field, Nathaniel)
Verlieb Dich Nicht in Eine Heilige (see Schäfer, Siegfried)
VERMOREL, Claude
    Un Jardin sur la Mer
    (In Plaisir de France, supplement theatral, no. 309, July
    1964)
Die Versöhnung (see Ziem, Jochen)
Very Social Service (see Church, Virginia)
Vial, Jean Baptiste Charles, 1771-1834
    **The Green-Eyed Monster (see Planche, James Robinson)
VIAN, Boris, 1920-1959
    The Empire Builders
    (In Plays of the Year, Vol. 25, 1961/62)
    L'Equarrissage pour Tous
    (In L'Avant-Scene du Theatre, no. 406, July 1, 1968)
    (In Plaisir de France, supplement theatral, no. 359, Sept.
    1968)
    The General's Tea Party
    (In Evergreen Playscript Series)
    Knackery For All
    (In Plays for a New Theatre)
Vian: Three Beach Plays (see Vodanovic, Sergio)
VIANA, Oduvaldo Filho
    O Castagnaro de Festa
    (In Revista de Teatro, no. 361, Jan./Feb. 1968)
    Chapetuba Futebol Clube
    (In Revista de Teatro, no. 311)
    Corpo a Corpo
    (In Revista de Teatro, no. 387, May/June 1972)
    Manhas de Sol
    (In Revista de Teatro, no. 319)
    Matador
    (In Revista de Teatro, no. 346)
VICENTE, Gill, 1470-1536
    Four Plays: "The Three Wise Men"; "The Serenade"; "The
    Sailor's Wife"; "The Widow's Comedy"
    (In Tulane Drama Review, Vol. 5, Mar. 1961)
VICENTE, Jose
    Teatro, Representacao Liturgica
    (In Revista de Teatro, no. 375, May/June 1970)
La Victime (see Fortuno, Claude)
Victims (see Lindenberger, Herbert)
Victor, Pierre-Edmond (see Bruno, Pierrette)
Victor, ou, Les Enfants au Pouvoir (see Vitrac, Roger)
Victoria, Queen of Great Britain, 1819-1901
    *The Queen's Highland Servant (see Home, William Douglas)
    *The Revolting Daughter (see Housman, Laurence)
    *Victoria Regina (see Housman, Laurence)
    *The Wicked Uncles; or, Victorious Virtue (see Housman,
        Laurence)
The Victors (see Sartre, Jean-Paul)

Victory Over the Sun   (see Kruchenykh, Alexei)
VIDAL, Gore, 1925-
  Barn Burning; a television script from the story by William
  Faulkner
    (In Visit to a Small Planet and Other Television Plays)
  The Best Man
    (In Evergreen Playscript Series)
    (In Best American Plays, Fifth Series, 1957-63)
    (In his Three Plays)
  Dark Possession; a television script
    (In Visit to a Small Planet and Other Television Plays)
  The Death of Billy the Kid
    (In Visit to a Small Planet and Other Television Plays)
  Honor
    (In Television Plays for Writers, 1957)
  On the March to the Sea
    (In Evergreen Playscript Series)
    (In his Three Plays)
  Romulus
    (In Esquire, Vol. 57, Jan. 1962)
  A Sense of Justice; a television script
    (In Visit to a Small Planet and Other Television Plays)
  Smoke; a television script from the story by William Faulkner
    (In Visit to a Small Planet and Other Television Plays)
  Summer Pavilion; a television script
    (In Visit to a Small Planet and Other Television Plays)
  Tom Jones   (see Osborne, John)
  The Turn of the Screw; a television script from the story by
  Henry James
    (In Visit to a Small Planet and Other Television Plays)
  Visit to a Small Planet
    (In Theatre Arts, Vol. 42, Feb. 1958)
    (In Best Television Plays)
    (In Evergreen Playscript Series)
    (In his Three Plays)
  Visit to a Small Planet; a television script
    (In Visit to a Small Planet and Other Television Plays)
Vidor, Charles, 1900-1959
  Over Twenty-One   (see Buchman, Sidney)
Vidor, King, 1894-
  The Citadel   (see Dalrymple, Ian)
La Vie de Chateu   (see Rappenau, Jean-Paul)
La Vie Est un Songe   (see Calderon de la Barca, Pedro)
La Vie Imaginaire de l'Eboueur Auguste Geai   (see Gateschi,
  Rossana)
La Vie Sentimentale   (see Velle, Louis)
Viet Rock   (see Terry, Megan)
Vietnam Campesino   (see El Teatro Campesino)
A View from the Bridge   (see Miller, Arthur)
VIGNY, Alfred Victor, comte de, 1797-1863
  Chatterton
    (In Chief French Plays of the 19th Century)

Vigny, Benno
 **Morocco (see Von Sternberg, Josef)
VIGO, Jean, 1905-
   Zero de Conduite
      (In L'Avant-Scene du Cinema, no. 21, Dec. 15, 1962)
VILALTA, Maruxa
   Un Jour de Folie
      (In Plaisir de France, supplement theatral, no. 369, July/
      Aug. 1969)
   La Ultima Letra
      (In L'Avant-Scene du Theatre, no. 314, July 1, 1964)
VILDRAC, Charles (Charles Messager), 1882-
   La Belette
      (In L'Avant-Scene du Theatre, no. 238, Mar. 1, 1961)
   Les Peres Ennemis
      (In Plaisir de France, supplement theatral, no. 312, Oct.
      1964)
      (In L'Avant-Scene du Theatre, no. 318, Sept. 15, 1964)
   The Steamer Tenacity
      (In Poet Lore, Vol. 32, 1921)
The Village Coquettes (see Dickens, Charles)
The Village Lawyer (Anon.)
      (In Cumberland's British Theatre, Vol. 27, no. 3)
Villiers, George, 2d duke of Buckingham (see Buckingham, George
   Villiers, 2d duke of)
Villikins and His Dinah (see Burnand, F. C.)
Vincent Van Gogh (see Hays, Hoffman R.)
Vincenzoni, Luciano
   Sacco and Vanzetti (see Roli, Mino)
Vindication (see Hines, Leonard)
Vinyl Visits an FM Station (see Tavel, Ronald)
The Violet under the Snow (see Cleugh, Dennis)
Violets (see Schehade, George)
Violett, Ellen
   Brewsie and Willie (see Stein, Gertrude)
Violons d'Ingres (see Brunius, Jacques B.)
VIOTTI, Sergio
   Vamos Brincar de Amor em Cabo Frio
      (In Revista de Teatro, no. 345)
Virgil (Publius Vergilius Maro), 70-19 B. C.
 **Pious Aeneas (see Baring, Maurice)
The Virgin Martyr (see Massinger, Philip)
Virginia, daughter of Virginius
 *Virginius (see Knowles, James Sheridan)
Virginie (see Andre, Michel)
Viridiana (see Buñuel, Luis)
VISCONTI, Luchino, 1906-
   Le Guepard (Il Gattopardo; The Leopard)
      (In L'Avant-Scene du Cinema, no. 32/33, Dec. 15-Jan. 15,
      1963/64)
   The Job
      (In Three Screenplays)

Rocco and His Brothers
   (In Three Screenplays)
Senso
   (In Two Screenplays, 1970)
La Terra Trema
   (In Two Screenplays, 1970)
La Terre Tremble
   (In L'Avant-Scene du Cinema, no. 32/33, Dec. 15-Jan. 15,
   1963/64)
White Nights
   (In Three Screenplays)
Visions of Sugar Plums   (see Pritchard, Barry)
The Visit   (see Castro, Juan Antonio)
The Visit   (see Dürrenmatt, Friedrich)
Visit to a Small Planet   (see Vidal, Gore)
Visit to a Small Planet; a television script   (see Vidal, Gore)
Uma Visita de Cerimonia   (see Santos, Miguel)
Les Visiteurs du Soir   (see Prevert, Jacques)
La Visiteuse   (see La Barge, Bernadette)
Visitor from Mamaroneck   (see Simon, Neil)
I Vitelloni   (see Fellini, Federico)
VITRAC, Roger, 1899-1952
   Der Coup von Trafalgar
      (In Theatre Heute, Jan. 1971)
   Victor, ou, Les Enfants au Pouvoir
      (In L'Avant-Scene du Theatre, no. 276, Nov. 15, 1962)
Viva la Muerte   (see Arrabal, Fernando)
Viva Maria   (see Malle, Louis)
VIVRAN
   Alizon
      (In Plaisir de France, supplement theatral, no. 305, March
      1964)
      (In L'Avant-Scene du Theatre, no. 306, Mar. 1, 1964)
Vivre sa Vie   (see Godard, Jean-Luc)
Vladimir Mayakovsky   (see Mayakovsky, Vladimir)
VODANOVIC, Sergio
   The Exiles
      (In Voices of Change in the Spanish American Theater)
   People Like Us
      (In Voices of Change in the Spanish American Theater)
   Vina: Three Beach Plays
      (In Voices of Change in the Spanish American Theater)
   The White Uniform
      (In Voices of Change in the Spanish American Theater)
VOGEL, Raymond, 1927-
   La Mer et les Jours
      (In L'Avant-Scene du Cinema, no. 68, 1967)
La Voie Lactee   (see Buñuel, Luis)
La Voix Humaine   (see Cocteau, Jean)
VOJNOVICH, Ino, 1857-1929
   A Trilogy of Dubrovnik: Allons Enfants; The Twilight; On the
   Terrace

(In Poet Lore, Vol. 56, Summer, Winter, Autumn, 1951)
Le Voleur de Bicyclette (see De Sica, Vittorio)
Volodia (see Mai, Fabiene)
Volpone; or, The Fox (see Jonson, Ben)
VON PFUHL, Oscar, 1916-
    Romao e Julinha, in the manner of Shakespeare's Romeo and
    Juliet
        (In Revista de Teatro, no. 382, July/Aug. 1971)
Von Rosow, Viktor (see Rosow, Viktor von)
VON STERNBERG, Josef, 1894-
    L'Ange Bleu (Der Blaue Engel), adaptation libre du roman de
    "Professor Unrath" Heinrich Mann, screenplay by Karl Zuck-
    mayer
        (In L'Avant-Scene du Cinema, no. 57, 1966)
    The Blue Angel; screenplay by Robert Liebmann, based on the
    novel "Professor Unrath" by Heinrich Mann, directed by Josef
    Von Sternberg
        (In Classic Film Scripts)
    Morocco; script by Jules Furthman, based on the novel "Amy
    Jolly" by Benno Vigny, directed by Josef Von Sternberg.
        (In Classic Filmscripts Series)
    Shanghai Express; script by Jules Furthman, directed by Josef
    Von Sternberg
        (In Classic Filmscripts Series)
VON STROHEIM, Erich, 1885-1957
    Greed, filmscript by Erich Von Stroheim, based on the novel
    "MacTeague" by Frank Norris
        (In Classic Film Scripts)
    Les Rapaces, by Erich Von Stroheim, d'apres le roman "Mac-
    Teague" by Frank Norris. Titre original "Greed."
        (In L'Avant-Scene du Cinema, no. 83/8, June 1968)
The Votary of Wealth (see Holman, Joseph George)
VOTEUR, Ferdinand
    My Unfinished Portrait
        (In Poet Lore, Vol. 56, Spring 1951)
Votre Silence, Cooper? (see Halet, Pierre)
Voyage (see Nemeth, Laszio)
Le Voyage (see Sussmann, C. Julien)
A Voyage Round My Father (see Mortimer, John)
Le Voyageur sans Bagage (see Anouilh, Jean)
La Voyante (see Roussin, Andre)
The Voysey Inheritance (see Granville-Baker, Harley Granville)
VOYSEY, Michael
    The Amorous Goldfish
        (In Television Playwright: 10 Plays for BBC)
La Vraie Nature de Bernadette (see Carle, Gilles)
Vrchlicky, Jaroslav, pseud. (see Frida, Emil Bohslav)
VULPIUS, Paul
    Youth at the Helm; English version by Hubert Griffith
        (In Famous Plays of Today, 1935)

Wages of Sin (see Holland, Norman)
WAGNER, Bernd
  "Das Hemd eines Glüchlichen" von Bernd Wagner nach Anatole
  France
  (In Theatre der Zeit, no. 9, 1971)
Wagner, Jack
  A Medal for Benny (see Butler, Frank)
Waiter! (see Box, Sydney)
Waiting for Godot (see Beckett, Samuel)
Waiting for Lefty (see Odets, Clifford)
The Waiting Room (see Baird, George M. P.)
WAJDA, Andrezej, 1926-
  Ashes and Diamonds
    (In Modern Film Scripts: A Trilogy)
  Cendres et Diamant, by Andrzej Wajda et Jerzy Andrzejewski.
  Titre original: "Popol I Diament. "
    (In L'Avant-Scene du Cinema, no. 47, 1965)
  Generation
    (In Modern Film Scripts: A Trilogy)
  Kanal
    (In Modern Film Scripts: A Trilogy)
A Wake for Me and Thee (see Costello, Ward)
Wakefield Cycle: Secunda Pastorum
  The Play of the Shepherds
    (In Religious Drama, Vol. 2)
Wakefield Master
  The Second Shepherd's Play
    (In Genius of the Early English Theater)
    (In Masterworks of World Drama, Vol. 2)
  A Wakefield Nativity
    (In Great English Plays)
Wakefield Mystery Cycle
  The Annunciation
    (In Representative Medieval and Tudor Plays)
  The Second Shepherd's Play
    (In Representative Medieval and Tudor Plays)
WALDAU, Roy S.
  A Cabin by the Lake
    (In Best Short Plays, 1954/55)
WALDMAN, Max
  The Constant Prince
    (In TDR/The Drama Review, Vol. 14, no. 2, Winter 1970)
WALKER, Stuart, 1888-1941
  The Medicine Show
    (In 50 Contemporary One-Act Plays)
  Six Who Pass While the Lentils Boil
    (In Short Plays by Representative Authors, 1920)
The Wall (see Caldwell, Ben)
WALLACE, Lewis, 1827-1905
  Commodus
    (In Harper's, Vol. 78, Jan. 1889)
Wallace, Richard, 1894-1951
  The Young in Heart (see Osborn, Paul)

WALLACH, Ira, 1913-
    Absence of a Cello, adapted by Albert Husson
      (In L'Avant-Scene du Theatre, no. 351, Feb. 15, 1966)
    Le Mal de Test
      (In Plaisir de France, supplement theatral, no. 329, March
      1966)
Wallenstein, Albrecht Wenzel Eusebius von, 1583-1634
    *The Death of Wallenstein (see Schiller, Johann Christoph
      Friedrich von)
Wallop, Douglas, 1920-
    **Damn Yankees (see Abbott, George)
Walpole, Sir Robert, Earl of Orford, 1676-1745
    *Walpole; or, Every Man Has His Price (see Lytton, Edward
      George Earle Lytton Bulwer-Lytton, 1st baron)
Der Walschrat (see Chekhov, Anton Pavlovich)
WALSH, Norman
    Let There be Farce
      (In Best Short Plays, 1955/56)
WALTER, Eugene, 1874-1941
    The Easiest Way
      (In Best Plays of the Early American Theatre, from the be-
      ginning to 1916)
WALTER, Nancy
    Rags
      (In Playwrights for Tomorrow, Vol. 7)
Waltz of the Toreadors (see Anouilh, Jean)
The Wandering Boys (see Le Pelerin Blanc)
WANDERLEY, Jose
    Amanha e'Dia de Pecar, by Jose Wanderley and Mario Lago
      (In Revista de Teatro, no. 377, Sept./Oct. 1970)
    Cupim, de Jose Wanderley e Mario Lago
      (In Revista de Teatro, no. 352)
    O Maluco da Familia, de Jose Wanderley e Daniel Rocha
      (In Revista de Teatro, no. 323)
Wann Kommt Ehrlicher? (see Kerndl, Rainer)
"Wanted, a Young Lady" (see Suter, W. E.)
Wantin' Fever (see Hughes, Elizabeth Wilson)
Wapping Old Stairs (see Savill, John Faucit)
War (see Artsybashev, Mikhail Petrovich)
War (see Van Itallie, Jean-Claude, 1935)
The War Woman (see Lovell, Caroline C.)
WARD, Douglas Turner
    Day of Absence
      (In New Black Playwrights)
    Happy Ending
      (In New Black Playwrights)
Wardock Kennilson; or, The Wild Woman of the Village (Anon.)
    (In Cumberland's British Theatre, Vol. 45, no. 5)
Ware, William Henry
    Peveril of the Peak (see Fitz-Ball, Edward)
Warren (see Bell, Neal)
WARREN, Robert Penn, 1905-
    All the King's Men

(In Sewanee Review, Vol. 68, Spring 1960)
Brother to Dragons
(In Kenyon Review, Vol. 15, no. 1, 1953)
The Warrens of Virginia (see De Mille, William Churchill)
Warwick, Richard Neville, Earl of, 1428-1471
    *The Earl of Warwick (see Francklin, Thomas)
WASHBURN, Deric
    Ginger Anne
    (In New American Plays, Vol. 1)
Washington, Booker Taliafero, 1859?-1915
    *Booker T. Washington in Atlanta (see Hughes, Langston)
Washington, George, pres. U.S., 1732-1799
    *George Washington Crossing the Delaware (see Koch, Kenneth)
    *I Know George Washington (see Phelps, Pauline)
    *Valley Forge (see Anderson, Maxwell)
The Wasps (see Aristophanes)
The Waste Disposal Unit (see Brophy, Brigid)
Watch on the Rhine (see Hellman, Lillian)
Watch on the Rhine; screenplay. (see Hammett, Dashiell)
The Watched Pot (see Munro, Hector Hugh)
The Watchmaker and the Doctor (see Romm, Gregory)
The Water Hen (see Witkiewicz, Stanislaw Ignacy)
WATERHOUSE, Keith, 1929-
    Billy Liar, by Keith Waterhouse and Willis Hall
    (In Theatre Arts, May 1962)
    The Sponge Room, by Keith Waterhouse and Willis Hall
    (In Modern Short Comedies from Broadway & London)
The Waterman; or, The First of August (see Dibdin, Charles)
The Waters of Babylon (see Arden, John)
Waters of the Moon (see Hunter, Norman Charles)
WATSON, George
    England, Preserved
    (In Modern Theatre, 1811, Vol. 8)
WATSON, Robert
    The Plot in the Palace
    (In First Stage, Vol. 3, Spring 1964)
The Waves of Sea and Love (see Grillparzer, Franz)
The Wax Engine (see Nichols, Robert)
The Wax Museum (see Hawkes, John)
The Way of the World (see Congreve, William)
A Way Out (see Frost, Robert)
The Way the Noise Began (see Knowlton, Don)
The Way to Get Married (see Morton, Thomas)
The Way to Keep Him (see Murphy, Arthur)
Ways and Means (see Coward, Noel Pierce)
We Are Three (see Fife, Evelyn Henderson)
We Commit This Body (see Dace, Wallace)
We Got Rhythm (see Ratcliff, Nora)
We Hold These Truths (see Corwin, Norman Lewis)
We Refuse to Die (see Shane, Maxwell)
We Speak for Ourselves (see Riggs, Lynn)
We Were Dancing (see Coward, Noel Pierce)

Weariness (see Rognoni, Angelo)
The Weather Breeder (see Denison, Merril)
The Weather Cock (see Allingham, John Till)
The Weavers (see Hauptmann, Gerhart)
WEBB, Alla
    Larnin'
      (In The One-Act Theatre, Vol. 1)
Webb, Chase Howard
    Manana Bandits (see Smith, Betty)
WEBBER, James Plaisted, 1878-1930
    The Golden Arrow
      (In Ten Fantasies for Stage and Study, 1932)
WEBER, Carl Maria von, 1786-1826
    Der Freischutz; or, The Bill! The Belle!! and the Bullet!!!
    (see Byron, Henry James)
    Der Freischutz; or, The Seventh Bullet
      (In Cumberland's British Theatre, Vol. 2, no. 5)
    Sylvana; adapted by C. A. Somerset
      (In Cumberland's British Theatre, Vol. 16, no. 1)
WEBSTER, Benjamin
    The Golden Farmer; or, The Last Crime
      (In Cumberland's British Theatre, Vol. 44, no. 2)
    High Ways and By Ways
      (In Cumberland's British Theatre, Vol. 29, no. 4)
    Paul Clifford; the Highwayman of 1770
      (In Cumberland's British Theatre, Vol. 35, no. 8)
WEBSTER, John, 1580?-1625
    Northward Ho (see Dekker, Thomas)
    Sir Thomas Wyatt (see Dekker, Thomas)
    The Tragedy of the Duchess of Malfi
      (In Masterworks of World Drama, Vol. 3)
    Westward Ho (see Dekker, Thomas)
    The White Devil
      (In Dodsley's A Select Collection of Old Plays, Vol. 6)
      (In Great English Plays)
The Wedded Husband (see Shen, Hung)
A Wedding (see Chekhov, Anton Pavlovich)
The Wedding Anniversary (see Smith, Marion Spencer)
The Wedding Day (see Fielding, Henry)
The Wedding Day (see Inchbald, Mrs. Elizabeth Simpson)
WEDEKIND, Frank, 1864-1918
    Der Kammersanger
      (In Das Deitsche Drama, 1880-1933, Vol. 1)
    King Nicolo; or, Such Is Life
      (In Genius of the German Theater)
    The Marquis of Keith
      (In From the Modern Repertoire, Series Two)
      (In The Modern Theatre, ed. by R. W. Corrigan)
  **Pandora's Box (Lulu) (see Vajda, Ladislaus)
    The Solar Spectrum
      (In Tulane Drama Review, Autumn 1959)
    Spring's Awakening

(In The Modern Theatre, ed. by Eric Bentley, Vol. 6)
The Tenor
  (In 50 Contemporary One-Act Plays)
Weekend (see Godard, Jean-Luc)
"Weiberhomödie" (see Müller, Heiner)
WEID, Gustau Johannes, 1858-1914
  Autumn Fires
  (In 50 Contemporary One-Act Plays)
Weidman, Jerome, 1913-
  Fiorello! (see Bock, Jerry)
WEIGER, Eugene
  The Set Up
  (In First Stage, Vol. 3, Spring 1964)
WEILL, Kurt, 1900-1950
  Johnny Johnson (see Green, Paul)
  Mahagonny, by Kurt Weill, Arnold Weinstein, and Bertolt
    Brecht
  (In Yale/Theatre, Vol. 1, no. 2, Summer 1968)
  The Three-Penny Opera (see Lania, Leo)
WEINGARTEN, Romain
  Alice dans les Jardins du Luxembourg
  (In L'Avant-Scene du Theatre, no. 461, Dec. 1, 1970)
  Comme la Pierre
  (In L'Avant-Scene du Theatre, no. 469/470, April 1-15,
    1971)
  L'Ete
  (In Plaisir de France, supplement theatral, no. 342, April
    1967)
WEINSTEIN, Arnold
  Mahagonny (see Weill, Kurt)
  Red Eye of Love
  (In Evergreen Playscript Series)
WEISENBORN, Günther, 1902-
  The Man without a Face (Das Verlorene Gasicht)
  (In Modern International Drama, Vol. 2, no. 2, 1968)
WEISS, Peter, 1916-
  Hölderlin
  (In Theater Heute, no. 11, Nov. 1971)
  The Investigation
  (In Partisan Review, Vol. 33, Fall 1966)
  Night with Guests
  (In Best Short Plays, 1968)
  The Persecution and Assassination of Jean-Paul Marat as Per-
    formed by the Inmates of the Asylum of Charenton under the
    Direction of the Marquis de Sade.
  (Atheneum Playscript, 1965)
  The Tower
  (In Best Short Plays of the World Theatre, 1958-67)
  Trotsky in Exile
  (In Partisan Review, Vol. 38, no. 1, 1971)
WEISS, Vsevolod
  The Gun-Site
  (In Soviet One-Act Plays)

WEISSE, Christian Felix, 1726-1804
    Rosamond, translated by Fanny Holcroft
        (In Theatrical Recorder, Vol. 2, no. 12, Nov. 1805)
WELCH, Rae
    Let's Get Out of Here
        (In Best Short Plays, 1958/59)
Welcome to Our Cities (see Wolfe, Thomas)
The Well of the Saints (see Synge, John Millington)
WELLER, Michael
    Cancer
        (In Plays and Players, Vol. 18, Dec. 1970)
    And Now There's Just the Three of Us
        (In Plays and Players, Vol. 17, no. 2, Nov. 1969)
WELLES, Orson, 1915-
    Citizen Kane, by Herman J. Mankiewicz et Orson Welles.
    Text in French.
        (In L'Avant-Scene du Cinema, no. 11, Jan. 1962)
    Citizen Kane; the shooting script by Herman J. Mankiewicz
    and Orson Welles.
        (In The Citizen Kane Book)
    Columbus Day, by Orson Welles in collaboration with Robert
    Meltzer and Norris Houghton
        (In Radio Drama in Action, 1945)
    The Invasion from Mars (see Koch, Howard)
    Le Proces, un film de Orson Welles, d'apres l'oeuvre de Franz
    Kafka. American title "The Trial."
        (In L'Avant-Scene du Cinema, no. 23, Feb. 15, 1963)
    The Trial, filmscript by Orson Welles, based on the novel by
    Franz Kafka
WELLINGTON, Barbara
    Is Romance Dead?
        (In Ten Fantasies for Stage and Study, 1932)
WELLMAN, Rita, 1890
    For All Time
        (In 50 Contemporary One-Act Plays)
Wellman, William A., 1896-
    The Ox-Bow Incident (see Trotti, Lamar)
    The Story of G.I. Joe (see Atlas, Leopold)
WELLS, Charles F.
    The Apothecary
        (In Ten Fantasies for Stage and Study, 1932)
Wells, Herbert George, 1866-1946
    **The Invasion from Mars (see Koch, Howard)
Wells Fargo (see Schofield, Paul)
The Welsh Embassador (see Dekker, Thomas)
Wen (see Bellow, Saul)
We're Due in Eastbourne in Ten Minutes (see Simpson, Norman
    Frederick)
WERFEL, Franz V., 1890-1945
    Goat Song
        (In Theatre Guild Anthology)
    Jacobowsky and the Colonel, adapted by Samuel Nathaniel

Behrman
   (In 20 Best European Plays on the American Stage)
Werner; or, The Inheritance (see Byron, George Gordon Noël
   Byron, 6th baron)
Werte des Vorsitzenden Mao Tse-Tung (see Albee, Edward)
Werter (see Reynolds, Frederick)
WESKER, Arnold, 1932-
   Chicken Soup with Barley
      (In New English Dramatists, 1959)
   Chips with Everything
      (In Theatre Arts, Vol. 47, Oct. 1963)
   La Cuisine
      (In Plaisir de France, supplement theatral, no. 348, Oct.
      1967)
   The Friends
      (In Plays and Players, Vol. 18, Oct. 1970)
   Des Frites, des Frites, des Frites... Titre original: "Chips
      with Everything"
      (In L'Avant-Scene du Theatre, no. 494, May 1972)
   The Old Ones
      (In Plays and Players, Vol. 20, no. 1, Oct. 1972)
   Les Quatre Saisons
      (In L'Avant-Scene du Theatre, Jan. 1, 1969)
   Roots
      (In New British Drama)
   Their Very Own and Golden City
      (In Plays and Players, Vol. 13, Aug. 1966)
WESLEY, Richard
   The Black Terror
      (In Scripts, Vol. 1, no. 2, Dec. 1971)
The West Indian (see Cumberland, Richard)
West Side Story (see Bernstein, Leonard)
Western Night (see Smith, Betty)
Western Star (see Benet, Stephen Vincent)
WESTMACOTT, C. M.
   Nettlewig Hall; or, Ten to One
      (In Cumberland's British Theatre, Vol. 28, no. 6)
WESTPHAL, Eric, 1929-
   Toi et Tes Nuages
      (In Plaisir de France, supplement theatral, no. 390)
      (In L'Avant-Scene du Theatre, no. 468, Mar. 15, 1971)
Westward Ho (see Dekker, Thomas)
Wetback Run (see Apstein, Theodore Emanuel)
Wetzel, Donald, 1921-
   **All Summer Long (see Anderson, Robert)
WEXLEY, John
   Comes the Dreamer
      (In First Stage, Vol. 2, Winter 1962/63)
   Running Dogs
      (In Best Short Plays of the Social Theatre, 1939)
WHARTON, Edith, 1862-1937
   Pomegranate Seed
      (In Scribner's, Vol. 51, Mar. 1912)

What Did You Learn in School?   (see Johnson, Wallace)
What Did You Say "What" for?   (see Dey, James)
The What D'ye Call It   (see Gay, John)
What Every Woman Knows   (see Barrie, Sir James Matthew, bart.)
What Happened   (see Stein, Gertrude)
What Is She?   (Anon.)
    (In Modern Theatre, 1811, Vol. 10)
What Men Live By   (see Church, Virginia)
What Never Dies   (see Wilde, Percival)
What Price Glory?   (see Stallings, Lawrence)
What Shall We Tell Caroline?   (see Mortimer, John)
What's in a Name   (see Grover, Harry Greenwood)
WHEELER, Hugh
    Big Fish, Little Fish
      (In Theatre Arts, Vol. 46, Sept. 1962)
    Look, We've Come Through
      (In Broadway's Beautiful Losers)
When Did You Last See My Mother?   (see Hampton, Christopher)
When the Bells Rang   (see Brighouse, Harold)
When the Ship Goes Down   (see McGuire, Harry)
When the War Was Over   (see Frisch, Max)
When the Willow Nods   (see Kreymborg, Alfred)
When Witches Ride   (see Lay, Elizabeth A.)
When You are Twenty-One!   (see Thoma, Ludwig)
Where Are You Going, Hollis Jay?   (see Bradford, Benjamin)
Where But In America   (see Wolff, Oscar M.)
Where E'er We Go   (see O'Dea, John B.)
Where Is de Queen?   (see Van Itallie, Jean-Claude)
Which Is the Man?   (see Cowley, Mrs. Hannah Parkhouse)
While the Sun Shines   (see Rattigan, Terence)
A Whisper in God's Ear   (see Birnkrant, Oscar)
Whistle, Daughter, Whistle   (see Kinoy, Ernest)
Whistler   (see Taylor, Peter)
WHITE, Bessie F.
    Life Begins at 84!
      (In The One-Act Theatre, Vol. 1)
WHITE, Edgar
    Dija
      (In Scripts, Vol. 1, no. 10, Oct. 1972)
    The Life and Times of J. Walter Smintheus
      (In Scripts, Vol. 1, no. 6, April 1972)
    The Rastifarian
      (In Scripts, Vol. 1, no. 10, Oct. 1972)
White, George
    Royal Gambit   (see Gressieker, Hermann)
White, Ida Alexa Ross, 1885-1959
    **The Young at Heart   (see Osborn, Paul)
WHITE, Joseph
    Old Judge Mose Is Dead
      (In TDR/The Drama Review, Vol. 12, Summer 1968)
WHITE, Kenneth
    Freight
      (In Best One-Act Plays of 1946/47, N.Y.)

WHITE, Leonard
    Lady Jemima's Weekly Thought
        (In Best One-Act Plays of 1936, London)
    The Perfect Marriage
        (In Best One-Act Plays of 1931, London)
WHITE, Lucy
    The Bird Child
        (In Plays of Negro Life)
A White Butterfly (see Roepke, Gabriela)
The White Devil (see Webster, John)
White Dresses (see Green, Paul)
The White Hawk (see Kemp, Harry Gibbard)
The White Liars (see Shaffer, Peter)
White Nights (see Visconti, Luchino)
The White Sheik (see Fellini, Federico)
The White Uniform (see Vodanovic, Sergio)
The White Whore and the Bit Player (see Eyen, Tom)
WHITEHEAD, William, 1715-1785
    Creusa, Queen of Athens, a recast of Euripides' "Ion" with the
    supernatural element omitted
        (In Bell's British Theatre, 1797, Vol. 34)
    The Roman Father; altered from Corneille's "Horace"
        (In Bell's British Theatre, 1797, Vol. 3)
        (In Cumberland's British Theatre, Vol. 37, no. 1)
    The School for Lovers
        (In Bell's British Theatre, 1797, Vol. 7)
WHITEMORE, Hugh
    Horrible Conspiracies
        (In Plays of the Year Special, 1972)
Whitest Elephant I Ever Saw (see Sims, Alan)
WHITING, John, 1917-
    Saint's Day
        (In Plays of the Year, Vol. 6, 1951)
WHITMAN, Robert
    Flower
        (In Theatre Experiment)
Who Are the Weavers (see Shore, Joseph)
Who Goes There! (see Dighton, John)
Who Is Harry Kellerman and Why Is He Saying Those Terrible
    Things About Me? (see Gardner, Herb)
Who Is Sylvia? (see Rattigan, Terence)
Who Wants a Guinea? (see Colman, George)
The Whore of Babylon (see Dekker, Thomas)
Who's Afraid of Virginia Woolf? (see Albee, Edward)
Who's Afraid of Virginia Woolf? Text in French. (see Albee,
    Edward)
Who's Happy Now? (see Hailey, Oliver)
Who's the Dupe? (see Cowley, Mrs. Hannah Parkhouse)
Whose Money? (see Dickson, Lee)
Why I Am a Bachelor (see Seiler, Conrad)
Why Marry? (see Williams, Jesse Lynch)
Why She Would Not (see Shaw, George Bernard)

WHYTE, Ron
    The National Enquirer
        (In Yale/Theatre, no. 2, Summer 1968)
The Wicked Cocks (see Grass, Günter)
The Wicked Uncles; or, Victorious Virtue (see Housman, Laurence)
The Widdy's Mite (see Totheroh, Dan)
WIDERBERG, Bo, 1930-
    Adalen 31
        (In L'Avant-Scene du Cinema, no. 124, Apr. 1972)
The Widow (see Jonson, Ben)
The Widow; or, Who Wins (see Allingham, John Till)
The Widow of Wasdale Head (see Pinero, Sir Arthur Wing)
The Widowing of Mrs. Holroyd (see Lawrence, David Herbert)
The Widow's Comedy (see Vincente, Gill)
The Widow's Tears (see Chapman, George)
WIECHERT, Ernst
    Das Spiel vom Deutschen Bettelmann
        (In Das Deutsche Drama, 1880-1933, Vol. 2)
WIENE, Robert, 1881-1938
    The Cabinet of Dr. Caligari; a film by Robert Wiene, Carl
    Mayer and Hans Janowitz
        (In Classic Film Scripts)
WIENER, Joel
    The End
        (In Soundings: Annual Student Literature Magazine, Vol. 6,
      1969)
Wiers-Jensen, Johanssen
    **Dies Irae (see Dreyer, Carl Theodor)
The Wife of Two Husbands (see Cobb, James)
WILBUR, Elene
    Mistletoe and Moonlight
        (In The Banner Anthology of One-Act Plays by American
      Authors)
Wild Decembers (see Ashton, Winifred)
The Wild Duck (see Ibsen, Henrik)
The Wild Man (see Dibdin, Charles)
Wild Oats; or, The Strolling Gentleman (see O'Keeffe, John)
Wild Strawberries (see Bergman, Ingmar)
WILDE, Oscar, 1854-1900
    **The Critic as Artist (see Marowitz, Charles)
    A Florentine Tragedy
        (In 24 Favorite One-Act Plays)
    A Florentine Tragedy; text in French
        (In L'Avant- Scene du Theatre, no. 138)
    The Importance of Being Earnest
        (In Genius of the Later English Theater)
        (In 16 Famous British Plays)
    Lady Windermere's Fan
        (In Great English Plays)
    Salome
        (In Representative One-Act Plays by British & Irish Authors)
        (In 30 Famous One-Act Plays)

WILDE, Percival, 1887-1953
  Blood of the Martyrs
    (In One-Act Play Magazine, 1937/38 Anthology)
  Confessional
    (In Dramas by Present-Day Writers)
  The Finger of God
    (In 50 Contemporary One-Act Plays)
  Mr. F.
    (In Best One-Act Plays of 1940, N.Y.)
  Pawns
    (In Plays as Experience)
  Refund (see Karinthy, Fritz)
  Salt for Savor
    (In Best Short Plays, 1953/54)
  What Never Dies
    (In Drama, Vol. 21, Jan. 1931)
WILDER, Billy, 1906-
  The Apartment, screenplay by Billy Wilder and I.A.L. Diamond
    (In The Apartment and The Fortune Cookie; two screenplays)
  Double Indemnity, a screenplay by Billy Wilder and Raymond
  Chandler, based on the book by James M. Cain.
    (In Best Film Plays, 1945, Vol. 2)
  The Fortune Cookie, screenplay by Billy Wilder and I.A.L.
  Diamond
    (In The Apartment and The Fortune Cookie; two screenplays)
  The Lost Weekend (see Brackett, Charles)
  Ninotchka (see Brackett, Charles)
  Some Like It Hot, screenplay by Billy Wilder and I.A.L. Dia-
  mond, based on the unpublished story by Robert Thoeren and
  M. Logan
    (New American Library Screenplays, 1959)
WILDER, Thornton Niven, 1897-
  Childhood
    (In Atlantic Monthly, Vol. 206, Nov. 1960)
  Drunken Sisters
    (In Atlantic Monthly, Vol. 200, Nov. 1957)
  The Happy Journey to Trenton and Camden
    (In The Long Christmas Dinner)
    (In A Search for Awareness)
    (In 24 Favorite One-Act Plays)
  **Hello, Dolly! (see Herman, Jerry)
  The Long Christmas Dinner
    (In The Long Christmas Dinner)
    (In American Drama)
    (In Reading Drama)
    (In Theatre Experiment)
  Love, and How to Cure It
    (In The Long Christmas Dinner)
  The Matchmaker, a revised version of his earlier play "The
  Merchant of Yonkers."
    (In Theatre Arts, Vol. 42, Apr. 1958)
  Mozart and the Gray Steward

(In Harper's, Vol. 157, Oct. 1928)
Our Town
    (In 16 Famous American Plays)
    (In Pulitzer Prize Plays)
Pullman Car Hiawatha
    (In One Act)
    (In The Long Christmas Dinner)
    (In The Modern Theatre, Vol. 4, ed. by Eric Bentley)
Queens of France
    (In Yale Review, Vol. 21, Sept. 1931)
    (In The Long Christmas Dinner)
The Skin of Our Teeth
    (In Modern Theatre, ed. by R. W. Corrigan)
WILKINS, George, fl. 1607
    The Miseries of Enforced Marriage
        (In Dodsley's A Select Collection of Old English Plays, Vol. 9)
        (In Dodsley's A Select Collection of Old Plays, Vol. 5)
The Will   (see Barrie, Sir James Matthew, bart.)
The Will   (see Reynolds, Frederic)
Will Somebody Please Say Something   (see Baxter, David)
Will Success Spoil Rock Hunter?   (see Axelrod, George)
Will This Earth Hold?   (see Buck, Pearl Sydenstricker)
WILLARD, John, 1885-
    The Cat and the Canary
        (In 13 Famous Plays of Crime and Detection)
William Conrad   (see Boulle, Pierre)
William Tell   (see Knowles, James Sheridan)
William Thompson; or, Which Is He?   (see Boaden, Caroline)
WILLIAMS, Arthur, 1930-
    The Poor Little Match Girl
        (In More Plays From Off Off Broadway)
WILLIAMS, Charles, 1886-1945
    The Death of Good Fortune
        (In Collected Plays)
    Grab and Grace; or, It's the Second Step
        (In Religious Drama, Vol. 3)
        (In Collected Plays)
    The House by the Stable
        (In Religious Drama, Vol. 3)
        (In Collected Plays)
    The House of the Octopus
        (In Collected Plays)
    Judgement at Chelmsford
        (In Collected Plays)
    Seed of Adam
        (In Collected Plays)
    Terror of Light
        (In Collected Plays)
    Thomas Cranmer of Canterbury
        (In Collected Plays)
    The Three Temptations
        (In Collected Plays)

WILLIAMS, Emlyn, 1905-
The Citadel (see Dalrymple, Ian)
The Corn Is Green
   (In Collected Plays, Vol. 1)
   (In 16 Famous British Plays)
He Was Born Gay
   (In Collected Plays, Vol. 1)
The Late Christopher Bean, based on "Prenez Garde a la
Peinture!" by Rene Fauchois
   (In Famous Plays of Today, 1933)
The Light of Heart
   (In Collected Plays, Vol. 1)
Le Monsieur Qui Attend
   (In L'Avant-Scene du Theatre, Jan. 1956)
A Month in the Country (see Turgenev, Ivan Sergeyevich)
Night Must Fall
   (In Collected Plays, Vol. 1)
   (In 13 Famous Plays of Crime and Detection)
   (In Famous Plays of Today, 1935)
Some One Waiting
   (In L'Avant-Scene du Theatre, no. 121)
WILLIAMS, George Llyonel
Snipe Hunt
   (In First Stage, Vol. 2, Summer 1963)
WILLIAMS, Heathcote
The Logical Stigmatic
   (In Evergreen Review, Vol. 11, no. 50, 1967)
WILLIAMS, Hugh
The Grass Is Greener, by Hugh and Margaret Williams
   (In Plays of the Year, Vol. 19, 1958/59)
The Irregular Verb to Love, by Hugh and Margaret Williams
   (In Plays of the Year, Vol. 23, 1960/61)
WILLIAMS, Jesse Lynch, 1871-1929
Why Marry?
   (In The Pulitzer Prize Plays)
Williams, Margaret
The Grass is Greener (see Williams, Hugh)
The Irregular Verb to Love (see Williams, Hugh)
WILLIAMS, Murray, 1939-
Willie the Germ
   (In More Plays From Off Off Broadway)
WILLIAMS, Tennessee, 1911-
Auto-Da-Fe
   (In 27 Wagons Full of Cotton)
Baby Doll, the script for the film based on the author's plays:
"27 Wagons Full of Cotton" and "The Long Stay Cut Short; or,
The Unsatisfactory Supper," directed by Elia Kazan
   (In New Directions, 1956)
Camino Real
   (In Theatre Arts, Vol. 38, Aug. 1954)
   (In Makers of the Modern Theater, 1961)
   (In 6 American Plays for Today)

The Case of the Crushed Petunias
   (In American Blues)
Cat on a Hot Tin Roof
   (In Theatre Arts, Vol. 41, June 1957)
   (In Best American Plays, Fourth Series)
The Dark Room
   (In American Blues)
The Demolition Downtown
   (In Esquire, June 1971)
The Glass Menagerie
   (In The Modern Theatre, ed. by R. W. Corrigan)
   (In Best Plays of the Modern American Theatre, Second
   Series)
   (In American Drama)
   (In Nine Modern American Plays)
Gnädiges Fräulein
   (In Esquire, Vol. 64, Aug. 1965)
Hello from Bertha
   (In 27 Wagons Full of Cotton)
I Can't Imagine Tomorrow
   (In Esquire, Vol. 65, Mar. 1966)
I Rise in Flame, Cried the Phoenix.   A play about D. H.
   Lawrence.
   (In Ramparts, Vol. 6, Jan. 1968)
Kingdom of Earth
   (In Esquire, Vol. 67, Feb. 1967)
The Lady of Larkspur Lotion
   (In Best One-Act Plays of 1941, N. Y.)
   (In 27 Wagons Full of Cotton)
The Last of My Solid Gold Watches
   (In Best One-Act Plays of 1942, N. Y.)
   (In 27 Wagons Full of Cotton)
The Long Goodbye
   (In 27 Wagons Full of Cotton)
The Long Stay Cut Short; or, The Unsatisfactory Supper
   (In American Blues)
Lord Byron's Love Letter
   (In English One-Act Plays of Today)
   (In 27 Wagons Full of Cotton)
The Milk Train Doesn't Stop Here Anymore
   (In New Directions Play Series, 1964)
Moony's Kid Don't Cry
   (In American Blues)
   (In Best One-Act Plays of 1940, N. Y.)
Mutilated
   (In Esquire, Vol. 64, Aug. 1965)
The Night of the Iguana
   (In Esquire, Vol. 57, Feb. 1962)
   (In Best American Plays, Fifth Series, 1957-63)
Orpheus Descending
   (In Theatre Arts, Vol. 42, Sept. 1958)
   (In Best American Plays, Fifth Series, 1957-63)

A Perfect Analysis Given by a Parrot
    (In Esquire, Vol. 50, Oct. 1958)
Period of Adjustment; High Point over a Cavern, a serious
comedy.
    (In Esquire, Vol. 54, Dec. 1960)
    (New Directions, 1960)
Portrait of a Madonna
    (In 27 Wagons Full of Cotton)
The Purification
    (In 27 Wagons Full of Cotton)
The Rose Tattoo
    (In Theatre Arts, Vol. 39, May 1955)
    (In Best American Plays, Fourth Series)
Something Unspoken
    (In Best Short Plays, 1955/56)
    (In 27 Wagons Full of Cotton)
The Strangest Kind of Romance
    (In 27 Wagons Full of Cotton)
A Streetcar Named Desire
    (In Best American Plays, Third Series)
    (In Plays of Our Time)
A Streetcar Named Desire, screenplay by Tennessee Williams,
adapted by Oscar Saul, based on the play by Tennessee Wil-
liams
    (In Film Scripts One)
Summer and Smoke
    (In Best American Plays, Third Series)
Sweet Bird of Youth
    (In Esquire, Vol. 51, Apr. 1959)
Talk to Me Like the Rain
    (In 27 Wagons Full of Cotton)
Ten Blocks on the Camino Real
    (In American Blues)
This Property Is Condemned
    (In 27 Wagons Full of Cotton)
27 Wagons Full of Cotton
    (In One Act)
    (In Best Short Plays, 1956/57)
    (In Best One-Act Plays of 1944, N.Y.)
    (In 27 Wagons Full of Cotton)
    (In 24 Favorite One-Act Plays)
The Unsatisfactory Supper
    (In Best One-Act Plays of 1945, N.Y.)
WILLIAMS, Thomas John, 1824-1874
    A Silent Protector
        (In 26 Short & Amusing Plays, 1871)
WILLIAMS, William Carlos, 1883-1963
    Many Loves
        (In Theatre Arts, Vol. 46, Feb. 1962)
WILLIAMS, William Henry, 1797?-1846
    The Wreck; or, The Buccaneer's Bridal
        (In Cumberland's British Theatre, Vol. 23, no. 4)

WILLIAMSON, Harold
    Peggy, a Tragedy of the Tenant Farmer
        (In Carolina Folkplays)
WILLIAMSON, Hugh Ross
    Cardinal's Learning
        (In Best One-Act Plays of 1948/49, London)
    Gunpowder, Treason and Plot
        (In Plays of the Year, Vol. 6, 1951)
    Heart of Bruce
        (In Plays of the Year, Vol. 20, 1959)
    Teresa of Avila
        (In Plays of the Year, Vol. 24, 1961)
WILLIAMSON, Scott Graham
    A Bed with the Others, by Scott Graham Williamson and Joseph
    Shore
        (In Best One-Act Plays of 1948/49, N.Y.)
Willie the Germ (see Williams, Murray)
WILLS, William Gorman, 1828-1891
    The Larboard Fin; or, Twelve Months Since
        (In Cumberland's British Theatre, Vol. 33, no. 2)
WILLSON, Meredith, 1902-
    The Unsinkable Molly Brown. Music and lyrics by Meredith
    Willson; book by Richard Morris
        (In Theatre Arts, Vol. 47, Feb. 1963)
WILMOT, Robert, fl. 1568-1608
    Tancred and Gismunda, composed by the Gentlemen of the Inner
    Temple
        (In Dodsley's A Select Collection of Old English Plays, Vol.
        7)
        (In Dodsley's A Select Collection of Old Plays, Vol. 2)
Wilmurt, Arthur, 1906-
    Noah (see Obey, Andre)
Wilson (see Trotti, Lamar)
WILSON, Donald
    Flight of the Dove
        (In Television Playwright: 10 Plays for BBC)
WILSON, Dorothy Clarke
    The Return of Chandra
        (In Best Short Plays, 1954/55)
WILSON, Edmund, 1895-
    Dr. McGrath
        (In Commentary, Vol. 43, May 1967)
WILSON, Frank H.
    Sugar Cane
        (In Plays of Negro Life)
Wilson, Harry Leon
    The Man from Home (see Tarkington, Booth)
Wilson, Harry Leon
    **Merton of the Movies (see Kaufman, George Simon)
WILSON, Lanford, 1937-
    The Great Nebula of Orion
        (In Best Short Plays, 1972)

The Madness of Lady Bright
    (In Eight Plays From Off-Off Broadway)
WILSON, Leila Weeks
    Like Father Like Son
    (In Drama, Vol. 13, Feb. 1923)
WILSON, Theodora Wilson
    Champion North
    (In Five Three-Act Plays)
Wilson, Thomas Woodrow, pres. U.S., 1856-1924
    *Wilson (see Trotti, Lamar)
Wily Beguiled (Anon.)
    (In Dodsley's A Select Collection of Old English Plays, Vol.
    9)
Wimperis, Arthur
    Mrs. Miniver (see Hilton, James)
WINCELBERG, Simon
    The Conqueror
    (In Best Short Plays, 1954/55)
The Wind (see Peterson, Agnes E.)
The Wind and Lady Moon (see Sheridan, Emma)
The Wind and the Rain (see Hodge, Merton)
Wind from the East (see Godard, Jean-Luc)
Wind in the Branches of the Sassafras (see Obalida, Rene de)
Wind o' the Moors (see Peach, Lawrence du Garde)
The Window (see Marcus, Frank)
Windows (see Schisgal, Murray)
Wine in the Wilderness (see Childress, Alice)
The Wingless Victory (see Anderson, Maxwell)
The Wings of the Dove (see Taylor, Christopher)
Winkelberg (see Hecht, Ben)
Winners All (see Ehrlich, Mrs. Ida Lublenski)
Winning a Husband; or, Seven's the Main (see Macfarren, George)
WINSLOE, Christa
    Children in Uniform
    (In Famous Plays of Today, 1932/33)
The Winslow Boy (see Rattigan, Terence)
WINTER, Mary
    The Ruling Class
    (In Drama, Vol. 15, Apr. 1925)
Winter Light (see The Communicants)
Winter Sunshine (see Marshall, Laura)
Winter's Night (see Boyce, Neith "Mrs. Hutchins Hapgood")
Winterset (see Anderson, Maxwell)
Wireless Can't Lie (see Brighouse, Harold)
Wirz, Henry, 1823?-1865
    *The Andersonville Trial (see Levitt, Saul)
Wisdom Teeth (see Field, Rachel Lyman)
The Wisdome of Doctor Dodypoll (Anon.)
    (In A Collection of Old English Plays, Vol. 3)
Wise Child (see Gray, Simon)
The Wise Men of the East (see Inchbald, Mrs. Elizabeth Simpson)
The Wish Shop (see Brighouse, Harold)

WISHENGRAD, Morton
    The Battle of the Warsaw Ghetto
        (In Radio Drama in Action, 1945)
    The Camel and I
        (In Best One-Act Plays of 1949/50, N.Y.)
    How They Knocked the Devil Out of Uncle Ezra
        (In Best One-Act Plays of 1946/47, N.Y.)
    The Last Inca
        (In Radio's Best Plays, 1947)
    The Rope Dancers
        (In Best American Plays, Fifth Series, 1957-63)
        (In Theatre Arts, Vol. 44, no. 1, Jan. 1960)
    To the American People
        (In Best One-Act Plays of 1945, N.Y.)
A Wishful Taw (see Hughes, Elizabeth Wilson)
The Witch of Edmonton (see Rowley, William)
The Witches' Sabbath (see Granick, Harry)
The Witching Hour (see Thomas, Augustus)
With Malice Aforethought (see Stranack, John)
Within the Law (see Veiller, Bayard)
Within Two Shadows (see Hair, Wilson John)
WITKIEWICZ, Stanislaw Ignacy, 1885-1939
    The Crazy Locomotive
        (In First Stage, Vol. 6, Fall 1967)
    The Madman and the Nun; or, There Is Nothing Bad Which
      Could Not Turn to Something Worse
        (In First Stage, Vol. 4, Winter 1965/66)
    The Pragmatists
        (In Drama & Theatre, Vol. 10, no. 1, Fall 1971)
    The Water Hen
        (In First Stage, Vol. 6, Summer 1967)
The Witness (see Frida, Emil Bohslav)
Witness for the Prosecution (see Christie, Agatha Miller)
The Wits (see D'Avenant, Sir William)
WITTLINGER, Karl
    Do You Know the Milky Way?
        (In Theatre Arts, Vol. 47, June 1963)
    The Night Nurse
        (In Best Short Plays, 1968)
Wives As They Were, and Maids As They Are (see Inchbald, Mrs.
    Elizabeth Simpson)
The Wizard of the Moor (see Gott, Henry)
Wodehouse, Pelham Granville, 1881-
    The Play's the Thing (see Molnar, Ferenc)
WOLF, Klaus
    Lagerfeuer
        (In Theater der Zeit, Vol. 24, no. 10, 1969)
WOLFE, Thomas Clayton, 1900-1938
    **Farewell to Altamount (see Lomax, Elizabeth)
    **Look Homeward Angel (see Frings, Ketti)
    Welcome to Our Cities
        (In Esquire, Vol. 48, Oct. 1957)

WOLFF, Oscar M.
    Where but in America
        (In Contemporary One-Act Plays, 1922)
A Woman Is a Weathercock (see Field, Nathaniel)
A Woman Killed by Kindness (see Heywood, Thomas)
A Woman Never Vext; or, The Widow of Cornhill (see Rowley,
    William)
The Woman of Andros (see Terence, Publius Terentius Afer)
Woman of Paris (see Becque, Henri)
The Woman of Samos (Samia) (see Menander)
The Woman of the World (see Coyne, Joseph Stirling)
Woman of Trachis (see Sophocles)
Woman Song (see Alexander, Hartley Burr)
The Woman Taken in Adultery (see Hegge Cycle)
The Woman Within the Cypress Fence (see Zeami Motokiyo)
The Woman-Killer and the Hell of Oil (Onnagoroshi Abura Jigoku)
    (see Chikamatsu Monzaemon)
A Woman's Place (see Yliruusi, Tauno)
A Woman's Privilege (see Hayes, Marrijane)
The Women (see Luce, Clare Boothe)
The Women; screenplay (see Loos, Anita)
Women Do Things Like That (see Brighouse, Harold)
The Wonder: A Women Keeps a Secret (see Centlivre, Susanna)
The Wonder of a Kingdom (see Dekker, Thomas)
WOOD, Charles
    Cockade
        (In Evergreen Playscript Series, no. 13)
    Dingo
        (In Plays and Players, Vol. 14, July 1967)
WOOD, Ellen (Price, Mrs. Henry Wood, 1814-1887)
    East Lynn
        (In S. R. O. , the Most Successful Plays...)
Wood, Sam, 1883-1949
    A Day at the Races (see Pirosh, Robert)
    Goodbye, Mr. Chips (see Sherriff, Robert Cedric)
    A Night at the Opera (see Kaufman, George Simon)
Wood Painting (see Bergman, Ingmar)
The Wooden Box (see O'Connor, Patrick)
WOODRESS, Frederick Albert, 1923-
    Impass
        (In Best One-Act Plays of 1948/49, N. Y.)
Wooing in Jest and Loving in Earnest (see Troughton, Adolphus
    Charles)
WOOLER, John Pratt, 1824-1868
    A Faint Heart Which Did Win a Fair Lady
        (In Lacy's Plays)
    Orange Blossoms
        (In Lacy's Plays)
Woollcott, Alexander, 1887-1943
    *The Man Who Came to Dinner (fiction) (see Hart, Moss)
The Word (see Dreyer, Carl Theodor)
A Word in Your Ear (see Goldschmidt, Walter)

A Word to the Wise (see Kelly, Hugh)
A Word with Sir Francis Drake During His Last Night in London
   (see Mansfield, John)
Words and Music (see Beckett, Samuel)
The Words upon the Window-Pane (see Yeats, William Butler)
The Workers at the Loom (see Dane, Essex)
The Workhouse Donkey (see Arden, John)
The Workhouse Ward (see Gregory, Isabella Augusta Persse, lady)
A World Elsewhere (see Riggs, Lynn)
The World of Paul Slickey (see Osborne, John)
The World Is What It Is (see Moravia, Alberto)
The World Tipped Over, and Laying on Its Side (see Feldhaus-
   Weber, Mary)
The World We Live In (The Insect Comedy) (see Capek, Josef)
The Worlde and the Chylde (Anon.)
   (In Dodsley's A Select Collection of Old English Plays, Vol.
   1)
   (In Dodsley's A Select Collection of Old Plays, Vol. 12)
WORMS, Jeannine
   Un Chat Est un Chat
      (In L'Avant-Scene du Theatre, no. 492, Apr. 1, 1972)
   Le Gouter
      (In L'Avant-Scene du Theatre, no. 492, Apr. 1, 1972)
   Un Gros Gateau
      (In L'Avant-Scene du Theatre, no. 440, Jan. 1, 1970)
   Lumieres de Boheme (see Valle-Inclan, Ramon Maria del)
   Les Pommes, Les Poires
      (In Plaisir de France, supplement theatral, no. 333, July
      1966)
   Puis-Je Me Permettre De?...
      (In Plaisir de France, supplement theatral, no. 333, July
      1966)
   Rever pour Vivre
      (In Plaisir de France, supplement theatral, no. 333, July
      1966)
   Tout a l'Heure
      (In L'Avant-Scene du Theatre, no. 492, Apr. 1, 1972)
WOSKOFF, Verna
   Castle in the Village
      (In Best Short Plays, 1958/59)
WOUK, Herman, 1915-
   The Caine Mutiny Court-Martial
      (In Best American Plays, Fourth Series)
The Wounded Highwayman (Teoi Yamadachi) (see Sakanishi, Shio)
The Wounds of Civil War (see Lodge, Thomas)
Woyzeck (see Büchner, Georg)
A Wreath and a Curse (see All Summer Long)
The Wreck; or, The Buccaneer's Bridal (see Williams, William
   Henry)
WRIGHT, Ethan Armstrong
   The Grass Grows Red
      (In The Banner Anthology of One-Act Plays by American
      Authors)

WRIGHT, James, 1643-1713
    Historia Histrionica: a Dialogue of Plays and Players
    (In Dodsley's A Select Collection of Old English Plays, Vol.
    15)
WUNDERLICH, Lawrence
    Prometheus Rebound
    (In First Stage, Vol. 3, Spring 1964)
WURLITZER, Rudolph
    Two Lane Blacktop, a screenplay by Rudolph Wurlitzer and
    Will Corry
    (In Esquire, Vol. 75, no. 4, April 1971)
Wuthering Heights (see Hecht, Ben)
Wyatt, Sir Thomas, 1503?-1542
    *Sir Thomas Wyatt (see Dekker, Thomas)
WYCHERLY, William, 1640?-1716
    The Country Girl; altered by David Garrick
    (In Bell's British Theatre, 1797, Vol. 13)
    The Country Wife
    (In Masterworks of World Drama, Vol. 4)
    The Plain Dealer
    (In Bell's British Theatre, 1797, Vol. 23)
Wyler, William, 1902-
    Mrs. Miniver (see Hilton, James)
    Wuthering Heights (see Hecht, Ben)
WYMARK, Olwen, 1929-
    Stay Where You Are
    (In Best Short Plays, 1972)

XXXXX (see Hoffman, William H.)
XY & Zee (see O'Brien, Edna)
X. Y. Z. (see Colman, George)
X. Y. Z. (see Lifchitz, Philippe)
Xanthippe, wife of Socrates
    *Barefoot in Athens (see Anderson, Maxwell)
    *Xantippe and Socrates (see Baring, Maurice)
    *Xanthippe on Woman Suffrage (see Osborne, Duffield)
Ximena, wife of El Cid
    *The Cid (see Corneille, Pierre)
    *Ximena; or, The Heroic Daughter (see Cibber, Colley)
Xmas in Las Vegas (see Christmas in Las Vegas)

YALTSEV, P.
    Circumstances Alter Cases
    (In Soviet One-Act Plays)
    The Ocean
    (In Soviet One-Act Plays)
    Success
    (In Soviet One-Act Plays)
YAMAMOTO Yuzo
    The Crown of Life

(In Three Plays of Yamamoto Yuzo)
Sakazaki, Lord Dewa
    (In Three Plays by Yamamoto Yuzo)
The Story of Chink Okichi
    (In Three Plays of Yamamoto Yuzo)
YANKOWITZ, Susan
    The Ha-Ha Play
        (In Scripts, Vol. 1, no. 10, Oct. 1972)
    Slaughterhouse Play
        (In New American Plays, Vol. 4)
        (In Yale/Theatre, Vol. 2, no. 2, Summer 1969)
    Terminal, by Susan Yankowitz and The Open Theater
        (In Scripts, Vol. 1, no. 1, Nov. 1971)
YARINGTON, Robert, fl. 1601
    Two Tragedies in One
        (In A Collection of Old English Plays, Vol. 4)
Yat Pak or the Hundredth Notch (see Bunje, Emil T. H.)
The Year the Yankees Lost the Pennant (see Damn Yankees)
YEATS, Jack Butler, 1871-1957
    La La Noo
        (In Genius of the Irish Theater)
YEATS, William Butler, 1865-1936
    Cathleen ni Houlihan
        (In Reading Drama)
        (In 24 Favorite One-Act Plays)
    Deirdre
        (In Three Anglo-Irish Plays)
    The Dreaming of the Bones
        (In 24 One-Act Plays, Revised edition, 1954)
    A Full Moon in March
        (In From the Modern Repertoire, Series One)
    The Land of Heart's Desire
        (In Atlantic Book of Modern Plays, 1921)
        (In Representative One-Act Plays by British and Irish Authors)
    On Baile's Strand
        (In The Modern Theatre, ed. by R. W. Corrigan)
        (In Makers of the Modern Theater, 1961)
    Purgatory
        (In Introduction to Literature: Plays)
        (In Makers of the Modern Theater, 1961)
        (In One Act)
        (In The Modern Theatre, Vol. 2, ed. by Eric Bentley)
    The Words upon the Window-Pane
        (In Genius of the Irish Theater)
        (In Introduction to Literature: Plays)
Yellow Jack (see Howard, Sidney Coe)
Yellow Jack; screenplay (see Chodorov, Edward)
YERBY, Lorees, 1930-
    The Golden Bull of Boredom
        (In New American Plays, Vol. 1)
Yerma (see Garcia Lorca, Federico)
"Yes!" (see Somerset, Charles A.)

Yes, I'm Going Away (see Brecht, Bertolt)
Yes, M'Lord (see Home, William Douglas)
Yes My Darling Daughter (see Reed, Mark White)
Les Yeux de l'Ete (see Sengissen, Paule)
YIRENCHI, Emmanuel
    The Firefly
      (In Yale/Theatre, Vol. 2, no. 2, Summer 1969)
YLIRUUSI, Tauno, 1927-
    Lucian (The Mark Twain of Antiquity)
      (In Modern International Drama, Vol. 3, no. 1, 1969)
    A Woman's Place
      (In Modern International Drama, Vol. 5, no. 1, Fall 1971)
York Butchers' Play
    The Crucifixion
      (In Religious Drama, Vol. 2)
York Cardmakers' Play
    The Creation of Man
      (In Religious Drama, Vol. 2)
York Cowpers' Play
    The Fall of Man
      (In Religious Drama, Vol. 2)
York Fullers' Play
    The Garden of Eden
      (In Religious Drama, Vol. 2)
York Locksmiths' Play
    The Temptation of Christ
      (In Religious Drama, Vol. 2)
York Mercers' Play
    The Last Judgement
      (In Religious Drama, Vol. 2)
York Saddlers' Play
    The Harrowing of Hell
      (In Religious Drama, Vol. 2)
York Skinners' Play
    Palm Sunday
      (In Religious Drama, Vol. 2)
York Tailors' Play
    The Ascension
      (In Religious Drama, Vol. 2)
York Tanners' Play
    The Creation of the Heavenly Beings: The Fall of Lucifer
      (In Religious Drama, Vol. 2)
York Tilemakers' Play
    The Second Trial before Pilate: the Scourging and Condemna-
    tion
      (In Religious Drama, Vol. 2)
York Tile-Thatchers' Play
    The Birth of Christ
      (In Religious Drama, Vol. 2)
A Yorkshire Tragedy (Anon.)
    (In Great English Plays)
Yosaku from Tamba (Tamba Yosaku) (see Chikamatsu Monzaemon)

You Can't Take It With You   (see Hart, Moss)
You Can't Take It With You; screenplay   (see Riskin, Robert)
You Know I Can't Hear You When the Water's Running   (see Ander-
     son, Robert)
YOUNG, Edward, 1683-1765
     The Brothers
          (In Bell's British Theatre, 1797, Vol. 30)
     Busiris, King of Egypt
          (In Bell's British Theatre, 1797, Vol. 29)
     The Revenge
          (In Bell's British Theatre, 1797, Vol. 8)
          (In Cumberland's British Theatre, Vol. 3, no. 3)
          (In The London Stage, Vol. 1)
YOUNG, Stanley
     A Bunyan Yarn
          (In Best One-Act Plays of 1945, N.Y.)
     Farmer Brown's Pig
          (In Best One-Act Plays of 1940, N.Y.)
     The Sound of Apples
          (In Best Short Plays, 1958/59)
YOUNG, Stark, 1881-1963
     At the Shrine
          (In Theatre Arts, Vol. 3, 1919)
     The Colonnade
          (In Theatre Arts, Vol. 8, Aug. 1924)
     George Dandin, or The Discomfited Husband   (see Moliere,
          Jean Baptiste Poquelin)
     The Queen of Sheba
          (In Theatre Arts, Vol. 6, 1922)
     Rose Windows
          (In Theatre Arts, Vol. 9, Oct. 1925)
     The Sea Gull   (see Chekhov, Anton Pavlovich)
     The Young and Fair   (see Nash, N. Richard)
The Young at Heart   (see Osborn, Paul)
The Young Hussar   (see Dimond, William)
A Young Lady of Property   (see Foote, Horton)
Young Mr. Santa Claus   (see Harris, Claudia Lucas)
The Young Quaker   (see O'Keeffe, John)
The Young Reefer   (see Soane, George)
The Young Wonder   (see Pillot, Joseph Eugene)
Young Woodley   (see Van Druten, John)
The Youngest Shall Ask   (see Shaber, David)
You're a Long Time Dead   (see Morgan, Elaine)
Youth at the Helm   (see Vulpuis, Paul)
Youth, Love, and Folly; or, The Little Jockey   (see Dimond,
     William)
The Youthful Queen   (see Shannon, Charles)
YUNG, Chun
     The Army and People Are One Family
          (In Chinese Literature, no. 9, 1968)

Z, or l'Anatomie d'un Assassinat Politique   (see Costa-Gavras)

Zabriskie Point (see Antonioni, Michelangelo)
Zadek, Peter
    Kleiner Mann, Was Nun? (see Dorst, Tankred)
ZAHN, Curtis
    An Albino Kind of Logic
        (In First Stage, Vol. 3, Summer/Fall 1964)
    Conditioned Reflex
        (In First Stage, Vol. 4, Summer 1965)
  **Sadco (see Pumphrey, Byron)
Zanet Kloubu (L'Arthrite) (see Foissy, Guy)
Zara (see Hill, Aaron)
Zarah (see Soane, George)
Zartian (see Savary, Jerome)
Zazie dans le Metro (see Malle, Louis)
The Zeal of Thy House (see Sayers, Dorothy Leigh)
ZEAMI Motokiyo, 1363-1444
    Akogi, a Noh Play
        (In Sewanee Review, Vol. 67, 1959)
    The Battle of Yashima
        (In The Old Pine Tree & Other Noh Plays)
    Haku Rakuten
        (In Genius of the Oriental Theater)
    Kagekiyo
        (In Plays of Old Japan)
    The Old Pine Tree
        (In The Old Pine Tree & Other Noh Plays)
    Tamura
        (In Plays of Old Japan)
    The Woman Within the Cypress Fence
        (In The Old Pine Tree & Other Noh Plays)
Zefa Entre os Hommens (see Pongetti, Henrique)
ZEIGER, Henry
    Five Days
        (In Best Short Plays, 1955/56)
Zeitgenossen (see Stolper, Armin)
The Zen Substitute (see Okamura Shiko)
ZENCHIKU Ujinobu, 1414-1499?
    Aoi no Uye
        (In Genius of the Oriental Theater)
Zenobia, Queen of Palmyra, 3rd cent. A.D.
  *Zenobia (see Murphy, Arthur)
ZERBONI, Roberto
    Antonio
        (In First Stage, Vol. 4, Winter 1965/66)
Zero de Conduite (see Vigo, Jean)
ZETTERLING, Mai, 1925-
    Jeux de Nuit, by Mai Zetterling et David Hughes d'apres le
      roman de Mai Zetterling
        (In L'Avant-Scene du Cinema, no. 67, 1967)
ZIEGELMAIER, Gregory
    A Common for All Saints
        (In First Stage, Vol. 4, Fall 1965)
ZIEM, Jochen

Die Versöhnung
(In Theatre Heute, no. 6, June 1971)
Zimmerman, Ingo
Levins Mühle (see Zimmerman, Udo)
ZIMMERMAN, Rolf
Connie und der Löwe
(In Theater der Zeit, Vol. 24, no. 6, 1969)
ZIMMERMAN, Udo
Levins Mühle, Oper in neun Bildern, frei nach gleichnamigen
Roman, von Johannes Bobrowski, Liberetto von Ingo Zimmer-
man, Musik von Udo Zimmerman
(In Theater der Zeit, no. 5, May 1972)
Die Zweite Entscheidung
(In Theatre der Zeit, Vol. 25, no. 5, 1970)
ZINDEL, Paul, 1937-
The Effect of Gamma Rays on Man-in-the-Moon Marigolds
(In Plays and Players, Vol. 20, no. 3, Dec. 1972)
ZOLA, Emile, 1840-1902
*The Life of Emile Zola (see Herald, Heinz)
Therese Raquin
(In From the Modern Repertoire, Series Three)
Zombi (see Scott, Natalie Vivian)
Zone of Quiet (see Lardner, Ring Wilmer)
Zoo, or, L'Assassin Philanthrope (see Ditt, Jean Bruller)
The Zoo Story (see Albee, Edward)
The Zoo Story; text in French (see Albee, Edward)
Zorinski (see Morton, Thomas)
ZUCCA, Pierre, 1943-
La Cage de Pierre; or, La Gouvernante Abusive
(In L'Avant-Scene du Cinema, no. 90, 1969)
ZUCKERMAN, Albert J.
Blobo's Boy
(In Best Short Plays, 1958/59)
Zuckmayer, Karl, 1896-
L'Ange Bleu (Der Blaue Engel) (see Von Sternberg, Josef)
Zweig, Stefan, 1881-1942
Volpone (see Jonson, Ben)
Zweipersonnenstück (see Kerndl, Rainer)
Die Zweite Entscheidung (see Zimmerman, Udo)

ANTHOLOGIES INDEXED

Agee, James. Agee on Film. New York: McDowell, Obolensky, 1958-1960.

Albee, Edward. The Box and Quotations from Chairman Mao Tsetung. New York: Atheneum, 1969.

_____. Zoo Story and Other Plays. London: J. Cape, 1962.

Aldington, Richard, ed. French Comedies of the 18th Century. London: Routledge, 1923.

Allen, John Piers, ed. Four Continental Plays. London: Heinemann, 1964.

Altenbernd, Lynn, ed. Introduction to Literature: Plays. New York: Macmillan, 1963.

Anderson, George Lincoln, ed. The Genius of the Oriental Theatre. New York: New American Library, 1966.

Anderson, Lindsay. In Making a Film; the story of "Secret People," chronicled and edited by Lindsay Anderson, with shooting script of the film by Thorold Dickinson and Wolfgang Wilhelm. London: Geo. Allen & Unwin, 1952.

Anderson, Maxwell. Eleven Verse Plays. New York: Harcourt, Brace, 1940.

Anouilh, Jean. Pieces Noires. Paris: Calman-Levy, 1942.

_____. Plays, 1958-59, 3 vols. New York: Hill & Wang, 1972.

Antonioni, Michelangelo Screenplays. New York. Orion, 1963.

Ashton, Winfred. Collected Plays of Clemence Dane, Vol. 1. London: Heineman, 1961.

Bailey, James Osler, ed. British Plays of the 19th Century. New York: Odyssey Press, 1966.

Ballet, Arthur H., ed. Playwrights for Tomorrow. 7 vols. Minneapolis: Univ. of Minnesota Press, 1966-1971.

Baring, Maurice. Diminutive Dramas. Boston: Houghton, Mifflin, 1911.

Barnet, Sylvan, ed. The Genius of the Early English Theatre.
     New York: New American Library, 1962.

_____. The Genius of the Irish Theatre. New York: New
     American Library, 1960.

_____. The Genius of the Later English Theatre. New York:
     New American Library, 1962.

Barnouw, Erik. Handbook of Radio Production. Boston: Little,
     Brown, 1949.

_____. Radio Drama in Action. New York: Farrar & Rein-
     hart, 1945.

Behan, Brendan. Quare Fellow and The Hostage. New York:
     Grove Press, 1964.

Bell, John. Bell's British Theatre. 34 vols. London: G. Caw-
     thorn, 1797.

Benedikt, Michael, comp. Theatre Experiment. Garden City,
     N.Y.: Doubleday, 1967.

Bens, John H. A Search for Awareness. New York: Holt, Rine-
     hart & Winston, 1966.

Bentley, Eric Russell, ed. The Classic Theatre. 4 vols. Garden
     City, N.Y.: Doubleday, 1958-1961.

_____. From the Modern Repertoire. Series 1: Denver, Colo-
     rado: Univ. of Denver, 1949; Series 2-3: Bloomington,
     Ind.: Univ. of Indiana, 1952, 1956.

_____. The Genius of the Italian Theatre. New York: New
     American Library, 1964.

_____. The Modern Theatre. 6 vols. Garden City, N.Y.:
     Doubleday, 1955-1960.

Bergman, Ingmar. Bergman: Persona and Shame. New York:
     Grossman, 1972.

_____. A Film Trilogy. New York: Orion Press, 1967.

Bermel, Albert. The Genius of the French Theatre. New York:
     New American Library, 1961.

Bertin, Charles. Two Plays. Minneapolis: Univ. of Minnesota
     Press, 1970.

Biutenen, Johannes Adrianus Bernardus van, comp. Two Plays

from Ancient India. New York: Columbia Univ. , 1968.

Bohemian Club, San Francisco. Grove Plays of the Bohemian Club.
     San Francisco, Calif. : H. S. Crocker, 1918.

Bond, Richard Warwick, comp. Early Plays from the Italian.
     New York: Benjamin Blom, 1967.

Booth, Michael R. , ed. Hiss the Villain. New York: Benjamin
     Blom, 1964.

Brancati, Vitaliano. Teatro. Milano: Bompiani, 1957.

Brandon, James R. , comp. Traditional Asian Plays. New York:
     Hill & Wang, 1972.

British Broadcasting Corporation. Television Playwright: 10 Plays
     for BBC. New York: Hill & Wang, 1960.

Browne, Elliott Martin, ed. New English Dramatists. Harmonds-
     worth, Middlesex: Penguin Books, 1959.

Bullen, Arthur Henry, ed. A Collection of Old English Plays.   7
     vols. in 4. New York: Benjamin Blom, 1964.

Buñuel, Luis. Three Screenplays. New York: Orion, 1969.

Burack, Abraham Saul. Television Plays for Writers. Boston:
     The Writer, 1957.

Byron, George Gordon Noel. Poems and Plays of Lord Byron.
     New York: T. Crowell, 1880.

Camus, Albert. Caligula and Three Other Plays. New York:
     Knopf, 1958.

Cantril, Hadley. The Invasion from Mars; a study in the psychology
     of panic, with the complete script of the famous Orson Welles
     broadcast by Howard Hoch, based on "War of the Worlds" by
     H. G. Wells. Princeton, N. J. : Princeton Univ. Press, 1940.

Caputi, Anthony Francis, comp. Masterworks of World Drama.
     Boston: Heath, 1968.

Carter, Leslie H. , comp. Banner Anthology of One-Act Plays by
     American Authors. San Francisco, Calif. : Banner Play
     Bureau, 1969.

Cartmell, Van Henry, and Bennett Cerf, eds. 13 Famous Plays of
     Crime and Detection. New York: Blakiston, 1946.

Cerf, Bennett Alfred, comp. Plays of Our Time. New York:
     Random House, 1967.

_____ . S. R. O. : The Most Successful Plays of the American Stage. New York: Blakiston, 1946.

_____ . Six American Plays for Today. New York: Modern Library, 1961.

_____ . 16 Famous American Plays. New York: Modern Library, 1941.

_____ . 16 Famous British Plays. Garden City, N. Y. : Garden City Pub. Co. , 1942.

_____ . 16 Famous European Plays. Garden City, N. Y. : Garden City Pub. Co. , 1943.

_____ . 30 Famous One-Act Plays. New York: Modern Library, 1943.

_____ . 24 Favorite One-Act Plays. Garden City, N. Y. : Doubleday, 1958.

Chapman, Robin, ed. The City and the Court: Five 17th Century Comedies of London Life. San Francisco, Calif. : Chandler Pub. Co. , 1968.

Chayefsky, Paddy. Television Plays. New York: Simon & Schuster, 1955.

Chikamatsu Monzaemon. Four Major Plays. New York: Columbia Univ. Press, 1961.

_____ . Major Plays of Chikamatsu. Cambridge, Mass. : Harvard Univ. Press, 1953.

Clair, Rene. Comedies et Commentaires. Paris: Gallimard, 1959.

_____ . Four Screenplays. New York: Orion, 1970.

Clark, Barrett Harper. Nine Modern American Plays. New York: Appleton-Century-Crofts, 1951.

_____ . Representative One-Act Plays by British and Irish Authors. Boston: Little, Brown, 1921.

_____ . World Drama. New York: D. Appleton, 1933.

Cocteau, Jean. Jean Cocteau: Five Plays. New York: Hill & Wang, 1961.

_____ . Nouveau Theatre de Poche. Monaco: Editions du Rocher, 1960.

_____ . Oeuvres Completes. 11 vols. Geneve?: Marguerat, 1946-1951.

_____ . Three Screenplays. New York: Grossman, 1970.

_____ . Two Screenplays. New York: Penguin, 1968.

Cordell, Kathryn Coe, ed. Pulitzer Prize Plays. New York: Random House, 1935.

Corrigan, Robert Willoughby, ed. Modern Theatre. New York: Macmillan, 1964.

_____ . New American Plays. 4 vols. New York: Hill & Wang, 1965-1971.

_____ . New Theatre of Europe. 2 vols. New York: Dell Pub. Co. , 1962-1964.

Couch, William, comp. New Black Playwrights. Baton Rouge: Louisiana State Univ. Press, 1968.

Coward, Noel. Curtain Calls. New York: Garden City Pub. Co. , 1940.

_____ . Tonight at 8:30. New York: Sun Dial Press, 1936.

Cox, Alva I. , ed. The Delinquent, the Hipster, the Square, and the Sandpile Series. St. Louis, Mo. : Cooperative Pub. Assoc. , Bethany Press, 1962.

Coyle, William, comp. Six Early American Plays. Columbus, Ohio: Merrill, 1968.

Cumberland's British Theatre, ed. by George Daniel. 45 vols. London: John Cumberland, 1825-1855.

Dekker, Thomas. Dramatic Works. 4 vols. Cambridge Univ. Press, 1953.

Dickens, Charles. Works: Vol. 18. New York: Bigelo, Brown, 19--.

Dietrich, R. F. , comp. The Art of Modern Drama. New York: Holt, Rinehart & Winston, 1969.

Dodsley, Robert, ed. A Select Collection of Old English Plays. 15 vols. in 7. New York: Benjamin Blom, 1964.

_____ . A Select Collection of Old Plays. 12 vols. , 1703-1764. London: Prowett, 1825-1827.

Downer, Alan Seymour, ed. American Drama. New York: Crowell, 1960.

Dreiser, Theodore. Plays of the Natural and the Supernatural. London: John Lane, 1916.

Dreyer, Carl Theodor. Four Screenplays. Bloomington: Indiana Univ. Press, 1970.

Duckworth, George Eckel, ed. The Complete Roman Drama. New York: Random House, 1942.

Eisenstein, Sergei-Mikailovitch. Que Viva Mexico!, with an introduction by Ernest Lindgren. London: Vision Press, 1952.

Eliot, Thomas Stearns. Complete Plays. New York: Harcourt, Brace & World, 1967.

Ernst, Earle, ed. Three Japanese Plays from the Traditional Theatre. London: Oxford Univ. Press, 1959.

Esslin, Martin, comp. The Genius of the German Theatre. New York: New American Library, 1968.

Famous Plays of Today: 1929, 1931, 1932/33, 1933, 1933/34, 1935, 1936, 1953, 1954. London: Gollancz.

Fellini, Federico. Early Screenplays. New York: Grossman, 1971.

Field, Rachel. Six Plays. New York: Scribners, 1924.

Fielding, Henry. Works: Vol. 1-4. London: Bickers & Son, 1902-1903.

Film: Book 1-2. New York: Grove Press, 1959, 1962.

Fitz John, Donald, comp. English One-Act Plays of Today. London: Oxford Univ. Press, 1962.

Five Three-Act Plays, with a foreword by W. G. Fay. London: Rich & Cowan, 1933.

Foote, Horton. Harrison Texas: Eight Television Plays. New York: Harcourt, Brace, 1956.

_____. Three Plays. New York: Harcourt, Brace & World, 1962.

Freedman, Morris, comp. Tragedy: Texts and Commentary. New York: Scribner, 1969.

Frisch, Max. Max Frisch: Three Plays. New York: Hill & Wang, 1962.

Fry, Christopher. Plays. London: Oxford Univ. Press, 1961.

Garrett, George P. , comp. Film Scripts One and Two. 2 vols. New York: Appleton-Century-Crofts, 1971.

Gassner, John, ed. Best American Plays, Third Series, 1945-1951. New York: Crown, 1952.

_____. Best American Plays, Fourth Series, 1952-1957. New York: Crown, 1958.

_____. Best American Plays, Fifth Series, 1958-1963. New York: Crown, 1963.

_____. Best American Plays, Sixth Series, 1963-1967. New York: Crown, 1971.

_____. Best American Plays, Supplementary Volume, 1918-1958. New York: Crown, 1961.

_____. Best Plays of the Early American Theatre, from the Beginning to 1916. New York: Crown, 1967.

_____. Best Plays of the Modern American Theatre, Second Series, 1939-1946. New York: Crown, 1947.

_____. Four New Yale Playwrights. New York: Crown, 1965.

_____. Three Plays from the Yale School of Drama. New York: Dutton, 1964.

_____. 20 Best European Plays on the American Stage. New York: Crown, 1957.

_____. 20 Best Film Plays. New York: Crown, 1943.

_____. 20 Best Plays of the Modern American Theatre, 1930-1939. New York: Crown, 1939.

_____. 25 Best Plays of the Modern American Theatre, Early Series, 1916-1929. New York: Crown, 1949.

Gassner, John, and Dudley Nichols, comp. Best Film Plays, 1945-1946. New York: Crown, 1946.

Gates, Marie Carmichael, and Joji Sakurai, eds. Plays of Old Japan. New York: Dutton, 1913.

Gibson, William. Dinny and the Witches: Two Plays. New York: Atheneum, 1960.

Giraudoux, Jean. Four Plays; Three Plays. 2 vols. New York: Hill & Wang, 1958.

Gogol, Nikolai Vasil'evich. Collected Tales and Plays. New York: Washington Square Press, 1957.

Golden, John. Three John Golden Plays. New York: Samuel French, 1925.

Grant, Eliott Mansfield. Chief French Plays of the 19th Century. New York: Harper, 1934.

Grass, Günter. Four Plays. New York: Harcourt, Brace & World, 1967.

Grillparzer, Franz. Plays on Classic Themes. New York: Random House, 1969.

Hampden, John. 24 One-Act Plays. London: Dent, 1954.

Handke, Peter. Kaspar and Other Plays. New York: Farrar, Straus, & Giroux, 1969.

Harrison's British Classiks. 8 vols. London: Harrison, 1785-1786?

Hartmann, Sadakichi. Buddha, Confucius, Christ: Three Prophetic Plays, ed. by Harry Lawton and George Knox. New York: Herder, 1971.

Hecht, Ben. A Treasury of Ben Hecht. New York: Crown, 1959.

Hellman, Lillian. Six Plays. New York: Modern Library, 1960.

Herlihy, James Leo. Stop, You're Killing Me. New York: Simon & Schuster, 1970.

Holcroft, Thomas. Theatrical Recorder, 1805. 2 vols. New York: Burt Franklin, 1968.

Housman, Lawrence. Palace Plays. London: Cape, 1930.

Howard, Clarence J. 26 Short and Amusing Plays for Private Theatricals; being Howard's "Drawing-Room Theatricals" and Hudson's "Private Theatricals for Home Performance" combined in one volume. New York: Dick & Fitzgerald, 1871.

Hrotsvit, of Candersheim. The Plays of Roswitha. New York: Benjamin Blom, 1966.

Inchbald, Elizabeth. Modern Theatre, 1811. 10 vols. New York: Benjamin Blom, 1968.

Inge, William. Eleven Short Plays. New York: Dramatists Play Service, 1962.

_____. Four Plays. New York: Random House, 1958.

Ionesco, Eugene. Amedee; The New Tenant; Victims of Duty. New York: Grove Press, 1958.

_____. Four Plays. New York: Grove Press, 1958.

_____. Hunger and Thirst and Other Plays. New York: Grove Press, 1968.

_____. The Killer and Other Plays. New York: Grove Press, 1960.

_____. A Stroll in the Air. New York: Grove Press, 1965.

Jodorowsky, Alexandro. El Topo, a Book of the Film. New York: Douglas Pub. Co., 1972.

Johnson, Theodore. Ten Fantasies for Stage and Study. Boston: Walter H. Baker Co., 1932.

Jones, Le Roi. Four Black Revolutionary Plays. Indianapolis, Ind.: Bobbs-Merrill, 1969.

Joyce, James. Passages from James Joyce's "Finnegans Wake." A film by Expanding Cinema. New York: Expanding Cinema, 1965.

Kaufman, William I., ed. Best Television Plays of the Year, 1949, 1950-1951, 1957. New York: Merlin Press, 1949; Harcourt, 1950-1951, 1957.

Keats, John. Complete Works. New York: AMS Press, 1970.

Keene, Donald, ed. Anthology of Japanese Literature. New York: Grove Press, 1955.

Kemble, Frances, ed. Plays. London: Longman, Green, Longman, Roberts, & Green, 1863.

Kemp, Harry. Boccaccio's Untold Tale. New York: Brentano's, 1924.

Kikuchi Hiroshi. Tojuro's Love and Four Other Plays. Tokyo: Hokuseido Press, 1925.

Koch, Frederick Henry. Carolina Folk-Plays. New York: Holt, 1922.

Koch, Kenneth. A Change of Hearts: Plays, Films, and Other Dramatic Works. New York: Random House, 1973.

Kopit, Arthur L. The Day the Whores Came Out to Play Tennis and Other Plays. New York: Hill & Wang, 1965.

Kozelka, Paul, ed. 15 American One-Act Plays. New York: Washington Square Press, 1961.

Kozlinko, William, ed. Best Short Plays of the Social Theatre. New York: Random House, 1939.

Lacy, John. The Dramatic Works of John Lacy, 1875. New York: Benjamin Blom, 1967.

Lacy, Thomas Hailes, ed. Lacy's Acting Edition of Plays, Dramas, Farces, Extravaganzas, Etc. London: T. H. Lacy, 1850.

_____. Lacy's Plays. London: T. H. Lacy, 1863?

Lahr, John. Showcase 1. New York: Grove Press, 1969.

Lass, Abraham Harold, ed. Plays from Radio. Boston: Houghton Mifflin, 1948.

Lawrence, D. H. Complete Plays. London: Heinemann, 1965.

Lee, Nathaniel. Works. New Brunswick, N. J.: Scarecrow Press, 1954-55.

Leonard, Sterling Andrus. Atlantic Book of Modern Plays. Boston: Little, Brown, 1921.

Lewis, Benjamin Roland. Contemporary One-Act Plays. New York: Scribner's, 1922.

Liss, Joseph. Radio's Best Plays. New York: Greenberg, 1947.

Littl, Frederic M., ed. Plays from Black Africa. New York: Hill & Wang, 1968.

Locke, Alain Le Roy. Plays of Negro Life. New York: Harper, 1927.

The London Stage, 1824-1827. 2 vols.

Loomis, Roger Sherman, ed. Representative Medieval and Tudor Plays. Freeport, N. Y.: Books for Libraries Press, 1970.

McGaw, Charles J. Acting is Believing. New York: Reinhart, 1955.

Machiz, Herbert, ed. Artists' Theatre: Four Plays. New York: Grove Press, 1960.

Maeterlinck, Maurice. A Miracle of Saint Anthony. New York: Boni & Liveright, 1917.

Manvill, Roger, ed. Three British Screenplays. London: Methuen, 1950.

Marion, Frances. How To Write and Sell Film Stories. New York: Covici, Friede, 1937.

Marriott, J. W., ed. Best One-Act Plays, 1931-1944/45; 1948/49; 1952/53.

Marshall, Herbert, ed. Soviet One-Act Plays. London: Pilot Press, 1944.

Matlaw, Myron, ed. The Black Crook and Other 19th Century American Plays. New York: Dutton, 1967.

Matthews, Brander, ed. Chief European Dramatists. Boston, New York: Houghton, Mifflin, 1916.

Mayorga, Margaret, ed. Best Short Plays, formerly Best One-Act Plays, 1937-1959/60; 1967/68-1972. New York: Dodd, Mead.

Menander. Plays of Menander, ed. by Lionel Casson. New York: New York Univ. Press, 1971.

Millett, Fred Benjamin. Reading Drama. New York: Harper, 1950.

Mishima, Yukio, pseud. Five Modern No Plays. New York: Knopf, 1957.

Montherlant, Henry de. The Master of Santiago and Four Other Plays. New York: Knopf, 1951.

Moon, Samuel, ed. One Act. New York: Grove Press, 1961.

Moore, Hortense, ed. Bread Loaf Book of Plays. Middlebury, Vt.: Middlebury College Press, 1941.

Munro, Hector Hugh. The Novels and Plays of Saki. New York: Viking Press, 1933.

New Plays for Women and Girls. Los Angeles, Calif.: Samuel French, 1935.

Newman, David. The Bonnie and Clyde Book. New York: Simon & Schuster, 1972.

Noble, Lorraine, ed. Four-Star Scripts. Garden City, N.Y.:
Doubleday, Doran, 1936.

Oates, Whitney Jennings, ed. The Complete Greek Drama. New
York: Random House, 1938.

Old Plays. Philadelphia: Bradford and Inskeep, 1810.

Oliver, William Irving, comp. Voices of Change in the Spanish
American Theatre. Austin: Univ. of Texas, 1971.

One-Act Play Magazine Anthology, 1937/38. New York: Contemporary Play Publications.

The One-Act Theatre. 2 vols. New York: Samuel French, 1936.

Orzel, Nick, and Michael Smith, eds. Eight Plays from Off-Off
Broadway. Indianapolis, Ind.: Bobbs-Merrill, 1966.

Pence, Raymond Woodbury, ed. Dramas by Present Day Writers.
New York: Scribners, 1927.

Pinter, Harold. Early Plays. New York: Grove Press, 1969.

_____. Five Screenplays. New York: Viking Press, 1973.

Plays for a New Theatre: Playbook 2. New York: New Directions,
1966.

Plays of the Year, 1948/49; 1951; 1954; 1956/57-1971/72. London:
P. Elek.

Plays of the Year Special. 2 vols. Television scripts of two
series "The Six Wives of Henry VIII" and "Elizabeth R," ed.
by J.C. Trewin. London: P. Elek, 1972.

Popkin, Henry, ed. New British Drama. New York: Grove Press,
1964.

Racine, Jean Baptiste. Jean Racine: Five Plays. New York:
Hill & Wang, 1960.

Rattigan, Terence. Collected Plays. 3 vols. London: H. Hamilton, 1953.

Reardon, William R., and Thomas D. Painley. The Black Teacher
and the Dramatic Arts. Westport, Conn.: Negro University
Press, 1970.

Religious Drama, selected and introduced by E. Martin Brown.
3 vols. New York: Meridian Books, 1957-59.

Richards, Stanley. Best Short Plays of the World Theatre, 1958-
1967. New York: Crown, 1968.

_____. Modern Short Comedies from Broadway and London.
New York: Random House, 1970.

Richie, Donald, ed. Six Kabuki Plays. Tokyo: Hokuseido Press,
1963.

Rose, Reginald. Six Television Plays. New York: Simon &
Schuster, 1956.

Rossen, Robert. Three Screenplays. New York: Doubleday, 1972.

Rowell, George, ed. Late Victorian Plays, 1890-1914. London:
Oxford Univ. Press, 1968.

_____. Three East European Plays. London: Penguin, 1970.

Rubenstein, Harold F., ed. Great English Plays. New York:
Harper, 1928.

Russak, Jon Ben, ed. Monte Cristo and Other Plays. Princeton,
N.J.: Princeton Univ. Press, 1941.

Rys, Ernest, ed. Modern Plays. London: Dent, 1937.

Sakanishi, Shio, tr. The Ink Smeared Lady and Other Kyogen.
Tokyo: Tuttle, 1960.

Sanchez, Florencio. Teatro de Florencio Sanchez. 2nd ed.
Buenos Aires: Editorial Sopena Argentina, 1942.

_____. El Teatro del Uruguayo. Barcelona: Editorial Cer-
vantes, 1926.

Sapegno, Natalino, comp. Scrittori d'Italia. Firenze: "La Nuova
Italia," 1964-1965.

Saroyan, William. Dogs, or, The Paris Comedy. New York:
Phaedra, 1969.

_____. Three Times Three. Los Angeles, Calif.: Conference
Press, 1936.

Satan, Socialites and Solly Gold; three new plays from England.
New York: Coward McCann, 1961.

Schevill, James Erwin. The Black President and Other Plays.
Denver, Col.: A. Swallow, 1965.

Schisgal, Murray. Five One-Act Plays. New York: Dramatists
Play Service, 1968.

_____ . Luv and The Typists and The Tiger; three plays. New York: New American Library, 1967.

Seldes, Gilbert Vivian. Writing for Television. Garden City, N. Y.: Doubleday, 1952.

Serling, Rod. Patterns: Four Television Plays. New York: Simon & Schuster, 1957.

_____ . The Season to Be Wary. Boston: Little, Brown, 1967.

Seven Plays of the Modern Theatre, with an introduction by Harold Churman. New York: Grove Press, 1962.

Shay, Frank, ed. 50 Contemporary One-Act Plays. Cincinnati, Ohio: Stewart & Kidd Co., 1920.

_____ . 50 More Contemporary One-Act Plays. New York: Appleton, 1928.

Shelley, Percy Bysshe. Complete Works. London: Oxford Univ. Press, 1933.

Simon, Neil. The Comedy of Neil Simon. New York: Random House, 1971.

Sims, Alan. Whitest Elephant and Four Other Heroic Comedies. London: French, 1950.

Sinclair, Upton. Plays of Protest. New York: M. Kennedy, 1912.

Smith, Alice Mary. Short Plays by Representative Authors. New York: Macmillan, 1920.

Smith, Michael Townsend. The Best of the Off-Off Broadway. New York: Dutton, 1969.

_____ . More Plays from Off-Off Broadway. Indianapolis, Ind.: Bobbs-Merrill, 1972.

Soyinka, Wole. Three Short Plays. London: Three Crowns Books, Oxford Univ. Press, 1969.

Sprinchom, Evert, ed. The Genius of the Scandinavian Theatre. New York: New American Library, 1964.

Stamm, Rudolph, ed. Three Anglo-Irish Plays. Freeport, N. Y.: Books for Libraries, 1970.

Stasio, Marilyn, ed. Broadway's Beautiful Losers. New York: Delacorte Press, 1972.

Steinhauer, Harry, ed. Das Deutsche Drama, 1880-1933. 2 vols. New York: W. W. Norton, Co. , 1938.

Story, the Yearbook of Discovery, 1968-1971. New York: Four Winds Press.

Strindberg, August. The Last of the Knights; The Regent; Earl Birger of Bjälbo; tr. and intro. by Walter Johnson. Seattle: Univ. of Washington Press, 1956.

_____. Queen Christina; Charles XII; Gustav II; tr. and intro. by Walter Johnson. Seattle: Univ. of Washington Press, 1955.

_____. World Historical Plays, tr. by Arvid Paulson with an intro. by Gunnar Ollen. New York: Twayne, 1970.

Sumarokov, Aleksandr Petrovich. Selected Tragedies, tr. by Richard and Raymond Fortune; intro. by John Fizer. Evanston, Ill. : Northwestern Univ. Press, 1970.

Swire, Willard, ed. Three Distinctive Plays about Abraham Lincoln. New York: Washington Square Press, 1961.

Theatre Guild. Theatre Guild Anthology. New York: Random House, 1936.

Theatre 1-4. New York: International Institute of the United States, 1969-1972.

Toller, Ernst. Seven Plays. London: John Lane of the Bodley Head, 1935.

Trussler, Simon. Burlesque Plays of the 18th Century. New York: Oxford Univ. Press, 1969.

Ueda, Makoto, tr. The Old Pine Tree and Other Noh Plays. Lincoln: Univ. of Nebraska Press, 1962.

Ulanov, Barry, ed. Makers of the Modern Theatre. New York: McGraw-Hill, 1961.

Van Itallie, Jean Claude. American Hurrah: Plays. New York: Coward-McCann, 1967.

_____. War and Four Other Plays. New York: Dramatists Play Service, 1967.

Vidal, Gore. Best Television Plays. New York: Ballantine Books, 1956.

_____. Three Plays. London: Heinemann, 1962.

_____ . Visit to a Small Planet and Other Television Plays.
Boston: Little, Brown, 1956.

Visconti, Luchino. Three Screenplays. New York: Orion, 1970.

Vreeland, Frank, ed. Foremost Films of 1938. New York: Pit-
man, 1939.

Wald, Jerry, and Richard Macaulay, eds. Best Pictures, 1939/40.
New York: Dodd, Mead, 1940.

Welles, Orson. The Citizen Kane Book. Boston: Little, Brown,
1971.

Wilder, Billy and I. A. L. Diamond. The Apartment and The Fortune
Cookie, two screenplays. New York: Praeger, 1970.

Wilder, Thornton. The Long Christmas Dinner and Other Plays.
New York: Harper & Row, 1963.

Williams, Charles. Collected Plays. London: Oxford Univ. Press,
1963.

Williams, Emlyn. Collected Plays. Vol. 1. New York: Random
House, 1961.

Williams, Tennessee. American Blues. New York: Dramatists
Play Service, 1948.

_____ . 27 Wagons Full of Cotton. Norfolk, Conn.: New Directions, 1953.

Woodyard, George William, ed. Modern Stage in Latin America:
Six Plays. New York: Dutton, 1971.

Wylie, Max. Writing for Television. New York: Cowles, 1970.

Yamamoto Yuzo. Three Plays. Tokyo: Hokuseido Press, 1957.

Zachar, Irwin, ed. Plays as Experience. New York: Odyssey
Press, 1944.

PERIODICAL TITLES AND PUBLISHERS' SERIES
SELECTIVELY INDEXED

Americas. Wash., D. C.

Anglo Saxon Review. London.

Arion. Austin, Texas.

Art of the Film Series. New American Library, New York.

L'Avant-Scene du Cinema. Paris.

L'Avant-Scene du Theatre. Paris.

Asia and the Americas. New York.

Atlantic Monthly. Boston.

Atlas. New York.

Bookman. New York.

Cahiers du Cinema. Paris.

Chicago Review.

Chinese Literature. Peking.

Cinema. Beverly Hills, Calif.

Classic Filmscripts Series. Simon & Schuster, New York.

Commentary. New York.

Cosmopolitan. New York.

Dial. New York.

Divaldo/Theatre. Prague, Czechoslovakia.

Drama. Chicago.

Drama & Theatre. Fredonia, N. Y.

Drama at Calgary. Calgary, Alberta.

Drama Survey. Minneapolis.

Educational Theatre Journal. Columbia, Mo.

Encounter. London.

Esquire. Chicago.

Evergreen Filmscripts Series. Grove Press, N. Y.

Evergreen Black Cat Playscripts Series. Grove Press, N. Y.

Evergreen Review. New York.

Everybody's Magazine. New York.

Film Focus Series. Prentice-Hall, Englewood Cliffs, N. J.

First Stage. Lafayette, Ind.

Fortnightly. London.

Forum. Philadelphia.

Golden Book. New York.

Grossman Library of Film Classics Series. Grossman, N. Y.

Harper's Magazine. New York.

Horizon. New York.

Hudson Review. New York.

Italian Theatre Review. Rome.

Kenyon Review. Gambier, O.

Life. Chicago.

Literary Review. Teaneck, N. J.

Little Review. Chicago.

Living Age. Boston.

London Magazine.

M G M Library of Filmscripts Series. Viking Press, New York.

Mademoiselle. New York.

Massachusetts Review. Amherst.

Modern Filmscripts Series. Simon & Schuster, New York.

Modern International Drama. University Park, Pa.

Modern Language Notes. Baltimore.

Music and Letters. London.

Negro History Bulletin. Wash., D. C.

New Statesman. London.

New Yorker.

North American Review. Mt. Vernon, Iowa.

Paris Review. New York.

Partisan Review. New York.

La Petite Illustration. Paris.

Plaisir de France, Supplement Theatral. Paris.

Players Magazine. De Kalb, Ill.

Plays and Players. London.

447

Poet Lore.   Boston.
Poetry.   Chicago.
Quarterly Review of Literature.
     Princeton, N. J.
Ramparts.   Menlo Park, Calif.
Review of English Literature.
     Oxford.
Revista de Teatro.   Rio de
     Janeiro.
Saturday Evening Post.   Phila-
     delphia.
Saturday Review.   New York.
Scribner's Magazine.   New York.
Scripts.   New York.
Seven Arts.   New York.
Sewanee Review.   Sewanee,
     Tenn.
Show.   Hollywood.
Show.   New York.
Soundings.   Stony Brook, N. Y.
Stage.   New York.
TDR/The Drama Review.   New
     Orleans.
Theater der Zeit.   Berlin.
Theater Heute.   Velber bei
     Hannover, Germany.
Theatre Arts.   New York.
Virginia Quarterly Review.
     Charlottesville.
Vogue.   New York.
Yale Literary Magazine.   New
     Haven, Conn.
Yale Review.
Yale/Theatre.